MAGILL'S
SURVEY
OF
WORLD
LITERATURE

MAGILL'S SURVEY OF WORLD LITERATURE

Volume 1

Achebe–Chekhov

REFERENCE

Edited by
FRANK N. MAGILL

Marshall Cavendish Corporation
New York • London • Toronto • Sydney • Singapore

Published By
Marshall Cavendish Corporation
2415 Jerusalem Avenue
P.O. Box 587
North Bellmore, New York 11710
United States of America

∞ The paper used in these volumes conforms to the American National Standard for Permanence of Paper for Printed Library Materials, Z39.48-1984.

Library of Congress Cataloging-in-Publication Data
Magill's survey of world literature. Edited by Frank N. Magill.
     p. cm.
  Includes bibliographical references and index.
  1. Literature—History and criticism. 2. Literature—Stories, plots, etc. 3. Literature—Bio-bibliography. 4. Authors—Biography—Dictionaries. I. Magill, Frank Northen, 1907-   .
PN523.M29 1992
809—dc20
ISBN 1-85435-482-5 (set)   92-11198
ISBN 1-85435-483-3 (volume 1)   CIP

Second Printing

PRINTED IN THE UNITED STATES OF AMERICA

PUBLISHER'S NOTE

The six volumes of *Magill's Survey of World Literature* present 215 writers from antiquity to the late twentieth century whose lives and work are of enduring interest. Articles in the set are arranged alphabetically by author. Highlighted ready-reference features guide the reader through each article, beginning with boxed introductory material and continuing with subheadings that aid the reader in retrieving information. Included with most of the essays is a photograph of the author being profiled.

The writers featured in these volumes represent an enormous diversity of cultural, historical, and linguistic experience and a wide range of genres: long and short fiction, poetry, drama, and nonfiction. The classical foundations of Western culture are explored in essays on the philosophy of Plato and Aristotle, the poetry of Homer and Vergil, and the drama of Aeschylus, Euripides, Sophocles, and Seneca. In addition to other major figures in the Western tradition, such as Dante Alighieri and Miguel de Cervantes, the set includes the classical Chinese poets Li Po and Tu Fu, the eleventh century Japanese novelist Murasaki Shikibu, and the master of haiku, Matsuo Bashō.

British writers of every period are featured, including such major figures as William Wordsworth, Jane Austen, George Eliot, and Charles Dickens, as well as twentieth century writers such as Evelyn Waugh, Graham Greene, and Iris Murdoch. Also appearing are English-language writers from Ireland, Canada, Africa, and the West Indies. American writers are covered in a companion set, the six-volume *Magill's Survey of American Literature*, but Latin American writers are included in this set, among them Jorge Luis Borges (Argentina), Carlos Fuentes (Mexico), Octavio Paz (Mexico), and Mario Vargas Llosa (Peru).

The major European literatures are strongly represented, with writers from France, Spain, Italy, Austria and Germany, and Russia. Writers in so-called minor languages are also covered—the Nobel Prize-winning Polish poet Czesław Miłosz, for example, and the novelist Aharon Appelfeld, who writes in modern Hebrew.

In addition to well-established figures, the set highlights some younger writers whose work has been widely noted—writers such as Martin Amis, Salman Rushdie, and the late Bruce Chatwin. Popular mystery writers (Sir Arthur Conan Doyle, Agatha Christie, Dorothy Sayers, and P. D. James) and authors of fantasy and science fiction (C. S. Lewis, J. R. R. Tolkien, and Arthur C. Clarke) are also included, as is the leading novelist of espionage, John le Carré.

Following the Magill reference tradition, each article begins with ready-reference top matter that presents the date and place of the author's birth and death. A separate boxed section then briefly encapsulates the writer's literary significance. The main text of the article begins with "Biography," a chronological overview of the author's life, with orientation toward his or her literary endeavors. In the "Analysis" section that follows, the author's style, themes, and literary characteristics are discussed; this section can be read independently as an overview of the author's work. Following the analysis are separate sections on individual works by the author. The ordering of these sections is first by genre, then chronological within the genre; each section is introduced by boxed information presenting the date of first publication and a capsule description of the work. The essay concludes with a brief "Summary" and a bibliography that directs the student to books and articles for further study.

Within the essays, literary works mentioned are accompanied by the date of first publication; dates given for plays represent the first major public performance of the work. When titles of foreign works appear in the text, the date of the original foreign publication is given, followed by the English translation title and the date of its first publication. A complete alphabetical List of Authors profiled in the set appears at the end of each volume. To aid the reader further, a Glossary of literary terms that appear in the set can also be found at the end of each volume. Unlike the Glossary that appears in the *Survey of American Literature*, the present Glossary—although perforce addressing many of the same terms—also defines literary styles and genres arising out of different cultures' literary traditions; thus, the entire Glossary was newly commissioned for the *Survey of World Literature*. At the end of volume 6 is an Author Index plus a Title Index that includes all works covered in separate sections within the articles.

We would like to acknowledge the work of the many fine academicians and other writers who contributed to this set. A list of their names and affiliations appears in the front matter of volume 1.

Photograph Credits

AP/Wide World Photos: *John Betjeman, Elizabeth Bowen, Italo Calvino, E. M. Forster, Kazuo Ishiguro, P. D. James, Franz Kafka, Stephen Leacock, Doris Lessing, C. S. Lewis, Wyndham Lewis, Hugh MacLennan, Yukio Mishima, George Orwell, Jean-Paul Sartre, Dorothy L. Sayers, Virginia Woolf.* Archive Photos: *Farley Mowat, Gabrielle Roy.* Archive Photos/Camera Press: *John Fowles.* Jerry Bauer, courtesy of Houghton Mifflin: *Muriel Spark*; courtesy of Viking: *Bruce Chatwin*; courtesy of Weidenfeld & Nicolson: *Aharon Appelfeld.* Copyright Jerry Bauer, courtesy of Alfred A. Knopf: *Margaret Drabble, Alice Munro*; courtesy of Farrar, Straus and Giroux: *Peter Handke, Mario Vargas Llosa*; courtesy of Grove Weidenfeld: *Eugène Ionesco*; courtesy of Random House: *J. M. Coetzee*; courtesy of Viking: *Robertson Davies, Salman Rushdie.* The Bettmann Archive: *Bertolt Brecht, Katherine Mansfield, Christopher Marlowe, Rainer Maria Rilke.* Jean-Claude Bouis, courtesy of Henry Holt and Company: *Yevgeny Yevtushenko.* Copyright 1991, Jane Bown, courtesy of Farrar, Straus and Giroux: *Ted Hughes.* Adapted from a portrait in the Itsuo Museum, Ikeda City, Osaka, reprinted by permission of Branden Press: *Matsuo Bashō.* Camera Press London: *Philip Larkin.* Copyright Nancy Crampton, courtesy of Random House: *V. S. Pritchett.* Culver Pictures, Inc.: *Federico García Lorca.* Maclean Dameron, courtesy of Alfred Appel, Jr.: *Vladimir Nabokov.* Kimberly Dawson: *Horace, Nikos Kazantzakis, Ovid, Barbara Pym, Tu Fu.* Courtesy of

CONTRIBUTORS

Michael Adams
Fairleigh Dickinson University

Patrick Adcock
Henderson State University

Anu Aneja
Ohio Wesleyan University

Raymond M. Archer
Indiana University at Kokomo

Stanley Archer
Texas A&M University

William Atkinson
Kennesaw State College

Bryan Aubrey
Maharishi International University

Charles Avinger
Troy State University

Jim Baird
University of North Texas

Carol M. Barnum
Southern College of Technology

Jane Missner Barstow
Hartford College for Women
University of Hartford

Melissa E. Barth
Appalachian State University

Stephen Benz
Barry University

Dorothy M. Betz
Georgetown University

Nancy Blake
University of Illinois at Urbana-Champaign

Julia B. Boken
State University of New York at Oneonta

Gerhard Brand
California State University, Los Angeles

Jean R. Brink
Arizona State University

Carl Brucker
Arkansas Tech University

Jeffrey L. Buller
Georgia Southern University

Edmund J. Campion
University of Tennessee

Warren J. Carson
University of South Carolina—Spartanburg

Hal Charles
Eastern Kentucky University

Cida S. Chase
Oklahoma State University

John Steven Childs
Polytechnic University

Daniel L. Colvin
Western Illinois University

George Craddock
Lindenwood College

John W. Crawford
Henderson State University

Lee B. Croft
Arizona State University

Laura Dabundo
Kennesaw State College

Bill Delaney
Independent Scholar

Carolyn F. Dickinson
Columbia College

Sarah Smith Ducksworth
Kean College of New Jersey

Margaret Duggan
South Dakota State University

Gweneth A. Dunleavy
University of Louisville

Robert P. Ellis
Worcester State College

Thomas L. Erskine
Salisbury State University

Charlene Taylor Evans
Texas Southern University

James Feast
Bernard M. Baruch College
City University of New York

John W. Fiero
University of Southwestern Louisiana

MAGILL'S SURVEY OF WORLD LITERATURE

Robert J. Forman
St. John's University

Carol Franks
Portland State University

Terri Frongia
University of California, Riverside

Jean C. Fulton
Maharishi International University

James Gaasch
Humboldt State University

Pat Ingle Gillis
Georgia Southern University

Erlis Glass
Rosemont College

Irene E. Gnarra
Kean College of New Jersey

Roy Neil Graves
The University of Tennessee at Martin

John L. Grigsby
Mississippi Valley State University

William E. Grim
Ohio University

Daniel L. Guillory
Millikin University

Natalie Harper
Simon's Rock of Bard College

Melanie Hawthorne
Texas A&M University

Terry Heller
Coe College

Pierre L. Horn
Wright State University

John Higby
Appalachian State University

E. D. Huntley
Appalachian State University

Archibald E. Irwin
Indiana University Southeast

Barry Jacobs
Montclair State College

D. Barton Johnson
University of California, Santa Barbara

Isaac Johnson
Pacific Union College

Jeff Johnson
Brevard Community College

Sheila Golburgh Johnson
Independent Scholar

Eunice Pedersen Johnston
North Dakota State University

Richard Keenan
University of Maryland—Eastern Shore

Douglas Keesey
California Polytechnic State University, San Luis Obispo

Steven G. Kellman
University of Texas at San Antonio

Rebecca Kelly
Southern College of Technology

Richard Kelly
University of Tennessee

Eugene S. Larson
Los Angeles Pierce College

Leon Lewis
Appalachian State University

Anna Lillios
University of Central Florida

James L. Livingston
Northern Michigan University

Dana Loewy
University of Southern California

Janet Lorenz
Independent Scholar

R. C. Lutz
University of the Pacific

James McCorkle
Hobart and William Smith Colleges

Andrew Macdonald
Loyola University, New Orleans

Gina Macdonald
Loyola University, New Orleans

Richard D. McGhee
Arkansas State University

Ric S. Machuga
Butte College

CONTRIBUTORS

Dennis Q. McInerny
Holy Apostles College

John L. McLean
Morehead State University

Dan McLeod
California State University, San Diego

Jennifer McLeod
California State University, Chico

Marian B. McLeod
Trenton State College

Victoria E. McLure
Texas Tech University

David W. Madden
California State University, Sacramento

Barry Mann
University of San Diego

Joss Lutz Marsh
Stanford University

Karen M. Cleveland Marwick
Independent Scholar

Charles E. May
California State University, Long Beach

Laurence W. Mazzeno
Mesa State College

Kenneth W. Meadwell
University of Winnipeg, Manitoba, Canada

Patrick Meanor
State University of New York at Oneonta

Vasa D. Mihailovich
University of North Carolina

Barbara Miliaras
University of Massachusetts at Lowell

Leslie B. Mittleman
California State University, Long Beach

John M. Muste
Ohio State University

Carolyn A. Nadeau
Pennsylvania State University

D. Gosselin Nakeeb
Pace University

William Nelles
Northwestern State University

Terry Nienhuis
Western Carolina University

Herbert Northcote
Temple University

George O'Brien
Georgetown University

Linda Rohrer Paige
Georgia Southern University

Margaret Parks
Independent Scholar

David B. Parsell
Furman University

Pamela Pavliscak
University of North Carolina

Larry H. Peer
Brigham Young University

Thomas Amherst Perry
East Texas State University

Lela Phillips
Andrew College

Susan L. Piepke
Bridgewater College

Victoria Price
Lamar University

Josef Raab
University of Southern California

Rosemary M. Canfield Reisman
Troy State University

Elizabeth Richmond
University of Texas at Austin

Claire Robinson
Maharishi International University

Bernard F. Rodgers, Jr.
Simon's Rock of Bard College

Peter S. Rogers
Loyola University, New Orleans

Carl Rollyson
Bernard M. Baruch College
City University of New York

Paul Rosefeldt
University of New Orleans

John K. Roth
Claremont McKenna College

CONTENTS

MAGILL'S SURVEY OF WORLD LITERATURE

MAGILL'S
SURVEY
OF
WORLD
LITERATURE

CHINUA ACHEBE

Born: Ogidi, Nigeria
November 16, 1930

Principal Literary Achievement

As the first African writer to win broad critical acclaim in Europe and America, Achebe has shaped the world's understanding of Africa and its literature.

Biography

Chinua Achebe was born in Ogidi, in the Eastern Region of Nigeria, on November 16, 1930, to Isaiah and Janet Achebe, who christened their son Albert Chinualumogu. Isaiah Achebe was a catechist for the Church Missionary Society, and he and his wife traveled through Eastern Nigeria as evangelists before settling in Ogidi, Isaiah's ancestral Igbo village, five years after Chinua Achebe's birth. Growing up in Ogidi, Achebe had contact with both Christian and Igbo religious beliefs and customs.

Achebe's first lessons were taught in Igbo at the church school in Ogidi. He began to learn English at the age of eight. An avid reader and an outstanding student, Achebe was chosen at age fourteen to attend Government College, a highly selective secondary school in Umuahia, where one of his classmates was the poet Christopher Okigbo. Upon graduation, Achebe accepted a scholarship to study medicine at University College in Ibadan but after one year decided to switch to English literature, forfeiting his scholarship. With the financial assistance of his older brother John, he was able to continue his studies.

Achebe and the Yoruban playwright Wole Soyinka, who were to become Nigeria's best-known authors, were undergraduates together at University College, and each published his first work in undergraduate publications. "Polar Undergraduate," a satire of student behavior that was later collected in *Girls at War* (1972), was Achebe's first published fiction. In his third year, he edited the *University Herald*. After graduation in 1953, he took a position as talks producer for the Nigerian Broadcasting Corporation (NBC).

In 1958, Achebe published *Things Fall Apart*, which won for him the Margaret Wrong Memorial Prize in 1959 for the novel's contribution to African literature. In 1960, the year of Nigeria's independence, Achebe published *No Longer at Ease* and was awarded the Nigerian National Trophy. He spent the remainder of 1960 and part of 1961 traveling through East Africa and interviewing other African writers. After his return to Nigeria, he married Christie Chinwe Okoli, with whom he was to have

1

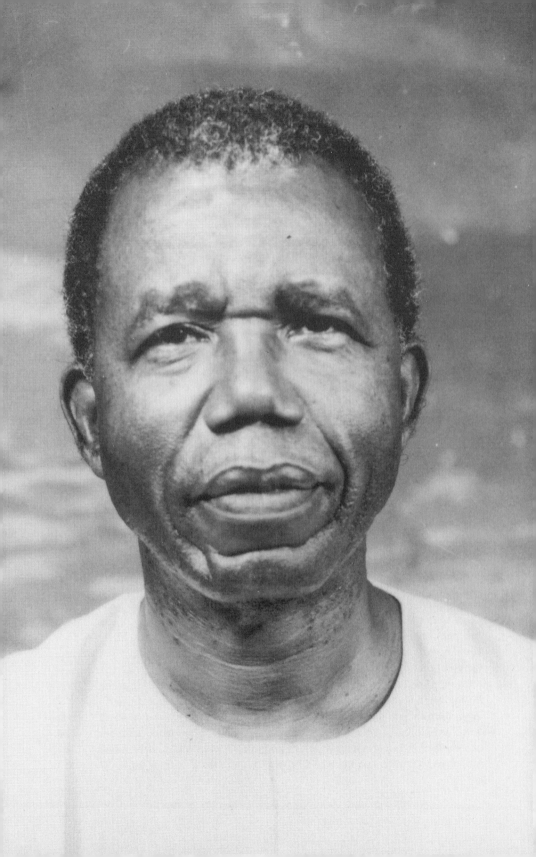

four children, and was appointed director of External Broadcasting for NBC.

In 1962, Achebe became the founding editor of Heinemann's African Writers series, and in 1963, he traveled in the United States, Brazil, and Britain on a UNESCO (United Nations Educational, Social and Cultural Organization) fellowship. Achebe published *Arrow of God* in 1964 and was honored with the Jock Campbell Award (*New Statesman*) in 1965 for his accomplishment. His publication of the prophetic *A Man of the People* (1966) was followed by successive military coups, massacres of Igbos, and the secession of Biafra in 1967. Achebe was forced to leave Lagos after the second coup, and during the Nigerian civil war he became a spokesperson for the Biafran cause in Europe and North America. He also served as a Senior Research Fellow at the University of Nigeria in Nsukka, which was renamed the University of Biafra during the war.

After three years of bitter struggle, Biafra surrendered, and Achebe, more dedicated than ever to the preservation of Igbo culture, began editing *Okike: An African Journal of New Writing.* He published his literary response to the war in *Beware, Soul Brother and Other Poems* (1971) and *Girls at War,* winning the Commonwealth Poetry Prize in 1972 for *Beware Soul Brother and Other Poems*, which was published in the United States as *Christmas in Biafra and Other Poems* (1973).

From 1972 to 1976, Achebe taught in the United States at the University of Massachusetts in Amherst, where his wife earned a doctorate, and the University of Connecticut. After the 1976 assassination of Murtala Muhammed, for whom Achebe had great respect, the author returned to teach at the University of Nigeria at Nsukka. In 1979, Achebe was elected chairman of the Association of Nigerian Authors and received the Nigerian National Merit Award and the Order of the Federal Republic. In 1982, he and Obiora Udechukwu edited *Aka Weta*, an anthology of "egwu" verse.

Disillusioned by President Shehu Shagari's failure to fight the corruption that was impoverishing Nigeria and saddened by the death of Mallam Aminu Kano, the leader of the People's Redemption Party (PRP), Achebe served as Deputy National President of the PRP in the election year of 1983. In *The Trouble with Nigeria* (1983), he presented his political prescription for improving Nigeria. After Shagari's reelection and removal from office by a subsequent military coup, Achebe once again concentrated his energies on artistic and cultural projects, editing the bilingual *Uwa ndi Igbo: A Journal of Igbo Life and Culture.* In 1986, Achebe was appointed pro-vice chancellor of the State University of Anambra at Enugu. The following year, Achebe published his first novel in twenty years, *Anthills of the Savannah* (1987), and returned to teach in the United States at the University of Massachusetts in Amherst, the City College of New York, and Bard College. In 1987, he published a collection of essays titled *Hopes and Impediments.*

Analysis

In his writings, Achebe affirms the educational function of literature and establishes a human context for understanding modern Nigerian history. He describes the first contacts between European and African cultures at the beginning of the twentieth century in *Things Fall Apart*; the subsequent institutionalization of European religious and political structures in *Arrow of God*; the uneasy years immediately preceding independence in *No Longer at Ease*; the excitement and disappointment of Nigeria's First Republic in *A Man of the People*; the suffering caused by the Nigerian civil war in *Girls at War* and *Beware, Soul Brother and Other Poems*; and the corrupt authoritarianism that has characterized Nigeria's Second Republic in *Beware, Soul Brother and Other Poems* and *Anthills of the Savannah*. Indeed, the title of his commentary, *The Trouble with Nigeria*, identifies a concern that has been central to all of his work.

As a corrective to European literature's stereotypical portraits of Africans as an unvarying, primitive force, Achebe strives to communicate the human complexity of Nigerian existence, to establish the independence of African literature, and to demonstrate the value of traditional Igbo culture. In "The Role of a Writer in a New Nation," he states that his first priority is to inform the world that "African peoples did not hear of culture for the first time from Europeans; that their societies were not mindless . . . that they had poetry and, above all, they had dignity." Achebe, however, does not idealize the precolonial past, for he knows that it cannot survive unaltered in a modern world; instead, he encourages his readers to explore continuities with the past that can coexist with modern society.

Achebe's protagonists, who are in conflict between self-realization and social responsibility, demonstrate the difficulty of reaching such a balance. Each character's movement toward communal acceptance is thwarted by the destructive pull of individual pride. In *Things Fall Apart*, Okonkwo overcomes personal humiliation to win the respect of his Igbo community, but his inflexible refusal to accommodate himself to the increasing influence of colonial government and Christianity alienates him from his clan and drives him to self-destructive violence. In *Arrow of God*, the priest Ezeulu earnestly wishes to be a good religious leader, but his proud refusal to adapt religious dictates to the necessities of circumstance leads to Christian dominance in his village and to his own madness. In *No Longer at Ease*, the idealistic Obi self-righteously resists the corruption of government service, alienating himself from his fellow civil servants and the clan members who funded his education; yet when his proud need to maintain an expensive life-style leads him to accept a bribe, his amateurish attempt results in his arrest. In *A Man of the People*, the cynical Odili, who collaborates in Nanga's political manipulation of rural people, learns to see the corrective value of traditional beliefs. *Anthills of the Savannah* offers the most hopeful view, with Beatrice showing that traditional values can exist in altered but viable forms in the present.

In his fiction, Achebe opposes interpersonal, political, cultural, and linguistic forms of authoritarianism. He associates inflexible refusal to recognize the validity of multiple viewpoints, which is the central flaw of his protagonists, with the cultural arrogance of colonial powers and the cynical greed of Nigerian officials. Stylistically, Achebe refutes this myopic authoritarianism through the use of multiple perspectives and irony. In *Anthills of the Savannah*, he repeats the Igbo proverb, "Where something stands, there also something else will stand," to indicate his belief in the fluidity of perception, the duality of existence, and the adaptability of Igbo culture. To represent this fluidity in his fiction, he mixes literary English, pidgin English, and a colloquial English that approximates the rhythms of Igbo speech; he mixes Igbo proverbs, songs, and rituals with allusions to European literature; he uses irony and unreliable narrators to emphasize his distrust of authoritarian voices. In his effort to create an open, nonauthoritarian view, Achebe uses one novel to balance another; thus, the naïvely idealistic Obi Okonkwo of *No Longer at Ease* is a tragicomic version of his grandfather, Okonkwo, in *Things Fall Apart.* Achebe's decision to write in English instead of his native Igbo allowed him to reach a worldwide audience but opened him to the charge that he was assisting in the demise of Igbo culture. He has moved toward the use of native languages by editing the anthology *Aka weta* (1982) and the bilingual journal *Uwa ndi Igbo.*

Achebe has been an active and visible public figure in Nigeria since the 1950's, and it is not surprising that his writings parallel his personal experiences. His early sympathetic portrayals of traditional Igbo culture were, in part, gestures toward expiating his own guilt over the rare educational privileges that he enjoyed. His skillful satire of the abuse of power and language in books such as *A Man of the People* is written against his own involvement in the development of Nigeria's mass media. After the Nigerian civil war, in which Achebe and many other Igbo writers took an active part, the author's writings became more directly utilitarian and political. After teaching in the United States and realizing that the most widely taught book concerning Africa was Joseph Conrad's *Heart of Darkness* (1902), Achebe became more sympathetic to African authors who renounced the use of colonial languages and became more aware of the extent to which Americans and Europeans misunderstand and ignore Africa's problems.

THINGS FALL APART

First published: 1958
Type of work: Novel

A violent opponent of colonialism's threat to traditional Igbo culture is destroyed by his failure to adapt.

Things Fall Apart tells the tragic story of Okonkwo, who, determined to overcome the example of his lazy and imprudent father, elevates himself to a position of respect in the Igbo community of Umuofia through acts of strength, courage, and endurance. Unfortunately, Okonkwo's obsessive fear of failure makes him a humorless and short-tempered man whose pride and violence undermine his reputation in the community. By erasing the effeminate from his character, Okonkwo makes himself into a man who is unable to enjoy his success fully, and by focusing for so long on his individual struggle to be successful, he distances himself from the communal life of Umuofia.

When Okonkwo accidentally kills a young boy, his clanspeople destroy his compound and exile him to live with his mother's clan for seven years. By the end of his exile, Okonkwo, who had earlier been known for his self-interest, has learned to appreciate the bonds of kinship and the comfort of speaking with one voice. Unfortunately, this awareness comes after the unity of Igbo culture has begun to deteriorate. Christianity has divided the community, and Okonkwo senses that this change threatens his connection to his family, his culture, and his spiritual existence after death. His eldest son's conversion to Christianity separates Okonkwo from his lineage, and when another young convert to Christianity desecrates a traditional religious totem, Okonkwo leads the Umuofians into destroying the missionaries' church. Like Okonkwo, the Umuofians face separation from their past and like him they face a future that will require difficult compromises; yet Achebe carefully shows that the decentralization and nonhierarchical structure of Igbo society allow for change.

Okonkwo's greatest flaw is his inability to adapt to cultural change. He is humiliated that Umuofia does not rise in his support and go to war against the white man. In a final, desperate act, he murders the District Commissioner's messenger and hangs himself. At the end of the novel, Okonkwo stands alone, a self-proclaimed defender of a rigid traditionalism that contradicts the true flexibility of his culture. He is an exceptional individual, but the heroism of his final act of defiance is undercut by his alienation from his clan. He does not understand that Umuofia is a living culture that has always adapted in order to meet new challenges. His effort to deny the reality of history condemns him while making a sad comment on the limitations of human endeavor. The novel dramatizes the situation of modern people and modern societies that are forced to adapt and compromise if they wish to survive. Its central theme, and the central theme of all Achebe's novels, is the tragedy of the individual or society that refuses or is unable to accommodate change.

In *Things Fall Apart*, Achebe effectively counters the persistent and self-serving European stereotypes of African culture, particularly the notion that traditional African cultures are authoritarian, amoral, and unsophisticated. In refuting this stereotype, Achebe carefully describes the complexity and fluidity of Igbo culture, disclosing its essential pluralism. It is, however, a society that cannot survive unaltered in a modern world. Like William Butler Yeats's "The Second Coming," from which the novel takes its title, *Things Fall Apart* presents an ironic and apocalyptic vision of the failure to maintain order and balance.

NO LONGER AT EASE

First published: 1960
Type of work: Novel

An idealistic young Nigerian bureaucrat, trapped between his traditional background and his European education, succumbs to the corrupting influences of government service.

No Longer at Ease opens and closes at the bribery trial of Obi Okonkwo, a young civil servant in the colonial Nigerian government and the grandson of the Okonkwo of *Things Fall Apart.* The novel provides a retrospective look at Obi's progress from the remote village of Umuofia to an English university and then to a position with the Nigerian Civil Service in Lagos, where he finally succumbs to the prevalent practice of bribery and is caught. Like a diminished version of his grandfather, Obi is crushed by cultural forces beyond his control, but the pettiness and ineptitude of his crime make him a paradoxical tragicomic hero. His innocence makes him a criminal; his coveted education does not provide him with wisdom; and the support of his clanspeople increases his sense of loneliness.

Obi is the first from his village to receive a European education; his expenses are paid by clan members who hope to enhance the status of their village and reap future economic dividends. Obi's life, however, is complicated by idealistic romance and his failure to manage his finances. He falls in love with a woman who is *osu*—marked by a traditional, hereditary taboo. Obi rejects the taboo as primitive superstition, but his naïve determination to be thoroughly modern places him in direct conflict with his family and his clan. At first, he eschews the customary practice of accepting bribes, self-righteously viewing it as an anachronistic behavior that the new generation of educated and idealistic civil servants will eradicate, but his obligation to repay the clan and his determination to maintain a life-style commensurate with his position as a civil servant eventually lead him to accept payments. When he does succumb to custom, he handles the bribery so amateurishly that he is caught and convicted.

Although Obi has been shaped by the traditional Igbo culture of Umuofia, the Christianity of his father, the idealism of English literature, and the corrupt sophistication of Lagos, he is at ease nowhere. As a child in Umuofia, he dreams of the sparkling lights of Lagos. In England, he writes pastoral visions of an idealized Nigeria. Disillusioned by the corruption of Lagos, he returns to his home village only to witness a truck driver attempting to bribe a policeman and to be greeted by his parents' rejection of his proposed marriage. Obi naïvely tries to maintain the idea of his own integrity as a detribalized, rational, thoroughly modern man, but his reintegration into Nigeria is a failure because he is unable to assimilate successfully any of the competing cultures through which he passes. He finds it impossible to mediate the conflicting duties that are thrust upon him, and his steady progress in the novel is toward despair and withdrawal.

No Longer at Ease is set on the verge of Nigeria's independence in Lagos, in an urban jungle that combines the worst of European and African cultures. Centralization has led to inefficiency and corruption; traditional Igbo communalism has devolved to the narrow pursuit of advantage. Having learned the Western desire for material goods without having sufficient income to satisfy them, the nation, like Obi, must choose between corruption and bankruptcy. It is therefore fitting that Achebe's title is drawn from Yeats's "Sailing to Byzantium," for like the wise men in Yeats's poem, Obi and the nation are trapped between two eras. As Okonkwo in *Things Fall Apart* stands for the vanishing traditional African, Obi in *No Longer at Ease* stands for the vanishing idealist in a world of compromise.

Summary

In many ways, Chinua Achebe's early fiction defined modern African literature, and it is impossible to overestimate the importance of his example. More than any other African author writing in English, Achebe has helped the world understand the value of African culture without ignoring the difficult problems that African nations face in the postcolonialist era. *Things Fall Apart* will undoubtedly remain the book for which Achebe is best known, but the entire body of his fiction, poetry, and essays makes a consistent and central contribution to the world's literature.

Bibliography

Carroll, David. *Chinua Achebe*. 2d ed. New York: St. Martin's Press, 1980.

Innes, C. L. *Chinua Achebe*. Cambridge, England: Cambridge University Press, 1990.

Innes, C. L., and Bernth Lindfors, eds. *Critical Perspectives on Chinua Achebe*. Washington, D.C.: Three Continents Press, 1978.

Killam, G. D. *The Writings of Chinua Achebe*. Rev. ed. London: Heinemann, 1977.

Njoku, Benedict Chiak. *The Four Novels of Chinua Achebe: A Critical Study*. New York: Lang, 1984.

Ravenscroft, Arthur. *Chinua Achebe*. Harlow, England: Longmans, 1969.

Turkington, Kate. *Chinua Achebe: "Things Fall Apart."* London: Edward Arnold, 1977.

Wren, Robert M. *Achebe's World: The Historical and Cultural Context of the Novels of Chinua Achebe*. Washington, D.C.: Three Continents Press, 1980.

Carl Brucker

AESCHYLUS

Born: Eleusis, Greece
525-524 B.C.
Died: Gela, Sicily
456-455 B.C.

Principal Literary Achievement

The earliest of the three great tragedians of ancient Athens, Aeschylus wrote grandiose and highly religious trilogies in which all three plays dealt with a single legend.

Biography

Throughout most of the ancient world, the city of Eleusis, fourteen miles northwest of Athens, was known primarily as the site of the Eleusinian Mysteries. Mysteries, in the religious sense, are sacred rites of initiation. The Eleusinian Mysteries honored the goddesses Demeter and Persephone, told the story of Persephone's abduction by Pluto, the god of the underworld, and offered their initiates a blessed afterlife. By the late sixth century B.C., the Eleusinian Mysteries were known in all parts of the Greek world, attracting worshipers both from Athens and from distant cities across the Aegean Sea. In 525-524 B.C., in this village filled with shrines, pilgrims, and the votive offerings of the faithful, there was born a playwright who was to reinterpret the ancient legends of his people from a profoundly religious perspective. He was the poet Aeschylus.

Aeschylus was a member of the Eupatridae, the ancient nobility that had once ruled Athens and all the cities of Attica. The Eupatridae were not a single family but rather a loose alliance of families, related by intermarriage, who shared an interest in preserving their wealth and aristocratic privileges. Aeschylus' father, Euphorion, had at least four sons: Cynegeirus, Ameinias, Euphorion the younger, and Aeschylus himself.

In 499 B.C., at the age of twenty-six, Aeschylus presented his first set of tragedies at the Festival of Dionysus (called the Great Dionysia) in Athens. The titles of these early tragedies have not been preserved and do not appear to have been among the poet's most successful works. During the fifth century B.C., prizes were awarded to playwrights who, in the opinion of ten judges, composed the finest tragedies performed during that year's festival. Aeschylus did not win the tragedy award in 499, and, indeed, he would not receive this prize until he was already forty years old.

9

From that time onward, however, Aeschylus would be victorious in tragedy competitions twelve more times. His works were also frequently revived, and frequently successful, after his death. That was a singular honor since few Greek playwrights had their tragedies revived until much later.

At about the same time that Aeschylus first began writing plays, the Greek cities of Ionia (the west central coast of Turkey) rebelled against the Persians, who had ruled them since 546 B.C. The rebellion of the Ionians received support from Athens, and that prompted the Persians to launch an extended series of punitive invasions into Greece. These invasions are known collectively as the Persian Wars. After reconquering Ionia in 494 and unsuccessfully attempting a northern invasion of Greece in 492, the Persians landed a huge army at a bay off the plain of Marathon, only twenty-six miles from Athens itself, in the late summer of 490. The Battle of Marathon became a source of Athenian pride for more than a century. In this battle, a small group of Athenians and their Plataean allies, together outnumbered ten to one by the Persians, inflicted a humiliating defeat upon the enemy. The Spartans, arriving too late for the battle, were amazed at the extent of the Greek victory. A total of about 6,400 Persians were killed at the Battle of Marathon, while only 192 Athenians lost their lives.

One of the Athenians who died at the Battle of Marathon was Aeschylus' brother Cynegeirus. According to the Greek historian Herodotus, Cynegeirus was killed during the fierce fighting around the Persian ships. Aeschylus, too, fought at Marathon, though he survived to participate in other battles of the Persian Wars. One of these battles, at Salamis in 480 B.C., was later commemorated in Aeschylus' tragedy the *Persai* (467 B.C.; *The Persians*), the only surviving Greek tragedy to deal with a historical, rather than a mythological, event.

The trilogy that contained *The Persians* won the award for tragedy for its year. Sometime later, the poet Sophocles won his first competition against Aeschylus. In the number of his tragedy victories, Sophocles was to become the most successful tragic playwright of the fifth century. Nevertheless, in about 429 B.C. when Sophocles' masterpiece *Oidipous Tyrannos* (*Oedipus Tyrannus*) was first performed, Sophocles did not receive the first prize. That victory was awarded to Philocles, a nephew of Aeschylus, whose works have not survived.

An obscure passage of Aristotle's *Ethica Nichomachea* (fourth century B.C.; *Nicomachean Ethics*, 1797) states that Aeschylus defended himself against the charge of divulging the mysteries by saying that he did not know that these were secrets. Clement of Alexandria interpreted that to mean that Aeschylus had unintentionally written a passage in one of his tragedies that resembled a sacred hymn of the Eleusinian Mysteries. Moreover, Clement suggested that Aeschylus had defended himself from the charge of exposing these secrets by proving that he had never been initiated. Nevertheless, a passage in the *Batrachoi* (405 B.C.; *The Frogs*) by the comic poet Aristophanes does seem to imply that Aeschylus had participated in the sacred rites of his native town (lines 886-887). The meaning of Aristotle's remark thus remains unclear.

In the years before his death, Aeschylus made at least two, possibly three, trips to

Sicily. For one of these trips, around 472 B.C. Aeschylus composed the tragedy *Aetnae*, honoring the foundation of the new city of Aetna by Hiero, the tyrant of Syracuse. In 456-455, during the last of these journeys, Aeschylus died in the city of Gela on Sicily's southern coast. The legend that arose concerning the death of Aeschylus is bizarre and almost certainly the invention of a later comic author. According to this legend, Aeschylus died when he was struck on the head by a tortoise that an eagle had been carrying off as prey. The eagle, it is said, had been searching for a place to smash the tortoise's shell and had mistaken Aeschylus' bald head for a stone.

The Greek traveler Pausanias states that Aeschylus composed his own epitaph, which, remarkably, contains no mention of his tragedies. "Beneath this monument lies Aeschylus of Athens, the son of Euphorion, who died in wheat-bearing Gela. The grove at Marathon could speak of his famed courage as could the long-haired Persians who learned of it there." Aeschylus left behind a number of relatives who also went on to become successful tragedians. In addition to his nephew Philocles, Aeschylus' sons Euphorion (who won first prize at the tragic festival of 431 B.C.) and Euaeon were famous dramatists.

Analysis

In Aristophanes' comedy *The Frogs* (lines 1019-1029), the poet Euripides challenges Aeschylus to explain what he did in his tragedies to make his audience more valiant and heroic. Aeschylus replies that he composed the *Hepta epi Thēbas* (467 B.C.; *Seven Against Thebes*, 1777), a play that filled everyone who saw it with a martial spirit. Aristophanes then goes on to say that Aeschylus' *The Persians* inspired young Athenians to imitate their elders' thirst for victory and contained a startling dramatic spectacle by bringing onstage the ghost of Darius, the dead king of the Persians.

These three elements—a spirit of heroism, a didactic tone, and lavish spectacle— were understood by Aeschylus' contemporaries to be the central features of his dramatic style. That style is already present in *The Persians*, the play that is considered to be the earliest of Aeschylus' seven extant tragedies. In *The Persians*, the Greeks' courageous defense of their homeland is coupled with a surprisingly sympathetic view of the Persians themselves. Moreover, while the Persians' defeat is presented in that play as due to the valor of the Greek warriors, Aeschylus attributes the Greek victory even more to the Persians' own hubris (excessive pride, over-confidence, and insolence). The didactic message of this play thus has meaning for the Greeks, as well as for their enemies: Pride can cause even a victorious army to be humbled; moderation is the safest path, even in success. That was a lesson that the Athenians would need to learn repeatedly throughout the fifth century B.C.

The lavish spectacle of Aeschylus' *The Persians* was due, in large part, to the magnificent costumes worn by the actors. In other plays, Aeschylus carried his interest in vivid spectacle even further. According to legend, at the first performance of the *Eumenides* (458 B.C.), pregnant women miscarried and children fainted at the horrifying appearance of the Furies. In the *Choēphoroi* (458 B.C.; *Libation Bearers*), the blood-drenched bodies of Aegisthus and Clytemnestra were displayed to the audience, and the robe in which Clytemnestra had entangled Agamemnon was unfurled in full view. These striking visual images, combined with the verbal imagery of Aeschylus' text, made these tragedies exceptionally vivid, at times even shocking, when they were first performed.

Aeschylus was also responsible for several important innovations in the staging and design of Greek tragedy. Born less than ten years after the victory of the tragic poet Thespis at the first Great Dionysia, Aeschylus invented many features that later ages would view as essential to Greek tragedy. Aristotle says in the *De poetica* (c. 334 B.C.- 323 B.C.; *Poetics*, 1705) that Aeschylus increased the number of actors from one to two, reduced the size of the chorus, and made dialogue prominent in his plays. Before Aeschylus' time, tragedy consisted of a single actor whose role was limited to exchanges with a large chorus. The introduction of a second actor permitted Aeschylus to explore different points of view, report new information from offstage, and create a more natural flow of dialogue. The character played by the second actor could question the protagonist about why a certain course of action was chosen. The second actor could also respond, either rationally or emotionally, to what the protagonist had said.

This questioning and interchange between the first and second actors was central to the dramatic purpose of Aeschylus. Unlike later playwrights such as Sophocles and Euripides, Aeschylus was interested in sweeping historical and religious forces more than in individual characters. This concern is also why Aeschylus preferred to write connected trilogies where a single theme or story was traced through all three plays. (The "trilogies" of Sophocles and Euripides were not trilogies at all in the modern sense. They were simply three plays performed on a single occasion.) In the *Oresteia* (458 B.C.; English translation, 1777), for example, Aeschylus traced the fulfillment of a curse through several generations of the same family. In the trilogy that contained the *Prometheus desmōtēs* (479 B.C.; *Prometheus Bound*, 1777), Aeschylus explored the nature of power and the development of justice among the gods.

Great theological questions, such as Why do people suffer? and How can a supremely good and supremely powerful deity permit evil in the world?, were never far from Aeschylus' mind. At times, the chorus deals with these issues explicitly as it comments upon the action of the play. At other times, the question is raised through the development of the plot itself.

Aeschylus' view is always panoramic, dealing with difficult questions and eschewing simple answers. While Euripides would later be criticized for his fascination with disreputable human impulses, Aeschylus could reinterpret even a base or primitive myth so as to give it a lofty religious and moral tone. In Aeschylus' treatment, for example, the slaying of Agamemnon and its consequences are transformed into an examination of retributive justice and its limits. In the *Seven Against Thebes*, the moral ambiguity of the encounter between Eteocles and Polyneices is eliminated: To Aeschylus, the defender of Thebes was right and the traitor to Thebes was wrong, and their situations were not at all comparable. As Aristophanes has Aeschylus say in *The Frogs* (lines 1053-1054, 1056), "It is the duty of the poet to hide the base, not to teach it or to display it in clear view. . . . Most of all, it is our duty to discuss what is noble." That is a value which may be seen in each of Aeschylus' plays.

Aeschylus' panoramic vision and his eagerness to address complex issues may also be seen in his frequent dramatic use of the "double bind." A double bind occurs when a character is doomed to failure no matter which alternative action is chosen. Nearly every Aeschylean tragedy presents at least one character who is caught in this type of situation. Thus, Orestes must either kill his mother or leave his father un-avenged, Eteocles must either face his own brother in battle or doom Thebes by leaving one of its gates undefended, and Pelasgus in the *Hiketides* (463 B.C.?; *The Suppliants*; also published as *Suppliant Women*) must either face war with the Egyptians or permit the Danaids to pollute his sanctuary with their suicide. In each of these cases, there is no simple solution, no solution at all that will avoid great suffering to the central characters. Yet the moral problems that interested Aeschylus were always ones in which this type of dilemma must be faced and somehow resolved.

The human characters of Aeschylus' plays seem entangled in forces far larger than themselves, in insoluble paradoxes, great curses and divine plans that may take several generations to be understood. This grand design of Aeschylean tragedy has also affected the language of his plays. Aristophanes has Aeschylus say in *The Frogs* (lines 1059-1061) that, "the poet must choose words equal to his great thoughts and ideas. God-like men should use more majestic words than ordinary men, just as their cloaks are more splendid than ours." As a result, the language used by Aeschylus is rich in compound words and difficult grammatical structures. For example, in the long opening chorus of the *Agamemnōn* (458 B.C.; English translation, 1777), the two sons of Atreus are described as "twin-throned and twin-sceptered" (line 43), the expedition to recover Helen of Troy is termed "a woman-avenging war" (lines 225-226), and the gag that bound Iphigeneia before her sacrifice is called "the guardian of her fair-prowed mouth" (line 235). Similar examples may be found in any of Aeschylus' tragedies. These difficult, often ponderous terms help maintain the spirit of grandeur that the poet is trying to evoke and elevate his language over that of everyday speech.

SEVEN AGAINST THEBES

First produced: *Hepta epi Thēbas*, 467 B.C. (English translation, 1777)
Type of work: Play

A curse upon the ruling house of Thebes is fulfilled as the king must do battle with his own brother, who is one of seven generals attacking the city.

The *Seven Against Thebes* was the third play in a 467 B.C. trilogy that also included the tragedies *Laius* and *Oedipus*, both of which are now lost. At its first performance, the *Seven Against Thebes* would have provided a climax, summarizing themes that the poet had been developing through two previous tragedies. In this way, the *Seven Against Thebes* would have been similar to the *Eumenides* (458 B.C.; English translation, 1777) in presenting the final results of a curse that had long afflicted a particular family.

The political situation of Athens in Aeschylus' own day had an important effect upon the *Seven Against Thebes*. First, though the tragedy is set in Thebes and deals exclusively with Theban characters, neither the word "Thebes" nor "Thebans" appears anywhere in the tragedy. Aeschylus is careful always to replace these terms with the Homeric expressions "city of Cadmus" and "Cadmeans," recalling the name of the mythical founder of Thebes. Aeschylus did that because Thebes had gone over to the enemy in the Persian Wars. Direct reference to the city was thus likely to offend his audience. The recent end of the Persian Wars also helps to explain why the chorus refers to the invading army as "foreign-tongued" (line 170, one of Aeschylus' characteristic compound adjectives), even though, according to legend, this army was composed of Argives and Thebans. Athens had recently emerged victorious over a "foreign-tongued" enemy, and the audience would naturally associate an invading army with alien speech.

The passions roused by the Persian Wars explain why Aeschylus sees the conflict between Eteocles and Polyneices as less morally ambiguous than did his successors. Both Sophocles, in the *Antigonē* (441 B.C.; *Antigone*), and Euripides, in the *Phoinissai* (c. 410 B.C.; *The Phoenician Women*), presented the two brothers as each having right on their sides, at least to some degree. Yet Aeschylus had fought in a battle caused by the treason of Hippias, the exiled tyrant of Athens who had led the Persians to Marathon. Unlike Sophocles and Euripides, therefore, Aeschylus could not present treachery to one's native city as justifiable for any reason. That is why only Eteocles' point of view is presented in this play and the audience is shown only the tragedy of a warrior who dies defending his country.

Since the original audience's memories of the Persian Wars were still fresh, the issues addressed by the *Seven Against Thebes* would have been particularly interesting when the play was first performed. Those issues, and the sheer grandeur of Aeschylus' language and the costumes worn by his characters, would also have made the play seem less "static" than it does when it is read today. It is sometimes said that the central episode of this tragedy, in which each of the seven generals of the invading army is first described and then paired with a defender of the city, resembles the catalog passages of epic poetry rather than the tense drama of most Greek tragedy. Nevertheless, it should be remembered that there is tension in this scene as Eteocles misses one opportunity after another to avoid meeting his own brother in battle. It should also be remembered that Greek audiences, far more than later audiences, enjoyed vivid description for its own sake and would have delighted in Aeschylus' account of the armor and blazons of the seven enemy generals.

ORESTEIA

First produced: 458 B.C.; includes *Agamemnōn* (*Agamemnon*, 1777);
                    Choēphoroi (*Libation Bearers*, 1777); *Eumenides* (English
                    translation, 1777)
Type of work: Play

As this trilogy begins, Agamemnon, king of Argos, is slain by his wife, Clytemnestra, after returning from the Trojan War; his son, Orestes, avenges the death by killing Clytemnestra and her lover, Aegisthus; haunted for this crime by the Furies, Orestes is freed when a new court is established at Athens.

The *Oresteia* is the only ancient Greek trilogy to survive. (Sophocles' Theban Trilogy consists of three plays that were actually written many years apart and never performed together during the poet's lifetime.) The three plays of the *Oresteia* are the *Agamemnon*, the *Libation Bearers*, and the *Eumenides* ("kindly ones" or "furies"). The *Proteus* (458 B.C.), the *Oresteia*'s satyr play (a humorous work traditionally performed at the end of a trilogy), has been lost; it is unclear whether the *Proteus* would have continued the plot of the *Oresteia* or, as is more likely, dealt with the encounter of Odysseus and Proteus described in the *Odyssey* (eighth century B.C.; first codified early second century B.C.; English translation, 1616).

A central motif of the *Oresteia* is the curse that has afflicted Agamemnon's family for several generations. Tantalus, Agamemnon's great-grandfather, had slaughtered his own son, Pelops, after divulging the secrets of the Olympian gods and stealing from them the nectar and ambrosia that conveyed immortality. Pelops, whom the gods later restored, betrayed and killed the charioteer, Myrtilus, by pushing him from a cliff. As Myrtilus fell to his death, he cursed Pelops and all of his descendants; that was the origin of the curse upon this household. Pelops' son, Atreus, butchered the children of his brother, Thyestes, and tricked Thyestes into eating the flesh of his own sons. When Thyestes learned what he unwittingly had done, he cursed Atreus and all of his children; the curse upon the house of Atreus was thus renewed. Atreus' son, Agamemnon, after whom the first play in this trilogy was named, sacrificed his own daughter, Iphigeneia, in order to obtain winds necessary to carry him to Troy. There, Agamemnon was responsible for the defeat of the Trojan army and the slaughter of many innocent victims.

This entire line of bloodshed, crime, and curse all devolves upon the single figure of Orestes, the son of Agamemnon who gives his name to the trilogy. Orestes must put an end to the curse, and he can do so only with the help of the gods. Moreover, Orestes stands at the end of another line, a line not of kinship this time, but of vengeance or retributive justice. The Trojan War began when Paris, the son of the Trojan king Priam, abducted Helen, the wife of Agamemnon's brother, Menelaus. To avenge this crime, Agamemnon and Menelaus were responsible for the deaths of many innocent victims, including Agamemnon's daughter, Iphigeneia. To avenge her death, Agamemnon is killed by his wife, Clytemnestra, in the first play of the *Oresteia*. Orestes is then bound by duty and honor to avenge his father, but to do so would entail killing his mother. Caught in this "double bind," Orestes can escape only with the gods' help. To end the cycle of retribution, the gods Apollo and Athena must intervene and create a new institution, a court that for all future time will replace endless reprisals with divine justice.

Seen from one perspective, therefore, the *Oresteia* traces the development of law from the time when its enforcement rested with the family to the poet's own day when the enforcement of law was overseen by the courts. The Areopagus, the court that Athena establishes in the *Eumenides*, was still operating in Aeschylus' lifetime. Though the court's charter had been restricted by the liberal statesman Ephialtes only four years before the *Oresteia* was first performed, the Areopagus still had jurisdiction in most murder trials, as Aeschylus suggests.

The development of the Athenian court is presented in the *Oresteia* as a necessary step in human progress. Without the court, justice would not be possible since law would be enforced according to the dictates of individual families, not the will of the city as a whole.

Aeschylus' religious perspective meant that the removal of the curse and the creation of the Athenian court were possible only through the intervention of the gods. Only a divine power, Aeschylus argues, has the perspective necessary to see larger issues at work. Ordinary mortals, living for only a single generation, are limited in terms of the experience upon which they can base their judgments. The gods, however, are detached from the passions that afflict the mortals in these plays. They can maintain a proper perspective, see "the big picture," and develop solutions that would never have occurred to the protagonists themselves. By writing connected trilogies such as the *Oresteia*, Aeschylus sought to convey some of this larger perspective to his audience, to encourage them to think, not merely in terms of their own time, but in terms of all of human history.

In order to provide some unity to sprawling trilogies such as the *Oresteia*, Aeschylus used repeated patterns of imagery that could remind the audience of earlier episodes. For example, in the opening scene of the *Agamemnon*, the image of light rising out of darkness is used repeatedly. The watchman is lying upon the roof of the palace at dawn, when a new light appears in the east. Rather than the rising sun, however, it is the beacon fire, arranged by Clytemnestra, which signals the end of the war at Troy. This "false dawn"—literally false, since the fire is man-made and not a natural light—creates a sense of foreboding that is soon fulfilled. The promise of a new dawn of peace goes unkept when Agamemnon, who survived ten years of fighting at Troy, is slain by his own wife upon his return home. This imagery of light and darkness occurs again at the very end of the trilogy when torches are lit for a procession guiding the Eumenides back to their subterranean home. The hope is that, this time, the "new dawn" really will bring peace to Argos and end the curse upon the house of Atreus. The Eumenides, addressed as the "children of night" (*Eumenides*, line 1034), are asked to bless all the earth and ensure that the long-awaited dawn of peace truly has arrived.

Another common source of imagery in the *Oresteia* is the imagery of blood. In Greek, as in English, the word "blood" (*haima*) has a number of different connotations: It may be used to symbolize the family ("bloodline," "blood relation"), violence ("bloodshed," "blood bath"), or miasma ("bloodstained," "bloodguilt"). The loss of blood may be seen as medicinal ("bloodletting") or violent ("blood spilling"). Because of these different impressions conveyed by the word "blood," Aeschylus uses this root repeatedly in describing the house of Atreus, a family afflicted by violence and miasma, a family where those related by blood so frequently shed one another's blood.

Imagery of animals also appears in the *Oresteia*, with many different connotations. For example, in the *Agamemnon*, the attack upon Troy by Agamemnon and Menelaus is compared first to an attack of eagles shrieking for their lost young (lines 49-51), then to birds of prey brutally seizing a pregnant hare (lines 114-120). Similarly, Orestes in the *Libation Bearers* refers to himself and Electra as "the orphaned offspring of their father, the eagle" (line 247). These images are useful in that they associate Agamemnon with both the regal splendor of the eagle and this bird's ferocious savagery. Other animal imagery is also common in the *Oresteia*: The watchman lies upon the palace roof "dog-like" (*Agamemnon*, line 3); Helen of Troy is like a lion cub who causes grief for those who had nurtured it (*Agamemnon*, lines 716-736); Aegisthus is a "powerless lion who rolls in his master's bed" (*Agamemnon*, line 1224); Clytemnestra and Aegisthus are twin snakes who have been slain by a single stroke (*Libation Bearers*, line 1047); and the god Apollo contemptuously calls the Furies "a herd of goats who lack a herdsman" (*Eumenides*, line 196). In this way, Aeschylus uses imagery of animals both to reinforce the nature of his characters and, by repeating and developing certain images, to provide a sense of continuity throughout his extended trilogy.

PROMETHEUS BOUND

First produced: *Prometheus desmōtēs*, after 479 B.C. (English translation, 1777)
Type of work: Play

At the order of Zeus, the Titan Prometheus is bound to a rock in the Caucasus as punishment for aiding humankind.

Prometheus Bound was the first work in a 479 B.C. trilogy that also included the plays *Prometheus Lyomenos* (*Prometheus Unbound*) and *Prometheus Pyrphoros* (*Prometheus the Fire-Bearer*), neither of which have survived. Since the final two dramas of the trilogy have been lost, it is difficult to determine Aeschylus' original intention for the work as a whole. This problem is intensified since the date of the trilogy is unknown. A reference (lines 363-372) to the eruption of Mount Aetna in 479 means that *Prometheus Bound* must date later than this event. Aside from that, however, scholars cannot agree whether the play was written early or late in Aeschylus' career or even whether it is a genuine work of Aeschylus.

The theme of *Prometheus Bound* is the conflict between force and justice. The supreme god Zeus has recently assumed control of the universe from the Titans and is ruling like a petty tyrant. He has bound Prometheus to a rock in a remote corner of the earth because Prometheus gave the gift of fire to humankind, a race whom Zeus had sought to destroy. To the original Athenian audience, which had expelled the tyrant Hippias only in 510 B.C., Aeschylus' references to tyranny in this play would have been topical. Moreover, it is surprising to find that these references are applied to the god Zeus, usually depicted in Aeschylean tragedy as the defender of justice and the patron of civil law.

The reason for the strange image of Zeus in this play was probably made clear in parts of the trilogy now lost. Justice, in Greek society, was frequently seen as a balance or a sense of proportion among conflicting demands. In the *Prometheus Bound*, Zeus, early in his reign, has not yet attained that balance. As the trilogy progressed, a sense of proportion must have been found between Zeus's excessive desire for order and Prometheus' extreme desire to benefit humankind. (Indeed, Prometheus is described as bestowing honors upon mortals "beyond what was just," at line 30. In the last line of the play, Prometheus states that Zeus has punished him "beyond what was just," line 1093.) Justice can only occur when there is a complete proportion of all things, including both discipline and mercy.

Like the *Seven Against Thebes*, *Prometheus Bound* has been criticized as being a "static" play. Indeed, once Prometheus has been bound to the rock in the opening moments of the tragedy, nothing "happens" on stage for the duration of the drama. Oceanos and his daughters arrive to give comfort to Prometheus. Hermes brings additional threats from Zeus. Beyond these, however, there is no movement in the tragedy. In the *Prometheus Bound*, this lack of movement intensifies the audience's sense of Prometheus' punishment. The drama becomes as motionless as the captive protagonist himself, and, even at the end of the tragedy, it is unclear how additional progress may be possible. The way in which Aeschylus solved this problem would only have been revealed in the next two plays of the trilogy.

Summary

The tragedies of Aeschylus are dramas of incredible grandeur. Their language is intentionally elevated over the common speech of everyday life. Their focus is upon the great struggles of gods and heroes from the remote past. Their interpretation of Greek mythology presents sweeping historical or religious patterns rather than dwelling upon individual characters. Unlike Sophocles, who focused upon individual heroes in his dramas, or Euripides, who sought to bring even the gods down to the level of ordinary mortals, Aeschylus presented figures who were larger than life, figures who were entangled by forces even greater than themselves.

One of the sweeping historical patterns frequently encountered in Aeschylean tragedy is that of the "double bind." In this situation, characters find that they are doomed no matter what they do. In some cases, as in the *Seven Against Thebes*, the double bind arises because of a curse placed upon the hero's family. In other cases, such as in the *Oresteia*, the intervention of the gods is necessary in order to prevent the hero's destruction and to see that justice is restored to the world.

Bibliography

Earp, F. R. *The Style of Aeschylus*. Cambridge, England: Cambridge University Press, 1948.

Herington, John. *Aeschylus*. New Haven, Conn.: Yale University Press, 1986.

Hogan, James C. *A Commentary on the Complete Greek Tragedies: Aeschylus*. Chicago: University of Chicago Press, 1984.

Kuhns, Richard. *The House, the City, and the Judge: The Growth of Moral Awareness in the "Oresteia."* Indianapolis: Bobbs-Merrill, 1962.

Owen, E. T. *The Harmony of Aeschylus*. Toronto: Clarke, Irwin, 1952.

Podlecki, Anthony J. *The Political Background of Aeschylean Tragedy*. Ann Arbor: University of Michigan Press, 1966.

Smith, H. Weir. *Aeschylean Tragedy*. Berkeley: University of California Press, 1924.

Spatz, Lois. *Aeschylus*. Boston: Twayne, 1982.

Taplan, Oliver. *The Stagecraft of Aeschylus*. Oxford, England: Clarendon Press, 1977.

Jeffrey L. Buller

Principal Literary Achievement

One of England's most gifted and versatile contemporary writers, Amis has distinguished himself as a poet and as an essayist but above all as a seriocomic novelist.

Biography

Kingsley William Amis was born in London on April 16, 1922. His father, William Robert, worked as a senior clerk in the export division of Colman's Mustard and fully expected his only child to enter commerce. His son's intention, however, was to be a writer—a poet, really—though it was not until the publication of his rollicking and irreverent first published novel, *Lucky Jim* (1954), that Amis received worldwide recognition, winning the W. Somerset Maugham Award in 1955. By Amis' own account, he had been writing since he was a child, but without notable success. To read his early poetry is an embarrassment for him, he has said; his first novel, "The Legacy," written while he attended St. John's College, Oxford, and rejected by fourteen publishers, was later abandoned altogether because it was boring, unfunny, and loaded with affectation. He also considered the novel derivative: He felt that he was writing someone else's book, while what he wanted to say needed a new story and a new style.

Several factors influenced Amis' development into a writer whose novels and style are unique and universally recognized. His comic proclivities were encouraged by his father—a man with "a talent for physical clowning and mimicry." Amis describes himself as "undersized, law-abiding, timid," a child able to make himself popular by charm or clowning, who found that at school he could achieve much by exploiting his inherited powers of mimicry. That was true not only at the City of London School—where he specialized in the classics until he was sixteen, then switched to English—but also at Oxford, where he earned his B.A. (with honors) and M.A. degrees in English.

School friends testified to Amis' capacity for making others laugh. Philip Larkin's description of their first meeting in the introduction to his own novel *Jill* (1946, 1964), suggests that it was Amis' "genius for imaginative mimicry" that attracted him: "For the first time I felt myself in the presence of a talent greater than my own." The

novelist John Wain recalled how, in the "literary group" to which both of them belonged, Amis was a "superb mimic" who relished differences of character and idiom. Later as a writer, like Charles Dickens, Amis sometimes acted out with his face and his body the appearances and the actions of his characters while creating them. More important, many of his fictional people would appear as fine mimics themselves, using masquerades, role playing, practical jokes, and faces of all kinds for sheer enjoyment, to cover up certain insecurities, or to defend themselves from boredom and other unpleasantness in their lives.

This period of "intensive joke swapping," as Larkin called it, continued when Amis entered the army in 1942. He became an officer, served in the Royal Signals, and landed in Normandy in June, 1944. After service in France, Belgium, and West Germany, he was demobilized in October, 1945. He later recalled how he and a friend wrote part of a novel based on "malicious caricatures" of fellow officers. This period also was to provide material for stories such as "My Enemy's Enemy," "Court of Inquiry," and "I Spy Strangers"; its immediate effect, however, was to open his eyes to the world, to all sorts of strange people and strange ways of behaving.

Amis' status as an only child also added to his development as a writer, for at an early age he found himself seeking "self-entertainment." He read adventure stories, science fiction, and boys' comics. During these years, Amis also became interested in horror tales. After seeing the Boris Karloff version of *Frankenstein* (1931) and *The Mummy* (1932), Amis became interested in what might be called the minor genres for reasons of wonder, excitement, and "a liking for the strange, the possibly horrific." He became aware that the detective story, various tales of horror or terror, and the science-fiction story provided vehicles both for social satire and for investigation of human nature in a way not accessible to the mainstream novelist.

In view of his early tastes in reading, then, it is not surprising that Amis went on to write genre novels of his own. In *The Green Man* (1969), for example, he would turn the ghost story into an examination of dreaded death and all of its imagined horrors. In *The Riverside Villas Murder* (1973), he would use the detective story to explore how a child perceives the world: The detective analogy lies in the idea that the world of the senses is a series of clues, from which people try to piece together reality. In *The Alteration* (1976), he would use the counterfeit world of science fiction to dramatize a boy's attempt to comprehend the consequences of adulthood and of his possible failure even to experience that stage in the sexual sense. In these instances and others, Amis would use contemporary literary genres as a means of exploring a world both absurd and threatening.

Along with his natural comic gifts and his interest in genre fiction, Amis' development was affected by his initial exposure to an English tradition that resisted the modernist innovations influential in America and on the Continent. His dislike for experimental prose, for mystification, is attributable in part to the influence of one of his Oxford tutors, the Anglo-Saxon scholar Gavin Bone, and to Amis' readings of certain eighteenth century novelists, whose ability to bring immense variety and plentitude to their work without reverting to obscurity or stylistic excess Amis found appealing.

Amis attributes his personal standards of morality to his readings in Charles Dickens, Henry Fielding, and Samuel Richardson and to the training in standard Protestant virtues that he received as a boy at home. Both of his parents were Baptists, but in protest against their own forceful religious indoctrination, their visits to church became less frequent as they grew older. Any reader of Amis' works—for example, *Russian Hide-and-Seek* (1980) and *The Old Devils* (1986), for which he won the Booker Fiction Prize—soon becomes aware that there is in his writings a clear repudiation of traditional Christian belief. Nevertheless, from his parents he received certain central moral convictions that crystallized a personal philosophy of life and art. Hard work, concientiousness, obedience, loyalty, frugality, patience—these lessons and others were put forward and later found their way into his novels, all of which emphasize the necessity of good works and of trying to live a moral life in the natural—as opposed to the supernatural—world.

Analysis

Like most novelists, Amis is interested above all in human nature, and for most of his life he has trained both eye and ear upon the exploration of that subject in all of its fascinating dimensions. From that exploration a primary theme emerges, one to which Amis himself refers when writing about G. K. Chesterton, whom he greatly admired, and Chesterton's novel *The Man Who Was Thursday* (1908). In that book, Amis senses "a feeling that the world we see and hear and touch is a flimsy veil that only just manages to cover up a deeper and far more awful reality." It is a feeling that the reader encounters in Amis' work as well, for the assumption underlying his novels is that people live in a broken world. The ever-increasing erosion of traditional values, the breakdown of communication everywhere, the seeming absence of any spiritual reality, the impossibility of the existence of any heroic figures—these are some of the painful conclusions following an imaginative investigation into the world as seen by Amis.

These bleak realities are not, of course, new to the evolution of the novel. What distinguishes Amis is that he communicates what could be an otherwise overwhelmingly black vision in such an engaging, entertaining, and readable way. His wit, his sense of style, his devotion to language and its revelation of character, the range of emotions that he elicits from his reader, and the richness of his invention all compel respect and critical attention.

Although at times his vision is bleak, his novels rarely make for bleak reading. For always, beneath the entertainment and eighteenth and nineteenth century fictional techniques for which he is known, there runs a consistent moral judgment that advocates the virtues of hard work, responsibility, decency, faith, and love—an enduring, if beleaguered, value system that defends the English language, traditions, customs, and freedoms against all of their assorted enemies.

The first public manifestation of his moral vision appears in *Lucky Jim* (1954). From that point, its development is clear and consistent. In his early novels—*Lucky Jim*, *That Uncertain Feeling* (1955), and *I Like It Here* (1958)—his fictional world is filled with verbal jokes, amusing or disturbing role playing, and outrageous incidents. Detached from political causes and the progress of their own lives, the protagonists of these stories are part rebels, part victims, part clowns who seek to compromise with or to escape from such facts of life as boredom, hypocrisy, and ignorance. Although each novel carries a serious moral interest, the mishaps encountered and sometimes caused by its unlikely heroes generate laughter instead of tears, because the reader is led to believe that through all of this chaos there is an ordering of events that will ultimately bring security and happiness.

Beginning with *Take a Girl Like You* (1960), however, Amis' view of life grows increasingly pessimistic. Now the world is an opportunistic, self-centered one in which the heroine must fend for herself; life for this character is more serious, more precarious, and less jovial. In *One Fat Englishman* (1963), *The Anti-Death League* (1966), and *I Want It Now* (1968), life is often an absurd game in which the characters are suffering, often lonely individuals, with little chance for leading the good life, a life free from anxieties, guilts, and doubts.

In his next four novels, Amis' characters live on a darkling plain in a nightmare world in which both young and old are victims of a predominating malevolent presence. *The Green Man* (1969), *Girl, 20* (1971), *The Riverside Villas Murder* (1973), and *Ending Up* (1974) are exemplars of Amis' increasing concern with the question of human depravity, the ambiguity of perfidy, and the existence of evil forces in a world that is driven supposedly by the forces of good.

The potency of evil, the destructiveness of guilt, the often uncertain quest for identity and peace of mind, the perils of old age—these are some of Amis' central philosophical concerns in *The Alteration* (1976), *Jake's Thing* (1978), and *Russian Hide-and-Seek* (1980). Amis once again finds a great many ways to convey the message that human beings suffer, life is difficult, and comic masks conceal great anguish. Only occasionally is this grim picture relieved by some sort of idealism, some unexpected attitude of unselfishness and tenderness. In these novels, the social fabric has given way completely, so that the old mores no longer apply and, indeed, have either been replaced by depraved ones or not replaced at all, leaving a moral vacuum.

Finally, in *Stanley and the Women* (1984), *The Old Devils* (1986), *Difficulties with Girls* (1988), and *The Folks that Live on the Hill* (1990), Amis moves away from the broad scope of a society plagued by trouble to examine instead the troubles plaguing one of that society's most fundamental institutions: marriage. His characters are not going to regain the old sense of security that their lives once held, and Amis does not pretend that they will. What success they manage to attain is always partial. What, in the absence of an informing faith or an all-consuming family life, could provide purpose for living? More simply, how is one to be useful? This is the problem that haunts Amis' characters, and it is a question, underlying all of his novels, that now comes to the forefront.

LUCKY JIM

First published: 1954
Type of work: Novel

In this satire on life in an English provincial university, a young lecturer lives a highly comic secret life of protest against the hypocrisy and pseudointellectualism of certain members of the British establishment.

Lucky Jim belongs to the genre of fiction known as the picaresque novel—with its episodic lurchings, its opportunistic hero, and its emphasis on satirizing various English character types. Although resourceful, the picaro is by tradition simple, a naïf who reveals, by his simplicity, the tattered moral fabric of a society based on pretension. It is Amis' great achievement in *Lucky Jim* that he has taken the ramshackle form of the traditional picaresque novel, centralized his moral theme (the firm value of being one's own person), and added the conventional plot element of lovers separated by evil forces.

To develop his moral stance in *Lucky Jim*, Amis divides his characters into two easily recognizable groups: generally praiseworthy figures, the ones who gain the greatest share of the reader's sympathy, and evil or at best worldly and corrupt characters who obstruct the fortunes of the good ones. Jim (the awkward outsider), Julius Gore-Urquhart (his benefactor or savior), and Christine Callaghan (the decent girl who accepts Jim despite his faults) are distinguished by moral honesty, personal sincerity, and a lack of pretense. Among the antagonists are Professor Welch (Jim's principal tormentor), Bertrand Welch (the defeated boaster), and the neurotic Margaret Peel (the thwarted "witch"), all of whom disguise their motives and present a false appearance. Gore-Urquhart functions as a mediator between common sense (Jim) and excess (the Welches), providing the norm by which to judge other frequently unstable personalities.

As the protagonist, Jim Dixon's character is established immediately with the description of his dual predicaments: He has a job that he does not want but for financial reasons is trying hard to keep, and he has become involved, without quite knowing why, with Margaret, a younger but better-established colleague. It becomes immediately apparent that academic life for Jim is little more than a running duel with his superior, a never-ending speculation as to whether he will be dropped at the term's end or continued on probation for another year.

The picaresque novel is commonly a novel of quest, and Jim's standby and salvation through his own journey is a strong sense of humor that enables him to make light of much very real distress and disaster. Although he hates the Welch family, he knows that deference to them is essential if he is to retain his job. In order to maintain self-respect, however, he resorts to a comic fantasy world in which he can express rage or loathing toward certain imbecilities of the social group that the Welch set represents. His rude faces and clever pranks serve a therapeutic function—a means by which Jim can express token resistance that will not seriously endanger his always-tenuous position.

Late in the novel, Jim is to deliver an important public lecture at the college honoring Welch. Once again, Jim is underwhelmed by the absurdity of the situation. He gets drunk, perfectly parodies Welch's mannerisms to the glee of some onlookers and the dismay of others, and passes out in front of the whole assemblage. The lecture could have been Jim's ticket to a secure future. Instead, it is somewhat less than Jim's shining hour.

Yet just when it seems that Jim's career is at its nadir, his horizons expand. He is offered a job as secretary to Christine's uncle, Julius Gore-Urquhart, a wealthy patron of the arts. When Christine breaks off with Bertrand, she and Jim are free to begin a new romance with the magical attractions of London before them. In the end, the novel affirms the importance of common decency over pretension, of honesty over duplicity, of good intentions over bad. Jim makes his own luck, it seems, through kindness, decency, and good humor in the face of great distress.

The imaginative core of the novel, then, is not the *fact* that Jim rebels or that he wins, but in the *way* that he rebels and wins. The ending is a satisfying conclusion to all the comic injustices that have occurred earlier. This happy ending is not contrived; it comes about naturally and can be explained in part as a convention of the novel, in part as the protagonist's wish-fulfillment, in part as his final nose-thumbing at the spiteful and malicious people whom Amis brings to life. The ending is based on the affirmation of a moral order, and as such it is both acceptable and laudable.

THE GREEN MAN

First published: 1969
Type of work: Novel

A seduction, an orgy, a homosexual parson, two exorcisms, and a monster are features of this powerful and moving parable of the limitations and dismay inherent in the human condition.

The Green Man is a medieval coaching inn at Fareham, Hertfordshire, and fifty-three-year-old Maurice Allington is its landlord. Plagued by anxiety, fears, depression, discontent, and an inner emptiness, Maurice seeks peace of mind under conditions that militate against it. His principal reaction to this unhappiness is to immerse himself in the mundane activities of life. There, the reader meets Maurice as a man on the run—from himself. Drink, women, and the tedious minutiae of the innkeeping business offer more satisfying—if only temporary—escapes. Add to this disquiet and revulsion the ever-growing urge toward self-destruction, and there begins to be felt in this novel a truly contemporary pulsebeat. Like the typical protagonist in the works of Albert Camus, Maurice emerges most convincingly as a complicated, self-divided, haunted man in a world that does not make sense.

Unlike Jim Dixon, Allington is given the unique opportunity to make sense of the world through supernatural intervention. The Green Man has its own special ghost, the wicked Dr. Thomas Underhill, who used his knowledge of the black arts for various evil deeds, including the conjuring of a powerful monster, the novel's other "green man," a creature of branches and twigs and leaves capable of rending an ordinary man. Underhill's final triumph is to reveal his power beyond the grave in pursuit of Maurice and his daughter.

While other characters cannot believe in the ghost, the intensity of Maurice's belief invites the reader to suspend that disbelief. Amis eases his readers into an acceptance of the supernatural by means of a variety of elements: the common sense and worldly character of the narrator, the characterization of the guests, the skillful use of incidental details to create the air of reality. People eat, drink, argue, reconcile, read, share, and make love with little or no expectation that anything out of the ordinary will (or can) happen.

As the tension grows, so does Maurice; he passes through various stages of awakening to the truth of himself and another world. Underhill, as a *Doppelgänger*, is evidence that evil is a real and active presence in the world and not just a concoction of the mind. His ghost is also a means by which Amis can credibly account for the forces that seek Maurice's destruction—all that afflicts, mystifies, and weighs on him.

The discovery of Underhill's power brings Maurice to a deeper consideration of the question of survival after death and prepares him for a conversation with still another supernatural agent, of quite a different kind from Underhill. Amis personifies God as a character in his own right, in the guise of a young man who expresses puzzlement and a certain degree of helplessness over the events unfolding in the world of his creation. Maurice's transformation from an alienated man to an unwitting hero who chooses to take on the responsibilities of an absentee God forms the dramatic core of the novel.

In his pursuit and eventual destruction of Underhill and the monster, Maurice gains self-knowledge. He begins to realize that his "affinity" to Underhill has taken many guises. Maurice has reduced people to mere objects, beings manipulated and controlled by a more powerful master, just as Underhill controlled his monster. For Underhill, further, sex and aggression and striving for immortality are all bound up together; it becomes clear, as Maurice struggles with the evil spirit, that the same holds true for him.

When the terrifying battle is finally over and the selfish Maurice has been softened by the closeness of disaster, he recognizes and responds for the first time to the love of his daughter, who agrees to look after him. Thus, the book is about moral education. Although the haunting was a terrifying experience, for Maurice it was also a rewarding one, for he has changed; he wants hereafter to be kind, not because social mores (in the shape of family and friends) tell him to do so, but because he has learned from facing his own potential for wickedness how destructive evil can be in any form. In exorcising Underhill and the monster, he has also exorcised the evil potential in his own character. The experience has ennobled him. He accepts the limitations of life and, most important, comes to an appreciation of what death has to offer—a permanent escape from himself.

JAKE'S THING

First published: 1978
Type of work: Novel

Jake Richardson holds a grudge against the world, a world of change and instability that is reflected on a personal level in his impotence.

In *Jake's Thing*, much more is going on with Jake Richardson than his loss of sexual control; the society in which he lives, the London and the Oxford of 1978, has also moved, subtly but surely, out of his range of understanding and/or desire, and Jake has responded by becoming bitter and cynical. A fifty-nine-year-old Oxford don, neither his career nor his other activities stimulate much interest in him, so that his desires—social, professional, emotional—have become as stultified as his sexual ones. Perhaps it is not coincidental that Jake's impotence comes at a time when Comyas College is debating the question of admitting women to its hallowed, previously all-male-inhabited halls. Jake, who is fighting for his psychic life on several fronts, inadvertently exposes his deep hostility to the project during a college meeting, where his colleagues had expected him to "speak for the ladies." At the end of his travail, and after nearly three hundred pages of unrelenting exposure to the incompetence and stupidity of professional therapists and the institutions that sustain them, Jake's desire for sex is gone, his dislike for women has intensified, and he decides that he would just as soon remain impotent.

Like Jim Dixon, Jake Richardson is an academic misfit who likes to drink, has a keen eye for hypocrites and phoneys, writes articles that bore even himself, copes with ferocious inner monologues on his own prejudices and irrational likes and dislikes, has a rollicking sense of fun, plays practical jokes, enjoys puns and wordplay, and talks to himself in voices that parody types whom he has encountered in books, television, movies, the army, and the academy. Like Jim, he suffers from the undesired attentions of a neurotic woman who stages a fake suicide attempt. Both characters manage to reconcile inner thoughts and outer statements in a public denunciation of a cause, delivered while they are drunk.

Many of the comic set pieces in *Jake's Thing* are reminiscent of some of the classic scenes in *Lucky Jim*, in that they serve to set the protagonist's role as an outsider to the contemporary world. That alienation often serves to parody the protagonist himself. Like Jim Dixon, Jake is caught in a snare of his own devising; his readiness to do battle with his foes and his gift for running into squabbles, fights, and embarrassments increase the chaos in a life that is already frustratingly out of control. Those frustrations are many, as they were for Jim, and signify the social and cultural impotence that Jake feels. The world around him is no longer to his liking, and everyday incidents painfully amplify that effect. Jake is no longer at home on his own turf, and that sense of foreignness compels him to withdraw further and further from the contemporary world. Jim's problems with his department chairman, with some of his students, and with a potential publisher for his essay on shipbuilding techniques are, of course, similar sources of frustration and outward signs that he is a man out of sync, immersed in the wrong culture for his personality.

In spite of the resemblances between the two novels, however, there is in fact a great conceptual jump from one to the other. Suffering from a general weariness, of which his loss of libido is but one indication, Jake has definite feelings about the modern world: He does not like it. There is no equivocation, no attempt to be "fair," to look at things from other angles as Jim was inclined to do. The world is going from bad to worse, changes that infuriate and baffle Jake. Included on his list of personal dislikes are airplanes, American tourists, psychologists, the working class, the young, strangers, sloppy language, wealthy Arabs, cocky youngsters, advertisements, telephones, architecture, cuisine—in other words, all facets of present-day England. Above all, he discovers that he despises women. His only real pleasure is in finding his expectations of dirt, decay, inefficiency, and boring and stupid behavior fulfilled. Amis' use of Jake's seething narration, his scathing internal commentary, and his sometimes vicious dialogue is instrumental in creating the universe of misogyny, prejudice, and dissatisfaction.

While *Lucky Jim* ends with a triumphant revelation to Jim of a new life, a new world, *Jake's Thing* ends with a closing down, a spurning of the world for which Jake feels at best indifferent—a retreat into TV dinners and TV movies. By the end of the novel, Jake has arrived at a stage of rejecting everything. Evidence points to a deepening misanthropy in Jake as he agonizes over his spiritual isolation, vainly attempts to recover his interest in sex, and learns to come to terms with impotence and acedia, the deathlike condition of not caring. In the end, readers see in Jake a gesture of impotence, puzzlement, anger, and eventual retreat from the contemporary world. All of this gives to the novel an overall mood of defeat and confusion far removed from the light comedy so much in evidence in *Lucky Jim*. Amis has come from the notion that one can choose to be happy (as in *Lucky Jim*) to the statement that there is no happiness possible in this world and one must accept powerlessness as a natural state.

THE OLD DEVILS

First published: 1986
Type of work: Novel

Through a microcosm of failed human relationships, Amis depicts the culmination of the decay of contemporary life.

The Old Devils tells of Alun Weaver, who has chosen to retire from his successful television career in London as a kind of "professional Welshman" and third-rate
poet and return after thirty years with his beautiful wife, Rhiannon, to South Wales.
The novel explores over a span of a few months the effect of this return on their
circle of old friends from university days.

The old devils—a group of Welsh married couples all in their sixties and seventies—
are retired. They do little else than reminisce about lost opportunities and a grander
Wales and grumble about slipping dentures, dietary restrictions, and dwindling physical energies while drinking steadily, ignoring the large role alcohol has played in the
mental, physical, and spiritual decay about which they complain. The men, however,
are not alone in their reverence for the bottle. At the same time, their spouses gather
elsewhere, ostensibly to drink coffee but more often to consume bottle after bottle of
wine, to chain smoke, and to pursue conversations about their marriages, sex, and
assorted other topics in an atmosphere reeking of alcohol fumes and stale cigarettes.

The physical ill health these cronies worry about extends to the spiritual health of
their marriages. With one major exception, the women in this novel are not only
plain, hard, sharp, critical, or cross but also lack any reasonable relation with their
husbands that would make significant communication possible. Only Alun and Rhiannon, married for thirty-four years, seem still to have an appetite for life and love as
well as drink, and most of their misunderstandings lead only to teasing, not to disaster. Yet their arrival arouses conflict among their old friends.

The conflict comes in part because their return revives memories of various youthful liaisons and indiscretions, and also because the egotistical Alun immediately sets
out to re-woo the three women with whom he had affairs in the old days. Alun plays
at adultery as if it were an idle pastime: His casual tone, however, is a poor disguise
for the emptiness and pain felt by his objects of attention, or by his wife, Rhiannon,
who tolerates his philandering, or by the husbands, who either suspect it or know of
it yet are resigned to doing nothing about it. Near the end of the story, Alun chokes
on his whiskey and water and falls forward, dead of a stroke. Given his reputation, it
is not surprising to find that there is no sadness over his death—only surprise, and a
thought or two that are quickly brushed aside by the others as a minor inconve-
nience.

The Old Devils is about more than an aging present; it is also very much about the past and its impingements upon everyone. Many of the characters in *The Old Devils* are carrying scars from bitterness and regret because of something that happened in their lives long ago, something they hide carefully from the world but on which their conscious attention is fixed. Past choices weigh heavily on all of them. These old devils are bedeviled by worries and fears of all kinds that deepen their uncertainty about life and increase their preoccupation with the past. Indeed, Amis points out that one of the reasons old people make so many journeys into the past is to satisfy themselves that it is still there. Yet when that, too, is gone, what is left? In this novel, what remains is only the sense of lost happiness not to be regained, only the awareness of the failure of love, only the present and its temporary consolations of drink, companionship, music, and any other diversions that might arise, only a blind groping toward some insubstantial future. Neither human nor spiritual comfort bolsters the sagging lives and flagging souls of the characters.

As in earlier novels, Amis finds in the everyday concerns of his ordinary folk a larger symbolic meaning, which carries beyond the characters to indict a whole country. In this story, unemployment is high, people lead purposeless lives, and the culture is dying. Buses are always late. Businesses suffer from staff shortages. There is an obvious absence of trade and enterprise, mines are closed, docks are dead. A local chapel has been deconsecrated and turned into an arts center; another has been converted into a two-screen pornographic theater, two extremes that underline the uselessness of the spiritual and its transformation from the divine into the mundane. Thus, the novel examines an often debilitating process of moral and spiritual decay, a lessening of these people as human beings as life goes on and how their hopes have dimmed along with their physical and mental powers.

Summary

In all of his novels, Kingsley Amis tries to understand the truth about different kinds of human suffering and then passes it on to the reader without distortion, without sentimentality, without evasion, and without oversimplification. Underlying all Amis' novels is the hero's quest for happiness, for meaning, for a life of morality and common sense in an ever-darkening world. In thirty-six years, he moved from fundamentally decent people who choose to act in a manner that has at least some significance, to utterly depraved ghosts, to people young and old stripped of their humanity, impotent and mad. The objects of his humor have broadened and deepened over the years, too.

No one can deny Amis' great technical gifts. He has never forgotton that the traditional first aim of most writers has always been to please the reader. The popularity of his art, the impressive body of critical literature, the review attention and honors given him—all testify to his continuing hold on the popular imagination. He is a writer for difficult, changing times.

Bibliography

Bradford, Richard. *Kingsley Amis.* London: Edward Arnold, 1989.

Gardner, Philip. *Kingsley Amis.* Boston: Twayne, 1981.

McDermott, John. *Kingsley Amis: An English Moralist.* Basingstoke, England: Macmillan, 1989.

Ritchie, Harry. *Success Stories: Literature and the Media in England, 1950-1959.* London: Faber, 1988.

Salwak, Dale, ed. *Kingsley Amis: In Life and Letters.* New York: St. Martin's Press, 1990.

_____. *Kingsley Amis: Modern Novelist.* London: Harvester Wheatsheaf, 1992.

_____. *Kingsley Amis: A Reference Guide.* Boston: G. K. Hall, 1978.

Dale Salwak

MARTIN AMIS

Born: Oxford, England
August 25, 1949

Principal Literary Achievement
Amis established himself as a master of satire by revealing the grotesque distortions of a world destroying itself with drugs, sex, crime—and environmental pollution.

Biography

Martin Louis Amis was born on August 25, 1949, in Oxford, England. He is the son of Kingsley Amis, the famous novelist, and Hilary Amis, daughter of a shoe-manufacturing millionaire. These parents would soon plunge young Martin into a kind of nomadic existence as they moved from one place to another, an odyssey that would require him to attend no fewer than fourteen different schools and live in at least three different countries. This heterogeneous background, in fact, may well account for his uncanny ability to appreciate various cultures, classes, and occupations.

Martin Amis, along with his older brother Philip and younger sister Sally, spent his early childhood years in Swansea, southern Wales, where the elder Amis held a teaching position at Swansea University. While in Swansea, Kingsley Amis published his most famous novel, *Lucky Jim* (1954), and the instant success of that novel initiated a string of new teaching appointments, including a crucially important year (1959) in Princeton, New Jersey. During that year, the ten-year-old Martin began to acquire his lifelong fascination with the exuberance of American slang, as shown much later in his brilliantly comic masterpiece *Money: A Suicide Note* (1984), which is set in both New York and London.

In 1960 the Amis family settled once more in England, this time in Cambridge, but the family unity was shattered the next year, when Kingsley and Hilary Amis were divorced. Young Martin spent the next year (1962) on the island of Majorca, Spain, in the company of his mother, sister, and brother. There he attended an international school with a wide variety of students. In 1963, he returned to England and briefly became a professional actor by landing a role in the film production of *A High Wind in Jamaica* (1965). During the next year, he attended school in London, where the primary focus of his life was social not academic, for he spent the bulk of his time investigating the lowlife of the city—not unlike the feckless ne'er-do-wells of *London Fields* (1989).

Around 1965, possibly under the influence of his stepmother-novelist, Elizabeth Jane Howard, Amis began to read serious literature and prepare himself for a university career by attending a series of "crammers" or preparatory schools. In 1968 he was admitted to Exeter College, Oxford; in 1971 he received a bachelor of arts degree with first-class honors in English.

Amis began his career as a man of letters in 1971, although at first he was operating strictly behind the scenes as a book reviewer for the *The Observer* and as editorial assistant and fiction and poetry editor of the London *Times Literary Supplement*. Simultaneously, public acclaim attached itself to the name of Martin Amis after the appearance of *The Rachel Papers* (1973), a largely autobiographical work about the detailed sexual exploits of a student named Charles Highway. Even though *The Rachel Papers* was Amis' first novel, it received unusually lavish praise from the demanding British reviewers and won the prestigious Maugham Award in 1974, exactly twenty years after his father had won the same award for *Lucky Jim*.

In 1975 Martin Amis became the assistant literary editor of the *New Statesman*, a magazine with which he would remain closely associated after becoming a full-time writer for that publication. In 1975 Amis also wrote his second novel, the controversial *Dead Babies* (1975), which explores the effects of drugs in a communelike setting that is destroyed by horrifying violence. This gruesome and realistic treatment of drug-induced madness caused the second American publisher to change the title to *Dark Secrets* (1977).

Success (1978), Amis' third novel, continues his preoccupation with sexual excess as well as with autobiographical elements. Certainly, it can be no coincidence that the narrative plot of *Success* revolves around the lives of two brothers (Terry and Gregory Riding) and one sister (Ursula). The additional element of incest caused quite a few reviewers to find the book repugnant or brutish, even though it clearly deals with the larger theme of old and new money—and of class warfare—in Britain.

In 1980 Amis became embroiled in a strange and celebrated case of literary plagiarism when he discovered that the American essayist and novelist Jacob Epstein had plagiarized some fifty passages from *The Rachel Papers* while composing *Wild Oats* (1980). Epstein later conceded his guilt, but the exact number of passages used was never established to Amis' complete satisfaction. Nor was Amis completely pleased by the revised edition of *Wild Oats* (with all of the plagiarized passages excised). It is worth noting that Amis took no legal action against Epstein; his primary concern, as always, was his integrity as an author.

Amis' fourth novel, *Other People: A Mystery Story* (1981), bears a close resemblance to *Success* in its use of the *Doppelgänger* or "double" motif—a pattern that has been underscored by scholars and critics of Amis' work. Instead of closely related brothers, *Other People* features the closely related sides or "halves" of a woman whose personality is split into two beings, one called Mary Lamb, the other Amy Hide.

Martin Amis married Antonia Phillips, an American professor specializing in aesthetics, in 1984. That same year he published *Money*, an extravagant, witty, and linguistically inventive book that began to reveal the extent of his maturing talent. The hero, John Self, an alcoholic self-abuser, looms as an obese figure of comic pathos. Yet his story is also the story of the failure to make art—even bad art in the form of a pornographic movie—in a culture of pure greed. One of the "characters" in *Money* happens to be a young British novelist named Martin Amis.

After the publication of *Money*, Amis turned his attention to the collecting and publishing of the various essays and occasional short stories he had written for periodicals and newspapers. *The Moronic Inferno and Other Visits to America* (1986) and *Einstein's Monsters* (1987) were the well-received results. *London Fields*, his biggest and most ambitious novel, somehow manages to combine journalistic precision with the kinds of literary invention that have made Amis a significant presence on the literary scene.

Analysis

On first reading Martin Amis' books, the reader will probably hear echoes of many twentieth century novelists. One perceives the zany, scatological world of Philip Roth, the skewed universe of Truman Capote, the meditative voice of Saul Bellow, the complicated plot lines of Thomas Pynchon or Kurt Vonnegut, and the high-voltage linguistic displays of Tom Wolfe, Vladimir Nabokov, and Anthony Burgess. Yet even though Amis has written about many of these famous novelists (especially in *The Moronic Inferno and Other Visits to America*), he remains stylistically unique. There is a certain blending of choppy British street slang, complicated literary allusions, playful puns or witticisms, and outrageously irreverent names that collectively brand each piece of fiction as belonging only to Amis. To read Martin Amis is to experience the literary equivalent of sky diving or deep-sea diving, where the most familiar objects become strange and surreal and where time itself slows down or speeds up in a fashion that is altogether unnerving.

Style ultimately means the way an author invents and manipulates language to suit his or her particular requirements. In Amis' satiric universe, the intent is always to poke fun at the colossal moral and social breakdown of the twentieth century. Like all good satirists, Amis is making the reader laugh at outrageous and illogical events that might otherwise be taken for granted. If Amis writes about sexual degradation, greed, trickery, and lying, he is not glorifying but denouncing these low points of human behavior. One of his favorite devices to call forth laughter is to create ridiculously appropriate—or inappropriate—names, as did the great British novelist Charles Dickens when he created such memorable figures as Pip, Scrooge, and Tiny Tim.

In *Money*, for example, a novel-length parable on greed and self-absorption, Amis gives these pecuniary names to certain appropriate characters: Buck Specie, Sterling Dun, Lira Cruzeiros, Anna Mazuma. In this monetary madhouse, automobiles have a high visibility and high status value and so receive names such as Torpedo, Boomerang, Culprit, Alibi, Jefferson, Iago, Tigerfish, Autocrat, and Farrago. The hero, improbably named John Self, drives an ultra-expensive Fiasco, which is perpetually breaking down and requiring more and more expensive parts. John Self is engaged in hiring actors for his new film, and again the satiric creativity of Amis produces such actors' names as Nub Forkner, Butch Beausoleil, and Lorne Guyland. The technical crew is composed of Micky Obbs, Kevin Skuse, and Des Blackadder. All of these characters in Money-land calm their nerves with the angelic tranquilizer Serafim. Amis actually makes a guest appearance in his own novel, and as the character "Martin Amis" reminds John Self near the end of the narrative, "Names are awfully important."

These unforgettable and oddly appropriate names are perhaps the most distinctive stylistic trait in all of Amis' novels: Charles Highway in *The Rachel Papers*, Terry Service in *Success*, Mary Lamb in *Other People*, and the gallery of characters in *London Fields*, including Guy Clinch, Nicola Six, Keith Talent, Lizzyboo, Marmaduke, Chick Purchase, and Trish Shirt, among others. Names are indeed important to the artistry of Martin Amis.

Closely akin to the making of names is the making of new words, or neologisms, and Amis delights in coining new terms or concocting hyphenated phrases in a manner that outdoes Tom Wolfe or Anthony Burgess. The antihero of *Money*, for example, crisscrosses the vast space over the Atlantic Ocean as he shuttles back and forth between London and New York, leaving behind a wake of "jetslime." In the latter portions of the narrative, this same peripatetic John Self begins to perceive the hollowness of his own existence and castigates himself for being no more than a "cyborg" or "skinjob."

When Amis is not inventing new words, he feels free to push every key on the linguistic keyboard, from technical, scholarly, academic, and literary English all the way down the scales to American and British slang. In all of his books, four-letter words abound, as do slang terms like "yob" (lower-class person), "bim" (short for "bimbo", an unflattering term for a woman), "rug" (hair), and "snappers" (teeth). Amis simply delights in any kind of linguistic artifact, especially those that help to define a culture or a character. He is amused by the American tendency to misspell just about everything, to use apostrophes with plural nouns (*light's* for *lights*) or to enclose nouns in unnecessary quotation marks (*"coffee"* for *coffee*).

This obsession with language allows Amis to develop memorable characters (like John Self and Keith Talent) because their personality is equivalent to the way they speak and write. This same preoccupation with language also facilitates the development of larger themes that organize the many strands of Amis' narrative designs. He tends to work with a small number of basic themes that he explores in different ways—and at different levels of complexity—in all of his novels.

The critic Karl Miller, in his important study titled *Doubles: Studies in Literary History* (1985), identified the principal theme in Amis' work as "doubling." Plot lines, characters, and situations always tend to be echoed in the universe according to Amis, such as the two brothers in *Success* or the characters "Martin Amis" and "Martina Twain" in *Money*. The two other major themes in Amis' work are planetary decay and the Muse-like woman. *The Moronic Inferno and Other Vists to America*, *Money*, and *London Fields* all presuppose a world on the brink of ecological disaster. In this world there is always a magnetic feminine presence, such as Selina Street or the inscrutable Nicola Six, whose blandishments and seductions literally keep the men moving through a world of smog, AIDS, and gamma rays.

MONEY

First published: 1984
Type of work: Novel

English film-director John Self tries unsuccessfully to launch a pornographic film in New York and in the process goes bankrupt.

Money: A Suicide Note (and its successor, *London Fields*) allows Amis to introduce a new kind of character, the corrupt or profane artist figure. In *Money* the would-be artist is John Self; he is echoed in *London Fields* by the figure of Keith Talent. Having made his mark by producing and directing pornographic commercials for British television, John Self, a rapacious and epically greedy human being, is approached by Fielding Goodney, a bisexual financier who volunteers to underwrite the full production costs of a new film to be made by Self in America. Goodney's proposal, of course, is an elaborate ruse, the first of many traps into which the obese Self will fall without any conscious deliberation.

In reality, Goodney is using Self's credit line to finance the entire project in New York, just as Self's partners in a London advertising agency are essentially living off Self's earnings. In the end, his credit cards become useless, he is evicted from a New York hotel, and he flies back to London, where he is evicted again (this time from his flat). Even his beloved Fiasco (a car as unreliable as all the people in his life) finally falls apart and refuses to run.

Before this collapse occurs and before he fails even in his own suicide, the pill-popping, alcoholic Self takes the reader on a grotesque binge of transatlantic hopping, slumming in New York's topless clubs and striptease joints, drinking impossibly large amounts (in taverns, bars, hotel rooms, and airplanes), and eating innumerable greasy American hamburgers and hot dogs (his favorite foods). The embodiment of greed, Self "feeds" on everything; he is never satisfied. Ultimately, he feeds upon himself and engineers his own destruction. Amis seems to be saying that John is a Self that has no "self" outside alcohol, drugs, sex, and money. He is the consummate consumer, an Everyman for twentieth century New York and London.

New York and London are depicted as polluted cities on both the spiritual and physical planes, and if the smog and drugs are not enough to confuse Self, there are doubles everywhere. Fielding Goodney doubles as a transvestite who follows Self everywhere. London and New York are the double locales of the book, and even the Muse-woman is doubled, taking the forms of sluttish, conniving Selina Street and cultured, elegant Martina Twain. Street satisfies the grossest physical needs of Self, but she, too, is greedy. While living with Self, she somehow manages an affair with Ossie Twain, an undertaking that makes virtually everyone unhappy. Only "Martin Amis" and Martina Twain tell Self the truth, namely that his film, *Good Money*, is abominable, just like his life. The tenderest and funniest moments in *Money* occur when Martina tries to reform John by taking him to concerts and by introducing him to the work of George Orwell. Yet since he is only half an artist, Self can never fully appreciate genuine art.

LONDON FIELDS

First published: 1989
Type of work: Novel

Nicola Six, an inscrutable temptress, involves three men in a complex scheme to make her suicide as artistic and destructive as possible.

Set in Margaret Thatcher's London, replete with smog, skinheads, and strange weather (the product of El Niño and other meteorological disturbances), *London Fields* is a grand novel that combines Amis' mature themes into a compelling synthesis that might be taken as a kind of parable for urban life. Artist-figures abound, including Sam (the American narrator who occupies the flat of an absent British writer named Mark Asprey), Keith Talent (the con man and philanderer extraordinaire who treats dart throwing as high art), and the Muse-woman, Nicola Six, who believes she will be murdered on her thirty-fifth birthday, which will occur on November 6 (hence her name, Nicola Six). Nicola is a jaded, listless symbol of the kind of dead-end to which glitzy, urban life inevitably leads. She is bored by everything, even by sex, which was once her forte (as documented in photographs once taken by Asprey and later discovered by Sam). Nicola doubles, triples, and quadruples herself in *London Fields*, adopting various disguises (social worker, groupie at a darts tournament) and playing different roles (demure virgin, schoolteacher, and whore), all the while manipulating the three men that come into her life at the Black Cross pub: Talent, Guy Clinch, and Sam.

Nicola and Keith conspire to defraud Guy, a rich businessman who is snugly ensconced in a world of upper-class privilege with a wife named Hope, a sister-in-law named Lizzyboo, and an obnoxious baby boy named Marmaduke (a veritable demon of the playpen). Keith prides himself on being a "cheat," a petty criminal who steals directly and indirectly from everyone, even his wife, who faithfully tends their daughter while Keith conducts open affairs with Nicola and a string of women with names such as Debbee, Trish, Analiese, Fran, Iqbala, and Petronella. Talent is one of Amis' supreme fictional creations, a lewd but dazzling figure who tries to write a book on darts and keep a journal even though he can barely spell. As Martina Twain did with John Self, Nicola Six does with Keith Talent, teaching him how to read Keats, the true artist of love and beauty. In the end, the only artistry Nicola experiences is that of Sam, who turns murderer and dispatches her in the front seat of his car on November 6, exactly as she predicted.

Summary

In an essay titled "Squares and Oblongs," the poet W. H. Auden noted that the true writer is one who enjoys "hanging around words listening to what they say." By that yardstick, Martin Amis is a genuinely successful writer because his fictions are built on the foundation of exquisite wordplay, from the use of symbolic names to the inclusion of slang and newly minted terms. Like all great satirists, Amis' ultimate goal is the redemption of society. If he portrays a sordid world of brutality, sex, drugs, greed, and pollution, it is only because he imagines—and desires—a more fitting scene for the human drama.

Bibliography

Bawer, Bruce. "Martin Amis on America." *The New Criterion*, February 5, 1987, 20-26.
Michener, Charles. "Britain's Brat of Letters." *Esquire* 107 (January, 1987): 108-111.
Miller, Karl. *Doubles: Studies in Literary History*. Oxford, England: Oxford University Press, 1985.
Pritchard, W. H. "Novel Reports." *The Hudson Review* 43 (Fall, 1990): 489-497.
Smith, Amanda. "PW Interviews." *Publishers Weekly* 227 (February 8, 1985): 78-79.

Daniel L. Guillory

AHARON APPELFELD

Born: Czernowitz, Bukovina, Romania
1932

Principal Literary Achievement
An escapee at age eleven from a Nazi concentration camp, Appelfeld made his way to Israel and began to write works that chronicle both the pre- and post-Holocaust periods.

Biography

Bukovina, the province of Romania into which Aharon (sometimes rendered "Aron") Appelfeld was born in 1932, was a part of the Austro-Hungarian Empire until 1918, when the nation of Romania was created. The area became, after World War II, a part of the Union of Soviet Socialist Republics (USSR). During the period between the two World Wars, most Jews in this area were assimilated. The Appelfelds spoke German within their household and did little to preserve their Jewish identity.

Czernowitz was overrun by German forces in 1939. Before long, the occupying intruders killed Aharon's mother. The boy and his father, along with other members of his family, soon were sent to the Ukraine, where they were interned separately in the Transnistria concentration camp. The train on which the frightened, blond-haired boy was taken to the concentration camp has become a pervasive symbol in Appelfeld's writing.

Young Aharon, alone, too young to understand the political ramifications of his displacement, was sucked into the forbidding freight car like a grain of wheat, a symbol that pervades his writing, obviously reflecting the helplessness that the boy felt at having his life snatched away from him in a way, and for reasons, that he could not comprehend, an object in the hands of a malevolent government.

For the next three years, Aharon lived at the whim of his captors in a setting where people dislocated solely on the basis of their ethnicity were robbed of their dignity, their self-determination, and, in many cases, their lives. The sensitive youth saw how cheap life was in such situations. Yet as his future writing demonstrates, he thought deeply about how his people could have come to such a pass in a country that was seemingly civilized. Such musing became the basis for his later writing about how European Jews, by encouraging assimilation and by acceding without protest to the growing inroads that the government was making upon their freedom, were parties to their own destruction.

When Aharon escaped from Transnistria in 1943, he did not emerge into a wel-

coming society. The Ukrainian peasants among whom he found himself were as anti-Semitic as the Nazis who controlled the area. Appelfeld, however, used his blond hair as a badge of Aryan lineage, albeit a misleading badge. He took whatever work he could find, sometimes as a farmer, sometimes as a shepherd. His adult friends were thieves and prostitutes. His younger friends were orphans enduring dislocations similar to his own.

When Germany surrendered in May, 1945, Appelfeld was the youngest of a band of boys who made their way to Italy, where Aharon was again able to pass as a Gentile. For a while, his group was permitted to live in a Roman Catholic church, where Aharon sang in the choir. Before long, however, the boy, remembering his ethnicity, went with his group to Naples, where they came into contact with the Youth Aliya, a group that urged them to go to Palestine, which would become Israel in 1948. In Palestine, Appelfeld spent mornings working in the fields and afternoons studying Hebrew, which he had to learn if he was to succeed in his adopted country.

In 1948, he was conscripted into the Israeli army, in which he served until 1950. Having met his military obligation and passed his entrance examination, he was able in 1950 to enroll in Hebrew University, from which he received both the bachelor's and the master's degrees with a specialty in Hebrew literature.

After studying briefly in Zurich and at Oxford, Appelfeld returned to Israel to teach Hebrew literature at Ben Gurion University in the desert town of Beersheba. During the 1950's, he wrote profusely, sending his poetry to an editor in Jerusalem, who, for three years, regularly rejected it.

In 1960, Appelfeld married an Argentinian woman, Yehudit. Along with their two sons and one daughter, they eventually made their home in Jerusalem. In the year that Aharon married, his father immigrated to Israel but declined to recognize Appelfeld as his son.

Appelfeld's ascendance as an Israeli writer was evident in the early 1960's, although his work had not yet been translated into English. In 1960, he won his first notable Israeli prize for poetry. Two years later, his first collection of short stories was published in Hebrew and, despite distribution problems, attracted favorable attention. He began to receive recognition outside Israel when he won Israel's Bialik Prize in 1978 and the Israel Prize for Literature in 1983, by which time his *Badenheim, 'ir nofesh* (1975; *Badenheim 1939*, 1980), *Tor-ha-pela'ot* (1978; *The Age of Wonders*, 1981), and *Kutonet veha-pasim* (1983; *Tzili: The Story of a Life*, 1983) had appeared in English translation.

The air of doom that stalks much of Appelfeld's work stems from the horrors and uncertainties of his formative years, although he does not write directly of the Holocaust, but rather of what preceded and followed it. He is passionately concerned with posing questions about what can happen to a people if they allow their own identities to be co-opted, their liberties eroded. Appelfeld is prolific, having produced eleven novels in Hebrew, several collections of his more than three hundred short stories, collections of essays, and an autobiography, *Ke'ishon ha-ayin* (1973; like the apple of my eye).

Analysis

Perhaps all writing is at heart autobiographical. Certainly no one who has read the work of Appelfeld would have difficulty accepting the thesis that his work is almost wholly a retelling of his life and of the philosophy that it has spawned. The overriding concern in nearly everything that he has written is the Holocaust, although he never writes in detail about it. Rather, it is a lurking presence, the more horrible because it is not broached directly or in detail.

The fact of his drawing from the same factual base for most of his work does not result in Appelfeld's being boringly repetitive. He has a remarkable ability to reshape constantly the images and details of what he is writing about, making each of them seem fresh and novel. He is a master of restraint in his writing, exhibiting a minimalism that allows him to make his most salient points vividly through understatement.

Appelfeld writes with consistently controlled objectivity about highly subjective matters. In a way, he writes about the Holocaust by not writing about the Holocaust: He depends upon his readers' memories of its horrors to fill in details too painful to relate. He writes about what led to this cataclysm and about its aftermath, never about the actualities, the gruesome events of this horrendous catastrophe that resulted in the deaths of over six million Jews between 1939 and 1945.

Realizing that the dimensions of the Holocaust are so huge as to beggar the human imagination, Appelfeld elects to write around, rather than directly about, this historical event. He constantly searches for an answer to the haunting, recurrent question, "How could such a thing have happened?"

He finds his answer partially in the major split that he detects in Jewish society and that surfaces in his stories. The rift lies between the intellectual Jews, who attached themselves to the mainstream culture of their societies by shedding most of the vestiges of their Judaic backgrounds and language, and the so-called *Ostjuden*. These were Jews from Eastern Europe, notably Poland, who were essentially philistines, merchants, and businessmen who preserved Jewish traditions but who were so bent on their remunerative business pursuits that they did not object to being excluded from the more genteel and powerful social milieus of their countries.

Both kinds of Jews were easily duped during the rise of Nazism in Germany and in Eastern Europe. The intellectuals wanted to be part of the mainstream culture, so they did not raise the objections that they should have when inroads began to limit their freedoms. The *Ostjuden*, on the other hand, did not want to jeopardize their financial security, so they overlooked what was gradually beginning to turn them into second-class citizens and, ultimately, for those who survived, into stateless people.

The two classes of Jews that Appelfeld identifies have little use for each other, so that the solidarity that might have been their salvation in the most critical time in their history was totally lacking. It was into such a milieu that Appelfeld was born. Among his earliest memories is one fundamental to *Badenheim 1939*, in which the Austrian resort being depicted is soon to be crowded with summer visitors. Dr. Pappenheim is to provide musical entertainment during the resort's high season.

Appelfeld uses Trude, the Jewish wife of the local pharmacist, who is not Jewish, metaphorically. She is manic-depressive, driven to distraction by her perception of the sick world that surrounds her and that she fears threatens the welfare of her daughter. There is about this book an air reminiscent of the atmosphere with which Thomas Mann infused *Der Zauberberg* (1924; *The Magic Mountain*, 1927), although the implications of the disease that Trude senses in the environment are much broader than were those posed by the tuberculosis in the Mann novel.

In *Badenheim 1939*, one also finds persistent overtones of paranoia like those found in Franz Kafka's *Der Prozess* (1925; *The Trial*, 1937), a work with which Appelfeld admits familiarity. In *Badenheim 1939*, the Sanitation Department erects fences and raises flags, steadily becoming an increasingly authoritarian factor in the lives of citizens, particularly of Jewish citizens. Against a backdrop of Rainer Maria Rilke's death poetry comes an announcement that all Jews must register with the Sanitation Department, presumably as a first step toward "sanitizing" the country of its Jewish citizens.

The intellectual Jews have petty disagreements with the *Ostjuden* about who has to register, while the Sanitation Department works quietly collecting dossiers on all the Jews in Badenheim. It forbids entry into, or exit from, the town and quarantines the Jews who are within it. Appelfeld writes of the "orange shadow" that hung over the town, a symbol that he uses in most of his stories. Trude's delusions become realities as the Jews become a marked people.

When trains arrive to relocate the captive Jews, Dr. Pappenheim speculates optimistically that they probably will not be taken too far because the boxcars in which they are to be transported are so filthy. The hapless Jews board the train, still thinking that their deportation to Poland is a transitional step, trying to minimize the import of what is happening to them.

Similar themes pervade most of Appelfeld's writing. He is obsessed with what the decadence of European Jews resulted in once Adolf Hitler came to power. Both of the groups of Jews about which he writes, the intellectual Jews and the *Ostjuden*, lapsed into decadence and sold out for their own gain. Both groups, in Appelfeld's view, felt an underlying self-hatred as Jews, ever alienated, ever shunned. In this self-hatred, fed certainly by the dominant society, were the seeds of the racial destruction that was inflicted upon most Jews east of France from the late 1930's until the end of World War II.

Appelfeld sustains this pervasive argument in his work by writing of the dispossessed, the abandoned, those who hide for fear of their lives, those who run from all that is dear to them because running is their only hope. He writes about dead mothers and unsympathetic fathers, about indifferent societies and vindictive institutions within those societies.

Mostly, though, Appelfeld writes about complacence and about the price it exacts in situations like that brought about by the Fascist rule of the period. He places responsibility for the Holocaust squarely on the shoulders of a passive Jewish community that might have rallied early to save itself.

TZILI

First published: *Kutonet veha-pasim*, 1983 (English translation, 1983)
Type of work: Novel

Tzili, daughter of a Jewish family that tries to deny its Jewishness, sustains her tie with her historic past and survives the Holocaust.

In *Tzili: The Story of a Life*, Tzili Kraus is in significant ways Appelfeld's female counterpart. As the story opens, she is the least favored of her parents' children because she is, unlike her older siblings, a poor student, something not to be encouraged in a Jewish-Austrian family with intellectual pretensions. The family, turning its back on its Jewish heritage, takes pride in its assimilation.

Tzili, a taciturn child, plays on the small plot behind her parents' shop, ignored by parents and siblings. She is abused because of her poor academic performance and is viewed as retarded. Her parents employ an old man to give their unpromising child lessons in Judaism, but she does poorly even in these lessons.

When it is apparent that Fascists are about to enter their town, the Krauses leave, but Tzili stays behind to guard their property. She sleeps through the slaughter that ensues, covered by burlap in a shed where no one thinks to look. Now Tzili is on her own. She must live by her wits, and part of what Appelfeld seeks to convey is that her inherent instinct for survival will serve her better than her family's intellectuality serves them. The family disappears, presumably victims of the Holocaust.

Appelfeld makes Tzili the symbol of a Judaism that survives through sheer pluck during a time of almost overwhelming difficulty. She consorts with prostitutes, works for peasants who abuse her physically, and struggles to hang onto what little hope there is. In time she links up with Mark, a forty-year-old who has left his wife and children in the concentration camp from which he escaped.

Like Aharon, Tzili looks Aryan and is relatively safe from identification as a Jew. She and Mark live by bartering, using some of his family's clothing that he had brought with him as a trading medium for food. By the time that Mark, now guilt ridden, defects, the fifteen-year-old Tzili is pregnant. She trades the clothing that Mark has left behind for food. When this source of sustenance is exhausted, the pregnant Tzili finds work with peasants, some of whom beat her unmercifully.

With the armistice, Tzili joins a group of Jews freed from their concentration camps and goes south with them. She delivers her baby stillborn near Zagreb, but she survives—and with her survives the Judaism that nothing can extinguish. As the novel ends, Tzili and Linda, a woman who had earlier saved her life, are on a ship presumably heading for Palestine.

The theme of this story is survival in the broadest sense—the survival of one woman to symbolize the survival of the Jews and their philosophy. Tzili survives because she has not allied herself with the Jews who allowed assimilation or with the *Ostjuden* and their mercantile ambitions. Tzili lives because her instincts, her sheer intuitions in time of crisis, serve her better than the artificial intellectuality of those who early shunned her and made her feel as though she was not part of her own family.

THE HEALER

First published: *Be-'et uve-'onah ahat*, 1990 (English translation, 1990)
Type of work: Novel

Helga Katz, the daughter of a Jewish family in Vienna, suffers from an illness that leads the family to a healer in the Carpathian Mountains.

In *The Healer*, the Katzes are bourgeois Jews who live in Vienna. When their daughter Helga begins to suffer from psychological problems, they seek help from every doctor available, but the treatment that she receives brings no permanent amelioration. Hearing of a healer in the Carpathian Mountains, the parents, Felix and Henrietta, decide that they must take Helga there in a desperate attempt to restore her health. Their son Karl accompanies them when, in October of 1938, they take Helga to the Carpathians for extended treatment. They stay there in an inn for six months.

The ironies that the story poses are not inherent but are a product of what readers know about the history of the period. This setting is the last year that Eastern Europe will be free from a Fascist tyranny that will lead to the annihilation of most of the people involved in Appelfeld's story.

As the story develops, one realizes that the healer, the innkeeper and his Yiddish-speaking wife, and the Katzes themselves are marked for destruction. They go about their daily tasks, engage in their petty conflicts, fill their lives with small details that in the long run have little meaning. Hovering darkly above the entire narrative is the specter of what is soon to happen to Eastern Europe and to every Jew connected with it.

In this story, Appelfeld reiterates the notion of self-hatred that he is convinced helped lead to the downfall of European Jews in the 1930's and 1940's. This theme is shown quite clearly in a discussion that Henrietta has with the healer about Helga's name. Henrietta had wanted to name her daughter Tsirl, after the girl's grandmother, who was born in this rural region.

She decided, however, that she could not give her daughter that name because of the ridicule that it would bring. Yet Henrietta, conditioned to the deceptions that Viennese society imposed upon its Jewish populace, does not rail stridently because she cannot give her daughter a Jewish name, saying merely that the name is "unusual" and would have caused people to laugh at the girl. In this exchange, Appelfeld expresses extremely well the insidiousness of the overwhelming Jewish repression of Jewish tradition, and the Jewish acceptance of conditions that would ultimately annihilate them.

Summary

 With masterful restraint, Aharon Appelfeld works consistently to make his point: The Holocaust was as much attributable to Jewish passivity as it was to Fascist activism. He presents the various faces of self-hatred that afflicted many European Jews during the rise of Naziism.

 Jews of the period blinded themselves to such discomfiting indignities as forced registration with the authorities and mandatory relocations, which resulted in the deportation of millions of Jews to concentration camps. They refused to admit the realities that surrounded them, and by the time that they were conscious of the implications of these realities, it was too late for them to save themselves.

Bibliography

Blake, Patricia. Review of *Tzili: The Story of a Life. Time*, April 11, 1982, 97.

Coffin, Edna Amir. "Appelfeld's Exceptional Universe: Harmony out of Chaos." *Hebrew Studies* XXIV (1983): 85-89.

Wisse, Ruth R. "Aharon Appelfeld, Survivor." *Commentary* LXXVI (August, 1983): 73-76.

Yudkin, Leon I. "Appelfeld's Vision of the Past." In *Escape into Siege*. Boston: Routledge & Kegan Paul, 1974.

R. Baird Shuman

ARISTOPHANES

Born: Athens, Greece
c. 450 B.C.
Died: Athens, Greece
c. 385 B.C.

Principal Literary Achievement
As sole surviving examples of Athenian Old Comedy, the eleven complete plays by Aristophanes provide the best clue to the nature of literary comedy as it developed and reached fruition in the later fifth century B.C.

Biography

Aristophanes was born in Athens, Greece, around 450 B.C., to parents Philippos and Zenodora. The date of Aristophanes' birth assumes that he was at least nineteen years old when his first play, *Daitaleis* (banqueters), was produced in 427 by Kallistratos. The notion is that he had to have been old enough to have had an understanding of the requirements of the competition and to have developed the literary skill requisite for the writing. That he was not yet old enough to have produced that play himself, a task assumed only in 424 with the production of *Hippes* (*The Knights*), after several successful plays, would seem to vouch for the assumption. Admittedly, for reasons no longer clear, several other plays, aside from those written earliest and latest in his life, were produced by others: in 414, the *Ornithes* (*The Birds*), again produced by Kallistratos, and the nonpreserved *Amphiaraos*, produced by Philonides. Aristophanes was already bald, however, when the *Eirene* (*Peace*) was produced in 421 (line 771).

Though born in Athens, Aristophanes had lived in Aigina, where his family presumably acquired property after the Athenian seizing of that island in 431. He was of the tribe or greater "district" of Pandionis, one of ten such districts created by the Athenian politician Cleisthenes with the constitutional reform of 508-507 B.C., and of the much older *deme*, the local or village "ward," of Kydathenaeus within the city. That was the same local ward of the famed politician Kleon, who receives considerable parody in *The Knights* and the *Sphekes* (*The Wasps*) of 422. The *Acharnes* (*The Acharnians*) of 425 implies that subsequent to his earlier prizewinning play, the *Babylonioi* (*Babylonians*) of 426, Aristophanes has been prosecuted for anti-Athenian propaganda by Kleon. While that trial was unsuccessful at its legal level, Aristophanes' reputation as comic playwright was established, and in Kleon, and the political structure of Athens, he had ample material for his buffoonery. That factor is par-

ticularly noteworthy considering the Peloponnesian War among the Greek city-states, especially Athens against Sparta, which dominated the historical epoch from 431 to 404 B.C.

Aristophanes was married, though his wife's name is not known. He had at least three sons, Araros, Nikostratos, and Philetairos, each of whom also wrote plays, which were staged among the Middle Comedy in the fourth century. Aristophanes had produced a play named *Ploutos* (*Plutus*) in 408, though it is not the one that survives under that name. Rather the surviving *Ploutos*, often considered the final example of Old Comedy, is a play staged in 388, though the occasion and achievement is not known; but it was produced by his son, Araros, who staged two other plays by his father, neither of which survive: the *Kōkalos* at the Greater Dionysia, and the *Aiolosikōn*, both of which were produced about 385. Aristophanes died in Athens sometime around 385 B.C.

Analysis

Aristophanes' plays can be studied as sources for political or social history, as works of literature, and as dramatic works. In antiquity, Plato recommended them to Dionysius I, tyrant of Syracuse, when the latter wished to learn more about Athens; and in the twentieth century, Viktor Ehrenberg employed them to write "a sociology of Old Attic Comedy." The distinction between the plays as literature and as drama rests upon the separation of poetic form from techniques of staging. Comic plays were produced normally but once; thereafter, they might be disregarded or studied as literature but were not "seen" again. The absence of staging instructions within the plays, as well as a frequent failure to differentiate the speakers clearly, meant that readers could become confused by the poetic content. It is no wonder that these masterpieces generated such an intensive study, since the comic poet was also a source of original and distinctive vocabulary needing clarification. The Greek biographer Plutarch, distinguishing the preferences of an elite, educated man from those of an ordinary, uneducated one, claims that Aristophanes suited the latter but not the former by virtue of "the vulgarity in speech," "the spectacle," and "the habits of a common laborer." The reader or student of Aristophanes must be prepared to enter a world filled with such material. Yet Plutarch's preferences also illustrate the changing tastes of another epoch and the lack of historical consideration for the development of comedy, as well as for the particular genius of Aristophanes.

In contrast to Plutarch, the observation made of Aristophanes by a fellow competitor speaks highly of his role. The Greek playwright Kratinos notes that "Aristophanes resembled Euripides in his concern for verbal precision and dexterity." The oldest manuscripts of Aristophanes date from the Byzantine empire of the tenth century A.D. An intensive study of the plays in the twelfth century noted his purity of language and quintessential example of the Attic dialect of the fifth century B.C. In spite of the changed environment of a Christianized Greek East, the coarseness of his humor is considered less a detriment than the positive value accorded to his opposition to war.

The obscenity charges against Aristophanes so frequently leveled by the literary critics of the nineteenth and early twentieth centuries are properly understood as reflections of changing societal tastes in different eras, as well as a failure to understand social history and satire, rather than actual indecency on the part of the comic poet. War and political machinations against people were the obscenities, not explicit sexual or scatalogical vocabulary; this truth is what Aristophanes knew. In his time the only thing forbidden in comedy was to resemble tragedy.

To understand specifics requires some attention to the history of comedy within Athenian life. The Greek philosopher Aristotle in his *De poetica* (c. 334 B.C.-323 B.C.; *Poetics*, 1705), provides a short history of the poetic arts. According to Aristotle, the "more serious writers" of dramatic tragedy imitated illustrious events involving illustrious persons. The "lighter-minded" imitated the more ordinary events and persons. He qualifies this general point by specifying that comedy does not include the full range of "badness," but that to be "ridiculous" or to be made "ridiculous" points to a kind of deformity: "The explanations of laughter are errors and disgraces not accompanied by pain or injury." Thus, for Aristotle, the comic mask, by which the characters in the play are identified and differentiated, is one of "deformity and distortion" within the proprieties required by the staging. Aristophanes was a master of the use of masks, though they also functioned to permit rapid switch of character on the stage as required by the limitation of three speaking actors.

While Aristotle could identify some of the development through which tragedy had passed, he wrongly concludes that "there are no early records of comedy, because it was not highly valued." Archaeological investigation has uncovered lists of the prizewinners within the history of the comedies. These lists evidence the connection of comedies to the history of festivals in the state and to the gods of the state. As Aristotle knew without exact chronological detail, "it was a long time before comic dramas were licensed by the magistrate; the early comedies were produced by amateurs." Yet he also knew that these productions were the outgrowth of phallic performances, which explains the perennial costuming within the plays.

From the remote past of the Greek world came wine making and celebrations of its accomplishment, associated with the god Dionysos. Specific developments are best understood within Athenian definitions. In the month Poseidion (December-January), following the picking of the grapes and their initial pressing, there was held "the Rural Dionysia." An explicit example from the Rural Dionysia, but slightly parodied, is preserved in *The Acharnians* (lines 237-279). In the next month, Gamelion (January-February), festivities (the "Lenaia") with phallic processions carrying the new wine shifted to the sanctuary within the city, where it was stored, and to the theater, where it was celebrated. Initially, "revelling songs" were part of the processions, from which evolved the more complex examples seen in the competitive series of comic plays, normally five except in some wartime years.

Festivities of the next month, Anthesterion (February-March), focused upon the tasting of the new wine and involved a great procession to the coastal marshes, where the god's arrival by ship, personified in the person of the king-archon, was dramatized. This event was followed in the month Elaphebolion (March-April) by further phallic processions from the walls of the city to a shrine and then back into Athens directly to the theater for the seasonal complex of plays (called "the City Dionysia" or the Greater Dionysia). This complex involved competitive trilogies of tragedies with a satyr play, plus another series of comedies. Remnants of the entering and exiting processionals, with their accompanying costumes, are imbedded within examples of the surviving comedies.

Recovered inscriptional lists from the festivities and the City Dionysia provide a sequence as far back as 487 B.C., associating many details with the particular festival and giving the names of competitors, their plays, and the winners. For fifth century Old Comedy, at least fifty-seven competitors have been identified, along with 374 lost play-titles. Of the latter, 30 are ascribed to Aristophanes, besides the 11 surviving examples.

The form of the comedy involves five elements, each with its own complexity: prologue, parodos (entrance of the chorus), episodic agon (formal "contest" or "debate"), parabasis (choral interlude), and exodos (final scene and exit). Insofar as comedy got beyond burlesque or slap-stick, which never completely disappeared, these elements constituted that structural integrity to which Aristotle gave the name "plot" and by which he evaluated the success of the poet.

Beyond these basic elements, Aristophanes employed a numerous variety of technically defined poetic meters and rhythms with brilliant skill. They are exceedingly difficult to reproduce in English, or in any other translation.

THE CLOUDS

First produced: *Nephelai*, 423 B.C. (English translation, 1708)
Type of work: Play

This play, a parody of the kind of intellectual development associated with Socrates, places such thinkers and their thoughts within the rarefied atmosphere of the "clouds."

The Clouds was staged at the City Dionysia of 423 B.C. and was awarded third place among the three competitors. Having taken first place with the *Acharnēs* (*The Acharnians*) and the *Hippēs* (*The Knights*) at the Lenaia, respectively in the two preceding years (425 and 424), Aristophanes was very disappointed. The preserved text is a revision of the original as staged, building in a variety of ingredients reflecting his effort not only to revamp the failure but also to incorporate observations on that failure. Lines 521-525 make the point specifically: "I thought you were a bright audience, and that this was my most brilliant comedy, so I thought you should be the first to taste it. But I was repulsed, worsted by vulgar rivals, though I didn't deserve that."

Aristophanes takes as his theme the contrast between an older educational mode and the new interrogative style, associated with the name of Socrates. Apparently his first play, the *Daitalēis*, had already exploited a similar theme. *The Clouds* begins with a prologue (lines 1-262), wherein is met the two principal characters, Strepsiades ("Twister"), worried by the debts accumulating by the propensity for chariot racing of his long-haired son, Pheidippides ("Sparer of Horses," or "Horsey"). The idea occurs, with the assistance of "a student," to have the son enter the school ("Think-shop") next door, operated by Socrates, wherein by the logic of the sophists one should be able to learn how to talk so as to evade one's debts. When the son refuses to go, lest his suntan be ruined, the father goes instead. He finds Socrates suspended in a basket from the roof, wherein rarefied thinking can be more appropriately done in the atmosphere of the clouds.

The parodos finally erupts with the entrance of the chorus of "clouds" singing and dancing (lines 263-509), following the incantations and chanted prayers of Socrates, to the alarm of Strepsiades. In brilliant repartee, the chorus is introduced as the goddesses, who, with wind, lightning, and thunder, patronize intellectual development. Yet the buffoonery that follows indicates that it is some weird intellect, for Socrates, in answer to questions about rain and thunder, assures Strepsiades that there is no Zeus, but only clouds displaying analogies to the human bodily functions of passing water or gas. Strepsiades is convinced, and the parodos ends with his agreeing to become a student and submit to the "hickory-stick" kind of educational technique.

A sequence of two parabases and two agon follow (lines 510-1452). The first parabasis (lines 510-626) provides the best evidence that the play in its present form has been rewritten; the second (lines 1113-1130) addresses the judges asking for the prize. Their function is typical, though they also serve as interludes between the episodic agon or scenes, and, whatever their present content, some similar kind of witty poetry addressed outside the play would have been present.

The first episode is the longer one (lines 627-1112). Strepsiades proves incompetent as a student, for he cannot memorize what is required but only wants to learn how to outwit creditors. Subsequent to his own dismissal, he forces Pheidippides to enroll under threat of expulsion from home. Included is the first agon (lines 889-1112), wherein Pheidippides is exposed to the debate between "Right" ("Just Logic") and "Wrong" ("Unjust Logic"), from which it is obvious that the argument of the latter will prevail.

The second episode is relatively short (lines 1131-1452). When Strepsiades comes to learn the result of his son's education, though assured of its great success, he discovers that success means that his son now knows how to whip him. The second agon (lines 1321-1452) argues for the validity of that action, making reference, as the comic poet's tended, to the tragic poets, the father preferring the older Aeschylus, characterizing older virtues, and the son siding with Euripides, whose newer notions are caricatured as immoralities. There are amusing anecdotes concerning child development in Strepsiades' argument to Pheidippides, but Strepsiades has been defeated by his own intentions.

The brief exodos (lines 1453-1510) involves Strepsiades getting revenge for his own sake and with reference to the displaced gods of ordinary life by setting fire to the "Think-shop" next door.

THE WASPS

First produced: *Sphēkes*, 422 B.C. (English translation, 1812)
Type of work: Play

In the midst of war and without definitive leadership, a democracy can be pulled this way, then that, eliciting a buffooning of its very structure.

Having failed in 423 B.C. with his "intellectual" parody, *The Clouds*, Aristophanes returned to the "more vulgar" arena of politics. Considered to be the most perfectly structured of Aristophanes' plays, *The Wasps* took second prize at the Lenaia. It provides a complete pattern against which other plays can be measured.

The prologue (lines 1-229) begins on an early morning before the house of Philokleon ("Lover of Kleon") and his son Bdelykleon ("Hater of Kleon") with two of their slaves, Sosias and Xanthias, discussing before the audience the peculiar illness of Philokleon, who has an obsession to serve daily on juries within the law courts— spelled out in a lengthy monologue (lines 85-135) by Xanthias—from which Bdelykleon is equally determined to prevent him. To get out of the house, Philokleon climbs the chimney pretending to be smoke, while Bdelykleon appears on the roof to stop him. The theme for the subsequent action is stated in lines 158-160: that Philokleon fears that the gods would punish him if any guilty defendant went unpunished.

The arrival of the chorus in the parodos (lines 230-315), spectacularly costumed as "wasps" so that they may "buzz" around, over which are the garb of the jurors whose action often "stings," signals the beginning of the play's action. They are exclusively old men of Philokleon's generation.

The agon is twofold: In a scene interlayered with irrelevant lyric that plays upon the nature of the wasp, the issue is defined (lines 316-525) by Philokleon and the leader of the chorus and formally debated (lines 526-727) by Philokleon and Bdelykleon before the chorus. Bdelykleon's argument prevails, convincing not only the chorus but also, intellectually if not emotionally, his father. The episode is extended (lines 728-1008), again with interlayered lyric, by dramatizing the agon, in a pretended domestic litigation intended to cure Philokleon of his illness by having him acquit a defendant. The context provides occasion to pan the actual politician Kleon, presumably in the audience.

The lengthy parabasis (lines 1009-1121), balanced between the leader and his chorus, and displaying the particular requirements of Attic lyric style with its highly technical linguistic components, serves to narrate the conflict that the playwright has had with his judges and audiences on previous occasions, who have failed to understand him. Considerable insight into biographical matters emerges.

The play intentionally "breaks down" in the episodes that follow, for much buffoonery and satire occur. Philokleon warns of excessive drinking (lines 1122-1264), anticipating his own drunkenness, illustrated in the final scene (lines 1292-1449). In between comes the second parabasis (usually lines 1265-1291), wherein Aristophanes places in the mouth of the chorus-leader, who is wearing a mask to represent the author, his bitter diatribe against Kleon for that earlier prosecution. Some translators prefer to switch this parabasis with the choral ode (lines 1450-1473) that would otherwise conclude these episodes, wherein Philokleon, apparently before his intoxication, could be envied for his change of character and his son praised for his wisdom. Others think that the intentional "diabolical irony" of Aristophanes would be best served by leaving the two sets of lines in their traditional places.

Either way, the exodos (lines 1474-1537) is also a dance routine with Philokleon executing a burlesque solo parodying those of various tragedies, including that from Euripides' Kyklōps (c. 421 B.C.; *Cyclops*).

THE BIRDS

First produced: *Ornithes*, 414 B.C. (English translation, 1824)
Type of work: Play

With the war in an apparent mode of Athenian victory, occasion for complex fantasy seemed in order, and this genius of a spectacle resulted with its utopian "cloud-cuckoo-land."

The longest of the surviving comedies by Aristophanes is *The Birds*. It was entered at the City Dionysia, where it was awarded second prize. It is without a doubt the singular achievement of Aristophanes for spectacle. Its brilliantly plumaged chorus of birds appears to be based on a genuine knowledge of birds in their great variety, for beginning at line 268 Aristophanes introduces each different bird in the chorus, commenting upon its respective dress.

Peace had been the concern of the state in the preceding decade, and *Eirēnē* (*Peace*) had been the theme of Aristophanes' play that took second prize at the Greater Dionysia in 421. Yet peace had not come in the continuing war between Athens and Sparta. While *The Birds* was presented in a moment of impending success, for Athens it was merely a matter of months before the most disastrous events of the war. It is hard to be certain how perceptive the poet was, yet there is a haunting underlying mood.

The prologue (lines 1-259) begins with Peisthetairos and Euelpides, Athenian citizens having abandoned the city, with its incessant penchant for litigation, earlier satirized in *The Wasps*, in search of some quieter country. Having been guided in their journey by birds, respectively a crow and a jackdaw, they call upon the mysterious Tereus, who, according to a tragedy by Sophocles, had been turned into a hoopoe (a multicolored bird with large crest). After some explanatory conversation, Peisthetairos has the idea that the birds should build a city-state between heaven and earth, where they can intercept the sacrificial smoke of offerings made by humans to the gods, reestablishing the original supremacy of birds over both. The prologue ends with the hoopoe's song, full of marvelous plays upon birdcalls, summoning the other birds.

A long parodos follows (lines 260-450), wherein the chorus of birds enters upon the stage one by one, to be introduced, to be descriptively identified, and to receive comic association with leading personalities of the day. Since humans regularly eat birds, the initial reaction by the birds is hostility, but the hoopoe intervenes. The parodos concludes with the hoopoe's instruction to Peisthetairos to explain his idea to the birds.

The agon (lines 451-675) provides the extended conversation involving the hoopoe and the chorus leader, a partridge, as the idea is expounded. The birds are gradually convinced. The establishment of the new land will require human assistance for structural details, but for the humans to participate in the construction enterprise it would be best if they grew wings. The agon ends with the hoopoe giving the humans a root to chew on that will produce wings, thereby preventing any threat that other birds might have against their former adversaries.

Parabases alternate with episodes. In the initial relatively brief parabasis (lines 676-800), the chorus of birds addresses the theater audience on the origin of birds and their value to humankind, concluding with an invitation to come live with them and an explanation of the advantage of having wings. The shorter first episode (lines 801-1057) brings back Peisthetairos and Euelpides, now with wings, of which they remain somewhat self-conscious. Yet it proceeds to the building of *Nephelo-kokky-gia* ("Cloud-cuckoo-land"), with Peisthetairos completely in charge. Both Euelpides and the hoopoe disappear from the play—a necessity of the limitation upon the number of speaking actors and of the large number of roles required in the two episodes. Various human personality types and bureaucratic functionaries appear looking for jobs in the new city-state, only to be driven off, with much good humor suggestive of the role that comedy had in the parodying of the pompous nature of local government. The second parabasis (lines 1058-1117) sees the chorus of birds proclaiming its divinity, reflecting upon the carefree life it leads, but concluding with the appeal to the judges to award the prize to it.

A long second episode (lines 1118-1705) follows. After a description of the completed structures, it becomes evident that the Olympian gods are being warned of this new competition, and there follows, with plays upon the control of opposition within the democratic political process, the necessity to effect some kind of truce with the gods. Prometheus, the well-known opponent of Zeus, assists Peisthetairos in the negotiations; Poseidon, Herakles, and a Triballian god who speaks an unintelligible form of Greek represent the peace envoys from Olympus. When terms are finally established, preparations are made for the wedding of Peisthetairos to Basileia ("Miss Sovereignty"), Zeus' housekeeper, who together will reign over all from the palace of Zeus.

The exodos (lines 1706-1765) combines the wedding hymns, sung by the adoring chorus of birds, with the departure of the royal couple to assume their regnal place.

LYSISTRATA

First produced: *Lysistratē*, 411 B.C. (English translation, 1837)
Type of work: Play

As the Peloponnesian War relentlessly continued, Aristophanes toyed with the notion that the women, by withholding their sexual favors to their men, might elicit peace.

One of the shorter plays, *Lysistrata* appears to have been produced at the Lenaia, with no surviving indication of its achievement. The most outrageously notorious scenes in all drama could only have been staged in the Greek theater, with its base in the phallic-oriented festivals of the city-state cult.

It is famous also for the role given to women, particularly noteworthy since there is no evidence for women attending Athenian theater, and since it entailed the somewhat comic difficulty of having men, already in their phallic-oriented costumes, play the roles of the women also. Yet that same year, 411 B.C., Aristophanes appears to have submitted for the City Dionysia another play with women as principal characters, the *Thesmophoriazousai (Thesmophoriazusae)*, and he returned to this theme several other times in subsequent plays.

The prologue (lines 1-253) introduces Lysistrata, an Athenian woman who seeks to achieve peace from prolonged warfare among the city-states, which the men have been unable or unwilling to accomplish. Her idea is to withhold all sexual relations from husbands or lovers until they agree to peace terms. In the opening scene, she must first persuade diverse women (some of whose discourse provides marvelous examples of what else women of the time had within their duties, as well as upon their minds). The scene closes with the women convinced. In agreement, they seize the Akropolis, site of Athena's temple.

Aristophanes employs two half choruses for this comedy, one of old men, the other of old women, to play off one another and as contrasts to the youthful feminine protagonists. The parodos (lines 254-386) involves their separate and successive entrances, first of men and then of women, each arriving to perform intended functions related to the war.

The episode (lines 387-466) begins with the abrupt entrance of the official Magistrate, who learns first from the chorus of men and then from Lysistrata and her companions what is transpiring. That leads into the agon (lines 467-613) between Lysistrata and the Magistrate, where the women's perspective upon war is made clear against the patriotic zeal of the government.

The parabasis (lines 614-705) juxtaposes in unusual fashion the two choruses against one another: the old men crying "tyranny," the old women responding "rights" even to advise the state. This interlude is designed to imply the passage of time, without which the subsequent episodes would be unintelligible.

First (lines 706-780), there is the threat to the movement by potentially disaffected women confronting their sex-starved men with permanent erection of their costumed phalluses. A choral interlude (lines 781-828) displays hatred of one another verbally and physically in the described actions. The second episode (lines 829-1013) magnifies the first with specific focus upon the married couple, Myrrine and her soldier-husband, Kinesias. As he, unsatisfied, exits, a herald from Athens' enemy Sparta arrives to report that the situation in his land goes badly in the same vein as in Athens. As a master of dialect, Aristophanes plays the two forms of Greek off each other; British translators have often relied on the ability to contrast English (for the Athenians) with a Scottish brogue (for the Spartans).

A second parabasis (lines 1014-1042) allows the choruses to be reunited with considerable sentiment in the lyric, first separately and then together addressing the audience. Throughout the remaining episodes, interlayered with lyric (lines 1043-1246), the chorus continues to tease the audience, while ranking delegates from Sparta and Athens agree to peace. Lysistrata makes the speech of "reconciliation" (lines 1112-1157) in such nearly tragic style that it has been hard for many critics to reconcile with the bawdiness of the play as a whole. Yet this is Aristophanes, perhaps at his best, suggesting to old enemies their more ancient common roots in Hellenism and their mutual obligations to one another.

The play ends with an exodos (lines 1247-1322) full of dancing revelry, yet with hymns of great beauty, even allowing the Spartan in his dialect to have the final song before all join in a four-line ode to Athena.

Summary

Over a forty-year period, Aristophanes wrote at least forty plays whose titles are known, and in five instances he rewrote examples. Of this number only eleven survive complete. Yet within these complete plays there are some of the finest examples of Greek lyric, so that alongside his contemporary, the tragic poet Euripides, Aristophanes is remembered as a master of Attic poetry.

Bibliography

Dearden, C. W. *The Stage of Aristophanes.* London: Athlone Press, 1976.

Dover, K. J. *Aristophanic Comedy.* Berkeley: University of California Press, 1972.

Ehrenberg, V. *The People of Aristophanes: A Sociology of Old Attic Comedy.* 2d ed. Cambridge, Mass.: Harvard University Press, 1962.

Harriott, Rosemary M. *Aristophanes: Poet and Dramatist.* Baltimore: The Johns Hopkins University Press, 1986.

Heath, M. *Political Comedy in Aristophanes.* Göttingen: Vandenhoeck & Ruprecht, 1987.

McLeish, K. *The Theatre of Aristophanes.* London: Thames & Hudson, 1980.

Pickard-Cambridge, Arthur W. *The Dramatic Festivals of Athens.* 2d ed. Revised by John Gould and D. M. Lewis. Oxford, England: Clarendon Press, 1968.

Stone, Laura M. *Costume in Aristophanic Comedy.* New York: Ayer Company, 1981.

Ussher, R. G. *Aristophanes.* Oxford, England: Clarendon Press, 1979.

Whitman, Cedric H. *Aristophanes and the Comic Hero.* Cambridge, Mass.: Harvard University Press, 1964.

Clyde Curry Smith

ARISTOTLE

Born: Stagirus, Chalcidice, Greece
384 B.C.
Died: Chalcis, Euboea, Greece
322 B.C.

Principal Literary Achievement
Known throughout the Middle Ages simply as "The Philosopher," Aristotle made significant contributions to a wide range of scientific, political, and philosophical topics.

Biography
Aristotle was born in 384 B.C. in Stagirus, a small colonial town on the northern coast of the Aegean Sea, in Chalcidice, Greece. His father, Nichomachus, was a physician to the court of the Macedonian king, Amyntas II. There is some speculation that being born into a physician's family led to Aristotle's later interest in biology, but that is at best only a partial account; both his parents died when he was quite young, and he was reared by an official in the Macedonian court.

At eighteen, Aristotle traveled south to Athens, where he became a member of Plato's Academy, where he spent the next twenty years. Many scholars have suggested that, during these years in close association with Plato, Aristotle imbibed his master's otherworldly and idealistic philosophy and that Aristotle was only able to develop his own naturalistic and empirically based philosophy when he left the Academy after Plato's death. Other scholars have argued that when Aristotle arrived at the Academy, it was already a large and world-famous institution engaged in all forms of intellectual and scientific investigation. While scholars can be sure that Aristotle spent much time working on a wide range of intellectual topics during his twenty years at the Academy, it is uncertain who influenced him. When Plato died in 347 B.C., Aristotle left the Academy. He spent the next five or six years teaching and doing biological research across the Aegean.

In 343 B.C., he received and accepted a request to return to Macedonia and tutor the young Alexander the Great. The relationship between the man who would be called simply "The Philosopher" throughout the Middle Ages and the future conqueror of the world was already an item for speculation when Plutarch wrote his profile of Alexander, which appears in *Bioi Parallēloi* (first transcribed c. A.D. 105-115; *Parallel Lives*, 1579), in the first century. Yet the political ambitions and ideals of the

ARISTOTELES.

*Apud Fuluium Vrsinum
in marmore.*

two men were so diverse that, whatever their personal feelings toward each other, it seems clear that Aristotle's three years of tutoring had little philosophical influence.

Once again he returned to Athens, and once again he was passed over when the presidency of the Academy became vacant. This time he opened a rival institution in the Lyceum, or gymnasium attached to the temple of Apollo Lyceus. Aristotle's reputation as a scholar was already sufficient to attract enough students, and even some teachers from the Academy, so that the Lyceum became the second viable institution of scientific and philosophical research in the West.

With Alexander's death in 323 B.C., a brief but intense anti-Macedonian mood swept through Athens. Aristotle's Macedonian origins and connections were well known. Being an astute judge of human nature, Aristotle knew that his life was in danger. Not wanting Athens to "sin twice against philosophy"—a clear allusion to Athen's execution of Socrates on the same charges many years before—Aristotle withdrew to his native province. He died the following year, in 322 B.C., in Chalcis, Greece.

Analysis

At the very heart of Aristotle's philosophy is the conviction that all things are teleologically ordered. There are two fundamentally different ways in which people explain events or things (understood in their broadest sense). Something is explained teleologically when its purpose or intention is made known. For example, a chair can be explained as an object made for sitting and a person's raised hand as an attempt to attract the teacher's attention. Alternately, something is explained causally when its physical antecedents are made known. For example, the crack in the brick wall can be explained as the result of a prior earthquake.

During the seventeenth and eighteenth centuries, there was a strong reaction against all teleological explanations because it was believed that all real knowledge gives power and control over nature. Since teleological explanations of nature do not typically help to prevent or predict natural phenomena, they were deemed to be sterile, as was Aristotle's philosophy as a whole. This period's rejection of Aristotle, however, was based largely on a misreading of his works. Aristotle did not ignore physical causes. The majority of Aristotle's work deals with topics and issues that today are considered scientific. Moreover, Aristotle's scientific investigations reveal a great care and concern for thorough observations and the collection of empirical evidence before reaching any conclusions.

Though Aristotle himself never ignored or belittled the investigation of physical causes, his view of nature and the modern scientific view of nature are quite different. The tendency today is to follow the seventeenth century's view of science as primarily an attempt to *control* nature. Aristotle, instead, emphasized science's attempt to *understand* nature, and that, he steadfastly insisted, would include both kinds of explanations. In his work *De anima* (c. 345 B.C.; *On the Soul*, 1812), Aristotle notes that some of his predecessors have tried to explain anger in terms of physical causes, while others have tried to explain it in terms of a person's intentions to seek retaliation. When asked whose explanation was better, Aristotle responded, "Is it not rather the one who combines both?"

According to Aristotle, an explanation is complete only if it has a place in a systematic and unified explanation of the whole of reality. The incredible range of topics on which Aristotle wrote is not simply the result of his wide interests. Rather, it is also the result of his conviction that all complete explanations must have their place in a systematic whole.

The goal of the special sciences—biology, physics, astronomy, for example—for both Aristotle and modern scientists is to deduce an explanation of as many observations as possible from the fewest number of principles and causes as possible. Yet Aristotle would add that the scientist's work is not complete until those principles and causes are themselves explained. If the "first principles" of a discipline are simply *assumed* to be true, then the whole discipline is left hanging in midair.

Aristotle's method of justifying first principles begins with the notion of dialectic. Aristotle's principal works start with a discussion of what his predecessors have said on the topic being studied. While such a review would always include conflicting opinions, Aristotle believed that if conflicting opinions are forced to defend themselves against their opponent's objections, the result is typically a distinction that allows the two partial truths to be unified into a larger and more complete truth.

Though Aristotle was always seeking to find some truth in conflicting opinions, he was neither a skeptic nor a relativist with regard to scientific or moral knowledge. He was never reticent to point out his predecessor's mistakes, and he oftentimes was convinced that his arguments demonstrated where these predecessors made their mistakes in such a way that all rational people would agree. Aristotle's *Organon* (335-323 B.C.; English translation, 1812) contains the tools of such demonstrations and, as such, is the first systematic formulation of the principles of deductive and inductive logic. While contemporary logicians have increased the power and versatility of Aristotle's logic, his analysis of fallacious reasoning has never been shown to be itself in error.

METAPHYSICS

First published: *Metaphysica*, fourth century B.C. (English translation, 1801)
Type of work: Philosophy

This work is an analysis of what it means to exist and a determination of the kinds of things that actually exist.

Twentieth century philosophers have distinguished between descriptive metaphysics and revisionist metaphysics. Aristotle's metaphysics is clearly an attempt to describe, analyze, and justify the common beliefs about humanity and the world, not an attempt to persuade people to revise their prephilosophical views of the world in some radical fashion. Unless the revisionist metaphysics of Aristotle's contemporaries is understood, however, it is impossible to understand Aristotle's own accomplishment.

Previous philosophers, such as Heraclitus, argued that the only source of knowledge is that which is observed through one of the five senses, and that since the testimony of the five senses reveals a continually changing world, it follows that absolutely nothing remains the same. A rock or a mountain may at first seem fairly stable, but close examination reveals that it, too, is continually being diminished by the winds and the rains. As Heraclitus said, it is impossible to step into the same river twice. Rocks and mountains may not change as quickly, but they change no less surely.

To be told that rivers, rocks, and mountains are continually changing appears to be relatively innocuous. Yet the logic of Heraclitus' argument makes it impossible to stop there. If the only source of knowledge is through the senses, then absolutely everything must be in a continual state of flux. A person who robs a bank, for example, can never be caught because whoever is charged with the crime is necessarily a different person than the one who actually committed it. Heraclitus' philosophical conclusions are clearly in radical opposition to the commonsense view of the world.

Other philosophers, such as Parmenides, argued for the exact opposite conclusion, namely, that all change is illusionary. While Heraclitus appealed to empirical data, Parmenides appealed to reason. Consider everything that really exists in the entire universe precisely as it is at this particular instance, he believed. Whatever that "everything" is, it is by definition the Real, and anything else must therefore be unreal. Now if the Real were to change, it would become something that it is not, that is, it becomes unreal. Yet the unreal does not exist. Thus, for anything to change is for it to become nonexistent. All change must therefore be unreal.

The radical opposition of Parmenides' philosophical conclusions are obvious from the start. What is not so obvious is exactly where his reasoning is mistaken. While the common people will be able to continue their daily tasks without ever addressing either Heraclitus or Parmenides' arguments, it would be inconsistent for Aristotle to insist that first principles must be dialectically justified and then simply ignore these revisionist arguments. Commonsense assumptions must be justified.

The three assumptions that Aristotle seeks to justify are, first, that things exist; second, that some things move and change; and finally, that the things in this universe that exist, move, and change are not totally unintelligible. The common element of all three beliefs is the notion of a "thing." What is a thing? Aristotle says that things have being (existence) and that a metaphysician's task is to make clear exactly what being is. In fact, he often defines the subject matter of metaphysics as the study of all things insofar as they exist.

Compare this definition with the definition of other disciplines. The subject matter of physics, says Aristotle, is things insofar as they are moving or changing objects. The subject matter of biology is things insofar as they are alive. The subject matter of ethics is things insofar as they are able to make rational choices between competing goods. One notices how the various subject matters of different disciplines constitute a hierarchical series from the particular to the general. Thus, a single person can be studied on at least three different levels. First, she can be studied by the moral philosopher as a "thing" capable of making rational choices. At a more general level, she can be studied by the biologist as a "thing" that is alive. At an even more general level, she can be studied by the physicist as a "thing" that moves.

The crucial metaphysical question for Aristotle thus becomes the following: Is there any more general level at which one can study things than at the level of the physicist? Aristotle thinks that there is, namely, at the level at which things are studied simply insofar as they exist. This way of defining the different disciplines ensures that no important questions are begged. In particular, it leaves open the question of whether anything exists apart from space and time. One of the important conclusions in the *Metaphysics* is that such a being, the unmoved mover or god, does exist. Yet before addressing such interesting and difficult theological questions, Aristotle wisely directs his attention to the more mundane, but almost as difficult, question, What is a thing?

Aristotle begins by cataloging the ordinary sorts of things that exist in this universe. There is *this* particular rock, *that* particular tree, and his friend Theaetetus. The point of any catalog is to organize different things into classes where all members of a class share something in common. People do this sort of thing all the time. The very act of speaking constitutes a kind of ordering of objects into classes. To say, "Theaetetus is snub-nosed," is to place a particular individual into one class of things as opposed to a different class. This ability to speak, and hence, classify, is grounded in two basic facts.

First, there are two fundamentally different sorts of words—substantives and words that describe substantives. In Aristotle's terms, there are subjects and predicates. Certain words or phrases are always subjects, and others are always predicates. For example, it makes sense to say, "This tree is tall," but it makes no sense to say, "Tall is this tree" (unless this statement is understood simply as a poetic way of saying, "This tree is tall"). This fundamental fact of language leads to Aristotle's distinction between form and matter. In the above sentence, "this tree" refers to some matter that one can see, touch, and perhaps even smell, and "is tall" refers to the shape or form of the matter. Pure matter, however, is inconceivable. No matter what one tries to picture, it always has some shape or form. Therefore, considered by itself, matter is mere *potentiality* as opposed to *actuality*.

Can one, then, conceive of pure form? That is difficult, though nonetheless possible according to Aristotle. It is possible, for example, to conceive of a particular song's melody without actually hearing the song. In fact, Ludwig van Beethoven conceived and composed his Ninth Symphony after he became totally deaf. In Aristotelian terms, he knew its form without ever experiencing its matter. Though Beethoven's is a special sort of case, it does help Aristotle make sense of god as pure form. In the vast majority of cases, though, Aristotle maintains that the matter and form of a thing always constitute a real unity and that they can only be separated conceptually.

People's ability to conceptually separate a thing's matter and form explains a second basic fact about language. A capacity with which all normal human beings are born is the ability to observe an incredible array of different sized, shaped, and colored objects and realize that they are all trees. Of course, the capacity to know that something is a tree presupposes much experience and instruction, but the fact remains—normal human beings are able to learn what makes an object a tree. Aristotle draws two conclusions from this fact. First, normal human beings are endowed with a capacity (*nous*) that enables them to abstract forms from matter. Second, nature is divided into *natural kinds* that humans discover and name when they abstract a thing's substantial form.

This last point leads to one final distinction—the difference between a thing's substantial form and what Aristotle calls its accidental form. A substantial form is that which makes a thing what it is. Change a thing's substantial form, and the thing becomes something else. Cut down an *actual* tree, and the mass of matter is no longer a tree but is *potentially* either a house, firewood, or compost, which will eventually turn to dirt. Yet a tree can undergo many changes and still remain a tree. Prune a limb from a tree or pick its fruit and the accidental form of the tree changes. Yet the tree remains a tree.

With these distinctions, Aristotle believes that he is able to justify commonsense beliefs about the world in the face of Heraclitus' arguments. While it is true that the five senses reveal that the accidental forms of things are continually changing, it is not true that a thing's substantial form is always changing. Thus, while there is a sense in which Heraclitus is correct, his failure to distinguish between matter and form, actuality and potentiality, and substantial forms and accidental forms invalidates his radical conclusion that everything is in a continual state of flux.

Having demonstrated that some things can remain the same, it remains for Aristotle to answer Parmenides and demonstrate how things can change. Aristotle begins by distinguishing two quite different uses of the verb "to be." To say, "The table is" (that is, "the table exists") says something quite different from saying, "The table is white." The former "is" asserts the existence of a thing; the latter "is" does not. "Whiteness" does not name a substantial form that itself exists; it only names an accidental form that cannot exist apart from actual things. While a table is actually white, it is also potentially red. Furthermore, if someone paints the table, and it becomes actually red, the table itself does not cease to exist while another table suddenly begins to exist. Parmenides' failure to distinguish between actuality and potentiality leads to his radical conclusion that nothing changes.

Aristotle is now in a position to analyze the commonsense notion of change by elucidating four ways that people use the word "cause." Consider, for a moment, a bronze statue. There are four different replies to the question of what makes that thing a statue: because it is made of bronze (material cause); because it is in the shape of a man (formal cause); because an artist shaped the matter the way that he did (efficient cause); or because an artist wanted to make a beautiful object (final cause). All four statements are true, yet no single one gives a complete explanation of the statue. According to Aristotle, any complete explanation of what a thing is, or why a thing changes, must mention all four kinds of causes.

The need for a final cause in all complete explanations has been the topic for much controversy, though there is no controversy that final causes play a central role in all Aristotle's thought. One important place is in book 12 of the *Metaphysics*. Aristotle repeatedly says that an infinite series of causes is impossible, but his words are somewhat misleading. He does not mean to assert that there is no infinite series of causes and effects. In fact, he believes that the universe itself must be infinite. What Aristotle means by his claim is that if such an infinite series of causes exists without a first cause, then the series as a whole is itself unintelligible. In any series of causes, until the stopping point can be ascertained, one cannot really determine who or what is responsible for any member of the series. Yet since Aristotle believes that the universe always existed in some form, its first cause cannot exist at some point of time prior to all others. Instead, the first cause must be conceptually first.

Not all answers to the question, Who or what is responsible for the some particular thing or movement?, refer to something that exists temporarily prior to the thing or movement being explained. A large bowl of food will cause a hungry dog to run toward it. In such a case, it is sufficient, says Aristotle, that the cause (the bowl of food) and the effect (the dog's running) exist simultaneously; the cause does not have to exist before the effect. Similarly, Aristotle argues that God's existence as the most perfect of beings is the final cause or end of all motion, even though both God and the universe have always existed.

Furthermore, the fact that God moves the universe as a final cause, rather than as an efficient cause, explains why God Himself does not require a cause. In Aristotle's metaphysics, God is conceived of as an unmoved mover. He is thus ultimately responsible for all movement and change in the universe without Himself moving. It makes no more sense to ask, What moves God? than it does to ask, Why is a vacuum empty?

NICOMACHEAN ETHICS

First published: *Ethica Nicomachea*, fourth century B.C. (English translation, 1797)
Type of work: Philosophy

Aristotle argues that happiness is the result of distinctly human activities performed well.

Aristotle believed that ethics was more a matter of character than of following rules. He was more concerned with what a person *was* than what he *did*. Of course, he realized that to a large extent a person's character is created by his actions. Yet making one's actions conform to rules was not the goal of morality. A person can obey all the rules of chess without being a very good chess player. So too, a person can follow all the rules of morality—never lie, steal, murder, or commit adultery—without being an especially good person.

The goal of morality, according to Aristotle, is human happiness. One of the questions that has received much attention by twentieth century moral philosophers—Why be moral?—never arose for Aristotle because he simply assumed that achieving a stable and lasting happiness was everyone's goal.

Of course, Aristotle understood that there is a wide divergence of opinion among people as to what constitutes happiness—some say it is wealth, others say it is power or honor, still others say it is pleasure. People will only know which of these, or which mix of these, really leads to a life well lived, says Aristotle, by first determining the proper work or function of a person *qua* person.

The function of a carpenter is to build houses, and the function of an author is to write books. Given these distinct functions, it is not unreasonable to assume that a carpenter would feel frustrated if forced to write a book, and conversely, that an author would feel frustrated if forced to build a house. Each of these would rather be doing that which he or she is uniquely suited to do. Aristotle takes this argument one step further and argues that human beings are happiest when they are acting in accordance with their essential nature.

The essential nature of anything is the thing's work or function, that is, that which it does better than anything else. Observation reveals that humans are superior to all other animals in two areas, reasoning and social organization. Aristotle does not say that only humans are capable of reasoning. A dog can infer from his master's facial expression that he is about to be punished. Yet dogs cannot discover, or understand, what is common to all punishments because they cannot know (*nous*) the essence of punishment. Dogs may be able to communicate with a series of growls and barks, but they are not able to create a language that defines and categorizes things according to their essential natures.

Similarly, while dogs live in packs and exhibit a rudimentary social nature, that social structure is determined by instinct. This tendency is evident by the invariant nature of that organization within a single species. Human social organizations are voluntary, and thus, they exhibit a wide variety of political structures ranging from the monarchical to the democratic.

Aristotle now becomes more specific as to exactly how human beings flourish. Since they are by nature rational, humans have a need and desire for knowledge. Only when this natural desire is fulfilled can humans be truly happy. Second, the nature of a person as a social animal means that men and women have a natural need and desire for friends. The *Nicomachean Ethics* devotes a fifth of its chapters to the nature and value of friendship.

In Aristotle's philosophy, a human being's rational and social nature feed and nourish each other. Their rational capacities, for example, must be developed by good parents and teachers, and good parents and teachers are only found in well-ordered societies. Conversely, well-ordered societies presuppose knowledgeable citizens. Thus, knowledge and virtue go hand in hand.

Aristotle defines virtue as "the mean relative to us, a mean which is defined by a rational principle, such as a man of practical wisdom would use to determine it." He explains himself with an example. Consider, he says, the different caloric needs of a heavyweight boxer in training and of a teacher during spring break. What may be too few calories for the boxer may very well be too many for the teacher. There is no set number of calories that all people ought to ingest. Similarly, consider the virtue of liberality. What may be a stingy contribution to charity by a rich man may be an overly generous contribution by a person of moderate means with a family to support.

Yet Aristotle is not a moral relativist. He is not saying that, since people in different cultures have different beliefs about what is right or wrong, there are therefore no moral absolutes. There is nothing in Aristotle's ethic that makes mere difference of belief a morally relevant factor in the determination of the mean. A society that believes that wealth is largely the result of individual initiative might believe that contributing 2 percent of one's income to charity is a worthy goal. A different society that believes that wealth is largely a gift of nature might believe that giving only 2 percent of one's income to the less fortunate would be unthinkably tight. Though these two cultures have different beliefs, that in itself, Aristotle would say, is morally irrelevant in determining the morally proper mean.

While the caloric needs of different people vary, what those needs are is not determined by majority opinion, but by the nutritional expert. So too, the mean in moral matters is not determined by popular opinion. Rather, it is determined by a rational principle, and that rational principle is in turn determined by the man or woman of practical wisdom.

The healthy individual has a desire for exercise and proper food. Regardless of what others say, his judgment in these matters is correct because of the obvious effect of his wholesome practices on his own life. According to Aristotle, one ought to reason similarly in ethical matters. Just as people know a physically healthy person when they see one, they also know a happy person when they see one. Of course, when Aristotle says a person is happy, he is not referring to an emotional state of someone who wins the state lottery. Such a condition is the result of external conditions and not the result of voluntary action. Rather, when he speaks of the happy woman, he is speaking of the woman who is happy largely as a result of what she has herself done. Her happiness is stable because it "feeds on itself" in the same way that a winning college basketball team continues winning year after year because it is able to recruit the best high school players. Similarly, a happy person is one who succeeds in the worthy things that she sets out to do. When she does, she receives satisfaction, and this in turn encourages her to set out to accomplish other worthwhile goals. That causes the cycle to repeat. It is this sort of person that Aristotle says determines the "rational principle" in moral matters.

POETICS

First published: *De poetica*, c. 334 B.C.-323 B.C. (English translation, 1705)
Type of work: Literary criticism

This is a work of theoretical and practical literary criticism, especially with regard to tragic drama.

Aristotle's *Poetics*, though short, has been widely influential outside philosophical circles. Yet it is doubtful that it can be fully appreciated outside Aristotle's philosophical system as a whole.

Central to all Aristotle's philosophy is the claim that nothing can be understood apart from its end or purpose (*telos*). Not surprisingly, the *Poetics* seeks to discover the end or purpose of all the poetic arts, and especially of tragic drama. Understood generally, the goal of poetry is to provide pleasure of a particular kind. The *Metaphysics* begins, "All men desire to know by nature," and the *Nicomachean Ethics* repeatedly says that the satisfaction of natural desires is the greatest source of lasting pleasure. The *Poetics* combines these two with the idea of imitation. All people by nature enjoy a good imitation (that is, a picture or drama) because they enjoy learning, and imitations help them to learn.

Of particular interest to Aristotle is the pleasure derived from tragic drama, namely, the kind of pleasure that comes from the purging or cleansing (catharsis) of the emotions of fear and pity. Though the emotions of fear and pity are not to be completely eliminated, excessive amounts of these emotions are not characteristic of a flourishing individual. Vicariously experiencing fear and pity in a good tragedy cleanses the soul of ill humors.

Though there are many elements of a good tragedy, the most important, according to Aristotle, is the plot. The centrality of plot once again follows from central doctrines of the *Metaphysics* and the *Nichomachean Ethics*. In the former, Aristotle argues that all knowledge is knowledge of universals; in the latter, he states that it is through their own proper activity that humans discover fulfillment.

For a plot to work, it must be both complete and coherent. That means that it must constitute a whole with a beginning, middle, and end, and that the sequence of events must exhibit some sort of necessity. A good dramatic plot is unlike history. History has no beginning, middle, and end, and thus it lacks completeness. Furthermore, it lacks coherence because many events in history happen by accident. In a good dramatic plot, however, everything happens for a reason. This difference makes tragedy philosophically more interesting than history. Tragedy focuses on universal causes and effects and thus provides a kind of knowledge that history, which largely comprises accidental happenings, cannot.

Summary

Aristotle's philosophy is not flawless. Even his most vigorous contemporary defenders are quick to point out his errors—for example, his belief that some people are slaves by nature and that women are naturally inferior to men. Many people today would argue that such pronouncements, made with complete confidence at the time, prove that what is true for one person may not be true for someone else. Rather than being patronized by those who would excuse his errors by relativizing truth, however, Aristotle would much prefer simply to be refuted with good arguments and careful observations. These are much more central to his philosophy than any particular conclusions that he reached on any particular topic.

Bibliography

Ackrill, J. L. *Aristotle the Philosopher.* New York: Oxford University Press, 1981.
Adler, Mortimer J. *Aristotle for Everybody.* New York: Macmillan, 1978.
Bambrough, Renford, ed. *The Philosophy of Aristotle.* New York: Mentor, 1963.
Barnes, Jonathan. *Aristotle.* New York: Oxford University Press, 1982.
Grene, Marjorie. *A Portrait of Aristotle.* Chicago: University of Chicago Press, 1963.
Ross, W. David. *Aristotle.* New York: Methuen, 1923.
Taylor, A. E. *Aristotle.* New York: Dover, 1955.
Veatch, Henry V. *Aristotle: A Contemporary Appreciation.* Bloomington: Indiana University Press, 1974.

Ric S. Machuga

MATTHEW ARNOLD

Born: Laleham, England
December 24, 1822
Died: Liverpool, England
April 15, 1888

Principal Literary Achievement
Arnold is preceded only by Alfred, Lord Tennyson, and Robert Browning as an important poet of Victorian England. His critical essays, emphasizing the role of literature in the amelioration of society, had a profound influence on twentieth century literary criticism.

Biography

Matthew Arnold was born in Laleham, England, on Christmas Eve, 1822, the second child and first son of Dr. Thomas and Mary Penrose Arnold. In December, 1827, Thomas Arnold was elected headmaster of Rugby School, where the family began residence in August, 1828. It was the beginning of an auspicious career for Thomas Arnold, who would distinguish himself as the foremost educational reformer of the English public school. In addition to a general enhancing of academic quality, Dr. Arnold's reforms for his new students specifically included the introduction of modern languages and mathematics into the center of the curriculum, the fostering of a higher moral tone, and the inculcation of a greater sense of social responsibility among the privileged Rugby students toward the lower classes of English society. Dr. Arnold's social and intellectual perspective had a pronounced influence on his son, who, although he did not begin studies at the school until 1837, lived at the center of the Rugby community.

Enrolled at Winchester School in August, 1836, for one year of preparatory study, Matthew Arnold subsequently entered Rugby in late summer of the following year. He was a desultory student, frequently late for class and poorly disciplined in his approach to his studies. It was an attitude that caused considerable concern for his parents, particularly his father, whose kindly but intimidating presence was clearly part of the problem. By 1840, his final year, Matthew had done much to redeem himself. He won the school poetry prize for "Alaric at Rome" and was successful in competition for a coveted scholarship to Balliol College, Oxford.

At Oxford, Arnold deepened his friendship with the poet Arthur Hugh Clough, who had been a friend of the family and a student of Dr. Arnold at Rugby. They

frequently disagreed on many of the leading issues of the day, but Clough, until his death in 1861, proved a steady and important influence. Their relationship is commemorated in Arnold's elegiac poem "Thyrsis," in which the poet reviews and re-examines the ideals, both spiritual and literary, that the two young men shared as Oxford undergraduates.

Although something of a "dandy," much preoccupied with fashionable dress and demeanor in his undergraduate years, Arnold managed to take a second-class honors degree in 1844 and, a year earlier, to win the coveted Newdigate Prize for his poem "Cromwell." In the following year, he won a fellowship to Oriel College, Oxford, which at the time was the storm center of the Tractarian controversy—the celebrated Oxford Movement—led by John Henry Newman. Along with Clough and Thomas Arnold, Newman was the third contemporary figure to have an important effect on the direction of Matthew Arnold's thinking. Although Arnold was now a firm adherent to the theological liberalism of his father, he nonetheless approved of many of the more salient points of Newman's conservative position, particularly the need to intensify religious feeling and sincere spiritual conviction and to counteract ambiguous religious liberalism.

In 1846, Arnold traveled in France and Switzerland, and he returned to England the following year to settle into gentlemanly employment as private secretary to Henry Petty-Fitzmaurice, marquis of Lansdowne. It was an undemanding position, offering considerable time for writing new poems and editing others. Between 1849, when he published his first collection, titled *The Strayed Reveller and Other Poems*, and 1855, the year that marked the appearance of *Poems, Second Series*, Arnold submitted to the world most of the poetry that he would write in his lifetime. In 1857, he was elected to the chair of professor of poetry at Oxford, a position that he held for the next ten years. His tenure at Oxford culminated in the publication of his final volume of verse, *New Poems* (1867), which contained the remarkable "Dover Beach." The position paid a small stipend and required only three lectures per year. Following a government appointment as inspector of schools in April, 1851, a position that he would hold simultaneously with the Oxford Poetry Chair, Arnold married Frances Lucy Wightman, daughter of Sir William Wightman, a judge of the Court of the Queen's Bench.

From the 1860's through the 1880's, Arnold's creative efforts shifted from poetry to prose. He concentrated on literary and social criticism and gave considerable attention to the improvement of public education in England. Much was to be learned, he believed, from a study of educational methods and procedures on the Continent. Toward this end, he toured in his official capacity the schools of France, Germany, and Switzerland and published his findings and observations in a series of essays: "The Popular Education of France"; "A French Eton"; and "Schools and Universities on the Continent." His literary criticism of the 1860's, particularly extended essays such as *On Translating Homer* (1861), *Essays in Criticism* (1865), and *On the Study of Celtic Literature* (1867), largely comprised lectures delivered at Oxford. *Culture and Anarchy*, his extended study of the ills of a materialistic, contemporary society, appeared in 1869. From October, 1883, until March, 1884, Arnold traveled in the United States and gave a series of lectures, which were published in 1885 under the title *Discourses in America.* In 1886, he made a second trip across the Atlantic to give additional lectures but returned to England that same spring, resigned his inspectorship, and effectively retired from public life. On April 15, 1888, Arnold died in Liverpool of a sudden heart attack. He was sixty-five.

Analysis

Although great poetry should transcend the limits of time, Arnold's poetry must be read in the context of his turbulent age if it is to be understood fully. He is a post-Romantic coming into full conflict with the British empire at the height of its expansion and industrialization. The effects of this conflict comprise the themes of his poetry: spiritual stasis and enervation, humankind as an alien figure in the cosmos, the absence in the modern world of spiritual and intellectual values, values largely subsumed by industrial growth and materialism. Arnold's poetry, however, offers no solutions, nor is it particularly articulate on the exact nature of the dilemma. Among the English poets, his mentors were William Wordsworth and John Keats, both of whom influenced his style and aesthetic perspective. His best work, exemplified in poems such as "Dover Beach," "The Scholar-Gipsy," "Rugby Chapel," "Thyrsis," "The Buried Life," and "Stanzas from the Grande Chartreuse," is outwardly calm and lucid, containing the same sincerity, dignity, and restraint that characterized his Romantic predecessors. It also pursues the same elusive serenity. It is a pursuit inherently complicated by the resulting tension between the temporal or "real" world of distracting sensory phenomena and the transcendent realm of the ideal.

Three social factors in the "real" world were largely responsible for the intellectual and spiritual division that Arnold felt so keenly and expressed in his poetry. Charles Darwin's *On the Origin of Species by Means of Natural Selection* (1859) brought new, scientific knowledge to the forefront, all but eclipsing the established authority of traditional beliefs. The Oxford Tractarians, following the lead of Newman, sought to bring English Christianity back to a more universal, conservative view, away from the "broad church" liberalism that, for many, threatened to become the secular bulwark of British Protestantism. The "Chartist" reform movements of 1832 and 1867, with recurrent calls for the expansion of suffrage, entailed a broadening of democracy that, for many, threatened the traditional stability of government guided by aristocratic values. In literature, the long popular Romanticism of novels by writers such as Sir Walter Scott, who extolled chivalric heroism, legend, and tradition, was gradually forced to give way before the realism of Charles Dickens, William Makepeace Thackeray, George Eliot, and Anthony Trollope.

To all of this Arnold responded with a poetry of general lament for the divisions of modern life, for the sense of fragmentation that now pervaded the age. In "Stanzas from the Grand Chartreuse," Arnold describes himself as "Wandering between two worlds, one dead,/ The other powerless to be born." The "dead" world of innocence and natural joy was the freely received gift of nature, a world in which emotion and intellect remained counterpoised on either side of a spiritual fulcrum. "We had not lost our balance then," he has the title character say in "Empedocles on Etna," "nor grown/ Thought's slaves, and dead to every natural joy." The world into which the poet is "powerless to be born" is a world of serenity characterized by unity and order. Its genesis lies in the pursuit of "culture," which Arnold defines in *Culture and Anarchy* as "a study of perfection, harmonious and general perfection which consists in *becoming* something rather than *having* something." The optimistic quest for perfection is an objective with which Arnold deals extensively in his critical essays, but in his poetry he remains immersed in melancholy. What little hope there is for the future lies in a vaguely intuitive recognition of truth, which is hopefully stimulated by those elements of culture that awaken humankind and enrich the human condition.

In his prose, Arnold examines the issue of England's societal malaise in even greater detail. Having all but abandoned poetry after the 1850's, he devoted the last thirty years of his life to prose criticism. His essays addressed four general areas: education, religion, literature, and society. His writings on education dealt with contemporary issues and are of interest primarily to historians concerned with curricula in English and Continental schools of the nineteenth century. On religious issues, Arnold produced four books: *St. Paul and Protestantism* (1870), *Literature and Dogma* (1873), *God and the Bible* (1875), and *Last Essays on Church and Religion* (1877). All are responses to the various religious controversies that swept through Great Britain in the latter half of the nineteenth century, which were spurred in part by the ferment caused by the Oxford Movement and the evolution theories of Darwin.

Of much greater interest to posterity than Arnold's writings on education and religion have been his critical examinations of society. In *Culture and Anarchy* and *Friendship's Garland* (1871), he expresses his growing concern with the suspect values of a Victorian middle class. This middle class, which he termed "Philistines," was, in Arnold's view, puritanical, inflexible, and selfishly individualistic. In short, it was wholly unprepared to confront the problems inherent in the combination of a growing industrialism, an expanding population, and an increasing and clamorous call for widespread democracy. To transform society, it would be necessary to eliminate the classes that divide it, an objective to be achieved through universal education. Central to this universal education would be the promotion and encouragement of culture.

The pursuit of culture is understandably at the center of his literary criticism. Nowhere is this more apparent than in his *Essays in Criticism* (1865). It is in the first essay, "The Function of Criticism at the Present Time," that Arnold offers most succinctly his critical manifesto. Criticism, as he defines it, is "a disinterested endeavor to learn and propagate the best that is known and thought in the world." It is this awareness, he further states—which the critic discerns and shares with the reader who pursues culture—that will nourish humanity "in growth toward perfection."

DOVER BEACH

First published: 1867
Type of work: Poem

As traditional beliefs are undermined by nineteenth century "progress," even the aesthetic verities of Love and Beauty are overwhelmed by doubt and despair.

"Dover Beach" is a brief, dramatic monologue generally recognized as Arnold's best—and most widely known—poem. It begins with an opening stanza that is indisputably one of the finest examples of lyric poetry in the English language. The topography of the nocturnal setting is a combination of hushed tranquillity and rich sensory detail. It is the world as it appears to the innocent eye gazing on nature: peaceful, harmonious, suffused with quiet joy. The beacon light on the coast of Calais, the moon on the calm evening waters of the channel, and the sweet scent of the night air all suggest a hushed and gentle world of silent beauty. The final line of the stanza, however, introduces a discordant note, as the perpetual movement of the waves suggests to the speaker not serenity but "the eternal note of sadness."

The melancholy strain induces in the second stanza an image in the mind of the speaker: Sophocles, the Greek tragedian, creator of *Oidipous Tyrannos* (c. 429 B.C.; *Oedipus Tyrannus*) and *Antigone* (c. 441 B.C.; *Antigone*) standing in the darkness by the Aegean Sea more than two thousand years ago. The ancient master of tragedy hears in the eternal flux of the waves the same dark note, "the turbid ebb and flow/ Of human misery." Thus, the speaker (like Sophocles before him) perceives life as tragedy; suffering and misery are inextricable elements of existence. Beauty, joy, and calm are ephemeral and illusory. The speaker's pessimistic perspective on the human condition, expressed in stanzas two, three, and four, undercuts and effectively negates the positive, tranquil beauty of the opening stanza; the *reality* subsumes the misleading *appearance*. In the third stanza, Arnold introduces the metaphor of the "Sea of Faith," the once abundant tide in the affairs of humanity that has slowly withdrawn from the modern world. Darwinism and Tractarianism in Arnold's nineteenth century England brought science into full and successful conflict with religion. "Its melancholy, long withdrawing roar" suggested to Arnold the death throes of the Christian era. The Sophoclean tragic awareness of fate and painful existence had for centuries been displaced by the pure and simple faith of the Christian era, a temporary compensation promising respite from an existence that is ultimately tragic.

The fourth and final stanza of "Dover Beach" is extremely pessimistic. Its grim view of reality, its negativity, its underlying desperate anguish are in marked contrast to the joy and innocent beauty of the first stanza. Love, the poet suggests, is the one final truth, the last fragile human resource. Yet here, as the world is swallowed by darkness, it promises only momentary solace, not joy or salvation for the world. The world, according to the speaker, "seems/ To lie before us like a land of dreams," offering at least an appearance that seems "So various, so beautiful, so new," but it is deceptive, a world of wishful thinking. It is shadow without substance, offering neither comfort nor consolation. In this harsh existence, there is "neither joy, nor love, nor light,/ Nor certitude, nor peace, nor help for pain."

Arnold closes the poem with the famous lines that suggest the very nadir of human existence. Humanity stands on the brink of chaos, surrounded in encroaching darkness by destructive forces and unable to distinguish friend from foe. The concluding image of the night battle suggests quite clearly the mood of the times among those who shared Arnold's intellectual temperament, and it is one with which they were quite familiar. Thucydides' *Historia tu Peloponnesiacon polemou* (431-404 B.C.; *History of the Peloponnesian War*, 1550) describes the night battle of Epipolae between the Athenians and the Syracusans. Dr. Thomas Arnold, Matthew's father, had published a three-volume translation of Thucydides' text in 1835; it was a favorite text at Rugby. Another ancillary source was John Henry Newman, who, in 1843, published a sermon, "Faith and Reason, Contrasted as Habits of Mind," in which he alludes to the growing religious controversy of the time, describing it as "a sort of night battle, where each fights for himself, and friend and foe stand together." Few poems have equaled its concise, sensitive note of poignant despair.

THE SCHOLAR-GIPSY

First published: 1853
Type of work: Poem

An Oxford student resists the increasingly materialistic emphasis of traditional university education, seeking instead inherent truths in the beauty of nature and in intellectual idealism.

For the central premise of "The Scholar-Gipsy," Arnold draws upon a legend of the area surrounding the university city of Oxford. The legend tells of a wandering scholar who rejects the material world of the academy to pursue a vague and idealistic objective. Arnold uses this story as a metaphor for his indictment of a world that is obsessed with materialism and individual advancement but is largely indifferent to culture and the pursuit of the ideal. In 1844, Arnold had purchased a copy of Joseph Glanvill's *The Vanity of Dogmatizing* (1661). Glanvill's book recounts the tale of an Oxford student who, with neither patron nor independent financial means, was forced to discontinue his studies and to make his way in the world. Increasing poverty leads him to join a band of roving gypsies, with whom he begins a new and very different education. From these vagabonds, who roam at will following rules and traditions that in no way answer to the world of "preferment," he discovers the power of the imagination stimulated by nature. Gradually he rejects the world of humanity and materialism. As the years become centuries, the increasingly mysterious scholar-gipsy continues his quest, a solitary figure always seen at a distance, carefully avoiding any contact with the corruption of modern civilization.

"The Scholar-Gipsy," with its bucolic setting, has many of the characteristics of the traditional pastoral elegy. These characteristics are clearly apparent in the first stanza. As, for example, John Milton does in "Lycidas," Arnold addresses the young poet, casting him in the role of the shepherd who has abandoned the "quest," the pursuit of the ideal, to go forth into the world of political change and turmoil. In 1848, Arnold's close friend the poet Arthur Hugh Clough left his post at Oxford in order to become more directly involved in the revolutionary social changes that were then restructuring all of European society. In the first stanza, the speaker calls upon the poet-shepherd to return, when the turmoil has settled, from leading the "sheep" of restless England. Return, he importunes the shepherd-poet, when "the fields are still,/ And the tired men and dogs all gone to rest." The speaker (Arnold) and his fellow poet will remain behind, in the natural setting, away from the din of the city. The third stanza is almost purely descriptive. It presents the speaker reclining amid the beauties of nature, which Arnold renders with true Keatsian sensuosity.

In the fourth through the seventh stanzas, Arnold relates the legend of the scholar-gipsy, drawn from "Glanvill's book." The secrets of the "gipsy-crew," the ultimate truth to be drawn from nature, remain elusive, the wandering scholar tells some former fellow students whom he encounters in the early days of his quest. When he has fully discovered that truth, he will impart it to the world; the skill to do that, however, "needs heaven-sent moments," divine or noumenal inspiration that lies beyond the knowledge and intellectual skills that one might develop at Oxford.

After the encounter with his former fellow students, the scholar becomes a ghostly figure. He is occasionally sighted, but as one draws close he disappears, becoming, as the years pass, more an enduring illusion than a tangible reality. Gradually, only those who inhabit the country, those associated with the outdoors and the rural life beyond the civilization of cities, see the scholar-gipsy.

In stanzas 10 through 13, Arnold traces the scholar's gradual integration with nature through the passage of seasons. The country people who encounter him at different times and in different places throughout the year remark upon his "figure spare," his "dark vague eyes and soft abstracted air." The scholar, on his singular mission, has forsaken the world of humanity and is gradually fading from humanity into the countryside that he inhabits. He seeks an ultimate truth that lies somewhere beyond the confines of university walls and the politics of modern society.

The scholar-gipsy's quest is presumably the same pursuit of the ideal that was so much a part of Romantic poetry in the early nineteenth century. While John Keats and William Wordsworth had a very pronounced influence on Arnold, the influence of Percy Bysshe Shelley and Samuel Taylor Coleridge should not be discounted. An important common element among these early nineteenth century poets was the concept of the division between the real and the ideal, between the tangible world of sensory phenomena and the noumenal, "ideal" world. The Romantic poet seeks to transcend the distractions, the demands, the profound limitations of the world "enclosed by the senses five," as William Blake termed it. He or she seeks to encounter, through the powers of the imagination, the world of synthesis, harmony, unity, and ultimate truth, in a world that is also beyond the limits of time and space. It is that transcendent condition, according to Wordsworth, when the poet is able to see "into the life of things," to perceive what Wordsworth calls "the hour/ Of Splendour in the grass, of glory in the flower." For the Romantics, the quest was continually interrupted by the demands of the material world. The poet inevitably plummets back to reality, falling, as Shelley said, "upon the thorns of life."

Arnold's pantheistic wandering scholar pursues the moment of Romantic inspiration and insight, waiting, as Arnold says in stanzas 12 and 18, for "the spark from heaven." In stanzas 15 through 17, Arnold praises the scholar-gipsy's single-mindedness, his pursuit of "*one* aim, *one* business, *one* desire." The legend has become the symbol for fidelity in the pursuit of a higher reality. The scholar-gipsy has not felt "the lapse of hours" but has become, like Keats's Grecian urn, "exempt from age."

In stanzas 20 through 23, Arnold characteristically gives full vent to his pessimistic view of the modern world. Life is "the long unhappy dream," one that individuals "wish . . . would end." Similar to the mood at the conclusion of "Dover Beach," this poem sees the mid-nineteenth century as a time when individuals "waive all claim to bliss, and try to bear." The aversion intensifies to the point where modern life is a contagious miasma, a veritable plague. The scholar-gipsy is right to avoid all social contact, to avoid "this strange disease of modern life/ With its sick hurry, its divided aims." He is warned to fly "our feverish contact," to save himself from the "infection of our mental strife." Not to heed this warning would mean that "thy glad perennial youth would fade,/ Fade, and grow old at last, and die like ours."

"The Scholar-Gipsy" effectively blends the Romantic sensibility of the late eighteenth and early nineteenth centuries with the Victorian reaction to the rapid growth of industrialism. It is one of Arnold's many poetic commentaries on a time when the "machinery" of the mind threatened the annihilation of both the soul and the artistically creative imagination.

CULTURE AND ANARCHY

First published: 1869
Type of Work: Essays

As widespread democratic reform follows technological progress and a growing emphasis on materialism, Arnold addresses the potential danger in the loss of traditional cultural values.

Culture and Anarchy, Arnold's masterpiece of social criticism, was the direct result of the turbulence leading up to the second reform bill of 1867. The book comprises six essays, which were published serially in the *Cornhill Magazine* between 1867 and 1868 under the title "Anarchy and Authority." At the time that Arnold was preparing these essays, anarchy in English society was very much in ascendancy. From 1866 through 1868, there were a variety of social disturbances: riots in Trafalgar Square, Fenian and trade union demonstrations, anti-Catholic rallies, and suffrage protests in the industrial cities of Birmingham and Wolverhampton.

There was a rising tide of anarchy in England, and for Arnold it seemed that the entire country was in a general state of decline. Chief among the faults leading to this condition was an appalling smugness and insularity in the English character. As Arnold saw it, the typical English citizen was narrow and circumspect in the appreciation of the higher qualities and virtues of life. The cities in which he or she lived and worked expressed no beauty in their architecture; they were sprawling, industrial conglomerations. People were smug and cantankerous, loud in their assertions of individualism and personal liberty and adamant in their dislike of centralized authority, church or state. They were, however, obsequious in their respect for size and numbers in the burgeoning Empire and in their acquiescence to the "machinery" of its ever-expanding bureaucracies. Arnold's "typical" English citizen worshiped the materialism that generally determined societal values, but in religious matters he or she emphasized the "protest" in Protestantism and generally abhorred centralized spiritual authority. The English citizen was puritanical and inflexible.

The character of the Victorian middle class, in Arnold's view, was woefully inadequate to meet the problems it was currently facing, problems such as a rapidly increasing population, the unchecked rise of industrialism, and the continued spread of democracy. In addition to the middle class, which Arnold identified as "Philistines," there were two other classes to be considered: the aristocracy, identifed as the "Barbarians," and the lower classes, termed the "Populace." All in varying degrees were in need of culture, which Arnold defines as the pursuit "of our total perfection by means of getting to know, on all matters that most concern us, the best which has been thought and said in the world." Culture is the means by which to achieve the general amelioration of English society and the general improvement of English character.

Central to the universal apprehending of "culture" are two elements that Arnold terms "Sweetness and Light," the title of the first chapter of *Culture and Anarchy*. These terms, borrowed from Jonathan Swift's "The Battle of the Books," are rather vague and abstract, but they suggest an analogy to beauty and truth as they are used by Keats's in "Ode on a Grecian Urn." "Sweetness," as Arnold uses it, is the apprehension and appreciation of beauty, the aesthetic dimension in human nature; "Light" is intelligence, brightened by open-mindedness, a full awareness of humankind's past, and a concomitant capacity to enjoy and appreciate the best works of art, literature, history, and philosophy. They are linked entities, aided in their development within the individual by curiosity and disinterestedness, the essential impartiality that dispels prejudice.

The successful infusing of Sweetness and Light into the individual and general character also requires a coalescence and a balance of two elements that are integral to the history of Western civilization. Arnold terms these elements "Hebraism and Hellenism," the title of chapter 4. Hebraism is the intellectual and spiritual heritage that is the basis of a Semitic and subsequently Judeo-Christian tradition. It is from the Hebraic influence that Western civilization derives a sense of duty, a work ethic, the value of self-control, and the importance of obedience to the will of God. This value of obedience is enforced by a strictness of conscience, a sense of imperfection rooted in a shared stigma of Original Sin. Hellenism, on the other hand, is an Indo-European rather than a Semitic heritage. Its worldview is largely the opposite of Hebraism. From Hellenism, humanity derives an open "philosophic" perspective, an ardor for thinking and knowing. It is characterized by a striving for an unclouded clarity of mind, an unimpeded play of thought among the questions of the universal order. It stresses a clear intelligence and a seeking to apprehend. In opposition to Hebraic strictness of conscience, Hellenism emphasizes a spontaneity of consciousness, a total intellectual and spiritual freedom in the pursuit of perfection. An inevitable collision, Arnold explains, occurred in the Renaissance, the period when Europe rediscovered Hellenic ideas and perspective. The result of this proximity and subsequent collision was the Hebraistic view that identified Hellenism with "moral indifference and lax rule of conduct." Hellenism, from the Hebraic perspective, was associated with a loss of spiritual balance, a weakening of moral fiber. The reaction solidified into Puritanism, bringing an end, in the seventeenth century, to the Renaissance in Europe.

Arnold's leaning in *Culture and Anarchy* is clearly toward Hellenism and away from the dominance of Hebraism; but he recognizes that the path to perfection, the theme and purpose of the book, is to be found in a coalescence of the two, an extracting of the best of both elements. Neither Hebraism nor Hellenism is a law of human development, but each is a contribution. He advocates a reintroduction of Hellenism to counteract the static inflexibility of Puritan influence in the English character. What is needed is a Hebraic-Hellenic central authority, the establishing of the state as an organ of society's collective "best" self. This authority would be guided by Sweetness and Light and "right reason," Western civilization's Hellenic legacy. Such a central authority would check self-serving, solipsistic individualism, would encourage culture, and would eventually transform society.

It is important to recognize that Arnold does not offer *Culture and Anarchy* as an active blueprint for the reconstruction of society. He was, in the strictest sense of the word, apolitical. The book is intended as a spiritual awakening, but spiritual in a far broader context than a strict adherence to the "machinery" of organized religion. There is a better self that lies within collective humanity that Arnold urges his readers to rediscover. To avert anarchy, humankind must pursue culture, must keep as an essential objective the achieving of perfection. In such pursuit alone lies the eventual salvation of humanity and society.

Summary

   Matthew Arnold's poetry and prose criticism are devoted to the themes of spiritual stasis, the absence of intellectual values, and the general diminution of humankind in the face of growing materialism and expanding industrialism. Arnold was not a social scientist and made no pretense at offering practical solutions to real problems. His responses are high-minded at best, often vague and idealistic to a fault. In a world that is fragmented and divided among many creeds and material objectives, he laments both the loss of and the failure to reachieve a world of serenity characterized by unity, order, right reason, and culture. In addition to his accomplishments in poetry, Arnold's remarkable achievements lie in the standards set by his literary criticism and in his perceptive analysis of England's social malaise in the latter half of the nineteenth century.

Bibliography

Allott, Kenneth. *Matthew Arnold.* London: Longmans, Green, 1955.

Brown, Edward Killoran. *Matthew Arnold: A Study in Conflict.* Chicago: University of Chicago Press, 1948.

Chambers, E. K. *Matthew Arnold: A Study.* Oxford, England: Clarendon Press, 1947.

Faverty, Frederic E. *Matthew Arnold, the Ethnologist.* Evanston, Ill.: Northwestern University Press, 1951.

Honan, Park. *Matthew Arnold: A Life.* Cambridge, Mass.: Harvard University Press, 1983.

Johnson, Wendell Stacy. *The Voices of Matthew Arnold: An Essay in Criticism.* New Haven, Conn.: Yale University Press, 1961.

McCarthy, Patrick J. *Matthew Arnold and the Three Classes.* New York: Columbia University Press, 1964.

Raleigh, John Henry. *Matthew Arnold and American Culture.* Berkeley: University of California Press, 1957.

Tinker, C. B., and H. F. Lowry. *The Poetry of Matthew Arnold: A Commentary.* London: Oxford University Press, 1950.

Trilling, Lionel. *Matthew Arnold.* New York: Columbia University Press, 1949.

Richard Keenan

MARGARET ATWOOD

Born: Ottawa, Ontario, Canada
November 18, 1939

Principal Literary Achievement

Canadian writer Atwood, who has focused on political themes such as feminism, censorship, and human rights, has achieved an international reputation as a novelist and poet.

Biography

Margaret Eleanor Atwood was born in Ottawa, Ontario, on November 18, 1939, the daughter of Carl and Margaret Killam Atwood. In 1945, her father, who was an entomologist specializing in forest insects, moved the family to northern Ontario, the bush country that is featured in many of her works. Though the family returned a year later to Toronto, Atwood, in later years, would often visit the rural parts of Ontario and Quebec and spend a considerable amount of time at her country place. She attended high school in Toronto, and when she began writing at the age of sixteen, she had the encouragement of her high school teachers and one of her aunts. While attending Victoria College of the University of Toronto, she read Robert Graves's *The White Goddess: A Historical Grammar of Poetic Myth* (1948), which she claims "terrified" her because, while women are at the center of Graves's poetic theory, they are inspirations, not creators, and are alternately loving and destructive. This view of women writers did not daunt the aspiring writer, who has since helped to "correct" Graves's view and has focused much of her writing on women's issues and the themes of identity and empowerment.

After graduating from Victoria College in 1961, the same year that *Double Persephone* (1961), her first volume of poems, appeared, she attended Radcliffe College, receiving her M.A. degree in 1962. She has also done graduate work at Harvard University, but she remains resolutely Canadian, and the United States and its citizens are frequent targets in her writing. After her graduate work, she worked briefly as a cashier, waitress, market research writer, and film-script writer, and her work experiences have been transformed into her fiction. Atwood's work is often autobiographical. She also taught at Canadian universities during the 1960's and later in her career served as writer-in-residence at such diverse institutions as the University of Alabama and Macquarie University in Australia.

In the 1960's, Atwood's work was primarily poetic, although she did write an un-

published novel before *The Edible Woman* (1969) appeared. In *Double Persephone* and *The Circle Game* (1966), Atwood establishes the images and themes that characterize all of her poetry. She uses images of drowning, journeys, mirrors, and dreams to develop the contrast between life and art and between humanity's creation and nature. In *The Edible Woman*, Atwood develops the theme of gender politics by focusing on the plight of an engaged young woman threatened by her "consuming" fiancé, who wishes to fix and limit her role. Although gender pervades her poems, her novel provides an early statement about women's rights and has established her as a somewhat reluctant spokesperson for feminism.

In the 1970's, despite the publication of five volumes of verse, Atwood's most significant works were novels. *Surfacing* (1972) is widely regarded as one of her best novels and has been the subject of numerous critical studies. As a story of a woman who returns to the past to heal herself, the novel uses myth and psychology as it explores the issues of language, family, love, and surviving—these issues also appear in her poems. *Lady Oracle* (1976) and *Life Before Man* (1979) also concern relationships, but they are notable for their humor, which is by turns satiric, parodic, wry, or broadly comic. Atwood's other prose achievement in the 1970's is her controversial *Survival: A Thematic Guide to Canadian Literature* (1972), a literary history of Canada that stresses the negative image of the victim in Canadian literature.

By the 1980's, Atwood's reputation was established; she had written three novels, twelve volumes of poetry, a collection of short stories, and a literary history. In addition, she had written poems, received numerous prizes, and become active in the Canadian Civil Liberties Association. In short, she had become, for the non-Canadian reading public, the most notable contemporary Canadian writer. During the 1980's, she published several more volumes of poetry, but her literary reputation during this decade rests on her fiction, notably *Bodily Harm* (1981), *The Handmaid's Tale* (1986), and *Cat's Eye* (1988). While in *Bodily Harm* Atwood uses the *Surfacing* pattern of alienation and subsequent healing through a journey into a more primitive, natural state, her *The Handmaid's Tale* is a radical break from the earlier novels. It is a dystopian science-fiction tale set in a future America, but it is also "fiction" that derives from Atwood's reading of contemporary totalitarian tendencies. With *Cat's Eye*, Atwood returns to her Canadian materials and themes as her painter-narrator journeys back to Toronto to rediscover herself. Some critics see the narrator as Atwood and regard the novel as her mid-life assessment, a guide to her own work, and as one of her best novels.

Since 1980, Atwood has also published two major volumes of short fiction: *Bluebeard's Egg* (1983) and *Wilderness Tips* (1991). Her short stories, which resemble her novels in content and style, are themselves of such quality as to assure her a prominent place in Canadian literature. Atwood has become, however, more than a successful writer; she is a spokesperson for her causes and, as an editor, an arbiter of what constitutes good literature. In her work for PEN International and Amnesty International, she has vigorously opposed censorship, and, as an editor of volumes containing the "best" American and Canadian short stories, she has shaped the standard of good writing. The many writing awards that she has received attest to her literary reputation, and her Woman of the Year award from *Ms*. magazine (1986) reflects her political importance to the feminist cause. As editor, writer, critic, and political activist, she is without peer in North America. Her awards include the Governor-General's Award, Canada's highest literary honor, for *The Circle Game* in 1966, the Bess Hokin Prize for poetry in 1974, the Canadian Bookseller's Association Award in 1977, and the Radcliffe Medal in 1980.

Analysis

Although she has written poetry, short stories, screenplays, and novels, Atwood's work is remarkably consistent in content and theme. In spite of her international reputation, she remains resolutely Canadian in residence and in temperament. She has become more political and certainly is a writer of ideas, but, with the notable exception of *The Handmaid's Tale*, she is not propagandistic and heavy-handed. Regardless of the forms, she is analytical, almost "anatomical," in her dissection of characters and relationships. For the most part, hers is a landscape of the mind, although her writing is also rooted in geography, whether it be Toronto or the Canadian wilderness. In many ways, *Survival*, her literary criticism of Canadian literature, is a key to not only Canadian writers but also Atwood herself. Much of her work is related to survival in an environment or relationship at once native and alien because, while ostensibly familiar, such contexts are also foreign to a character's sense of wholeness. For the most part, her characters live defensively, creating superficial, ordered lives that enable them to live in modern urban settings, but there is another, darker side that they repress. That darker, irrational self is associated with the wilderness, with nature, in almost an Emersonian sense.

In the novels, Atwood's protagonists are usually young women who have roots in the wilderness but who currently live in an arid urban (or suburban) environment characterized by materialism, consumerism, exploitation, and male chauvinism—all of which are seen as products of the United States. The landscapes, both literal and symbolic, of her novels shape the lives of her female characters, who are both women and products, objects in a society where everything is for sale. Ill at ease, uncomfortable, half-aware of their problems, they leave a society that ironically seems safe, despite the psychological and spiritual threats that it poses, for another environment, a more primitive and dangerous one; it is, nevertheless, a healing environment, because the journey, in Atwood's novels, is mythical, psychological, and literal. In *Surfacing*, the protagonist travels to a wilderness island; in *Bodily Harm*, she goes to the Caribbean. In both cases, the new environment seems alien or foreign, but in the new environments the characters confront the realities that they had repressed and emerge or "surface" as re-created people. The healing process is spiritual, usually related to a culture seen as more primitive. In *Surfacing*, the Native American culture aids the heroine.

Part of the healing process concerns regaining control of one's body and one's language. In *Edible Woman*, the protagonist sends her lover a woman-shaped cake as a substitute for herself; in *Surfacing*, the narrator uses her lover to replace the baby whom she had aborted; and in *The Handmaid's Tale*, Offred flees her role as breeder. In the novels, Atwood equates language with power; the protagonist must articulate her feelings in gender-bound language—in *Surfacing*, language erodes as the narrator returns to the "primitive," irrational side of her nature. By "reporting" their experiences, her protagonists gain power and expose the ruling culture.

In her fiction, Atwood uses language as a poet would; she uses puns ("Offred" is "of Fred," but also "off red" with many meanings in *The Handmaid's Tale*), images (particularly water), and recurrent motifs. Moreover, she is aware, and hence suspicious, of the limits of language, of the problem of narration and voice. Her *Murder in the Dark* (1983) explores the issue of writing, the relationship between writer and reader, but it also reflects the ease with which she moves from poetry to short fiction and blurs the distinction between the two genres. In fact, her short stories, as a group, are "poetic" in the way that she used images and experiments with form to explore human relationships.

Atwood's poetry also concerns human relationships that are played out against geographical and psychological landscapes. Her early *The Circle Game* establishes the "garrison mentality" of adults under emotional siege; they construct abstract patterns or maps that appropriate reality and keep others at a safe distance. The volume also develops the images of water/drowning suggestive of the descent into one's repressed self, of mirrors that entrap those more concerned with image than reality, and of violence that characterizes human relationships. In *Power Politics* (1971), she makes explicit the themes developed in *The Circle Game*; the myth of romantic love is exposed as a sham. "Love" is a power struggle in which partners victimize, exploit, and consume (as in *The Edible Woman*) each other. The "Circe/Mud" poems of *You Are Happy* (1974) reinforce the idea of exploited women, who are shaped like clay to suit their lovers.

The feminist politics of *Power Politics* and *You Are Happy* become more global in *Two-Headed Poems* (1978) and in *True Stories* (1981). In "Two-Headed Poems," Atwood uses two speakers to explore Canadian complicity in the "Americanization" process, and in *True Stories*, she attacks national "circle games" that enable Canadians to shield themselves from the harsh realities of international famine, violence, and terrorism. Atwood's poetry, like her fiction, has become increasingly political, but in neither form has she abandoned literature for propaganda. She remains committed to form and to experiments with narrative and language; she also has the ability, despite the seriousness of content, to use humor, ranging from puns to irony, to convey her vision of human relationships.

SURFACING

First published: 1972
Type of work: Novel

In her search for her missing father, the narrator retreats to the literal and psychological wilderness of northern Quebec, where she reexamines her life and symbolically re-creates herself.

Surfacing, Atwood's second novel, recapitulates many of the themes and images from both her poems and *The Edible Woman* (1969), her first novel. In both novels, for example, a young woman finally rebels against a technological society that would mold and shape her life and then experiences a psychological breakdown before emerging as a survivor with an integrated or whole personality. *Surfacing*, however, is a richer, denser novel because the journey that the unnamed narrator undertakes is literal, psychological, and mythical; the novel is further complicated by the unreliable narrator, who not only acknowledges "fictionalizing" her story but also must use the very rational language that she comes to distrust because it is the language of the Americanized culture that she rejects.

In the first part of the novel, the unnamed narrator (her lack of a name suggests a lack of real identity and implies that she does not belong in her culture) leaves the city and travels to the Canadian wilderness to find her missing father, who is perhaps dead. Her companions are David, a would-be cinematographer; Anna, his passive doll/girlfriend; and Joe, the narrator's shaggy lover and a frustrated potter. As they travel north, the narrator suggests that "either the three of them are in the wrong place or I am" and calls her "home ground," "foreign country." When she later adds, "I don't know the way any more," it seems clear that she has become alienated from her parents (she also did not attend her mother's funeral) and from her past. She is alienated from "them," the companions whom she comes to see as exploitive "Americans" with the technology, pollution, and violence that slowly creep northward. As she narrates the story, she mentions her husband and a child, as well as a drowned brother. The brother, however, is not dead; he "surfaced," foreshadowing her own surfacing. The husband and child are also part of her "fiction"; she aborted the baby whom she conceived with her married lover, and that abortion, cutting her off from nature, still haunts her. She is an incomplete person, a point that Atwood makes by having her mention that Anna thought she was a twin; later, the narrator states, "I must have been all right then; but after that I'd allowed myself to be cut in two," obliquely referring to the abortion.

The narrator returns to the divided self at the beginning of part two and maintains that the language that divided the body and the head is "wrong," that she is "translating badly, a dialect problem." Atwood's concern with the limitations of language continues throughout the novel and reflects the growing distrust of the rational and the embracing of less conscious, more instructive modes of knowing. What the narrator comes to know is that David and Anna are in a mutually destructive relationship, which David attempts to capture on film, thereby defining Anna as object rather than person. The narrator, who had believed that she and David were similar in their lack of love, comes to understand that he is incapable of surfacing or becoming real: "He was infested, garbled, and I couldn't help him; it would take such time to heal, unearth him, scrape him down to where he was true." (This process is what occurs to the narrator in part 3.) David is an exploiter, like the "Americans"—ironically, real Canadians, who shot the heron "to prove they could do it," who wish to develop her father's island property, and who want to flood the area. In fact, part of David's problem is that, despite his clichéd attacks on the Americans, he has himself become "Americanized."

As time passes, the narrator discovers her father's drawings and her mother's scrapbook, two "guides" that lead her to the cliff where she hopes to find the Native American paintings and clues about her father's fate. When she dives, she finds instead "a dark oval trailing limbs," a vision that makes her confront the truth about her abortion. Since she describes the vision as a "chalice, an evil grail," the narrator's vision or epiphany becomes the answer, the end of the mythical quest or journey, although she cannot yet interpret it correctly. The vision, however, does radically alter her, setting her apart from her companions, who have "turned against the gods" and yet would persecute her for "heresy." "It was time for me to choose sides," she writes, but her choice is seen ironically as "inhuman." Part 2 concludes with her decision to immerse herself "in the other language," the language not associated with the dominant culture.

Part 3 of the novel begins with the narrator being impregnated by Joe, who has already been described as more "animal" than David or Anna and hence is the appropriate father foreshadowed in her childish picture of the moon-mother and horned man. While their union might reinforce the stereotypical gender roles that she has rejected, the narrator's description of their coupling is devoid of feeling; he is only a means of restoring the "two halves" separated by her complicity in the abortion: "I can feel my lost child surfacing within me, forgiving me." She then unwinds the film, symbolically denying David and Joe the power to capture their vision of reality and freeing Anna from her passive celluloid image, though Anna remains trapped in her compact that shapes her appearance and life to the masculine will. The narrator hides when the others leave, turns the entrapping mirror to the wall, discards her wedding ring and clothes, leaves the cabin, and enters her parents' world. Language breaks down as she breaks "down" and then "through"; she sees both parents, who then return to nature, one as a jay, and one as a fish. When she wakes the next morning, the ghosts have been exorcised and she is free. At the end of the novel, she states that the most important thing is "to refuse to be a victim," but she must decide whether or not to go back with Joe. If she does, her description of him as "half-formed" implies that she, not he, will be the creator and shaper.

THE HANDMAID'S TALE

First published: 1986
Type of work: Novel

In a postnuclear war society governed by repressive, puritanical men, a young woman recounts on tape her survival and escape.

Set in the near future, a time just prior to the year 2000, *The Handmaid's Tale* is science fiction but also an indictment of the present, since Atwood's future is the reader's present. It is an atypical Atwood novel, her only novel not rooted in Canada and the only one to be so blatantly propagandistic. In it, she fulfills the promise of her narrator protagonist in *Lady Oracle* (1976): "I won't write any more Costume Gothics. . . . But maybe I'll try some science fiction." Atwood prefers the term "speculative fiction" because of the blending of future and present and maintains that all the events in the novel have a "corresponding reality, either in contemporary conditions or historical fact." Since the novel is set in Cambridge, Massachusetts, Atwood also indicts the "American" culture, which contains the "corresponding reality."

The novel begins with a quotation from the Book of Genesis about a barren Rachel encouraging her husband Jacob to have children by her maid, Bilhah. In the aftermath of nuclear war, a new North American republic called Gilead (another biblical reference to fertility) attempts to correct a declining birthrate, caused by nuclear radiation and pollutants, by relegating fertile women to the role of Bilhah-like Handmaids, the breeders of society. (In fact, all Gilead women are assigned to one of eight roles, each distinguished by its own "uniform.") In such a patriarchal society where religion, state, and military are combined, women's identities are controlled by men. Offred, the narrator, has lost her real name; she is "of Fred," in reference to the commander whom she services in a perverse, impersonal sexual coupling with his wife, Serena Joy, at the head of the bed. At the beginning of the novel, Offred recounts her training under the aunts—also a perverse parody of the training that nuns and sisters (Offred's uniform, though red, resembles a nun's habit) undergo.

Despite her indoctrination, Offred chafes under the repressive regime, and, when her commander gives her access to his library, a male preserve—reading is dangerous for women—she becomes even more rebellious. She meets Moira, an old friend, at a brothel where the males circumvent their own repressive sexual roles and discovers that there is a revolutionary organization named Mayday, which suggests fertility and anarchy. Her rebellion is fueled by her illegal affair with Nick, the chauffeur, who restores her identity (she tells him her real name), liberates her sexually, and ultimately aids in her escape via the Underground Femaleroad, reflecting, through its parody of the slave underground railroad, the slavish position of women in Gilead.

Offred survives to tell her tale, not in traditional epistolary form, but in tapes that have been edited by scholars in the year 2195. Atwood's account of the tapes (similar to traditional accounts about finding ancient manuscripts) is appended as "Historical Notes on *The Handmaid's Tale*" to the text of the novel, but, in suggesting that two centuries have not altered female/male relationships, the "notes" continue the novel's indictment of current culture. In keeping with Utopian tradition, Atwood's site for the scholarly proceedings is the University of Denay, Nunavit (or the university of deny, none of it). Atwood's wry denial of the validity of the proceedings calls into question the male editing of female discourse; Professors Pieixoto and Wade have arranged "the blocks of speech in the order in which they appeared to go." Since Offred frequently alludes to the problem of articulating her feelings and experiences, the professors' presumptuous efforts are open to question.

While the proceedings are chaired by a woman, Professor Maryann Crescent Moon (perhaps a criticism of academic tokenism), the keynote speaker is a man, Professor Pieixoto whose comments hardly represent an improvement over current male chauvinism. In his opening remarks, he alludes to "enjoying" Crescent Moon, "the Arctic Chair." His further comments about the title of the book (the "tale"/"tail" being a deliberate pun by his male colleague) and his joke about the "Underground Frailroad" reveal the same chauvinistic condescension that characterizes current academic discourse. His unwillingness to pass moral judgments on the Gileadean society, because such judgments would be "culture-specific," reflects not scientific objectivity, which he already has violated by his editing, but his moral bankruptcy.

The Handmaid's Tale does survive, however, despite the male editing, as a "report" on the present/future; similarly, in *Bodily Harm*, the radicalized protagonist becomes a "subversive," who vows to "report" on the repressive society. The novel, like *Brave New World* (1932) and *Nineteen Eighty-Four* (1949), serves as an "anatomy" of current society, as an indictment, and as a warning about current society. Among her targets are religious fanaticism, nuclear energy, environmental waste, and antifeminist practices. Like other Utopian novels, however, *The Handmaid's Tale* is weakened by its political agenda, which creates one-dimensional characters and somewhat implausible events; the propaganda, however, also gives the novel its power, relevance, and appeal. Because of its popularity, it was adapted to film in 1990.

THE CIRCLE GAME

First published: 1964
Type of work: Poem

The speaker explores the emotional barriers that children and adults erect to remain separate and alienated.

The title poem of Atwood's *The Circle Game* (1966) develops the circle motif that pervades her poetry and represents the patterned, structured world that both controls and shelters individuals who seek and fear freedom from conformity. The seven-part poem juxtaposes the children's world and the adult world but suggests that childhood circle games, ostensibly so innocent, provide a training ground for the adult circle games that promote estrangement and emotional isolation. In the first part of the poem, the children play ring-around-a-rosy; but despite the surface appearance of unity, each child is separate, "singing, but not to each other," without joy in an unconscious "tranced moving." As they continue going in circles, their eyes are so "fixed on the empty moving spaces just in front of them" that they ignore nature with its grass, trees, and lake. For them, the "whole point" is simply "going round and round," a process without purpose or "point." In the second part, the couple plays its own circle games as the lover remains apart, emotionally isolated despite sharing a room and a bed with the speaker. Like the children, his attention is focused elsewhere, not on the immediate and the real, but on the people behind the walls. The bed is "losing its focus," as he is concerned with other "empty/ moving spaces" at a distance or with himself, "his own reflection." The speaker concludes that there is always "someone in the next room" that will enable him to erect barriers between them.

Part 3 moves from the isolation of part 1 to an abstract defensiveness that unconsciously enforces that isolation. The innocent sand castles on the beach are comprised of "trenches," "sand moats," and "a lake-enclosed island/ with no bridges," which the speaker sees as a "last attempt" to establish a "refuge human/ and secure from the reach/ of whatever walks along/ (sword hearted)/ these night beaches." Since the speaker has earlier equated "sword hearted" with the adult world, she implies that the adult world poses the real or imagined threat. Protection from "the reach" becomes the metaphor for the lover's unwillingness to have her "reach him" (part 2 described her as "groping" for him) in part 4. The lover's fortifications are more subtle verbal and nonverbal games ("the witticisms/ of touch") that enable him to keep her at a "certain distance" through the intellect that abstracts and depersonalizes reality. As the lover has been a "tracer of maps," which are themselves the abstraction of physical reality, he is now "tracing" her "like a country's boundary" in a perverse parody of John Donne's map imagery in his Metaphysical love poetry. For the lover, she becomes part of the map of the room, which is thus not real but abstract, and she is "here and yet not here," here only in the abstract as she is "transfixed/ by your eyes'/ cold blue thumbtacks," an image that suggests distance, control, and violence.

The last three parts of the poem draw together the children's world and that of the adults. In part 5, the speaker observes the contrast between the children's imaginative perception of violence (the guns and cannons of the fort/museum) and the adult perception of the domestication of that violence as the "elaborate defences" are shifted first to the glass cases of the museum and then, metaphorically, to their own relationship. The defenses become the "orphan game" of part 6, in which the lover prefers to be "alone" but is simultaneously attracted and repulsed by the family games in which parents "play" their roles. Metaphorically, he is on the outside looking in, observing but separated by the window barrier. In the last part of the poem, it is "summer again," itself a circle of the seasons, and the children's outside circle games are again mirrored by the adult's inside circle games. The earlier images—the "observations," the noises in the next room, the maps, the "obsolete fort"—resurface as the couple are neither "joined nor separate." The speaker, "a spineless woman in/ a cage of bones" (another image of entrapment), wants to break the circle, to erase the maps, to break the glass cases, to free herself from his "prisoning rhythms." The speaker, frustrated as the speaker in Amy Lowell's "Patterns," recognizes and articulates the problem, but she cannot free herself of the circles.

TWO-HEADED POEMS

First published: 1978
Type of work: Poem

Two speakers conduct a "duet" about the complex love-hate relationship between Canada and the United States.

The title poem of *Two-Headed Poems* is, according to the speaker, "not a debate/ but a duet/ with two deaf singers." In fact, the poem concerns the problems of being a Canadian neighbor to a world power whose corrupt values are expressed in the "duet." Like the Siamese twins, described as "joined head to head, and still alive," the United States and Canada are awkwardly joined: "The heads speak sometimes singly, sometimes/ together, sometimes alternately within a poem." At times, it is clear which country speaks, but not always, for the two countries do share, however reluctantly, some characteristics. The leaders of both countries are criticized, though the leader who "is a monster/ sewn from dead soldiers" is an American president of the Vietnam era, a recurrent motif in the poem. Yet Atwood is as concerned about language as she is with actions, the nonverbal gestures. One "head" asks, "Whose language/ is this anyway?" The corruption of Canadian English, itself a political act, stems from the passive nature of a people content to be Americanized, to shut down "the family business" that was "too small anyway/ to be, as they say, viable." The Canadians whose identity comes from "down there" in the United States are associated with "nouns," but they are also hostile (the candy hearts become "snipers") and impatient to act on their own:

> Our dreams though
> are of freedom, a hunger
> for verbs, a song
> which rises double, gliding beside us
> over all these rivers, borders,
> over ice and clouds.

The Canadian head calls for action to complete the sentence by combining with nouns, and the resultant language should not be a political statement, but a celebratory song, a "double" that transcends borders. The dreams of freedom are, however, only futile dreams, and the closing images are of being "mute" and of "two deaf singers." Communication between the two "heads" is, by definition, impossible, and Atwood clearly implies that the American/Canadian coupling that impedes both countries is an aberration of nature.

Summary

As novelist, poet, literary critic, editor, and spokesperson for women's rights, Margaret Atwood is an international figure whose ideas and beliefs about consumerism, environmental damage, censorship, militarism, and gender politics pervade her writing. Though most of her work is set in Canada and reflects the survival theme that she claims is distinctly Canadian, her dissection of human relationships transcends national boundaries. She focuses on geographical and emotional landscapes in which her protagonists journey, usually to nature or to the wilderness, in order to shed civilization's influence, confront themselves, rediscover their true identities, and survive. Atwood's style is, regardless of the genre, poetic, in that her delight in language is revealed through puns, metaphors, allusions, and ambiguous words and phrases that resonate with meaning. Though there is pessimism and despair in her work, there is also a wry sense of humor that is almost inevitably satiric.

Bibliography

Browne, Pat, ed. *Heroines of Popular Culture*. Bowling Green, Ohio: Bowling Green State University Popular Press, 1987.

Davidson, Arnold E., and Cathy N. Davidson, eds. *The Art of Margaret Atwood: Essays in Criticism*. Toronto: Anansi, 1981.

Grace, Sherrill E. *Violent Duality: A Study of Margaret Atwood*. Montreal: Véhicule Press, 1980.

McCombs, Judith, ed. *Critical Essays on Margaret Atwood*. Boston: G. K. Hall, 1988.

Regney, Barbara Hill. *Madness and Sexual Politics in the Feminist Novel: Studies in Bronte, Woolf, Lessing, and Atwood*. Madison: University of Wisconsin Press, 1978.

Van Spanckeren, Kathryn, and Jan Garden Castro, eds. *Margaret Atwood: Vision and Forms*. Carbondale: Southern Illinois University Press, 1988.

Thomas L. Erskine

W. H. AUDEN

Born: York, England
February 21, 1907
Died: Vienna, Austria
September 29, 1973

Principal Literary Achievement
Auden's considerable body of work is remarkable for its uniqueness: Employing the poetic forms of a wealth of literary periods, no other twentieth century poet so successfully blended, and stood apart from, prevailing modernist styles.

Biography
Wystan Hugh Auden was born on February 21, 1907, in York, England. He was the youngest son of George and Constance Auden. His father and mother belonged to a very distinct niche of early twentieth century Edwardian society—that of the politically liberal, scientific intelligensia. He came, nevertheless, from a very devout Anglo-Catholic home, and his early experiences with the Church would remain with him when he returned to it later in life. As a child, he was fascinated by the "magic" of Church of England rites, and this enchantment with the magical and the mystical also remained a lifelong characteristic. Auden's father was a distinguished physician and professor of medicine; his mother was a nurse. By all accounts, his family environment was loving, intelligent, clear-thinking—traits that were foremost in Auden as an adult. He received the standard schooling of an upper-middle-class male child in early twentieth century England. Beginning his education at St. Edmund's preparatory school at eight years of age, he attended Gresham's School at age thirteen.

At first, Auden intended to become a scientist, like his father. He was principally interested in both engineering and biology and planned to become a mining engineer. This career path was soon overtaken by another, however; while he was still at Gresham's, he began to write poetry. His first poem was published when he was seventeen. This early publication foreshadowed the fame that would come to him just a few years later while he was still in college. He entered Oxford in 1925 and very soon afterward had acquired a faithful clique. Those who knew him during his university years remember him as a rising star, someone who would clearly make a name for himself as a poet and thinker. A group of men who would later also be important poets formed around him—Stephen Spender, Cecil Day Lewis, and Louis MacNeice. Spender privately printed the first collection of Auden's poems in 1928,

the year that Auden graduated from Oxford.

After graduation, he spend a year abroad, the traditional *Wanderjahr* of upper-class young Englishmen. When his parents asked in which European city he would like to spend his year, Auden surprisingly answered that he wanted to live in Berlin. Germany in the years before Adolf Hitler came to power (the time of the Weimar Republic) was an exciting place—stimulating, racy, intellectually bold. There, Auden became acquainted with the politically charged plays of Bertolt Brecht and the sexy, witty songs of the Berlin cabarets. He perfected his German during his year abroad, and throughout his life he would be influenced by German literature, both classical and modern.

When he returned to England, he became a schoolmaster, first at Larchfield Academy, in Scotland, then at Downs School, near Malvern, England. At the same time, however, his literary reputation was growing. His *Poems* appeared in 1930, firmly establishing his reputation as the most brilliant of England's younger generation of poets. Perhaps under the influence of Brecht, he had begun writing works that were broadly "dramatic." *Paid on Both Sides: A Charade* (pb. 1930) reinforced the literary world's opinion of Auden as an important young writer.

Auden's adult life has frequently been divided into four segments—a division suggested by the poet himself in an introduction to his *Collected Shorter Poems, 1930-1944* (1950). The first segment runs from his undergraduate days through 1932, the second comprises the period from 1933 to 1938, and the third extends from 1939 to 1946; the fourth segment began in 1948. The first segment entails the period of his early fame—his notoriety as a brilliant, precocious undergraduate and the publication of his first important poems. This era of Auden's life might also be viewed as his "Freudian period"; in part, he viewed the work of this era as a kind of therapy, giving free play to fantasy and uncovering hidden impulses. Yet even this early poetry shows the social and political awareness that would infuse his poems throughout the 1930's.

By 1933, partly under the influence of Brecht and in reaction to the collapse of his beloved Weimar Republic, Auden became an outspoken critic of the political establishment—his life's second, political, segment. He became increasingly committed to left-wing causes and in 1937 journeyed to Spain as a stretcher-bearer in the struggle of the Loyalist Left against the forces of fascism. He also made use of theater as a way to gain wider public expression of his beliefs; he was a cofounder of the Group Theatre in 1932 and collaborated with Christopher Isherwood, a longtime friend, on several dramatic works. Moreover, he wrote film scripts for the General Post Office film unit, a government-sponsored creative effort that, among other subjects, frequently made movies about working-class life in Britain.

Auden traveled widely during the 1930's, not only to Spain but also to Iceland (his family name, as "Audun," is mentioned in the Icelandic sagas), China, and the United States. His experience with the Spanish Loyalist armies had left him disillusioned with the Left, and his fame in England apparently meant little to him by this time. Thus, in 1939, he moved to the United States, marking the third period in his life story. Once again, he became a teacher—this time on the university level, as a member of the faculties of the New School for Social Research, the University of Michigan, and Swarthmore, Bennington, Bryn Mawr, and Barnard Colleges. The war years were a time of inward-turning for Auden: He returned to the Anglo-Catholicism of his youth and wrote several long poems that explore this newly found meditative introspection. The last of these, *The Age of Anxiety* (1947), won for him the Pulitzer Prize in 1948.

During the last period of his life, from 1948 until his death in Vienna on September 29, 1973, Auden divided his time between the United States, Italy, and Austria. Eventually, in 1972, he established residence in Oxford, where he had earlier been named professor of poetry. He continued to write prolifically, although no long poems appeared after 1948. He published two volumes of prose, *The Dyer's Hand and Other Essays* (1962) and *A Certain World* (1970), translations, and he collaborated on the librettos of several operas.

Many students of Auden's biography are struck by the series of enthusiasms that colored his life. Marxist, Freudian, Anglo-Catholic—a lover of Icelandic sagas, William Shakespeare, and Johann Wolfgang von Goethe—Auden continued until his last years to hold strong beliefs that are often central to his poetry. On the other hand, he was also a very private, introspective man: His love lyrics are among the twentieth century's most celebrated. His later Anglo-Catholicism revealed a powerful inward-turning element in his character, and his religious poems are obviously the result of much soul-searching.

Analysis

Having come to fame early, Auden had the close attention of critics throughout his adult life, far longer than most poets. Being in the literary spotlight from young manhood clearly affected his own perspective of his work; in fact, in his later years, he rewrote, abandoned, and cannibalized many of his earlier poems because he felt this youthful work was "untrue." Essentially, he attempted to remake the outlines of his own body of poetry. Another effect of his early fame—or notoriety, as the case may be—was his fairly substantial audience (for a poet). Conscious of this loyal readership, he broadcast his political and social ideas throughout the 1930's. The effort was made in good conscience: He was only attempting to persuade his readers of what he felt was right. Yet perhaps in reaction, as the 1930's drew to an end, Auden withdrew from the spotlight. Having come to literary fame early, he tired of it; having spent nearly a decade fighting for a just society, he turned inward.

That is not to say that Auden's poetry had not had a strong streak of inward-turning from the outset. The early poems often have as their setting a wild, make-believe landscape concocted from a rich variety of sources: Icelandic sagas, Old English poetry, boys' adventure stories, and surreal fantasies that he had found in reading the Austrian neurologist Sigmund Freud. Throughout Auden's poetry, during all four literary states into which he divided his career, his work would have this same curious division between a highly personal mythology and the clear, logical setting forth of an argument. Many readers find the introspective level of Auden's poetry very obscure, although his poems are no more difficult that other twentieth century masters such as T. S. Eliot, Ezra Pound, or Wallace Stevens. Throughout his career, Auden was clearly fascinated by dreams and imaginative fantasies, and the drive to express this highly personal inner world contributes to his poetry's thorniness.

At the same time, Auden's poetry consistently presented to the world another outward face. Like any intelligent, sensitive young person, Auden lamented social and political injustice. In response, his work at this time is apocalyptic. The landscape portrayed in his early dramatic work *Paid on Both Sides* is a violent, confused one, populated by vindictive raiding parties armed with up-to-date weaponry and a medieval siege mentality. Critics at the time noted Auden's thorough familiarity with contemporary ideologies such as Marxism and capitalism, Freudianism, sexual freedom, and feminism. His youthful work attempts to employ these schools of thought to diagnose a diseased society, but, most scholars agree, the results are often confusing and amateurish. His short lyric poems, such as "Since You Are Going to Begin Today," remain his most lasting work of this period, a harbinger of the gifted lyric voice that he sustained throughout his career. The lyric poetry is open, candid, heartfelt, showing a young man alive to the world and to himself.

Actually, Auden was typical of many authors during the late 1920's and early 1930's, as writers moved from creating introspective works bound by personal symbolism toward socially committed poems, novels, and stories. The shift was natural: Benito Mussolini, Adolf Hitler, and Joseph Stalin had risen to power during this period, and the world was once again threatened by world war. Economically, too, the international community was entering a severe depression; while smaller nations continued to suffer poverty, the great powers also began to see widespread deprivation. Thus, it was natural for Auden, already politically aware, to strive, through poetry and drama, for a better world. He began consciously to aim his verse at a wide readership, chiefly through the poetic dramas staged by the Group Theatre. The 1930's saw the production of several Auden plays, of which the three most important—*The Dog Beneath the Skin: Or, Where Is Francis?* (1935), *The Ascent of F6* (1936), and *On the Frontier* (1938)—were written with close friend Isherwood. Although spoken in verse, these plays were similar to the songs and skits of English music halls and German cabarets and sought to stir a large audience to action.

His poetry of the 1930's breathes fellow feeling, an eager love for humanity, and a conviction that universal harmony was not far away. Yet throughout the decade he continued to write personal poems, often love lyrics contemplating the brevity and fragility of emotions. A celebrated example is "As I Walked Out One Evening," which uses the well-worn rhythms and phrases of popular love songs to picture love's uncertainty. Even a poem such as "Spain 1937," which offers a panorama of the people engaged in civil war, has an introspective side; at the same time as the speaker explores each person's social motivation, he also looks forward to a peaceful future where the participants may rediscover "romantic love." Although it would be inaccurate to say that Auden had been "embittered" by his experience in the Spanish Civil

War, by 1939 he had, however, begun to express weariness with the state of the world. He had moved to the United States, and in "September 1, 1939," he sits in "one of the dives" on New York's "Fifty-Second Street," watching as the "clever hopes expire/ Of a low dishonest decade." In "The Unknown Citizen," written a few months earlier, his tone is bitterly sarcastic as he describes the faceless, obedient automaton/ citizen of the modern state.

In 1940, Auden to an extent put aside his political commitments and embraced religious and purely artistic ones. He returned to the Church of his boyhood, and his Christmas oratorio, *For the Time Being* (1944), expresses this spiritual culmination. He also returned to his English literary roots through a careful study of William Shakespeare. The long poem *The Sea and the Mirror* (1944) explores the meaning of Shakespeare's *The Tempest* (c. 1611-1612) as a parable of the artist and his creations. Finally, *The Age of Anxiety* investigates the psychic landscape of the postwar years, as Western culture struggled to recover from the traumas of the 1930's and 1940's. These later, longer poems are unquestionably difficult in language and theme, a far cry from the accessible, socially committed verse plays of the preceding decade.

By 1950, Auden was widely recognized as one of the two or three most important poets writing in English. Among his many other honors, he was awarded the Pulitzer Prize in 1948, the Bollingen Prize for Poetry in 1954, and the National Book Award in 1956. The poetry of his later years is brief, highly symbolic, but still recognizably his own—the old concerns with society are there, but filtered through an intensely personal lens. During the 1950's and 1960's, Auden also produced a number of translations from many literatures, including works by Johann Wolfgang von Goethe, Bertolt Brecht, St.-John Perse, and the young Russian poet Andrei Voznesensky.

SPAIN 1937

First published: 1937
Type of work: Poem

The Spanish Civil War signals the imminent collapse of the peacetime world—its art, learning, culture—and the ordinary lives of men and women.

"Spain 1937"—tells a story that is partly autobiographical. As a sympathizer with the socially progressive forces of the Spanish Loyalists, Auden had gone to Spain to participate in the war as a stretcher-bearer. Once there, he witnessed the viciousness of civil conflict, not only between the opposing armies but also among the Loyalists themselves. He returned to England embittered with politics, especially the European variety, and would soon leave to establish residence in the United States.

Yet the tone of "Spain 1937" is generally elegiac—sad and wistful. In the poem's first six stanzas, Auden recalls the often-glorious history of this peninsular country, surveying its ocean-borne exploration of the world, its expansion of global trade, and its building of cathedrals. In the more recent past, he notes the more obvious "advances" in Hispanic civilization, the engineering of machines and the building of railroads. At the same time, he does not ignore Spain's darker past, such as the "trial of heretics" during the Inquisition. The distant past of discovery and religious feud and more recent signs of progress are erased, however, by the coming conflict: "But today the struggle" overtakes Spain. In stanzas 9 through 11, Auden suggests the causes of war, or at least the condition of the country as war begins. He pictures Spain's impoverished citizens in the "fireless lodgings" as they read the evening news and realize that they have nothing left to lose. Emboldened by the promises of Marxism, the poor invest their hope in the action of history and the forces of change. In response, the forces of reaction, the "military empires," "descend" on the fledgling progressive nation.

Yet Auden avoids portraying the Spanish Civil War as a simple struggle of good against evil. He foretells that this particular conflict will symbolize a greater horror to come. In stanzas 12 through 14, "life" answers the combatants, saying that it is their servant, that it will shape itself to fill their desires, whatever these may be. Auden personifies the common life of the Spanish nation—and by implication the nations of the world—as a "bar-companion," willing to go along with anything. The peoples of Europe propose, according to the personified life, the building of the "just city" in Spain, a free and equal commonwealth. Life, however, knows that the proposal is based on illusion, a kind of "suicide pact" born of romanticism. Nevertheless, it accepts the people's decision.

Driven by this romantic vision, people from all over flock to the civil war. In Spain itself, they "migrate" to the struggle like birds; in Europe, they rush to war on express trains; others farther away "float" over the oceans. All are drawn to Spain like moths to the flame, which Auden imagines as a giant "arid square" rather "crudely" slapped onto Europe. As people arrive to give their lives to the cause, to the ideology of Loyalist or Rebel, their bodies become the guarantees of their beliefs. Their emotions are now all channeled into warfare, and even their "moments of tenderness blossom/ As the ambulance and the sandbag."

Mirroring the poem's opening stanzas, the last seven stanzas also survey time—in this case, however, the future. Auden imagines the harmless, even slightly silly activities of humankind during peacetime: dog-breeding, bicycle races, or walks by the lake. This sort of "fun" is in desperate contrast to the present, where idealistic young people "explode like bombs" and pleasures are limited to badly rolled cigarettes and quick sex. The result is a debacle of which even the animals are ashamed: They look away from human evil. Meanwhile, the history that the poor hoped would redeem them may or may not turn in their favor. In any case, although history may lament those defeated in the war, it does not have God's power to pardon the evil that people do.

W. H. Auden   105

AS I WALKED OUT ONE EVENING

First published: 1940
Type of work: Poem

Telling his story in a ballad, the poet overhears a lover's song, which begins traditionally enough with vows of eternal fidelity but soon turns to stranger, less hopeful images.

Most readers of "As I Walked Out One Evening" will quickly notice something familiar about the rhythm of this poem: Auden has chosen to tell this apparently simple story in a simple, traditional poetic form, the ballad. The poem's rhythm and the rhyme strongly echo folk songs, and, in fact, the work's first line is a standard opening phrase in scores of variations on this old English and American love ballad. Yet right from the first, the poet suggests that this poem will not be as conventional as one may think: As he takes his evening walk among the London crowds, the people seem like a field of wheat—a comparison not likely to be found in the ordinary folk song. In the poem's second stanza, though, the image is once again typical: The poet overhears a lover singing under a railway arch and reproduces the song for us.

In stanza 3 (the first stanza of the repeated song), the lover makes the age-old lover's commitment: He (or perhaps she) will remain faithful for eternity, until the impossible comes to pass—"till China and Africa meet," until "the ocean/ Is folded and hung up to dry." Some of the images are whimsical and original; salmon "sing in the street" and the "seven stars go squawking/ like geese about the sky." These curious figures suggest that this lover is not like the usual ballad singer; he seems to have a quirky imagination. In any case, he is unafraid of time because he holds "the first love of the world" in his arms throughout the ages. The lover's song ends, and the poet hears the "whirring" of London's clocks, replying to the lover's grandiose claims about time. "You cannot conquer Time," the clocks warn the lover. The clocks describe a sinister Time, one that lurks in shadows and nightmares and that carries cruel justice.

In stanza 8, the clocks portray life as it is actually lived; life, they say, is "leaked away" in worry and "headaches." Time's chief purpose, they stress, is to banish life's springtime pleasures, to disrupt the dance of love. It is better, they counsel, to "plunge your hands" in cold water and wake up to reality. The clocks, who know how time works better than the lover, say that the real image of eternity is the "glacier," whose presence is always near, as near, in fact, as the kitchen cabinets, where it "knocks on the cupboard" door. Real life is grim, the clocks say, and love is, as often as not, merely sex. Love is not a fairy tale. In actual day-to-day existence, the fairy-tale hero, Jack, is actually attracted to the cruel giant, and Jill is nothing more than a prostitute. Take a look in the mirror, the clocks advise the lover, and understand life's sadness.

Strangely, they say, "life remains a blessing," nonetheless, even though human beings eventually find it difficult to bless their existence. True redemption comes from loving one's disreputable neighbor, despite the neighbor's flaws, because both the lover and the neighbor are equally "crooked," equally wounded by time.

The last stanza is left to the poet to speak. By now it is very late, and the lovers have departed. Even the clocks have ceased their "chiming," and he perhaps feels as though time itself has finally stopped. Yet even so, the river continues to run beside him, reminding him of the impersonal passage of the hours.

MUSÉE DES BEAUX ARTS

First published: 1939, as "Palais des Beaux Arts"
Type of work: Poem

A painting by an old master of the fall of Icarus sparks an appraisal of its theme by the poet-viewer: These painters knew all about life, especially the role of human suffering.

The much-anthologized "Musée des Beaux Arts," whose main subject is a painting by Bruegel, is itself a small "portrait," a tightly bound image of how people react to the suffering of others. The dramatic situation in the poem is easily imaginable: The poet is visiting an art gallery, the "Musée" of the title, and has drawn to a halt in front of *Icarus* by the early Renaissance Flemish painter Pieter Bruegel (the Elder). The speaker has very likely just viewed a series of other paintings by old masters, in which traditional subjects such as the Crucifixion or a saint's martyrdom, are prominent. *Icarus*, however, gives him pause: After he has studied it for a while, one may imagine, he reveals his thoughts.

Although the painting's theme is drawn from Greek mythology—the flight of Icarus too near the sun and his subsequent fall—the treatment is typical of Bruegel. This early modern painter delighted in the depiction of rural people in real-life settings: Many of his works show peasants farming, going to market, celebrating the harvest. Bruegel's people are hardworking, not too pretty, and full of life. Renaissance painters, of course, devoted thousands of canvases to imagined scenes from Greek myths, like the one the Flemish artist has chosen for this picture. Ordinarily, however, a painter of this period would have placed Icarus in a restrained, "classical" setting, showing the noble tragedy implicit in the story. The myth relates how the inventor, Daedalus, and his son, Icarus, are imprisoned and escape using two sets of wings constructed by Daedalus of wax and feathers. Icarus, in his joy and pride, flies too near the sun, the wax melts, and he plunges into the sea. Thus, there is an irony implicit in Bruegel's painting: This grand, classical theme is placed in a humble, contemporary setting. Moreover, as Icarus falls into the sea in the background, everyone else continues going about his or her business.

The speaker finds great truth in this contrast between high tragedy and everyday life. As he contemplates the painting, he concludes that the old masters, Renaissance painters such as Bruegel, had a profound knowledge of human experience. The central fact of that experience, the masters show, is life's enormous variety: There are so many people in the world, feeling so many emotions and doing so many things, that moments of great significance pass by unnoticed. In another painting the speaker has seen, for example, the "aged" Magi "reverently, passionately [wait] for the miraculous birth" of Christ. Yet at the very same time, children are playing nearby, oblivious to the impending Event. In another painting, a holy person is martyred in the foreground while a dog wanders in the background and a horse rubs against a tree.

Similarly, in *Icarus*, life continues while the young man drowns. The fall of Icarus takes place in the background—it is only one event in a very busy canvas. A peasant, for example, continues to plough his field, even though he may have heard Icarus' faint cry. The people on a "delicate" ship think that they may have seen something amazing—a "boy falling out of the sky"—but they are not sure, and, in any case, they have to be on their way. The point of the painting is not that people are cruel or even particularly indifferent. Rather, Bruegel, the speaker says, wants to show how suffering and death, which is understandably center stage in the life of the people to whom these things happen, are really merely trivial episodes in the greater scope of human existence. Is this how things must be? The speaker refrains from saying: His interest is not really in passing judgment on human conduct. Instead, he simply wishes to praise the unerring eye and wise judgment of masterful painters.

THE SEA AND THE MIRROR

First published: 1944
Type of work: Poem

The characters and situations from William Shakespeare's play *The Tempest* (c. 1611-1612) are used to cast a new light on this drama's themes.

Beginning where Shakespeare's play ends, *The Sea and the Mirror* exploits the ironic vein implicit in the drama. In the Shakespearean work, the magician Prospero is about to leave his exile on an island in the New World. The old man and his daughter, Miranda, had been cast adrift by his brother, Antonio, and left to die. The castaways reach an island inhabited by Ariel, a fairylike spirit, and Caliban, who is half human, half brute. Years later, King Alonso of Naples and his followers (including Antonio) are shipwrecked by Prospero's magic. His son, Ferdinand, falls in love with Miranda, Caliban plots with other followers to assassinate Prospero, and various other subplots arise. Yet Prospero is reconciled to his brother in the end, Ferdinand and Miranda are married, Ariel (who has been held captive) is freed, and Caliban is left "ruler" of the island.

It is at this point that Auden's long poem commences. The work begins with the play's stage manager addressing unnamed "critics." The manager points out that, although there are reasonable, scientific explanations for many human motives, only art can truly mirror the mystery of life. He suggests in the last stanza of the preface that Shakespeare was a supreme master of this truth.

In the poem's second section, Prospero bids goodbye to his spirit-servant, Ariel. His learning and the arts of magic now seem futile to him as he prepares to leave his solitude. He knows that he will soon return to "earth"; death is near. The aged magician reveals himself as something of a cynic, but he is critical of no one more than himself. He even forgives the treachery of Antonio. He realizes that his own treatment of Caliban and Ariel, holding them as spiritual slaves, is unforgivable. Still, his mood is thoughtful and even mellow. Although he is happy that he is too old to feel the extremes of romantic love, he can view the love between Miranda and Ferdinand with equanimity.

In the second section, several of the "supporting cast" from the play speak soliloquies, beginning with Antonio. As the ship carrying them moves out to sea, he notes how contented everyone is—the result, he claims, of Prospero's spell. Yet he remains embittered and resists his brother's enchantment. Ferdinand's speech is to Miranda, his bride. He emphasizes his joy and their oneness. In the final italicized stanza (a device that will be repeated at the end of all the speeches to come), he asserts his individuality to Prospero while contrasting his own identity with Antonio's. Stephano, the drama's drunken butler, declares his allegiance to his "belly," to things of the flesh. He concludes that his "nature" is "inert," and, like Ferdinand, he cannot know Antonio's kind of solitude. Gonzalo, the king's honest counselor, analyzes his own failure to understand the passions of the other characters. In his final stanza, he acknowledges that at least the power of the word, his "language," is "his own," even though he cannot understand the subtleties of Antonio's interior dialogue. King Alonso addresses his son, Ferdinand. He explains the pitfalls and complexities of rule. His individuality is in his worldly "empire." Two sailors, the Master and the Boatswain, then describe their lives at sea, their homesickness and their simultaneous need to explore. Sebastian and Trinculo, two relatively minor characters, deliver similar speeches. The last short monologue is Miranda's. Prospero's daughter rejoices in her love for Ferdinand and her departure from her father's enchanted island.

Part 3, the poem's longest section, is an address by Caliban to the drama's audience. In Shakespeare's play, Caliban is virtually subhuman; in the world of this drama, he is clearly fitted to be a slave. Yet like many slaves, he revolts and tries to kill his master. Thus, the Shakespearan Caliban is crude, murderous, beastlike. In contrast, Auden's Caliban, as he reveals himself in this soliloquy, is erudite, subtle, even perhaps overly intellectual. He is also inexplicably modern: Throughout the monologue are references to the twentieth century—fighter pilots or contemporary home furnishings. In fact, Caliban recalls Shakespeare's play as at once a distant part of his own life and a quaint, old-fashioned relic. Nevertheless, he draws the audience's attention to the parallels between his former situation and the modern world's grim conflicts: "whipping," slavery, and torture, of the kind that he received at the hands of Prospero, have not vanished. Instead, these things have become institutionalized, government sanctioned. Caliban's final message is grim: "There is nothing to say. There never has been."

The poem's final section, a postscript, is spoken by Ariel to Caliban. Now that Prospero, Miranda, and the other alien intruders have left their island, these two strange beings can reveal their true feelings: She announces her love for Caliban and accepts him as he is. She loves him for his flaws, those same flaws that Prospero used as an excuse to enslave him. Now that the play's busy, complex characters are gone (presumably to continue with their mixed motives and subplots), Ariel and Caliban can return to a kind of motiveless paradise until their spirits are mixed in "one evaporating sigh."

Summary

W. H. Auden's work in many ways contradicts the Romantic view that a poem should be an emotional outpouring, a sincere expression of pure subjectivity. Instead, he said, poetry is a "game of knowledge," a clear-eyed way of approaching objective truth.

In his own poems, this truth often adopted a moral or social guise: "Poetry," Auden wrote, "is a way of extending our knowledge of good and evil." Many of his poems are intended to help men and women make good moral choices, even though the way by which the poems do this is not always clear. Nevertheless, the body of Auden's poetry is exemplary for its vivid and strongly felt social conscience. Also marked in his work is his fine ear, his instinct for rhythm and structure and sound. This seamless joining of intelligence and verbal music signal that Auden is one of the master craftsmen of modern poetry.

Bibliography

Blair, J. G. *The Poetic Art of W. H. Auden.* Princeton, N.J.: Princeton University Press, 1965.

Bloomfield, B. C. *W. H. Auden: A Bibliography.* Charlottesville: University Press of Virginia, 1964.

Hoggart, Richard. *Auden: An Introductory Essay.* New Haven, Conn.: Yale University Press, 1951.

Replogle, J. M. *Auden's Poetry.* Seattle: University of Washington Press, 1971.

Spears, Monroe K. *The Poetry of W. H. Auden.* Oxford, England: Oxford University Press, 1963.

Untermeyer, Louis. *Lives of the Poets.* New York: Simon & Schuster, 1959.

Wright, G. T. W. *W. H. Auden.* New York: Twayne, 1969.

John Steven Childs

JANE AUSTEN

Born: Steventon, Hampshire, England
December 16, 1775
Died: Winchester, England
July 18, 1817

Principal Literary Achievement

One of English literature's greatest writers, Austen captures the subtleties of human nature and social interaction with satiric wit and a precise, elegant style.

Biography

Jane Austen was born on December 16, 1775, in the tiny village of Steventon, where her father, the Reverend George Austen, served as the town rector. Her mother, Cassandra Leigh Austen, was herself the daughter of a rector, and Jane was the seventh of the couple's eight children. An older brother, George, suffered from epilepsy and did not live with the family, and the couple's third son, Edward, was adopted by wealthy, childless relatives who took a strong interest in the boy throughout his childhood. The remaining six children, however, lived with their parents in the plain, comfortable village rectory.

George Austen was a scholarly man, and the household included a large library, from which Jane read extensively throughout her life. Much of the children's education took place under their father's tutelage, with two of Jane's brothers, James and Henry, both of whom attended the University of Oxford, assisting their father with the younger children's periods of schooling at home. Jane and her sister Cassandra received several years of formal education, first at private schools in Oxford and Southampton and later at the Abbey School in Reading.

The Austens were a lively, close-knit family. Literature was a shared family interest, and evenings in the rectory were often spent discussing works by the leading novelists of the day. Among Jane's favorite authors were Henry Fielding, Samuel Richardson, and Fanny Burney, and references to their work appear in both her letters and her own novels. Amateur theatricals were also a much-loved family pastime, and friends and neighbors were frequently recruited to participate in plays staged in the rectory barn. This interest, too, later found its way into Austen's work, most notably in *Mansfield Park* (1814). Indeed, family life itself is a frequent theme in Austen's work, and her heroines' relationships with parents and siblings are as fully developed as the romantic alliances on which their stories turn.

Jane's closest ties within her family were to her adored older sister, Cassandra. Three years apart in age and the only girls among the eight children, the two were close companions from childhood onward. Although Cassandra was engaged once, to a young man who died of yellow fever, and Jane entered into several brief romantic attachments, neither sister married, and the two lived together with their mother until Jane's death in 1817. Many of Austen's wittiest, most informal—and therefore most revealing—letters were written to Cassandra during their occasional separations, and it was Cassandra who most often had early glimpses of Jane's novels in progress. A less fortuitous result of the sisters' close bond, however, was Cassandra's decision following Jane's death to edit or destroy any of her sister's letters and papers that she feared might cast Jane in an unfavorable light. For Austen scholars, Cassandra's loyalty has been a source of much speculation and regret.

In 1801, George Austen retired as rector of Steventon and moved with his wife and two daughters to Bath, where he died in 1805. The family's years in the city were difficult ones; in addition to Mr. Austen's death, Mrs. Austen suffered a serious illness, and Jane herself is thought to have begun a romance with a man who died soon afterward. Following her husband's death, Mrs. Austen moved with her daughters to Southampton. In 1809, Jane's brother Edward, who had inherited the estates of the wealthy relatives who had adopted him years before, offered his mother and sisters a permanent residence at one of his properties, a house in the village of Chawton. It was there that Jane Austen would live until her death, from what is believed to have been Addison's disease, at the age of forty-one.

Austen's writing life is less easily chronicled. Inspired by her own love of reading, Austen began writing at the age of twelve. Now termed "the Juvenilia" by Austen scholars, three volumes of her early writings, dated between 1787 and 1793, remain in existence. Her first mature work, an epistolary novel titled *Lady Susan*, was written in 1794 or 1795. Around that same time, she also began work on a second novel of letters, "Elinor and Marianne" (completed between 1795 and 1797), which she would rewrite two years later as *Sense and Sensibility* (1811). Between the two versions, Austen wrote a third epistolary novel, "First Impressions," which would later become *Pride and Prejudice* (1813). In 1798 or 1799, following the initial rewriting of "Elinor and Marianne," Austen began work on "Susan," which would later be retitled and published as *Northanger Abbey* (1818), her satire on gothic novels. Because of the frequent lapses in time between each novel's earliest drafts, completion, and eventual publication, the publication dates of Austen's work are no indication of when the books were actually written.

In 1803, two years after the move to Bath, "Susan" was sold to the publishers Crosby and Company for ten pounds. The book was never published, however, and was bought back for the same amount by Austen six years later. Austen also began *The Watsons* in 1803, a novel she put aside and never resumed after her father's death two years later. In the difficult years following Mr. Austen's death, Jane appears to have abandoned her writing entirely, resuming it only after the family was at last settled at Chawton in 1809, where she embarked on a period of tremendous productivity.

The years between 1809 and 1811 Austen devoted to *Sense and Sensibility*, and in 1811 the book became her first published work. That same year, she began work on *Mansfield Park*, which continued throughout the next two years. The following year, 1812, Austen began extensive revisions on "First Impressions," abandoning its episto-lary form for that of a traditional novel. The book was published in 1813 as *Pride and Prejudice*. *Mansfield Park* appeared the following year, shortly after Austen began work on *Emma*, which was published in 1815. Over the next two years, Austen wrote *Persuasion* (1818) and began work on *Sandition* (1925), which remained unfinished at the time of her death on July 18, 1817, in Winchester, England. Both *Persuasion* and *Northanger Abbey* were published posthumously in 1818.

Analysis

In a letter written to her nephew several months before her death, Austen referred to her writing as "the little bit (two Inches wide) of Ivory on which I work with so fine a Brush," a description of her work that conveys its essence with remarkable precision. Austen is not a writer whose books are characterized by sweeping dra-matic action unfolding against a vivid historical backdrop; nor are her novels trea-tises on social ills or controversial contemporary issues. Austen wrote instead about the world she knew—a world of country villages, of polite middle-class society, of family life, of love and courtship—and her books offer a portrait of life as it was lived by a small segment of English society at the end of the eighteenth and the beginning of the nineteenth centuries.

Yet so great is her talent and her insight into the complexities of human nature that the seeming simplicity of her books belies the universality of their perceptions. In turning her writer's gaze on the world around her, Austen reveals deeper truths that apply to the world at large. Her portraits of social interaction, while specific to a particular and very carefully delineated place and time, are nevertheless the result of timeless human characteristics. If one looks beneath the details of social manners and mores that abound in Austen's novels, what emerges is their author's clear-eyed grasp of the intricacies of human behavior.

What is also readily apparent is that human behavior was a source of great amuse-ment to Austen. Her novels are gentle satires, written with delicate irony and incisive wit. The famous opening lines of *Pride and Prejudice* capture her style at its best: "It is a truth universally acknowledged, that a single man in possession of a good fortune must be in want of a wife." Courtship and marriage are the subject of all six of Austen's completed novels, and she treats the topic with a skillful balance of hu-mor and seriousness. The elaborate social ritual of courtship and the amount of time and energy expended on it by the parties involved provide Austen with an ideal target for her satirical portraits. Dances, carriage rides, and country walks are the settings for the romances that unfold in her books, and the individual's infinite capacity for misconceptions and self-delusions provide the books' dramatic structure. Her heroes and heroines misjudge each other, misunderstand each other, and mistake charm for substance and reserve for lack of feeling with a determination that seems likely to undermine their chances for happiness—until at last they find their way through the emotional mazes they have built for themselves and emerge with the proper mate.

Yet while Austen is happy to amuse her readers with her characters' foibles and missteps, she brings an underlying empathy to her creations as well. Her heroines are never figures of fun—that role is left to the stories' supporting characters—but are instead intelligent, sensitive, amiable young women who are eminently likable despite the flaws they may exhibit. It is human nature in all its complexity that fascinates Austen, and she is capable of providing her novels with interesting, well-developed central characters who are believable precisely because they are flawed. Her amusement is not scorn but rather a tolerant awareness of the qualities, both good and bad, that constitute the human character. It is this awareness that lends Austen's work its relevance and contributes to her stature in the hierarchy of English literature.

Also central to the high critical regard in which she is held is Austen's extraordinarily eloquent and graceful literary style. Austen's use of language is as sure and as precise as her character development; indeed, the two are inseparable. Whether she is depicting the selfish, greedy Mrs. John Dashwood in *Sense and Sensibility*, who says of a proposed yearly allowance for her widowed mother-in-law, "people always live forever when there is any annuity to be paid them," or characterizing Edmund Bertram's pursuit of Fanny Price in *Mansfield Park* with the observation, "She was of course only too good for him; but as nobody minds having what is too good for them, he was very steadily earnest in the pursuit of the blessing," Austen sketches her characters and relates their stories with the elegance and wit that are the unmistakable hallmarks of her style.

Jane Austen's work offers ample proof that, in the hands of a gifted writer, stories of ordinary lives filled with everyday events can transcend their outward simplicity and capture the intricacies of human nature. Austen's ironic portraits of the world she knew are both a revealing look at her own time and a perceptive examination of the workings of the human heart and mind.

SENSE AND SENSIBILITY

First published: 1811
Type of work: Novel

Two sisters, very different in nature, face obstacles as they find love.

Sense and Sensibility is a novel that is best understood within the context of the era in which it was written. Jane Austen lived in that period of English history when eighteenth century rationalism was giving way to the increasing popularity of nineteenth century romanticism, as typified by William Wordsworth and the Romantic poets. The open embrace and deliberate cultivation of sensibility—deep feelings and passionate emotions—were perhaps a natural reaction to the admiration of reserve and practicality that had typified the preceding decades.

Austen's novel, her first published work, offers a portrait of two sisters, Elinor and Marianne Dashwood, who embody the two qualities set forth in the title. Elinor, the elder of the two, is intelligent, loving, and wise enough to see the potential folly in failing to temper emotion with good sense. Marianne, although sharing many of these qualities, lacks her sister's wisdom; she is, as Austen describes her, "everything but prudent."

Marianne's insistence on giving her emotions free rein leads her into an unhappy romance with the fortune-hunting Willoughby when she mistakes his false expressions of sentiment for love. Although Marianne's own excessive displays of emotion spring from genuine feeling, they blind her to the realization that less fervently expressed emotions may also be heartfelt and true. Waiting patiently throughout the book is the quiet, steadfast Colonel Brandon, a man of deep but reserved feelings who loves Marianne and whose true worth she comes to recognize only after she is forced by her failed romance with Willoughby to reassess her views.

Elinor remains her sister's mainstay throughout her unhappy first love, assisting her toward maturity with patience and tenderness. She, too, is in love, with her selfish sister-in-law's brother, Edward Ferrars. Both are restrained in their expressions of their feelings, Elinor out of modesty and a sense of propriety and Edward because he is secretly and unhappily engaged to another woman favored by his snobbish mother. Yet adherence to principles of rational thought and good sense does not prevent Elinor from suffering greatly when she believes that her hopes of marrying Edward are impossible. Their eventual union is as happy and full of emotion as that of any two people in love.

Although her own sympathies are perhaps most closely aligned with those of Elinor, Austen writes with affection for both sisters and her message is one of compromise. She is careful to show that a balance of both heart and intellect is necessary for a full life—a blending of sense and sensibility that both Elinor and Marianne possess by the novel's close.

PRIDE AND PREJUDICE

First published: 1813
Type of work: Novel

A man and woman must reassess their first impressions of each other before they are able to find love.

Pride and Prejudice is the best known of Austen's six novels and ranks among her finest work. As in *Sense and Sensibility*, its story centers on two sisters, Jane and Elizabeth Bennet. Jane falls in love early in the book with the amiable, wealthy Charles Bingley. Bingley returns her sentiments but is temporarily persuaded to abandon the romance at the urging of his friend, Mr. Darcy, who does not detect love in Jane's discreet manner.

The book's true center, however, is the complex relationship between Elizabeth and Darcy. Both are intelligent and forthright, but their initial impressions blind them to the qualities in each other that will eventually form the basis for their love. Darcy is indeed proud and does feel himself above the less refined country families in whose company he finds himself during his visit to Bingley. Elizabeth's mother, a vain, silly woman who is often a source of embarrassment to her daughter, is also an object of Darcy's scorn. When she overhears Darcy's assessment of her and her family, Elizabeth's own pride is wounded; she dismisses him as a proud, disagreeable man and is more than willing to believe the lies she is told about him by the charming, deceitful Wickham. For his part, Darcy's pride in his position and his family cause him at first to resist his attraction to Elizabeth and later to propose to her in a manner that she finds even more offensive than his initial hauteur.

Yet as time passes and their interest in each other continues, both Elizabeth and Darcy begin to see beyond their original judgments of the other's personality and character. Both possess a measure of pride and prejudice that must be overcome before they will fully understand one another, and Elizabeth's younger sister, Lydia, is unintentionally a catalyst for the change. Foolish and headstrong, Lydia runs away with Wickham, and it is only through Darcy's intervention that the two are married and the Bennet family is saved from disgrace. Elizabeth has already learned the truth behind Wickham's slander toward Darcy, and Darcy's willingness to help her family despite her own stinging refusal of his proposal offers her a glimpse of the true nature of his character. Darcy, too, has changed, losing some of the stiffness and pride that accompanied his wealth and social standing.

The substantial emotional shift experienced by Darcy and Elizabeth is indicated by Mr. Bennet's reaction to the news of Darcy's second proposal: " 'Lizzy,' said he, 'what are you doing? Are you out of your senses, to be accepting this man? Have you not always hated him?' " Mr. Bennet's reaction is understandable, given the disdain with which Elizabeth had expressed her initial reaction to Darcy. What her father has not been witness to—and the reader has—is Austen's gradual revelation of the qualities that Darcy and Elizabeth share and the manner in which each has come to appreciate these qualities in the other.

That theirs is a meeting of the mind and heart is clear, and those qualities that at last draw them to each other and impel them to overcome their early misunderstandings will form the basis for a strong and happy marriage.

MANSFIELD PARK

First published: 1814
Type of work: Novel

A timid young girl living with wealthy relations falls in love with her cousin.

There are several points that set *Mansfield Park* apart from the rest of Austen's work. Chief among them is Austen's depiction of her heroine, Fanny Price, a frail, quiet young woman who has none of the high spirits or wit of Elizabeth Bennet or Marianne Dashwood. Reared from the age of ten among wealthy relatives, Fanny is an unobtrusive presence in the household at Mansfield Park, useful and agreeable to everyone and steadfast in her secret affection for her cousin, Edmund Bertram.

Fanny's manner contrasts sharply with the livelier, sometimes careless behavior of her cousins and their friends. Only Edmund spends time with the gentle Fanny, although his own affections have been captivated by the sophisticated Mary Crawford. With Fanny's uncle, Sir Thomas Bertram, away on an extended stay in the West Indies, the cousins and their friends decide to put on an amateur theatrical production of a scandalous French play. Only Fanny refuses to participate, out of natural modesty and a certainty that her absent uncle would not approve. Sir Thomas returns unexpectedly and does not approve, much to his children's chagrin, but Fanny quickly falls from his favor when she refuses the proposal of Mary Crawford's brother, Henry, who had begun an unwelcome flirtation with her after Fanny's cousin Maria married another man.

Distressed by her uncle's disapproval, Fanny visits her parents and her eight brothers and sisters, only to discover that her years at Mansfield Park have left her unable to fit easily into her noisy, often vulgar family. She is summoned back by Sir Thomas when Maria leaves her husband for Henry Crawford and Maria's sister, Julia, elopes. Now fully appreciated by her uncle, Fanny comes into her own, winning the love of Edmund Bertram.

Because Austen's novels often adopt the tone of their heroines, *Mansfield Park* is a more somber, less satirical book than *Pride and Prejudice*. Fanny is a young woman who has been shaped by both her separation from her family and her awkward position as a poor relation in a wealthy household. Yet, it is her alienation from her cousins that has perhaps saved her from taking on their faults. They have been spoiled while she has been grateful; she has grown in sensitivity and moral strength while they have been indulged. In Austen's world, true worth is always recognized in the end, and Fanny's resistance to the more worldly pursuits of her cousins and their friends wins for her the love of her adored Edmund.

Fanny is also alone among Austen's heroines in her uncertainty as to her position in society. Catherine Moreland of *Northanger Abbey* may visit wealthy friends, but she enjoys a secure place in her own family, as do the Dashwood and Bennet sisters and Emma Woodhouse of *Emma*. Only Anne Elliot of *Persuasion*, unappreciated by her self-centered father and sister, somewhat approximates Fanny's experience. It is a situation that lends great poignancy to Fanny's experiences and one which Austen conveys with great feeling and perception.

Mansfield Park is perhaps the most controversial of Austen's novels. While some critics fault its author for abandoning the irony and elegant wit that characterize most of her work, others praise her for her willingness to undertake a variation on her usual themes. In Fanny Price, Austen has created a heroine who must engage the reader through her gentleness rather than her spirit; that Fanny does with admirable success.

EMMA

First published: 1815
Type of work: Novel

A goodhearted but indulged young heiress misguidedly plays matchmaker for her friends.

The forces that shape the dramatic action in *Emma* are described by Austen in the book's opening paragraphs; they are the qualities possessed by Emma Woodhouse herself. In this novel, Austen turns her satiric talents to a portrait of a wealthy young woman with "a disposition to think a little too well of herself," who has yet to acquire the sensitivity to realize that the emotional lives of her companions are not toys for her own amusement.

With an adoring, widowed father and an indulgent companion, Emma has reached early adulthood secure in the belief that she knows what is best for those around her. When her companion marries, Emma replaces her with Harriet Smith, an impressionable young girl from a local school, and quickly decides that the girl's fiancé, a farmer, is beneath her. Persuading Harriet to break off the engagement, despite the misgivings of Emma's admiring friend, Mr. Knightley, Emma sets in motion a chain of romantic misunderstandings that will come close to ruining Harriet's chances for happiness. After playing with the romantic futures of several of her acquaintances, Emma at last recognizes the dangers of her interference and realizes that her own chance for happiness has existed within her grasp for some time in the person of Mr. Knightley.

Emma is one of Austen's best novels, with some critics holding it in higher regard than *Pride and Prejudice*. In Emma Woodhouse, Austen has created one of her most memorable heroines, a willful, headstrong, yet fundamentaly well-intentioned young woman whose intelligence and energy need the tempering of experience before she can be judged truly mature. She gains this experience through her relationship with

Harriet, when her manipulations backfire and she finds that Harriet believes herself to be in love with Mr. Knightley. With the force of a revelation, the truth of what she has done comes to Emma, along with the realization that she loves Knightley herself. As Austen writes, "Her own conduct, as well as her own heart, was before her in the same few minutes." Seeing herself and her actions clearly for the first time, Emma is forced into difficult but necessary self-doubt and self-examination, a new but ultimately valuable experience for a young woman who has never before had cause to doubt her own judgment.

That Emma will learn from her mistakes is clear, and her happiness with Knightley, who has known and admired her since childhood, seems assured. *Emma* is Austen's commentary on how little anyone knows about the workings of another's heart and affections, and her heroine's painful lesson is evidence of her creator's wisdom.

Summary

Although she completed only six novels, Jane Austen has retained a position of great critical acclaim among English novelists. A writer of great wit and elegance of style, she depicts her characters' strengths and weaknesses with tolerance and sympathy.

Finding, as she once noted in a letter to her niece, that "3 or 4 Families in a Country Village is the very thing to work on," Austen examines the world she knows with delicate irony and wry humor, revealing in the process a grasp of the subtleties of human nature that transcends the books' deceptively ordinary settings and events.

Bibliography

Austen, Jane. *Jane Austen: Selected Letters*. Edited by R. W. Chapman. Oxford, England: Oxford University Press, 1985.

Grey, J. David. *The Jane Austen Companion*. New York: Macmillan, 1986.

Honan, Park. *Jane Austen: Her Life*. New York: St. Martin's Press, 1987.

Jenkins, Elizabeth. *Jane Austen: A Biography*. London: Victor Gollancz, 1986.

Odmark, John. *An Understanding of Jane Austen's Novels*. Totowa, N.J.: Barnes & Noble Books, 1981.

Tanner, Tony. *Jane Austen*. Cambridge, Mass.: Harvard University Press, 1986.

Williams, Michael. *Jane Austen: Six Novels and Their Methods*. New York: St. Martin's Press, 1986.

Janet Lorenz

HONORÉ DE BALZAC

Born: Tours, France
May 20, 1799
Died: Paris, France
August 18, 1850

Principal Literary Achievement

Balzac developed the novel into a superb instrument for the realistic depiction of contemporary life and created a gallery of characters that have become part of the mythology of French culture.

Biography

Honoré Balzac was born in Tours, southern France, on May 20, 1799. His father, Bernard-François, was a government official of peasant origin. His mother, Anne Laure Sallambier, from a family of similar background but higher status, was twenty-two years younger than her husband. Honoré, the first of their four children, felt closest to his sister Laure in his childhood and early youth. Educated at boarding schools, he was a voracious reader and showed an early interest in philosophy. In 1814, the Balzac family moved to Paris.

From 1816 to 1818, Honoré Balzac attended the Sorbonne, studying law and philosophy. He was apprenticed to a lawyer but resolved to pursue literature as his profession. For seventeen months between 1818 and 1820, supported by his parents, Balzac lived in a tiny garret in Paris and dedicated himself to learning the craft of writing. The first product of this apprenticeship was a five-act tragedy, *Cromwell* (1925; written, 1819-1820), inspired by the neoclassical dramas of Pierre Corneille and Jean Racine. The verdict of both family and outsiders was unanimous: Balzac should give up writing. He left his garret and returned to his family but continued to write.

Balzac now experienced a second literary apprenticeship, producing numerous anonymous potboilers and writing popular fiction and self-improvement manuals in collaboration with pulp novelists and journalists. He did not, however, neglect the cultivation of more serious literary interests; even the potboilers show the growing influence upon Balzac of his great predecessors François Rabelais, Molière, and Jean-Jacques Rousseau, as well as the leading writers of the Romantic movement, whose early growth paralleled Balzac's lifetime. A watershed year for this movement was 1830, which saw revolutionary upheavals across Europe and the ascendance of such Romantic luminaries as Victor Hugo, Stendhal, George Sand, and Alfred de Vigny.

In 1824, Balzac's parents left Paris, and Honoré was on his own again. He experienced a renewed interest in philosophy, meditated on politics and religion, and absorbed the new literary trend toward satirical and topical realism. Yet he still lacked recognition as a writer, and was regarded as a man without a real career. His parents urged him to plunge into the world of business with their financial backing. Thus between 1825 and 1828, with ingenuity and enthusiasm but little patience for detail, Balzac pursued the commercial side of book production. All of his investments in publishing, bookselling, and printing went bankrupt. The experience, however, bore fruit in his understanding the economic forces of society, thus enriching his novels though not his bank account.

In 1828, Balzac rededicated himself to writing and at last had a modest success with the first novel to which he later signed his name *Les Chouans* (1829; English translation, 1890). For the next nineteen years, Balzac wrote steadily and enjoyed a growing success. (His self-confidence led him to add "de" to his name by 1831.) By 1831, Balzac had the concept (put into effect later) of intertwining most of his works into *La Comédie humaine* (1829-1848; *The Comedy of Human Life*, 1885-1893; also known as *The Human Comedy*).

The novels of this cycle that have become an integral part of French culture, their heroes and heroines seen as virtual archetypes, include: *La Peau de chagrin* (1831; *The Magic Skin*, 1888), *Le Médecin de campagne* (1833; *The Country Doctor*, 1897), *Eugénie Grandet* (1833; English translation, 1859), *Le Père Goriot* (1834-1835; English translation, 1860), *La Cousine Bette* (1846; *Cousin Bette*, 1888), and *Le Cousin Pons* (1847; *Cousin Pons*, 1880).

Even more than most writers, the concrete and sensual Balzac felt that his talent was nourished by beautiful, exotic, and delicious things. His pursuit of social success showed a thirst for the sumptuous and aristocratic—not out of simple materialism but rather to satisfy an appetite for what he called the "Arabian nights" atmosphere of Parisian high life. Thus his extravagances outstripped his income, and debt was a constant goad both to produce more and to improve his social contacts. He was fortunate in his friends and protectors, above all Mme Laure de Berny, his most important woman friend.

Beginning in 1832, almost two years before actually meeting the Polish-born Countess Eveline Hanska (née Rzewouski), Balzac conceived an idealized passion for her in the course of an exchange of letters that she had initiated. Their eventual meeting and liaison were complicated by the necessity that Balzac stay on good terms with Hanska's husband. When Hanska became a widow in 1847, the planned marriage with Balzac was postponed until Hanska's affairs could be put in order. Marrying a foreigner meant that Hanska had to transfer ownership of her huge estate at Wierzchownia, located in the Ukraine, to her daughter. That she was willing to do, as Hanska, like Balzac, greatly preferred Paris.

In 1848, numerous misfortunes struck at once. New revolutions flared across Europe. Apart from more serious destruction, the sale of books virtually ceased, at the very moment when Balzac was most in need of money. Also at that time, Balzac's health, long abused, collapsed. His heart and digestion were beyond repair. He enjoyed a few months of happiness on Hanska's estate, whose beauty he began to describe in unfinished notes, called the *Lettre sur Kiev* (1847). Thereafter, his health rapidly declined. On March 14, 1850, Balzac and Hanska were married in Berdichev, Ukraine. With Balzac gravely ill, he and Hanska made an excruciatingly difficult journey back to Paris, where Balzac died days later, on August 18, 1850.

Analysis

The fullest expression of Balzac's vision is *The Human Comedy*. Although it comprises more than fifty novels and stories, it was never completed. Enough is in place, however, to allow one to grasp the outer limits and inner workings of a complete universe. As Napoléon Bonaparte set out to conquer Europe—a parallel of which Balzac was well aware—Balzac set out to conquer the world that he envisioned by capturing it in words. Province by province and realm by realm, Balzac added to his universe of human types, occupations, and conditions.

The idea of using recurring characters—coming to the foreground in some works, receding to the background in others, thus creating an effect of multidimensional reality—came to Balzac spontaneously, indeed as an organic outgrowth of his work. Yet he found philosophical support for his method in the thinking of French naturalist Geoffroy Saint-Hilaire regarding the unity-in-diversity of all creation.

Balzac bases his compelling vision upon portraits of physically and psychologically convincing individuals. The reader is made to care enough about Balzac's individual characters to absorb even the most prosaic details of their occupations and, eventually, the workings of the social forces that buffet them.

One of Balzac's most moving characters is Father Goriot, in the novel of the same name. At first, Balzac reveals little more of him than that he is a retired pasta maker—a thoroughly prosaic profession. Before the story began, when Goriot had first moved to Mme Vauquer's boardinghouse, he was rotund and portly and wore a coat of cornflower blue. Then Goriot goes into a decline, which is depicted only through humble, concrete details. Both the reader and Goriot's fellow boarders are brought to an extreme pitch of suspense as Balzac withholds all explanation. At last, clues surface that suggest a hypothesis: A girl comes to visit Goriot, gliding into his room like a snake, with "not a speck of mud on her laced cashmere boots."

Balzac was one of the first great literary realists of the nineteenth century to discover that the most prosaic details of real life are themselves poetry. It requires an unobtrusive mastery and poetic inspiration to make such unlikely material as "laced cashmere boots" speak to the reader's emotions. Yet while Balzac could have created beauty with an unrelieved inventory of prosaic details, he does not limit himself in that way. His portraits of girls and young women shine with a luminous charm. In creating such portraits, which always have an element of the ideal, Balzac combines realistic detail with metaphor. His range of memorable characters includes the spiritual Eugénie Grandet and the worldly Mme de Beauséant.

An important organizing element of Balzac's world, one which raises it to a higher aesthetic pitch than the real world it resembles, is contrast. The author shows wealth side by side with poverty, the ascetic beside the profligate, beauty beside ugliness, the ideal and the cynical, the urbane and the rustic, virtue and vice. Such contrasts abounded in his own life and in the city that he loved—Paris, the "ocean that no line can fathom," the world within a world. Just as no quality can exist without its opposite, proud Paris cannot exist without the provinces. Yet, paradoxically, the extremes can sometimes change places or masquerade in each other's raiment.

Balzac, who began his literary career by following the tragedies of Racine and Corneille, reached for a higher insight in *The Human Comedy*. To call it "comedy" was not a facile decision, though "tragicomedy" might have been more accurate; time and again, Balzac's heroes make great sacrifices that are unnecessary, unappreciated, misunderstood, or, worst of all, drive out of reach the very goal that they are seeking. The "human" side of Balzac's epos is in the universals of human nature that he reveals. In a world where the real and illusory are intertwined, simple human love endures as the great, and only nonillusory, value.

While Balzac's psychological insight is the foundation of his realism and enduring interest for the reader, his understanding of the political and economic workings of his society add depth to the picture. Ideologically, Balzac was Roman Catholic, conservative, and at times an avowed monarchist. He was too keenly aware of the opportunism in human nature to put much faith in radical political ideology. He also expressed an almost visceral aversion to the "mud" in which the lower classes lived and with which his heroes dread being spattered. Yet in the heyday of Romantic contempt for the "Philistine" (in other words, everyone who was not an artist, from the humblest tradesmen to upper-class professionals), Balzac had a generous, democratic acceptance of so-called ordinary people. A human being, to Balzac, was by definition never ordinary, and the distinctions of class had no effect on the universal human dilemmas of how to live, whom to love, and what choices to make.

Despite his humanistic spirit, Balzac was acutely aware of the pervasive role of money throughout the French society of his day. It was a glue binding all together, from the lowest to the highest. Its power to corrupt provides the saddest, most pessimistic, and most ironic pages of *The Human Comedy*.

With Balzac, creative fiction comes of age, and the outer parameters of the realistic novel are clearly indicated even if Balzac did not live to fill them in completely. Later novelists who proudly acknowledged their debt to him include Fyodor Dostoevski, Henry James, and Balzac's compatriots Guy de Maupassant and Marcel Proust.

EUGÉNIE GRANDET

First published: 1833 (English translation, 1859)
Type of work: Novel

The selfless goodness of Eugénie Grandet survives the harshness of her miserly father and the treachery of her lover, but her moral triumph is not accompanied by any hope of happiness.

Eugénie Grandet shows Balzac at his most idealistic. He presents three characters who are completely incorruptible in the face of the greed that surrounds them. Eugénie Grandet, her mother, and their servant Nanon all lead lives that are virtually monastic in their self-denial. Despite the fabulous wealth that has been accumulated by the shrewd and unscrupulous winemaker, Monsieur Grandet, his family lives in a wretched house, under strict and despotic rules enforced by him.

While Grandet, a miser who doles out candles and sugar cubes one at a time, keeps his wife and daughter ignorant of their enormous fortune, the local townspeople are very well aware of it. Indeed, talk of Grandet's millions is the chief subject of gossip. While everyone in town is well aware that Grandet is a most unsavory character, he is regarded with awe and forgiven every trespass because of his millions of francs. As Eugénie turns twenty-three, her father assumes that he will marry her off to the candidate of his choosing. Two local figures vie for her hand, with no thought of anything but her father's money. As all the principals are gathered for Eugénie's birthday, an unanticipated guest arrives from Paris like a magnificent peacock descending on a barnyard.

The peacock is Eugénie's cousin Charles, the son of old Grandet's younger brother. Young Charles is visiting the poor country cousins to humor his father, from whom he is bringing a letter to old Grandet. Unbeknown to Charles, the letter contains news of his father's bankruptcy and intended suicide.

In the few days that the young man is allotted to mourn, before he is sent to "the Indies" to make his fortune, he and his cousin fall in love. The worldly Charles has loved before; but as Balzac describes this first love of Eugénie, it is as if she were truly seeing the world for the first time. Eugénie is constantly accompanied by the imagery of light. As light is the first thing that we love, asks Balzac, then is not love the very light of the heart?

In one of many plot ironies anticipating the stories of de Maupassant, Eugénie gives Charles all of her gold coins (mainly gifts from her father). As a pledge of both his own and the money's return, Charles gives her a golden case with two exquisite portraits of his parents. Charles, however, uses Eugénie's money to pursue trade yielding the quickest profit, including traffic in slaves. He stays away for seven years, forgets all about her, and becomes utterly corrupt and cynical. Eugénie has to face a terrible day of reckoning when her father, who craves the sight of gold as if addicted to it, discovers that she has given all of her coins away. She refuses to tell her father anything.

The struggle of wills between father and daughter is as epical, in its own way, as any struggle in the House of Atreus (Balzac's analogy). Drama is created not by the object of contention but by the clash of principles. On Grandet's side, there is the individual's sense of absolute ownership, mastery, will, and desire. On Eugénie's side, there are moral and religious principles: fidelity, charity, pity, respect for family bonds, and love. Eugénie's mother, long ago reduced to psychological slavery by Grandet, is crushed by Grandet's harshness—he refuses for weeks on end to allow her to see her daughter. The mother suffers a decline that results in her death.

Grandet's obsession with self-enrichment and the physical possession of gold never flags. Balzac's ultimate miser differs significantly from Harpagon, Grandet's great seventeenth century French predecessor, in *L'Avare* (1668; *The Miser*, 1672) of Molière. Molière used his archetype to provoke ridicule and pity. Yet Grandet, who has his own sardonic sense of humor, dupes others to the very end and dies almost contentedly, with his millions intact. The contrast between Grandet and his daughter can be compared to that between Shylock and Portia in William Shakespeare's *The Merchant of Venice*; it is more stark than that between Molière's miser and his children.

PÈRE GORIOT

First published: *Le Père Goriot*, 1834-1835 (English translation, 1860)
Type of work: Novel

A young provincial makes his choice to pursue the vanity of the world, while an old man sacrifices himself so that his two daughters may have a glittering life.

Père Goriot is a novel of beautifully balanced ironies. A young provincial, Eugène de Rastignac, comes to Paris and finds lodging in the same boardinghouse as a decrepit former pasta maker, Père Goriot. While the other lodgers make Goriot the butt of their jokes, Eugène feels an instinctive sympathy for him. Goriot, formerly wealthy, has inexplicably fallen upon hard times; for no visible reason, his fortune has melted away. He bears his humiliation with a seemingly imbecilic meekness. Yet he reveals a sense of honor and compassion when he hears of the misfortunes of another lodger, Victorine Taillefer, a young girl who has been callously disinherited by her wealthy father. Another mysterious lodger, Vautrin, takes a liking to young Eugène and shocks him with a cynical offer to help him escape poverty. Vautrin eloquently states the philosophy that the ends always justify the means.

The setting is Balzac's Paris, a semimythic place that foreshadows the Paris of Charles Baudelaire's *Les Fleurs du mal* (1857, 1861, 1868; *Flowers of Evil*, 1931). The evil and the angelic live side by side and wrestle in this setting. Evil, with the unbridled power of money on its side, appears to have the upper hand. Eugène, from motives of wishing to help his family (especially his two sisters), decides to put aside the drudgery of his law studies and apprenticeship and take a shortcut to easy wealth. He persuades his mother and sisters, back home in the provinces, to sell their modest stock of jewels in order to outfit him for his great adventure of storming high society. While only a poor relation, he wishes to exploit his family connection with the socially powerful Mme de Beauséant.

Meanwhile, it comes to light that Père Goriot has sacrificed all that he had, down to the last silver memento from his late wife, in order to keep his two spoiled daughters in a blaze of glory. In particular the elder daughter, Mme Anastasie de Rastignac, has exploited Goriot in order to pay the bills run up by her young lover, Maxime des Treyes. She haughtily rejects Eugène, who tries to insinuate himself into her good graces, being himself irresistibly drawn to the luxury for which she has sold her father.

Goriot's only slightly less ruthless younger daughter, Delphine, then becomes the object of Eugène's relentless pursuit, initially in order to spite Anastasie and Maxime. Eugène, however, then falls in love with Delphine. Like her adoring father, Eugène sees Delphine's total selfishness but is blinded by her goddesslike beauty and the need to feel that he pleases her. Rather than being able to make use of them, Eugène becomes as much the sisters' victim as their old father.

With no more left to give, Père Goriot, as pitiful as King Lear, is dying. He is barred from both his daughters' homes. In any event, they have been so profligate that they have not the wherewithal to help him. Yet so long as he is allowed simply to love them, Goriot experiences happiness. Eugène uses the last of the money that he has received from home to pay for Goriot's burial. Then he heads for the house of Delphine, still dreaming of his future conquest of society.

Summary

Honoré de Balzac is an almost pure example of the creative inpulse at work. Founded in the author's broad knowledge of society, his characters grow, interact, and pursue their trades as if they had a life of their own. Balzac acknowledged their autonomy, which he believed was limited only by the basic laws of his lifelike world. While a higher justice occasionally intervenes in Balzac's world, it is primarily human choices that determine the ironic course of the myriad individual lives in *The Human Comedy*.

Bibliography

Festa-McCormick, Diana. *Honoré de Balzac*. Boston: Twayne, 1979.
Hunt, Herbert J. *Honoré de Balzac: A Biography*. London: Athlone Press, 1957
Marceau, Félicien. *Balzac and His World*. New York: Orion Press, 1966.
Maurois, André. *Prometheus: The Life of Balzac*. New York: Harper & Row, 1966.
Oliver, E. J. *Honoré de Balzac*. New York: Macmillan, 1964.

Prendergast, Christopher. *Balzac in Fiction and Melodrama.* New York: Holmes & Meier, 1978.

Pritchett, V. S. *Balzac.* New York: Alfred A. Knopf, 1973.

Rogers, Samuel. *Balzac and the Novel.* Madison: University of Wisconsin Press, 1953.

Stowe, William W. *Balzac, James, and the Realistic Novel.* Princeton, N.J.: Princeton University Press, 1983.

D. Gosselin Nakeeb

CHARLES BAUDELAIRE

Born: Paris, France
April 9, 1821
Died: Paris, France
August 31, 1867

Principal Literary Achievement

Baudelaire's innovative use of poetic imagery in *Flowers of Evil* laid the stylistic groundwork for the Symbolist poets, while his prose poems expanded the form of poetry.

Biography

Charles-Pierre Baudelaire was born on April 9, 1821, in Paris, France. His father, François Baudelaire, was thirty-four years older than his mother, Caroline Dufayis. Born in 1759, François was ordained a priest prior to the French Revolution but was compelled to renounce his clerical order in 1793, the year of the most intense persecution of the clergy. François was already sixty years old at the time of his marriage to Caroline and he died in 1827 when their only child, Charles, was not yet six years old. The poet's father left him a heritage of Catholic faith that may have influenced both the moral preoccupations and the choice of imagery in Charles's later work and a financial inheritance that would come into Charles's control when he turned twenty-one. This money guaranteed the poet minimal subsistence in his adult years but became the source of a bitter dispute between him and his family.

After a year during which she devoted herself largely to her son, Caroline remarried in 1828. Her husband, Jacques Aupick, was very successful in his military career, rising eventually to the rank of general, but had virtually nothing in common with Charles, who resented Aupick's relationship with Caroline. Perhaps in rebellion against the authoritarian Aupick household, Baudelaire led an increasingly bohemian lifestyle in Paris. He had won prizes for his studies at the Collège Louis-le-Grand but was dismissed from it on disciplinary grounds. After earning his *baccalauréat*, he was supposed to study law but turned instead to the various temptations of Paris.

Fearing that when Baudelaire came into his inheritance in 1842 he would quickly squander it, his family sought to separate him from his Parisian companions. In May, 1841, he was forced to embark from Bordeaux on a voyage that would keep him out of France until the following February. The ship aboard which Baudelaire took passage was bound for India, but after a particularly rough rounding of the Cape of

Good Hope, he abandoned it at the island of Mauritius in the Indian Ocean. After two months on this island and the neighboring Reunion, Baudelaire found passage on a ship returning to France. While this trip had been involuntary, Baudelaire having returned from it as soon as possible, the exotic, tropical images that he had encountered would play a central role in his subsequent poetry.

Back in France, Baudelaire justified his family's fears. During the two years following his coming-of-age, he spent much of the money that his father had left him and contracted numerous debts. To protect him from absolute poverty, his family instituted a legal procedure to have him effectively declared a minor and incapable of handling his own financial affairs. While this arrangement did preserve for Baudelaire a modest income from his remaining funds, he greatly resented this curtailment of his freedom. His correspondence for many years is filled with bitterness toward the lawyers administering his estate and pleas to his mother for additional money.

Soon after his return from his travels, Baudelaire began a lengthy affair with Jeanne Duval, a onetime actress of mulatto Caribbean origins, whose exotic appearance may have reminded him of his memories of Africa. Given his mother's ardent opposition to this relationship, there was no question of Baudelaire marrying Jeanne. They stayed together for a number of years, but even after their eventual separation, Baudelaire sent money to Jeanne when his meager resources permitted it. Jeanne Duval survived Baudelaire. The last record of her comes from a friend of Baudelaire's, who recorded seeing her on a Paris street in 1870, obviously suffering from poverty and ill health. She was probably crippled by the same venereal disease that Baudelaire had contracted even before his departure for India.

How much of Baudelaire's physical suffering came from his syphilis and how much from the unhealthy conditions in which he lived is impossible to determine. Indeed, the two causes were linked because, unlike his contemporary, the novelist Gustave Flaubert, who suffered from the same illness but had numerous medical contacts, Baudelaire was never able to afford treatment for his disease. The chief form of his suffering, documented in his letters, concerned digestive complaints. His diet, however, was never healthy and often simply inadequate.

Living on what he regarded as a pittance from his inheritance and only occasional income from his writings, Baudelaire could afford no more than a series of rooms in residential hotels. He moved often, at one point six times in the course of barely a month, to avoid his creditors. In addition, Paris at that time lacked central heating, and there was often no money for firewood. Baudelaire wrote of one three-day period during a particularly cold December, when he spent the entire three days in bed as the only means of warming himself. Restaurants would extend only limited credit, and he had no other access to food. Even when he had money for food, however, much of it went to buy wine or opium.

Given the circumstances of his life, Baudelaire's ill health is understandable. What has amazed his readers is that, amid this stress and discomfort, he was able to produce a literary work that stands as a milestone in modern literature. His poetry was not initially accepted. While a number of individual poems had been welcome in periodicals, the first collected edition, *Les Fleurs du mal* (1857, 1861, 1868; *Flowers of Evil*, 1909), was suppressed in 1857 when a famous lawsuit attacked its immorality. Eventually, all but six of its poems reached the public in a second edition of 1861, together with a large number of new works that have made the second edition the standard version now generally reprinted with the censured poems as an appendix.

Baudelaire yearned for acceptance as a poet, but during the height of his poetic productivity, he was read as an art critic for his commentaries on the annual Salons, the art exhibitions. When he died in Paris on August 31, 1867, at the age of only forty-six, his fame and influence were just beginning.

Analysis

In terms of the evolution of literary style, Baudelaire was very much a man of his time, but his time was one of transition. The Romantic poets of the generation before him had taken the essential first steps to free poetic expression from neoclassical constraints. Victor Hugo declared in his 1829 preface to *Les Orientales* (1829; *Les Orientales: Or, Eastern Lyrics*, 1879) that "the poet is free." Hugo linked poetic expression to political liberty, a public dimension of the poet's role that Baudelaire would not follow, but he also adopted the varied poetic forms and wide range of nature images that would provide Baudelaire with the building blocks of his own style. Later, Symbolist poets such as Stéphane Mallarmé would in turn draw on Baudelaire's work to create a more complex and abstract poetic style. Later still, after Sigmund Freud transformed the view of the human mind, psychologists would explore subjective resonances of the images that Baudelaire had raised to the role of symbols. Baudelaire provided the link between two very distinct forms of expression.

The concept of "symbol," as it was to evolve in the works of the Symbolist poets, differs greatly from the allegorical use of an image to represent one, specific, other idea. Allegory has been a rich form of expresson since even before Christian tradition began to posit a link between bread and wine (the objects) and the body and blood of Christ (the idea represented). With the effusive nature description of the Romantic poets, quantities of images multiplied, but their applications remained simple. Alphonse de Lamartine's poem "Le Lac" ("The Lake") repeatedly invoked nature through lists of images—"Oh lake! mute rocks! grottoes! shadowy forest!"— but these objects represented only their own role in the scene that he described.

With his sonnet "Correspondances" ("Correspondences"), Baudelaire defined a new way of seeing objects in nature. The poem opens with the assertion that a voice within nature speaks: "Nature is a temple where living pillars/ Sometimes let forth confused words." Although the description of Nature as a temple posits some form of religious revelation, the "confused words" that issue forth from it are not at once intelligible. They are symbols that must be interpreted: "Man passes through forests of symbols."

The reader is left to wonder how to interpret the mysterious symbols, but in these lines Baudelaire has provided a key. The image of the forest joins the "living pillars" of the first line to clarify that the living trees of the forest provide the pillars of

Nature's temple. Images that share a physical resemblance, trees and pillars, fuse to form a new concept, that of the place of worship displaced to the outdoors. The "correspondences" of the poem lie in the ways that various things resemble one another. The poet, who can perceive these affinities, can understand the mysterious unity of nature: "Like long echoes that fuse in the distance/ Into a dark, deep unity." The first similarity noted in the poem, that of trees and pillars, is based on their visually observed forms. Now, Baudelaire changes to a fusion of sounds as the echoes merge, and the sestet of his sonnet finds affinities in perfumes. This appeal to diverse senses characterizes Baudelaire's verse, where perfumes, especially, play a major role.

The most important function of the senses, however, lies in their interrelationships: "Perfumes, colors and sounds answer each other." The verb "to answer," with its implication of spoken language, recalls the "confused words" through which nature originally communicated. In the sense in which "response" implies exchange between participants, however, the verb posits a similarity between the messages of the senses. Thus, with "there are perfumes as fresh as the flesh of children/ Sweet as oboes, green as fields," the perfumes are in turn likened to the texture of children's skin, the sound of oboes, and the color of fields. For Baudelaire, the perception of these messages of the senses, messages "containing the expansion of infinite things," allows the poet to understand mysteries hidden to the casual observer.

The role of the poet at this point is crucial. Baudelaire shared with many of his contemporaries the concept of the poet as a person of uncommon insight, whose perceptions went far beyond those of the masses. Attaining this vision, however, resulted from painful experience. Baudelaire's version of this suffering closely parallels the Fall of Man, as the poet, led astray from the beauties of the world largely by temptations associated with women, discovers that he has lost his transcendent vision.

A second sonnet much later in *Flowers of Evil*, "Obsession," returns to the images of "Correspondences" but in a much more negative context. The temple of nature remains, but it terrifies the poet: "Great woods, you terrify me like cathedrals." Conscious of his fallen state, the poet now flees those elements in nature that offer meaning: "How you would please me, oh Night, without these stars/ Whose light speaks a known language." The language of the stars testifies to what he has lost. Another sonnet documenting the poet's recognition of his fall places the reason for it clearly on his own debauchery. In "L'Aube spirituelle" ("Spiritual Dawn"), the enlightenment of his spirit corresponds to dawn awakening a reveler: "When in the house of debauchery the white and crimson dawn/ Enters together with the gnawing Ideal." The memory of the Ideal torments him, because it has now become "the unreachable azure."

The contrast between the spiritual ideal and fallen man parallels the radiant imagery that Baudelaire adopted from his trip of 1841 set against the depression of his life in Paris. Opposing images contrast the two ideas: "The sun has blackened the flame of the candles" (from "Spiritual Dawn"), but the dynamic element is the interaction between the two. The sun of the Ideal serves to darken the candles that light the debauchery.

THE TRIP

First published: "Le Voyage," 1859 (English translation, 1931)
Type of work: Poem

 After retracing the frustration of the journey of his life, the poet posits the ultimate new beginning in the departure of death.

Baudelaire added "The Trip" to the second edition of *Les Fleurs du mal* (1857, 1861, 1868; *Flowers of Evil*, 1909) in 1861 and found in it the ideal poem with which to conclude his work. The overall structure of *Flowers of Evil* is loosely autobiographical, beginning with the birth of the poet in the initial "Bénédiction" ("Benediction") and progressing through the emotional; the work also addresses the spiritual experiences of his life. "The Trip" begins again with the poet's childhood and serves as a final summary of the work before it offers a new, concluding hope.

The initial image is that of the child who can travel only in his imagination: "For the child who loves maps and engravings/ The universe satisfies his vast appetite." Yet immediately, the voice of the poet's experience intrudes to declare that this naïve enjoyment surpasses the reality of actual travel: "Oh how big the world is in lamplight/ How small the world is in the eyes of memory." The contrast of the vast and narrow perceptions of the world coincides with Baudelaire's dual vision. The poet perceives the vastness, while the fallen man sees the world close in around him.

The first section of the poem narrates a joyful departure: "One morning we leave, our minds enflamed." While the experience seems quite comfortable, the travelers find their will lulled to sleep: "Rocking our infinite nature on the finite seas." The physical limits of the ocean are contrasted this time with the unlimited potential of the human soul, lulled into unconsciousness. Baudelaire's choice of the verb "to rock" recalls his prefatory poem to *Flowers of Evil*, "Au Lecteur" ("To the Reader"), where the devil rocks the human soul before seducing it down to hell. As if this analogy were not warning enough, the following quatrain introduces the image of Circe, the seductress who sought to lure Ulysses to his doom in Homer's the *Odyssey* (c. 800 B.C.). In "The Trip," however, Circe represents the danger inherent in all women, as men are "drowned in the eyes of a woman/ Tyrannical Circe with her dangerous perfumes."

A technique basic to Baudelaire's symbolism involves the progressive refinement of the definition of his central images as the same object or idea is repeated in varied contexts. In this final poem of his collection, much of the vocabulary has already acquired multiple connotations through previous usage. Thus, the woman's eyes and dangerous perfumes have become negative in the sense of contributing to the poet's seduction but remain positive in the appeal of their beauty. Such ambiguities caused the confusion that led the poet to lose sight of his ideal.

The travelers recognize the danger inherent in Circe, and "so as not to be changed into beasts, they become drunk/ On space and light and burning skies." To avoid the woman's domination, the "being changed to beasts" that threatened Ulysses and his crew, they become drunk. Yet this drunkenness, too, has been predefined in Baudelaire's lexicon as a source of danger. Already in "Benediction" the child-poet "disinherited becomes drunk on sunlight" as he enters the hazardous world, and the clustering of images of sun and drunkenness has been in several poems linked to dangers. Thus, while "The Trip" recapitulates to some extent the life of the poet, it draws on the poems that have gone before to give very precise definitions to its terms.

The central segment of the poem narrates the voyage, first, in part 2, still in Baudelaire's voice, and then in parts 3 through 6 in a dialogue between the naïve child and the experienced travelers. In response to the child's repeated questions, the travelers finally declare that all that they have seen has been "the boring spectacle of immortal sin." Again, the language carries multiple meanings. While sin, especially oft-repeated, may indeed be boring, "Boredom" was also the name of the monster who, in "To the Reader," seduced men into losing their souls. Parts 7 and 8 return to the poet's own voice, providing in these two final sections a symmetry with the two opening sections of the poem. Baudelaire's conclusion concerns that "bitter knowledge that is gained from travel," and he compares the long frustration of travel to the story of the Wandering Jew. After relying on his own symbol vocabulary in the earlier parts of the poem, Baudelaire now expresses himself through traditional myth.

His last scene, paralleling the earlier use of Circe, is that of the Lotus Eaters, another of the perils that faced Ulysses. Their song invites the poet once again, "Come to get drunk," but he recognizes the danger: "By the familiar accent we recognize the specter." This ghost is that of the seductive woman: "Swim toward your Electra!/ Says the woman whose knees we used to kiss."

The voyage ends with the poet seemingly alone, though he still speaks in a plural "we" that potentially incorporates all humankind. In the final section, composed of only two quatrains, the poet invites death: "Oh Death, old captain, it is time! raise the anchor!/ This country bores us, oh Death! Let us set sail!" The maritime imagery redefines death. It will be a departure like any other, and as such it is nothing to be feared.

The vocabulary continues to draw on Baudelaire's previous usage, where sea voyages have been numerous and "boredom" has acquired multiple associations. Similarly, the next lines draw on the contrasts of light and darkness that have characterized Baudelaire's dual view of the world—"If the sky and the sea are as black as ink,/ Our hearts, you know, are filled with light"—and his call for poison in the last quatrain repeats another recurring motif. All of this repletion of the familiar seems to reassure the reader that there is nothing new in this latest voyage.

BY ASSOCIATION

First published: "Parfum exotique," 1857 (English translation, 1931)
Type of work: Poem

A woman's perfume inspires the poet to see a vision of an earthly paradise.

· "By Association" details one of the many forms of departure that tempted Baudelaire throughout *Flowers of Evil* prior to his ultimate departure in "The Trip." The poem, situated between two others, "Hymne à la Beauté" ("Hymn to Beauty") and "La Chevelure" ("The Head of Hair"), on the general subject of the beauty of women, also exemplifies Baudelaire's technique of developing both ideas and imagery through a sequence of related poems.

"Hymn to Beauty" addresses beauty in general, though clearly in female form, and reflects the dualism that Baudelaire recognized in this subject. The opening lines, "Do you come from deep heaven or from the abyss/ Oh Beauty?" recognize the danger of woman. Yet by the end of the poem, the poet willingly takes whatever risk that he must: What does it matter, if you—velvet-eyed fairy/ Rhythm, perfume, light, my only queen—you make the universe less ugly and time less heavy?" The attributes that Baudelaire ascribes to the woman reflect her duality. The allusions to "rhythm, perfume, light" recall the multiple sensory stimuli that contributed to the poet's vision in "Correspondences." Yet the reference to her eyes, the instruments by which women often overpower the poet elsewhere in *Flowers of Evil*, alludes to her potential dominance and links this poem to the one that is to follow.

"By Association" begins with the poet's eyes closed, in contrast to those of the woman, which are presumably open: "When with closed eyes on a warm autumn evening/ I breathe the odor of your warming breast." The poet's closed eyes imply that he is abandoning himself to the sensations provided by the perfume, sensations that still evoke, as they had in "Correspondences," a visionary experience: "I see stretched out before me happy shores/ Dazzled by the fires of a monotone sun." The vision, drawing on the suggestion of "exotique" in the title of the sonnet, conjures a setting frequent in Baudelaire's imagery. The "shores" suggest a sea voyage, while the dazzling sun suggests a tropical destination.

Dangers lurk even in this idyllic landscape. The sun described as "monotone" recalls Baudelaire's negative "boredom," and the second quatrain describing "a lazy island" anticipates the Lotus Eaters of "The Trip." The island is also inhabited by "women whose eyes astonish by their frankness." Yet the poet does not take warning from the power expressed in the women's eyes. The sestet describes an earthly paradise to which he is "guided by your perfume." In describing this paradise, Baudelaire briefly abandons the contradictory images that have rendered many of his visions ambiguous: "While the perfume of the green tamarind trees/ That circulates through the air and widens my nostrils/ Combines in my soul with the song of the sailors." The fusion of perfume and music returns to the experience of "Correspondences." This imaginative departure inspired by the woman continues in the following poem, "The Head of Hair," where the perfume of her hair carries the poet as far as "languorous Asia and burning Africa." Yet in the following, untitled poem "I adore you as the vault of night," the danger of passion reappears, as Baudelaire realizes that his experiences with the woman "separate my arms from the blue immensity."

Baudelaire's linking of themes and development of ideas from poem to poem through *Flowers of Evil* invites the reader to approach the work as a unit, both for the story that it traces of the poet's life and for the progressive development that it makes possible for his slowly evolving symbols.

THE SWAN

First published: "Le Cygne," 1861 (English translation, 1931)
Type of work: Poem

Images of exile cause the poet to meditate on his own solitude.

In "The Swan," a poem appearing much later in *Flowers of Evil* than "By Association," Baudelaire's perspective has considerably evolved. Numerous disappointing experiences with women and other distractions have persuaded him that what he has lost through his dissipation has been of more lasting importance than what he has enjoyed. He now finds himself removed from his once-clear vision of his ideal.

The imagery of "The Swan" functions on two levels of complexity. The surface meaning remains deceptively simple. Baudelaire enumerates several examples of exile, Victor Hugo, Andromache, and the swan, and proposes them as simple analogies for his own separation from "old Paris." Hugo's name appears only in the dedication, but it would have been sufficient to remind the readers of Baudelaire's time that Hugo was in exile on the island of Guernsey. Andromache appears in the poem as she was after the fall of Troy, widowed and captive in a strange land: "Andromache, I think of you! This little river/ Poor, sad mirror where once shone/ The immense majesty of your widow's pain." The sad mirror of the river reflects not only Andromache's present suffering but also her former, happier life. The analogy of the river with the Seine, by which Baudelaire stands, "Suddenly fertilized" his "fertile memory," and he regrets, as he walks by the place du Carrousel near the Louvre, that the city of Paris is changing around him. As he passes a place where "animals were once sold," he meets "a swan that had escaped from its cage."

With the appearance of the swan, the complexity of the imagery changes. The bird suffers superficially because, in strange surroundings not adapted to its needs, it cannot find water to drink: "Rubbing the dry pavement with his webbed feet/ On the rough ground dragged his white plumage/ By a dry gutter the beast open[ed] his beak." Yet the wings dragging on the pavement convey the degree to which this animal is out of place in its surroundings. Baudelaire imagines the emotions of the swan, "his heart filled with the beautiful lake of his birth." The water that he needs is not merely what is necessary to drink but that of his homeland. The swan thus becomes the "strange and fateful myth" that figures Baudelaire himself. Yet Baudelaire remains in his native Paris. The nature of his exile becomes clear only through suggestions begun with the exotic webbed feet and "beautiful lake of his birth" of the swan that suggest the more tropical climates emblematic of Baudelaire's ideal.

Baudelaire sees himself like "the man in Ovid," an allusion to Ovid's distinction that man looks toward heaven and animals toward earth. Yet he looks at "the ironic and cruelly blue sky," cruel because it now mocks the poet's futile aspiration. In the second part of the poem, Baudelaire repeats this revelation, detailing the suffering of each creature in exile and adding the image of the Negress: "I think of the skinny and consumptive Negress/ Tramping in the mud, and seeking, with haggard looks/ The absent coconut trees of proud Africa." The plight of the woman, perhaps inspired by the example of Jeanne Duval, reinforces the haunting presence of tropical nature contrasted at the end of the poem with "the forest where my Spirit is exiled."

A VOYAGE TO CYTHERA

First published: "Un Voyage à Cythère," 1855 (English translation, 1931)
Type of work: Poem

A traveler sees on the island of Cythera an emblem of his own fate.

"A Voyage to Cythera" shows the full evolution of the motif of departure in Baudelaire's work. In earlier poems, the poet shared the innocence exemplified by the child at the opening of "The Trip." Thus, in "By Association" he saw no reason not to abandon himself to the imagined departure inspired by the woman's perfume. "The Swan" reflects his recognition of separation from the ideal, but in a context of sadness rather than despair. The images of death in "A Voyage to Cythera" finally document the extent of the poet's fall.

Baudelaire borrowed the circumstances of this poem from a story that Gérard de Nerval had told of his own visit to Greece in his *Voyage en Orient* (1851; *Journey to the Orient*, 1972). The poem opens with the familiar scene of a happy sea voyage: "My heart, like a bird, fluttered joyfully/ And soared freely around the rigging." The joyful bird representing the poet's heart recalls the use of the same image in "Elévation" ("Elevation"), a poem at the beginning of *Flowers of Evil*, and serves to show from what heights the poet has fallen. Immediately, the imagery of this joyous scene suggests the fall: "The ship rocked under a cloudless sky/ Like an angel drunk on radiant sunlight." The negative implication appears, not in the literal meanings of the words, but in special nuances that Baudelaire has attached to them. The rolling ship echoes the rocking action by which "Boredom" rocked humanity's will, and the drunken angel recalls the angel of "Benediction" who observed the child's drunkenness.

When the island of Cythera, once sacred to Venus, becomes visible to the travelers, it is devoid of its former charms, "proud ghost of the antique Venus." Baudelaire recalls the island's past, "Where the sighs of adoring hearts/ Roll like incense on a rose garden," and the perfume recalls Baudelaire's own seduction. Like Baudelaire, the island has changed. On its banks now stands a gibbet, upon which hangs the body of a man already being devoured by beasts of prey. Faced with this grotesque image, Baudelaire recognizes in it the emblem of his own condition: "On your island, oh Venus! I found standing/ Only a symbolic gibbet where hung my own image." His spiritual death was linked to women, even as this man's death was to the island that represented love. In his fallen state, the poet can only reach out to God: "Oh Lord! give me the strength and courage/ To contemplate my heart and body without distaste." The strength for which he prays may indeed provide the courage with which he will face death in his ultimate departure in "The Trip."

Summary

Charles Baudelaire's personal evolution paralleled the evolution of his language. He came to recognize within his own life the signs of his spiritual fall, and the reader learns to attach special nuances to his often-repeated images. These evocative emblems finally become complex literary symbols. Baudelaire's major achievement lay in part in the creation of this symbol vocabulary through which each object may convey much more than simply its own identity.

The corollary to Baudelaire's symbol system was to become as important as the symbol itself. He persuaded his readers to analyze meaning in a new way, a process that would become fundamental to modern poetry.

Bibliography

Bloom, Harold, ed. *Charles Baudelaire*. New York: Chelsea House, 1987.

Carter, A. E. *Charles Baudelaire*. Boston: Twayne, 1977.

Hemmings, F. W. J. *Baudelaire the Damned: A Biography*. New York: Charles Scribner's Sons, 1982.

McLees, Ainslie Armstrong. *Baudelaire's "Argot Plastique": Poetic Caricature and Modernism*. Athens: University of Georgia Press, 1989.

Ruff, M. A. *Baudelaire*. Translated by Agnes Kertesz. New York: New York University Press, 1966.

Sartre, Jean-Paul. *Baudelaire*. Translated by Martin Turnell. London: Hamish Hamilton, 1964.

Turnell, Martin. *Baudelaire: A Study of His Poetry*. New York: New Directions, 1972.

Ward Jouve, Nicole. *Baudelaire: A Fire to Conquer Darkness*. New York: St. Martin's Press, 1980.

Dorothy M. Betz

SAMUEL BECKETT

Born: Foxrock, Ireland
April 13, 1906
Died: Paris, France
December 22, 1989

Principal Literary Achievement

Writing in both English and French, Beckett emerged during his forties as a master of both drama and fiction, his bleak vision of humanity often offset by the beauty of his prose.

Biography

In 1906, Good Friday happened to fall on the thirteenth day of April, bringing religion and superstition into rare conjunction. Samuel Beckett, whose writings contain more than their share of both, favored that date when citing his birth, although several of his biographers and commentators suggest a more likely birthdate later in the spring, citing a midsummer baptismal certificate as evidence. In any event, Samuel Barclay Beckett was born in the "comfortable" Foxrock district of Dublin sometime during the first half of 1906, the second son of William Beckett, who had prospered as an estimator of construction costs, and the former Mary Roe. William Beckett, born in Ireland of French Huguenot stock, thus bequeathed to his sons a mixed heritage that Samuel would often return in kind through his works, resulting in perplexity on both sides of the Channel.

Privately educated at Earlsfort House School, Portora Royal Schoool, and Trinity College, Dublin, in keeping with his Protestant background, Samuel Beckett emerged during adolescence as a skilled student athlete, showing talent also in those academic areas that happened to interest him. It was not until his years at Trinity, however, that he truly distinguished himself as a student, having discovered French literature and thought under the tutelage of Trinity's Professor Thomas Rudmose-Brown. Graduating first in his class of 1927, apparently destined to succeed Rudmose-Brown at Trinity, Beckett received an exchange fellowship for 1928 to 1930 at the prestigious École Normale Supérieure in Paris. Before leaving for Paris, Beckett taught briefly at a boys' boarding school in Belfast, finding teaching a bore but not yet prepared to abandon his plans for an academic career. During the summer of 1928, Beckett visited relatives then vacationing in Germany, falling briefly and somewhat disastrously in love with his first cousin Peggy Sinclair, who, destined to die young of tuber-

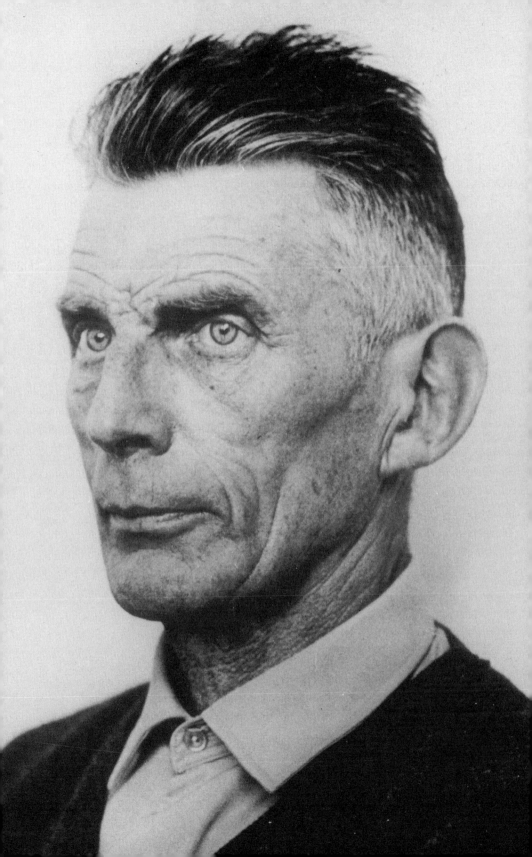

culosis, would figure prominently in such later Beckett works as *Krapp's Last Tape* (1985).

Already acquainted with most of the serious artists and writers then living in Dublin, who accepted him as their equal, Beckett lost little time developing similar acquaintances upon his arrival in Paris, helped by the friendship and "connections" of the writer Thomas McGreevy, the Trinity Fellow whom he had technically been appointed to replace. Mingling freely among French and expatriate writers, Beckett soon joined the "circle" of would-be writers surrounding Paris' most famous Irish expatriate of the period, James Joyce, who was then putting the finishing touches on the "work in progress" soon to be known as *Finnegans Wake* (1939). Although the exact extent and depth of Beckett's involvement in Joyce's life and career remain in dispute among both men's various commentators, it is clear in any case that the older writer, Joyce, influenced and inspired the younger one, Beckett; it is a matter of record, also, that Beckett was the object of a postadolescent "crush" on the part of Joyce's emotionally disturbed daughter Lucia, one year younger than Beckett. During the course of his two-year fellowship, involving minimal teaching duties, Beckett tried his hand at both poetry and prose, attracting the attention of several publishers and "little magazines" then serving English-speaking expatriates in Paris. By 1930, he had a contract from Hours Press to prepare a brief monograph on the Parisian novelist Marcel Proust, who, then as later, ranked with Joyce as a master of the modernist novel; significantly, Beckett's study of Proust would often be reprinted over six decades to follow, of interest to students of Beckett as well as to students of Proust.

Returning as planned to Trinity College after his fellowship ran its course, Beckett soon decided once and for all that teaching did not agree with him, claiming both that his students (mostly female) knew nothing and that he himself knew even less. While returning to the Continent in a sort of panic, he sent in a letter of resignation from Germany, thus sparing his mentors the unpleasant task of firing him for inattentive or, at best, "eccentric" teaching. Following the death of his father in 1933, Beckett moved to London, where he may or may not have undergone psychoanalysis, living on the proceeds of a share in his father's estate while working on the manuscript of *Murphy* (1938), his first completed novel. Beckett then traveled the British Isles and the Continent for two years in search of a publisher for the novel, finally finding one in 1937, the year that he settled permanently in France.

Barely surviving on commissions from writing and small portions of the family heritage sent to him from Dublin, Beckett soon "blended in" among the artists and writers then at work in Paris, and by late 1937 he had begun an amatory affair with the American heiress and art dealer Peggy Guggenheim. Early in 1938, Beckett, returning to his lodgings late at night, was accosted and stabbed by a local hoodlum whom he recognized on sight and who apparently was out to beg, borrow, or steal money that Beckett denied having on his person. The stabbing might well have proved fatal: Beckett spent weeks in the hospital, his lungs permanently damaged and susceptible to illness; only his thick, old overcoat had prevented the blade from reaching his heart. His rescuer on the scene was the musician Suzanne Deschevaux-Dumesnil, who applied first aid and arranged for his transportation to the Hôpital Broussais, where she later visited him. Before long, Suzanne, like Peggy Guggenheim some seven years Beckett's senior, would displace Guggenheim as the writer's companion of choice and would remain in that position for life, eventually becoming the first and only Mrs. Samuel Beckett.

Visiting his relatives in Ireland when war broke out on the Continent in 1939, Beckett returned home in haste to Paris out of loyalty to French and Jewish friends, a recent trip to Germany having confirmed his worst suspicions about Nazism. By late 1940, he was actively engaged in espionage activities with the French Resistance, working not for the French, as he later made clear, but against Hitler and all that he stood for. For the rest of his life, Beckett would remain resolutely apolitical, tending to downplay his Resistance activity as simple "Boy Scout stuff," keeping secret even from his closest friends the Croix de Guerre awarded to him in 1945 on the basis of his Resistance activities.

Late in the summer of 1942, after several close calls, Beckett and Suzanne (who by then was a Resistant herself) learned that their room had been infiltrated and that arrest was imminent. Little more than one step ahead of their pursuers, the two fled Paris with only the clothes on their backs, eventually finding their way to the small southern town of Roussillon, where they would wait for the war to end and where Beckett, facing enforced idleness, would write the novel later published as *Watt* (1953). After the war, Beckett returned to Ireland to check on his aging mother and other relatives, only to run into problems reentering France as a resident alien. In time, he found a workable solution, attaching himself as interpreter-storekeeper to an Irish Red Cross unit dispatched to the bombed-out city of St. Lô in Normany. After several months of service, Beckett found his way back to his old apartment in Paris, where he soon embarked upon the most productive phase of his literary career. With Suzanne to look after his daily needs and, in general, to protect his privacy, Beckett soon produced the three novels known as the Trilogy, published starting with *Molloy* in 1951. By that time, Beckett had already written *En attendant Godot* (pb. 1952; *Waiting for Godot*, 1954), which would bring him worldwide recognition almost immediately after its first performances early in 1953. From that point, Beckett lived and wrote as a rather reluctant celebrity, finding even his lesser works received with enthusiasm by scholars and critics. Awarded the Nobel Prize in Literature in 1969, Beckett died shortly before Christmas, on December 22, 1989, in Paris, having left instructions in his will that news of his death not be released until a week or so thereafter.

Analysis

"I can't go on, I'll go on." Those last words of *L'Innommable* (1953; *The Unnamable*, 1958), the final volume of Beckett's Trilogy, tend to summarize the author's mature output both in prose fiction and in drama, in which human life and aspirations are reduced to bare essentials; in the short novel *Comment c'est* (1961; *How It Is*, 1964), two "characters," presumably the last remnant of the human species, crawl toward each other through mud, subsisting on a diet of canned sardines left behind by a now-vanished civilization. In the memorable *Fin de partie: Suivi de Acte sans paroles* (1957; *Endgame: A Play in One Act; followed by Act Without Words: A Mime for One Player*, 1958), a Beckettian mime tries all possible human options, including suicide, only to end in apathy, waiting—for what? It is perhaps no accident that Beckett's creative "breakthrough" came in midlife with the first performances (in Paris) of *Waiting for Godot* a visible illustration, three-dimensional when staged, of the "waiting" that, in Beckett's developing vision, was characteristic of all human life. Is all of humanity, as one of his characters would later say in *Endgame*, waiting for "it," meaning life, to end? If not, then what is humankind awaiting?

Born with the verbal instincts of the traditional Irish poet, Beckett defined himself early in life as a writer and apprenticed himself to James Joyce, arguably the outstanding Irish writer of his own time or any other and a leading exponent of high modernism. Unfortunately, Beckett's early work remains not only hopelessly derivative of Joyce but also quite immature in its convoluted jokes, puns, and mannerisms. Indeed, it was not until after World War II, when Beckett began writing originally in French, that he would discover and assert a truly original talent that would forever distance him from Joyce's direct influence.

When asked, the normally reticent, even taciturn Beckett would give various cryptic explanations for his choice of writing idiom, perhaps the best-remembered of which is that it was easier for him to write "without style" in French. At the very least, the works composed originally in French are notably spare and deceptively simple, refreshingly free of the mannerisms that had marred Beckett's early works in English. Significantly, the new spareness of style would carry over into Beckett's own English versions of his works, as well as into those few later efforts, most notably *Krapp's Last Tape*, composed originally in English. Arguably, the evolution of Beckett's mature style had as much to do with his wartime experiences as with his change of language: *Waiting for Godot*, although set at no specific time, was assumed by many early commentators to be taking place in France during the Nazi occupation; indeed, the moral and psychological "landscape" of his late work suggests the "ground zero" of a world laid waste by postatomic war.

At once simple and complex, Beckett's plays and novels of the 1950's attracted many would-be interpreters; by the time Beckett won the Nobel Prize in 1969, his work had spawned a major academic "industry," with dozens of books and articles already in print and dozens more to follow. Not infrequently, the various "readings" of Beckett tended to contradict one another; Beckett himself, maintaining a nearly reclusive silence that may or may not have been a "pose," refused most requests to discuss or to explain his work, allowing critics of all persuasions to interpret his texts however they chose. By his middle sixties, Beckett, renowned as the creator of antiheroes for the stage, had himself become an anticelebrity of sorts, rarely seen, heard, or photographed yet assured that even the slightest of his new publications would attract enthusiastic attention. By the time of his death at eighty-three, only twenty years after he had received the Nobel Prize, Beckett's work and the "legend" generated by his reputation had become inextricably fused, making it more difficult than ever to separate, as his character Krapp had said, "the grain from the husks."

Although Beckett had written and published several volumes of prose fiction before the publication and performance of *Waiting for Godot*, it is doubtful that his "novels" would have drawn much attention, critical or otherwise, were it not for the runaway success of that first completed play; the subsequent successes of *Endgame* and *Krapp's Last Tape* would prove that *Waiting for Godot* was no fluke. Readers and spectators attracted to Beckett by his plays would then begin to discover his prose, in which the form of "the novel" is repeatedly questioned and tested. To be sure, most of the themes and concerns common to Beckett's plays are also to be found in his fiction, albeit in more concentrated, less readily accessible form: The narrator(s) of the Trilogy, for example, can be seen as one or more of the stage tramps in stationary pose, quite literally composing himself/themselves offstage, facing only a blank sheet of paper. Fortunately or unfortunately, the physical demands of the stage would force Beckett to be somewhat less cryptic in his dramatic efforts than in his fiction, and his plays continue to attract a somewhat wider audience.

In theater and fiction alike, Beckett stresses the essential solitude of humankind, whose efforts to discern meaning in life vacillate between pathos and bathos, often approaching a kind of grim humor. Most of Beckett's characters, whether on the stage or on the page, tend to share their creator's intense, even perverse preoccupation with mathematics and measurement, a concern that many commentators have traced back to Beckett's close study, during his fellowship years in Paris, of the life and career of the philosopher-scientist René Descartes and of Descartes' Belgian disciple Arnold Geulincx. The urge to count and to measure, leading as it does toward science and technology, may be seen as one of humankind's earliest and most abiding responses to the apparent chaos of the human condition, an effort to establish order. Hugh Kenner, in the first of his reliable studies of Beckett's work, isolated the theme and symbol of the "Cartesian centaur"—a man on a bicycle—as central to nearly all the author's basic texts. The bicycle, combining humankind's upright stance with the invention of the wheel, yet subject to frequent breakdowns and flat tires, shows both the ingenuity and the limitations experienced by Beckett's most memorable characters.

Even with technology (as represented by the bicycle), Beckett's human figures remain thwarted in their hopes and desires, more often carrying or pushing the bicycle than using it for extended locomotion as originally planned. In *Krapp's Last Tape*, the two wheels of a bicycle become the two reels of an early tape recorder, on which the striving but failed writer known only as Krapp had attempted to extend his mental locomotion, keeping track of time—and memory—through technology. Inevitably, he fails, falling back on the unreliable human memory that he abandoned years before. "What's to say?" he wonders aloud, preparing a "fresh" tape. "Not a squeak." Yet he keeps speaking, or squeaking, into a machine that has already failed him and will surely do so again.

WAITING FOR GODOT

First produced: *En attendant Godot*, 1953 (first published, 1952; English translation, 1954)
Type of work: Play

Two tramps wait by the roadside for someone who never appears, meeting instead a peculiar "master" and his equally strange "slave."

Arguably, *Waiting for Godot* provides an optimum point of entry not only into Beckett's enigmatic body of mature work but also into the antirational theater that emerged on the European continent during the decade following World War II, permanently altering the expectations of spectators (and playwrights) all over the world. In Beckett's first performed and published play, as in contemporary (but quite different) plays by Eugène Ionesco, Arthur Adamov, Max Frisch, and Friedrich Dürrenmatt, plot is all but discarded as a necessary element of drama, the tension residing instead in metaphysical concerns and in interaction (or noninteraction) among the characters.

The play is set on a desolate roadside, requiring little in the way of scenery. Two aging tramps, Vladimir (Didi) and Estragon (Gogo), reminiscent of the film comics Laurel and Hardy gone to seed, exchange desultory conversation as they wait for the arrival of a man called Godot, who in fact never appears. Vladimir, like Laurel, is spare of build; Estragon, like Oliver Hardy, considerably stouter. "Nothing to be done," says Estragon in the play's first line, which in fact summarizes all the ensuing dialogue and action, although Estragon, at that moment, refers only to the act of taking off his shoes. Beckett's lines, even when translated into English from the original French, tend thus to send ambivalent messages and meanings that continue to reverberate long after the curtain falls. Like most of Beckett's marginal characters in both plays and fiction, "Didi" and "Gogo," as they address each other with childlike nicknames, have obviously known far better days; both are well educated, as their dialogue soon makes clear, yet education proves to be of little help in their current predicament.

Shot through with philosophical speculations and learned references to Holy Scripture, the prolonged interchanges between the two tramps have prompted many commentators to find in the play religious overtones that may or may not have been intended; more to the point, it seems, is the simple act of waiting, and the basically human instinct to talk (or keep busy or both) in order to stave off boredom.

Divided into two approximately equal acts, the action of *Waiting for Godot* twice relieves Vladimir and Estragon of boredom through encounters with two additional characters, the arrogant, autocratic Pozzo and his mute (or at least tongue-tied) manservant Lucky, attached to Pozzo's body with a rope. Pozzo, like Estragon, is portly of build; Lucky, like Vladimir, is almost painfully thin. All four of the main characters are well past middle age, with ailments and impediments to suit. Pozzo, a caricature of the self-important rich man, will have lost his sight between his first and second encounters with the tramps; Lucky, although mute, will suddenly deliver himself, toward the end of act 1, of a "learned" but incomprehensible monologue that, for later generations of spectators, would "recall" the printouts of an ill-programmed computer gone berserk.

Apparently unexpected and quite unpredictable, *Waiting for Godot* would soon achieve landmark status in the history of Western drama, drawing upon the familiar (stock characters from silent film or British music hall, Bowler-hatted and stiff-gaited), yet leading toward unexplored territory, in concept as well as in location. Still contemplating suicide, as they have more than once in the past, Vladimir and Estragon decide to leave because Godot has yet to shown himself. As the curtain falls, however, they are both still in place, waiting.

ENDGAME

First produced: *Fin de partie*, 1957 (first published, 1957; English translation, 1958)
Type of work: Play

Four characters wait for the end of the world in an isolated room that resembles the inside of the human skull.

If *Waiting for Godot* recalls France during the Nazi occupation, where people waited in desolate spots for others who might or might not appear, *Endgame* recalls a bizarre bomb shelter in the wake of Hiroshima and worse disasters, or perhaps the post-Freudian human skull. In the center, at his own request, sits Hamm, a ham-actor or failed Hamlet, often confusing himself with King Lear, now blind and immobile, confined to a makeshift wheelchair that more closely resembles a throne mounted on casters. Downstage, contained in trash cans, are Hamm's parents Nagg and Nell, left legless after a tandem-bicycle accident years earlier in the Ardennes. The only character left standing is Clov, who suffers from an ailment that keeps him from sitting down and who may or may not be Hamm's son.

In many ways, Hamm recalls Pozzo of *Waiting for Godot*. Used to the exercise of power, turning blindness to his own advantage as he spins his dreams and memories into delusions of grandeur, Hamm rules his shrinking domain with the endless "mind games" alluded to in the play's title, drawn from the game of chess. "Me to play," says Hamm in the first line of the English version, delivered after nearly five minutes of illuminated stage-business on the part of Clov. Using his own French original, Beckett might better have translated the line as "It's *my* turn, now," to be delivered in a childish, churlish tone.

Throughout the action of *Endgame,* Hamm does indeed take his turn, doing most of the talking and insisting on a "turn" around the room, in his chair pushed by Clov, after which he must return "to the center." A seemingly endless monologue, interrupted only by the nagging of his father, Nagg, recalls or imagines a time when Hamm, like Pozzo, was truly in control, sufficiently rich and influential to control far more than the space to which his questionable influence is now limited. There are no more bicycle wheels, indeed no more bicycles, a luxury that Hamm never afforded Clov as a boy. "The light is sunk," planted seeds will never sprout, and Hamm is looking at "the end" even as Clov jauntily seeks to make "an exit."

Even more self-conscious of the stage than *Waiting for Godot, Endgame* is still—for good or for ill—considered by many of Beckett's commentators to be his finest play, perhaps more satisfying for actors than for spectators. Technology, although much in evidence—the makeshift wheelchair, an invisible telephone long past usefulness, the defunct bicycles, a keywound alarm clock that still rings loud enough "to wake the dead" but not the deaf—offers no exit or salvation to those held captive in the "end game," perhaps the game eternally played inside one's own skull. At the end of the play, with Hamm having staged his own death—but perhaps having really died—and his parents presumed dead, Clov, bags in hand, moves downstage as if to make good on his threat or promise. Like Vladimir and Estragon, however, he remains poised but, as the curtain falls, still does not move. Where, indeed, would he go?

KRAPP'S LAST TAPE

First produced: 1958 (first published, 1958)
Type of work: Play

A failed, aging writer replays a "memoir" taped thirty years earlier, finding neither the truth nor the beauty for which he had aimed.

No doubt the best known of Beckett's mature efforts written originally in English, *Krapp's Last Tape* carries his theatrical experiment one step further, reducing the "cast of characters" to a single human actor, supplemented by a tape recorder playing back the same voice at a much earlier age, with references to still earlier recordings. Going well beyond the usual dramatic monologue, the interaction of the aging Krapp with his former self (or selves) raises *Krapp's Last Tape* to the dimension of full-scale theater.

Set "in the future"—tape recorders being relatively new at the time of the play's composition—*Krapp's Last Tape* presents the title character under the strong, merciless light of his workspace, light demanded by his increasingly poor eyesight. Light and shadow, sight and blindness figure prominently in Beckett's attempt to examine, and possibly correct, Marcel Proust's often-misinterpreted concept of "involuntary memory." Krapp has apparently intended to surprise himself with memories kept "fresh" on tape, but there are few surprises to be found. Krapp, like Proust, is a writer by choice, albeit a most unsuccessful one whose major publication has only sold seventeen copies, "to free circulating libraries beyond the seas." He is also, like Hamm and Pozzo, something of a *poseur* whose carefully phrased speeches, here recorded solely for his own benefit, ring hollow when heard across the gulf of time.

Like Vladimir and Estragon, Krapp is rather clownish in appearance and dress, prone to a variety of ailments no doubt inflicted by his life-style. A heavy drinker who interrupts the tape more than once to take a "nip" offstage, Krapp is also hopelessly addicted to bananas, despite chronic constipation. While onstage, Krapp eats at least two bananas and starts to eat more, stuffing them absently into his pockets as he prepares to leave the room. Both scatological and sexual in their symbolism, the bananas serve also to generate much interesting stage "business," as does the near-sighted Krapp's continual fumbling with keys, locks, reels of tape, and ledgers, Even when he can read his own writing in the ledger where he has cataloged his tapes, the cryptic notations make little or no sense to him. Choosing spool five from box three, Krapp must play the tape through in order to make sense of such references as the "black ball" and the "dark nurse." It soon becomes clear, though, that he has chosen that particular tape because of the final notation, "farewell to love."

Recorded some thirty years earlier on the occasion of his thirty-ninth birthday, the tape that occupies Krapp's attention on the evening in question itself refers back to even earlier tapes that the younger Krapp played just before recording his latest message to himself. His taped "journals," an evident attempt to subvert the fallibility of human memory through the "wonders" of modern technology, prove even more fallible than his own failing memory, which holds fast to a narrated love scene involving himself and a girl in a boat, no doubt the "farewell to love." Increasingly drunk and dispirited, Krapp will keep replaying that portion of the tape, fast-forwarding past sequences in which his thirty-nine-year-old self proudly holds forth on his literary ambitions and career. Clearly, the girl in the boat soon fell victim to those same ambitions, abandoned in favor of Krapp's "vocation." During the course of the play, however, Krapp becomes painfully aware that he has managed to save neither career nor memories, and that love has managed to pass him by, if only because he sidestepped it at the time. In his French version of the play, *La Dernière Bande*, Beckett substitutes a sexual allusion—implying arousal—for the scatological one implicit in the English title. Both elements are foregrounded in the play itself, leaving little doubt that Krapp has selfishly, if unconsciously, chosen the excremental over the erotic, and in old age has little choice but to lie in the bed that he has prepared for himself. Abandoning his attempt to record a fresh tape, the old man replays the love "scene" again, gazing blankly toward the audience as the tape continues, in silence.

Despite its unorthodox form, *Krapp's Last Tape* remains among the more explicit and accessible of Beckett's works, yet somewhat more complex than it appears at first glance or hearing. In this work, more than in any other, Beckett seriously questions the interrelationship of life and art, wondering aloud if art is worth the candle—or the ultimately blinding light above Krapp's table, described on his earlier tape as "a great improvement" that makes him feel "less alone. In a way."

THE TRILOGY

First published: *Molloy*, 1951 (English translation, 1955); *Malone meurt*, 1951 (*Malone Dies*, 1956); *L'Innommable*, 1953 (*The Unnamable*, 1958)
Type of work: Novels

A narrative consciousness writes itself into—and out of—existence, calling into serious question the convention of the "novel" as known to the reader of the 1950's.

"I am in my mother's room. It is I who live there now. I don't know how I got there." The narrative voice first known as Molloy calls himself into existence with such utterances and tries to sustain the reader's interest as he describes his observation of two possible pursuers noted only as A and C (Abel and Cain, perhaps). He directs his faltering moves back toward his elderly mother, with whom he can communicate only with knuckle-blows to the head, one number for yes, another for no, yet another for "money." "Composing" himself as he writes, or speaks, Molloy recalls a ritual of sucking pebbles, careful to rotate each of the small rocks through the pockets of his seedy overcoat so as not to suck the same one twice in one day. On another occasion, Molloy pulls from his pocket a miniature sawhorse in silver or silverplate with no recollection of its intended function, as a knife-rest at formal dinners in a long-gone bourgeois society.

Riding with increasing difficulty on a bicycle possibly less functional than himself, Molloy runs down a small dog belonging to a woman known only as "Lousse," who then detains him for reasons unspecified. Not long thereafter, the narrative viewpoint shifts to that of a certain Jacques Moran, whose fruitless search for Molloy will constitute the second half of the "novel." Like Pozzo and Hamm, Moran is authoritative, even cruel, treating his adolescent son much as Pozzo treats his slave, Lucky. Just as Pozzo loses his sight between the acts of *Waiting for Godot*, so, too, will Moran lose his mobility and equilibrium during the course of his search, in effect *becoming* Molloy, or Molloy's double, carried about on the handlebars of the bicycle that Molloy once rode. The final sentence of Moran's narrative neatly negates the first, and incidentally all that has passed between.

"Malone is what I am called now," says the narrator at the start of *Malone Dies*, implying soon thereafter that the various Murphys, Molloys, and Morans were creatures of his own imagination, brought to life, abandoned or killed at will. Like Hamm, the octogenarian Malone is a compulsive storyteller, calling to life a father and son known as Saposcat (Sapo for short), later to be known as Macmann. Alone in a room save for the creatures of his own devising, the invalid Malone dreams of poling his bed down a circular staircase as one would pole a raft downriver; regretting his eventual inability to record his own death, Malone contents himself with "killing off" characters in his endless narrative, meanwhile dropping hints that he might actually have committed murder at an earlier stage of his life. Malone presumably dies as his recorded monologue trails off into nothingness; yet in *The Unnamable* the narrative continues, presumably delivered by a legless man confined to a jar, just as Nagg is confined to a trash can in *Endgame*. The narrator may or may not be called Mahood, or perhaps Mahood is yet another "fictional" creature summoned into existence in order to be discarded at will. The narrative runs on and on as if self-driven, almost without punctuation, proceeding toward—and perhaps beyond—the outer limits of the fictional form.

Summary

Although first expressed in the experimental fiction that he continued to write until his death, Samuel Beckett's lyrical pessimism found its strongest and most memorable expression in his plays, which represent both a landmark and a turning point in the history of world drama. Notable for their "accessibility" despite an apparent complexity, *Waiting for Godot*, *Endgame*, and *Krapp's Last Tape* remain in the worldwide dramatic repertory decades after they were first performed, challenging actors and audiences alike with their haunted, haunting "humanity."

Bibliography

Alvarez, Alfred. *Samuel Beckett.* New York: Viking Press, 1973.

Bair, Deirdre. *Samuel Beckett.* New York: Harcourt Brace Jovanovich, 1978.

Barnard, G. C. *Samuel Beckett: A New Approach.* New York: Dodd, Mead, 1970.

Ben-Zvi, Linda. *Samuel Beckett.* Boston: Twayne, 1986.

Cohn, Ruby. *Just Play: Beckett's Theater.* Princeton, N.J.: Princeton University Press, 1980.

Fletcher, John. *The Novels of Samuel Beckett.* New York: Barnes & Noble Books, 1970.

Kenner, Hugh. *A Reader's Guide to Samuel Beckett.* New York: Farrar, Straus & Giroux, 1973.

_____. *Samuel Beckett: A Critical Study.* New York: Evergreen Press, 1961.

Mercier, Vivian. *Beckett/Beckett.* New York: Oxford University Press, 1977.

David B. Parsell

ARNOLD BENNETT

Born: Shelton, near Hanley, Staffordshire, England
May 27, 1867
Died: London, England
March 27, 1931

Principal Literary Achievement

Bennett's reputation rests upon his novels of "the Five Towns," a re-creation of the Staffordshire of his youth, as well as on his later, intensely realistic portrayals of English life.

Biography

Enoch Arnold Bennett was born in Shelton, near Hanley, Staffordshire, on May 27, 1867, the son of Enoch and Sarah Ann Longson Bennett. The eldest of nine children, Bennett descended from a long line of Methodists whom he portrayed in his novels *Anna of the Five Towns* (1902) and *Clayhanger* (1910). His father, after working long days as a master potter, draper, and pawnbroker and spending his nights studying the law, qualified as a solicitor at the age of thirty-four, when Arnold was nine. The wealth of precise notation about such occupations in Bennett's novels seems to stem from his early years. He was also fortunate enough to observe the interaction of different social classes as his family's status steadily improved under the sway of his father's autocratic direction (depicted in *Clayhanger*) and his mother's pliable consent.

Bennett attended local schools, but his father determined that his son should be a clerk, and thus he had to forgo the opportunity of a college education. Almost immediately, Bennett resolved to get out of this clerkship, chafing at the life of the "Pottery towns," the filth and provincialism he delineates in *The Old Wives' Tale* (1908) and in other novels.

Bennett's first literary efforts (gossipy notes) appeared in the *Staffordshire Sentinel* while he was educating himself by reading English, French, and Russian authors. He eventually began a job as a clerk with a firm of lawyers in London, where he escaped forever the towns of his youth.

The sometimes gloomy and temperamental Bennett did not like the law, and to supplement his poor pay he turned to secondhand bookselling, which he put to good use in his evocation of Henry Earlforward in *Riceyman Steps* (1923). Soon he established a circle of friends, organizing musical evenings in which he would

sing without a trace of the stammer he could not otherwise control. Honing his schoolboy French, he began to consort with artists, musicians, and writers and to publish stories in prestigious London literary magazines. He found his first novel, *A Man from the North* (1898), an agony to write and a commercial failure.

Enoch Bennett's purchase of shares in a periodical, *Woman*, provided Arnold with an assistant editorship, and under the pseudonym "Barbara" he published weekly reviews. As "Marjorie," he supplied gossip and advice in "Answers to Correspondents," later crediting this assignment as contributing to his knowledge of women's apparel, housekeeping, and their most intimate thoughts. Advancing to the position of editor, Bennett managed also to write reviews for other important journals and to thrust himself into the fads of his age: cycling and painting watercolors.

Perhaps because of his experience with so many different sorts of newspapers and journals, Bennett quickly showed his mastery of both serious and superficial literature, producing in the same year (1902) *Anna of the Five Towns* (one of his best novels) and a slight but enjoyable comic thriller, *The Grand Babylon Hotel* (published in the United States as *T. Racksole and Daughter*). The latter formed part of a series of novels that did nothing to enhance Bennett's literary stature but instead enabled him to procure income to satisfy a long-held ambition: to live in Paris, to which he dispatched himself in 1903.

Paris was the center of Bennett's literary universe, where he could commune with fellow writers and openly address subjects—particularly sex—that were prohibited in London. There was also the *demimonde* of Paris, the world of the theater and of women who were much freer in their sexual habits than those he had known in England. A young American woman rejected his marriage proposal, but in 1907, Marguerite Soulié, once connected with the theater, a proprietor of a dress shop, married him. The early years of the marriage in Paris may have been Bennett's happiest, for it is where he conceived and wrote most of his masterpiece, *The Old Wives' Tale*, drawing quite directly on his experience of provincial England and cosmopolitan France.

Bennett continued his prodigious output into the next decade. He published short fiction: *The Grim Smile of the Five Towns* (1907); novels: *Clayhanger and the Card* (1911; published in the United States as *Denry the Audacious* 1911); plays: *Milestones: A Play in Three Acts* (1912) and *The Great Adventure: A Play of Fantasia in Four Sets* (1913); nonfiction: *The Human Machine* (1908) and *Mental Efficiency and Other Hints to Men and Women* (1911); and criticism: *The Price of Love* (1914) and *Books and Persons: Being Comments on a Past Epoch* (1908-1911). As he drove himself relentlessly, his income increased and his health deteriorated. He experienced sleeplessness, exhaustion, and intermittent depression. After bouts of gastroenteritis, Bennett would dose himself with various pills and nerve tonics. Yet he had an enviable reputation as a sweet-tempered and generous man, which is somewhat belied by his later relations with his wife, from whom he separated in 1921.

During World War I, Bennett worked hard and without pay at a five-day-a-week schedule in the Ministry of Information, later basing an important novel, *Lord Raingo* (1926), on his experience. Continuing to write journalism, novels, and other books that would swell his total output to more than eighty titles, Bennett was lionized, feted, and offered titles he refused—always careful to remember his social roots, eschewing snobbery, and taking a line sympathetic to working men and women.

Toward the end of his career, he was often regarded as a relic. His reputation in eclipse, after coming under the heavy literary guns of Virginia Woolf and Rebecca West, Bennett died on March 27, 1931, in London, a prosperous writer mourned even by his severest critics, who noted the power of his kind and sympathetic personality and art.

Analysis

Bennett's highest literary ambition was to become the English Flaubert. Profoundly influenced by *Madame Bovary* (1857), Bennett set out to record a faithful, intensely accurate, and scrupulously realized account of English provincial life in the second half of the nineteenth century and the early twentieth century. Flaubert had shown that the single most important factor in literature was the writer's imagination, his ability to plumb the milieu and the minds of his characters. Rendering their worlds in meticulous detail, creating the canvas of human nature, would yield a God-like mastery of social reality and individuality and issue into an art that could stand by itself.

Flaubert's appeal to Bennett is obvious, for here was a man who wanted to transcend his place in the dirty pottery towns of the north of England, who in his early years had to bow to the authority of his strong-willed father. To create his own world for himself and to project that world into literature seemed to him to be the noblest and most exciting goal he could conceive.

The key to Bennett's success lay in his efforts to amass a densely organized and detailed view of social reality. In his best work he set a geographical boundary to his fiction, the territory of the five towns in Staffordshire—Tunstall, Burslem, Hanley, Stoke-on-Trent, and Longton—that he called in his fiction Turnhill, Bursley, Hanbridge, Knype, and Longshaw. Within these environs, Bennett could map and plot and analyze human character and society with virtually exhaustive completeness. Thus in a "Five Towns" novel he could describe in riveting detail the transportation network, the items in the shops, the dress of men and women, the character and quality of their furniture, the local politics, the announcements and gossip in the newspapers, and the seemingly glacial, reluctant emergence of these provincial places into the modern world.

If Bennett found his first novel painful to write, it is not difficult to see why. His novels are stocked with a profusion of data about social mores and material culture that are almost anthropological in their completeness. When Bennett describes the interior of a home, there is no doubt that he has fully imagined these features and must have found the creation of them arduous. The discipline of a mind capable of such extraordinary specificity, however, produced a magnificent storehouse of imagined environments that Bennett could quickly call upon, for he wrote his greatest and one of his longest works, *The Old Wives' Tale*, in less than a year.

Although Bennett's prodigious output varies in quality, even his least accomplished novels, plays, and criticism reflect his incredible inventory of subjects, which he would recycle throughout his long career. Thus *The Grand Babylon Hotel* initiated his writing about hotels, a characteristic that would appear regularly throughout his fiction. A miser appears in *Anna of the Five Towns* and then is given definitive treatment in *Riceyman Steps*. His women tend to split between the homelike and the unruly—Constance and Sophia in *The Old Wives' Tale*, Alice Challice and Hilda Lessways in *Buried Alive* 1908). Knowing Paris almost as well as his Five Towns, he turned to it in *The Old Wives' Tale*, *The Pretty Lady* (1918), and *Lilian* (1922).

Bennett's understanding of human nature is founded on the strong material basis of his fiction. His characters' minds and hearts are as plentifully filled as his houses, shops, and streets. A character's mind in Bennett's imagination has as much of a geography as does the locality in which he or she resides. For example, Constance in the *The Old Wives' Tale* has a mind like the draper's shop in which she was reared. She is dull, used to the dirt in the square that invades her household, and positively panicked by her sister Sophia's proposal that they live abroad. Constance has outfitted her life to suit the narrow confines of her provincial setting and knows that the strength and interest she can muster depends upon her devotion to local values.

THE OLD WIVES' TALE

First published: 1908
Type of work: Novel

Two sisters, Constance and Sophia Baines, choose opposite ways of life (accepting and rejecting their provincial roots) and reunite in their difficult, yet happy, last years.

The Old Wives' Tale is generally considered to be Benett's masterpiece. It captures both the provincial and cosmopolitan worlds that were the basis of both his life and his fiction. In this work, Bennett attained an exquisite balance between his two homes, England and France, and between his romantic and realistic sides, that are mirrored in the lives of his two heroines, Constance and Sophia.

Constance and Sophia are the daughters of a well-known draper in Bursley. Constance finds it no trouble at all to accustom herself to the drab atmosphere of the shop, to obey her mother in every respect, and to wait upon her invalid father. The beautiful Sophia dreads commerce and is bored by it, preferring a career as a teacher, which her parents strictly forbid her to pursue. Of a romantic disposition, Sophia is quickly taken with Gerald Scales, a traveling salesman who persuades her to elope with him.

Book 1 of the novel is finely balanced between Constance and Sophia, so that the claims of the family and the desires of the individual are both given their due. The characters of Sophia and Constance come to the fore in a hilarious scene involving Samuel Povey, the chief assistant of the shop, who has fallen into a stupor induced by the drug he has taken to deaden the pain of an aching tooth. As his mouth drops open, Sophia deftly inserts a pair of pliers, extracting what she deems to be the offending tooth, only to discover that she has pulled the wrong one. Naturally, Constance is shocked by her sister's boldness, for she cannot imagine taking such liberties or behaving so recklessly. She can be neither as assertive nor as certain as her sister.

Book 2 is devoted to Constance's life, her marriage to Samuel Povey, the birth of her darling son, her management of the shop after the death of her parents, and her retirement to the rooms above the shop when she is bought out by a female assistant and her new husband, the family's dour attorney, Mr. Critchlow. Sophia largely disappears as a character, with Constance receiving only a few postcards that tell her that Sophia is still alive. It is to Bennett's credit that he manages to make Constance an interesting character when her personality is so clearly drab in comparison with her sister's. Bennett is successful because he is so well informed about the details of Constance's life and can show her inner feelings, making what would appear trivial matters to an outside observer important events in Constance's inner life. Bennett demonstrates how Constance makes her marriage and her career in the shop successful, so that within her limitations she performs admirably and heroically. At the same time, the intermittent mentions of Sophia whet the curiosity. What has she made of her life?

Book 3 shifts to Sophia, showing that Gerald Scales never meant to marry her. A spoiled young man with an inheritance, he planned only to make sport with Sophia, but her stolid refusal to have an affair with Scales forces him to marry her. Yet the marriage is a failure, a fact that Sophia prudently acknowledges when she takes advantage of her husband by stealing several hundred pounds to set aside for the day he leaves her.

After recovering from a serious illness occasioned by Gerald's departure, Sophia finds that she is a Baines after all; that is, she has a gift for business, setting herself up with a pension and gaining a reputation as an industrious, no-nonsense proprietor. She rejects various male suitors, saving both her money and her energy for business, paying little attention to the Paris to which her husband has taken her and in which she expects to remain, having given up all thoughts of contacting her family.

At fifty, life changes for Sophia when she is recognized by a family friend who is visiting Paris. Contact is initiated by Constance, who overwhelms Sophia with her sweetness. Sophia is impressed and gratified by her sister's generosity and her complete lack of criticism. Constance, in short, welcomes her sister home, and Bennett shrewdly conveys the way in which each must adjust to the habits of the other, sharing the Baines propensity for efficient household management but remaining divided on their views of the best way of spending their remaining years.

Book 4, titled "What Life Is," sums up what the novel is ultimately about: how the sisters come to terms with their mortality and measure the way they have lived. Constance dies, appropriately enough, by exhausting herself in a long walk to the polling booth to vote against the referendum that would unite the five towns and put an end to the provincial life she has treasured. Sophia dies at the shock of seeing her presumably dead husband, who has finally returned home in penury, a feeble old man whose presence floods her with memories of her youth, of her wayward romantic feelings that have given way to a much safer, if narrower, life.

RICEYMAN STEPS

First published: 1923
Type of work: Novel

Henry Earlforward, proprietor of a secondhand bookshop, gradually allows his miserly habits to overwhelm his life, causing the death of himself and his wife.

Riceyman Steps is a bleak novel about a miser. It is a tribute to Bennett's art that the novel is both enjoyable and moving. There is something about knowing a character so well that there is no human fault that cannot be sympathetically understood, if not condoned. So it is with Henry Earlforward, a neat, mild, and fastidious man. When he marries Elsie Sprickett, an equally fastidious and shrewd shop owner, he defeats her efforts to behave more generously and to spend more on life, and though she rails at him, she loves him, softening to his tender voice and his obvious devotion to her.

Bennett contrives a plot and a setting that mercilessly bear down upon the characters yet give them full play to express their individuality. They are not merely the victims of circumstances, but they are also not quite strong enough to alter their lifelong habits and prejudices. There is no area of life, for example, that Henry does not submit to his austere notions of economy. When Elsie attempts to surprise him by having his shop and home cleaned on their honeymoon day (they have agreed it is to be only one day), he insists on cutting the honeymoon short, not wanting to spend more money on what he sees as the extravagance of dinner and a motion-picture show. When they return home and he discovers the vacuum cleaners, he interviews one of the workers, asking him what they do with the dirt.

Does it have a market value? Henry wants to know.

Henry denies himself and his wife food, trying to live without heat and light in his home as he does in his business. His mind measures virtually every act by what it costs, so that eventually he turns his own body into an emaciated version of his parsimonious temperament. Where he lives, Riceyman Steps, is but the external manifestation of Henry's reluctance to live a full, expended life. It is a neglected part of London that has not kept pace with the present and has little to recommend itself in the way of culture. Having inherited the book business from a relative, T. T. Riceyman, Henry becomes known by the place he inhabits: He is Riceyman, the human representation of the square, and the twenty Riceyman steps that mark the limit of his enterprise.

Neglecting himself and his wife, Henry does see the signs of their physical deterioration. He will not spend money on a doctor, attributing his increasing pain to indigestion and his wife's ill health to needless worry when in fact he is suffering from cancer and she will eventually die following an operation.

Riceyman Steps is perhaps Bennett's final word on the extremity of a certain kind of provincial mind that so starves itself that it cannot recognize the approaching death of the mind and the body. Yet Henry, like so many of Bennett's provincial characters, is likable, for he has an inner harmony, a fullness within the context of his own limitations (such as his full, almost sensual lips)—a surprising feature in such a deprived figure.

Summary

For all of his criticism of the provincial character, Arnold Bennett's fondness for figures such as Constance Baines and Henry Earlforward is apparent, for they are presented in loving detail and often exhibit a stalwart, dependable integrity that he much admires. They also represent the power of the past, of the status quo, and of the masses of people who content themselves with life as it is. Though Bennett himself did not choose to live a conventional life, he understood and sympathized with those who made such decisions, because he realized that there were certain compensations for them—chiefly, a sense of comfort and security that his more flamboyant and romantic characters could not achieve.

Bibliography

Barker, Dudley. *Writer by Trade: A View of Arnold Bennett.* London: Allen & Unwin, 1966.

Broomfield, Olga. *Arnold Bennett.* Boston, Twayne, 1984.

Drabble, Margaret. *Arnold Bennett: A Biography.* New York: Alfred A. Knopf, 1974.

Hepburn, James G. *The Art of Arnold Bennett.* Bloomington: Indiana University Press, 1963.

Swinnerton, Frank. *Arnold Bennett.* London: Longman, 1950.

———————. *Arnold Bennett: A Last Word.* Garden City, N.Y.: Doubleday, 1978.

Wright, Walter F. *Arnold Bennett: Romantic Realist.* Lincoln: University of Nebraska Press, 1971.
Young, Kenneth. *Arnold Bennett.* Harlow, Essex, England: The Longman Group, 1975.

Carl Rollyson

JOHN BETJEMAN

Born: London, England
August 28, 1906
Died: Trebetherick, Cornwall, England
May 19, 1984

Principal Literary Achievement

Dedicated to making poetry accessible to, and understood by, the general reading public, Betjeman, with his indelible portraits of English towns, villages, and people, is a significant, modern literary voice.

Biography

Born in London, England, on August 28, 1906, John Betjeman was the only child of Mabel Bessie Dawson and Ernest Betjeman, a prominent businessman of Dutch ancestry and supplier of fine furnishings for exclusive shops. Betjeman's early years, especially those of his childhood, are recounted in his verse autobiography, *Summoned by Bells* (1960). Growing up in the North London Edwardian suburbs, Betjeman became painfully aware of class differences, the seemingly small but inexorable distinctions of income and status. He developed, even at an early age, a profound sensitivity to subtle forms of snobbery. Betjeman's family relations were somewhat strained, even perverse. His father, from whom the author later became estranged, figured into his poetry as a formidable reminder of his son's "inadequacies," not only because the younger Betjeman did not enjoy hunting and fishing, as his father did, but also because he refused to continue in the family business. Betjeman's guilt for disappointing his parent was obsessive, extending to his imagining that he also had disappointed his father's employees.

Feeling the magnetic draw of poetry, Betjeman recognized even as an adolescent that his future lay in verse: "I knew as soon as I could read and write/ That I must be a poet" (*Summoned by Bells*). The young poet attended preparatory school at Highgate, London; his teacher there, T. S. Eliot, was a profound force in modern poetry. To Eliot, the young Betjeman would bind and submit his first poetic attempts in a volume, titled "The Best of Betjeman." Eliot never commented, however, upon the scholboy's verses. At Marlborough public school, which Betjeman entered in 1920, bullies teased and terrorized the youngster. One of Betjeman's classmates mocked his poem about a city church, thus humiliating the already sensitive and lonely adolescent. This experience traumatized the fifteen-year-old and contributed to his an-

tipathy toward abusive criticism.

In 1925, Betjeman entered Magdalen College, Oxford, with plans of earning a degree in English, but, to his father's disappointment and to his own dismay, his irresolute life-style prohibited him from attaining academic success: "For, while we ate Virginia hams,/ Contemporaries passed exams" (*Summoned by Bells*). For the most part, Betjeman's memories of Oxford, however, were pleasant. There, he developed many friendships, most notably with Evelyn Waugh, who later became one of England's most prodigious novelists. Betjeman's talents did not go unnoticed at Oxford, as C. W. Bowra, a renowned scholar, applauded his verse, as well as his knowledge of architecture. Accolades were not to be showered on Betjeman at Oxford, despite Bowra's admiration and affection for him. Having neglected his studies, Betjeman won the distaste of his tutor, C. S. Lewis, distinguished critic and author, whom the poet later satirized in some of his poems. Failing repeated attempts to pass a simple qualifying exam, Betjeman was forced at last to leave Oxford. Stunned and saddened by his failure, the poet left college disillusioned, having fallen short of his dream of becoming a university don: "Reading old poets in the library,/ Attending chapel in an M.A. gown/ And sipping vintage port by candlelight" (*Summoned by Bells*). Despite his aversion to sports, Betjeman obtained, and held for a short time, a teaching post at Heddon Court School, in Barnet, Hertfordshire, a post secured, ironically, under the auspices of his mastery of cricket.

The 1930's saw Betjeman's popularity increase as he gained visibility and recognition. In 1931, the poet published his first book of poetry, *Mount Zion; Or, In Touch with the Infinite*, whose poems contained many of his major themes and revealed his interest in topography. That same year, Betjeman became assistant editor of the *Architectural Review*, a position that granted him exposure to many of England's prominent architects and architectural historians of the day. Betjeman left his position in 1933 and began editing a series of topographical guides to Britain. To her mother's chagrin, Penelope Chetwode, daughter of Field Marshal Sir Philip Chetwode, commander-in-chief, India, accepted Betjeman's proposal of marriage in 1933. The couple had two children, Paul and Candida. In a few short years, Betjeman's second volume of verse, *Continual Dew: A Little Book of Bourgeois Verse* (1937), with its light and whimsical tone, appeared and immediately enjoyed success. Betjeman, however, wanted to be regarded as a serious poet, not merely a popular one, though the ambiguity of some of his best images and the complexity of his tone lay buried beneath his copious iambics. Nonetheless, the public flocked to buy his unpretentious verse. Not since George Gordon, Lord Byron, and Alfred, Lord Tennyson, had a poet been so embraced by the masses.

When World War II broke out, Betjeman's penchant for writing found various forms of expression: He served as a press attaché in Dublin for the United Kingdom Press, he functioned as a broadcaster for the British Broadcasting Corporation in 1943, and he worked in the Books Department of the British Council from 1944 to 1946. These years saw the publication of *Old Lights for New Chancels: Verses Topographical and Amatory* (1940), as well as a new collection of poems, *New Bats in Old Belfries*

(1945). Partly because of his enormous success as a writer of books on topology and architecture, such as *Ghastly Good Taste: Or, A Depressing Story of the Rise and Fall of English Architecture* (1933), *An Oxford University Chest* (1938), *Antiquarian Prejudice* (1939), and *English Cities and Small Towns* (1943), Betjeman's widespread reputation as a poet seemed almost overshadowed by his prose. Indeed, he had become a spokesperson for the preservation of English architecture, especially Victorian architecture. When the war ended, Betjeman resumed his journalistic career, extending it to the increasingly popular medium of television, at which he won further notoriety.

The poetry of Betjeman's last forty years, though more overtly pessimistic than his previous work, reiterates many of the author's earlier themes, as exemplified in his volume *A Few Late Chrysanthemums* (1954). His continued acclaim, however, as a poet, as a broadcaster, and as a critic of modernity gained him widespread recognition, precipitating his being knighted in 1969 and appointed poet laureate in 1972, a position that he held until his death on May 19, 1984, in Cornwall, England.

Analysis

Beside the erudite, and often enigmatic, verse of many of his contemporaries, Betjeman's poetry seems simple and natural. It lacks the features of fragmentation and austere intellectualism that typify much modern poetry, though Betjeman does recurrently embrace themes of alienation and guilt, common twentieth century themes. Eschewing obscurity, Betjeman embraces a conversational style, replete with narrative elements, and utilizes traditional meter and rhyme, though occasionally he employs metrical variations or substitutions. He borrows his forms especially from his nineteenth century predecessors. Because his verse is so natural, in fact, most critics fail to notice his penchant for ambiguity, evident in some of his better poems, "The Arrest of Oscar Wilde at the Cadogan Hotel," in *Mount Zion*, or "On a Portrait of a Deaf Man," in *Old Lights for New Chancels*. Betjeman's major themes underscore the defects of modernity, with its disregard for the aesthetic and its disrespect for the environment. They also highlight the author's spiritual doubt, his obsession with class, with guilt, and with death, as well as divulge his affinity for topography.

The verses of *Mount Zion*, demonstrate the young author's interest in topography, especially English suburbia, with such memorable sketches as "Croydon" and Oakleigh Park of "The Outer Suburbs," with its "blackened blocks" and stained-glass windows. Betjeman's verse fuses reds and greens, oranges and blacks on his canvas of neighborhood sidewalks, churches, railways, and trams. *Mount Zion* also reveals Betjeman's genius for mild satire and for humor, perhaps most noticeable in "The 'Varsity Students' Rag."

Though Betjeman figures as a significant modern poetic force, his exceptional prose writings are also a hallmark of his enormous productivity: works on England's cities and towns, churches and architecture, even a book on his friend, abstract painter John Piper. These prose works, like Betjeman's poetry, are marked by their readability and friendly, intimate tone.

Most of what is known of Betjeman's childhood, through his stay at Oxford and up to the beginning of his first teaching position, is captured in his blank-verse autobiography, *Summoned by Bells*. This work, written toward the middle of Betjeman's career, not only demonstrates the poet's proclivity for detail but also reiterates many of his earlier themes and preoccupations. Sharing some similarities with the confessional poets of the mid-twentieth century, Betjeman's verse in this volume is surprisingly candid, revealing the poet's fears and embarrassments, his defeats, as well as his victories.

Many of Betjeman's later volumes of verse, notably *A Few Late Chrysanthemums* (1954), *High and Low* (1966), and *A Nip in the Air* (1974) deal, in part, with the present impinging upon the past and the results of that friction. Edwardian drawing rooms are replaced by abstruse monstrosities. Thus, Betjeman often establishes a series of antitheses, not only of artificial cities, belted in concrete, but also of artificial people, who, in the name of progress, awkwardly tread on the beautiful and the sacred, in flagrant abandon. The poet frequently illustrates this abrasive combination humorously, as in "Inexpensive Progress," from *High and Low*:

> Encase your legs in nylons,
> Bestride your hills with pylons
> O age without a soul;
> Away with gentle willows
> And all the elmy billows
> That through your valleys roll.

Betjeman likens the industrialized present's encroachment upon the landscape of the past to the human body, stripped of the gentle curves that signal its beauty, inevitably resulting in barrenness, ugliness. In the above passage, Betjeman shows his keen faculty even for spacing of the lines: The indentations of the third and sixth lines imitate the once-rolling hills and gentle breezes that soon will vanish. Emphasizing the passing of a life-style that is continuously eroding, the poet's images of modern impatience and disregard are typically characteristic of his verse, perhaps best epitomized in the picture of the "Executive," from *A Nip in the Air*: "I've a scarlet Aston-Martin—and does she go? She flies!/ Pedestrians and dogs and cats— we mark them down for slaughter./ I also own a speed-boat which has never touched the water." In this light social satire, the poet plays with the ambiguous image of the speedboat, whose acceleration seemingly allows it to defy gravity. Simultaneously, the image speaks of the artificiality of an age, whose leaders relish acquiring material goods for the sake of appearance, rather than for their intrinsic value or usefulness: The boat has, after all, "never touched the water."

Though the verdict on Betjeman's importance as a poet is still yet to be determined—he has spawned no imitators—his artistry has been appreciated by a generation of readers and poets alike. Modern poets, such as England's Philip Larkin, have lauded his verse, whereas his critics have complained of its sentimentality. Perhaps his greatest tribute has been the English poet W. H. Auden's dedication to him of *The Age of Anxiety* (1947), a verse dialogue reflecting man's isolation.

ON A PORTRAIT OF A DEAF MAN

First published: 1940
Type of work: Poem

The poem wryly contrasts the reality of death's putrefaction with a dead man's lifelong exuberance.

"On a Portrait of a Deaf Man," written in ballad stanza form (four line stanzas of alternating iambic tetrameter and iambic trimeter, rhyming *abcb*) and published in *Old Lights for New Chancels: Verses Topographical and Amatory* (1940), exemplifies Betjeman at his best. Approaching the theme of death through images of the five senses, the persona juxtaposes the dead man's past vitality and productivity with his present idleness and deterioration, "his finger-bones/ Stick[ing] through his fingerends." The poet blithely blends understatement, ambiguity, and paradox, revealing death, the eternal silencer, as the ultimate sign of "deafness":

> And when he could not hear me speak
> He smiled and looked so wise
> That now I do not like to think
> Of maggots in his eyes.

The comic, yet tragic, portrait of the man may be that of Betjeman's own father, whom he once described as "deaf" in *Summoned by Bells* (1960).

Pointing out the dead man's peculiarities, including his fondness for "potatoes in their skin," "old City dining-rooms," the smell of the Cornish air after a rain, and even his penchant for knowing "the name of ev'ry bird," the poet wryly juxtaposes images of life's activity with death's passivity. The allusion to the man's preference for potatoes is more complex than might initially appear. Betjeman's father reportedly got angry if his potatoes were not cooked until tender. Ironically, now the man has become, metaphorically, a sort of "potato" in his "skin," the mush of his decaying body only loosely encompassed by his exterior layer of skin: "But now his mouth is wide to let/ The London clay come in." Betjeman's fusion of the macabre with the comic seems a bit perverse, yet frightfully funny, nonetheless. The image of humanity in this vegetative state bears some kinship to Andrew Marvell's lady in "To His Coy Mistress" (a seventeenth-century English poem), whose virginity ultimately will be violated by worms in the grave.

Betjeman means his reader to appreciate the incongruity of humanity's seeming importance with its final insignificance. Though the tone of the poem, on the surface, appears light and humorous, it is not without seriousness. The reader comes to realize, paradoxically, that the dead man, who appeared so vivid and alive, was "deaf" even in life, having failed to "hear" the voice of the persona and the "song" of the bird.

SUMMONED BY BELLS

First published: 1960
Type of work: Poem

In this autobiographical verse, spanning Betjeman's youth, up to and including his leaving Oxford and securing a teaching position, the poet recollects his experiences.

Summoned by Bells, a blank verse autobiography, recollects Betjeman's childhood, marred by the abusive treatment of a nursery maid, Maud, who instilled in him the dread of damnation, more terrifying than any fiery rhetoric from any preacher's pulpit. It was she who preached to him about hell, rubbed his face in his own messes, and punished him for his tardiness: " 'You're late for dinner, John.' I feel again/ That awful feeling, fear confused with thrill,/ As I would be unbuttoned, bent across/ Her starchy apron." Surprisingly, Betjeman's choice of meter, unrhymed iambic pentameter, heightens, rather than diminishes, the tension of the scene. The regular iambic rhythm with which the nurse delivers her matter-of-fact remark exposes her inflexibility. Maud's influence on Betjeman's themes of guilt and fear of death should not be overlooked.

Though the abusive relationship with Betjeman's nurse is easily discernible, more complex is the mental torment that the author suffered as a result of his relationship with his father. The poet admits that he could never please his "dear deaf father," especially after refusing his request to continue the family business: "Partly it is guilt:/ 'Following in Father's footsteps' was the theme/ Of all my early childhood." With each glance, Betjeman's father's eyes accused his son of failure. Even to his dying day, the elder Betjeman had a gaze that seemed to assail the poet, smarting like stinging nettles. Not surprisingly, Betjeman recounts his childhood years as being lonely: His remembrances include lost loves, childhood betrayal, insensitive remarks of a teacher who called him "common," and childhood bullies at his various schools. Trapped and beaten by two "enemies" at Highgate Junior School, then hurled into the bushes, the adolescent Betjeman emerged from the attack humiliated.

> There in the holly bush they threw me down,
> Pulled off my shorts, and laughed and ran away;
> And, as I struggled up, I saw grey brick,
> The cemetery railings and the tombs.

The reader need not be a psychologist to understand from this episode Betjeman's interconnected associations of fear, pain, and death; yet, the poet's stance in relaying this experience appears neutral, that of an unbiased observer.

It would be incorrect to assume that *Summoned by Bells* contains merely embarrassing or tragic accounts of Betjeman's early life. For the most part, the book is a kaleidoscope of colorful topographical portraits of English landscapes and seasides, of city and country dwellings, and of the English people. Nor does Betjeman's volume lack good nature or compassion. When, as a child, the author fabricated an excuse to avoid fighting a schoolfellow, pleading that he had "news from home" that his "Mater was ill," his would-be combatant, Percival Mandeville, gingerly clasped him on the shoulder comfortingly and said, "All right, old chap. Of course I understand." This touching account, revealing the ease and spontaneity with which young boys may reverse their adversarial positions and exhibit signs of friendship, is one of the most memorable portraits of *Summoned by Bells*. The book is not without humor, either: In describing his mother's complaints about her tooth pain, Betjeman presents Mrs. Betjeman comically, as she charges that her infection is "just the same" as Mrs. Bent's, who "nearly died" of the disease, though the other lady's infection was "not, of course, so bad" as Betjeman's mother's own ailment.

Summary

Ironically, John Betjeman's local color, his greatest strength, is the aspect of his poetry most often criticized: His lyrics are decidedly English, not universal. Whether he explores the mystery of faith, satirizes the imperfections of himself, his family, or the middle classes, or whether he nostalgically describes the countryside of Cornwall or a bath at Marlborough, Betjeman exhibits his wry compassion and demonstrates his facility for strict observation. Betjeman, the deliberate traditionalist, presents a discerning, not myopic, view of the world, his world, England. Indeed, his triumph lies in his partisanship.

Bibliography

Bergonzi, Bernard. "Culture and Mr. Betjeman." *Twentieth Century* 165 (1959): 130-137.

Brooke, Jocelyn. *Ronald Firbank and John Betjeman*. New York: Longmans, Green, 1962.

Gibson, Walker. "Summoned by Bells." *Poetry* 97 (1961): 390-391.

Stapleton, Margaret L. *Sir John Betjeman: A Bibliography of Writings by and About Him*. Metuchen, N.J.: Scarecrow Press, 1974.

Wiehe, R. E. "Summoned by Nostalgia: John Betjeman's Poetry." *Arizona Quarterly* 19 (1963): 37-49.

Linda Rohrer Paige

MARIE-CLAIRE BLAIS

Born: Quebec City, Quebec, Canada
October 5, 1939

Principal Literary Achievement

Only nineteen when she published the first of more than twenty novels, Blais, also a poet and playwright, is one of the most prolific and important French-Canadian authors.

Biography

Marie-Claire Blais was born on October 5, 1939, in Quebec City, Quebec, Canada, the first of five children of Fernando and Veronique Nolin Blais. She began writing at the age of ten, an obsession that was discouraged both at home and at school. As the oldest child in a large working-class family, she was burdened by the need to help her family financially. She began her secondary education at a Catholic convent school but left at the age of fifteen, at her parents' request, to attend a secretarial school. From the age of fifteen to age eighteen, Blais worked as a stenographer for many different employers. Writing, though, was her passion and solace, and she continued to work in the evenings at her parents' home, which was always crowded and noisy. At nineteen, Blais moved to a rented room in Quebec City. She studied French literature at the Université Laval, reading Honoré de Balzac, Marcel Proust, Jean Genet, and the surrealists and symbolists, such as Arthur Rimbaud. She also made the acquaintance of Jeanne Lapointe and Père Georges-Henri Lévesque, both of whom would be instrumental to the success of her literary career.

Lévesque was impressed with Blais's early stories and urged her to continue writing. Blais completed *La Belle Bête* (1959; *Mad Shadows*, 1960), and through Lévesque's influence and belief in her promise as a writer, Blais's controversial novel was published in Canada. Because she was so young at the time of her first success, Blais was considered something of a precocious schoolgirl. *Mad Shadows* elicited both admiration and outrage in Quebec. A nightmarish fable, the violent emotions of envy and hatred and the consequences of the failure of maternal love are vividly dark and poetic. *Tête Blanche* (1960; English translation, 1961) is another story embracing the theme of a childhood of isolation and despair, told in rich, poetic language.

Blais received a fellowship from the Conseil des Arts du Canada in 1960 and spent the following year in Paris, where she continued her education through literature and film. In 1962, she returned to Quebec and completed *Le Jour est Noir* (1962; English

169

translation, 1967; published in *The Day Is Dark and Three Travelers: Two Novellas*, 1967). In 1963, with the support of the highly respected American critic Edmund Wilson, she was awarded the first of two Guggenheim Fellowships, which allowed her to move to Cambridge, Massachusetts, where she lived and wrote for several years. While in Massachusetts, Blais wrote *Les Voyageurs sacrés* (1966; English translation, 1967; published in *The Day Is Dark and Three Travelers: Two Novellas*, 1967), an attempt to combine music, poetry, and sculpture. *L'Insoumise* (1966; *The Fugitive*, 1978) chronicles the disintegration of a family; *David Sterne* (1967; English translation, 1973), influenced by her feelings about the war in Vietnam, is a cry against violence. Neglected by critics, these novels reflect the troubled decade of the 1960's, a time when Blais's vision moved from the tormented inner world to the outside political and social realm. In Cambridge, Blais met the painter Mary Meigs. A deep friendship developed, and Blais moved to Wellfleet, Massachusetts, to form a community with Meigs, who was living with her companion Barbara Deming. Meigs's life-style and work were to have a profound effect on Blais; at the refuge in Wellfleet, she produced *Une Saison dans la vie d'Emmanuel* (1965; *A Season in the Life of Emmanuel*, 1966). Translated into thirteen languages, it established her international reputation and was considered her most original and important work. It is a bleak, often humorous story about the lives of damaged children in church-dominated, impoverished rural Quebec, and in 1966 Blais was awarded both the Canadian Prix-France Quebec and the French Prix Médicis for *A Season in the Life of Emmanuel.*

She received critical acclaim again in 1969, when she won her first Governor-General's Literary Award and *Livres et Auteurs Canadiens* magazine's Best Book award for *Manuscrits de Pauline Archange* (1968; *The Manuscripts of Pauline Archange*, 1970). During the same year, she published one of her four plays, *L'Exécution* (1968; *The Execution*, 1976).

Deeply troubled by the war in Vietnam, Blais and Meigs moved to France in 1971, where they lived for four years. Dividing her time between Montreal and Paris, Blais explored homosexual love as a literary theme. In *Le Loup* (1972; *The Wolf*, 1974), she explores love and cruelty in her young male characters' homosexual relationships. She returned to the theme of homosexual love with *Les Nuits de l'underground* (1978; *Nights in the Underground*, 1979), in which she explores the "sacred," self-liberating aspects of lesbian love.

During the 1970's, Blais's themes shift focus again, from the inner world of emotions and the suffering of individuals to the conflicts of national identity, long a struggle in provincial Quebec. While in France, she wrote *Un Joualonais, sa joualonie* (1973; *St. Lawrence Blues*, 1974); it is written in Montreal's French street slang, *joual*. She continued to explore these political themes in *Une Liaison parisienne* (1975; *A Literary Affair*, 1979). *Le Sourd dans la ville* (1979; *Deaf to the City*, 1980) earned for Blais a second Governor-General's Literary Award. Part poetry, part prose, it is another study of anguish and of art as a means of salvation. Continuing to move her vision outward and to combine poetry and prose, Blais produced *Visions d'Anna: Ou, Le vertige* (1982; *Anna's World*, 1985). Another dark vision of the modern world,

Pierre, la guerre du printemps 81, appeared in 1984. Blais's work centers on the complexity and inherent pain of human life, as she searches for a vision of the ideal, exposing the harshness of the reality that she has lived and observed. Blais was awarded the Prix David in 1982 in recognition of the major contribution she has made to the literature of Quebec.

Analysis

The power of Blais's fiction lies in her thematic obsession with the forces of evil and the suffering of children. Blais treats her characters with tenderness in their solitude, however, and they find, as she did in her own life, that art—language—is the only escape from madness and death. Her writing has been characterized as bold and inventive, but her vision is profoundly bleak. Her work is in the tradition of the existentialists who explore the consequences of psychological abandonment and abuse of the young as the crucible in which evil is created.

Her characters' capacity for evil and cruelty, and particularly the pathological relationships between mothers and children, shocked critics in the late 1950's. Although it was less of a sensation elsewhere, *Mad Shadows*, Blais's first book, created a furor of both admiration and outrage in Quebec because of its macabre and violent story. The theme of both *The Day Is Dark* and a novella, *La Fin d'une enfance* (1961; published in *Chatelaine*, 1961), is the suffering and powerlessness of children, trapped in emotional and spiritual isolation even when surrounded by family and dominated by the cult of religious authority. The overbearing influence of religion, always negative and suffocating, is perceptible in the lives of all Blais's characters; the awakenings of adolescent sexuality, sensuality, and curiosity are the beginnings of an irrevocable "fall from grace." Poor families, however devout, are overburdened with many children and live in depravity, lovelessness, and intellectual and creative starvation.

Her later novels, especially *A Season in the Life of Emmanuel*, have been described as "typically Canadian" in their evocation of rural poverty and hopelessness, of the harsh northern winters, and in the sense of dislocation in a country populated by a defeated people. Her passionate, poetic voice is original in its relentlessly realistic exposure of a repressed, dispirited, and intellectually deprived underclass.

Although her first work was dismissed by many American critics as the exaggerated fantasy of an adolescent author, it was regarded as a great phenomenon in France. Wilson was responsible for bringing Blais to the American literary audience. The most ardent and outspoken of her American supporters, Wilson included Blais in his study *O Canada: An American's Notes on Canadian Culture* (1965):

> Mlle Blais is a true "phenomenon"; she may possibly be a genius. At the age of twenty-four, she has produced four remarkable books of a passionate and poetic force that, as far as my reading goes, is not otherwise to be found in French Canadian fiction.

Wilson wrote the foreword for her second book, *A Season in the Life of Emmanuel*, a disjointed, often humorous story with a constantly changing point of view, about the material and emotional poverty of a large, Catholic, lower-class Quebec farm family. All the children are devastated by the evil in the adult world. Their innocence is betrayed by predatory priests, they are brutalized by their family and crushed by the dreary lives to which they are resigned.

Blais was disappointed when many reviewers of this novel focused on its bleakness and the depravity of the characters, missing its ironic humor. She treats her characters with tenderness as they struggle, some with great vitality and creativity, against the wretchedness of their lives. Her style is greatly influenced by the French surrealists and symbolists and was regarded as a great phenomenon by the French critics.

Deeply affected by the political climate in the United States during the Vietnam War, Blais found it troubling that people could not see or take action against the clear dangers arising in the world's social conflicts and ecological disasters, or the destruction of the earth. In the 1970's, Blais's landscapes changed from those of an undefined time and place to a world inhabited by real people who are struggling to find their vision in contemporary society. Her art is a prophetic cry for sanity and peace in a violent world.

During her time in France, Blais wrote two books exploring and celebrating homosexual love. *The Wolf* is a study of cruelty and love in male relationships, and *Nights in the Underground* concerns the sacred and "self-liberating" aspects of lesbian relationships. Blais drew her characters from life in the gay bars and the streets of Montreal and Paris. They live for love and sex and talk about both without inhibition or shame, celebrating this freedom in otherwise unhappy lives.

Moving further from the gothic inner world of *Mad Shadows* and some of her earlier works, Blais addressed the condition of Quebec as a "colony" of France and the need for a separate French-Canadian national identity in *St. Lawrence Blues*. Written entirely in *joual*, a form of French street slang, *St. Lawrence Blues* is a satiric novel about an illegitimate orphan's life among outcasts in Montreal's down-and-out working class. Dedicated to the memory of Wilson, it was regarded by American critics as her best work to date when the English translation was published in 1974. Quebec critics were less impressed and were especially hostile toward her use of a literary form of *joual* as an expression of "nationalist pride."

Deaf to the City is an observation of travelers and exiles suffering yet surviving through art. It is another experiment with language, written as a long paragraph in wild poetry and prose. Blais again fused these two styles in *Anna's World* in the drugged, suicidal torment of a young woman living in an uninhabitable world. Blais's vision of the world as a truly terrifying and desperate place is also the subject of *Pierre, la guerre du printemps 81*, which was critically acclaimed.

MAD SHADOWS

First published: *La Belle Bête*, 1959 (English translation, 1960)
Type of work: Novel

A surreal tale of tortured relationships between a mother obsessed with her son's beauty and the unattractive daughter doomed by envy and the shallow nature of her mother's love.

Mad Shadows, Blais's first published work, created considerable controversy in Quebec. Many Canadian critics disliked it intensely; others thought it was astonishingly original and brilliant. Set in an unidentified time and place, the story begins on a train, as a young girl watches strangers become captivated by her brother's beauty. The grotesque, erotic pleasure that the mother takes in her son's physical beauty is matched only by her indifference toward her daughter, and it sets the tone for the tortured relationships that develop. In *Mad Shadows*, Blais explores what will become a theme in much of her later work: the creation of evil and the suffering of children caused by the failure of maternal love. The world that Blais's characters inhabit is dark and loveless. The first critics and readers were shocked by the utter depravity of the relationships between the mother, her lover, and her children and the starkness of the young author's vision. Yet the power of her vision and poetic style were undeniable; she was awarded the Prix de la Langue Française from L'Académie Française for *Mad Shadows* in 1961.

The mother, Louise, an attractive, vain widow, adores and spoils her simple-minded son, Patrice, a reflection of herself. Dimly aware of his own beauty, Patrice seeks his unformed self in every mirrored surface, pond, and window. His sister, Isabelle-Marie, is not beautiful; wounded by her mother's indifference, her feelings of envy toward her brother begin to overwhelm her. Louise is afflicted by a lesion on her face, a cancerous growth symbolic of the malignancy of her soul. She meets Lanz, an elegant, declining dandy, who becomes her lover; her attentions and affection now go to him, and Patrice, abandoned, rides his horse in a frenzy of jealousy, killing Lanz. In death, Lanz's shallowness is revealed as his wig and false beard disintegrate around him. Even so, Louise feels little rancor toward her son, the "beautiful beast."

Among Blais's recurring themes is the end of innocence and the fall from grace inherent in sexual awakening. For her characters, all consequences of love are tragic; in *Mad Shadows*, there is a sense that human beings are doomed at the moment of awareness and that happiness is illusory. For a short time, miraculously, Isabelle-Marie finds happiness in the love of a young blind man, Michael. Sight, symbolic of truth, would not allow the illusion of love to survive in Blais's nightmarish world; fearing rejection, Isabelle-Marie deceives Michael into believing that she is beautiful. They marry and have a daughter, Anne, and for a time enjoy a kind of simple happiness. When his sight suddenly returns, Michael discovers his wife's deception. Unable to hide his anger, he cruelly abandons Isabelle-Marie and their child, and in misery, they return to Louise's farm.

Driven by her rejection and envy, Isabelle-Marie disfigures her brother by pushing his face into a pot of boiling water. No longer a beautiful object, Patrice is rejected by his mother and sent to an asylum, proving the shallowness of her love. Seeing his grotesque face in a lake's surface, Patrice is horrified and drowns in his own reflection. His suffering gives Isabelle-Marie some satisfaction; but even this does not bring her peace. *Mad Shadows* ends in a final act of suicidal despair, as Isabelle-Marie sets her mother's farm on fire and waits to throw herself under a train, leaving her young daughter to wander alone on the tracks.

A SEASON IN THE LIFE OF EMMANUEL

First published: *Une Saison dans la vie d'Emmanuel*, 1965 (English translation, 1966)
Type of work: Novel

Newborn Emmanuel, sixteenth child of an impoverished Quebec farmer, is witness to the suffering of his siblings and the ways in which each rebels against fate.

A Season in the Life of Emmanuel was declared by critics to have been both "written by the devil" and among the best French-Canadian novels. Blais moves her character from an earlier imaginary, gothic world into the recognizable world of French-Canadian culture. The story takes place during the first year in the life of Emmanuel, the sixteenth child of a materially and emotionally impoverished farm family. Bleak, disturbing, and full of biting humor, this depiction of Quebec's church-dominated lower-class life is considered Blais's masterwork.

Blais begins the story with a constantly changing point of view, as the mother of this brood of children (some called only by their birth order number) gives birth to Emmanuel and then returns to work in the fields. The strongest influence in the lives of the children is their grandmere, the rigid and traditional caretaker of their futures. The mother has no name, no presence in the book, though her absence and failure are clearly felt as she moves through life exhausted and resigned to her wretched state. Maternal failure is a theme common to Blais's work, which often presents a world where children are limited and defined by their emotional and physical deprivation.

The main character in this novel is not Emmanuel but four of the older children. It is through his eyes that one sees their suffering, and none escapes the evil in the world. Heloise, believing that the sensuality that she experiences in adolescence is a religious calling, goes first to a convent, then to a brothel. Two of Heloise's brothers are sentenced to life in a reformatory, where they are molested by predatory priests and then made to suffer the stupefying life of factory work, accepting the inevitability of their fate. Jean-Le-Maigre, the most alive and creative of the brood, ends his short life in a sanatorium; his journal is the only evidence of his existence, as his death, like his life, becomes nothing more than another family burden.

Obsessed with death, the repression of children, and the perversion of religious authority, Blais's vision is one of stifled lives and the responses of suffering children, suffering sometimes with great joy and grace, to the constant evil that they encounter in the adult world. Her realistic style fascinated French critics in particular. Playing with language, often with biting and ironic humor, she renders both depravity and grace with naturalistic detail, which is especially poignant in the emotional expression of the suffering of fragile children. For many of Blais's characters, as in her own life, language and the act of writing are symbolic paths to salvation, forestalling spiritual death and madness. The humorous and touching autobiographical writings of Emmanuel's brother Jean-Le-Maigre are part of the structure of the book. Dying of consumption, his poems express his vitality and symbolize his rebellion against fate.

Summary

Marie-Claire Blais has said that life for her would be unbearable without the solace of writing. The characters in her novels suffer so deeply that escape is possible only through death of the body or through salvation in the language of art. Her love of language and experimentation with form and style are a unique expression of her passionate, poetic vision of the suffering in a bleak and terrifying world.

The sum of Blais's work is a complex expression of the subjects that obsess her. Sometimes with the cold eye of a realist, often with ironic humor and great compassion, she writes in an unmistakable voice, in pursuit of the intangible.

Bibliography

Brazeau, J. Raymond. *An Outline of Contemporary French-Canadian Literature.* Toronto: Forum House, 1972.

Meigs, Mary. *Lily Briscoe: A Self-Portrait.* Vancouver: Talonbooks, 1981.

Stratford, Philip. *Marie-Claire Blais.* Toronto: Forum House, 1971.

Margaret Parks

WILLIAM BLAKE

Born: London, England
November 28, 1757
Died: London, England
August 12, 1827

Principal Literary Achievement

Blake's unique work combines poetry and painting in a compelling vision of humanity attaining its most blissful, creative, and enlightened condition. His work exemplifies the goals of the English Romantic movement.

Biography

William Blake was born on November 28, 1757, in London, the second of five children of James Blake, a hosier, and his wife, Catherine Blake. Blake was schooled at home until he was about eleven, after which he was sent to a drawing school, where he studied until 1772. He was then apprenticed for seven years to James Basire, a well-known engraver. In 1779, Blake began to study at the Royal Academy and also did commercial engravings for the bookseller Joseph Johnson. In 1782, Blake married Catherine Boucher, the illiterate daughter of a market gardener. Blake taught her to read and write, and eventually she helped him color his designs.

Blake had been writing poetry since the age of twelve, and by the early 1780's he was beginning to acquire a reputation among his friends as a poet and painter. Two friends, John Flaxman and the Reverend A. S. Mathew, paid the expenses for the publication of Blake's first volume, *Poetical Sketches*, in 1783. The following year, Blake wrote *An Island in the Moon* (wr. 1784), a satire on contemporary ways of thinking, but it was never published.

Three years later, Blake suffered a major blow when his younger brother Robert, to whom Blake was devoted, died of consumption at the age of nineteen. Blake, who from his childhood had revealed a capacity for visionary experience, said that, at the moment of death, he saw his brother's spirit ascending, clapping its hands for joy. Blake felt that Robert's spirit remained with him throughout his life. Indeed, it was Robert, Blake claimed, who gave him the idea for an original method of engraving, in which he etched poems and illustrations together on a copper plate, then printed them and colored them by hand.

His first experiments in this new method of illuminated printing were in the form of three tractates, in two versions, titled *There is No Natural Religion* (1788) and *All*

Religions Are One (1788). About this time, Blake first came under the influence of Emanuel Swedenborg, a Swedish scientist turned mystic philosopher. Blake attended the first General Conference of the Swedenborgians' New Jerusalem Church in London in April, 1789.

In the same year, Blake published his first masterpieces in illuminated printing, *The Book of Thel* and *Songs of Innocence*. The latter celebrates a childlike state of spontaneity and joy, in which the divine world interpenetrates the natural world. The following year, 1790, Blake began work on his great satire *The Marriage of Heaven and Hell*, which is at once a spiritual testament and a revolutionary political manifesto in support of the French Revolution.

Throughout the 1790's, Blake continued working as a commercial engraver, as well as completing artistic commissions from his patron, the civil servant Thomas Butts. For the most part, Blake saw this work as daily drudgery, undertaken solely to provide for his few worldly needs; his real interests lay in giving form to his own creative vision, which he did in a stream of illuminated books: *Visions of the Daughters of Albion* (1793), *America: A Prophecy* (1793), *Songs of Innocence and of Experience* (1794), *Europe: A Prophecy* (1794), *The [First] Book of Urizen* (1794), *The Song of Los* (1795), *The Book of Los* (1795), and *The Book of Ahania* (1795). In 1797, he commenced an ambitious long poem, *Vala: Or, the Four Zoas* (wr. 1795-1804) which he kept revising over a ten-year period, retitling it *The Four Zoas* but eventually abandoning it unfinished. Few people, if any, in Blake's time understood these obscure books, and they attracted almost no buyers. This lack of public recognition set a pattern for the remainder of Blake's life. His one-man exhibition of sixteen of his paintings in 1809-1810 was a complete failure. Although he was embittered by his inability to find an audience, he did not allow his disappointment to weaken his dedication to his art.

Blake spent all of his life in London, except for the period 1800 to 1803, when he lived at Felpham, a village on the Sussex coast in southern England. There, he was under the patronage of William Hayley, a minor poet who was also, in his time, a well-respected man of letters. Hayley provided Blake with some hack work, but Blake resented his patronizing attitude and eventually the two men quarreled. Blake's stay at Felpham is also notable for an incident in which Blake evicted a drunken soldier from his cottage garden. The soldier then accused him of uttering threats against the king. Blake was charged with sedition, tried, and acquitted in 1804. Blake had returned to London the previous year, 1803, and, in addition to working on some watercolors for one client and some designs for Hayley's *A Series of Ballads* (1802), he began work on his two lengthy masterpieces, *Milton: A Poem* (1804-1808) and *Jerusalem: The Emancipation of the Great Albion* (1804-1820). These were years of increasing obscurity for Blake, although in the last period of his life he gathered around him an admiring group of young painters, who recognized his genius. Blake's last great works were his engravings in *Illustrations of the Book of Job* (1825) and his *Illustrations of Dante* (1827), on which he was still working at his death on August 12, 1827, in London.

Analysis

Blake stated his poetic and philosophical principles early in his career and never wavered from them, although there were some changes of emphasis as his work developed. He formed his imaginative world in opposition to the prevailing materialist philosophy, which he saw embodied in three English thinkers, Francis Bacon, John Locke, and Isaac Newton. Bacon was one of the founders of modern experimental science, but Blake detested this method of acquiring knowledge because it relied solely on objective criteria and encouraged the principle of doubt. In "Auguries of Innocence," Blake points out that this is not the way that the rest of the universe functions:

> He who Doubts from what he sees
> Will ne'er Believe do what you Please
> If the Sun and Moon should doubt
> Theyd immediately Go out.

In Locke, the philosopher who exerted an extremely powerful influence on eighteenth century thought, Blake found another opponent. In *An Essay Concerning Human Understanding* (1690), Locke argued against the belief that there are in the human mind "innate ideas," universal truths stamped on the mind at birth. For Locke, the mind was a *tabula rasa*, a blank tablet. Knowledge was gained only through sense experience and the mind's reflection on the data provided by the senses. Locke's views were anathema to Blake, for whom the first principle of knowing was not through the senses but through the mind. The mind is not a *tabula rasa*; it is fullness itself, the Divine Imagination, the eternal container of the permanent realities of existence. As Blake put it when he annotated the *Discourses* (1769-1791) of Sir Joshua Reynolds, president of the Royal Academy, who attempted to apply Lockean principles to art: "Reynolds Thinks that Man Learns all that he knows. I say on the Contrary that Man Brings All that he has or can have Into the World with him. Man is Born Like a Garden ready Planted and Sown. This World is too poor to produce one Seed."

For Blake, it is the mind that shapes the way that one perceives the object. He called this seeing *through*, not *with*, the eye. Different minds see in different ways:

> The Sun's Light when he unfolds it
> Depends on the Organ that beholds it.

This is a key idea in Blake, and he repeats it again and again. For Blake, the more imagination that is applied to the act of perception, the more true the perception will be. The world of sense, by itself, is illusory. Only the imagination, the formative power of the mind, can penetrate beyond surface appearances to the divine nature of existence, which permeates this "Vegetable Glass of Nature" and is also the true nature of the human self.

That was Blake's answer to the third member of his unholy trinity, Newton, the great seventeenth century scientist who not only discovered gravity but also synthesized many other contemporary theories into a grand system that appeared to explain all the laws that governed the physical universe. The problem with Newton's philosophy of nature, from Blake's point of view, was that it made the universe into a vast and impersonal machine that had no vital connection with human consciousness. By creating a split between subject and object, it had left humans alone and isolated in a universe over which they had no control. Against this dehumanizing tendency of natural philosophy, Blake opposed a universe in which joy, delight, and bliss are the essential constituents of both the human and nonhuman world. In his poem "*Europe*," for example, in answer to the poet's question, "what is the material world, and is it dead?" a fairy sings, "I'll shew you all alive/ The world, when every particle of dust breathes forth its joy." In such a universe humanity is not subject to an impersonal, mechanical order, presided over by a God who sits in judgment on it beyond the skies. On the contrary, when humanity exercises its imaginative powers to the full it becomes the Divine Humanity, the creator of a visionary time and space that reveals rather than obscures the eternal, immaterial essence of life. The universe becomes as close to humankind as its own heartbeat, as precious to it as its own blood.

Armed with this vision, Blake set himself the task of waging war on ignorance, on everything that he believed diminished or obscured the Divine Humanity. He developed a complex mythology, pieced together not only from his own visionary experiences but from a wide variety of sources. In addition to the Bible and the works of John Milton, which were a constant inspiration to him, he delved deeply into the Western esoteric tradition, including Neoplatonism, Hermeticism, Kabbalah, and individual mystical thinkers such as Swedenborg and the seventeenth century German seer Jacob Boehme. However, Blake was never a slave to the thoughts of others; whatever he borrowed from his sources was put through the crucible of his own imaginative power and transformed into a vision that was uniquely his own.

AMERICA: A PROPHECY

First published: 1793
Type of work: Poem

This poem celebrates the American Revolution, which is seen as a victory over British tyranny and the birth of a new age of freedom for humanity.

America: a Prophecy was Blake's first attempt to present historical and contemporary events in mythological form so as to draw out their universal significance. The Preludium introduces two mythological characters, the "shadowy daughter of Urthona," who is nature in an unfruitful time, and Orc, who embodies both the life-giving return of spring and the liberating, revolutionary energy that is about to be unleashed in the world through the American Revolution. Since Orc's birth fourteen years previously, the shadowy female has been bringing food to him. Throughout this period Orc has been chained to a rock, although his spirit soars and can be seen in the forms of eagle, lion, whale, and serpent.

Having reached the age of sexual maturity, Orc breaks free of his chains, seizes and ravishes the shadowy female. She erupts in joy, exclaiming that she recognizes him—Orc stimulates the periodic renewal of earth's procreative power—and declares him to be the image of God that "dwells in darkness of Africa" (perhaps an allusion to Emanuel Swedenborg's belief that the Africans understood God better than the Europeans). The shadowy female then says that she sees the spirit of Orc at work in America, Canada, Mexico, and Peru (all these places had seen recent outbreaks of rebellion against established authority).

The poem itself begins on Plate 3. As war-clouds, fires, and tempests gather, some of the leading American rebels—including George Washington, Tom Paine, and Benjamin Franklin—gather together. Washington makes a speech warning of the dangers the colonists face, and as he finishes, King George III and the British government— referred to as the Guardian Prince of Albion, or Albion's Angel (Albion is the ancient name of England)—appear to the rebels as a fiery dragon rising up from England. But this apparition is countered by the appearance of Orc over the Atlantic Ocean. In Plate 6, in one of the most impressive passages in all of Blake's work, Orc announces the imminent outburst of freedom at all levels: political, spiritual, and cosmic.

Albion's Angel responds by denouncing Orc as a "Lover of wild rebellion, and transgressor of God's law." Orc replies that he is the "fiery joy" of life itself, which Urizen (the fallen god of reason in Blake's mythology and similar in function to the God of the Old Testament) imprisoned at the proclamation of the ten commandments. Now these commandments are to be abrogated.

In Plate 9, Albion attempts to rally support from his "Thirteen angels" (the colonial governors), but they refuse to respond to his call. "Boston's Angel" makes a speech in which he refuses to continue obeying an unjust system. In Plate 13, war breaks out and the British suffer defeats. Albion's Angel responds to these reversals by dispatching a deadly plague to America, but driven by the flames and fiery winds of Orc, the plague recoils upon the sender. The effects on England are devastating. Soldiers desert, rulers sicken, and priests are overthrown. In Plate 16, Urizen weeps as he beholds his world crumbling. For twelve years he manages to restrain the energies of Orc, until Orc breaks free once more in the French Revolution. The thrones of Spain and Italy shake; the restrictive moral law is burnt up by Orc's fires and a new age begins.

THE [FIRST] BOOK OF URIZEN

First published: 1794
Type of work: Poem

This work is a myth of Creation and the Fall as a result of the limiting activity of the rational intellect, embodied in the figure of Urizen.

The [First] Book of Urizen is an unorthodox version of the Creation and Fall, written to satirize the traditional accounts in Genesis and John Milton's *Paradise Lost* (1667, 1674). In *The [First] Book of Urizen*, the creator, Urizen, is neither all-powerful nor benevolent; his creation is not "good" as in Genesis, but flawed from the beginning. As a product solely of the unenlightened rational intellect, his world is incomplete. Cut off from the creative power of the imagination, which is personified in the poem by Los, Urizen can only create a world full of suffering and death.

After a preludium, in which Blake gladly accepts the call of the Eternals to dictate their story, chapter 1—the poem is divided, like Genesis, into chapter and verse—describes Urizen's activity in wholly negative terms. He is "unknown, unprolific," and "unseen"; he broods introspectively; he is "self-clos'd" and a "self-contemplating shadow." That is exactly the withdrawn, abstract type of mental activity that, in Blake's view, was responsible for many of the ills that he saw in contemporary society. By retreating into a void within himself, Urizen is beginning to close himself off from the primal joy of existence.

In chapter 2, it transpires that Urizen's activity is taking place before the creation of the world, before the existence of death, and before there are any material restrictions placed around the fiery delights of eternal existence. Urizen now reveals himself as the lawgiver, the Jehovah of the Old Testament, whom Blake associated with tyranny. Because Urizen cannot enjoy the free-flowing and joyful clash of opposite values in eternity, he attempts to create for himself "a joy without pain,/ . . . a solid without fluctuation." To his eyes, the Eternals live in "unquenchable burnings," when in fact these are the fires of the creative imagination as it constantly fulfills its desires. Failing to understand this, Urizen tries to fight with the fire and sets himself up as lord over all the other faculties. With his laws of "One command, one joy, one desire," he attempts to impose a false unity on the infinite diversity of existence. For Blake, this is the sign of a tyrant.

Throughout the poem, the Eternals are horrified by Urizen's self-defeating actions, which open up a series of separations between Urizen and eternity: "Sund'ring, dark'ning, thund'ring,"/ Rent away with a terrible clash,/ Eternity roll'd wide apart." As Urizen is forced out of (or expels himself from) eternity, he undergoes a gradual process of materialization. In a parody of the seven days of creation in Genesis, Urizen acquires a material body, which is also the material world. His awareness of eternal life vanishes. Horrified at what is taking place, Los, the creative imagination, watches the process and throws nets around Urizen and binds him with chains to stop him from descending even further into the darkness of ignorance. In his later work, Blake regarded creation as an act of mercy because it put a limit to the fall and so allowed the possibility of redemption.

In this poem, however, the emphasis is entirely on the pervasive negative consequences of Urizen's acts, which also affect Los, Urizen's counterpart in eternity. Los forgets his true creative function and allows himself to feel pity for Urizen, which in Blake's work is usually a negative emotion ("For pity divides the soul"). Los, like Urizen, is now a divided being, and the female portion of himself (which Blake calls the emanation) now takes on an independent life, separate from him. This first female form is named Enitharmon. The Eternals, who are androgynous beings, are appalled at this division into sexes, which is yet another sign of the Fall—an idea that Blake borrowed from his spiritual mentor, the German mystic, Jacob Boehme.

In chapter 6, Los and Enitharmon give birth to a child, Orc, who elsewhere in Blake's work symbolizes revolutionary, redemptive energy. Los becomes jealous of Orc, and in an act that suggests at once the Crucifixion of Christ, the binding of Isaac by Abraham, and the chaining of Prometheus, Los and Enitharmon chain Orc to a mountain.

In the next chapter, Urizen explores his grim new world, trying to understand it by dividing and measuring, which is all that the rational intellect, cut off from the unifying power of the imagination, can do. Urizen can only discover "portions of life." Nothing is whole or healthy, and Urizen sickens at the sight of it. As he traverses the cities of earth, he curses his creation and realizes that no being can keep his "iron laws one moment." A net stretches out behind him, born from the sorrow in his soul. Everything in creation is trapped by this net, which is named the net of religion. This image expresses Blake's dislike of conventional religion, based on moral laws and human reason alone. As Urizen's religion spreads across the earth, human beings find their senses, which in eternity are expansive; human are able to perceive delight in everything, narrowing and shrinking, until, like everyone else in this poem, they "forgot their eternal life."

MILTON: A POEM

First published: 1804-1808
Type of work: Poem

In this epic poem, Blake corrects the errors of his predecessor, John Milton, and assumes the Miltonic mantle of poet and prophet of England.

In *Milton: A Poem*, Blake continues the argument with Milton that he had begun in *The Marriage of Heaven and Hell* (1790). In that book, Blake had identified the

Christ of *Paradise Lost* (1667, 1674) with the restrictive values of reason and conventional morality, and Milton's Satan, whom Christ casts out, with the passionate energies of humankind, which to Blake were the sources of creativity. Blake thought that, although Milton was a great poet, he had put himself in service of a bad theology, and this had divided him against himself. In *Milton: A Poem*, which was written more than one hundred years after Milton's death, Milton is in heaven but unhappy. He decides to return to earth to redeem his errors and be reunited with his "sixfold emanation," the feminine aspect of himself, which is still wandering in torment in the earthly sphere. Historically, the emanation represents Milton's three wives and three daughters; symbolically, they are the aspects of his creative imagination that he repudiated in his earthly life.

Milton's decision to return to earth is prompted by his hearing of the Bard's Song, a key passage that occupies Plates 3 to 13 of this 43-plate, two-book, poem. It is based on an episode in Blake's life, when he was living at Felpham under the patronage of William Hayley. Hayley urged Blake to pay more attention to earning a living, to put his artistic talents in service of the commonsense world of "good taste." Blake thought that Hayley was a spiritual enemy who was trying to deflect him from his true artistic and prophetic path. In *Milton: A Poem*, Blake creates a cosmic allegory out of the conflict between them. Hayley becomes Satan; Blake is Palamabron, one of the sons of Los, the imagination. When the quarrel is brought out into the open, Hayley/Satan, whose crime is to assume a role that is not his own, reveals the tyrannical and arrogant self that hides behind his surface appearance of benevolence. He is the enemy of true poetic inspiration.

When Milton hears the Bard's Song, he recognizes himself in Hayley/Satan and resolves to return to earth, to cast off this false selfhood in an act of "self-annihilation." He passes through the different levels of Blake's cosmology, from Eden, the highest realm of imaginative activity, to Beulah, a feminine, sexual paradise, to the abyss of Ulro, the material world. There, in Plate 19, he encounters Urizen, the personification of the unenlightened rational intellect, who attempts to freeze Milton's brain. As they struggle with each other, Milton works like a sculptor, creating new flesh on the bones of Urizen; the shaping, enlivening vision of the artist strives to impart life to the Urizenic death principle.

A crucial moment now follows: The spirit of the descending Milton, like a falling star, enters Blake's left foot one day as he binds on his sandals. Blake becomes aware that in this tremendous instant, Los, the imagination, has also entered and taken possession of him, and he knows that he is ready to fulfill his destiny as the poet-prophet of England, the seer whose task it is to awaken his country to the reality of the divine, and fully human, life. Much of the remainder of the first book of the poem is devoted to a transfigured vision of the time and space world, seen as the creative work of Los, whose task is accomplished in the single, eternal moment of poetic inspiration.

In book 2 of *Milton: A Poem* a female character named Ololon descends from Beulah to Ulro. It later transpires that she is Milton's emanation. She descends to

Blake's cottage in Felpham, and he perceives her as a young girl. Ololon's sudden appearance in what Blake calls the Mundane Shell (the physical world) is another crucial moment in the poem. Like Blake's union with Milton and Los in book 1, it occurs in a timeless moment of mystical illumination, which Blake associates with the song of the lark and the odor of the wild thyme. In this moment of heightened perception, eternity streams into time, and the effect is so powerful that it cancels out all the mistakes and perversions of the entire span of Christian history. A new era is at hand.

All the remaining events of the poem take place in this one instant. Milton, still continuing his descent into the physical world, appears in Blake's garden as the Covering Cherub, a symbol derived from the Bible and, in Blake's mythology, signifies the final manifestation of all the errors of the Christian churches. The Covering Cherub is closely linked with Satan the selfhood, who also now appears; the inspired Milton, who is hidden within the Covering Cherub, recognizes the false selves to which he formerly surrendered. In a great speech in Plates 40-41, he casts them off in an act of self-annihilation, giving his allegiance solely to the truth of poetic inspiration. Hearing Milton's speech, Ololon is cleansed also, and in a purified form she is able to unite with Milton. The poem ends on a note of apocalyptic hope for the reawakening of the entire humanity.

THE TYGER

First published: 1794
Type of work: Poem

In awe, wonder, and puzzlement, the speaker asks a series of questions about the nature of the being who could create such a fearsome beast.

"The Tyger," from the *Songs of Innocence and of Experience* (1794), is probably Blake's most famous poem. Its artful simplicity and pounding repetitions make a strong impression when the poem is read aloud. The meaning of "The Tyger," however, is not so easy to ascertain, and it has provoked a wide range of interpretations. The poem consists of six quatrains, each of which asks at least one question about the nature of the tiger's creator. None of the questions are answered. The central question of the whole poem appears in the fifth quatrain, "Did he who made the Lamb make thee?" This question recalls the poem "The Lamb," from the same collection, in which the question, "Little Lamb, who made thee?" is answered clearly. The lamb is made by Christ and is an obvious symbol of the mild and gentle aspects of Creation, which are easy to associate with a God of love. But what about the more fearsome, destructive aspects of creation, symbolized by the tiger? Do they proceed from the same God? Under what circumstances? Is the tiger only a product of the Fall of humankind? Or are there, perhaps, two Gods?

Crucial to interpretation are the first two lines of the fifth quatrain: "When the stars threw down their spears,/ And water'd heaven with their tears." This event appears to take place, from the evidence of the following line ("Did he smile his work to see?"), at the moment of the tiger's creation. It may be a reference to the fall of the rebel angels in Milton's *Paradise Lost:* "they astonished all resistance lost,/ All courage; down their idle weapons dropped." In Christian tradition, the stars are said to be the tears of the fallen angels. In *The Four Zoas*, Blake uses a phrase almost identical to the one in "The Tyger" in the context of Urizen's account of the fall: "The stars threw down their spears and fled naked away/ We fell." In Blake's mythology, the immediate result of the Fall was the creation of the physical world. This cluster of associations suggests that the tiger is a product only of the Fall, a suggestion that is strengthened by the phrase "forests of the night" in the first quatrain, which symbolizes Blake's fallen world of Experience.

Yet this does not seem to provide the whole answer to the riddle of the poem. The fire that burns brightly, if destructively, in the state of Experience is still the divine fire, the stupendous creative energy that can frame the "fearful symmetry" of the tiger. In the fallen world, however, it cannot be fully appreciated for what it is. In quatrain 3, for example, the awestruck speaker lapses into incoherence as he tries to fathom the mystery of the fierce aspect of Creation. As Blake puts it in one of the proverbs in *The Marriage of Heaven and Hell*, "The roaring of lions, the howling of wolves, the raging of the stormy sea, and the destructive sword, are portions of eternity, too great for the eye of man." The speaker in "The Tyger" cannot understand that, if there is a lamb, there must also be a tiger; opposites are necessary for the full manifestation of divine creativity.

Yet another possibility is that Blake was drawing on the teachings of the Gnostics, who flourished in the early years of the Christian era. For the Gnostics, the created world was a dark prison; it was not created by the true God but by an inferior power, the demiurge, who was often likened to the God of the Old Testament. If Blake indeed had this in mind—and elsewhere in his work he expresses a very similar view—the answer to the poem's central question, "Did he who made the Lamb make thee?" would be "no." The tiger would then be associated with the Old Testament God of fire and judgment, not the New Testament God of love, embodied in Christ.

Summary

Ignored in his own time, William Blake has come into his own in the twentieth century, and his status as one of the six greatest English Romantic poets is unlikely to be challenged. His intense spiritual vision, embodied alike in simple lyrics and complex prophetic books, amounts to a manifesto of the art, psychology, philosophy, and religion of human enlightenment. Creating his own mythology of the creation, fall, and redemption of humankind, Blake offers a vision of the "Human Form Divine" that transcends the conventional wisdom regarding the nature of the human condition.

Bibliography

Blackstone, Bernard. *English Blake.* Reprint. Hamden, Conn.: Archon Books, 1966.

Bloom, Harold. *Blake's Apocalypse: A Study in Poetic Argument.* Garden City, N.Y.: Doubleday, 1965.

Damon, S. Foster. *A Blake Dictionary: The Ideas and Symbols of William Blake.* 1965. Rev. ed. Hanover, N.H.: University Press of New England, 1988.

_____. *William Blake: His Philosophy and Symbols.* Reprint. Gloucester, Mass.: Peter Smith, 1958.

Erdman, David E. *Prophet Against Empire: A Poet's Interpretation of the History of His Own Times.* 3d ed. Princeton, N.J.: Princeton University Press, 1977.

Frye, Northrop. *Fearful Symmetry: A Study of William Blake.* Princeton, N.J.: Princeton University Press, 1947.

Hagstrum, Jean. *William Blake: Poet and Painter.* Chicago: University of Chicago Press, 1964.

Percival, Milton O. *William Blake's Circle of Destiny.* Reprint. New York: Octagon Books, 1977.

Bryan Aubrey

GIOVANNI BOCCACCIO

Born: Florence or Certaldo, Italy
June or July, 1313
Died: Certaldo, Italy
December 21, 1375

Principal Literary Achievement

Although an erudite Latin humanist, Boccaccio is known primarily for *The Decameron*, which reflects the medieval world, influenced such writers as Geoffrey Chaucer, and was a precursor of Renaissance thought.

Biography

Giovanni Boccaccio was born in June or July of 1313 in Florence or Certaldo, Italy, the illegitimate son of Florentine merchant Boccaccio di Chellino. The identity of his mother is uncertain. He spent his early childhood in Florence, but in 1327 he moved with his father to Naples, where he studied banking, trade, and canon law. Boccaccio eventually abandoned his pursuit of a vocation in commerce and law for a literary life.

The years spent in Naples were crucial to Boccaccio's social, intellectual, and literary development. Because of his father's connections with the aristocracy of Naples, Boccaccio enjoyed the carefree and privileged life-style of the court of King Robert of Anjou. There, his passion for poetry and his superior aptitude in literature, both classic and medieval, flourished and formed the basis of his literary works. It was there that he began his early original poetry, which evidences a gift for narration: *Il filocolo* (c. 1336, *Labor of Love*, 1566), *Il filostrato* (c. 1335, *The Filostrato*, 1873), *Teseida* (1340-1341; *The Book of Theseus*, 1974).

In this body of work, Boccaccio introduces a female character, Fiammetta, whose charms are extolled throughout his early poetry. His first encounter with her is described in *Labor of Love*, where the poet sees her for the first time on Easter Sunday in the Franciscan Church of San Lorenzo in Naples. It is notable that the manner in which this encounter is described is consistent with Italian poet Dante Alighieri's description of Beatrice, and also remarkably similar to the reported meeting of Boccaccio's revered idol, Petrarch, and his beloved Laura.

Boccaccio encountered during this period a man who would influence his life and his work considerably. While studying the law, he met Cino da Pistoia, a prestigious lawyer of the time, who was also a friend of Dante, author of *La divina commedia*

(c. 1320; *The Divine Comedy*). Cino da Pistoia was a poet in his own right and a disciple of *il stil nuovo*, the "sweet new style," a school of poetry in the Tuscan idiom. Cino da Pistoia became a link to Dante, and through him Boccaccio acquired an appreciation for poetry in the vernacular. Similiarly, Boccaccio made acquaintance with Dionigi da Borgo san Sepolcro, who had close ties with the Italian poet Petrarch. Petrarch was to become something of a mentor to Boccaccio, and his influence is evident throughout his works. During this time, Boccaccio was also surrounded by scholars who inspired a reverence for classical literature and a fascination with Greek culture, which would influence many of his future literary works. This appreciation of the classics would become one of the salient characteristics of the imminent Humanist movement.

Boccaccio's years in Naples were his happiest, and it was against his will that he returned to Florence in 1341 because of his father's financial difficulties. During the first years in Florence, Boccaccio sought work and contact with the northern aristocracy, while continuing to write more mature literary works such as *Il ninfale fiesolano* (1344-1346; *The Nymph of Fiesole*, 1597), and the *Elegia di Madonna Fiammetta* (1343-1344; *Amorous Fiammetta*, 1587), which reflected cultural and spiritual situations of the era.

In 1348, Boccaccio was in Florence when it was struck by the Black Death, an event that inspired the writing of *Decameron: O, Principe Galeotto* (1349-1351; *The Decameron*, 1620). His father, stepmother, and many friends died during this horrifying episode, and Boccaccio offers a vivid description of this deadly plague in the introduction to the work. The bulk of his writing on *The Decameron*, considered his masterpiece, was completed in the years during which Boccaccio was compelled to remain in Florence to administer his father's estate.

In 1350, Boccaccio finally had the opportunity to cultivate a deep, long-standing personal friendship with his most revered contemporary literary figure, Petrarch. When Boccaccio learned that Petrarch was expected to visit Florence, he arranged to welcome the poet to the city personally. A strong personal bond developed between the two men, which lasted until Petrarch's death in 1374. It has been said that, in his later years, Boccaccio questioned the validity of *The Decameron* and that it was Petrarch who persuaded him not to destroy the manuscript.

The last twenty years of Boccaccio's life are characterized by profound introspection, reflection on moral values, and his spiritual evolution. He shared with Petrarch the belief in the spiritual value of poetry and classical literature as being the highest expression of human civilization. During these years, Boccaccio composed his most erudite Latin treatises, which earned for him fame as one of the great scholarly Humanists of the fourteenth century: *De mulieribus claris* (c. 1361-1375; *Concerning Famous Women*, 1943), *Genealogia deorum gentilium* (c. 1350-1375; genealogies of the Gentile gods), and *De casibus virorum illustrium* (1355-1374; *The Fall of Princes*, 1431-1438).

Following the political downfall and consequent exile of some of his most powerful friends in Florence in 1360, Boccaccio spent most of the last thirteen years of his life on his farm in Certaldo. He made two return visits to Naples and several trips to see Petrarch. After his last trip to Naples in the autumn of 1370, Boccaccio returned home to recopy and revise *The Decameron*. At the invitation of the city of Florence, he also gave public lectures on *The Divine Comedy*. He retired to Certaldo in 1374, where he died after a long illness on December 21, 1375.

Analysis

An appreciation of the numerous and varied works of Boccaccio must begin with an understanding of the historical and cultural milieu in which they were conceived. Boccaccio was an innovative artist whose development as a writer sprang from a solid foundation on traditional medieval rhetoric and classical models. Evidence of medieval philosophy and literary devices, as well as those of ancient classical writers, pervades all of his works. Boccaccio was also engaged, however, in a new endeavor: the development of an Italian literary language comparably suitable for literary purposes, as Latin had been. Although vernacular Italian had been developed and utilized in the area of poetry by such authors as Dante and Petrarch, Boccaccio was the first Italian writer to employ the models of past classical traditions and style to develop a rich vernacular prose for fiction. This singular achievement, coupled with his masterful development of the narrative, places him among the greatest of Italian writers. His remarkable skill in characterization and his unparalleled status as a consummate raconteur influenced writers throughout the world.

A summary glance at the works of Boccaccio tempts the novice to categorize his literary efforts simply into three distinct phases. His first works, both poetry and prose, clearly reflect the conventional medieval treatment of the subject of idealistic courtly love. Characteristic emphasis on rhetorical eloquence, the heavy use of allegory and theological symbolism, and the ever-present influence of Dante as well as classic Greek writers are common threads throughout the writings preceding *The Decameron*.

At least superficially, *The Decameron* itself seems to stand out among the works of Boccaccio as an anomaly. This period in his life as a writer is markedly distinct from any other. In his later years, scholarship replaced creativity in the author, and the object of his efforts was to service the needs of those devoted to erudition. *The Decameron*, however, was neither the exposition of ideals of a romantic young poet nor work written for the consumption of scholars. Rather, it served, by the author's own admission, as a diversion for the new flowering class of the bourgeois public, particularly women. It is a unified collection of tales, many comic, some rather bawdy, written strictly to delight from the perspective of an open-minded realist, with winking tolerance of the flaws of human nature that motivate the actions of his various colorful protagonists.

An adequate analysis of Boccaccio's works must also address the fruits of his labor in an integrated manner. Numerous stylistic, thematic, and structural traits unique to the times and the author himself appear throughout his youthful works as well as his most advanced literary endeavors. The influence of Dante, Petrarch, and other poets who claimed allegiance to *il stil nuovo* (the sweet new style), a popular style of poetry of the time, is evident in the majority of Boccaccio's works, as well as the use of "tertiary rhyme," a rhyming device popularized by Dante. Also borrowed from these poets were the conventional themes of courtly love, the dedication to a particular lady and her heavenly beauty, and the ennobling power of love.

Perhaps the most significant Dantean influence in the works of Boccaccio is the use of allegory, whether under the guise of fictitious narrative, portraying a moral (*Amorous Fiammetta* and *The Decameron*) or as a representation of the refining effects of sensual love (*The Filostrato, The Book of Theseus, The Decameron*). Erotic allegory and the use of history as allegory were also characteristic of Boccaccio's early works.

Boccaccio, like his colleagues, inherited and utilized the thematic resources of Old French ballads and traditions, as evidenced by *Labor of Love, The Filostrato,* and *The Decameron,* with their themes of star-crossed lovers confronting adversity in the form of social or class distinctions and consequent disapproval.

Although Boccaccio incorporated into his writings the vast legacy of literary forms and devices provided by his predecessors, he fashioned these elements into a new style, a new perspective, and created an art form that was to become uniquely his own. Boccaccio's greatest distinction lies in his vivid narrative style and strategy in his prose fiction. It is first evidenced in embryonic form in *Labor of Love,* which is considered a plot model for *The Decameron.*

It is notable that, in both works, the author himself intrudes to explain his purpose in writing the book: to please the fair sex. *Labor of Love,* like *The Decameron,* begins with a group of characters who escape unpleasant reality by fleeing to a world of fantasy. The stories are told within a certain structure. As in *The Decameron,* there is a presiding officer to order and control the episodic events, and certain problematic questions to be addressed and established at the outset.

The technique of writing a narrative that contains within it many narratives is characteristic of Boccaccio. It is present in the *The Decameron* and *Labor of Love;* hints of it had also appeared in such earlier works as the *Nymph of Fiesole* and the *L'amorosa visione* (1342-1343; English translation, 1986). Numerous dominant themes and motifs so richly portrayed in *The Decameron* were cultivated in his earlier writings. The pathetic, abandoned, or scorned lover is one such figure; it inhabits *The Decameron* but was introduced in such early works as *The Filostrato, Amorous Fiammetta,* and *L'amorosa visione.* The theme of adultery is present throughout Boccaccio's writings, without necessarily a moral judgment.

The Decameron, however, views such things from a totally new perspective for the Middle Ages: a perspective that shrugs at human indecencies and failings and portrays them in a comic light. It is this unique, delightful perspective that has prompted literary critics to compare *The Decameron* to Dante's *The Divine Comedy.*

THE DECAMERON

First published: 1349-1351 (English translation, 1620)
Type of work: Novel

Ten young people escape the city of Florence together during the Black Death and amuse each other by telling stories.

Contemporary Florence, during the terrible Black Plague, is the setting chosen by Boccaccio for *The Decameron*, which historians generally agree was written between 1349 and 1351. A desire to escape the horrors of the city prompts a group of ten young people (seven women and three men) to retreat to a country villa. There, they amuse themselves by telling each other stories.

The structure of *The Decameron* begins with a frame. The author addressed his readers, whom he presumes to be women, in his prologue, declaring his intent. He offers *The Decameron* as a pleasant distraction to those tormented lovers whose woes are more difficult to endure. He then apologizes to the "charming ladies" for the book's unpleasant but necessary beginning. A graphic description in realistic detail of the devastation of the plague in the city of Florence follows. The device of the frame was used by Boccaccio in earlier works, but on a smaller scale, as in *Labor of Love*. The frame in *The Decameron* provides a specific location and date to the story, while offering a realistic and reasonable explanation for such a collection of unchaperoned young people in a remote place. It further serves to unify what would otherwise be a loose collection of seemingly unrelated tales. The frame characters are the ten narrators, each endowed with intelligence, breeding, charm, and some distinguishing feature. Once settled in their country villa, it is proposed that each of the ten preside as queen or king for one day, choose a topic for that particular day, and invite everyone to recount an appropriate tale: thus, the significance of ten by ten, or one hundred stories, which explains the title and also satisfies medieval numerology.

The first day is ruled by Pampinea, the oldest, who assumes throughout the book a somewhat mature, motherly stance. There is no appointed topic of the day, but many of the stories told represent the tenor of the book as a whole. The tale of the debauched and irreverent Ciappelletto, who confesses falsely on his deathbed with such seemingly deep contrition to sins so minor as to render him a saint in the perception of those around him, is one of the most famous stories in *The Decameron*. Vice and virtue intertwine in the work as in life, and Boccaccio chooses to begin with a symbol of ultimate evil.

Filomena rules the second day, and her theme is those who overcome adverse fortune to their advantage. Representative is the story of Andreuccio, a simple-minded horse trader from Perugia, whose misfortunes in the city of Naples teach him to sharpen his wits—an apt lesson for any merchant.

The third day, under the reign of Neifile, is dominated by stories of lust, although the proposed theme is the successes of people who seek to achieve through their own efforts. The use of ingenuity and guile to achieve seduction is common to most of the stories of the day, and members of the clergy are not spared as protagonists in this collection of characters.

The theme of the fourth day, ruled by Filostrata, is in striking contrast to its predecessor. The theme of unhappy loves is designated, and the stories that follow are, for the most part, of a pathetic, if not tragic, nature. One example is the story of Ghismonda, who eloquently defends her love of a man of low breeding to her disapproving father by stating that his is the only true nobility, one of character. Ghismonda ultimately kills herself after her father has the lover's heart cut out and sent to her in a goblet.

The fifth day is ruled by Fiammetta, who calls for stories of lovers whose trials have ended happily. The most moving is that told by Fiammetta herself: the story of Ser Federigo and his beloved falcon, which he ultimately sacrifices to please his lady. The focus in this episode is utmost chivalry, a reminder of the traditions dominating contemporary literature, and perhaps a personal comment on nobler times.

The theme for the sixth day, announced by Elissa, is the use of clever retort as a means of avoiding danger or embarrassment. The witty Filippa, who avoids the death penalty for adultery by eliciting an admission from her husband that he was never denied her charms and by exclaiming that she should not be punished for donating her leftovers to others, is exemplary.

The seventh, eighth, and ninth days, ruled by Dioneo, Lauretta, and Emilia, are devoted to tricksters: women who try to fool their husbands or men who play tricks on others. Human astuteness is praised, even if the emphasis seems to be on the comic. Many of the tales concern the Bruno-Buffalmaco pranksters, who never tire of victimizing their simple-minded companion, Calandrino, who is even duped at one point into thinking that he is pregnant.

The stories of the tenth day, according to Panfilo, are to be of those who acted liberally or magnanimously, in love or other matters. The theme on the tenth day is to treat only those actions motivated by generosity or lofty ideas. The last story is that of Griselda, who appears as a symbol of womanly virtue, of humility and goodness, and who thereby offers a poignant contrast to the very first tale and the figure of Ser Ciappelletto.

Viewing *The Decameron* as a whole, it is not surprising that critics have referred to it as "The Human Comedy" while comparing it to Dante's masterpiece. Human nature is examined and reexamined throughout, from the tragic to the comic, from noble to base, but always with a tolerance that is the force behind the comic spirit that only Boccaccio could create.

Summary

Although influenced by past literary traditions and the classics, Giovanni Boccaccio developed a style and language uniquely his own in the area of prose fiction. A review of his earlier works reveals his gradual development toward the skilled use of vernacular Italian in narrative prose form. His masterpiece, *The Decameron*, was written at the pinnacle of his career as a literary artist, displaying without restraint his refined gifts for narration and rich characterization. *The Decameron* not only was an innovation in Italian literature but also became a fertile source of reference for authors throughout the world for centuries to come.

Bibliography

Bergin, Thomas G. *Boccaccio*. New York: Viking Press, 1981.

Branca, Vittore. *Boccaccio: The Man and His Works*. Translated by Richard Monges. New York: New York University Press, 1976.

Cottino-Jones, Marga. *An Anatomy of Boccaccio's Style*. Napoli: Cymba, 1968.

Dombroski, Robert S., ed. *Critical Perspectives on "The Decameron."* New York: Barnes & Noble Books, 1977.

Hollander, Robert. *Boccaccio's Ten Venuses*. New York: Columbia University Press, 1977.

Marino, Lucia. *"The Decameron" "Cornice": Allusion, Allegory, and Iconology*. Ravenna, Italy: Longo, 1979.

Wright, Herbert G. *Boccaccio in England, from Chaucer to Tennyson*. London: Athlone Press, 1957.

Victor A. Santi

HEINRICH BÖLL

Born: Cologne, Germany
December 21, 1917
Died: Merten, West Germany
July 16, 1985

Principal Literary Achievement

A Nobel laureate in literature, Böll was known worldwide as the conscience of postwar Germany, attacking evils and advocating the humane through his speeches, essays, short stories, and novels.

Biography

Heinrich Theodor Böll was born December 21, 1917, in Cologne, Germany, to Victor and Marie Hermanns Böll, solidly middle-class, liberal Catholics from old Rhineland families. Henrich's native region, the time of his birth, his parents' class, and their moral and religious convictions all were strong influences on Böll's character and his works. Although the parents suffered from the inflation of the 1920's and the Depression of the 1930's, so that Böll sometimes identified his background as middle class, sometimes as proletarian, the Bölls provided their children with security, understanding, and freedom but did not hide social problems from them. Devout but independent-minded Catholics, the elder Bölls taught their children the tenets of Christian love but never forced formal practices on them. Consequently, young Böll realized the injustice when many of his proletarian friends could not attend *Gymnasium* (college preparatory school) with him.

An adolescent in the 1930's when Adolf Hitler rose to power, Böll never embraced Nazi teachings or activities, mainly because of the influence of his family. After *Gymnasium*, Böll worked in a bookstore, where he read such proscribed thinkers as Karl Marx and Sigmund Freud, until he was conscripted for compulsory labor in 1938-1939. Later in 1939, shortly after entering the University of Cologne (with difficulty, since he was not a Nazi Party member), he was drafted into the army. Always opposed to war and Nazism, Böll suffered wounds three times; he deserted, forged passes, and devised his capture by Americans. He witnessed atrocities of Hitlerism but also enough incidents of compassion to reject the doctrine of collective guilt.

Returning to a bombed-out Cologne in November, 1945, Böll reentered the university to acquire a ration card, worked in the family carpentry shop and, later, for the city, and wrote; but his wife, Annemarie Cech, an English teacher whom he had

197

married in 1942, virtually supported the family. A voracious reader, Böll had written six novels before the war. In 1947, he began publishing stories in periodicals. Two of these stories, about the difficulties of the postwar years, led Middelhauve, a publisher of technical books, to contract for Böll's fiction. In 1949, Middelhauve published the novella *Der Zug war punctlich* (*The Train Was on Time*, 1956) and in 1950 *Wanderer, kommst du nach Spa . . .* (*Traveller, If You Come to Spa*, 1956), short stories about wartime and postwar dreams of a better world.

In 1951, *Wo warst du, Adam?* (*Adam, Where Art Thou?*, 1955), a novel about the absurdity of war, established Böll with critics. The same year, Gruppe 47, a prominent coterie of writers who met to read, criticize, and encourage one another's work, awarded its annual prize to Böll's humorous story "Die schwarzen Schafe" ("The Black Sheep"). In 1952, with a new publisher, Kiepenheuer and Witsch, and a new novel about postwar poverty, hypocrisy, and bigotry, *Und sagte kein einziges Wort* (1953; *Acquainted with the Night*, 1954), Böll achieved financial and popular success. Throughout the 1950's, he produced a steady stream of novels, stories, radio plays, essays, humor, satire, and the pleasant *Irisches Tagebuch* (1957; *Irish Journal*, 1967), an account of his visits to Ireland, which he admired for its genuine Catholicism and its antimaterialism. These works won a steady stream of literary prizes.

Billard um halbzehn (1959; *Billiards at Half-Past Nine*, 1961) and the 1963 bestseller *Ansichten eines Clowns* (*The Clown*, 1965) contrast the evil, materialistic, institutional, opportunistic "buffaloes" with the persecuted, sensitive "lambs." *The Clown* shows the influence of American novelist J. D. Salinger, whose *The Catcher in the Rye* (1951) Böll had translated in 1962. In the 1960's, Böll was also active in public life. His *Brief an einen jungen Katholiken* (1961; letter to a young Catholic) criticizes the position of the Church in Nazi and postwar Germany. In four lectures given at the University of Frankfurt in 1963-1964 and published in 1966, Böll identifies love, language, and commitment as defining human qualities and advocates an "aesthetic of the humane." In 1968, having witnessed the invasion of Czechoslovakia while visiting writers in Prague, Böll protested Soviet policies. In 1969, he campaigned for Willy Brandt and the Social Democrats against the authoritarian government of Konrad Adenauer's Christian Democrats.

Elected president of PEN, an international association of writers, in 1971, Böll in this position aided a number of Soviet dissidents, among them the novelist Aleksandr Solzhenitsyn. In 1972, the Swedish Academy gave Böll the Nobel Prize in Literature, citing especially *Gruppenbild mit Dame* (1971; *Group Portrait with Lady*, 1973), a recapitulation of the social and moral criticism that had filled his earlier works.

Although in poor health, Böll remained active in the 1970's and 1980's. His advocacy of due process for the terrorist Baaden-Meinhoff gang, which had been tried and condemned in the press, initiated a long controversy between Böll and the establishment. Böll's novels *Die verlorene Ehre der Katharina Blum: Oder, Wie Gewaltentstehen und wohin sie führen kann* (1974; *The Lost Honor of Katharina Blum: Or, How Violence Develops and Where It Can Lead*, 1975) and *Fursorgliche Belagerung* (1979; *The Safety Net*, 1982) depict, respectively, the "public violence" of journalistic slander and the horrors of both terrorism and systematic protection. In 1981, Böll joined the Bonn peace demonstration, a last straw, perhaps, that made Christian Democrats oppose making the social critic, but not the "great writer," an honorary citizen of Cologne. Böll responded that the two were one.

Böll died in Merten, West Germany, on July 16, 1985. *Frauen vor Flusslandschaft. Roman in Dialogen und Selbstgesprächen* (*Women in a River Landscape*, 1988), about life in West Germany's capital, was published the next month.

Analysis

In an interview given in 1976, Böll remarked: "There are authors whose immediate impulse to write is political. Mine was not." Indeed, he asserted, perhaps denying the salutary effects of didactic literature, perhaps denying the effects of circumstances on character, "I am of the conviction that what comes to one from outside does not change one very much. . . . Everything history throws at one's feet, war, peace, Nazis, communists, the bourgeois, is really secondary." Nevertheless, sociopolitical criticism, even satire, plays a primary part in his writings—so much so that Böll-scholar Robert Conrad warns critics against denying that Böll's work is "motivated by the challenge to gain aesthetic control over the experience of Nazi Germany, postwar guilt, and the inadequacies of West German democracy." Moreover, at the end of *The Lost Honor of Katharina Blum*, Böll's narrator affirms, though ironically: "Art still has a social function."

Böll's art indeed has a social function. In the early war story, *Traveller, If You Come to Spa*, Böll discredits classical education that encourages war by emphasizing the martial: A mutilated soldier evacuated to his old *Gymnasium*, now a field hospital, observes the schoolroom ornaments—statues of a hoplite, Julius Caesar, Frederick the Great—and a war memorial. *Acquainted with the Night* shows the inequities in the currency revaluation and the Economic Miracle: A middle-aged husband working full-time cannot earn a decent living for his family. *Das Brot der frühen Jahre* (1955; *The Bread of Our Early Years*, 1957), shows another side: An up-and-coming young employee, whose former poverty has made him acquisitive, at last rejects the capitalist system, its excess profits, and its callousness, which is manifested in his fiancée, the boss's daughter. *Haus ohne Hüter* (1954; *Tomorrow and Yesterday*, 1957) shows poverty almost naturalistically determining the choices of one war widow, whereas another lives in inherited wealth not redistributed in the postwar democracy. *The Clown* castigates the cooperative establishment—the government, economic system, and Church—which lacks concern for the little people. *Group Portrait with Lady* criticizes the Communist Party for failure to live by its principles and Christian Democratic capitalism for its very tenets: profit, private ownership, self-interest, the exploitation of natural and human resources. The novel offers an alternative: direct antiexploitation action, rejection of excess profit taking, moderate work, and informal socialism. Böll's last book, about corruption in the Bonn government, "the only state we have," is certainly political.

Böll also said that he considered writing primarily a craft, but some critics have found his diction flat and his narration neither craftsman-like nor inspired. Most, however, have recognized that Böll, like Günter Grass and other contemporaries, solved the problem of writing with a language, which Nazi usage had made depraved and untruthful, by using elementary diction and syntax to reflect elemental or indifferent conditions, by playing ironically on Nazi perversions of the language, and by "bring[ing] something from a foreign terrain" into German by translating foreign literature. Böll has proven able to use diction and syntax to create many individual voices in his complex and sophisticated narrative structures.

In Böll's style and structure, critic J. H. Reid has found a number of the "marks of modernism": the disappearance of the " 'omniscient,' commenting narrator" and his assumed audience; the reduction of chronological plot; "a tendency to spatialize . . . through montage, leitmotifs, and the reduction of narrated time." In *Acquainted with the Night*, for example, the husband and wife narrate alternate chapters, apparently as interior monologues with no communication between the two or with the reader. Though the narration of *Tomorrow and Yesterday* and *Billiards at Half-Past Nine* is in the third person, the narrator is rarely apparent; both novels are told from multiple viewpoints of unreliable characters, in two cases those of confused adolescents. In *Billiards at Half-Past Nine*, the account of three generations of a German middle-class family is refracted in the characters' memories in the course of ten hours. One character's daily billiard playing serves as a leitmotif; his random creation of geometric patterns by rolling the balls over the table symbolizes the apparently random structure of the novel. (Böll, of course, had to plan the structure carefully; he often did so with complex spatial color graphs.)

These practices create an autonomous aesthetic structure detached from literary traditions and, in many modern novels, an autonomous subjective world detached from the external world. In *The Clown*, for instance, the world is presented exclusively as Hans Schnier understands it. Yet, in *The Clown*, as in most Böll works, the real world and real time are the objects of the narrator's perceptions, and Böll's social criticism seldom gets lost in the narrator's psyche.

In his later works, Böll employs numerous postmodern (or premodern) techniques, as in *Entfernung von der Truppe* (1964; *Absent Without Leave and Other Stories*, 1965). Commentator Hans Magnus Enzenberger has enunciated the duty of the postmodern writer to take direct action or to document the struggles of the oppressed; Böll did both.

THE CLOWN

First published: *Ansichten eines Clowns*, 1963 (English translation, 1965)
Type of work: Novel

In postwar Germany, a professional clown condemns materialism, opportunism, hypocrisy, and the Church and society's subordination of people to regulations.

Although both its artistry and its themes have drawn contradictory evaluations, *The Clown* artfully reveals the perceptions of the title character, Hans Schnier. Hans's past-tense narration of three crucial hours creates the immediacy of stream of consciousness, punctuated with telephone conversations that trigger Hans's opinionated memories of his childhood in World War II and his life as an outsider in the postwar period.

Returning to his Bonn apartment, failed, drunken, and penniless after an injury on stage, Hans, the scion of the "brown-coal Schniers," who has separated himself from his wealthy family and their values, grieves that his companion, Marie Derkam, the Catholic daughter of an old socialist, has left him after seven years to marry Heribert Züpfner, a Catholic lay functionary. Hans telephones his family and Marie's circle of Catholics to seek money and news of Marie. In conversations with the Catholic officials, Hans espouses the spiritual and sensual marriage in which the lovers "offer each other the sacrament" and rejects the validity of legal and ecclesiastical marriage if it lacks reciprocal grace. Denying the virtue of Hans's relationship with Marie, the Catholics defend submission to "abstract principles of order" and reveal that Marie and Züpfner are honeymooning in Rome.

A call to Hans's socially prominent mother, a nationalist racist who in 1945 urged a last stand of children against the "Jewish Yankee" but now directs the Societies for the Reconciliation of Racial Differences, points up the hypocrisy of many rehabilitated Nazis in postwar Germany—as do Hans's recollections of Herbert Kalick, his Hitler Youth leader who has been decorated for popularizing democracy among the youth of postwar Germany. Hans cannot forget or forgive Kalick's responsibility for the death of a little orphan boy. Nor can Hans forgive his mother's sending her adolescent daughter, Henrietta, to death on antiaircraft patrol in the last days of the war.

Informed that Hans is in Bonn, his father, the industrialist whose fine looks and manner have made him a television spokesman for German economic renewal, visits the apartment and offers to support Hans if he will train with a "famous" mime recommended by a "famous" critic. Hans rejects his father's philistinism and his reverence for "money in the abstract." Although he remembers gratefully his father's having saved two women from execution in 1945, Hans rebuffs the old capitalist who accommodates himself to whatever political and social authority is current.

In other telephone conversations and memories, Hans condemns a popular preacher, Somerwild, and through him the Church, for pseudointellectualism, sophistry, and worldly self-aggrandizement; his brother, Leo, a seminarian, resists breaking curfew to bring Hans companionship and money—further evidence of legalism's inhibiting the Church's mission of consolation and charity. In reverie Hans foresees a stultifying conventional middle-class life for Marie and Züpfner.

A call from his agent and meditations on his profession, especially his memory of having refused to play satires on the West German democracy in East Germany, reveal Hans to be an artist in the tradition of the German cabaret clown: an entertainer whose satire reveals society to itself. After the three hours' traffic that passes in his mind, Hans, integrity intact but completely isolated from both groups and individuals, returns in cracked white face to the train station. There, still looking for a few coins and Marie, he sings a ballad of Catholic politics in Bonn with small hope that his performance may yet make church and state see itself. Yet if Marie, he says, sees him like this and remains with Züpfner, then she is dead and they are divorced. Institutional religion will have killed reciprocal love.

GROUP PORTRAIT WITH LADY

First published: *Gruppenbild mit Dame*, 1971 (English translation, 1973)
Type of work: Novel

An investigator researches the life of a naïve, sensual, generous woman who survives the vicissitudes of German history from 1922 to 1970.

Group Portrait with Lady, the comprehensive novel that earned for Böll the Nobel Prize, is written as the report of an investigator, identified only as the Author ("Au."), on the lady, Helene Marie ("Leni") Gruyten Pfeiffer, forty-eight in 1970, who has lived in but not with the Third Reich, the occupation, and the growth of the Federal Republic in Cologne. Au.'s informants and others whose lives touch Leni's constitute the 125-member group in the portrait. Although Au. professes to be an absolutely objective seeker of facts, he appears instead to be an advocate of Leni as a contemporary humanist saint, an alternate to the ambition-driven heroes of "Christian" capitalism.

Although the first half of the book recounts Leni's life chronologically from 1938 to 1945, it is distractingly composed of short testimonies from the informants and longer analytic commentary of Au. Named "Most German girl" in her elementary school for her blondness, Leni, mystically sensual but not cerebral, leaves convent school in 1938 at sixteen to work for her father, a building contractor. In 1940, when her brother and her sweetheart, Cousin Edward, are executed for selling an antitank gun to the Danes in reaction to serving in Hitler's army, Leni grieves terribly. Yet the next year she marries Alois Pfeiffer, a crude soldier whose lewd dancing she has mistaken for sensual love. When he dies in battle, she does not grieve but renews her association with the sensual, mystical Jewish nun from her convent school, Sister Rahel. In 1942, Sister Rahel dies of malnutrition; Leni's father is imprisoned for defrauding the government and distributing wealth by means of a dummy company, and all of his property, except Leni's house, is confiscated. Making an easy transition from middle class to proletarian, Leni in 1943 takes the job that she will hold for twenty-seven years. Indifferent to social class, race, or nationality, Leni makes wreaths in a microcosm: Pelzer, the nursery owner, is an opportunist forgivable because of terrible memories of childhood poverty; Leni's fellow workers include Nazis, neutrals, a disguised Jew, a Communist, and a Russian prisoner of war.

The structural and thematic center of *Group Portrait with Lady* recounts the love of Leni and Boris, the joyful Germanophile Russian prisoner. It begins with Leni's spontaneous act of humanity: On his first day in captivity, she offers Boris a cup of her precious coffee. The ecstasy of their first touch, hand on hand, illustrates spiritual sensuality. Their lovemaking in the cemetery during air raids demonstrates the power of life in the face of death; their fidelity, the true marriage that occurs when the lovers offer each other the sacrament.

With the birth of Boris and Leni's son, Lev, during the Allies' nine-hour raid on Cologne, the mode of narration changes. Au. records fluent accounts of 1945 in the words and voices of the informants: Boris in German uniform is captured by the Allies and dies in Lorraine; Leni, a natural communist who instinctively shrinks "from every form of profit-thinking," wants to join the Communist Party, but the institution cannot understand her.

Having sold her house for a pittance to Otto Hoyser, her father's old bookkeeper, Leni from 1945 to 1970 rents an apartment in it and sublets rooms to old acquaintances and foreign "guest workers," each according to his needs, and charges each even less than his ability to pay. When the Hoysers try to evict Leni in the name of progress, a Committee sends a blockade of garbage trucks to delay the evacuation until the eviction order can be reversed. A model of classless solidarity, the Committee includes a music critic, civil servants, a small-business owner, German and foreign laborers, and Au. himself.

Although in the span of the book, Leni and members of the group portrayed have suffered dictatorship and war, and capitalism and evil have often triumphed, Au.'s report ends as a saint's life should: with a miracle. Leni's lodgers are secure. Leni herself is pregnant by a Moslem guest worker. Her brilliant son Lev, a garbage collector who practices "deliberate underachievement" to combat capitalism's excesses of ambitious overachievement, will soon join her. Even Au. has found happiness with a former nun. At least temporarily, "that which society has declared garbage" has triumphed over capitalistic exploitation.

Summary

Although Heinrich Böll insisted that his characters were "compositions," not psychological creations, they have psychological reality. Hans, the reification of the clown metaphor, is actually an opinionated, sensitive, sentimental, narcissistic, nonintellectual man. Leni, an archetype, is real in generosity, sensuality, and will. "As an author," said Böll, "only two themes interest me: love and religion." With a dichotomous cast of "compositions," the evil self-servers and the persecuted pure, a contemporary sociopolitical setting, and a repertory of symbols Böll condemned the sin of exploitation wherever it occurred and preached a religion of love made manifest in forbearance, generosity, and grace.

Bibliography

Conrad, Robert C. *Heinrich Böll*. Boston: Twayne, 1981.

Friedrichsmeyer, Erhard. *The Major Works of Heinrich Böll: A Critical Commentary*. New York: Monarch Press, 1974.

Heinrich Böll, on His Death: Selected Obituaries and the Last Interview. Translated by Patricia Crampton. Bonn: Inter Nationes, 1985.

MacPherson, Enid. *A Student's Guide to Böll*. London: Heineman, 1972.

Reid, J. H. "Heinrich Böll: From Modernism to Post-Modernism and Beyond." *The Modern German Novel*. Edited by Keith Bullivant. Leamington Spa, U.K.: Oswald Wolff Books, 1987.

Sokel, Walter Herbert. "Perspective and Dualism in the Novels of Böll." *The Contemporary Novel in German*. Edited by Robert R. Heitner. Austin: University of Texas Press, 1967.

Thomas, R. Hinton, and Wilfried van der Will. *The German Novel and the Affluent Society*. Toronto: University of Toronto Press, 1968.

Waidson, H. M. *The Modern German Novel*. 2d ed. London: Oxford University Press, 1971.

Pat Ingle Gillis

JORGE LUIS BORGES

Born: Buenos Aires, Argentina
August 24, 1899
Died: Geneva, Switzerland
June 14, 1986

Principal Literary Achievement

Borges' labyrinthine, esoteric short fiction and his innovative style have gained for him an international reputation as one of the most significant contributors to twentieth century literature.

Biography

Born in Buenos Aires, Argentina, on August 24, 1899, to Jorge Guillermo Borges and Leonor Acevedo de Borges, Jorge Luis Borges belonged to a well-off family. His father was of English descent. The young Borges appears to have enjoyed a relatively happy childhood and the security of a close-knit Latin American family. Under the nurturing influence of his family, Borges began to write at a very early age. He read voraciously from his father's personal library, which was rich in adventure tales by English authors such as Rudyard Kipling. Stories about distant lands and wild animals of the East shaped Borges' childhood imagination. This curiosity was later to develop into more serious pursuits of study in the areas of Eastern religions and philosophies. Borges was introduced to the benefits of private study from the beginning, not receiving any formal public education until the age of nine. This faith in self-education was to remain with him until he died.

In 1914, the Borges family was traveling in Europe when World War I began and was forced to extend its stay in Geneva for four years. It was there that Borges attended secondary school and was first introduced to French and German languages and literatures, as well as to the works of European authors such as Heinrich Heine, Charles Baudelaire, and Arthur Schopenhauer. Between 1919 and 1921, Borges and his family spent much of their time in Spain, where Borges produced his first poems and also met a group of young Spanish writers and poets who called themselves the *Ultraístas*. The *Ultraístas*, reacting against the Romanticism of the nineteenth century, had formed their own literary movement known as *Ultraísmo*. This movement was to be of some influence both in Borges' own career and in Argentina's literary growth during the 1920's. In 1921, the family returned to Buenos Aires, where Borges resumed his writing career. His early publications consisted mainly of poetry, mani-

festos, literary reviews, and a collection of essays. Some of these works exhibit traces of the tenets of *Ultraísmo*, such as the central use of metaphor, an art-for-art's-sake attitude, and an apolitical public stance, which Borges espoused for most of his life.

In the mid-1920's, Borges was closely associated with another avant-garde literary group known as the *Martinfierrista* group. Like the *Ultraístas*, this new group professed a disengaged aesthetic attitude, viewed literary activity mostly as an intellectual game, and was opposed by a more committed, leftist group of writers. Although Borges seems to have maintained an aloofness from political events, there is not enough evidence available to prove that he was personally detached from political reality, since he exhibited a characteristic reserve and shyness in discussing personal or political subjects.

Throughout the 1920's and the 1930's, Borges continued to write and publish poetry and essays. At this time the subjects that seem to have absorbed him most are love, time, and memory, and some of his early poems are nationalistic and romantic in flavor. The economic depression of the early 1930's and the major political changes that were sweeping Argentina under a conservative regime, however, seem to have left their mark on Borges. He dealt with the crisis by developing an art that was self-absorbed and evasive of political reality. His writing became increasingly intellectualized and esoteric, and at the same time he grew interested in mystic belief systems such as Gnosticism and the Kabbala. Through his study of these systems of thought he developed a personal ethos of philosophic mysticism, which is often reflected in his fiction.

The 1940's are probably the most significant decade in Borges' career, for it was during this period that he published much of the short prose fiction that was to bring him international fame in his later years. His first collection of stories arrived in 1941 and was later included in a larger anthology, *Ficciones, 1935-1944* (1944; English translation, 1962). The short stories (some critics prefer the term "essayistic fiction" to describe Borges' short fiction) for which Borges is now renowned are to be found in *Ficciones* and in a later collection, *El Aleph* (1949, 1952; translated in *The Aleph and Other Stories, 1933-1964*, 1970).

Because of a difference of views with the Perón regime that had come into power in 1946, Borges lost his job as a librarian in Buenos Aires and was forced to spend the following decade as a teacher and lecturer at private institutions. Once Perón was removed from power in 1955, Borges' career opportunities improved considerably. He was offered the directorship of the National Library in 1955 and in 1956 was appointed professor of English literature at the University of Buenos Aires. In the same year he was also awarded the coveted National Prize for Literature; in 1961, he won the Fomentor Prize, which he shared with Samuel Beckett in a tie. By the mid-1960's he had won worldwide acclaim, and his work was being widely published in translation. In 1968, Borges returned from his travels abroad to life in Buenos Aires and was married for a period of three years to Elsa Astete Millán. The marriage ended in a divorce in 1970.

In 1960, Borges had embarked on a new phase of his career with the publication of a collection of prose and poetry called *El hacedor* (1960; *Dreamtigers*, 1964). Throughout the 1960's and the 1970's, Borges repeatedly turned to poetry as a medium of expression and published a number of collections of both poetry and prose. His literary production began to wane during the last decade of his life, but he continued to travel and lecture. In 1984, he again visited Europe, this time accompanied by his traveling companion, María Kodama, whom he married in 1986. Already suffering from almost complete blindness, he had developed cancer of the liver as well. He died in Geneva on June 14, 1986.

Analysis

Borges is often included among writers described as postmodernists. Postmodernism, a literary movement whose influence has steadily increased since the middle of the twentieth century, is characterized by literature that meditates upon the processes of its own construction. Because of their inherent self-reflectiveness and circularity, Borges' stories provide a good example of such "metafiction." Borges is also known for his innovative literary techniques and an austere, polished craftsmanship.

The avant-garde intellectuals of early twentieth century Argentina, among whom Borges was one, conceived of literary activity as intellectual play. In Borges' "La Lotería en Babilonia" ("The Babylon Lottery"), for example, the lottery is an intellectual construct, conceived by an unknown brain, which seduces people into risking their fates by playing with chance. Stories such as this one seem to emphasize that life—like its fictional counterpart, literature—is an arbitrary construction based purely on coincidence. Many of Borges' detective-type stories, such "El jardín de senderos que se bifurcan" ("The Garden of Forking Paths") and "La muerte y la brújula" ("Death and the Compass"), emphasize equally the gamelike nature of everyday reality by their insistence on a mysterious relationship between life and accident. In such stories, Borges spoofs spy fiction and parodies other literary genres.

Borges repeatedly draws attention to the fact that literature is imitation and can be nothing but inventive repetition. In a typical story, "Examen de la obra de Herbert Quain" ("An Examination of the Work of Herbert Quain"), the narrator discusses the work of a fictitious writer whose experiments lead him to invent plots that repeat themselves in symmetrical structures. Borges uses stories such as this one in a dual way: He displays his interest in symmetry, invention, and the story-within-the-story structure and at the same time adopts a tongue-in-cheek critical attitude toward academic critics by mimicking them through his erudite, pretentious narrators. He thus combines serious meditations on the nature of fiction with a subtle and refined sense of humor.

In a more serious vein, Borges explores the relationship between the real world and its more fabulous counterparts. Two major metaphors that allow him to intermingle reality with imagination are the labyrinth and the mirror. Both of these appear in many of the stories included in *Ficciones* and *The Aleph and Other Stories*. In "Los dos reyes y los dos labertinos" ("The Two Kings and Their Two Labyrinths"), which appeared in *The Aleph and Other Stories*, the labyrinth is both a maze and a desert—a space within which one can lose one's way, or perhaps an intellectual problem that can be resolved only with great difficulty.

While the labyrinth suggests artifice, the mirror invokes duplication. In one of the stories from *Ficciones*, "La biblioteca de Babel" ("The Library of Babel"), a large library becomes an allegory of the universe. At the entrance to the library hangs a mirror, which may suggest the illusory nature of the universe or the possibility of having access to a duplicate world such as that of fiction. Such aspects of Borges' stories point to the influence of Hindu and Buddhist philosophies, in which the world is viewed as "Maya" or delusion, something ephemeral that can be shattered at any time.

What is paradoxical about much of Borges' philosophy is that it offers a two-pronged system of conception. On the one hand, Borges insists that twentieth century writers can do nothing but repeat ideas and plots that have already been presented in one form or another. Like literary activity, reality is for Borges both repetitive and cyclical. Paradoxically, however, repetition does not imply monotony, for the human being has the ability to be infinitely inventive in the rearrangement of previously acquired patterns of knowledge. Therefore, the possibilities available in any one lifetime are rich and multitudinous, even though the choosing of any one path may imply the foregoing of others.

The cyclical nature of the universe and of time is represented in many of the stories in *Ficciones*. In "Las ruinas circulares" ("The Circular Ruins") the protagonist discovers that the reality in which he envisioned another being is in fact a dream in which he himself has been projected by some greater dreamer. Such patterns of infinite regression are represented through the idea of the Creator-behind-the-Creator. In "El acercamiento a Almotásim" ("The Approach to Al-Mu'tasim"), the narrator's search for an omniscient God leads him to the idea that "the Almighty is also in search of Someone, and *that* Someone in search of some superior Someone (or merely indispensable or equal Someone), and thus on to the end—or better, the endlessness—of Time, or on and on in some cyclical form."

Borges' fascination with dreams and magic and with their power to lend a mythic quality to reality is not surprising, since he is the inheritor of a Latin American literary tradition that has had an ongoing interest in the fantastic as well as the occult. Concurrently, Borges' fiction has had its impact on other major Latin American writers, such as Gabriel García Márquez and Julio Cortázar, as well as on writers as far removed geographically from Borges as Salman Rushdie. Borges' interest in the occult was more than a playful diversion. He undertook serious study of mystic belief systems such as the Kabbala and Gnosticism and adopted many of these ideas in his own writing. In Borges' fiction, the world of the fantastic duplicates and interrupts the real world. Yet he never lets the reader lose sight of the fabricated quality of fiction and, by extension, of reality. The intellectual and sometimes esoteric density that is thus created forces the reader to participate actively in the process of fabrication.

Finally, for Borges myth and mystery are never very far from philosophy. The allure of some of the mystical aspects of Middle-Eastern and Eastern traditions seems to lie in the fact that they reinforce his own conception of the universe as a chance happening. Such a universe has all the qualities of a well-constructed dream and, like a dream, is susceptible to disappearance if left to the whims of a capricious God.

TLÖN, UQBAR, ORBIS TERTIUS

First published: 1940 (English translation, 1962)
Type of work: Short story

An imaginary universe called Tlön, based on an idealistic philosophy, begins to rule everyday reality.

"Tlön, Uqbar, Orbis Tertius," which first appeared in the literary magazine *Sur* in 1940, is one of Borges' best known stories. Because of its documentary style, which provides detailed "facts" about an imaginary universe, the text defies the term "short story" and, like many of Borges' other texts, verges on essayistic fiction. The story begins with the first-person narrator describing a conversation that he has had with his friend, Bioy Casares, during which his friend mentions a place called Uqbar, presumably discussed in the *Anglo-American Cyclopaedia*, a reprint of the *Encyclopædia Britannica*. After some futile searching, the unusual article is found in a deviant and pirated copy of the same encyclopedia. The description of Uqbar, a mysterious city supposedly located in Asia Minor, seems deliberately vague. The narrator and his friend fail to establish whether such a place really exists, and the problem remains unresolved for two years. After this period, the narrator comes across another, equally mystifying encyclopedia that tells of a planet called Tlön, describing in some detail its culture, philosophy, language, and literature.

In the description of the planet and its idealistic philosophy, the reader can find some typically Borgesian ideas. The language spoken on Tlön includes verbs and adjectives but no nouns, because the existence of nouns would point to a materialistic and empirical conception of the universe, something that is anathema to the inhabitants of Tlön. Because the inhabitants also deny the possibility of reduction or classification, the only science that flourishes on the planet is psychology. Similarly, various schools of thought have redefined the notion of linear time, either rejecting it completely or injecting a fantastic aspect into it. One school of thought conceives of time as a vague memory of the past, while another insists that all people live in two duplicate time zones simultaneously. In many such examples, Borges is playing with some of the idealistic notions proffered by the eighteenth century philosopher George Berkeley. As is usual in any reading of Borges, the seriousness of these ideas is undercut through the use of irony and playfulness.

An idea that appeals especially to Borges is the possibility of creating objects through force of imagination, which is what the people of Tlön are able to do. These objects, or "hrönir" as they are called, at first the products of absentmindedness, are later deliberately created in order to modify reality. Through the concept of the "hrönir" Borges delves into the powers of intellectual activity. By imagining objects, the people of Tlön are able to transform their environment to suit their idealistic conception of reality. This activity, then, is very similar to that of writers, who also create fantastic environments that supplement the one available in the real world.

This association between the inhabitants of Tlön and writers of fiction becomes apparent in the postscript to the story. In this final summation the narrator describes how, some years later, forty volumes of an encyclopedia of Tlön are discovered. Among the facts revealed is that Tlön is the fabulous brainchild of a seventeenth century secret society, which has circulated the idea of Tlön's supposed existence through literature. In nineteenth century North America, an atheistic millionaire named Ezra Buckley expands on the original idea of a utopian city and turns it into an entire planet. Through these documentary details the narrator dissembles the mystery of Tlön and the various encyclopedias. In a typically Borgesian conceit, however, one enigma is unveiled only to posit another. For the dissemination of rational explanations occurs simultaneously with the discovery of certain mysterious objects that have secretly entered the real world. These include a magnetic compass from Tlön found among the table service of a princess and a heavy metal cone discovered by the narrator himself. The thought products or "hrönir" of a fictional world have begun to impinge upon the smooth rationalism and empiricism of reality. Finally, fiction and reality merge, first because it is impossible to keep them distinct, but second because reality welcomes the intrusion of an idealized world into its seamy present.

THE GARDEN OF FORKING PATHS

First published: "El jardín de senderos que se bifurcan," 1941 (English translation, 1946)

Type of work: Short story

In this spoof of a spy story, the labyrinthine plot becomes the symbol of a mazelike universe where multiple time zones and destinies coexist.

In "The Garden of Forking Paths," Borges indulges in one of his common literary pastimes, the writing of spoof detective fiction. The story has all the necessary elements of a spy story: secret agents, guns, murder, mystery, drama, and an intricate plot that rushes the reader toward the resolution of the puzzle. Borges, however, is not as concerned with writing good spy fiction as he is with showing how an imitation of a spy story can be used for purposes other than the final demystification of the plot.

The plot concerns the escapades of its Chinese protagonist, Yu Tsun, a German spy. His task, while on a secret mission in England in the middle of World War I, is somehow to communicate to his German chief the name of a British town that is to be targeted by the Germans. Yu Tsun devises a clever plan that leads him to murder a man by the name of Stephen Albert, the last name of the murdered man being the name of the British town to be bombed. Pursuing Yu Tsun is a British agent, Richard Madden, who arrests him immediately after the murder but is unable to prevent the information from reaching Berlin.

Most of the story is told in the first person by the narrator, Yu Tsun, who is awaiting his execution at the end of the story. What adds to the intrigue of this interesting scheme of events are a series of coincidences and a labyrinth to be found at the heart of the story. Stephen Albert, the victim of the plot, happens to be a sinologist who lives in surroundings reminiscent of China. When Yu Tsun reaches his house in the countryside, he is mistakenly identified by Albert as a Chinese consul and so welcomed inside the house. Albert also happens to have occupied himself with unraveling the mystery of a labyrinth, whose construction is credited to Ts'ui Pen, an illustrious writer and the ancestor of the narrator. Albert has resolved the enigma of the maze by discovering that the maze is not a building but the large, chaotic novel authored by Ts'ui Pen. In this novel, characters live not one but multiple destinies. Refuting the fact that every choice presented to the human being in one lifetime presumes the abandoning of all other alternative choices, the Chinese writer has tried to create a work in which all possibilities coexist in a multiplicity of time zones. The inspiring image for the novel is a garden of forking paths, in which bifurcating paths lead to different places but also sometimes converge.

Both the labyrinthine book and the garden become symbolic of a chaotic universe in which all possibilities are available. Various destinies are realized in overlapping time zones. The metaphor of the labyrinth is a central one in much of Borges' fiction. It represents the idea of wandering and being lost in an unfathomable universe, sometimes following paths that converge with those already known, at other times re-treading previously familiar tracks. The labyrinth incorporates the richness of endless possibilities available in infinite lifetimes. Seemingly dissatisfied with the definition of Time as uniform and absolute, Borges attempts in this story, as he does in "Tlön, Uqbar, Orbis Tertius," to dwell on other possible ways of conceiving of it. The plot of Borges' own story is also a maze. The reader resolves the puzzle by following at the heels of the narrator and the writer of the tale. These cerebral journeys that make up literary activity form the backbone of Borges' aesthetic.

PIERRE MENARD, AUTHOR OF THE *QUIXOTE*

First published: "Pierre Menard, autor del Quijote," 1939 (English
translation, 1962)
Type of work: Short story

This work is a tongue-in-cheek story about a fictitious twentieth century writer
who uses memory and imagination in his attempt to rewrite *Don Quixote de la
Mancha* in its original form.

In "Pierre Menard, Author of the *Quixote*," Borges combines a sophisticated sense
of humor, directed toward the scholasticism of the academic, with one of his favorite
images—that of the simulacrum. The story begins as a eulogy written in the first
person and dedicated to the memory of an admirable French author, Pierre Menard.
The narrator first provides a list of the author's visible works in a rather pompous,
academic style and often invokes his (the narrator's) literary authority by dropping
names of famous writers or providing documentary proof through the citation of
very real authors or journals in his footnotes. The insertion of footnotes for the purpose of creating an impression of assumed authority is a much-used technique in
Borges' stories. In this story the footnotes add to the general irony, since Borges uses
them to mock academic critics. He mimics the style of bookish scholars who catalog
literary works and associate themselves with reputable names in order to give themselves some stature as literary critics. Borges implies that such critics remain well on
the outskirts of literary activity. Through such spoofs of literary techniques and genres, he invites the reader to participate in a playful activity that exposes the pretentiousness of some brands of scholasticism.

From the imitation of bombastic critics and styles, Borges proceeds to another
form of imitation. The eulogized writer, Pierre Menard, is credited with another set
of "subterranean" works, one of which is an attempted imitation of Miguel de Cervantes' *El ingenioso hidalgo don Quixote de la Mancha* (1605, 1615; *Don Quixote de
la Mancha*, 1612-1620). The reader is led to another typically Borgesian idea. Since,
according to Borges, everything that seeks to amaze has already been said before,
there are no longer any new stories left to narrate. Rearrangement of old plots in new
patterns is the only available type of creativity that writers in the twentieth century
can enjoy. Therefore, he suggests the fabrication of simulacrums, or copies, of original tales. These copies will be different from the originals because they will rearrange facts, color them, or throw a new light on them through the use of an ironic or
humorous tone.

The fictitious French author, Pierre Menard, who decides to rewrite *Don Quixote
de la Mancha* three hundred years after its original publication, takes this Borgesian

device even further. Menard does not want to rearrange the story of Quixote or to imitate its style in a modern tale. Rather, he wants to succeed at creating an identical story, a book that will duplicate the original in every minute detail. Any thought of creating a mechanical transcription is of course rejected at the outset. At first, Menard conceives the plan of immersing himself completely in the seventeenth century world of Cervantes. He decides to learn Spanish, become a Catholic, and fight the Moors and the Turks—in other words, experience the life of Cervantes in order to become Cervantes. This plan, however, does not seem challenging enough to the rather eccentric French writer, who then conceives an even more difficult method. Since by being Cervantes it would be relatively easier to write the book that Cervantes had written, Menard undertakes the task of creating a copy of the original work while he remains Pierre Menard. Having read the original work in childhood, he will depend entirely on his hazy memory of the work and his imaginative powers to reconstruct *Don Quixote de la Mancha* word for word. He succeeds, according to the narrator, at creating an exact replica of two complete chapters and a fragment of a third one.

The narrator then provides excerpts from Menard's and Cervantes' works and comments that Menard has created a new text that is infinitely richer and subtler than the original. Considering the fact that Menard's sentences are exact duplicates of those of Cervantes, the suggestion that Menard's work differs so radically from the original is funny yet not completely gratuitous. Although the passages to be compared are identical, the narrator draws the reader's attention to the fact that the more recently composed text is the work of a man who was culturally, geographically, and historically removed from his predecessor. The same words, written in the twentieth century, are bound to lead to new critical interpretations as well as the presumption of different authorial intentions. The narrator, placed in the role of a reader, is thus able to perceive subtle differences between excerpts that on the surface are exact replicas of each other. The reader's perception and interpretation, then, is as important a tool in the construction of fiction as is the ability of the writer to fabricate these texts. In this very postmodern story, Borges undoes the traditional opposition between reader and writer, showing how both can achieve new variations of a text and how both play a role in the creation of fiction.

FUNES, THE MEMORIOUS

First published: "Funes el memorioso," 1944 (English translation, 1962)
Type of work: Short story

The relationship between memory and abstract thought is invoked through a character who develops an infallible photographic memory.

Ireneo Funes, in the short story "Funes, the Memorious," is a young Uruguayan lad with an unusual gift. Known to be rather eccentric in his personal life-style, Funes is also famous in his province for always being able to tell the exact time without looking at a watch. After an accident in which he slips from his horse and sustains a concussion, Funes is crippled. This tragic loss of his physical capacities, however, does not seem to bother him, because he has been compensated in a rather amazing way. After his concussion, Funes develops the startling intellectual capacity for memorizing an infinite number of facts, names, and images that he has seen or read. This photographic memory includes the ability to reconstruct his own dreams in minute detail. In other words, Funes is unable to forget anything that his mind has observed even once.

The powers of his infallible memory are recounted to the first-person narrator when the narrator visits Funes in order to reclaim several Latin texts that he had earlier lent to Funes. With absolutely no prior knowledge of Latin, Funes is able to read and memorize the texts in their entirety. He provides other prodigious examples of his gift: He can perceive and remember exact changes in moving scenes—a herd of cattle in a pass, an innumerable number of stars in the sky, all the details of a stallion's mane, every leaf on every tree that he has ever seen. The burden of such an infinite memory, however, turns Funes into an insomniac. Although he can remember every precise detail from his past experience, he is unable to generalize about facts or to abstract himself from reality in any way. Finally, the narrator relates that Funes, who used to spend most of his time lying on a cot in a dark room, meditating upon his marvelous memories, dies of a pulmonary congestion.

Through the strange character of Funes, Borges dwells on the nature of language and the relationship between memory and thought. Funes' ability to remember everything presupposes his inability to forget anything. The gift of memory is thus at once a curse, its ominous aspects suggested through the funereal and unfortunate associations of the name "Funes." Borges indicates that imagination and creativity begin with the ability to think in abstract terms, to rise above precise details, and to condense impressions into thought. These things Funes is never able to do, for his photographic mind keeps him firmly entrenched in detail. He is unable to perform reductions, to idealize or to abstract other realities from the ones at his disposal. In fact, he compares his own mind to a garbage bin into which all kinds of useful and useless facts get thrown together. Borges suggests that in order to be able to create, one must first be able to select certain items and forget others, so that imaginary situations can be posited. It is thus an imperfect memory that lets the writer become a fabricator, someone who can forget and, subsequently, create.

Summary

Combining some unusual literary techniques with a refined wit, Jorge Luis Borges insisted on the fictionality of fiction—something fabricated and artificial. Many of Borges' stories are true "artifices," carefully wrought intellectual exercises that involve clever conceits. Borges is thus a truly postmodern writer, as interested in the process of construction as in the final product itself. Through the use of metaphors such as the labyrinth and the mirror and a highly cerebral style, Borges offers the reader a unique philosophy that denies the division between the real and the unreal worlds.

Bibliography

Barrenechea, Ana María. *Borges: The Labyrinth Maker*. Translated by Robert Lima. New York: New York University Press, 1965.

Bell-Villada, Gene H. *Borges and His Fiction: A Guide to His Mind and Art*. Chapel Hill: University of North Carolina Press, 1981.

Lindstrom, Naomi. *Jorge Luis Borges: A Study of the Short Fiction*. Boston: Twayne, 1990.

Rodríguez Monegal, Emir. *Jorge Luis Borges: A Literary Biography*. New York: Dutton, 1978.

Stabb, Martin S. *Borges Revisited*. Boston: Twayne, 1991.

_____. *Jorge Luis Borges*. New York: Twayne, 1970.

Sturrock, John. *Paper Tigers: The Ideal Fictions of Jorge Luis Borges*. Oxford, England: Clarendon Press, 1977.

Wheelock, Carter. *The Mythmaker: A Study of Motif and Symbol in the Short Stories of Jorge Luis Borges*. Austin: University of Texas Press, 1969.

Anu Aneja

ELIZABETH BOWEN

Born: Dublin, Ireland
June 7, 1899
Died: London, England
February 22, 1973

Principal Literary Achievement

Known best for her novels, Bowen was an astute and subtle student of human nature, especially in conflicts between young people and adults.

Biography

Elizabeth Dorothea Cole Bowen was born in Dublin, Ireland, on June 7, 1899. Her parents were Henry Cole Bowen and Florence Isabella Pomeroy (Colley) Bowen. Both of them were Anglo-Irish, giving Elizabeth a Protestant, landowning heritage. Her father, a barrister, inherited Bowen's Court, which was built in the eighteenth century and in which Elizabeth lived as a young girl. In 1930, upon the death of her father, she inherited the family estate. When Elizabeth was thirteen years old, her mother died. After her father's health deteriorated, she spent several years living with various relatives. Her mother's death, her father's precarious health, and her lack of a permanent, stable home all had a strong impact on the way that Elizabeth developed, both as a person and as a writer.

Bowen's education began at Downe House, Kent, England. She also studied at the London County Council School of Art, and she soon began to write short stories. Her first collection, *Encounters*, was published in 1923. In the same year, she married Alan Charles Cameron, a graduate of Oxford and a World War I veteran. He began a long career in educational administration through his appointment, in 1925, as secretary for education in the city of Oxford.

By 1927, Bowen was an established writer and spent part of each year in one of her three residences: London's Chelsea section, Bowen's Court, and a home in Italy. In addition to writing ten novels and several collections of short stories, Bowen lectured and taught in Italy, England, and the United States. She also wrote literary criticism, book reviews, radio scripts, and autobiographical pieces, while also working for the Ministry of Information and as an air-raid warden in London during World War II.

Bowen's novels include *The Hotel* (1927), *The Last September* (1928), *Friends and Relations* (1931), *To the North* (1932), *The House in Paris* (1935), *The Death of the Heart* (1938), *The Heat of the Day* (1949), *A World of Love* (1955), *The Little Girls*

(1964), and *Eva Trout* (1968). Among her short story collections are *Encounters* (1923), *The Demon Lover* (1945; published in the United States as *Ivy Gripped the Steps*, 1946), and *A Day in the Dark and Other Stories* (1965). Her work in forms other than fiction includes *Bowen's Court* (1942), *English Novelists* (1946), *Seven Winters* (1942), and *AfterThought: Pieces About Writing* (1962). Most of Bowen's works were published in the United States shortly after they appeared in England.

Some of the many honors that she received include being named Commander, Order of the British Empire, receiving honorary degrees from Trinity College, Dublin, and from Oxford, and being designated a Companion of Literature of the Royal Society of Literature.

Having returned to Ireland after the end of World War II, Bowen and her husband lived at Bowen's Court for only a brief time. Alan Cameron died in 1952. Bowen continued to live there for a few more years and wrote *A World of Love* there. She could not afford to maintain the old place, however, and returned to England in 1960. She died on February 22, 1973, in London, after one last trip to Ireland, in 1973.

During her lifetime, Bowen enjoyed generally favorable, although by no means unanimous, critical acclaim. Rose Macaulay, reviewing *A World of Love*, wrote that it was "rather fascinating, though not to everyone." Many critics thought *The Death of the Heart* was her best novel; some even considered it one of the best English novels of the twentieth century. Victoria Glendinning, who wrote a biography of Bowen in 1978, thought that she was one of the ten most important fiction writers in English. Even before her death, however, Bowen's popularity had begun to decline and her books had been hard to find. In the 1970's, though, they were reissued in paperback, and a new generation of readers found at least some of them fascinating and entertaining.

Analysis

In Bowen's novels and short stories, certain subjects and themes are represented, though with a variety of viewpoints and plots. Bowen was interested in the ways in which the past—persons and events—affect, control, and even destroy the living. Her Anglo-Irish heritage gave her a special understanding of this subject. She was particularly sensitive to displacement, a feeling of alienation, a helplessness in the face of what has occurred before. Bowen's "romances" contained the usual elements of love, conflict, and mystery, but the dramas that unfold in her works contain both tragedy and comedy.

Adolescence is a frequent subject in Bowen's fiction; many of her characters are young persons struggling to become adults and often struggling *with* adults, who represent the past. The older generation has usually come to terms with the past and attempts to impose its own worldliness on those who are yet in a state of hope and faith, in the kind of innocence that Bowen describes in *The Death of the Heart*. At one point, she says that the innocent are "incurable strangers to the world, they never cease to exact a heroic happiness." That could also be said of Jane in *A World of Love* and of the young characters in Bowen's other novels.

Bowen's use of houses and landscape is a predominant feature of her narratives. The ramshackle house in *A World of Love* is exactly the right setting for the unfolding of this romance, which is almost a ghost story, in which the past imposes itself on all the main characters. In *The Death of the Heart*, two sharply contrasting houses form the essential background for Portia's struggle. The elegantly furnished, immaculate house in London is a place where feelings are unexpressed and where frank, open communication is unknown. In sharp contrast is Waikiki, the seaside house to which Portia has been sent while Thomas and Anna take an April holiday in Capri. Life at Waikiki is noisy, spontaneous, and as common as the life in the London house is formal and aristocratic. In both houses, Portia is an outsider; her separateness is emphasized by the alien atmosphere of each house.

In Bowen's books, the characters talk to one another rather than act; there is very little real action in her fiction. Rather, through conversations that are often ambiguous and restrained, hiding as much as they are revealing, the story unfolds with a delicate subtlety that challenges the reader to discover what the story really means. Irony is another characteristic of Bowen's style. The wit and humor in her novels depend on the discrepancies between what the characters think and say and what other characters reveal about them. There is irony, too, in what they expect and what they receive. For example, the cruel irony of Eddie's betrayal of Portia is typical of the way that Bowen resolves her characters' fates. She does not, however, always use irony to highlight disappointment. In *A World of Love*, Jane gives up her ghostly lover just before falling in love with a real young man when she least expects that to happen.

Bowen's style is highly descriptive; her scenes are visible, and the atmosphere in which they take place is palpable. Objects are important images of the emotions being felt but not expressed. At Montefort, the setting of *A World of Love*, rooms are described meticulously and vividly, not in long passages but in carefully selected and telling details.

Another aspect of Bowen's style is her occasionally convoluted sentence structure. Her tendency to twist syntax was a delight to some of her readers and an affectation and annoyance to others. For example, in *A World of Love*, the author, in describing Maud, the younger sister, says, "Nothing, or almost nothing, made Maud not young, not a child throughout." That is the kind of sentence that may leave the reader confused as to what the author means. On the other hand, Bowen's work has a poetic quality that many critics and other readers have noticed. Her language is allusive, precise, suggestive, and highly dependent on the implied, the unspoken but intensely felt truth.

The psychological insight that is perhaps Bowen's most notable characteristic is suggested by a remark made by St. Quentin, a Bowen character and a novelist, quite obviously speaking for Bowen, the novelist: "I swear that each of us keeps, battened down inside himself, a sort of lunatic giant—impossible socially, but full-scale—and that it's the knockings and batterings we sometimes hear in each other that keeps our intercourse from utter banality."

THE DEATH OF THE HEART

First published: 1938
Type of work: Novel

An orphaned sixteen-year-old girl goes to London and, through cruel betrayal, loses her innocence.

Portia Quayne is the sixteen-year-old heroine of *The Death of the Heart*, which begins soon after she arrives in London. Her father and mother having died within a few years of each other, Portia must now live with her father's son, Thomas Quayne, and his wife Anna. Thomas is a middle-aged, successful, reserved businessman who is unable to form close personal relationships with anyone, although he does love his wife in his own aloof and undemonstrative way. Anna is a stylish, elegant woman whose principal interest is making herself and her house beautiful. She entertains frequently, but she, too, has no close relationships, though she appears to have a certain cool, impersonal attachment to her husband. Both are embarrassed and uncomfortable at the appearance of Portia, the child of the elder Quayne's disgrace and second marriage.

Into this house comes Portia, who does everything that she can to please the Quaynes, being obedient, well-mannered, and quiet. She observes them minutely and records in a diary her thoughts about them, as well as the uninteresting events of her life, which consist primarily of attending an expensive, exclusive establishment where French lessons, lectures, and excursions are offered to a small group of girls. Portia does not know that Anna has discovered her diary. Worse, Anna discusses the diary with St. Quentin, a novelist and one of her several bachelor friends. Anna is upset by Portia's insights and candid observations, but she is too resentful of the slight disruption caused by Portia's presence to feel any real pity or concern for her.

Portia is bewildered by the lack of open, shared feeling in this household. She believes that she is the only one who does not understand what is beneath the genteel, snobbish surface of the Quaynes' lives. Two other characters add to Portia's puzzlement. One is Matchett, the housekeeper, a woman who worked for the first Mrs. Quayne and who knows a considerable amount about the family but who reveals only as much as she chooses to reveal in response to Portia's attempts to make a connection with the only family left to her. Matchett is a perfect servant—conscientious, discreet, authoritarian, and snobbish. Her principal interest is the house and maintaining it in perfect order as she has always done. Like the Quaynes, she does not open herself to receive the affection of the lonely, seeking girl. The other character who is important to Portia, and who also disappoints her by being too self-centered, too manipulative, is Eddie. At twenty-three, he recognizes Portia's innocence but is unmoved by her need for love; he has too many needs of his own.

Portia encounters a very different household when she is sent to Seale-on-Sea to stay with Anna's former governess while Thomas and Anna escape to Capri. Mrs. Heccomb is kind and her two stepchildren, young adults Dickie and Daphne, are as cool and self-centered as the Quaynes and Eddie are, but at Waikiki life is full of events, and Portia is allowed to participate in the activities of the family. She shops and goes to church with Mrs. Heccomb; she goes walking, dancing, and to the movies with the two young people. When Eddie comes, quite surprisingly, to visit Portia at Waikiki, he is immediately accepted by the others, but Portia is still just an observer. Just as she is imagining that her love for Eddie is reciprocated, she observes him holding hands with Daphne at the movies. Disillusioned, she returns to London, where she is further betrayed by learning that Anna has not only read her diary but also discussed it with St. Quentin; in fact, it is he who tells Portia about this duplicity.

The betrayals by Eddie and Anna push Portia to run away from the Quaynes. She goes to the hotel of Major Brutt, another bachelor friend of Anna; he is an honorable, sensible, responsible man and convinces her that he must let the Quaynes know where she is. Whether or not she will return to them, she says, depends on what they do. They send Matchett in a cab to retrieve her, and the book ends as Matchett arrives at the door of the hotel.

The reader is not told what Portia decides, but one can assume that she will return because she has nowhere else to go. The question of what will eventually become of Portia is also left unanswered. The real point of the story is that Portia's ignorance of the world—her innocence—has ended. It remains only for the reader to discover the meaning of the novel's ambiguous title. One can be fairly sure that Portia's heart is not "dead," for her sense of hurt and disillusionment is too intense to suggest that she no longer yearns for understanding and love. On the other hand, one can easily see that the adults around her *have* undergone a "death of the heart." Each one has shut himself or herself off from others, has refused to acknowledge the deep needs of others, is self-protective and deceitful. These people—Thomas, Anna, Eddie, St. Quentin, and Matchett—have all played a part in what happens to Portia, and one can only speculate on whether the damage that they have done to her through their lack of real concern and caring will result in Portia becoming like them.

A WORLD OF LOVE

First published: 1955
Type of work: Novel

In a small country house in Ireland, five related characters live in a world of illusion and fantasy dominated by a ghostlike presence.

Bowen wrote *A World of Love* a few years after returning from England to Bowen's Court, her ancestral home in Ireland. A dilapidated and deserted farmhouse nearby served as a model for Montefort, the setting of *A World of Love*. The owner of Montefort is Antonia Montefort, a photographer in her fifties, who lives in London and only occasionally visits the house that she inherited from her cousin Guy. Killed in World War I when he was twenty, Guy had been loved by Antonia as well as by Lilia, his seventeen-year-old fiancée, and quite possibly by one or more other women. Out of pity for Lilia, who should have inherited the house, Antonia arranged Lilia's marriage to Fred Danby, an illegitimate cousin of Guy and Antonia. Feeling responsible for this marriage, Antonia gave Lilia and Fred the use of the "manor" in return for its maintenance, an obligation that Fred diligently though not very successfully tries to fulfill. Meanwhile, Lilia, ostensibly the housekeeper, dreams of escaping from her dull, discontented, and stifling life. The Danbys have two children, both girls. Jane is now twenty and Maud is twelve.

The action of the novel takes place during two days in the summer of the early 1950's. Life in this isolated, seemingly half-asleep house is dreamy, unreal, and filled with fantasy, especially to Jane and Maud. They are not alike or close to each other, but they share a tendency to live in their imaginations, and the house gives them plenty of material with which to get through the uneventful days. Jane, who has completed her education under Antonia's sponsorship, is uncertain what she will do next. In the attic one day, she finds a bundle of love letters written by Guy to an unnamed lady. There is also a beautiful Edwardian dress, which Jane wears as she wanders in and out of the house, reading the letters, imagining that she is the one to whom they were addressed. This fantasy is the central "event" of the novel, affecting each of the three women at Montefort in terms of their relation to Guy. Their relations with each other and with the past form the subject of the book.

The sense of Guy's presence dominates the lives of Antonia, Lilia, and Jane in the days after Jane's discovery of the letters. Jane's imagined love of Guy becomes more real to her than the life that actually surrounds her. When she goes to a dinner party at a neighboring castle, she gulps her first martinis and then, seeing a spare place at the table, imagines that Guy is sitting there. To her, Guy is more real than the hostess and the guests, who seem to be merely actors in a drama performed for her benefit. Jane returns to reality when she learns that Guy did not write the love letters to her mother, as she had suspected, nor to her, as she had imagined.

Guy also appears to Antonia, who experiences a moment when Guy seems to be near her, thus restoring to her an awareness of herself; that, in turn, gives her the ability to make her presence felt by the others in the house, restoring to her a sense of importance that she had lost during her years of feeling abandoned by her beloved cousin. She now feels reunited with Guy instead of separated from him. The moment does not last, of course, but its effect does.

Lilia, whose life was made most uncertain and dependent by Guy's loss, also has a moment when she senses that Guy has returned. The house has been pervaded by this feeling that an apparition is present. When she goes out to the garden to meet him, she finds her husband, Fred, who, by handing her Guy's letters, makes it possible for her to renounce her dead and faithless lover and accept a real love.

Even Maud falls under the spell for a while. With her ever-present imaginary companion, Gay David, Maud unconsciously parodies the experiences of the three women. By stealing the letters from the place where Jane has hidden them, Maud sets the course of the novel back toward reality, which is fully realized when the two girls are driven by a chauffeur to meet a young man, a friend of the neighboring Lady Latterly, who gave the dinner party. Maud is very much in present reality as she sees for the first time an airplane landing. Yet it is left to Jane to go beyond the present moment and, without realizing it, into the future, as she and the young man catch sight of each other and immediately fall in love.

Summary

Elizabeth Bowen was a prolific writer from the time that she published her first fiction. She was considered an important and original author by readers who shared her taste for the understated and the poetic. They admired her patient probing of the psychological aspects of her characters. Speaking through her characters, she revealed her insights through such images as "the lunatic giant" mentioned by St. Quentin of *The Death of the Heart*. That noisy, crazy, internal figure is the one to which Bowen paid the most attention.

The American scholar and critic Edwin J. Kenney pointed out that all Bowen's books deal with the isolated and self-destructive capacities of innocent heroines in disordered circumstances. The crisis of identity recurs in all of her work and makes a unified whole of the novels and short stories. A somewhat eccentric and oblique style set her apart from all but a few writers of her time, notably the novelists Virginia Woolf and Henry James. Her affinity with them in style, structure, and subject matter placed her in very distinguished company, among the outstanding writers of the twentieth century.

Bibliography

Austin, Allan, ed. *Elizabeth Bowen*. Boston: Twayne, 1989.

Bloom, Harold, ed. *Elizabeth Bowen*. New York: Chelsea House, 1987.

Bowen, Elizabeth. *The Mulberry Tree: Writings of Elizabeth Bowen*. Edited by Hermione Lee. London: Virago, 1986.

Coles, Robert. *Irony in the Mind's Life*. New York: New Directions, 1974.

Craig, Patricia. *Elizabeth Bowen*. New York: Penguin Books, 1986.

Glendinning, Victoria. *Elizabeth Bowen*. New York: Alfred A. Knopf, 1988.

Kenney, Edwin J. *Elizabeth Bowen*. Lewisburg, Pa.: Bucknell University Press, 1975.

Lassner, Phyllis. *Elizabeth Bowen*. New York: Macmillan, 1990.

Natalie Harper

BERTOLT BRECHT

Born: Augsburg, Germany
February 10, 1898
Died: East Berlin, East Germany
August 14, 1956

Principal Literary Achievement

Brecht was Germany's leading modern dramatist and a central influence on Western drama since World War II.

Biography

Even though Eugen Berthold Brecht composed several ballads in his early twenties that told of his having been descended from shrewd, ruthless peasants, his genealogy was solidly middle class and could be traced back to the sixteenth century. He was born on February 10, 1898, in Augsburg, Germany. His father, Berthold Friedrich Brecht, was managing director of a paper mill in Augsburg. The father was Catholic, and his wife, Sophie, was Protestant; both Berthold and his younger brother, Walter, were reared in their mother's faith and primarily by her. Brecht's boyhood and adolescence were marked by self-confidence, quick-mindedness, cunning, and vitality—all characteristics that kept him in good stead throughout his life. His skill in manipulating people and his suppleness in pursuing his goals were also evident from his youth.

During World War I, Brecht began medical studies at the University of Munich to delay an early conscription call-up; however, the only medical lectures that he attended were those dealing with venereal diseases. Instead, he studied theater history and met Frank Wedekind, who not only wrote notorious, expressionistic plays advocating sexual liberation, but also composed and sang ballads with aggressive bravado. Imitating Wedekind, Brecht performed his own ballads in the coffeehouses and cabarets of Munich. In 1918, he wrote a play, *Baal* (pb. 1922; English translation, 1963), about an amoral, bohemian bard-balladeer who cruelly exploits, and then discards, friends and lovers of both sexes. Baal's only care is for the natural world, whose beauty he celebrates in raw, eloquent lyrics. That same year, Brecht also wrote *Trommeln in der Nacht* (1922; *Drums in the Night*, 1961), a powerful pacifist drama whose protagonist is a disillusioned veteran returning to à Berlin dominated by war profiteers.

Perhaps the best of Brecht's early works was *Im Dickicht der Städte* (1923; *In the*

226

Jungle of Cities, 1961). Two men, Shlink and Garga, engage in a seemingly motiveless duel of wills. Shlink, a Malaysian lumber dealer, seeks to buy Garga's soul but is himself shown to be a victim—one whose skin has been so toughened by life that he can no longer feel. He stages his battle with Garga to penetrate his own shell of indifference.

Brecht moved to Berlin in 1924 and became a celebrated personality in that city's culturally brilliant postwar jungle. He shortened his first name to "Bert," and established for himself a part-intellectual, part-proletarian, persona. His trademarks were a seminarian's tonsorial haircut, steel-rimmed spectacles, two days' growth of beard, a leather jacket, a trucker's cap, a cheap but large cigar, and chronic rudeness. People found him either charismatic or repulsive; many women found him irresistible. He charmed the beautiful singer-actress Marianne Zoff in the early 1920's. They married in November, 1922, had a daughter in 1923, but separated that year and divorced in 1927. He was to have many mistresses, of whom the most cherished were Elisabeth Hauptmann, Margarete Steffin and Ruth Berlau.

The most important woman in Brecht's life was the Vienna-born actress Helene Weigel. She was Jewish, strongly Marxist, and staunchly feminist. They met in 1923, married in 1929, and had a son, Stefan, in 1924, and a daughter, Barbara, in 1930. Weigel's marvelously expressive face and superbly disciplined acting skills caused many theater critics to call her the best actress of her time on the German-speaking stage. Her greatest successes were in the title roles of Brecht's *Die Mutter* (1932; *The Mother*, 1965) and *Mutter Courage und ihre Kinder* (1941; *Mother Courage and Her Children*, 1941).

A central problem for students of Brecht is his adherence to Communism and its effect on his work. Clearly, from youth onward, he revolted against the middle-class values that led Germany to a wasteful war, bitter defeat, extreme socioeconomic disorder in the 1920's, and Adolf Hitler's rise to power in the early 1930's. What drew Brecht to Marxism was largely its antagonism toward Germany's business and military circles. His adherence to Communism remained, nonetheless, consistently idiosyncratic—equally distasteful to the official Soviet cultural apparatus, to the House Committee on Un-American Activities, and to the rigid party-liners who ran East Germany after World War II.

In his best plays, Brecht rises above his mixture of cynicism-cum-Communism. For example, in *Der gute Mensch von Sezuan* (1943; *The Good Woman of Setzuan*, 1948) the heroine, Shen Te, is naturally loving, selfless, and motherly; she finds fulfillment in giving and thrives on sharing her feelings and goods. Unfortunately for her, the world repays her virtues with greed, betrayal, envy, spite and ruthless exploitation. Hence she needs to call, with increasing frequency, on the services of her calculating male "cousin," Shui Ta, who meets the world on its own level of meanness and deception. Shui Ta turns out to be Shen Te masked, the other half of her personality, which she needs to protect her interests, yet also the half that denies Shen Te her essential identity.

When the National Socialists, commonly called Nazis, took over Germany's regime in 1933, Brecht had to flee for his life. In fifteen years of exile, he, his wife, their two children, and always at least one of his mistresses lived in various Central European countries, then in Denmark, Sweden, Finland, and from 1941 to 1947, Southern California's Santa Monica. Remarkably, wherever he was and however scant his circumstances, Brecht continued to produce plays and occasional poems at full pressure. He dragged his ménages after him, ruthlessly exploited the devotion of his intimates, cut his losses, and wrote his most masterful plays in exile: *The Good Woman of Setzuan, Herr Puntila und sein Knecht Matti* (1948; *Mr. Puntila and His Hired Man, Matti,* 1976), *Mother Courage and Her Children,* and *The Caucasian Chalk Circle* (1948).

By and large, the United States failed to impress, let alone inspire, Brecht. He frequented a narrow circle of German and Austrian refugee writers and performers and made only two important friends outside that orbit: The British-born actor Charles Laughton, who collaborated closely with him on a revised version of *Leben des Galilei* (1943; *Life of Galileo,* 1947), and the critic-scholar Eric Bentley, who became the authorized American translator and occasional director of Brecht's works. In October, 1947, Brecht was forced, by way of a subpoena, to testify before the House Committee on Un-American Activities. Accused of having composed Communist poems, he was cleared of pro-Communist charges by the committee. A few days later, Brecht returned permanently to Europe.

Arriving there as a stateless radical, he soon surrounded himself with safeguards: Austrian citizenship, a West German publisher, and a Swiss bank account. Then he accepted the leadership of East Berlin's repertory troupe, the Berliner Ensemble, and fashioned it into possibly the world's finest theatrical company of the late 1940's and 1950's. Brecht supervised a unit of more than 250 actors and supporting staff and directed his own plays in productions rehearsed from three to five months. He became the grand old man of East German culture.

On June 17, 1953, workers in East Berlin demonstrated against increased production norms; Russian tanks quickly quelled the unrest. Brecht thereupon wrote a letter to Walter Ulbricht, first secretary of the East German Communist Party, generally siding with the strikers but also declaring his fundamental loyalty to the Communist regime. Ulbricht published only the sentence expressing Brecht's attachment to the party, thereby causing Brecht to be widely attacked in the West as a burned-out coward of questionable integrity. Increasingly disillusioned with East Germany's course, worn out by the enormous strains to which he was subjected, Brecht died of coronary thrombosis on August 14, 1956, in East Berlin.

Analysis

Brecht's status as Germany's greatest twentieth century playwright is by now securely established. He joins the pantheon of his country's most commanding dramatists, which includes Friedrich Schiller, Heinrich von Kleist, Johann Wolfgang von Goethe, Georg Buechner, and Gerhart Hauptmann. Moreover, he is also a distinguished poet, with an astonishingly wide lyric range spanning folk ballads, Rimbaudesque prose poems, political epistles, and luminously concrete sonnets. Additionally, he is a provocative theorist of drama, whose concept of theatrical presentation has had enormous influence.

To address Brecht's dramaturgy first: He had nothing but contempt for what he called illusionist, bourgeois, Aristotelian theater. He scorned all devices of composition and production that sought to seduce an audience into responding empathically to the events on stage, into identifying with one or more of the characters. He sought to produce the opposite effect, one of estrangement or distancing, which he called *Verfremdung*, the process of alienating. He wanted the audience not to identify strongly with the characters, not to be transported emotionally by the actions on stage. Instead, he wished to initiate contemplation and critical judgment in his spectators, to have them remain aware that they were witnessing "nothing but" a play on whose meaning they were invited to exercise their critical intelligence during the performance rather than after it.

To deliver his audience from what he regarded as the captivity of illusion and bring it to a state of social reform, Brecht rejected many of the hitherto unquestioned criteria of dramatic art. He sought to avoid a firmly coherent and climactic structure in his plays, instead unfolding the action in numerous loosely connected episodes that he termed "epic form." He instructed his actors to remain detached from the personages that they portrayed, instead telling them to play openly to the public in the theater, making their roles commentaries rather than representations. He had brief synopses, often songs, at the beginning of each scene; they were intended to empty the following action of suspense. Instead of eliciting strong emotions to purge the spectators of pity and terror, Brecht sought to stress the unheroic, the grotesque, the farcical, with his characters often speaking in colloquial, and even low, language.

Nonetheless, despite Brecht's intense efforts to achieve distance and estrangement, to make his theater a school for educating the audience to revolutionary acts, he usually succeeded as a dramatist in proportion to his failure as a didactic theoretician. The differences between illusionist and epic theater turn out to be ones of degree rather than direct opposition. After all, in no theater does complete identification of the spectators with the characters occur, or they would rush on stage to save Desdemona from Othello. In no theater can there be complete detachment of the spectators from the drama, or they would doze off or walk out.

Brecht's plays, despite his strenuous efforts to circumvent the emotional response of his audience by the negation of illusion, are charged with the energies of his moral and political passions. They have the effect of enthralling and, at best, deeply moving those who witness them. In his finest dramas, though he wished only to hone his audience to critical keenness, he also moved it to tears and wonder and laughter. Though he sought to shock his audience with sardonic humor and savage indignation, he could not help letting his compassion flood through self-imposed dikes of ferocious cynicism. Though he concentrated on such vices as greed, envy, brutality, and disloyalty in many of his works, he also rose above these pessimistic indictments. In such great achievements as *The Good Woman of Setzuan, Mother Courage and Her*

Children, The Caucasian Chalk Circle, and *Life of Galileo*, he presented immortal images of vulnerability, decency, and sacrifice; he dramatized a world where sold souls do not always stay sold, and where the promptings of humaneness sometimes conquer the dictates of ideology. The disproof of much of Brecht's theorizing, then, came through his art as a playwright—an art that richly gratified the audience's hunger for sympathy, identification, and, thus, illusion.

Brecht is a divided, often enigmatic, writer whose works, for all of their extreme left-wing ideology, remain enticing and elusive. His basic vision of life is harrowing, fascinated by, in his early plays, cruelty, determination, bestiality, irrationalism, blind instinctualism. A hysteria of violence hovers at the margins of his early dramas (as well as poems) an awareness that humankind's will is weak and malleable and that its nature is savage, brutal, and often uncontrollable. Should a character speak of love, loyalty, friendship, honor, progress, or religion, the chances are that he is merely masking a corrupt and greedy deal.

Yet Brecht's works also often have a raffishly humane aspect that charms and beguiles his public. Almost all of his characters find themselves repelled by their base instincts and seek a state of calm beyond the turmoil of their appetites. All of Brecht's later characters, such as Galileo, Courage, Shen Te and Shui Ta, the two Annas in *Die Sieben Todsünden der Kleinbürger* (1933); *The Seven Deadly Sins*, 1961), and Puntila drunk and Puntila sober, are split, vacillating between reason and instinct, the true self and the pseudoself, survival, and self-sacrifice. The mature Brecht often shows human impulses as healthy, kindly, courteous, and loving, while reminding the audience that society is selfishly competitive and ultimately evil.

THE THREEPENNY OPERA

First produced: *Die Dreigroschenoper*, 1928 (first published, 1929; English translation, 1949)
Type of work: Play

This work is a Marxist reinterpretation of John Gay's ballad opera, starring a businessman-gangster.

The Threepenny Opera, written exactly two hundred years after John Gay's *The Beggar's Opera* (1728), follows its model closely in plot and in the names of its characters. Like Brecht's Berlin, Gay's eighteenth century London underwent a period of expansion and consolidation, with a Whig government rotten with corruption. Gay's opera chiefly satirizes the aristocracy's manners and morals, although it also mocks marriage, politics, theatrical conventions, the prison system, and many professions. By providing the highwayman Macheath with the dash of a courtier, and whores with the grace of ladies, Gay indicts the vices of the upper class without needing to bring a single upper-class personage on stage.

Brecht adopts Gay's ironic inversion of high and low life but aims, in place of the no-longer-vital aristocracy, at Germany's triumphant, smug, powerful bourgeoisie. The criminal highwayman Macheath is called "Mac the Knife" (Mackie Messer), and while he is a thief, arsonist, rapist, and murderer, he also has the habits of a middle-class entrepreneur, keeping books, worshiping efficiency, and insisting on business discipline by his gang. His thieves are in competition with big business and the banks; they are defeated by the more predatory, shrewder, better-financed Jonathan Peachum. As he stands before the gallows, in what seems to be his farewell address, Mackie laments that he is a small fish about to be swallowed by a bigger one:

> Ladies and gentlemen. You see before you a declining representative of a declining social group. We lower-middle-class artisans who work with humble jemmies on small shopkeepers' cash registers are being swallowed up by big corporations backed by the banks. What's a jemmy compared with a stock certificate? What's breaking into a bank compared with founding a bank?

In Brecht's cynical, Marxist equation, the petty bourgeois equals the petty larcenist, while the tycoon finds his counterpart in Peachum, who licenses all the beggars in London and forces them to pay him 70 percent of their weekly take. Peachum transforms healthy men into deformed and pitiful creatures through the application of artificial limbs, eye patches, and the like—all carefully calculated to evoke the limited charitable impulses of the rich. Thus, if Mackie exemplifies the relationship between crime and business, Peachum highlights the relationship between the selfish capitalist ethic and the sacrificial morality of Christianity. Both Mackie and Peachum agree, in one of Brecht's most famous statements, that eating comes first, then morality. Brecht suggests that Christianity and capitalism are really in the same ultimately corrupt league.

Brecht's satiric attack on the bourgeoisie extends to its conventions of marriage, romantic love, and male camaraderie. Mac the Knife's wedding to Polly Peachum is a typical middle-class banquet, featuring toasts, gifts, bad jokes, and gorging guests—except that it takes place in a stable and all the furnishings are stolen. Romantic love is reduced to lust and betrayal, with the relationship of Mackie and Jinny Jenny replete with pimping, whoring, sexual disease, and betrayal.

The play's action follows a complicated network of double crosses: Macheath betrays Polly, Lucy Brown, and his gang; the whores betray Macheath twice; Peachum not only informs against Macheath but also sabotages his daughter's chances for romantic bliss; and the plot climaxes with Mackie's betrayal to the authorities by his supposed friend, the high sheriff of London, Tiger Brown. The Brown-Macheath friendship, added by Brecht to Gay's plot, features a Kiplingesque ballad of their army bonding but is actually based on commercial advantage: Mackie gives Brown the goods on other criminals, while Brown, collecting a third of the reward, in turn provides police protection for Macheath.

Brecht sees every individual betrayed by an aggregation of other individuals, as well as by his own nature. Mackie, after all, commits consistent self-betrayals by following his compulsive libido and is brought down by his womanizing.

The Threepenny Opera is a second-rate achievement on Brecht's part: Macheath is too winning a charmer to persuade the audience that he is a reprehensible criminal. More significantly, Brecht's play fails to resolve a fundamental dilemma: Does human evil stem from an evil system (capitalism), or are there fundamental evils in human nature that systems merely reflect? The work's glory is Kurt Weill's brilliant music, which displays a high level of wit and rhythmic vitality. Thanks mainly to Weill, *The Threepenny Opera* is probably Brecht's most frequently mounted play.

MOTHER COURAGE AND HER CHILDREN

First produced: *Mutter Courage und ihre Kinder*, 1941 (first published, 1949; English translation, 1941)

Type of work: Play

Anna Fierling, nicknamed Mother Courage, lives by the war as a small trader but pays her dues by losing all three of her children.

Brecht completed *Mother Courage and Her Children* in November, 1939, with its theme of the harrowing and devastating effects of a European war paralleling the outbreak, in September of that year, of World War II. Its world premiere did not take place until 1941, in Zurich, Switzerland, starring the fine actress Therese Giehse. In 1949, an even finer actress, Brecht's wife Helene Weigel, assumed the central role for what was to be her most celebrated triumph. The work's subtitle, "A Chronicle of the Thirty Years' War," indicates that it deals with the feast of death that bore down on much of Europe from 1618 to 1648, solving no problems, settling no issues.

Having identified business with gangsterism in *The Threepenny Opera*, Brecht now identifies business with war. He seeks to present a relentlessly Marxist indictment of the economic causes of war. In his production notes, he states that the work is designed to demonstrate that "war, which is a continuation of business by other means, makes the human virtues fatal even to their possessors." In the drama's atmosphere of rape, pillage, and meaningless killing, with Protestants and Catholics slaughtering one another for a generation, all human ideals degenerate into hypocritical cant, while heroism shatters into splinters of cruelty, madness, greed, or absurdity. The play is bitterly pacifist, with all the featured characters living off the war yet remaining blind to the penalties that it demands, as most of them pay with their lives.

The play's protagonist, Anna Fierling, is a canteen owner known more familiarly as Mother Courage. Brecht took the name from a picaresque novel, *Lebensbeschreibung der Ertzbetrügerin und Landstörtzerin Courasche* (1670; *Courage: The Adventuress*, 1964), by the German novelist Hans Jakob Christoffel von Grimmelshausen. Whereas Grimmelshausen's heroine is a seductive, hedonistic, childless harlot of illegitimate but aristocratic birth, Brecht's Courage is a salty, opportunistic, self-serving businesswoman, a shameless profiteer who cashes in on the troops' needs for alcohol and clothing; another character calls her "a hyena of the battlefield." Shrewd, sardonic, skeptical, she is a full-blooded personification of her creator's antiheroic view of life.

For twelve scenes, from 1624 to 1636, the reader/spectator follows Anna Fierling's wagon as she makes her living from the war yet believes that she can keep her grown children out of it. Each child is by a different father, each represents one virtue in excess and is consequently killed by it. Swiss Cheese, honest but stupid, is entrusted with the cashbox as paymaster of a Protestant regiment; when he is captured by the Catholics, he refuses to surrender the money and is riddled by eleven bullets. His mother could have saved him, but only at the price of pawning her wagon, on which she and her daughter depend for their livelihood. The mother concludes prolonged bouts of bargaining with the realization, "I believe—I haggled too long."

The other son, Eiliff, is brave—a virtue in wartime, but a liability during an interlude of peace, when he murders innocent peasants who wished only to protect their cattle. He discovers that law and morality are relative, shifting their ground to accommodate society's needs.

Fierling's daughter, Kattrin, mute and disfigured, is the incarnation of kindness, compassion, and love, achieving allegorical grandeur. Yet in this merciless war she is shot down from the wagon's roof by soldiers attempting a surprise attack, as she beats her drum to warn the besieged town and thereby save children's lives. Her grand gesture succeeds, but at the cost of her life. The scene dramatizing Kattrin's heroism has the prolonged excitement and suspense of melodrama, substituting passionate persuasion and spectator empathy for Brecht's satiric dialectic and strategy of distancing.

Courage herself is one of Brecht's most contradictory and perplexing characters. She is in turn admirable and despicable, with more extreme traits than any other of his protagonists. As Eric Bentley has pointed out, she is tough, honest, resilient, courageous, but also cold, cunning, rigid, and cowardly. She concludes business deals in the back room while her children die, yet all of her transactions are undertaken for their sake. Her philosophy is to concede defeat on such large issues as the war itself, while trying to prosper as a small business entrepreneur. Brecht intends her as a vice figure in a morality play but cannot control his affection for her as she transcends his design. He tries to condemn her as a vicious Falstaff, yet his drama stresses her single-minded determination to survive.

While it is true that Courage has haggled while her children die, it is also true that her loss of them is desolately tragic. A pathetic victim of wrong dreams, she must end the play by harnessing herself to her inhuman fourth child—her wagon—to trudge after the troops as the stage begins to turn in an accelerating vortex of crazed misery. Both her smallness and her greatness are memorable in the last scene of this masterpiece.

LIFE OF GALILEO

First produced: *Leben des Galilei*, 1943 (first published, 1955-1956; English
translation, 1947)
Type of work: Play

One of history's greatest scientists exhibits both admirable strengths and de-
plorable weaknesses.

Life of Galileo is the most heavily reworked of Brecht's plays, occupying his interim attention during the last nineteen years of his life. He first wrote it in German
in 1938 while in Denmark, with the great physicist Niels Bohr checking the accuracy of
Brecht's astronomical and physical descriptions. This version was the one produced
in Zurich in 1943. After he had moved to Southern California, Brecht befriended the
actor Charles Laughton, and from 1944 to 1947 they collaborated on a new version in
a unique mixture of mostly German and some English. This new text changes Galileo's character from that of a guileful hero who recants to safeguard his scientific dis-
coveries to a coward who betrays the truth and later castigates himself for having
compromised his scientific calling. The explosion of the first nuclear bombs over Japanese cities strongly affected Brecht's characterization of his protagonist. The Laughton version, starring Laughton in the central role, was produced in Los Angeles and
then in New York in 1947, though with small success. In 1953, Brecht and some members of the Berliner Ensemble created a third version in German, using what they
considered to be the best portions of previous texts. This construction was the one
staged in 1955; it is generally regarded as the standard text.

Life of Galileo is written in chronicle form, with fifteen scenes taking the scientist
from 1609, when he is forty-five, to 1637, when he is seventy-four. In the first scene,
he is a lecturer at the University of Padua, living with his daughter Virginia and
housekeeper, Mrs. Sarti, whose intelligent son, Andrea, becomes his favorite pupil.
Frustrated because he is underpaid, Galileo accepts better conditions at the court of
the Medici in Florence. There his findings tend to prove the heliocentric theories of
Nicolaus Copernicus, while the Church insists on adhering to the earth-centered Ptolemaic cosmology. The Holy Office forbids Galileo to pursue his research, but when
a liberal mathematician becomes the next pope, Galileo resumes his work. His hopes
for the dissemination of his theories are short-lived: He is summoned before the
Inquisition, threatened with torture, and recants his views. For the rest of his life,
Galileo remains the Holy Office's prisoner. When Andrea Sarti visits him in 1637,
however, Galileo gives him the "Discorsi" to smuggle out of Italy, while also bitterly
denouncing himself for his cowardice.

Galileo tells Andrea that, had he resisted the Inquisition, "scientists might have developed something like the physicians' Hippocratic oath, the vow to use their knowl-

edge only for the good of mankind." This unequivocal self-condemnation sharpens the split nature of the great scientist. For Brecht, Galileo is not only a masterly scholar and teacher, an intellectual locksmith picking at rusty incrustations of Ptolemaic tradition, but also a self-indulgent sensualist who loves to gorge himself with food and wine. After his recantation, his disciples are disillusioned with their master. Responds Galileo drily, "Unhappy the land that needs a hero." Such a view echoes Brecht's own sentiments, and his Galileo is in important respects a canny self-portrait. Like Galileo, Brecht employed all of his cunning and compromised with the authorities so that he could persist in his work. Moreover, the Galileo who lashes himself for his failure of nerve may represent Brecht's self-evaluation and self-condemnation. For one brief stage in his foxy life, Brecht may have been seized by the seductive notion of absolutely intransigent morality. It did not last.

Life of Galileo is the subtlest of Brecht's dramas, challenging readers and audiences with its muted, yet constrained, force and its divided focus: It is a play about both the suffocation of free intellectual inquiry and the alleged sociopolitical irresponsibility of purely scientific inquiry. Next to Courage, Galileo is the most complex of Brecht's creations, compassionate to his students yet brutal to his pious daughter, brilliantly charismatic yet also selfishly opportunistic, driven by a Faustian passion for knowledge yet gluttonous for personal comforts. The play is marvelously organic, with each scene serving an indispensable purpose, each character integrated meaningfully into its structure, while the language unites historic accuracy with elegant irony. It is one of the wonders of the modern theater.

THE CAUCASIAN CHALK CIRCLE

First produced: 1948 (first published, 1949)
Type of work: Play

In this mellow morality play, virtue and justice triumph in an otherwise harsh world.

The Caucasian Chalk Circle is Brecht's most cheerful and charming play, offered as a moral lesson with deference to the techniques of both the Oriental and the Elizabethan theater. Its structure is intricate, and more distanced, or epic, than that in any other Brechtian play. Several plots run like as many tracks, all merging at the end.

Plot 1 is set in the Russian province of Georgia, where members of two collective farms meet to resolve a dispute about a tract of land. Plot 2 is a story of flight. The peasant Grusha is forced to flee a Caucasian city as a result of usurpation and revolt. Having saved the abandoned child of the dead governor's wife, she risks her life for her maternal instinct, passing over dangerous bridges, marrying an apparently dying man (who then revives to plague her), and almost sacrificing her lover, Simon, who is returning from the civil war. After two years, a counterrevolt returns the governor's party to power, and the governor's widow claims her estate, which she can only obtain as the mother of the legal heir. Her soldiers find Grusha and the infant and bring them to trial. As the storyteller, who distances the text in epic fashion, sings, "She who had borne him demanded the child./ She who had raised him faced trial./ Who will decide the case?"

The judge is Azdak, one of the finest rogues in dramatic literature. Plot 3 features him as a brilliant Lord of Misrule. Having been appointed magistrate as a consequence of a prank, he used bourgeois, Marxist legal chicanery to pass down antibourgeois, Marxist legal decisions. He is a drunk, lecher, and monumental bribe taker, yet he always manages to arrive at humane and fair decisions, acting according to the spirit of justice while ignoring the letter of the law.

In plot 4, the play's separate actions neatly converge, finding their moment of impact in a marvelous courtroom scene. Azdak awards Grusha the child in a chalk-circle test that enacts the biblical legend with inverse results: The woman who has been a nurturing mother obtains custody over the biological but unfeeling mother; moreover, Azdak divorces Grusha from her husband so that she and Simon can marry. The disputed land is awarded to the fruit growers, who can use it better than its previous, goat-breeding owners.

The play is a parable that poses and resolves a set of basic issues: legal justice versus practical justice, morality versus expediency, reason versus sentiment, and, as stated, the claims of the adoptive mother versus those of the natural mother. Yet the work is singularly lacking in didacticism and offers a wealth of theatrically striking episodes, while the lyrical language of the storyteller's narration is suitably balanced by starkly realistic, earthy idioms.

Summary

Like his greatest characters, Shen Te, Grusha, Azdak, Puntila, Courage, Galileo, Bertolt Brecht is a survivor. He survived fifteen years of exile in the 1930's and 1940's; he survived harrowing stresses of migration, poverty, personal crises, grubby internecine rivalries, the whole bitter pathos of Adolf Hitler's demonic enmity toward culture and Joseph Stalin's betrayal of left-wing idealism. Wherever he was, however sour his circumstances, he managed to produce an impressive volume of distinguished plays, poems, and provocative essays on dramaturgy at full steam. Like his literary/scientific alter ego, Galileo, he employed his sly tenacity to persist in his work.

No theatrical writer since Henrik Ibsen, August Strindberg, and Anton Chekhov has achieved as many masterpieces as Brecht: *The Good Woman of Setzuan, The Caucasian Chalk Circle, Mother Courage and Her Children*, and *Life of Galileo* are assuredly among modernism's dramatic peaks. Bertolt Brecht's only rival as the leading Western playwright of the middle and late twentieth century is Samuel Beckett.

Bibliography

Bentley, Eric. *The Brecht Commentaries: 1943-1980.* New York: Grove Press, 1981.

Demetz, Peter, ed. *Brecht: A Collection of Critical Essays.* Englewood Cliffs, N.J.: Prentice-Hall, 1962.

Esslin, Martin. *Brecht: The Man and His Work.* 1960. Rev. ed. Garden City, N.Y.: Doubleday, 1971.

Gray, Ronald. *Bertolt Brecht.* New York: Grove Press, 1961.

Hayman, Ronald. *Brecht: A Biography.* New York: Oxford University Press, 1983.

Lyons, Charles R. *Bertolt Brecht: The Despair and the Polemic.* Carbondale: Southern Illinois University Press, 1968.

Morley, Michael. *Brecht: A Study.* London: Heinemann, 1977.

Gerhard Brand

CHARLOTTE BRONTË

Born: Thornton, Yorkshire, England
April 21, 1816
Died: Haworth, Yorkshire, England
March 31, 1855

Principal Literary Achievement

In isolated circumstances, Brontë produced *Jane Eyre*, a work that was to have tremendous influence on the Victorian reading public.

Biography

Charlotte Brontë was born in Thornton, England, on April 21, 1816, the third daughter of Maria Branwell Brontë and the Reverend Patrick Brontë. The family rapidly increased to include a son, Branwell, and two more daughters, Emily and Anne. Shortly after moving to the village of Haworth, situated high in the moors of West Yorkshire, the children experienced the first of many tragedies: In September, 1821, their mother died of a lingering illness. To help take care of the children, Maria Branwell's older sister Elizabeth came to live with the family; her strict Methodist ways and somewhat unsympathetic nature were a gloomy influence on the grieving, lonely youngsters.

Finding some sympathy in one another's company was not to provide solace for long. The two oldest Brontë daughters, Maria and Elizabeth, were sent to school, followed soon after by Charlotte and Emily. Weakened by bouts of measles and whooping cough and subjected to the poor diet of the school, Maria and Elizabeth were particularly susceptible to the illnesses that were epidemic at the time. Within months, both had been sent home from school, and by June of 1825, both had died. The younger children remained at home, being schooled by their father and forging the close literary relationships that were to inform their future endeavors.

In June of 1826, Patrick Brontë brought home a set of twelve wooden soldiers as a gift for Branwell. Already accustomed to making up stories in the style of *Blackwood's Magazine*, the children quickly named the soldiers after popular heroes and began to identify with their favorite characters. They created an imaginary land over which they ruled as the four "Genies." The two older children, Charlotte and Branwell, began collaborating on stories about the land of "Angria," about which they wrote every day in minuscule books. From these early productions came Charlotte's desire to be a novelist and Branwell's belief that he would become a great poet in the style of Byron.

In 1831, Brontë again went to school, this time at Roe Head, a happy environment where she made lifelong friends with two other pupils, Ellen Nussey and Mary Taylor. She was fond of her teacher, and she seemed to accept the occupation for which she was being trained, that of governess. By the time she was nineteen, she had been offered the opportunity to teach at Roe Head, thereby earning free schooling for one of her sisters. Her letters from this period indicate her frustration with teaching; her only real pleasure seemed to come from the continued collaboration with Branwell. Yet Brontë suspected that even this satisfaction was temporary after she received a response to a letter that she had written in 1836 to Robert Southey, the poet laureate of England. He was discouraging about a literary career and warned her that she might become unfit for any other work if she spent too much time daydreaming. Brontë seemed to accept this advice, and she left Roe Head vowing to put her fantasy-world behind her.

By 1839, Brontë herself was realizing the dangers of indulging for too long in imaginative escapism. After turning down two marriage proposals from men for whom she was temperamentally unsuited, she began to reject the extravagant romanticism of her imaginary characters and turned to the question of how to support herself. Much of the discretionary income of the Brontë family went to support Branwell's education and desire to become an artist or poet, and Emily seemed emotionally incapable of living away from her home and familiar moors, so Charlotte was determined to find practical employment. She took a position as private governess to a wealthy family but found the situation exhausting and degrading. Her experiences with the Sidgwick family provided much of the material for *Jane Eyre* (1847) but were otherwise unproductive.

Realizing that her education was insufficient to obtain a first-class teaching position, Brontë traveled to Brussels in 1842 to study French at the Pensionnat Heger, a small private school. Her lessons were interrupted by her aunt's death in November of that year, but she made enough progress to be asked to return to the Pensionnat as a teacher in 1843. She soon developed romantic feelings for the master of the school, Clementin Heger. She expressed her passion for him in letters that she wrote after her return to Haworth in 1844, but Heger, married, could not respond. Ironically, her depression over this unrequited love was deepened by the disturbing behavior of Branwell, who left a tutoring job in disgrace after having an affair with his employer's wife. Other aspects of Branwell's behavior—his bragging, his drunken carousing, his experiments with opium—all seemed evidence of the dangerous romanticism inherent in his adolescent aspirations to a poetic life.

Nonetheless, it was in 1844 that Brontë began her most productive period as a writer. With new maturity and seriousness of intent, she wrote her first novel, *The Professor* (1857), which was destined to be rejected by six publishers. Using the pseudonym Currer Bell, she published a collection of poetry with her sisters, *Poems by Currer, Ellis, and Acton Bell* (1846), and then, while Anne and Emily worked on their novels, she produced *Jane Eyre*. This book, extremely popular at the time, was to gain for her the fame that she experienced in later life.

The year 1848 included Brontë's supreme enjoyment at reading good reviews of *Jane Eyre* and the pleasure of making herself known to her London publishers. This public triumph, however, was countered by private tragedy: Branwell, weakened by his intemperate behavior, contracted tuberculosis and rapidly died. Charlotte collapsed emotionally and physically after his death, and, though needing care herself, she began to observe signs of tuberculosis in Emily. Emily refused to discuss her obvious illness or accept medical care. Before the year was over, she, too, had died, and there were suspicions that Anne was infected with the disease as well.

In 1849, Charlotte published *Shirley*, a novel whose main character reflects aspects of Emily Brontë's personality. In an attempt to save Anne's life, Charlotte traveled with her to Scarborough, where the air was deemed healthy for victims of tuberculosis. The effort came too late, and Anne died while visiting the seaside resort. She traveled again to London and met William Makepeace Thackeray, the leading literary figure of the time, and in 1850 she became friends with Elizabeth Gaskell, a significant Victorian novelist who was to become Charlotte's first biographer. Throughout this period of mourning, Charlotte kept writing.

Villette, Brontë's last complete novel, was published in 1853. In 1854, she decided to marry Arthur Bell Nicholls, who worked as her father's curate. After taking a wedding trip to Ireland to meet Nicholls' relatives, she began work on another novel, *Emma*, which was published in *Cornhill Magazine* in 1860 (it is often reprinted in editions of *The Professor*). Brontë found great satisfaction in her marriage to Nicholls, despite having resisted his proposals for years. They seemed destined for a happy future, until she became ill. Already worn out by pregnancy, Brontë took a poorly timed walk on a stormy day, and her condition rapidly worsened. She died in Haworth on March 31, 1855, leaving her husband to see to the long-delayed publication of *The Professor*.

Analysis

Brontë learned her craft from the available literature of the day and through practice. In childhood, she imitated the style of literary magazines and popular fiction while writing stories, plays, and poems with her brother and sisters. In these collaborative productions, she often chose to create the persona of a historical hero—a particular favorite was the Duke of Wellington—and tried to speak in the elevated, stylized language that she imagined was appropriate to such distinguished public figures. The effort, although a considerable amount of imaginative fun, resulted in characters who sounded bombastic and unnatural.

In her mature fiction—four novels and an unfinished fragment of a fifth—Brontë found greater success creating narrators who shared a measure of her life experience. The most autobiographical of her novels, *Jane Eyre* and *Villette*, focus on the private world of women and their restricted choices in male-dominated Victorian society. Narrated by female characters, both *Jane Eyre* and *Villette* make use of the popular nineteenth century motif of the orphaned child who must make his or her own way in an antagonistic world. Brontë also successfully exploited elements of the romance novel and the gothic novel when she constructed her plots. Jane Eyre discovers a madwoman concealed in the attic of her employer's mansion, and Lucy Snowe (the narrator of *Villette*) is frightened by the recurrent appearance of a ghost who haunts her school.

Feminist critics have been extremely interested in Brontë's work because it exposes the limitations placed on women's lives in the nineteenth century. Women of the respectable middle class had very few ways of earning their keep. Marrying, teaching, or serving as secretary-companion to a wealthy woman were nearly the only choices that a moderately educated woman could expect to have. Brontë, though not an outspoken feminist, regretted that women were not encouraged to make the same kinds of contributions as men and were often treated as intellectually inferior. Her characters, male or female, demand respect as individuals and strive to work in conditions where their potential will be fully realized.

Brontë's ideas about nature were shaped by the Romantic poets and her life in the Yorkshire moors. In her novels, cities tend to be places of corruption, where human beings conspire against or neglect one another. Outdoors, there is a purifying element that allows people to approach one another honestly, and natural forces often act to promote correct moral behavior. Brontë makes use of the pathetic fallacy— nature mimicking human feeling—and personifies nature in various ways, most notably when the moon becomes a mother-figure in *Jane Eyre*. Both techniques emphasize Brontë's view that the landscape plays an important role in determining human action.

JANE EYRE

First published: 1847
Type of work: Novel

An orphaned, friendless governess achieves independence and finds contentment in marriage to her former employer.

Jane Eyre appealed to the Victorian reading public on both sides of the Atlantic. Published under a pseudonym, the novel had its London enthusiasts at first speculating about the real author, then marveling at the achievement of a little-known, isolated vicar's daughter from Yorkshire. In America, the plot and narrative technique of *Jane Eyre* were quickly imitated by women writers hoping to capitalize on the novel's popularity. The plot contains many elements to capture and maintain the reader's attention: an abused orphan who rebels successfully against her oppressors, a mystery involving screams in the attic and a burning bed, a marriage stopped at the altar, sensual temptation and moral victory, and the reformation of a good man gone wrong.

The appeal of the book is not dependent solely on a lively plot; Jane Eyre herself is an engaging character. Unwilling to accept others' definitions of her as an unattractive, dependent relation, Jane asserts herself against those who treat her badly. With her unpleasant cousins and oppressive schoolteachers Jane fights for what she thinks is right. She is made to feel that her passionate responses are a character flaw, but the reader is made to see that her rebelliousness is appropriate.

In a book that explores the conflict between individual and society, it is not surprising that there are a number of structural oppositions as well. Jane's worldly cousins, the Reeds, are countered by her intellectual cousins, the Riverses. The tyrannical schoolmaster, Mr. Brocklehurst, is paired with the soothing headmistress, Miss Temple. Most important is the contrast between the two proposals of marriage that Jane receives, and the men who make them: Mr. Rochester recognizes Jane's true character, but he would pamper and oppress her with riches; St. John Rivers respects Jane's intellectual capabilities and self-control, but he would withhold true love and expect Jane to destroy her health doing difficult missionary work in India. Jane is able to resist both of them, because she has developed a healthy sense of self-worth and has risen above the abuse she received as a child. Her emotional independence is matched by an unexpected inheritance, which alleviates Jane's need to work in subservient positions. Thus strengthened, Jane can return to Rochester after his first wife dies. The physical mutilation he has undergone—blinding and loss of an arm—makes him dependent on Jane for more than amusement. In a marriage of mutual respect and support, Jane's self-image can continue to prosper.

VILLETTE

First published: 1853
Type of work: Novel

Orphaned and nearly friendless, a young Englishwoman seeks to earn a living by teaching in a Belgian school.

In *Villette*, Brontë once again tells the story from the point of view of an autobiographical narrator. Unlike Jane Eyre, however, the narrator of *Villette*, Lucy Snowe, is neither entirely reliable nor likable. Her unpleasant nature and habit of withholding information from the reader is responsible for the lack of critical consensus about *Villette*. While some literary scholars see the novel as a well-constructed discourse on the repressive nature of Victorian society, others view it as a disordered representation of a neurotic character. The mixed response to *Villette* was evident in the first reviews it received, and it never achieved the popularity of *Jane Eyre*.

There are marked similarities between *Villette* and *Jane Eyre*: Both narrators are orphans, both teach to earn their livings, and both consider themselves unattractive. In both novels, Brontë drew on her own experience to create a realistic setting; indeed, *Villette* is placed in the same Belgian territory as Brontë's first novel, *The Pro-*

fessor. Yet *Villette* differs from the previous novels in a number of important ways. Formally, the shifting focus, plot coincidences, and length of time that passes between Lucy's narration and the events that she recounts all challenge the conventions of the realistic novel. This departure is particularly evident in the ending, when Lucy Snowe refuses to explain what has happened to her fiancé, Paul Emanuel, and instead tells the reader to imagine that she has been reunited with him and has embarked on a blissful life. The reality, which Lucy condescendingly assumes the reader is too sentimental to accept, is that Paul Emanuel has been drowned in a violent storm at sea.

Lucy Snowe's open ending of her story points to another important difference between *Villette* and earlier Brontë novels: The delineation of the narrator's character is such that she cannot be trusted. Like Jane Eyre, Lucy feels that her inner self is not expressed or evident in her passive, public existence. Unlike Jane, however, she does not rebel against this disjunction; instead, she manipulates it in order to satisfy her voyeuristic impulses. Powerless, Lucy gains perverse pleasure in thinking that she is more observant about others than they are about her. She works at disguising her true character, an effort that fails only with Paul Emanuel, the man whom she eventually comes to love.

Lucy Snowe, named carefully by Brontë to suggest her cold personality and buried life, emphasizes those experiences that support her assertion that fate has deprived her of any kind of happiness. She hastily summarizes her childhood, spent happily with a godmother, and begins a detailed account of her life at the time of her first employment as companion to an old woman who has mourned a dead lover for thirty years. From this melancholy position, Lucy takes a job as teacher to the youngest children in a Belgian girls' school. Strongly biased against Catholics, she finds herself alone in a Catholic country with an imperfect grasp of the language and contempt for the moral corruption that she perceives in her pupils and fellow teachers. Isolated in such a way, it is small wonder that she has an emotional and physical breakdown.

Her illness serves to reunite her with her godmother and former friends, who now live in Villette, and Lucy is tempted to enjoy the life of ease that they offer. Instead, she returns to the company of Madame Beck, the director of the school, who spies on Lucy, and Paul Emanuel, a sarcastic, small man who seems to discern Lucy's true nature. He recognizes her passivity for what it is, a condescending voyeurism, and he stimulates Lucy to bring her true talents to the surface. Under his sometimes savage tutelage, Lucy demonstrates significant intellectual and dramatic capabilities, and she seems less afraid of expressing her feelings. Yet Brontë was not content to write another novel with the conventional happy ending; Paul Emanuel and Lucy never do marry, and Lucy, writing the book near the end of a long life, is careful not to revise her initial self-portrait as someone whom fate has deprived of happiness. What Brontë allows the reader to see, however, is that Lucy's psychological inability to act on her own behalf, her repressed anger at what she calls fate, have partially created her circumstances. At the same time, Lucy has survived with a measure of dignity as the director of her own school. With both financial and emotional independence, Lucy Snowe suggests that there are possibilities for women other than marriage or degrading subservience to an employer.

Summary

Charlotte Brontë's contribution to the Victorian novel was one of character, not one of plot or technical innovation. Her most vivid creation is the autobiographical narrator of *Jane Eyre*, a character who relates her story in an entertaining fashion and establishes that it is personality, rather than wealth or physical appeal, that makes an interesting heroine. By the time she wrote *Villette*, Brontë was more overt in her challenges of literary convention, a tendency that makes that novel more problematic and promising for contemporary literary scholars.

Bibliography

Alexander, Christine. *The Early Writings of Charlotte Brontë*. Oxford, England: Basil Blackwell, 1983.

Eagleton, Terry. *Myths of Power: A Marxist Study of the Brontës*. London: Macmillan, 1975.

Gérin, Winifred. *Charlotte Brontë: The Evolution of Genius*. Oxford, England: Oxford University Press, 1967.

Gilbert, Sandra, and Susan Gubar. *The Madwoman in the Attic*. New Haven, Conn.: Yale University Press, 1979.

Knies, Earl A. *The Art of Charlotte Brontë*. Athens: Ohio University Press, 1969.

Martin, Robert. *The Accents of Persuasion*. New York: W. W. Norton, 1966.

Moglen, Helene. *Charlotte Brontë: The Self Conceived*. New York: W. W. Norton, 1976.

Gweneth A. Dunleavy

EMILY BRONTË

Born: Thornton, Yorkshire, England
July 30, 1818
Died: Haworth, Yorkshire, England
December 19, 1848

Principal Literary Achievement
Known chiefly for her inspiring novel *Wuthering Heights*, Brontë is also recognized for her imaginative poetry.

Biography

Emily Jane Brontë was born on July 30, 1818, in Thornton, Yorkshire, England, the fifth of six children, five of whom were girls. Her father, Patrick Brontë, was an industrious Irish clergyman who accepted a permanent post at St. Michael and All Angels Church when Emily was two years old. Her mother, Maria Branwell, a Cornish merchant's daughter, died shortly after the move to Haworth, after which her devout and capable sister, Elizabeth Branwell, joined the family to care for the Brontë children.

Growing up in the parsonage shaped Brontë's life enormously. She was secluded from all but her family. The few accounts to be had of Brontë's character confirm that she was outwardly reserved, almost incommunicative, but inwardly she experienced a freedom and power of imagination that was anything but reserved. Brontë was attached to few things in her lifetime—her household, the moor, and her own imaginative world—but from these she was inseparable.

Brontë had little formal education. The few times that she left home were injurious to her. In 1824, at the age of six, Brontë and her sister Charlotte followed the two eldest girls, Maria and Elizabeth, to the Clergy Daughters' School at Cowan. Within a year, all had returned, Maria and Elizabeth subsequently dying of typhoid and consumption caused by the harsh conditions experienced at the school (a period later described in Charlotte's novel *Jane Eyre*, 1847). After that, Brontë was tutored at home in her father's study and exposed to a wide variety of literature, including the works of William Shakespeare, John Milton's *Paradise Lost* (1667, 1674), the novels and poetry of Sir Walter Scott, and the works of the Romantic poets, such as William Wordsworth, Percy Bysshe Shelley, and George Gordon, Lord Byron. She also had access to the Border country ballads from Scotland, political journals (*Blackwood's Magazine*), and local tales.

Walker & Boutall ph.sc.

Emily Brontë

from a painting of a family group by Branwell Brontë.

Published by Harper & Brothers, New York.

Brontë's first efforts as a writer began at the age of eleven. Her muse came to her in the form of a wooden toy soldier brought home in a box for her brother, Patrick Branwell. Together, the Brontë children began the ongoing creation of imagined worlds and the adventures of their newfound heroes. Brontë's was the world of "Gondal," an island kingdom in the South Pacific, complete with a history of political struggle and passionate intrigue. Many of her 193 poems originated in this imaginative but highly developed kingdom.

In 1831, Brontë briefly attended Roe Head School, where her sister Charlotte was governess. Intensely homesick, she was soon replaced by her younger sister, Anne. Seven years later, Brontë left home again to teach at Law Hill near Halifax, this time enduring only six months away from home. She left for a final time in 1842 to attend a school in Brussels with Charlotte, as part of their dream to open a school of their own in Haworth. Brontë's faculty for both music and languages proved enormous in Brussels, but she was forced to leave abruptly after a year, when Elizabeth Branwell died. Brontë chose never to return, remaining at Haworth until her death in 1848.

Brontë's poetry was first published in 1845, more than fifteen years after she began writing, and long since the girls had stopped sharing their work. A manuscript of her Gondal poems was discovered by Charlotte, who was delighted and stirred by the unusually bold style of her sister's work. Emily herself stormed at the invasion of her privacy and only gradually was persuaded to contribute the poems to a joint publication of all three sisters' poetry, *Poems by Currer, Ellis, and Acton Bell* (1846). Pseudonyms neutral in gender were used so that the sisters' work could not be judged solely on that basis, and all ties to the world of Gondal were omitted, erasing any possible aspects of childishness from the poems. Only two copies sold, despite the careful preparation and hard work put into the venture. Stimulated, rather than disheartened, by the experience, the three women began writing novels.

Between October of 1845 and June of 1846, Brontë wrote her great, and only, novel, *Wuthering Heights* (1847), a romance that has its roots in the Gondal poetry. Unfortunately, *Wuthering Heights* received attention mainly in connection with Charlotte's novel, *Jane Eyre*, whose simultaneous appearance led to public confusion about the authorship of both novels. Some critics maintained that *Wuthering Heights* was a previous, inferior effort of Currer (Charlotte) Bell, condemning it as rough and brutal next to the more refined and humane *Jane Eyre*.

Brontë did not live to write another novel or see the strength of her one work acknowledged by more than her family and perhaps one critic. In 1848, her brother, Patrick Branwell, who had already succumbed to alcohol and opium, died of consumption. Brontë caught cold at her brother's funeral and never recovered. She died on December 19, 1848, in Haworth, Yorkshire, England.

Analysis

Emily Brontë shared much with the Romantic poets, whose works she had read during childhood. Underlying all of her own poetry and prose is the Romantic ideal of transcendence, the desire to rise above the domain of time and space that encompasses ordinary human experience. Brontë's works are filled with human passion and longing that drive toward this goal. In its emotional turmoil, the love between Heathcliff and Catherine (*Wuthering Heights*) exceeds the boundaries of the mortal world and endures beyond the grave. This lack of established borders between life and death provides much of the excitement in the novel, as characters communicate as ghosts and in dreams through the veil of time, in a setting that simultaneously assumes supernatural qualities.

Brontë's poetry expresses the longing for freedom from the chains of mortality, depicting life as "cold captivity" ("The Caged Bird") and death as liberation of the soul. The subject of one of her most renowned poems, "No Coward Soul Is Mine," is her Romantic desire for a mystical union with the deity, whom Brontë saw as the God both within and without her. In Brontë's poetry, crossing over the lines of the mortal world establishes a resonance, exemplified in "Remembrance," where speakers, events, and audience exist in different realms: for example, in the distant past, in the present, and in the realm beyond death. All Brontë's poetry and prose are highly imaginative, which points to a final means to freedom in her work: the world of imagination, a gift more highly prized by the Romantics than reason.

Another important Romantic element in Brontë's work is nature. Growing up in the stormy northern England countryside, Brontë knew the great potential of the tempestuous moorland weather to communicate the vast range of human emotions. Brontë uses the outer world of nature as a metaphor for human nature, that is, as something heavily symbolic, carrying an equivalence to a person's inner world. There is interplay and even interchange between Brontë's characters and the natural elements. Lockwood's surreal dream of Catherine Earnshaw's ghost on a stormy night is prompted by the wildly knocking branch against the window pane, which becomes a "little, ice-cold hand!" when he reaches for it (*Wuthering Heights*). Heathcliff himself assumes enough aspects of the moor in his brutal, remorseless nature that he becomes inextricable from it. The dynamic role of nature also adds much excitement to the action in the drama, continually energizing the characters.

For all the passionate overflow of Brontë's created worlds, her presentation is highly controlled, giving her work unexpected power and intensity. This aspect of her writing stems not only from the nature of the themes that she explores but even more so from her own skill in delivering the material. The narrative of *Wuthering Heights* is a complex chronological layering, yet Brontë delivers it cleanly and ingenuously, as the narrator is brought under Heathcliff's roof by the storm and, in a single night, brings three names, three dates, and the ghost of Catherine Linton into view. Likewise, Nelly, the housekeeper who relates the tale to Lockwood, quotes the characters directly without encumbering interpretation or embellishment. Brontë's own description is always vivid and striking, with no extra words spent, moving her plot forward at a delightfully exciting pace.

Brontë's poetry exhibits the simplicity and austerity inherent in her style. She uses ordinary, uncomplicated language, direct address, and subtle methods, such as the repetition of single words or alliteration, to create moods and deepen their effects, often achieving a profound lucidity. Even the pauses in her lines work to expand or command a mood: for example, her words to the immortal deity ("No Coward Soul Is Mine") who "Changes, sustains, dissolves, creates, and rears." These singly delivered, sibilant words demand the slow pace of deliberation and awe. Likewise, Brontë constructs her literature from natural materials. As a result, her images endure humbly yet vividly in the memory. The correspondence posited in Brontë's poem "Love and Friendship" between love and the seasonal rose-briar and between the evergreen holly and friendship is simple, yet powerfully effective. A single bluebell ("The Bluebell") that can remedy homesickness for the more passionate "purple heath" of the moor quietly persists in miniature.

Brontë communicates her own fierce independence, as well as her well-known mystical yearning for transcendence, in all of her work, from her young poems of the childhood world of Gondal to the rich harvest of her single novel, *Wuthering Heights*. In all Brontë's work, it is apparent that her attachment to the natural world is always as strong as her desire to transcend it. This enigma of individuality that seeks to go beyond itself was the one that Brontë chose to write from and live through. It is this concern that haunts her poetry and lives unsettled and restless in her novel.

WUTHERING HEIGHTS

First published: 1847
Type of work: Novel

A jilted lover's passion becomes a storm of vengeance in the wild moorland of northern England.

First published in 1847, *Wuthering Heights* is an enduring Gothic romance filled with intrigue and terror. It is set in the northern England countryside, where the weather fluctuates in sudden extremes and where bogs can open underfoot of unsuspecting night venturers. Under this atmospheric dome of brooding unpredictability, Brontë explores the violent and unpredictable elements of human passion. The story revolves around the tempestuous romance between Heathcliff, an orphan who is taken home to Wuthering Heights on impulse, and Catherine Earnshaw, a strong-willed girl whose mother died delivering her and who becomes Heathcliff's close companion.

The setting is central to the novel. Both action and characters can be understood in terms of two households. Wuthering Heights, overtaken by the sinister usurper, Heathcliff, becomes a dark, winter world of precipitous acts that lead to brutality, vengeance, and social alienation. What Wuthering Heights lacks in history, education, and gregariousness is supplied by the more springlike Thrushcross Grange, where the fair-haired Lintons live in the human world of reason, order, and gentleness. Unfortunately, these less passionate mortals are subject to the indifferent forces of nature, dying in childbirth and of consumption too easily. They are subject to Heathcliff's wrath, as well, losing all assets and independence to him.

Brontë uses the element of unpredictability to spur the action in *Wuthering Heights*, which adds excitement and suspense at every turn and enlivens the characters by infusing them with the characteristic storminess of the moorland weather. Seemingly chance events gather like ominous clouds to create the passionate tale of Heathcliff and Catherine. They are brought together by chance and are left to roam the moor together, far from the world of shelter and discipline, when Catherine's father dies, leaving her tyrannical brother, Hindley, in charge. Accident also accounts for Catherine's introduction to the more refined world of Thrushcross Grange, when she is bitten by a watchdog while spying on her cousins, who then rescue her. Even Heathcliff's angry departure and vowed vengeance is the result of eavesdropping, hearing only what he could mistake for rejection, and not Catherine's true feelings for him.

In Heathcliff's character, Brontë explores the great destructive potential of unrestrained passion. In him, human emotion is uncontrollable and deadly. In the ghostly union of Catherine and Heathcliff beyond the grave, however, Brontë suggests the metaphysical nature of love and the potential of passion to project itself beyond the physical realm of existence.

The ending of *Wuthering Heights* depicts Brontë's final answer to the theme of destructive passion—the answer of mercy and forgiveness, which Brontë holds to be the supreme quality in human beings. Hareton, whom Heathcliff once unwittingly saved from death and then forever after abused, forgives his captor for everything. This forgiveness is accompanied by the mercy that Catherine Linton shows Hareton, teaching him to read after years of mocking his ignorance. Together, these acts of grace nullify the deadly effects of their keeper, who dies soon afterward. The passion of winter becomes the compromise of spring; the storm has passed, and life continues in harmony at last.

REMEMBRANCE

First published: 1846
Type of work: Poem

A woman mourns the death of her lover, fifteen years later.

"Remembrance" is one of Brontë's well-known poems, one originally from the world of Gondal that Brontë created with her sister Anne at a young age. This poem is an elegy, a sorrowful lament for the dead. Queen Rosina Alcona speaks directly to her lost love, the emperor Julius Brenzaida, fifteen years after his assassination, in yearning that does not recognize the limits of time and space. Such an emotional state is typical in Brontë's poems, as is the simplicity and earnestness of the lines. The key feature of her style is repetition:

> Cold in the earth—and the deep snow piled above thee!
> Far, far removed, cold in the dreary grave!

Have I forgot, my Only Love, to love thee,
Severed at last by Time's all-severing wave?

Brontë repeats single words, such as "cold," throughout the poem, insisting on their effect, but only subtly. When the repetition occurs in each line ("cold," "far," "love," and "sever"), a resonance is established that expresses the unfilled span of fifteen years through which the speaker's words must travel.

Brontë also uses assonance, the less obvious repetition of vowel sounds, as in the second stanza line, "Over the mountains, on that northern shore." She uses alliteration to unify the speaker's experience of life and death, sorrow and joy, as well. In the sixth stanza, "days of golden dreams" are tied to the "despair [that] was powerless to destroy" by strong consonant alliteration. To further the emotional effect of joy turned to sorrow, "destroy" is rhymed with "joy" in the last line of the stanza.

The pauses that occur at the ends of the lines are unusually long. This effect certainly adds to the resonance and feeling of words that must travel a long way, perhaps never reaching the listener except by the web of quiet persistence that exists in repetition. This is the memorableness of Brontë's poems, that they linger like faint strains of music.

Summary

Emily Brontë is a master at exploring human emotion. In the annals of world literature, her status is unique. Her standing as a major novelist rests on the merits of *Wuthering Heights*; yet no examination of English fiction can afford to ignore it. The book's character and settings are embedded within the heritage of Western culture. Her poetry, infused with the Romantic ideal of transcendence, depicts the soul's desire to travel beyond the limits of time and space in order to find liberation.

The moorland in which she grew up gave her a language of expression that is powerful, as well as beautiful. Charlotte Brontë best expresses the originality and power of Emily's work:

> With time and labour, the crag took human shape; and there it stands, colossal, dark, and frowning, half statue, half rock: in the former sense, terrible and goblin-like; in the latter, almost beautiful, for its colouring of mellow grey, and moorland moss clothes it; and heath, with its blooming bells and balmy fragrance, grows faithfully close to the giant's foot.

Bibliography

Brontë, Emily. *Wuthering Heights: Authoritative Text.* Edited by William M. Sale and Richard J. Dunn. New York: W. W. Norton, 1990.

Duthie, Enid Lowry. *The Brontës and Nature.* New York: St. Martin's Press, 1986.

Frank, Katherine. *A Chainless Soul: A Life of Emily Brontë.* Boston: Houghton Mifflin, 1990.

Gerin, Winifred. *Emily Brontë: A Biography.* Oxford, England: Clarendon Press, 1971.

Knoepflmacher, U. C. *Emily Brontë: Wuthering Heights.* New York: Cambridge University Press, 1989.

Pinion, F. B. *A Brontë Companion: Literary Assessment, Background and Reference.* London: Macmillan, 1975.

Pykett, Lyn. *Emily Brontë.* Savage, Md.: Barnes & Noble Books, 1989.

Winnifrith, Tom J., and Edward Chitham, eds. *Brontë Facts and Brontë Problems.* London: Macmillan, 1983.

Jennifer McLeod

RUPERT BROOKE

Born: Rugby, Warwickshire, England
August 3, 1887
Died: On a ship in the Aegean Sea
April 23, 1915

Principal Literary Achievement

A poet and writer of some prominence before World War I, Brooke wrote war poems, particularly "The Soldier," that captured the patriotic idealism of the generation of young soldiers who died in the early months of that conflict.

Biography

Rupert Chawner Brooke was born in Rugby, England, on August 3, 1887. His father, William Parker Brooke, was an instructor of classics at Rugby School, one of the most prestigious of England's public schools, but it was Mary Ruth Cotterill, Rupert's mother, who dominated the family. Young Brooke, the middle child among three brothers, attended Rugby School, pursuing cricket and football, excelling in English, winning prizes for his poetry, an becoming Head Boy. Many of his contemporaries were attracted to his personality; others noted his tall, blond physique, reminiscent of a young Apollo.

From Rugby, Brooke entered King's College, Cambridge, where, under the influence of more modern writers and intellectuals, he abandoned some of the Decadent *fin de siècle* postures found in his earlier poetry. He also made friends among some of England's most famous political and artistic families: the Asquiths, Darwins, Oliviers, and Stracheys. Freed from the day-to-day influence of his family, he joined the socialist Fabian Society and university dramatic groups; he also began writing for the *Cambridge Review*, a university journal with a national reputation. During his Cambridge years, from 1906 to 1909, he wrote at least sixty poems, about a third of which were printed in his first volume of poetry, *Poems*, in 1911.

Failure to receive a first-class degree and the complications of emotional exhaustion prompted Brooke to leave Cambridge for the small village of Grantchester, just a few miles distant but far enough from the attractions of the university city. His friends and acquaintances congregated around him there, and his time at the Old Vicarage, his principal residence in Grantchester, assumed almost mythic proportions, although he lived there principally for only two years. In addition to his poetry, Brooke became an accomplished literary critic; he particularly admired Robert Browning and

John Donne, and although always opposing free verse, he praised the poetry of Ezra Pound. He also wrote a dissertation on the Elizabethan dramatist John Webster. Virginia Woolf, a friend, noted Brooke's wide literary knowledge and disciplined work habits.

Poems included fifty poems from both his younger years and after his university days. The volume was widely reviewed and well received, considering that it was the author's first book. In early 1912, however, Brooke suffered a breakdown, compounded by both personal and professional considerations. His literary career, his dependency on his changing circle of acquaintances, his relationship with his mother, and his other emotional attachments led him to fear that he was becoming insane. Nevertheless, during this period he wrote one of his most famous poems, "The Old Vicarage, Grantchester." By the end of the year, apparently recovered, he was again engaged in several literary projects.

In 1913, Brooke traveled to Canada, the United States, and the islands of the South Pacific. Initially, his response to the culture of the Western Hemisphere was mainly dismissive, but the California cities of San Francisco and Berkeley pleased him, and his three months in Tahiti led to some of his best love poems. He had also begun working with Edward Marsh on the first of a series of anthologies of modern poets. Known as "Georgian Poetry," the first volume appeared in 1913. Later, the term came to denote a certain artificial vacuousness, but the initial volume included, in addition to Brooke, D. H. Lawrence, John Masefield, Robert Graves, Isaac Rosenberg, and Siegfried Sassoon.

By the time of his return to England in the spring of 1914, Brooke's circle included not only his university friendships at Cambridge and Grantchester but also the major writers and artists of the day. In addition, he was on close terms with the prime minister, Herbert Asquith, and Winston Churchill, first lord of the admiralty. Still young, his future seemed bright as a poet or literary critic, even perchance a politician. On the day after his twenty-seventh birthday, however, Great Britain entered World War I, and Brooke soon sought an officer's commission. During the winter of 1914-1915, he wrote a series of sonnets on the war, published in *1914 and Other Poems* (1915), in which he idealized sacrificing one's life for one's country. Many of his contemporaries had already gone to the Western Front, where thousands were dying in what came to be called "no man's land," and in early 1915 Brooke's Royal Naval Division was ordered to take part in the Dardanelles campaign against Turkey, Germany's ally. In spite of his robust appearance, Brooke's health had always been problematic, and before his unit entered combat he became ill with fever and died on a hospital ship in the Aegean Sea on April 23, 1915, England's St. George's Day. Even before his death, his poem "The Soldier" had been read during services in Westminster Abbey. Churchill wrote of Brooke's death and sacrifice in Brooke's obituary in *The Times* of London. Brooke's apotheosis had begun.

Analysis

Brooke's facility with verse manifested itself early in his youth, and his technical abilities were fully developed before leaving Cambridge. Influenced by Browning's use of common language and ordinary personalities, so unlike the poetry of fellow Victorians Alfred, Lord Tennyson, and William Morris, Brooke freely borrowed from and parodied the style and content not only of Browning and Tennyson but also of A. E. Housman and Algernon Charles Swinburne. He mastered the dramatic sonnet form and wrote numerous poems in what has been called a narrative idyll style. Whatever his form, Brooke chose to write in traditional meter rather than experiment in the free-verse approach of Pound and T. S. Eliot. Brooke's reliance upon such forms is perhaps one reason why his reputation declined among critics, but it also explains in part why he remained popular among general readers.

Brooke's mature literary life was relatively brief. If he early mastered the forms of poetry, the subject matter of his works and the "voice" of his poems evolved from his boyhood days at Rugby and his years at Cambridge until his death while still in his twenties. Although he worked and reworked his material, his willingness to exclude so many of his early efforts from his first published volume of poetry in 1911 suggests that he realized that many of his poems were not of the highest quality. The collected poems form a rather slight volume, and in terms of mere quantity Brooke could be categorized as a minor poet.

Yet critics have also complained that Brooke too often intruded sentimentality and artificiality into many of his poems. In poems such as "Ante Aram," Brooke resorts to archaic diction, convoluted syntax, and vague, romantic description. The resulting language is more Victorian, more Tennysonian, than expected, given Brooke's avowed aim of a new poetry for the new century, and hardly reflects his praise of Browning's use of the common speech of the common people.

One of the most apparent elements throughout Brooke's work is his preoccupation with death, particularly the death of the young. His idealized notion of the sacrificial death appears out of place in the violent historical context of the twentieth century, but it could have resulted from Brooke's youth: Death can hold a morbid fascination for the young, who have no sense of their own mortality. Perhaps he was also influenced by the Decadent writers who interested him while still a schoolboy. Yet the paradigm for this theme may be Brooke's own personality; among his last poems, "The Soldier" can be seen as a culmination of his quest for death.

Brooke's poems also frequently connect death with love. In "Mummia," he describes the ancient Egyptians drinking the dust of mummies to achieve a state of sexual ecstasy. In the same way, he says that the poet has "sucked all lovers of all time/ To rarify ecstasy," citing famous lovers such as Helen, Juliet, and Cleopatra, whose tragic lives immortalized their passion. This romantic vision of death as the culmination of love contrasts with poems such as "The Funeral of Youth: Threnody," where Brooke tells in allegorical fashion the sad lament of those friends of Youth who came to his burial. He includes among these such figures as Laughter, Pride, Joy, Lust, Folly, Grief, Sorrow, Wisdom, Passion, and others who met again at Youth's funeral, "All except only Love. Love had died long ago." Death, in this poem, brings the loss of love, rather than its ultimate fulfillment. At other times, death results in the transmutation of love into a kind of Platonic ideal, as in "Tiare Tahiti," written during his travels in the South Pacific. He notes that, after death,

> Instead of lovers, Love shall be;
> For hearts, Immutability;
> And there, on the Ideal Reef,
> Thunders the Everlasting Sea!

Brooke, however, was not always the youthful romanticist or idealist ruminating about death and love. Like Browning, he could also be very much the realist, sometimes punctuating this realism with humor and irony, too much so for some of his contemporaries. Both his publisher and Edward Marsh, his close friend and adviser, objected to the inclusion of two of his sonnets in his first book of poems. In "Libido," where Brooke writes of sexual conquest, not romantic love, the phrase "your remembered smell most agony" was felt by Marsh and others to be in bad taste. In "A Channel Passage," the narrator tries to remember his lover in order to avoid becoming physically sick while crossing the English Channel.

Finally, if critics have often rightly criticized Brooke for idealizing the sacrificial death of youth, he could also write of the end of youthful idealism brought about by age. In a reference to Homer's tale of the Trojan Wars, Brooke shows, in "Menelaus and Helen," husband and wife at the end of their lives:

> Often he wonders why on earth he went
>   Troyward, or why poor Paris ever came.
> Oft she weeps, gummy-eyed and impotent;
>   Her dry shanks twist at Paris' mumbled name.
> So Menelaus nagged; and Helen cried;
> And Paris slept on by Scamander side.

Brooke never reached the age of Helen and Menelaus, dying, at age twenty-seven, to be immortalized like Achilles or the young Apollo whom so many believed that he resembled.

THE OLD VICARAGE, GRANTCHESTER

First published: 1912
Type of work: Poem

The poem records the exiled poet's reflections and remembrances of his home in England.

"The Old Vicarage, Grantchester" was written by Brooke while in Berlin in 1912. Initially titled "Home" and then "The Sentimental Exile," the author eventually chose the name of his occasional residence not far outside Cambridge. One of Brooke's most famous poems, its references can be overly obscure because of the many specific Cambridge locations and English traditions to which the poem refers. Some have seen it as sentimentally nostalgic, which it is, while others have recognized its satiric and sometimes cruel humor.

Using octosyllabics—a meter often favored by Brooke—the author writes of Grantchester and other nearby villages in what has been called a seriocomic style. It is very much a poem of "place," the place where Brooke composed the work, Berlin, and the contrast of that German world ("Here am I, sweating, sick, and hot") with his home in England. Yet it is more than just the longing of an exile for his home, nostalgically imagined. The landscape of Cambridgeshire is reproduced in the poem, but Brooke, the academic, populates this English world with allusions and references from history and myth. He compares the countryside to a kind of Greek Arcadia, home to nymphs and fauns, and refers to such famous literary figures as George Gordon, Lord Byron, Geoffrey Chaucer, and Tennyson. Homesick for England, a land "Where men with Splendid Hearts may go," it is Grantchester, in particular, that he desires.

If the poem is nostalgic and sentimental, however, it is also satiric in its treatment of the Cambridgeshire landscape. In wishing to be in Grantchester, Brooke compares its virtues with those of other nearby towns and villages. In a series of wry couplets, Brooke pokes sly fun at the inhabitants of neighboring villages, whom he contrasts with those in Grantchester. The people of Cambridge are said to be "urban, squat, and packed with guile," while oaths—or worse—are flung at visitors to Over and Trumpington. He complains that "Ditton girls are mean and dirty,/ And there's none in Harston under thirty," but Grantchester is described as a place of "peace and holy quiet." Even the residents of Grantchester, however, are not immune to Brooke's teasing; in a line that is perhaps only half in jest, given his own bouts of depression, he adds that "when they get to feeling old,/ They up and shoot themselves, I'm told."

Yet there is also a seriousness in the poem underneath its comedic elements. In his conclusion, Brooke asks a series of rhetorical questions:

> Say, is there Beauty yet to find?
> And Certainty? and Quiet kind?
> Deep meadows yet, for to forget
> The lies, and truths, and pain? . . . oh! yet
> Stands the Church clock at ten to three?
> And is there honey still for tea?

The poet longs for the remembered, if imagined, permanence of Grantchester, but he also sadly and whimsically recognizes even its ultimate impermanence and transience. Written only two years before the outbreak of World War I, the poem foreshadows the world that will be forever lost as a result of that conflict.

THE SOLDIER

First published: 1915
Type of work: Poem

Envisioning the narrator's probable death in war, the poem reflects his idealism and patriotic self-sacrifice.

"The Soldier" was one of five sonnets that Brooke composed shortly after the beginning of World War I and published in 1915 with the title *1914 and Other Poems.* Written in two stanzas, an octet of eight lines and a sestet of six lines, it is by far his most famous poem, expressing the idealism common throughout the nations of Europe as they eagerly marched to battle in 1914 and felt by Brooke before his own death in April, 1915.

The well-known opening lines represented this romantic notion of consecration through sacrifice by showing the speaker's transformation after death: "there's some corner of a foreign field/ That is for ever England." In retrospect, to others the poem came to epitomize the misguided and self-satisfied naïvete that died in the trenches of "no man's land." The real war of ugly and often futile death was captured not in Brooke's work but in the poems by his English contemporaries, such as Wilfred Owen's "Dulce et Decorum Est."

Yet "The Soldier" is more an elegy of sacrifice than a poem about modern war. It is true that Brooke died before going into battle, but his friendships with English statesman Winston Churchill and other high-ranking politicians had given him knowledge about the destructiveness that industry and technology would bring to the battlefield. There is nothing of that kind of war in the poem. There is also nothing about the reality of dying; the first-person narrator ignores the stench of corpses on the battlefield, instead envisioning a death that transfigures him into an idealized world.

This is not simply any world, however, for "The Soldier" is a poem about Brooke's feelings for England, particularly the rural English countryside of Cambridgeshire. His burial place, though in some foreign land, will become a part of England, but not the England of cities and factories. It was the landscape of natural England that made and formed the poet, and he waxes lyrical about the beauties of English flowers, rivers, and sunshine, elements that have formed him in his youth.

Brooke believed that his England was worthy of sacrifice. This patriotic element in "The Soldier" reflects the strong strain of nationalism existing throughout Western civilization in the late nineteenth and early twentieth centuries. As traditional religion had become more personal and individual, nationalism and patriotism had become the religion of the public community, and "The Soldier" reflects those passions. In the second stanza, Brooke refers to "the eternal mind," a Platonic reference, where the dust of the narrator had become a mere "pulse," but a pulse that

Gives somewhere back the thoughts by England given;
.Her sights and sounds; dreams happy as her day;
And laughter, learnt of friends; and gentleness,
In hearts at peace, under an English heaven.

Brooke's soldier—as Brooke himself—was eagerly willing to sacrifice everything, even his life, for the Eden of England. It struck a strong chord in the early days of World War I. By the end of the war in 1918, with ten million dead, other poets were striking other chords, less idealistic, less self-sacrificing, and less patriotic.

Summary

Unfortunately, perhaps, Rupert Brooke is remembered primarily for one poem, "The Soldier," a poem that most critics agree was not among his finest accomplishments. His patriotic elegy to sacrifice, coinciding with his youthful death, turned Brooke into a monument to youth, to idealism, to a past that no longer existed after the Great War was over. Brooke saw himself and his poetry as a progressive step beyond that of his Victorian predecessors. Paradoxically, he now too often seems part of a world of rural innocence that has long since disappeared. If Brooke had lived, it is impossible to say that he would have become a major poet, but his early death obscured his legacy of poetic realism, irony, humor, intelligence, and passion, which is also found in his writings.

Bibliography

Delany, Robert. *The Neo-Pagans*. London: Macmillan, 1987.

Hassall, Christopher. *Rupert Brooke: A Biography*. London: Faber & Faber, 1964.

Lehmann, John. *Rupert Brooke: His Life and His Legend*. London: Weidenfeld & Nicolson, 1980.

Marsh, Edward. *Rupert Brooke: A Memoir*. London: Sidgwick & Jackson, 1918.

Pearsall, Robert Brainard. *Rupert Brooke: The Man and the Poet*. Amsterdam: Rodopi, 1974.

Ross, Robert H. *The Georgian Revolt*. Carbondale: Southern Illinois University Press, 1965.

Eugene S. Larson

ELIZABETH BARRETT BROWNING

Born: Durham, England
March 6, 1806
Died: Florence, Italy
June 29, 1861

Principal Literary Achievement

As a nineteenth century English poet, Barrett Browning is recognized as a major literary artist and is considered an originator of a feminine poetic tradition.

Biography

Elizabeth Barrett was born on March 6, 1806, the eldest child of Mary Graham Clark and Edward Barrett Moulton-Barrett. She spent her childhood at Hope End, an estate owned by her parents, located in Herefordshire, England. She was a bright, intelligent child who grew up with the advantages of living in an upper-middle-class family, advantages made possible by her father's plantations in Jamaica. According to an essay she wrote when she was fourteen, she claims to have wanted to be a poet from the age of four. Poetry remained her lifelong ambition.

Elizabeth's early life revolved around her family. Her mother was a submissive Victorian wife dedicated to her husband and children. She encouraged Elizabeth by copying and saving her daughter's early attempts at writing. Her father was a man with a tyrannical nature who imposed his will on the family. At the age of eight, Elizabeth wrote two birthday odes, one to her mother and one to her father. She portrayed women as loving and kind, but without power, and men as powerful and God-like. Although she remained devoted to her parents, neither parent served as a model for an aspiring female poet. She had to look elsewhere for the inspiration that she required to reach her goal.

Barrett found three main sources of encouragement through her commitment to reading and studying: the Romantic poets, especially Lord Byron, the radical feminist writings of Mary Shelley, and Greek language and literature. Her success in teaching herself the Greek language was one of the most extraordinary accomplishments of her early years. Since Victorian girls were not sent to school, all Barrett's knowledge was gained by self-study and her desire to learn. The two subjects to which she

263

committed herself were poetry and Greek, although she taught herself other subjects, including Latin. Through her efforts, she became an acknowledged expert in her favorite subjects. Her first major poem, *The Battle of Marathon* (privately published by her father in 1820), written at the age of fourteen, is modeled after the Greek Homeric epic poem form. Its subject is an early Greek battle.

At fifteen, Barrett and two of her sisters became ill. It was feared that Elizabeth would die. She was sent to Gloucester for medical treatment and remained there for a year. She did not fully recover. The cause of her illness has never been determined. For many years, it was believed to be an emotional rather than a physical disorder, although it has been suggested that she suffered from tuberculosis. Her family blamed a fall from a horse, which injured her back. Whatever the cause, she became an invalid and a recluse. More than ever, her life was restricted to her family circle and to the books that she loved. She devoted herself to writing.

In 1826, Barrett published her first serious book of poetry, *An Essay on Mind, with Other Poems* (1826). Although published anonymously, it marked her first attempt to address a larger audience. The book also resulted in two important friendships. In response to *An Essay on Mind, with Other Poems*, she received a letter from Uvedale Price, an eighty-year-old man who asked her to review the proofs of his book on ancient Greek pronunciation. He praised her poems and approved of her latest work, "The Development of Genius," a poem to which her father objected and which she did not finish. Price encouraged her and provided the support that she needed to overcome her father's displeasure. Hugh Stuart Boyd, a blind classical scholar, also sent her a letter of praise. She began spending her time reading Greek to him, and he helped her to continue her study of the language and literature.

The years 1828 thru 1832 were marked by setbacks in Barrett's personal life and a curbing of her literary production. In 1828, her mother died. Price died the following year. In 1832, her father had to sell his Hope End estate due to losses experienced in his Jamaican plantations. The family began a series of moves to various rented houses, ending in Wimpole Street, London, in 1838. With her mother's death and the loss of her friendships with Price and Boyd, Barrett became even more reclusive. In 1833, she published *Prometheus Bound, Translated from the Greek of Aeschylus: And Miscellaneous Poems* (1833). With the publication of *The Seraphim and Other Poems* (1838), she finally achieved critical and popular acclaim. The reviewers found the poems intelligent and learned. Her ballads were particularly popular. It was this book that established her reputation in America.

In 1844, she published *Poems, by Elizabeth Barrett Barrett.* The four years that Barrett spent writing the poems were filled with sickness and sorrow. She had contracted a disease of the lungs and was forced to lived in Torquay, France, because of its milder climate. In 1840, her brother Sam died from a fever, and her favorite brother, Edward, died in a sailing accident in the bay of Torquay. Her father believed that his eldest son's death was caused by Elizabeth, since he had been visiting her. She suffered intense grief, sorrow, and guilt. In 1841, she returned to Wimpole Street, where she retreated to her room to live the life of an absolute recluse. She refused to see anyone. Her doctors advised her not to change her clothes, so she continually wore a black dress, silk in the summer, velvet in the winter. During this period, she wrote the poems that established her as one of the major poets of her time.

Perhaps even more important than the acclaim that she achieved with the publication of *Poems, by Elizabeth Barrett Barrett* was a letter of admiration that she received from a fellow poet. In January, 1845, Robert Browning wrote Elizabeth, "I love your verse with all my heart . . . and I love you too" (*The Letters of Robert Browning and Elizabeth Barrett Barrett*, published in 1899). This letter was the beginning of one of the most romantic love stories of all time. They continued to correspond until May, when he came to visit her. They were secretly married in September, 1846, and left England to establish their home in Italy.

Their marriage was a happy one. They influenced each other's poetry. Elizabeth Barrett Browning's *Poems* (1850), which includes *Sonnets from the Portuguese*, is a sonnet sequence of forty-four poems representing their relationship. During her married years, she continued writing poetry, including her epic poem of feminine struggle *Aurora Leigh* (1856). In 1849, at the age of forty-three, she bore her only child, Robert Weidemann. Elizabeth Barrett Browning died from a lung disorder, probably tuberculosis, in Florence, Italy, on June 29, 1861.

Analysis

Elizabeth Barrett Browning is a poet remembered for all the wrong reasons. Reclusive for most of her life, publicity shy, extremely reserved, she is primarily known today as the heroine of an unbelievably romantic and public love story, *The Barretts of Wimpole Street* (a book, and a 1934 film and its 1957 remake, have been released under that title). A serious poet aspiring to her own place in Western poetic tradition, she is regarded as the conventional love poet of *Sonnets from the Portuguese* who celebrates the power of conjugal love and monogamous marriage. As an advocate for women's rights, she is seen as a mere appendage of her more famous husband. Politically conservative, born into aristocracy, and appalled by what she considered the inhumanity of modern industrial society, she has been viewed as a spokeswoman for radical political upheaval. Finally, though a woman who believed in the natural superiority of men, Barrett Browning is admired as an early proponent of equal rights for women.

These discrepancies between the person, the poetry, and the reputation are not merely the result of confusion or ignorance. Barrett Browning is an extremely difficult author, whose work is complex, experimental, and individual. Her use of poetic form to subvert poetic expectation and tradition makes her work interesting and significant but requires reflective readers and critical examination if it is to be understood. The study of her work is important for an understanding of the time in which she wrote and for her poetic achievement.

Barrett Browning was an extremely prolific author who began writing prose and poetry as a child and continued actively writing until she died at the age of fifty-five. She demonstrates a serious concern for the world around her, an unflinching ability to analyze her own feelings and motivation, a love of language, a desire to experiment and create a new poetry, and a conception of poetry as a moral force in the affairs of men and women.

Barrett Browning is also one of the first major poets to articulate the themes and concerns of Victorian England and the developing industrial world. The value of work, the awareness of alienation and human isolation, the loss of conventional religious faith, the conflict between religion and science, the function of art, the ambiguous relationship between society and nature, the conflict between free will and fate, the relationship between men and women, and the place and value of culture are subjects that absorbed Victorian writers and intellectuals. These themes are found throughout Barrett Browning's poetry. She anticipates the emptiness and feelings of alienation expressed by Matthew Arnold, writes medieval ballads and experiments with epic and sonnet forms, as did Alfred, Lord Tennyson, and Dante Gabriel Rossetti, uses dramatic monologues much like Robert Browning, and addresses the political and social issues of her time, as did many of her male contemporaries. Yet she is an original, innovative poet who presents her own well-considered, informed views in a highly developed, artistic form.

Barrett Browning's most lasting contribution to poetry and literature is her imaginative adoption of traditional poetic forms to new subject matter, her struggle and final success in establishing the female voice as a poetic possibility, her belief in poetry as a moral agent in the affairs of men and women, and her persistency in the belief that life has meaning and purpose. Poems such as "Rhyme of the Duchess May," "Lady Geraldine's Courtship," and "Bertha in the Lane" extend the ballad form to include the ambivalent position of women rather than the traditional subject of masculine heroism. *The Cry of the Children* (1844), "Crowned and Buried," and "The Runaway Slave at Pilgrim's Point" address the controversial topics of child labor, Napoleon's return from exile, and slavery. They extend the province of poetry to contemporary political issues. In *Sonnets from the Portuguese*, she not only adopts a form previously reserved for the male expression of love but also creates one of the most accomplished and beautiful sonnet sequences in the English language. Finally, in *Aurora Leigh*, she creates a successful epic poem about the struggle of a woman to achieve a life of her own on equal terms with society and men.

Barrett Browning believed that a poet was an important moral influence in the world. Accepting the Romantic vision of the poet as prophet, she appropriated the vision and resolved restoration of values destroyed by the marketplace. She saw the underside of an industrial society in the prevalence of ignorance, crime, prostitution, and exhaustion. For Barrett Browning, the poet served as the link between the everyday values of commonplace life and the possibility of transcendent consciousness. In the materialistic world of Victorian England and the modern industrial world, she believed that there was a desperate need for a contemporary prophet-poet to restore the values preempted by the factories and the mines. Humanity required a poet who would embrace the joy and pain of human existence and confront the conditions and reality of the world. Barrett Browning saw herself as the prophet-poet in a debased, lost, industrial world, crying, like the children in her poem *The Cry of the Children*, for hope and compassion.

THE CRY OF THE CHILDREN

First published: 1844
Type of work: Poem

The plight of Victorian children working in a factory is exposed by their lament of the drudgery and hopelessness of their lives.

The Cry of the Children is representative not only of Barrett Browning's political poetry but also of her work in general. It contains themes and images that can be found throughout her work. The use of language, meter, and rhyme in the poem demonstrates her innovative poetics and singular style.

It is problematic that Barrett Browning actually heard the cry of the children whom she so eloquently laments in her poem. She wrote *The Cry of the Children* after reading a report on the employment of children in mines and manufactories. A master of language, she evokes its emotional power to engender a response of outrage in her readers. The poem is intentionally didactic, political in purpose, as well as subject matter. It is an expression of her own alienation and abhorrence of industrial society seen through the eyes and feelings of factory children, represented as innocence betrayed and used by political and economic interests for selfish purposes.

Throughout the poem, demonic images of a Factory Hell are contrasted with the Heaven of the English countryside, the inferno of industrialism with the bliss of a land-based society. The children are implored to leave the mine and city for the serenity of meadow and country. The grinding, droning mechanism of industrial society destroys the promise and hope of human life. Barrett Browning was concerned with the fate of a society that exploited human life for profit, and she ends her poem with an indictment of industrial society.

The reader is made to experience the dreariness of the factory inferno by Barrett Browning's use of language, as she describes the harrowing reality of the "droning, turning" factory wheels, relentlessly grinding the children's spirit and life as it molds its goods. The factory is depicted as a perversion of nature, a literal Hell seen as the absence and corruption of the natural world. Instead of the world revolving around the sun, the sky turns—as the wheels, similarly, turn. Barrett Browning's use of words ending in "ing" and containing long vowel sounds—"moaning," "droning," "turning," "burning"—invokes the monotony and despair of this awful abyss of industry.

The "Children" of the poem are silenced by the sound of the wheels turning, seek the silence of death as their only means of escape, and, finally, are reduced to a mere "sob in the silence" in a vain effort to curse. The struggle to speak is a constant theme in the poem, a motif that vies with the oppression of the factory and the plight of the children. The repetition of the phrase, "say the children" makes it a key element in the very structure of the poem. Words of speech and silence are used throughout—"hear," "ask," "listen," "sing," "answer," "quiet," "silent," "still," "words," "speechless," "preach," "stifle." The hopelessness of the children's plight is partially caused by their inability to be heard or to express themselves. They are oppressed and exploited because they are not authorized to speak. In the end, even God is unable to hear their feeble attempts at prayer.

SONNETS FROM THE PORTUGUESE

First published: 1850
Type of work: Poems

This sequence contains forty-four sonnets written in the Petrarchan sonnet form and treating romantic love in a long poem from a woman's perspective.

Sonnets from the Portuguese is Barrett Browning's most enduring and popular poem, although it has been undervalued by critics. The sequence of sonnets was new and experimental when it was written. It adopted a poetic form and subject matter reserved for the expression of male amatory experience and depicted modern life and domestic events in a traditionally high literary form used to express the pursuit of ideal love and the poet's failure to translate it into the actual world. Instead, Barrett Browning replaced the male poetic voice with her own and related the feelings that she experienced during Robert Browning's courtship. The sonnets bring together the voice of a woman and the voice of the poet and make them one. They not only relate a courtship between a man and a woman but also relate the transformation of a woman into a poet. They authorize the woman to be a poet and ponder the problem of being both the object and the subject of love and poetic thought.

For a full understanding of the poems, it must be remembered that they are a sequence that forms a complete work describing a process that ends with achieved love and realized poetic power. Helen Cooper, in *Elizabeth Barrett Browning: Woman and Artist* (1988), divides the poems into three groups: woman seen as the object of a man's desire and love (Sonnets 1 and 2), the woman struggling to free herself from being objectified and maintaining her own subjectivity (Sonnets 3 thru 40), and the woman achieving her own subjectivity while accepting the man's love (Sonnets 41 thru 44). This grouping reveals the two themes addressed in the sonnets: the development of a mature love based on mutual respect and the quest of the poet-artist for her own voice and authority.

Barrett Browning wrote the sonnets to record her feelings during her courtship. At the time, she was living in her father's house and subject to his will. He had forbidden any of his children to marry, and, as a dutiful daughter, Elizabeth obeyed him until she married Robert at the age of forty. The sonnets are an honest portrayal of her struggle with the prospect of love and marriage, which were not easily accepted by her because of age and her father's demands. Many critics in her own time and later consider the poems too personal. They view them as a form of private love letters that should not have been published. In large part, their popularity is due to Barrett Browning's lack of pretense and sincere expression of her own experiences of love. Many readers have shared these experiences with her and find joy in their poetic expression. Although the emotions in the sonnets validate their sincerity, and though they are based on her own courtship, these considerations hide the true achievement that she accomplished in writing the sonnets. They are complex, crafted, artistic poems, written in a difficult form, employing original conceits and metaphors. They are not the simple emotional writings of a woman in love but the realized work of an accomplished poet performing at the height of her powers.

Summary

Elizabeth Barrett Browning is a preeminent poet of the nineteenth century whose work belongs in the mainstream of Western poetic tradition. Her work is more significant and influential than is generally accepted. She is a pivotal writer in the transition from a Romantic to a modern sensibility, appropriating the outlook and perspective of her precursors, adapting them to her own time and situation, and preserving them for the future. Not only is she the first poet in a tradition of female poets, but she has also earned her place in the larger tradition of English poetry, which includes men and women.

Bibliography

Besier, Rudolf. *The Barretts of Wimpole Street: A Comedy in Five Acts.* Boston: Little, Brown, 1930.

Cooper, Helen. *Elizabeth Barrett Browning: Woman and Artist.* Chapel Hill: University of North Carolina Press, 1988.

David, Deirdre. *Intellectual Women and Victorian Patriarchy.* Ithaca, N.Y.: Cornell University Press, 1987.

Gilbert, Sandra M., and Susan Gubar. *The Madwoman in the Attic.* New Haven, Conn.: Yale University Press, 1984.

Leighton, Angela. *Elizabeth Barrett Browning.* Edited by Sue Roe. Bloomington: Indiana University Press, 1986.

Lupton, Mary Jane. *Elizabeth Barrett Browning.* Long Island: Feminist Press, 1972.

Mander, Rosalie. *Mrs. Browning: The Story of Elizabeth Barrett.* London: Weidenfeld & Nicolson, 1980.

Mermin, Dorothy. *Elizabeth Barrett Browning: The Origins of a New Poetry.* Chicago: University of Chicago Press, 1989.

Radley, Virginia I. *Elizabeth Barrett Browning.* Boston: Twayne, 1972.

Taplin, Gardner B. *The Life of Elizabeth Barrett Browning.* New Haven, Conn.: Yale University Press, 1957.

Herbert Northcote

ROBERT BROWNING

Born: Camberwell, England
May 7, 1812
Died: Venice, Italy
December 12, 1889

Principal Literary Achievement

Widely recognized as one of the two greatest poets of Victorian England (with Alfred, Lord Tennyson), Browning produced some of the best dramatic poetry of all time and influenced modern poets.

Biography

Robert Browning was born on May 7, 1812, in Camberwell, a suburb of London, England, to Robert and Sara Anna Wiedemann Browning. His father was a senior clerk in the Bank of England and a conservative, unambitious, bookish man closer in temperament to a scholar than to a businessman. His mother, a Scottish gentlewoman, reared her son to love the Church, music, gardening, and nature. Growing up in the urban middle class, Browning had one sister, to whom he paid a lifelong devotion. From 1820 to 1826, he attended a boarding school. In 1828, he enrolled in the recently opened University of London, but he withdrew after only a few months. His main education came from tutors and his father's ample library.

In the view of many, Browning's young adulthood was an essentially irresponsible time, as he preferred to stay at home rather than work or attend school. At home, he read Alexander Pope's *The "Iliad" of Homer* (1715-1720), the romantic poets in general, and a favorite who became his idol, the poet Percy Bysshe Shelley. Around 1824, Browning wrote "Incondita," a volume of poetry in imitation of Lord Byron. When his parents could not get the manuscript published, he destroyed it. Only two poems from this collection have survived.

Thus, Browning's occupation became that of poet. His whole family seemed to indulge him. When his first poem, *Pauline*, finally appeared in 1833, his aunt paid for its publication. Anonymously printed, the poem received little notice, and no record can be obtained proving that it sold a single copy. In fact, most critics view *Pauline* as a typical Romantic poem characterized by excessive self-indulgence.

During the next few years, Browning journeyed to Russia (1834) and produced two long poems—*Paracelsus* (1835), set in the Renaissance, and *Sordello* (1840), set in medieval Italy. Although both poems were critical failures, taken together with his

272

trip they indicate that Browning was learning to move beyond himself, to develop aesthetic distance from his subject.

From 1837 to 1847, Browning turned to playwriting. Determined to make a career change to dramatist and inspired by actor-manager William Charles Macready, Browning threw himself into his ambition. In 1837, *Strafford* was performed for five nights before closing, and in 1846 *Luria* appeared. None of his plays made money, and he finally abandoned the theater. That is not to say, however, that the period was wasted. During that time, William Shakespeare replaced Shelley as Browning's literary guiding light, and Browning mastered some of the basic dramatic techniques that later made his poetry great.

In 1841, concurrent with his outpouring of drama, Browning began writing a series of eight "shilling" pamphlets. Titled *Bells and Pomegranates* (1841-1846; includes *Dramatic Lyrics*, 1842, and *Dramatic Romances and Lyrics*, 1845) after the hem of a Hebrew high priest's garment, all were issued at his father's expense. Originally intending to make each pamphlet a play, Browning had such faith in his newly acquired dramatic ability that he included a few poems. *Pippa Passes* (1841), the first of these poems, eventually became very popular. The poem, complete with monologues and scenes, tells the tale of a factory girl's yearly holiday and her song, which influences others into action and morality.

The strength of the ensuing poems was the dramatic monologue, a form that Browning did not invent but that he did perfect by adding a psychological dimension. *Dramatic Lyrics* contains his first real successes in this format, with such notable poems as "My Last Duchess," "Porphyria's Lover," and "Soliloquy of the Spanish Cloister." *Dramatic Romances and Lyrics* delivered "The Bishop Orders His Tomb at Saint Praxed's Church." Although few of these volumes sold well immediately, critics and a segment of the public began to appreciate his psychological insights into people and his grasp of historical periods. Influenced, too, by John Donne, Browning had achieved objectivity, ridding himself of his indulgent Romantic angst.

The most famous portion of Browning's life also occurred during this period, and it was directly occasioned by his new type of poetry. One person expressing admiration for his talents was the famed English poet and invalid Elizabeth Barrett. Thus began one of the great factual love stories in Western culture. Her father, dedicated to keeping his children unmarried, dominated her, using her poor health to make her into a recluse. In January of 1845, Browning began to correspond with her. Elizabeth expressed herself and her growing love for Browning poetically in *Sonnets from the Portuguese*, published in *Poems* (1850). After more than a year and a half of courtship, Browning secretly married her—without her father's permission—in St. Marylebone Church on September 12, 1846. With his new wife, her dog, and her maid, Browning hastened to Italy, their new home.

Flourishing in the society of Rome and Florence, Elizabeth seemed healthier, and Browning began to publish his finest work. *Men and Women*, which many people consider to be his best single volume, appeared in 1855 and became his first popular success. *Dramatis Personae* was published in 1864. During this period, Elizabeth produced a son, and, utilizing Italian materials, Browning himself achieved great fame. Yet tragedy struck as the sickly Elizabeth died in 1861. Browning buried her in Florence, took his son, Robert "Pen" Browning, home, and never returned to the city that he loved.

For the next two decades, Browning continued to produce collections of poetry at the rate of one every year and a half. Socially, he gave dinners for many of the literary luminaries of his day, and he had a great many honorary degrees conferred upon him. His poetry lost some of its freshness, and his voice occasionally weakened. Yet his poems still sparkled with moments of greatness.

From 1888 to 1894, he saw published his *Poetical Works* in seventeen volumes, supervising the last edition himself. In 1889, his last work, *Asolando*, appeared, and in the fall of that same year he journeyed back to Italy. While walking on the Lido in Venice, where he was staying with Pen and his wife, he caught a cold. He died on December 12, 1889, in Venice. His body was returned to England, where he received his most prestigious honor, burial in the Poets' Corner of Westminster Abbey. Born into the heyday of Romanticism, he died at the time that the Victorian era was itself expiring.

Analysis

During his lifetime, Browning was probably appreciated most for his optimistic themes about humankind in a pessimistic era. Typically, Browning offers this self-portrait at the end of the epilogue to *Asolando*: "One who never turned his back but marched breast forward/ Never doubted clouds would break./ Never dreamed, though right were worsted, wrong would triumph." Retrospect, however, reveals a greater legacy and a more profound influence, especially on later generations of poets. When Browning began writing, Romanticism dominated poetry with all of its effusive self-indulgence, its confessional nature, its overwhelming *Weltschmerz*—its supreme subjectivity and preoccupation with the individual poet's emotional state of being. By the time he died, Browning had demonstrated that poetry could be intensely dramatic, profoundly psychological, and simultaneously insightful.

The enduring legacy for, and the greatest influence on, future poets (for example, T. S. Eliot) is Browning's insistence on the poet's detachment and devotion to the dramatic ideal. In his advertisement published on the second page of *Dramatic Lyrics*, Browning announced his credo, his preference for "poetry always dramatic in principle, and so many utterances of so many imaginary persons, not mine." More precisely, Browning refined, though he did not invent, a poetic genre called the dramatic monologue. Browning's poems of this type are essentially speeches by a single person. Unlike a soliloquy, however, a listener/audience is present, though never speaking. As a result, as in real life, the speaker offers no guarantee of telling the truth. As with all drama, the speech is set at a particular place, is about a specific subject, and contains a conflict with some opposing force. The ultimate thrust of a Browning monologue is character insight; the speaker, no matter what the apparent subject of the monologue, always reveals the essence of his or her personality. Thus, there is usually a sense of dramatic irony. Browning's major contribution to the dramatic monologue, then, is to demonstrate its psychological potential; the chief motives, the very soul of the speaker, are laid bare.

Browning, then, is the harbinger of the modern literary preoccupation with the mysteries of the psyche. He reveals both the breadth and the depth of the human mind, and these insights range from the normal to the abnormal. Browning, for example, originally classified one of his earlier poems, "Porphyria's Lover," under the heading "Madhouse Cells." The poem, coldly narrated by a man who has only a moment ago finished strangling his lover, shows Browning's willingness to explore that other side of the human mind, the dark side. Moreover, Browning is willing to plumb the depths beyond the conscious mind. Occasionally, when his poems seem incomprehensible, his characters are gripped by irrational impulses and speak from their unconscious.

Of course, not all Browning's seemingly obscure lines can be traced to the minds of his characters. After the hours in his father's library and his journeys to Italy, his knowledge was immense, and he frequently uses allusions to history, the Bible, and the classics. In "The Bishop Orders His Tomb at Saint Praxed's Church," for example, Browning displays an awareness of church ritual, Greek mythology, and marble. Also, he was a great experimenter. He used metrical variations and often unnatural syntax. He was fond of beginning his poems in mid-speech and situation. "My Last Duchess" commences as the Duke of Ferrara is only fifty-six lines from finishing a long interview with the count's emissary. Browning shuns logical transitions, preferring to jump from one thought to the next as most people do in everyday speech. He often discards pronouns.

Another notable characteristic of Browning's verse is his detachment. Like many of the realists of his day, he refrained from the moral judgment of his characters, thus eschewing the didactic theory of art. Nowhere in "Porphyria's Lover," for example, does Browning intrude to pronounce the homicidal lover evil or a sociopath. If there are judgments to be made, Browning leaves that task to his readers. Thus, Browning occasionally went against the oversimplified Victorian morality of art.

As both Browning's intense love affair with Elizabeth Barrett and the title of one volume, *Men and Women*, suggest, he was very much interested in the relationship of the sexes, especially in the high plane of love. Perhaps partially because he was forced to woo Elizabeth at first from a distance, Browning became profoundly reflective about romantic love. Even a cursory reading of his poetry reveals that he had several theories about man-woman relationships, and these theories, combined with the intense psychological reality of his characters, suggest why he is viewed as one of the great love poets in English. Interestingly, some of his great love lyrics were written before he met his wife and after she had died. When the eponymous speaker of "Rabbi Ben Ezra" argues, "Grow old along with me!/ The best is yet to be," one must realize that the lines were composed after Elizabeth had died and therefore express wishful thinking. Also, Browning's love lyrics express not only the joy of love but also its failures. "Meeting at Night" is coupled with "Parting at Morning," wherein the male lover must leave the woman whom he loves to return to the "world of men."

One notable idea often finding expression in Browning is how often love can be replaced by a preoccupation with material things. In "My Last Duchess," the Duke of Ferrara has reduced the woman whom he had married to a work of art, where she is now even less treasured than a bronze statue. In "The Bishop Orders His Tomb at Saint Praxed's Church," the dying Bishop has replaced his original love of God with things—a wine press, classical manuscripts, and villas.

Another typical theme in Browning is the supremacy of romantic love. Perhaps the best example of this idea occurs in "Love Among the Ruins." The place of the prince and the prince's power are in ruins, the soldiers and their war machines have vanished, and Browning concludes that despite their "triumphs" and "glories," "love is best." True love for Browning was part and parcel of spiritual love.

What, then, is the poet's role in the midst of love and psychology? Perhaps Browning best states his poetic credo in "Fra Lippo Lippi" by using the persona as his mouthpiece: "this world . . . means intensely, and means good." In his "Essay on Percy Bysshe Shelley," Browning elaborated upon this notion of the poet finding the "good." The poet must have a "great moral purpose," must search the world around him, for, paradoxically, the greatest spiritual elevation occurs when the poet immerses himself in the things of this world. Often Browning's optimism is misunderstood. Good comes not in the actual attainment of higher things, often love, but in the attempt. Failure and disappointment are secondary if the attempt is made.

MY LAST DUCHESS

First published: 1842
Type of work: Poem

The Duke of Ferrara reveals himself to be a selfish, jealous man desiring to control other people's lives.

"My Last Duchess" is probably Browning's most popular and most anthologized poem. The poem first appeared in 1842 in *Dramatic Lyrics,* which is contained in *Bells and Pomegranates* (1841-1846). Perhaps the major reason for the fame of "My Last Duchess" is that it is probably the finest example of Browning's dramatic monologue. In it, he paints a devastating self-portrait of royalty, a portrait that doubtless reveals more of the Duke's personality than Ferrara intends. In fact, the irony is profound, for with each word spoken in an attempt to criticize his last duchess, the Duke ironically reveals his utterly detestable nature and how far he is from seeing it himself.

Before the subtleties of "My Last Duchess" can be grasped, the basic elements of this dramatic monologue must be understood. The only speaker is the Duke of Ferrara. The listener, who, offstage, asks about the smile of the last duchess in the portrait, is silent during the entire poem. The listener is the emissary of a count and is helping to negotiate a marriage between the count's daughter and the Duke. The time is probably the Italian Renaissance, though Browning does not so specify. The location is the Duke's palace, probably upstairs in some art gallery, since the Duke points to two nearby art objects. The two men are about to join the "company below" (line 47), so the fifty-six lines of the poem represent the end of the Duke's negotiating, his final terms.

Since the thrust of a Browning dramatic monologue is psychological self-characterization, what kind of man does the Duke reveal himself to be? Surely, he is a very jealous man. He brags that he has had the Duchess' portrait made by Fra Pandolf. Why would he hire a monk, obviously noted for his sacred art, to paint a secular portrait? The Duke admits, "t'was not/ Her husband's presence only, called that spot/ Of joy into the Duchess' cheek" (lines 13-15). Then he notes that "perhaps/ Fra Pandolf chanced to say" (lines 15-16) and provides two exact quotations. The suggestion is strong that he observed the whole enterprise. He gave Fra Pandolf only a day to finish the expensive commissioned art. Pandolf is a painter so notable that the Duke drops the artist's name. Probably, he chose Pandolf because, as a man of the cloth, the good brother would have taken a vow of chastity. Yet the Duke's jealousy was so powerful that he observed this chaste painter with his wife in order to be sure. Later, the Duke implies that the Duchess was the kind of woman who had to be watched, for she had a heart "too easily impressed" (line 23), and "her looks went everywhere" (line 24). Yet the evidence that he uses to corroborate this charge—her love of sunsets, the cherry bough with which she was presented, her pet white mule—suggests only that she was a natural woman who preferred the simple pleasures.

The Duke's pride and selfishness are also revealed. He is very proud of his family name, for, as he describes his marriage to his last duchess, he states that he gave her "My gift of a nine-hundred-years-old name" (line 33). Yet he never once mentions love or his willingness to emerge from his own ego. Instead, he emphasizes that it is his curtain, his portrait, his name, his "commands" (line 45), and his sculpture. Tellingly, within fifty-six lines he uses seventeen first-person pronouns.

Undoubtedly, though, the most dominant feature of the Duke's personality is a godlike desire for total control of his environment: "I said/ 'Frà Pandolf' by design" (lines 5-6). Browning reveals this trait by bracketing the poem with artistic images of control. As noted above, the painting of the Pandolf portrait reveals how the Duke orchestrates the situation. Moreover, even now the Duke controls the emissary's perception of the last duchess. Everything that the listener hears about her is filtered through the mind and voice of the Duke. The emissary cannot even look at her portrait without the Duke's opening a curtain that he has had placed in front of the painting.

The final artistic image is most revealing. The last word in the Duke's negotiations is further evidence of his desire for control. He compels the emissary to focus attention on another commissioned objet d'art: "Notice Neptune, though,/ Taming a sea-horse, thought a rarity/ Which Claus of Innsbruck cast in bronze for me!"

(lines 54-56). Once again, the commissioned art is a sort of Rorschach test—it reveals a great deal about the personality of the commissioner. The thrust of the art object is dominance—the Duke desires to be Neptune, god of the sea, taming a small, beautiful sea creature in what would obviously be no contest. In other words, the Duke sees himself as a god who has tamed/will tame his duchess.

As earlier indicated, the Duke has always associated his last duchess with beautiful things of nature. Like Neptune, the Duke rules his kingdom, Ferrara, with an iron fist. When he grew tired of his last duchess, he says, "I gave commands" (line 45), and her smiles "stopped together" (line 46). Since the Duke says that in her portrait the last duchess is "looking as if she were alive" (line 2), the suggestion is strong that, like the god that he would be, the Duke has exercised the power over life and death.

The key critical question in "My Last Duchess" focuses on the Duke's motivation. Why would a man so obviously desiring marriage to the count's daughter reveal himself in such negative terms? Critics take opposing views: Some characterize him as "shrewd"; others, as "witless." A related critical question considers the Duke's impending marriage: Why would a man who has had so much trouble with his first duchess want a second wife?

The answers to both questions seem to lie in the Duke's godlike self-image. Interestingly, for a man preoccupied with his nine-hundred-year-old name, nowhere does he mention progeny, and without children there will be no one to carry on the family name. Importantly, he uses a series of terminative images, all emphasizing the end of the cycle of life, to describe his last duchess—the sunset ends the day, the breaking of the bough ends the life of the cherry (also a sexual reference), the white mule is the end of its line (mules then could not reproduce within the breed), and whiteness as a color associated with sterility. Could it be that the Duke, since he uses these images, employs his last duchess as a scapegoat and that he is the one who is sterile? Thus, his object in procuring the "fair daughter's self (line 52) is children. No doubt, for a man who likes commissioned art work, the "dowry" (line 51) will help defray his expenses. Perhaps the Duke, like another Renaissance figure, Henry VIII, will run through a series of brides because he is unable to see the flaws in his own personality.

Stylistically, Browning has written a tour de force. The fifty-six lines are all in iambic pentameter couplets. The couplet form is quite formal in English poetry, and this pattern suggests the formal nature of the Duke and control. Interestingly, unlike the traditional neoclassic heroic couplet, where lines are end-stopped, Browning favors enjambment, and the run-on line suggests the Duke's inability to control everything—his inability to be a god.

Historically, readers have wondered about two things. Is the Duke based on a real person? Some have suggested Vespasiano Gonzaga, duke of Sabbioneta, while others favor Alfonso II, fifth and last duke of Ferrara. Second, in his lifetime Browning was often asked what really happened to the Duke's last duchess. Finally, Browning was forced to say, "the commands were that she should be put to death . . . or he might have had her shut up in a convent."

THE BISHOP ORDERS HIS TOMB AT SAINT PRAXED'S CHURCH

First published: 1845
Type of work: Poem

The dying Bishop reveals himself to be more concerned with maintaining his materialism than admitting his many sins.

"The Bishop Orders His Tomb at Saint Praxed's Church" was printed in 1845 in *Hood's Magazine* and later that same year in *Dramatic Romances and Lyrics*, which is contained in *Bells and Pomegranates* (1841-1846). It was probably suggested by Browning's visit to Italy the previous year. Although an actual Saint Praxed's church exists in Rome, no bishop from "15—," the poem's dateline, is buried there, but the Bishop in the poem typifies the bishops of the era.

The poem is another fine example of Browning's mastery of the dramatic monologue form. The speaker is the church's Bishop, who is "dying by degrees" (line 11). His silent audience is his "Nephews—sons mine" (line 3). Actually, "nephews" is a historic euphemism for illegitimate sons, and only on his death is the Bishop finally willing to acknowledge his paternity. The setting is Saint Praxed's church: More specifically, the Bishop seems to be lying up front, to the right of the pulpit, and near the choir loft. The situation is simple: With not much time left, the Bishop is negotiating with his "sons" to do something that he cannot—to assure that he will be buried in a marble tomb as befits his position in the church hierarchy.

As with "My Last Duchess," the speaker ironically creates a self-portrait very different from what he intends. Because the Bishop nears death, he can no longer control his words and thus reveals a man somewhat less than a paragon of virtue, a very flawed human who has hypocritically violated his clerical vows. As a representative of the Roman Catholic church, he suggests that the institution has failed, having been corrupted by materialistic, secular concerns.

One measure of a cleric's righteousness has always been how he avoids the seven deadly sins. Browning provides an ironic "confession" in which the Bishop admits to them all. Wrath is one of the deadly sins. Dying, the Bishop is still angry at Gandolf, his predecessor, who has claimed a better burial site in the church. As his negotiations with his sons prove unsuccessful, the dying Bishop becomes increasingly angry at them. He also asks God to curse Gandolf.

Another sin is pride. Though he begins his 122 lines with a warning about vanity, he is proud of many things, especially his possessions, and the fact that he won his boys' mother away from Gandolf. Yet he still envies (the third sin) his predecessor for that burial site.

Gluttony is manifest in a general sense by the sheer number of his possessions and in a gustatory sense by the way that he depicts the sacrament of communion; once dead, he will feast his eyes on a perpetual banquet, "God made and eaten all day long" (line 82). Greed is revealed with his last wish and his possessions. He desires his tomb to be made of basalt (a hard, dark-colored rock), as compared to his predecessor's cheap and "paltry onion-stone" (line 31). The Bishop's legacy is mostly materialistic. Seeing that his sons are not acceding to his dying wishes, he offers his possessions as a bribe. He has accumulated a vineyard, a huge lapis lazuli stone, villas, horses, Greek manuscripts, and mistresses. Of course, as a priest he at one time took a vow of poverty.

Perhaps his greatest sin, however, is lechery. Having also taken a vow of chastity, he has also taken several mistresses and by at least one of them has fathered children. Quite often he commingles the sacred and the sexual. The lapis lazuli is described as "Blue as a vein o'er the Madonna's breast" (line 44). On the horizontal surface of his tomb, he wants etched in bronze a bas-relief of pans and nymphs, Christ delivering the Sermon on the Mount, Moses with the Ten Commandments, and "one Pan/ Ready to twitch the Nymph's last garment off" (lines 60-61). Furthermore, Browning emphasizes the ironic distance between the Bishop's sexual activity and what the cleric should be by the name of the very church that the Bishop serves and represents. St. Praxed was a second century virgin martyr who converted to Christianity and gave her worldly possessions to the poor. The Bishop is a sixteenth century nonvirgin who has never practiced self-sacrifice and has unofficially converted from Christianity to mammonism. He now obviously worships all the worldly goods that he can accumulate.

One helpful way of reading this poem is as an ironic sermon. After all, the Bishop typically begins his address with a biblical quotation, the words from the Book of Ecclesiastes 1:2, and the rest of the poem is an ironic portrayal of his own vain self-estimation, complete with moral illustrations. As a religious person, the Bishop should doubtless consider this moment as an occasion for confession—to explain what he did, to acknowledge its sinfulness, and to ask for forgiveness. Instead, he dies as vain and as self-deluded as he has lived. His final thoughts dwell upon the carnal beauty of his mistress and the envy that that evoked in his arch-rival. Browning's final irony, then, is overwhelming. The Bishop is not a servant of God but of Dionysus, the pagan god of fertility and sexuality.

MEETING AT NIGHT and PARTING AT MORNING

First published: 1845
Type of work: Poems

Romantic passion is brief, and lovers must return to the real world.

"Meeting at Night" and "Parting at Morning" are companion poems that are best read as one poem. They were first published in *Dramatic Romances and Lyrics* under the general title "Night and Morning," which suggests that Browning saw them as part of a natural, inevitable cycle.

When the poems first appeared, they were criticized as being immoral because they describe lovers rendezvousing for a night of passion, then going their separate ways. Early critics worried that the man and woman, because of the clandestine nature of the tryst, are not married. In any event, there is much of Browning in this poem, for, like its lovers, Elizabeth Barrett and he had to meet secretly.

Although early critics debated the poems' use of pronouns, Browning said that in both poems the man—the "me" of "Parting at Morning," line 4—is speaking, detailing his night with his lover. The real strength of the poems is Browning's mastery of imagery. Every line in both poems employs some specific image in an attempt to stimulate a particular sense. Browning's subject is a favorite, love between men and women, but only a close examination of the imagery reveals the exact nature of that love.

What Browning meticulously communicates in these poems is the physical nature of love. The images constantly refer to the sense of smell, taste, touch, and hearing, as well as sensations of heat, light, and kinesthesia. Browning's artistry lies in his indirection. Never does the speaker say that their relationship is deeply sexual; he implies it. The description of the journey becomes a sort of emotional topography. Life apart for the lovers is like the land, black and gray with only a little light. They are each halves of the moon. Yet as he gets closer to the woman, his senses come alive, even commingle: the "warm sea-scented beach" (line 7) appeals to three senses simultaneously. When they join, like the boat's prow in the "slushy sand" (line 6), there is a sudden spurt of love.

While he communicates the emotions of the ecstatic moment, Browning also suggests that they are fleeting, like the night, and inevitably the male must return to the "world of men" ("Parting at Morning," line 4). Browning said that the first poem argues that "raptures are self-sufficient and enduring," while the second contends "how fleeting" is that belief.

Summary

Robert Browning stands as the transitional English poet between the supreme subjectivity of the Romantics and the subtleties of modern poetry. He masterfully showed the dramatic and psychological possibilities of verse. In the Victorian era of sexual reticence and profound doubt, he demonstrated the power of human passion and the prevalence of the human spirit.

Bibliography

Blythe, Hal, and Charlie Sweet. "Browning's Ferrara: The Man Who Would Be Neptune." *Studies in Browning and His Circle* 7, no. 2 (1979): 17-20.

DeVane, William. *A Browning Handbook.* 2d ed. New York: Appleton-Century-Crofts, 1955.

Drew, Philip. *The Poetry of Browning: A Critical Introduction.* London: Methuen, 1970.

Irvine, William, and Park Honan. *The Book, Ring, and the Poet: A Biography of Robert Browning.* New York: McGraw-Hill, 1974.

King, Roma, Jr. *The Focusing Artifice: The Poetry of Robert Browning.* Athens: Ohio University Press, 1968.

Orr, Sutherland. *Life and Letters of Robert Browning.* Rev. ed. Boston: Houghton Mifflin, 1908.

Hal Charles

JOHN BUNYAN

Born: Elstow, England
November, 1628
Died: London, England
August 31, 1688

Principal Literary Achievement
A master of the plain style, Bunyan enriched English literature by producing allegorical prose works on the theme of religion and a spiritual autobiography.

Biography
John Bunyan was born in the village of Elstow, near Bedford, England, in November, 1628, the son of Thomas Bunyan and his second wife, Margaret Bentley. Although his ancestors had been English yeoman farmers and small landowners in Bedfordshire, his father was a whitesmith or metal craftsman, suggesting that the family fortunes had declined over generations. Bunyan himself was apprenticed at his father's craft, though the designation changed to tinker, or mender of metal implements, and for many years he earned his living through his skill. The Bunyans were not destitute, nor were they forced to become itinerant craftsmen, for both Bunyan and his father owned a forge and workshop in Elstow. In his confessional autobiography, Bunyan lists activities of his youth as dancing, playing tip-cat, ringing church bells, and swearing—all of which he solemnly condemned.

He attended school, either in Elstow or nearby Bedford, but it appears that he learned little beyond the ability to read and write English. His actual lifelong education was obtained through the King James Bible (1611), which he knew well enough to recall hundreds, perhaps thousands, of verses at will. He absorbed its style, its metaphors and symbols, its cadences, and its themes. In addition, he possessed a broad knowledge of Protestant religious works, including John Foxe's *The Book of Martyrs* (1563) and Martin Luther's *In epistolam sancti Pauli ad Galatas commentarius* (1519; *Commentary on St. Paul's Epistle to the Galatians*, 1575). Throughout Bunyan's lifetime, England was undergoing sweeping changes in its society, politics, economics, and religion. Although these changes affected Bunyan's life profoundly, except for the movement toward religious freedom, he hardly noted them.

In 1644, following the death of his mother and his father's remarriage, Bunyan enlisted in the parliamentary army in a regiment garrisoned at Newport Pagnall and commanded by Sir Samuel Luke. Historians have established that parliamentary ar-

mies of the time had religion as their main interest, with units expounding the scriptures, reading, and debating points of doctrine; Bunyan probably encountered a wide range of viewpoints among the Dissenters. A plan to send his company to Ireland failed to occur, and he had experienced no military engagements of importance when he was demobilized in 1646.

Bunyan married soon afterward, perhaps in 1648, and his wife's small dowry included two religious handbooks, *The Plaine Man's Pathway to Heaven* (1601), by Arthur Dent, and *The Practice of Piety* (1612), by Lewis Bayley. The Dent book employed the biblical journey metaphor that became prominent in Bunyan's own prose. Following a prolonged period of religious angst, narrated in his autobiography *Grace Abounding to the Chief of Sinners* (1666), Bunyan joined the Baptist Congregation at Bedford in 1653 and began evangelical preaching and religious tract writing, the first of these being pamphlets directed against the Quakers. Following the death of his first wife, who left him with four small children, he married again in 1659 and, with his devoted second wife, had two additional children.

A successful preacher who never prepared his sermons in advance, Bunyan attracted large crowds through his obvious sincerity, plain style, and fervor. After his fame spread, he was invited to preach in towns throughout the Midland counties and even in London. Barred from preaching in the established church, he addressed congregations in fields, barns, chapels, and forests. As he was not licensed, he was arrested in 1660 and imprisoned in the Bedford county jail, where he remained until 1672, sustaining himself and his family by making laces. Imprisonment was not a stern ordeal for him, and it is plain from his own account that his jailers sought to release him, provided that he would agree not to preach. This Bunyan steadfastly refused to do. He pointed out that while none could be absolutely certain of correctness in biblical interpretation, his own views were as plausible as the official ones. During his imprisonment he was permitted visits from friends and family, wrote prolifically, and was released for brief periods to visit others. The record shows that he attended unauthorized religious meetings during some of his leaves from prison. Following his release in 1672, he became the minister of the Bedford Congregation; he was then imprisoned again for several months, probably in 1676-1677. It is generally accepted that during this imprisonment he wrote his masterpiece *The Pilgrim's Progress from This World to That Which Is to Come* (Part I, 1678). *The Pilgrim's Progress from This World to That Which Is to Come the Second Part* was published in 1684.

For the remainder of his life, Bunyan continued his ministry and prolific writing. In August, 1688, while riding horseback from Reading to London after attempting to settle a dispute between a father and son, he experienced a chill. He died in London on August 31, 1688, and was buried in Bunhill Fields, the principal cemetery for Dissenters.

Analysis

Beginning with the publication of *Some Gospel Truths Opened* (1656), a tract directed against the Quakers, Bunyan was to produce approximately sixty published works during his lifetime. All were religious in nature, though there is considerable variety within the general subject. Some are polemical and controversial, and a few concern broad religious doctrines; some are handbooks or guides for adults, while others instruct children. Since Bunyan did not publish his sermons, little evidence remains of his preaching, though two of his published titles appear to be sermons. Literary historians agree that only four of his works are of lasting interest, and three of these—*The Pilgrim's Progress*, *The Holy War* (1682), and *The Life and Death of Mr. Badman* (1680)—are allegories of religious life that center on the plight of the individual soul.

Bunyan's first significant prose work was his spiritual autobiography, *Grace Abounding to the Chief of Sinners*, a prominent example of a genre that goes back to the fifth century *Confessiones* (397-400; *Confessions*) of Saint Augustine. In simple and muscular prose, Bunyan gives an account of his spiritual development, his conversion, and the beginning of his ministry. Details of his daily life are scant, and his autobiography serves to illustrate the workings of God on Earth. To Bunyan, salvation is essentially a gripping drama featuring God and the Devil struggling for the individual soul. In accounting for his spiritual development, Bunyan lists evidences of his wickedness, actually trivial infractions, and attempts to elucidate the stages of his conversion.

At the center of Bunyan's narrative lies a recurring cyclic pattern of psychological interest, for life's journey does not occur in a direct line. Always anxious about salvation, the narrator falls into a deep depression, convinced that he is lost or, in one memorable instance, that he has committed the unpardonable sin. These periods last for days, weeks, or months. He sometimes hears voices telling him to sell Christ or urging him to doubt or curse God. Occasionally he hears a stern and wrathful voice from Heaven issuing a warning. Efforts to find support and reassurance from others prove fruitless. On one occasion he confesses to a wise old Christian man that he believes he has committed the unpardonable sin, and the old man agrees. After a period of profound gloom, however, he reads or recalls a biblical verse that gives him hope or relieves his anxiety. The depression passes, and he is reassured for a time, only to experience a later recurrence of the entire cycle. Finally, sometime during his late twenties, the cycles end. Assured of salvation, he begins his ministry.

With the publication of *The Pilgrim's Progress*, a richly imaginative depiction of the quest for salvation, Bunyan achieved lasting fame. The work saw numerous editions within his lifetime and through translations into many languages attained the status of a world classic.

In contrast to Christian's successful journey to Heaven in *The Pilgrim's Progress*, Bunyan's next allegorical work chronicles the destruction of a sinner. *The Life and Death of Mr. Badman* is cast in the form of a dialogue between Mr. Wiseman and Mr. Attentive, who does not simply listen but injects comments of his own and asks pointed questions. A notorious sinner from childhood, Mr. Badman seeks wealth through marriage, defrauds others throughout his life, and betrays all who trust him. A clear example of Bunyan's view of a hardened sinner, he grows increasingly vicious in his personal life. Following the death of his first wife, he marries a woman as evil as himself, but they soon part in acrimony. As if to stress that he no longer struggles against sin, he is granted a peaceful death.

In their narration, Mr. Wiseman and Mr. Attentive enrich the plot with brief sensationalized accounts of other sinners and their fates. Drawn from actual events of the time or from current stories, they emphasize the disastrous consequences of evil, and their authenticity is never questioned. In one account, a man is borne away violently by evil spirits after publicly drinking a toast to the Devil. In other accounts, a despondent man's suicide is recounted in vivid detail, while a poor village woman, having stolen two pence, swears that she is innocent and invites the ground to swallow her, whereupon witnesses see the ground open and bury her twelve feet deep. To supplement the instructional intent of the allegorical and brief stories, Mr. Wiseman quotes biblical verses directed toward Christian behavior and ethics, reinforcing the moral message.

The Holy War features a more complex allegorical plot than Bunyan's earlier works; scholars have demonstrated that the meaning of the work operates on several levels. On one level, Bunyan alludes to contemporary events in Bedford, where Puritan officeholders were being replaced by Royalists. In its description of sieges and drills, the work also reflects the English Civil War and Bunyan's experience as a soldier. Yet fundamentally the book presents a sweeping, comprehensive depiction of God's Providence as it applies to the world at large and the individual soul. The city, Mansoul, with five gates named for each of the senses, is established by El Shaddai (God). Diabolus besieges and captures the city, endowing it with a new charter and replacing the old city recorder, Mr. Conscience, with Mr. Forget-Good. El Shaddai dispatches an army to besiege and retake the city, at length placing Emmanuel (Christ) in command. Supported by a host of important personages—such as Mr. Alderman Atheism, Mr. Lustings, and Mr. Fornication—Diabolus mounts a strong resistance, but eventually the city falls. Once the rule of El Shaddai is restored, however, the city relapses into its evil ways, and Diabolus renews the war. Although he recaptures most of the city, he fails to retake the citadel at the center, which is defended by Emmanuel and his supporters.

THE PILGRIM'S PROGRESS

First published: Part 1, 1678; part 2, 1684
Type of work: Religious allegory

Rejecting his existence in the City of Destruction, Christian makes the long and arduous journey to the Heavenly City.

The Pilgrim's Progress, Bunyan's best-known work, narrates the protagonist Christian's journey to salvation. Made aware of his own mortality, Christian abandons the

City of Destruction and begins his journey to the Heavenly City. The narrative takes the form of an allegorical dream vision and develops the theme of individual salvation through a highly consistent allegorical framework.

Urged on by Evangelist, Christian abandons his wife and children, stopping his ears with his fingers to silence their pleas, an indication that the journey to salvation must be an individual experience. The two companions whom he encounters along the way, Faithful and Hopeful, are actually facets of his own character. Once he has begun the journey, he reflects the character of the wayfaring, warring Christian disciple, often tempted and often struggling but never abandoning the path.

Christian is not tempted by the worldly pleasures of Vanity Fair or by any pomp and ceremony associated with riches. Nor is he swayed by the erroneous reasonings of Obstinate, Pliable, Sloth, or Mr. Worldly Wiseman or the shallow optimism apparent in characters such as Hypocrisy, Formality, and Ignorance. His serious temptations concern fear, doubt, and despair. At the journey's beginning he is mired in the Slough of Despond, escaping only after difficult exertions. He meets frightening monsters such as Pope and Pagan and battles the demonic warrior Apollyon. Cast into a dungeon at Doubting Castle by Giant Despair, he can free himself only with a key called Promise. He must maintain constant vigilance in order to avoid being distracted from his goal in places such as the Valley of Ease and the Valley of Deceit.

Yet the journey is not without its rewarding pauses and encouragements. At the outset his burden drops when he reaches the Cross, and at the House Beautiful he receives instruction and grace. In the vicinity of Beulah Land, he meets the shepherds Knowledge, Watchful, Experience, and Sincere. As he approaches the River of Death near the end of the journey, he can see the Heavenly City beyond and is confident of his safe arrival.

The style of *The Pilgrim's Progress* makes the work accessible to readers of all levels. Bunyan employs simple diction and language, biblical images and metaphors, and repetition, all of which are suitable to his didactic purpose. In 1684, Bunyan published a second part of *The Pilgrim's Progress*, narrating the journey of Christian's wife Christiana, her maid, and children to heaven. They are guided by the magnanimous Mr. Greatheart, whose presence makes the perils of the journey less intense.

Summary

John Bunyan's writings brought him fame as a master allegorist and exponent of the plain style. While his works are informed with a powerfully consistent mythic vision, his arresting theme of individual salvation remains their most striking feature, a theme developed through strain and angst. His individualism, denying all but arbitrary grace, places the entire burden of salvation on the individual human. Even while realizing that most people would not play their part in the great drama successfully, he sought to illustrate how the individual's journey through life might best be made.

Bibliography

Furlong, Monica. *Puritan's Progress.* New York: Coward, McCann, and Geoghegan, 1975.

Hill, Christopher. *A Tinker and a Poor Man: John Bunyan and His Church, 1628-1688.* New York: Alfred A. Knopf, 1989.

Sadler, Lynn Veach. *John Bunyan.* Boston: G. K. Hall, 1979.

Sharrock, Roger. *John Bunyan.* London: Hutchinson's University Library, 1954.

Talon, Henry A. *John Bunyan.* London: Longmans, Green, 1956.

Tindall, William York. *John Bunyan, Mechanick Preacher.* New York: Columbia University Press, 1934.

Winslow, Ola Elizabeth. *John Bunyan.* New York: Macmillan, 1961.

Stanley Archer

Born: Manchester, England
February 25, 1917

Principal Literary Achievement

One of the most prolific twentieth century British writers, Burgess is known for his linguistic prowess, his engaging plots, and his parodic, sometimes vicious, humor.

Biography

Anthony Burgess, christened John Burgess Wilson (Anthony was his confirmation name), was born on February 25, 1917, in Manchester, England, to Joseph and Elizabeth Burgess Wilson. In early 1919, an influenza epidemic killed Burgess' mother and his only sibling, a sister. In 1922, Burgess' father remarried. Anthony Burgess faulted his stepmother, Maggie Dwyer, with "an emotional coldness" that he believed marred his work and which many of the female characters in his novels exhibit.

Burgess attended a Catholic elementary school and did well enough on his examinations to win two scholarships to the Catholic preparatory school Xaverian College, where he flourished, both artistically and intellectually. Though he attended Catholic schools, by sixteen he had rejected the Catholic church and its teachings (Catholicism remains, however, a recurrent subject of his fiction). Because he failed a physics course, Burgess was unable to enroll in music studies as he had wished, but he received his bachelor of arts, with honors, in English language and literature, from the University of Manchester in June, 1940.

In October, 1940, Burgess joined the army, serving first in the Army Medical Corps, then in the Army Educational Corps. In January, 1942, he married Llewela Isherwood Jones, a Welsh economics student at the University of Manchester and a cousin of writer Christopher Isherwood. Throughout their long marriage, Llewela, or Lynne, as Burgess called her, was unfaithful, engaging in numerous casual affairs. This behavior, and Burgess' attitude toward it, undoubtedly contributed to the portrayal of faithless wives and to the misogynism that appear in his fiction. In 1944, while Burgess was stationed in Gibraltar, he received word that Llewela had been assaulted, according to her, by American soldiers, resulting in her miscarriage and in physicians' orders that she never become pregnant again. Somewhat simplistically, Burgess blamed this attack for Llewela's increasing alcoholism and for her death (of cirrhosis of the liver), twenty-four years later. This attack was transformed into the attack on

the fictional writer and his wife in Burgess' novel *A Clockwork Orange* (1962).

From 1946 to 1959, Burgess held various teaching posts, including one as education officer in Malaya. His stay in Malaya was a turning point in his career: It is in Malaya that he began writing fiction. In 1956, his first novel, *Time for a Tiger*, was published. Since colonial servants were discouraged from writing fiction, he used the pen name Anthony Burgess. *The Enemy in the Blanket* (1958) and *Beds in the East* (1959) became the second and third installments in the Malayan Trilogy, *The Long Day Wanes* (1965; includes *Time for a Tiger*, *The Enemy in the Blanket*, *Beds in the East*).

In 1959, Burgess collapsed while lecturing to his students, was sent back to London, and was diagnosed (so Burgess consistently claimed) as suffering from a fatal brain tumor, with only a year to live. During this "terminal" year, his first year as a full-time writer, Burgess wrote five novels: *The Doctor Is Sick* (1960), *The Right to an Answer* (1960), *Devil of a State* (1961), *The Worm and the Ring* (1961), and *One Hand Clapping* (1961), two of which he published under the pseudonym Joseph Kell. Burgess later complied with a request to review one of Kell's novels, claiming to have "assumed that the editor wanted a bit of a joke." Burgess' review created a controversy about the fact that an author had "deceitfully" reviewed his own book, but Burgess' literary career was now firmly established. No sign or symptoms of a brain tumor ever subsequently appeared.

In 1962, Burgess published his most famous novel, *A Clockwork Orange*, as well as *The Wanting Seed*. In 1963, he published two additional novels under the pseudonym Joseph Kell: *Honey for the Bears* and *Inside Mr. Enderby*. Burgess' fictional biography of William Shakespeare's love life, *Nothing Like the Sun* (1964), and *The Eve of Saint Venus* (1964), appeared in the same year that Liliana Macellari, a linguist at Cambridge, and Burgess had a son, Andrew. Several books appeared the following year, including *A Vision of Battlements* (1965). His parody of Ian Fleming's James Bond series, *Tremor of Intent*, was published in 1966.

The year 1968 was another momentous one for Burgess. In March, his wife Llewela died. In October, Burgess married the mother of his son, Liliana Macellari. He published *Urgent Copy*, *Enderby Outside*, and, in the United States, *Enderby* (which contained both *Mr. Enderby*, and *Enderby Outside*). Burgess also permanently left England. From 1969 to 1973, Burgess continued his prolific writing career, also serving as writer-in-residence and teaching creative writing at several universities in the United States. Burgess' novel *MF* (1971) and Stanley Kubrick's brilliant and faithful adaptation of Burgess' *A Clockwork Orange* appeared in the same year. From 1974 to 1986, Burgess published many books, among them *The Clockwork Testament: Or, Enderby's End* (1974), *Abba Abba* (1977), *Man of Nazareth* (1979), and *Enderby's Dark Lady* (1984). During this same period, Burgess wrote *Napoleon Symphony* (1974), his most experimental novel, which is elaborately patterned after Ludwig van Beethoven's *Eroica* symphony, a work that Beethoven dedicated to Napoleon. *Earthly Powers*, Burgess' treatment of Roman Catholicism, appeared in 1980. In 1987, Burgess published *Little Wilson and Big God*, the first volume of his projected three-volume autobiography. *The Devil's Mode*, a collection of short stories, appeared in 1989; in 1991, the second installment of Burgess' autobiography, *You've Had Your Time*, was published.

Analysis

Burgess seems not only fascinated with language but also obsessed with it. Though he claims to have avoided "overmuch word play and verbal oddity" in deference to his reading public, his novels are nevertheless filled, occasionally distractingly so, with wordplay. Sometimes, as in *A Clockwork Orange*, this playing with language creates a new language, one that becomes more powerful than English could have been for portraying the subject matter. When *A Clockwork Orange's* gang member-narrator, Alex, describes "a bit of the ultra violence" as fine and "horrorshow," or describes as "sophistoes" two adolescent girls intent on seduction, the language defines Alex as much as, if not more than, his behavior does. In fact, in *A Clockwork Orange*, language is a character. Burgess also uses language effectively in *Nothing Like the Sun*, his fictional biography of Shakespeare. In this novel, Elizabethan language and idiom create a Shakespeare that no other rendering of language could have produced. The language of WS, whom Burgess calls a "word-boy," involves the reader more intensely than traditional usage of English. In *The Eve of Saint Venus*, Burgess parodies overinflated poetic language, with language again becoming one of the characters of the novel. Burgess' Malayan Trilogy has been called "not so much plotted as it is orchestrated," and the integration of music with language is vital in Burgess' most experimental novel, *Napoleon Symphony*, in which he attempts to synthesize the language of the novel and the musical elements of Beethoven's *Eroica*. Though Burgess often calls unnecessary attention to his play with language and can overdo his linguistic games, he manages, in most of his work, to make language powerful, effective, and noticeable.

Burgess' work often deals with the duality of nature: good and evil, free will and determinism, romanticism and realism, comedy and tragedy. His characters constantly have to grapple with their own behavior in terms of these dualities. Hillier, in *Tremor of Intent*, has many debates with several other characters on the nature of good and evil in his attempt to discover his own beliefs. The conflict and paradox of opposing forces are abundant in the three novels that constitute the Malayan Trilogy. Kenneth Toomey, the homosexual narrator of *Earthly Powers*, wrestles with the question of good and evil. Toomey and the pope's discussions of good and evil, and of free will and determinism, form the philosophical backbone of the novel. Zverkov, of *Honey for the Bears*, represents philosophy and thought; Karamzin, of the same novel, represents force and physical strength. Like the characters in T. S. Eliot's *The Waste Land* (1922), the characters in Burgess' *One Hand Clapping* are confronted with the predicament of living a meaningful life in a spiritual and cultural desert. Alex, the narrator of *A Clockwork Orange*, complains about all the discussion and debate over good and evil; since no one ever tries to determine the essential source and nature of goodness, Alex claims that he does not understand the insistence on dissecting the nature of evil. Burgess seems as much a philosopher as a novelist, with his constant analysis of the duality of the nature of life, but it is these philosophical ruminations that lend depth to his work.

Sometimes subtle, but more often blatant if not slapstick, the comic elements of Burgess' work are essential Burgess. The violence and depravity of *A Clockwork Orange* are made palatable by its narrator's irrepressible sense of irony, lending humor to the most gruesome aspects of the novel. In the Malayan Trilogy, Burgess' engaging representation of life transforms depravity into comedy. The narrator of *The Right to an Answer* is cynical and ironic. *Devil of a State* is a farce, while *Honey for the Bears* is comic throughout. The comic elements of both *Earthly Powers* and *Tremor of Intent* are interwoven with philosophical musings on the nature of good and evil. The humor of Burgess' work is sometimes grotesque, often cynical, but usually integral to the fiction.

Sexuality, especially homosexuality, seems to be another obsession of Burgess. Many of the wives in his fiction are unfaithful: Hortense in *Earthly Powers*, Sheila in *The Doctor Is Sick*, Anne in *Nothing Like the Sun*, Mrs. Walters in *Tremor of Intent*, Belinda of *Honey for the Bears*, Beatrice-Joanna of *The Wanting Seed*. Incest, and the potential for incest, appear also. Toomey often ponders the possibility of a sexual liaison with his sister Hortense. Shakespeare's brother Richard has an affair with Shakespeare's wife, which constitutes a type of incest since she is Richard's sister-in-law. Hillier, in *Tremor of Intent*, often ruminates on his paternal yet sexual feelings toward Clara, with whom he does eventually have sex. *MF* also deals with the incestuous. Homosexuality often appears in Burgess' work. WS in *Nothing Like the Sun* becomes involved with his beautiful male sponsor. While in prison, Alex of *A Clockwork Orange* is forced to fend off an inmate to protect himself from homosexual advances. Alan, in *Tremor of Intent*, submits himself to a homosexual encounter in order to receive a stolen gun. The husband and wife of *Honey for the Bears* have an open marriage but are basically homosexual. Derek, the high government official of *The Wanting Seed*, is homosexual. Kenneth Toomey of *Earthly Powers* is a homosexual, and his homosexuality is as much a concern of the novel as is the role of the church and God.

A CLOCKWORK ORANGE

First published: 1962
Type of work: Novel

In an unidentified future society, teenage Alex recalls his violent gang activities, his imprisonment, and his reformation.

Burgess' most memorable novel, *A Clockwork Orange*, cannot be discussed without addressing its language, "nadsat," a combination of Russian, English, and slang, which was invented for the novel and which catapults its narrator, Alex, into the reader's consciousness as few other books can. Alex invites us along with him and his "droogs" (buddies) as they sit in a bar, eyeing the "devotchkas [girls] . . . dressed in the heighth of fashion" and wearing "make-up to match (rainbows round the glazzies [eyes], that is, and the rot [mouth] painted very wide)." He narrates their adventures as they do a bit of ultraviolence: They "razrez" a teacher's books to bits, then "tolchock" him and treat him to the "old bootcrush"; they come across Billyboy and his five droogs, which leads to a gang fight with "the nozh [knife], the oozy [chain], the britva [razor], not just fisties and boots"; they beat to death an old woman and her "pusscats." Throughout part 1, the extreme violence of the novel is made palatable by the unusual language, which presents repulsive acts with strange, new words, drawing the reader into the book and into the violence itself. The language of the novel captures the reader and makes him or her one of Alex's "droogs," maintaining sympathy for Alex throughout his violent activities. When he rapes two ten-year-old girls in his room, he tells the reader that "this time they thought nothing fun and stopped creeching with high mirth, and had to submit to the strange and weird desires of Alexander the Large which . . . were choodessny and zammechat and very demanding. . . . But they were both very very drunken and could hardly feel very much." When he hints at his brutality toward his father and mother, he reveals that his father was "like humble mumble chumble." In addition to making the violence more acceptable, Alex's inclusion of biblical language, "Oh, my brothers," makes the narrator more than just an uneducated criminal; at times, in fact, Alex sounds suspiciously like a preacher addressing his congregation on the nature of good and evil. The language of *A Clockwork Orange*, innovative, powerful, and original, becomes almost like a character in the novel. The language not only distances the violence being described but forces the reader to reevaluate that violence. Indeed, the language is one of the things that makes *A Clockwork Orange* so powerful.

The novel opens with the line "What's it going to be then, eh?" and this question, which serves as the structure to open each of the novel's three sections, introduces the reader not only to the "humble narrator" Alex but also to one of the novel's major themes: the nature of free will. In part 2, Alex, who is only fifteen and who has been incarcerated for murdering the old woman with the cats, is subjected to reconditioning by the State. In this, "the real weepy and like tragic part of the story," the State tries to take away Alex's free will by making him ill when he views sex and violence, and also when he listens to Ludwig van Beethoven's Ninth Symphony, which had been a favorite of Alex after his violent activities. The nature of free will and determinism is one of Burgess' most oft-repeated themes; Alex and the prison chaplain, who constantly addresses Alex as "little 6655321" rather than by his name, discuss the fact that Alex is going "to be made into a good boy." Burgess' attack on behaviorists and on totalitarian states is obvious: Alex is made ill by drugs, is forced to view nauseatingly violent films, and is reduced to a sniveling, whining victim. Part 3 presents the reader with a new, reformed Alex, an Alex without free will or freedom of choice, an Alex who has become a victim, and an Alex who ultimately tries to commit suicide. Something of a celebrity after his reconditioning by the State, Alex views a photograph of himself in the newspaper, looking "very gloomy and like scared, but that was really with the flashbulbs going pop pop all the time." Upon arrival home, Alex learns that his parents have rented his room to a lodger and that he is no longer welcome there. All of his personal belongings were sold to pay for the upkeep of the orphaned cats of the woman Alex had murdered. Alex staggers away, only to encounter some of his former victims, who beat him and subject him to the same treatment to which he had originally subjected them.

Throughout, Burgess makes it clear that without freedom of choice and free will, even when that choice is used to commit evil, people become helpless victims of society and life. In his despair at his life without choice, Alex tries to commit suicide, leading the State to be accused of failure in its "criminal reform scheme" and to be accused of figurative murder, since the State has, indeed, murdered the real Alex. Alex's attempted suicide makes him feel "filled up again with clean." It also makes his parents repent for their abominable treatment of him after his release from prison. The government authorities try to restore Alex to his former, unreconditioned self. Until 1987, the American edition of the novel excluded the final chapter, as did Stanley Kubrick's 1971 film, and the second to the last chapter ends with Alex's imagining himself doing some ultraviolence and his ironic comment, "I was cured all right." The final chapter, however, though often considered weak by American audiences or critics, reveals another of Burgess' important themes: an essentially optimistic view of humankind. Alex chooses to reject his formerly violent ways. He tells his audience, "And all it was was that I was young." Alex decides to grow up and have a family. Just as he had chosen to commit violence, with free will Alex can choose to avoid evil.

NOTHING LIKE THE SUN

First published: 1964
Type of work: Novel

Set in Elizabethan England, and using Elizabethan language and idiom, this fictional account of William Shakespeare's love life concentrates on his sexual encounters.

In *Nothing Like the Sun: A Story of Shakespeare's Love-Life*, Anthony Burgess freely imagines the sexual exploits and love life of William Shakespeare. The protagonist, identified as WS throughout the novel, is seduced and forced into marriage by Anne Hathaway. WS does not believe the child is his, and this establishes some of the themes of the novel: sexual infidelity, manipulation, and coercion. WS's relationship with his wife is not a happy one, and, despite the birth of twins, whom WS does claim as his own, he goes to London to work and live, rarely returning home to his wife and children, who live with WS's parents and siblings. Away from home, WS becomes involved with his beautiful male sponsor, the Earl of Southampton, Henry Wriothesly, to whom the poem "Venus and Adonis" and the sonnets are dedicated. As WS's wife will prove to be, Southampton is unfaithful to WS, which forces WS to seek the love of his "dark lady" in the arms of Fatimah, an island beauty whom WS describes as neither black nor white, but "gold." Fatimah is greatly interested in WS's friends and acquaintances: She eventually has an affair with Wriothesly. When WS discovers her infidelity, he returns to his home in Stratford, only to find himself cuckolded by his own brother. WS returns to London. After a time, he takes Fatimah back. From her, WS contracts syphilis, which Fatimah contracted from Wriothesly. According to Burgess, this disease affects WS's worldview, leading, by implication, to the darker artistic vision of the tragedies.

Interwoven with WS's sexual exploits and disappointments is the milieu of Elizabethan England. Burgess shows his readers the effects of the plague, the struggles of the theaters, and the tempests of the playwrights and their players, all in the idiom and language of the Elizabethans. Burgess abundantly displays his linguistic ability and playfulness in *Nothing Like the Sun*. Many of the characters speak lines from Shakespeare's plays, and Burgess describes the environment, characters, and behavior in language that approximates that of the time period, lending a richness and complexity to the novel that would not have been comparable with contemporary English. The usage of language is also of great importance to the "word-boy" WS, so the Elizabethan English in the novel becomes an appropriate metaphor for WS's struggles to form language that fits his view of the world and to express his deepest beliefs. To emphasize this importance of language, a few parts of the novel are written as a journal or as if they were excerpts from a drama.

As a sort of prologue (though not identified as such) before the novel proper, these words appear: "Mr. Burgess's farewell lecture to his special students . . . who complained that Shakespeare had nothing to give to the East. (Thanks for the farewell gift of three bottles of *samsu*. I will take a swig now. Delicious.)" In the epilogue, the reader is again introduced to this *samsu*-swigging persona, who enters the narrative of the novel only once or twice. The point of view in the epilogue immediately returns to that of WS, however, who is now dying, attended by his physician son-in-law. The viewpoint in *Nothing Like the Sun* is almost consistently that of WS, so it is unclear why Burgess' persona intrudes into the narrative, especially since Burgess does it so infrequently and inconsequentially.

TREMOR OF INTENT

First published: 1966
Type of work: Novel

In this parody of the spy genre, secret agent Hillier is sent to reclaim a British scientist named Roper, and he encounters the villainous Theodorescu.

In the first part of Burgess' *Tremor of Intent*, the protagonist is a secret agent named Hillier, who wishes to retire and who suffers from the "two chronic diseases of gluttony and satyriasis." He recounts his memories of his childhood and young adult relationship with Roper, a British scientist. Hillier has been sent, on this last mission before retirement, to recover Roper from the Soviet Union. Many of Burgess' standard themes appear in this part of the book: the role of the church and religion, the duality of good and evil, the nature of free will, and the infidelity of wives. Roper and Hillier engage in many of these discussions themselves, but Roper also discusses the philosophical issues with others. Roper's wife, a German girl whom he married after World War II, is unfaithful, and Hillier, ostensibly in the name of Roper's honor, beats up her lover (just before Hillier has sex with her himself). Though Hillier is on a cruise ship on his way to recover the scientist, Roper, at the beginning of the novel, it is not until part 2 that the action of the novel actually takes place on the cruise ship.

In part 2, where the parody of the spy genre begins in earnest, Hillier meets the siblings Alan and Clara Walters, who will aid him in his attempt to get Roper and who will save Hillier's life. Young Clara represents the innocent female in the novel, and, though Hillier will ultimately have relations with her, he spends much of the novel avoiding sexual contact with her, trying to convince himself that his feelings toward her are paternal. He readily admits his sexual feelings for Miss Devi, however, the wicked woman of the genre; she is employed as secretary to the novel's villian, Mr. Theodorescu, a gluttonous, obese pederast. Hillier engages in a gluttony contest with Theodorescu, and Burgess catalogs the foods that they eat with great detail. Hillier also indulges in sexual antics with Miss Devi, which leads to his being tricked (by drugs) into giving Theodorescu information, which the villain, as a neutral, plans to sell to the highest bidder. Burgess clearly condemns the villain Theodorescu for being a neutral. Apparently, not choosing sides, or choosing to be on all sides, is a crime in this novel; many of the other characters, but especially the young boy Alan, despise such neutrality.

In part 3, after Hillier finds Roper, he discovers that he himself is the one who has been duped: He has not been sent to rescue Roper after all, but to be killed. True to the genre, however, Hillier is saved. Burgess has the assassin engage in a philosophical discussion with Hillier and Roper, which allows them the time to be rescued.

Hillier then finds Theodorescu, gorges the villain with information, and eliminates him. Hillier also has his long-anticipated sexual rendezvous with Clara. Even while parodying the genre, Burgess presents a plot with sufficient twists and surprises to retain the reader's interest. Though the sometimes lengthy discussions on good and evil or on the nature of choice may seem inappropriate, they could also be interpreted as Burgess' parody of the genre: His spies and villains deal with major philosophical issues even while they practice their craft.

In part 4, Burgess has Clara and Alan, who were essential components of Hillier's success in surviving his last assignment, come to visit Hillier, and the three of them briefly discuss some of the philosophical issues present in the early parts of the novel. Hillier, former spy, glutton, and satyr, has now, in the ultimate parody of the spy genre and in the ultimate representation of Burgess' essentially optimistic worldview, become a priest. Burgess does not play with language excessively in *Tremor of Intent.* His characters discuss his usual themes in great detail.

EARTHLY POWERS

First published: 1980
Type of work: Novel

Against a backdrop of international events of the twentieth century, the homosexual author Kenneth Toomey narrates the story of his life.

Earthly Powers contains many of Burgess' favorite themes: the duality of nature, good versus evil, free will versus determinism, sexuality, and infidelity. The narrator, homosexual author Kenneth Toomey, becomes related, through the marriage of his sister Hortense, to the Catholic family Campanati, whose adopted son Carlo will one day become pope. Though future pontiff Carlo Campanati is rarely in the novel, when he is present, he and the narrator often argue about such philosophical issues as free will, choice, and the nature of a God who creates homosexuals and whose church condemns homosexuality. Toomey is eighty-one years old at the start of the novel. When Toomey tries to end the relationship with his unfaithful lover-secretary Geoffrey, Geoffrey threatens blackmail. Geoffrey, however, is then forced to flee to avoid criminal prosecution for some crime he has committed. Early in the novel, Toomey is asked to corroborate a "miracle" supposedly performed by Carlo years earlier; to rid himself of Geoffrey, Toomey sends Geoffrey to Chicago to investigate the miracle.

The novel then explores Toomey's long life, including his various affairs and betrayals: with Val, who leaves him and who will one day become a poet; with Sir Richard Curry Burt, who involves Toomey in a bizarre homosexual situation at a dock; with Ralph, an African American, who leaves Toomey to return to Africa and his black heritage; with physician Phillip Shawcross, a platonic relationship that Toomey claims is his greatest love. Like the wives in Burgess' other works, the male lovers of Toomey in this novel are often unfaithful and frequently cruel. Toomey, like many of Burgess' characters, is obsessed with sexuality and often has incestuous thoughts about his sister Hortense, who seems to be the only woman with whom he would consider having a physical relationship. After her divorce, Hortense has a lesbian relationship, despite the fact that she had previously reviled Toomey for his homosexuality. At the end of the novel, Toomey and his sister Hortense are living together, as Mr. and Mrs. Toomey, and sleep in the same bedroom, though in separate beds.

Woven into the story of Toomey's relatively unhappy love life are the stories of his sister Hortense, who marries the pontiff's brother Domenico Campanati, and who is unfaithful in order to give her sterile husband children; of Toomey's brother Tom, a comedian who dies, apparently from smoking-induced cancer; of Toomey's nephew John, who is killed in Africa, along with his wife, after Toomey helps finance a research trip for them; and of John's twin sister, Ann, whose own daughter Eve will become tragically involved with the person whom Carlo Campanati saved in the miracle performed so long ago. Toomey's life intersects not only with these characters but also with various literary and historical personages, some of whom are actually presented in the plot of the novel, and others who are mentioned only in passing: James Joyce, T. S. Eliot, George Orwell, Heinrich Himmler, and Joseph Goebbels, to name a few.

By the end of the novel, in a bizarre twist of the characters' fates, Toomey learns that the child miraculously saved by Carlo Campanati grew up to become Godfrey Manning, or God for short, a cult figure who poisons his entire congregation with cyanide but does not join his flock in this ultimate communion. Burgess' irony is deftly presented, especially in the final chapters of the novel. His homosexual narrator remains a relatively sympathetic character throughout *Earthly Powers*, and Burgess' plot successfully weaves the stories of all the characters together. Burgess does not engage in extensive linguistic wordplay or invent new language for this novel, as he does in so many of his other books, but he does explore in depth his usual philosophical and theological issues: the nature of good and evil and the nature of free will and choice.

Summary

The fiction of Anthony Burgess is a unique concoction of language and linguistic wordplay, philosophical discussions, grotesque details, comedy, and tragedy. Burgess' work is not of a consistently high quality; some of his novels are flawed, and his obsession with language can become intrusive and distracting. Nevertheless, Burgess' body of work shows a wide range of philosophical interests and diverse treatment of his subject matters, and it is a worthy representative of British literature. At his best, Burgess creates language that becomes a character in the fiction and that is greater than the characters or themes contained in the novels.

Bibliography

Aggeler, Geoffrey. *Anthony Burgess: The Artist as Novelist.* Tuscaloosa: University of Alabama Press, 1979.

Bloom, Harold, ed. *Modern Critical Views: Anthony Burgess.* New York: Chelsea House, 1987.

Burgess, Anthony. *Little Wilson and Big God.* New York: Weidenfeld & Nicolson, 1987.

Coale, Samuel. *Anthony Burgess.* New York: Frederick Ungar, 1981.

Mathews, Richard. *The Clockwork Universe of Anthony Burgess.* San Bernardino, Calif.: Borgo Press, 1978.

Morris, Robert K. *The Consolations of Ambiguity: An Essay on the Novels of Anthony Burgess.* Columbia: University of Missouri Press, 1971.

Stinson, John J. *Anthony Burgess Revisited.* Boston: Twayne, 1991.

Sherri Szeman

ROBERT BURNS

Born: Alloway, Ayrshire, Scotland
January 25, 1759
Died: Dumfries, Scotland
July 21, 1796

Principal Literary Achievement

As the greatest of the Scottish poets, Burns composed lyrics, ballads, satires, and occasional verse that advanced the Romantic movement and remain part of the permanent literary heritage.

Biography

Robert Burns was born on the family farm in the Ayrshire district of Scotland on January 25, 1759, to William Burnes (as the father spelled his name) and Agnes Broun. William, a poor tenant farmer, struggled to keep his family from poverty. At Mount Oliphant, Lochlie, and Mossgiel, as the family moved from one farm to another, the story of failure was the same, in spite of back-breaking toil. In every case, rents for the land were too costly. To supplement the family income, Robert tried to dress flax in Irvine, but he eventually returned to the farm in Mauchline parish, where his father died in 1784. In "The Cotter's Saturday Night," Burns romanticizes the nobility of his father in a nostalgic, deeply felt remembrance.

Burns's earliest schooling was from John Murdoch, a competent teacher hired by the farmers of the district; at Dalrymple, he studied at the parish school. Briefly in 1773, he was again a pupil at Murdoch's school at Ayr. In spite of the interruptions in his education, Burns was an apt scholar and was fortunate to have sound educators as his masters. He learned French well enough to read but not to speak in that language, studied mathematics with his uncle at Ballochneil in 1777, and studied elements of surveying under Hugh Rodger, schoolmaster at nearby Kirkoswald.

Before that time, Burns had been writing verse to various young women, among them Mary Campbell ("Highland Mary"), with whom he was having an affair, and who died in 1786. He married Jean Armour, of Mauchline, in 1788, with whom he had four children. As early as 1785, he had begun "The Jolly Beggars." By 1786, he collected enough early verse to publish his first book, *Poems, Chiefly in the Scottish Dialect* (1786, 1787, 1793), printed at Kilmarnock.

At first, Burns achieved a local reputation, but his fame as a supposedly unlettered bard soon grew. In Edinburgh, where he was lionized as a country genius by the

Robert Burns

aristocrats, he conducted himself with dignity. Two reprintings of his poems, with additions, appeared in Edinburgh in 1787. The volume was also published in London; within two years, pirated editions appeared in Dublin, Belfast, Philadelphia, and New York.

For the first edition of the Kilmarnock poems, he had received only twenty pounds, but for the second he earned the princely sum, to him, of four hundred pounds. With this money, he was able to travel briefly, buy property of his own, and settle down with Jean and his four children on a farm at Ellisland, near Dumfries. After a last unsatisfactory attempt to make the farm pay, Burns left with his family to Dumfries, where he accepted another appointment as an excise (tax) officer in 1791; he remained there for the rest of his life.

In spite of malicious gossip, his last five years were those of a respected townsman and celebrated poet. Yet these years were burdened as well by illness, the toll of his early plowman's labors. Nevertheless, he continued writing and contributed three hundred songs to two collections of Scottish songs, James Johnson's *The Scots Musical Museum* (1787-1803) and George Thomson's *A Select Collection of Original Scottish Airs* (1793-1805). Burns died in Dumfries from rheumatic heart disease at the age of thirty-seven, on July 21, 1796.

Analysis

In a letter to Reynolds, July 13, 1818, Keats wrote of Burns:

> One song of Burns's is of more worth to you than all I could think for a whole year in his native country. His misery is a dead weight upon the nimbleness of one's quill—I tried to forget it—to drink toddy without any care—to write a merry sonnet—it won't do—he talked with bitches—he drank with blackguards, he was miserable—We can see horribly clear, in the works of such a man his whole life, as if we were God's spies.

Keats admires in Burns his humanity, an expansiveness that elevates Burns's vision to those who, in William Shakespeare's words from *King Lear* (c. 1605-1606), are "God's spies." In his range, Burns indeed may be compared with such English poets of tolerance and humanity as Geoffrey Chaucer and Robert Browning; although his psychology and depth of understanding is less acute than those writers, his lyrical gifts are possibly purer. Burns's scope includes a wide range of types and literary conventions, from sketches on the "bitches" and "blackguards" in taverns or in churches, to the most elevated love songs, to rallying choruses for democratic solidarity. A poet of the people, Burns wrote so that "his whole life" became the subject of his art.

Burns's major poetry generally falls into five convenient groupings: drinking songs, love songs, satires, usually on Calvinistic rigors, democratic chants or songs, and verse narratives. In addition, he wrote miscellaneous verse epistles, mostly moralistic but sometimes aesthetic, and occasional pieces, usually to commemorate a particular event or to praise (sometimes flatter) a particular person. Among his most notable drinking songs are "The Jolly Beggars" and "Willy Brew'd a Peck of Maut." Examples of his love lyrics include "Ae Fond Kiss," "Highland Mary," "A Red, Red Rose," and "O, Once I Lov'd a Bonie Lass." Examples of the satires are "Holy Willie's Prayer," "Address to the Unco Guid," and "Address to the Deil." Among Burns's patriotic or democratic songs are "Scots, Wha Hae," "Is There For Honest Poverty," and the more Jacobean "A Dream" and "The Twa Dogs." His most famous verse narrative is "Tam O'Shanter." A good example of Burns's didactic verse treating his aesthetic is "Epistle to J. Lapraik." Taken together, these varieties of poetic subjects or types share the Burns signature of spontaneity, wit, freshness, sincerity, and vigor.

Usually classed among the "Pre-Romantic" writers of the late eighteenth and early nineteenth centuries, Burns is in most regards a true Romantic. Like such major early Romantics as William Wordsworth, Samuel Taylor Coleridge, Lord Byron, and Percy Bysshe Shelley, Burns demonstrates in his verse extemporaneous effusion, directness, and lyricism; like them, he exalts the common man, delights in the rustic (or natural) beauties of the open countryside, and celebrates his own ego. To the extent that Burns is also influenced by neoclassical literary conventions, his verse is generally more tersely epigrammatical (except in comparison with much of Byron's work), less innovative in terms of experimentation with new meters or forms, and less directly concerned with transcendental emotions. Unlike the major Romantics who followed him, Burns eschewed blank verse and never attempted to write for the theater. These distinctions aside, Burns rightly takes his place with the still-greater poet William Blake as both forerunner and shaper of the Romantic impulse in Western literature.

THE JOLLY BEGGARS

First published: 1799
Type of work: Poem

> Subtitled "A Cantata," this poem is a medley of rowdy, sometimes ribald, joyous drinking songs.

In "The Study of Poetry," Matthew Arnold, a severe critic of Burns in general, could not resist describing "The Jolly Beggars" favorably as a "puissant and splendid production." Literary antecedents of the work, which combines a medley of songs in a loose dramatic structure, go back to John Fletcher's *The Beggar's Bush* (before 1622) or to John Gay's *The Beggar's Opera* (1728). Slightly more than a generation after Burns, the French poet Pierre-Jean de Béranger would write song-comedic productions such as "Les Gueux" ("The Beggars") and "Le Vieux Vagabond" ("The Old Vagabond"). But nothing in Western literature can match Burns's production for energy, sly wit, and lyricism.

Suggested by a chance visit by the poet with two friends to the "doss house" (brothel) of Poosie Nansie (her real name was Agnes Gibson) in the Cowgate, Mauchline, "The Jolly Beggars" transforms the sordid reality of the original scene into a baudy, lighthearted comedy. Challenging the prudery of his own day, Burns exalts a kind of rough, natural sensuality, without a trace of sniggering. Although joyous sex is a theme of the poem, its real message is that people must have liberty to live in the way that they wish. No more defiant yet witty lines have been written in defense of freedom:

> A fig for those by law protected!
> Liberty's a glorious feast!
> Courts for cowards were erected,
> Churches built to please the priest!

A RED, RED ROSE

First published: 1796
Type of work: Poem

The speaker in this well-beloved lyric bids his sweetheart farewell but promises to return to her.

"A Red, Red Rose," also titled in some anthologies according to its first line, "O, my luve is like a red, red rose," was written in 1794, printed in 1796. The song may be enjoyed as a simple, unaffected effusion of sentiment; or it may be understood on a more complex level as a lover's promises that are full of contradictions, ironies, and paradoxes. Yet the reader should keep in mind the fact that Burns constructed the poem, stanza by stanza, by "deconstructing" old songs and ballads to use parts that he could revise and improve. For example, Burns's first stanza may be compared with his source, "The Wanton Wife of Castle Gate": "Her cheeks are like the roses/ That blossom fresh in June;/ O, she's like a new-strung instrument/ That's newly put in tune." Clearly, Burns's version is more delicate, while at the same time audaciously calculated. By emphasizing the absolute redness of the rose—the "red, red rose"— the poet demonstrates his seeming artlessness as a sign of sincerity. What other poet could rhyme "June" and "tune" without appearing hackneyed? Yet in Burns the very simplicity of the language works toward an effect of absolute purity.

Readers who analyze the poem using the tools of New Criticism or other twentieth century critical approaches will observe, on the other hand, contradictory elements that seem to work against the speaker's innocent protestations of love. The first two lines of the second stanza do not complete an expected (or logical) thought: "So deep in luve am I" (that I cannot bear to leave my beloved). Instead, the speaker rhetorically protests his love through a series of preposterous boasts. His love will last until the seas go dry, until rocks melt with the sun; he will continue to love while the sands of life (in an hourglass) shall run. Yet so steadfast a lover, after all, is departing from his beloved, not staying by her side. For whatever reason, he is compelled to leave her rather than remain. His final exaggerated promise, that he will return to her, though the journey takes a thousand miles, seems farfetched, even ironically humorous: Instead of such a titanic effort, why should he not simply stay with her?

These paradoxical reflections, however, which change a reading of the poem from one of "pure" lyric to one of irony, are not so difficult to reconcile on the level of common sense. What lover has not exaggerated his or her emotions? Are these exaggerated promises of Burns's speaker any less sincere for being illogical? No matter how the reader resolves this issue, he or she cannot help but admire Burns's art in revising the meter of his source for the last stanza, an old song titled "The True Lover's Farewell": "Fare you well, my own true love/ And fare you well for a while,/ And I will be sure to return back again/ If I go ten thousand mile." Although Burns's revisions are minor, they reveal the difference in technique between a merely competent poet and a master.

HOLY WILLIE'S PRAYER

First published: 1789
Type of work: Poem

The poet satirizes Willie, who is far from "holy," caught in the act of prayer.

"Holy Willie's Prayer," written in 1785, was printed in 1789 and reprinted in 1799. One of the poet's favorite verses, he sent a copy to his friend, the convivial preacher John M'Math, who had requested it, along with a dedicatory poem titled "Epistle to the Rev. John M'Math" (published in 1808). To M'Math he sent his "Argument" as background information:

> Holy Willie was a rather oldish bachelor elder, in the parish of Mauchline, and much
> and justly famed for that polemical chattering which ends in tippling orthodoxy, and for
> that spiritualized bawdry which refines to liquorish devotion.

The real-life "Willie" whom Burns had in mind was William Fisher, a strict Presbyterian elder of the Mauchline church.

In his satire on religious fanaticism, Burns cleverly allows Willie to witness against himself. Willie's prayer, addressed to the deity of Calvinist doctrine, is really a self-serving plea to be forgiven for his own sins of sexual promiscuity (with Meg). Willie's God—more cruel than righteous—punishes sinners according to the doctrine of predestination of saints: Only a small number of "elect" souls, chosen before their births, will enter Heaven; the others, no matter their goodness, piety, or deeds, are condemned (predestined) to Hell. Willie exults in thoughts of revenge toward the miserable souls who are doomed to such eternal torment. The victims over whom he gloats are, from the reader's point of view, far less deserving of hellfire than Willie, a hypocrite, lecher, and demon of wrath.

In the "Epistle to the Rev. John M'Math," Burns defends his own simple creed as one superior to self-styled "holy" Willie's: "God knows, I'm no the thing I should be,/ Nor am I even the thing I could be,/ But twenty times I rather would be/ An atheist clean/ Than under gospel colors hid be,/ Just for a screen." His argument, he avers, is not against a benign doctrine of Christianity with its reach of forgiveness for sincerely repented sins, but against the hypocrites and scoundrels "even wi' holy robes,/ But hellish spirit!"

IS THERE FOR HONEST POVERTY

First published: 1795
Type of work: Poem

This celebrated democratic poem advances claims for the simple dignity of the common man over those for class and caste.

"Is There For Honest Poverty" (also sometimes anthologized under the title "For A' That and A' That") was written in 1794, printed in 1795, and reprinted in 1799. Burns adapted the meter and the phrase "for a' that" from older songs. A Jacobite song published in 1750 has the following chorus: "For a' that and a' that,/ And twice as muckle's a' that,/ He's far beyond the seas the night/ Yet he'll be here for a' that." Also, in "The Jolly Beggars," Burns had used the popular refrain, although in a different context.

Although the poem is clear enough in its general outline—that the honest worth of men of goodwill, no matter what their social class, rank, or financial condition, outweighs the pretentions of caste or privilege—readers often have trouble understanding Burns's elliptical phrasing. His argument is that "honest poverty" has greater worth than the false pride of high social position. Symbols of rank—ribbons, stars, "and all that"—are superfluities. True merit is based upon "sense and worth," the "pith o' sense, and pride o' worth," not upon the "tinsel show" of fine clothing or the pretentiousness of fine dining.

Because Burns wants his reader to grasp the implied meanings of his poem, he often omits logical connectives between ideas. The beginning lines, with suggested additions, may be paraphrased as follows: (What) is there for honest poverty, that it hangs its head and all that (meaning, all that humility, all that false shame because of supposedly low status)? We pass by the coward slave (who lacks the authentic dignity of self-esteem); we dare to be poor for all that (in spite of "all that" lowly position implied by our poverty).

Throughout the poem, Burns invites the reader to participate in interpreting the poem. He wants the reader to understand the elliptical expression "and a' that" in terms of one's own experiences with the class system. As for Burns's point of view, that is unambiguous. He hopes that men and women of goodwill in time will unite, so that "man to man, the warld o'er/ Shall brithers be for a' that!"

TAM O'SHANTER

First published: 1791
Type of work: Poem

In this sustained narrative poem, a drunken befuddled Scottish farmer encounters witches, but he survives.

"Tam O'Shanter" was a favorite with Burns who described the work in a letter to Mrs. Dunlop (April 11, 1791): "I look on *Tam O'Shanter* to be my standard performance in the poetical line." He goes on to say that his "spice of roguish waggery" shows a "force of genius and a finishing polish that I despair of ever excelling." The idea for the story came from several legends popular in the neighborhood of the poet's birthplace, which is within a mile of Alloway Kirk (church). One of Burns's friends, Francis Grose, sent him a prose account of the legend, one upon which Burns probably drew. Yet if a reader compares the flat style of Grose with Burns's jolly version, he or she can better assess the poet's talent. The conclusion of Grose's narrative is as follows: "the unsightly tailless condition of the vigorous steed was, to the last hour of the noble creature's life, an awful warning to the Carrick farmers not to stay too late in Ayr markets." Burns's rendering is: "Now, wha this tale o' truth shall read,/ Each man and mother's son take heed;/ Or cutty-sarks rin in your mind,/ Think! ye may buy the joys o'er dear;/ Remember Tam O'Shanter's mare."

Tam himself may have been based loosely upon the character of Douglas Graham, whose father was a tenant at the farm of Shanter on the Carrick shore. Noted for his habits of drunkenness, Graham was, like Burns's hero, afflicted with a scolding wife. According to D. Auld of Ayre (whose story was taken from notes left at the Edinburgh University Library), a local tradition held that once, while Graham was carousing at the tavern, some local humorists plucked hairs from the tail of his horse, tethered outside the tavern door, until it resembled a stump. As Auld's account has it, the locals swore the next morning that the unfortunate horse had its tail depilated by witches.

Burns's narrative is that oxymoron, a rollicking ghost story. With gentle, tolerant humor, the poet moralizes over the foibles of Tam, commiserates with his good wife, Kate, and philosophizes on the brevity of human happiness. Most of the narrative is perfectly clear to readers, so long as they follow notes on the Scottish words glossed from a well-edited text. Yet the matter of the "cutty-sark" confuses some. Burns has in mind, first, the short skirt worn by the most audacious of the witches; then he refers to the witch herself, when Tam blurts out, "Weel done, Cutty-sark"—meaning the hag who dances wearing the clothing. At this point in the narrative, Tam upsets the witches' frolic dances, and witches and warlocks chase after the hard-riding Tam to the keystone of the bridge. Why cannot the witches pursue Tam over the bridge?

Because they must not approach water, symbol of Christian baptism and grace. So Nannie, leading the witches' riotous pursuit, can grasp only at poor Meg's tail as the horse reaches the safety of the bridge. Horse and rider are saved, but not the tail. So ends, with an appropriate moral, Burns's homily on the dangers of "inspiring bold John Barlycorn"—hard alcohol.

Summary

In his "Epistle to J. Lapraik," Robert Burns modestly denies any pretentions to the highest ranks of poetry: "I am nae poet, in a sense,/ But just a rhymer like by chance./ An' hae to learning nae pretence;/ Yet, what the matter?/ Whene'er my Muse does on me glance,/ I jingle at her." Critics who have taken these casual words seriously, as a valid expression of Burns's aesthetic, have done the poet an injustice. His artistry is by no means that of "jingling" rhymes. Burns is a thinking sentimentalist, a writer who combines rationality with passion. Even his sentimentality is usually controlled by wit, irony, or plain common sense, so that his love poetry not only seems genuine, it is indeed a genuine expression of the poet's larger love of freedom—freedom to live honestly and to love openly, without the constraints of religious bigotry, social prudery, or political subjugation. In his love of freedom, Burns remains—over the centuries—a defiant voice against hypocrisy and cant, against meanness of spirit. Through his art, he shows us that freedom is joyous.

Bibliography

Bentman, Raymond. *Robert Burns.* Boston: Twayne, 1987.

Crawford, Thomas. *Burns: A Study of the Poems and Songs.* Stanford, Calif.: Stanford University Press, 1960.

Daiches, David. *Robert Burns and His World.* London: Thames & Hudson, 1971.

Ferguson, John DeLancey. *Pride and Passion: Robert Burns, 1759-1796.* 1939. Reprint. New York: Russell & Russell, 1964.

Grimble, Ian. *Robert Burns: An Illustrated Biography.* New York: P. Bedrick Books, 1986.

Keith, Christina. *The Russet Coat: A Critical Study of Burns' Poetry and Its Background.* London: Hale, 1956.

Lindsay, John Maurice. *The Burns Encyclopaedia.* New York: St. Martin's Press, 1980.

McGuirk, Carol. *Robert Burns and the Sentimental Era.* Athens, Ga.: University of Georgia Press, 1985.

Stewart, William. *Robert Burns and the Common People.* New York: Haskell House, 1971.

Leslie B. Mittleman

LORD BYRON

Born: London, England
January 22, 1788
Died: Missolonghi, Greece
April 19, 1824

Principal Literary Achievement

One of the major English Romantic poets, Byron, as satirist and as creator of the Romantic figure of the "Byronic hero," also had a significant impact on nineteenth century European culture.

Biography

George Gordon, later to become the sixth Lord Byron, was born January 22, 1788, in London, England, the son of Captain John "Mad Jack" Byron and Catherine Gordon of Gight, Scotland. Catherine was heiress to a small fortune, which her husband soon squandered. After the couple fled from creditors to France, Catherine left her philandering husband and moved to London. George Gordon was born with a clubbed right foot, an ailment that caused him much humiliation throughout his life but for which he attempted to compensate through athletic endeavors. The Byrons soon moved to Aberdeen, where Catherine could better afford to live on her modest allowance. Captain Byron died in France in 1791 at the age of thirty-six. His son would die at the same age.

After years of attending grammar schools in Aberdeen, George Gordon became the sixth Lord Byron upon the death of his granduncle in 1798. He moved to Newstead Abbey, Nottinghamshire, the Byron family seat, and the Byrons' life-style changed considerably. From 1801 to 1805, young Byron attended Harrow School, spending his vacations with his mother, who was alternately abusive and tender. In 1804, he began a correspondence with his half sister, Augusta Leigh, from whom he had been living separately since his infancy, thus forming a close and complicated relationship that outlasted many others and that became the source of considerable scandal, in part accounting for the failure of his marriage and in part prompting Byron's self-exile to Europe. Entering Trinity College, Cambridge, in 1805, Byron formed other lasting alliances, most notably those of his dear friends John Cam Hobhouse and John Edleston. It was during this time that Byron began to form his ideals of the sanctity of political and personal liberty. In 1807, he published his first volume of poems, *Hours of Idleness*, which was attacked in the *Edinburgh Review*. An undistinguished stu-

dent, Byron left Cambridge in 1808 with a master's degree.

In 1809, Byron took his seat in the House of Lords, often supporting liberal, un-popular causes. In this year, he also discovered and exploited his unrivaled knack for satire, publishing *English Bards and Scotch Reviewers*, in which he lashed out at the *Edinburgh Review* and criticized contemporaries Robert Southey, William Words-worth, and others of the "Lake School" of poetry. Later in 1809, Byron left with his friend Hobhouse on a tour, not the customary Grand Tour of Western Europe, but a tour of Portugal, Spain, Albania, and Greece. This trip inspired him to begin *Childe Harold's Pilgrimage* (1812-1818; 1819), and he finished the first canto in Athens. In 1810, Byron finished the second canto of *Childe Harold's Pilgrimage*, traveling fur-ther in Turkey and Greece. Inspired by the Ovidian story of Hero and Leander, he swam the Hellespont on May 3, 1810, an accomplishment of which he boasted in a poem "Written After Swimming from Sestos to Abydos." He returned to England in 1811, shortly before his mother's death. Despite her unstable and often cruel treatment of him, the son mourned her loss, which was closely followed by the loss of two school friends.

In 1812, *Childe Harold's Pilgrimage* was published. "I awoke one morning and found myself famous," Byron wrote. Byron's fame, his extraordinary personal beauty, and the intriguing, dangerous image created by the public's insistence upon confus-ing the character of Harold with Byron himself attracted the attention of many women, and he engaged in numerous indiscreet affairs, notably with Lady Caroline Lamb, whose obsession with him would provoke him to escape into an ill-suited marriage with Annabella Milbanke in 1815. Meanwhile, in 1813, Byron also began an affair with Augusta Leigh, his half sister; he also published the first of his Oriental tales, *The Giaour* and *The Bride of Abydos*, and in the following year he published *The Cor-sair* and *Lara*. Annabella, who was intellectual but priggish, was frightened and ap-palled by Byron's cruelty, his sexual and behavioral eccentricities, and his excessive attention to Augusta. Seriously doubting his sanity, Lady Byron left her husband af-ter only a year of marriage, taking their only daughter, Augusta Ada. In April of 1816, Byron again left England, this time never to return.

Byron spent the summer of 1816 in Switzerland with Percy Bysshe Shelley, the Romantic poet, Mary Godwin (later known as Mary Shelley, the author of *Franken-stein*, 1818), and her stepsister, Jane "Claire" Clairmont, with whom Byron had had a brief affair in England. He traveled some more through Italy and Switzerland with Hobhouse and published canto III of *Childe Harold's Pilgrimage* and *The Prisoner of Chillon, and Other Poems* (1816). The trip through the Alps inspired him to begin *Manfred* (1817), the darkest treatment of his "Byronic hero." In 1817, Claire Clair-mont and Byron had a daughter, Allegra. Byron spent most of 1817 traveling and living in Venice and other parts of Italy, completing *Manfred* and working on the fourth and final canto of *Childe Harold's Pilgrimage*. It was also during this time that Byron luckily discovered the Italian poetic form of *ottava rima*, with which he ex-perimented in writing *Beppo: A Venetian Story* (1818), a comic tale set in Venice.

In 1818, Byron began *Don Juan* (1819-1824; 1826). In 1819, he began his last major love affair, with Teresa, Countess of Guiccioli. The first two cantos of *Don Juan* were published in July of 1819. Public reception was one of outrage and cries of indecency and slander. In 1820, Byron lived in the Guiccioli palace in Ravenna, Italy, and wrote *Marino Faliero, Doge of Venice* (1821), the first of his political dramas based on the five-part classical models. After the pope permitted Teresa's legal separation from her husband, Byron became more closely involved with her family's political activities, most significantly with the radical society known as the Carbonari, who conspired to revolt against Austrian dominance in Italy. This struggle was unsuccessful, and in 1821 the family was exiled to Pisa. Byron then turned his attention to the Greek cause of independence from Turkey.

In 1821, Byron also published *Cain: A Mystery* (1821) and cantos 3 through 5 of *Don Juan*, which, amid continued public disapproval, enjoyed tremendous sales. Joining Teresa and her family in Pisa, Byron was the source of extensive scandal back in England, and his friends, though admiring his genius, became increasingly concerned and admonishing about the license of his work. Disgusted with his publisher's reluctance to publish *Cain*, Byron changed publishers, allowing John Hunt to include *The Vision of Judgment* (1822) in the first issue of the literary journal *The Liberal*. In 1822, Byron mourned the death of both his daughter, Allegra, and his close friend Shelley. In 1823, Byron left for Greece with Teresa's brother, Pietro Gamba. He soon became severely ill, but left for Missolonghi, Greece, convinced of its strategic importance in the revolution. John Hunt published *Don Juan*, cantos 6 through 14. On his thirty-sixth birthday, Byron wrote "On This Day I Complete My Thirty-sixth Year." In Missolonghi, on April 19, 1824, Byron died, to this day a national hero in Greece. Denied burial with fellow great poets in Westminster Abbey because of his profligate life-style, Byron's body is buried in the family vault at Hucknall Torkard Church in Nottinghamshire, near Newstead.

Analysis

Byron's popularity has not always corresponded to his critical appraisal. He stands apart from his fellow Romantic poets—William Wordsworth, Samuel Taylor Coleridge, Percy Bysshe Shelley, and John Keats—in his stubborn reverence for the poetic style of eighteenth century writers such as John Dryden and Alexander Pope. Indeed, it was the eighteenth century propensity for wit and satire that was also Byron's forte. It is ironic, then, that Byron is in many ways considered to represent the epitome of the Romantic figure. Both personally and in many of his dark, tormented Romantic heroes, Byron created a cultural icon that had a significant impact on his society and the literary movement of his time, though it must be noted that, although the Byronic hero is certainly in part autobiographical, it represents only one aspect of a complex personality.

Perhaps the salient characteristic of Byron's work that assures his label as a consummate Romantic is his creation of the so-called Byronic hero. This character type appears in many variations in Byron's works but is generally based on such literary characters as Prometheus, John Milton's Satan, Johann Wolfgang von Goethe's Faust, and many popular sentimental heroes of the age—and, of course, on Byron himself. Though there are variations on this type—Harold, Cain, Manfred, the Giaour, Lara, Selim, and others—generally, the Byronic hero is a melancholy man of great and noble principles, with great courage of his convictions, and haunted by some secret past sin—usually a sin of illicit love, occasionally suggested to be incestuous. He is alienated, proud, and driven by his own turbulent passion.

Recurrent themes in Byron's work can be said to be subsumed under the larger category of nature versus civilization. Political oppression, military aggression, sexual repression, even the superficial restraints of a frivolous, silly English society—all go against the Romantic aspiration that Byron sees as inherent in human nature, and such oppression always yields disastrous results.

Byron, who appears to have had an almost innate love of liberty, was exposed in his extensive travels to markedly diverse cultures and experiences, thus giving him a unique perspective (and certainly a broader one than his contemporaries) on human nature and civilization. Witnessing the ravages of war, the demoralization of political oppression, and the violence of prejudice and hypocrisy particularly afforded Byron a rare insight into the weaknesses of his own English society. These political and societal flaws Byron exposed in many of his works, particularly in *Childe Harold's Pilgrimage*, *Don Juan*, and *The Vision of Judgment*, at the risk of great public disapproval and alienation and at great personal cost. The extent and the exotic nature of Byron's travels, in addition to his vivid descriptions of his experiences and his retelling of colorful folktales, additionally account for much of the popularity of Byron's works. His accounts of the virtually unexplored, mysterious land of Albania, for example, captivated the imagination of his insular English readers.

A common theme in Byron's work is certainly that of love in its many manifestations: illicit love, idyllic love, sexual repression, sexual decadence, thwarted love, marriage. Yet in all of its variations, this theme, too, is one of civilization and the discontentment it creates when it denies natural expressions of love. Probably the most touching of Byron's love stories is that of Don Juan and Haidee in canto 1 of *Don Juan*. The affair is innocent, natural, primitive, and therefore by society's standards immoral and unsanctified. Similarly, Don Juan's lack of proper sex education, despite his mother's otherwise vigorous intellectual rigors, in denying what is natural and inevitable, ironically destroys lives.

Byron also repeatedly rails against tyranny and political oppression of any kind. The recent turn of events resulting from the French Revolution and the despotic reign of Napoleon, all of which in the beginning offered such promise, provided Byron with much fodder for condemning such acts of aggression. Yet in war Byron finds inspiration in those who fight to retain or protect their freedoms. His knowledge of political and military history—European, American, Oriental, Mediterranean—was vast, his understanding profound.

Byron was a versatile poet, if not always an accomplished one. In addition to skillfully and poignantly handled romantic lyrics such as "She Walks in Beauty," "When We Two Parted," and the more famous epics, *Childe Harold's Pilgrimage* and *Don*

Juan, Byron also completed lyrical dramas, a number of popular exotic and romantic tales, and satirical works on the literary and political foibles of his time. In terms of both style and structure, his indebtedness to his eighteenth century heroes Dryden and Pope has been given much critical attention. His philosophical and literary faith lay more in reason than in emotion; his preferred delivery was more often one of wit and satire than sentiment and self-indulgence.

CHILDE HAROLD'S PILGRIMAGE

First published: Cantos 1 and 2, 1812; canto 3, 1816; canto 4, 1818; 1819 (the four cantos published together)
Type of work: Poem

Attempting to escape the pangs of guilt resulting from his mysterious past, self-exiled Childe Harold flees to Europe and witnesses the beauties and horrors of other cultures.

Byron began *Childe Harold's Pilgrimage* on his first trip abroad, when he and Hobhouse toured Spain, Portugal, Albania, and Greece. It was originally titled "*Childe Burun*"; "Childe" refers to a young nobleman who has not yet officially taken his title, and "Burun" is an earlier form of Byron's own name. Inspired by his recent reading of Edmund Spenser's *The Faerie Queene*, Byron chose to employ the nine-line Spenserian stanza for the major part of this work.

The first two cantos were published in 1812, and Byron's ensuing popularity among the social and literary circles of London was unprecedented, in part because the public insisted—with some accuracy and despite Byron's prefatory disclaimer to the contrary—upon identifying the intriguing Harold as Byron himself. Byron's own confusion of the two, however, is evident in his frequent dropping of the story line of the work to engage in repeated authorial digressions, which themselves intrude on the almost gratuitous plot. Harold is a young, though not inexperienced, Englishman who is compelled to flee Britain, although, the reader is told, it is in fact his own psyche he is trying to escape. The young man has a mysterious background, an unspeakably painful secret in his past. Perhaps, it is suggested, the secret is of some illicit love. With Harold, Byron introduces the first of his many Byronic heroes.

In canto 1, Harold leaves England, having lived a life of sensuous indulgence. He bids farewell to no friends or family, not even to his mother and sister, although he loves them both deeply. Landing in Portugal, Harold proceeds to visit various battlegrounds across Europe, thus giving Byron as narrator the opportunity to digress on historical, political, and even moral issues of the recent Peninsular War in which England served to help the Spanish resist the French invasion, an event that portended the end of Napoleon's tyranny. As he looks upon the towns that were devastated by Napoleon's army, Byron laments the loss of life and champions those who nobly fought for the preservation of liberty. Byron praises the courageous women of the Spanish province of Aragon who joined the men in resisting an invading French army. Though these women were not trained to be warriors, like the mythological Amazons, but were taught to love, they nevertheless proved themselves to be strong and brave; thus, Byron suggests, they emerge far more beautiful than the women of other countries such as England.

In Spain, Harold witnesses a Sunday bullfight in one of the most famous passages from *Childe Harold's Pilgrimage*, in which Byron is clearly at the same time fascinated and repelled by this violent yet graceful sport. Though Harold is moved by the beauty and song of the festivities around him, he cannot participate, for his pain alienates him from the joys of human activity. He remains a spectator. Singing a ballad, "To Inez," Harold mourns the futility of running away when it is his own "secret woe" that he is attempting to escape. Comparing himself to the "Wandering Jew" of medieval legend who, having mocked Christ, is doomed to roam the earth eternally, seeking the peace of death, Harold bemoans the "hell" that lies hidden in the human heart.

Canto 2 opens with a meditation upon the contributions of classical Greece, a salute prompted by Harold's visit to the Acropolis. As Harold views the ruins of Greece's high achievements, Byron interprets them as reflections of the present loss of Greek freedom, thus foreshadowing his later involvement in the cause of Greek independence. Descriptions of the mysterious land of Albania in this canto represent one of the earliest authentic representations of this exotic country by an Englishman.

Canto 3 begins with Byron's sadly recalling his daughter, Ada, whom he has not seen since the breakup of his marriage. Byron returns to the story of Harold, first warning readers that the young hero has greatly changed since the publication of the first two cantos. During the interim, Byron has endured the painful separation and the scandal concerning his relationship with Augusta, all of which essentially forced him to leave England. His bitterness is evident in the far darker tone of canto 3, and the character of Harold and that of the narrator, never strikingly different in temperament, now are more clearly merged.

Still unable to completely detach himself from feeling the pangs of human compassion, Harold flees to the solitude of natural surroundings, finding nature to be the one true consoler. He feels a communication with the desert, the forest, the ocean, the mountains. Finding Harold at the site of the Battle of Waterloo, "the grave of France," Byron resumes the theme of Napoleon's despotism and takes the opportunity to examine tyranny in general. Praising the heroes of that fateful and momentous battle, Byron blames Napoleon's extremism, arguing that moderation would have prevented the disastrous results of a once noble plan. Harold then travels to Germany, where he still is not immune to feelings of love and joy, however fleeting.

Visiting the Swiss Alps leads Harold to the sites of other battles. Lake Leman (Lake Geneva) recalls to Byron the great French philosopher Jean-Jacques Rousseau, one of the forerunners of the Romantic movement. This section, it has often been noted, has a distinctly Shelleyan mood, and indeed Byron wrote it while visiting

Shelley. Byron explores the pantheistic philosophies of Wordsworth, Shelley, and Rousseau, and expresses feelings of oneness with nature, though he ultimately rejects their ideas. These feelings, furthermore, lead him to consider his feelings of alienation in the world of humankind. Insisting that he is neither cynical nor completely disillusioned, Byron insists that he believes that there are one or two people who are "almost what they seem" and that happiness and goodness are possible. Byron concludes the canto as he begins it, lamenting his absence from Ada, imagining what it would be like to share in her development, to watch her grow.

Canto 4 takes Harold to Italy, at first to Venice, decaying yet still beautiful because its spirit is immortal. Byron confesses that he still has some love for his native country and that he hopes that he will be remembered there. If he dies on foreign soil, he confesses, his spirit will return to England. The canto concludes with Byron's famous apostrophe, or address, to the ocean.

DON JUAN

First published: Cantos 1 and 2, 1819; cantos 3 through 5, 1821; cantos 6 through 14, 1823; cantos 15 and 16, 1824; 1826 (the sixteen cantos published together)

Type of work: Poem

Forced to flee his homeland, the ingenuous Spanish rogue finds love, tragedy, violence, hypocrisy, and wisdom on his world travels.

Don Juan is a unique approach to the already popular legend of the philandering womanizer immortalized in literary and operatic works. Byron's Don Juan, the name comically anglicized to rhyme with "new one" and "true one," is a passive character, in many ways a victim of predatory women, and more of a picaresque hero in his unwitting roguishness. Not only is he not the seductive, ruthless Don Juan of legend, he is also not a Byronic hero. That role falls more to the narrator of the comic epic, the two characters being more clearly distinguished than in Byron's *Childe Harold's Pilgrimage*.

In *Beppo: A Venetian Story* (1818), Byron discovered the appropriateness of *ottava rima* to his own particular style and literary needs. This Italian stanzaic form had been exploited in the burlesque tales of Luigi Pulci, Francesco Berni, and Giovanni Battista Casti, but it was John Hookham Frere's *Whistlecraft* (1817-1818) that revealed to Byron the seriocomic potential for this flexible form in the satirical piece he was planning. The colloquial, conversational style of *ottava rima* worked well with both the narrative line of Byron's mock epic and the serious digressions in which Byron rails against tyranny, hypocrisy, cant, sexual repression, and literary mercenaries.

Byron opens *Don Juan* with a dedication to his old nemesis, Robert Southey, who was at the time poet laureate. Byron hated Southey for his turncoat politics, for his spreading of rumors about Byron, and for his weak verse. The publication of the first two cantos in 1818 created scandal and outrage for the author. Although the names of publisher and author did not appear on the title page, Byron's identity was unmistakable. Even Byron's friends—Hobhouse and others—though admiring the genius of the work, were shocked and concerned about its language and content. The invectives against contemporaneous writers and against Lady Byron smacked of slander; his comments on political and theological issues bordered on sedition and blasphemy. Byron, arguing that this was in fact "the most moral of poems," remained steadfast against editing and censoring. The work, however, also received significant critical praise from such noteworthy giants as Shelley, German poet Johann Wolfgang von Goethe, and John Gibson Lockhart (Sir Walter Scott's son-in-law, writing under the pen name of "John Bull"). Byron found much strength and determination in these encouragements.

Byron's avowed purpose in *Don Juan* was to be "quietly facetious on everything." The narrative opens with sixteen-year-old naïf Don Juan, who innocently falls in love with Dona Julia, the young wife of Don Alfonso, a gentleman of fifty who has been linked romantically with Juan's mother, Dona Inez. Although Byron's poem is "epic" and he promises to observe the epic conventions of Aristotle and the classical authors, his hero is modern, of ordinary proportions and weaknesses. The plot follows a line of at times almost stock farce, the lovers being discovered by Alfonso's spotting Juan's shoes under Julia's bed. At the end of the canto, Juan must flee Spain, the divorced Julia enters a convent, and the picaresque adventures of the young hero begin. Byron's narrator takes the opportunity during the story to comment on love, education, and marriage.

Juan is shipwrecked in canto 2 and, after a shocking encounter with cannibalism, is washed ashore in the Greek Cyclades and is rescued by the beautiful maiden, Haidee, with whom he shares an idyllic love in canto 3 until her pirate father, Lambro, returns in canto 4 and Juan is sold into Turkish slavery. Haidee dies of a broken heart. The Haidee passage is one of Byron's most poignant, his depiction of innocent love thwarted by external, evil forces one of his most touching. Canto 5 finds Juan accompanied and befriended by Johnson, an English soldier of fortune, and the two are bought by a black eunuch who dresses Juan in women's clothes and takes him to the harem queen, Gulbayez, whose advances Juan rejects in deference to Haidee's memory. In Canto 6, however, Juan spends a sensuous and loving night in the harem with Lolah, Katinka, Dudu, and the other odalisques but is unfortunately sentenced to death in the morning.

The epic takes on a more serious tone with cantos 7 and 8, in large part as a result of the significant changes in Byron's own life since the publication of the previous cantos. Juan and Johnson, who have managed to escape, join the Russian army, and Byron vehemently condemns war and military aggression. In cantos 9 and 10, Juan, now a war hero, meets Catherine the Great, who sends him to England. In the remaining cantos, 11 to 16, Byron satirizes English society. As a guest at the country estate of Lord Henry Amundeville, Norman Abbey (based on Byron's own Newstead

Abbey), Juan is pursued by three women: Lord Henry's wife, the sophisticated and intellectual but self-centered Lady Adeline; the mysterious, gracious, graceful Countess Fitz-Fulke; and the silent but emotionally deep Aurora Raby. Much of the final canto concerns a social gathering and the identity of the mysterious ghost of the Black Friar, whom Juan sees at night.

At the time of his death in 1824, Byron was still working on *Don Juan* but had completed only a fragment of canto 17, which does not continue the story line.

THE PRISONER OF CHILLON

First published: 1816
Type of work: Poem

Imprisoned for religious and democratic sentiments, a priest watches his brothers die beside him but is inspired by a songbird and his own strong spirit.

The Prisoner of Chillon is a dramatic monologue written after Byron and Shelley visited the Castle of Chillon in Switzerland, where a priest, François Bonivard, was imprisoned for six years for expressing democratic ideals rooted in his religious doctrine. Impressed by Bonivard's courageous and principled struggle against the cruelty and tyranny of his captors, Byron used the story to comment further on his already characteristic themes of isolation, liberty, oppression, and conviction.

The poem opens with the "Sonnet on Chillon," which reveals, both in content and in style, the influence of Shelley on Byron's work and thought at this time in his career. Byron celebrates the site of Bonivard's imprisonment as consecrated ground, and he praises in exalted and idealistic tones the futility of attempts to constrict the true and free spirit.

The remainder of the poem is told from the first-person perspective of Bonivard himself. Although Byron deviates somewhat from the historical record, this poem represents the first example of Byron using a real person as his protagonist. Bonivard's father and five of his brothers have already perished as a result of this persecution of their faith. Two of them were imprisoned with Bonivard: the youngest brother, sweet of disposition, with tears only for the pain of others; the older brother an active man, strong and courageous. Both of the brothers died while the three of them were chained to huge pillars in the dark Gothic dungeon. Alone and the last survivor of his family, Bonivard then fell into a deep despair, his senses dulled, losing any concept of time, unaware of darkness or light.

In an almost conventional Romantic moment, Bonivard's despair is interrupted by the arrival of a songbird. The prisoner speculates, with last vestiges of optimism, that the bird may also have been imprisoned in a cage and has managed to escape. Perhaps, he speculates, the bird might in fact be his brother's soul visiting him with messages of hope. When the bird flies away, however, Bonivard feels more alone than ever. Yet miraculously, his captors begin to treat him with more compassion, allowing him to walk around in his cell unchained. He climbs up the wall, not to try to escape but merely to get a glimpse through the barred windows of the mountains once again. The beauty of this sight again makes his imprisonment seem even more unbearable. After an indeterminate length of time—days, months, even years—Bonivard is released. The freedom is a hollow victory, however, since he has lost all that is dear to him, and he had come to consider the prison his home. Even the chains and the spiders seemed to be his friends.

THE VISION OF JUDGMENT

First published: 1822
Type of work: Poem

Upon the death of King George III, Satan and the Archangel Michael debate over possession of the tyrant's soul.

Byron had already mocked Robert Southey in *English Bards and Scotch Reviewers* (1809) and in his dedication to *Don Juan*, but his ridicule of Southey is at its pinnacle in *The Vision of Judgment*. Byron hated Southey for many reasons. He disapproved of the poetry of Southey and even the greater "Lake School" poets, William Wordsworth and Samuel Taylor Coleridge. He also resented Southey's turn to conservatism later in life, marked by his being made poet laureate in 1813. Moreover, Southey had spread vicious rumors about Byron's personal life. Upon the death of King George III, Southey, in his role as poet laureate, wrote a sycophantic celebration of George's glorious entry into heaven, *A Vision of Judgment* (1821). In this work, Southey lashed out at Byron, ascribing him to the "Satanic" school. Byron retorted with *The Vision of Judgment*. John Murray, Byron's publisher, was becoming increasingly fearful of the British disapproval of Byron's work, so Byron published the poem in the new literary journal *The Liberal*, edited by Byron and John Hunt, later Byron's new publisher.

In Byron's poem, Saint Peter waits, bored, by the gates of Heaven, his keys rusty and the lock dull with disuse. The angels have nothing to do but sing. Only the angel who records the names of souls lost to hell is overworked, even requesting additional help. Satan is so busy that his thirst for evil is almost quenched. The death of George III brings hypocritical mourning on earth, people drawn to the pomp without really caring about him. Upon hearing that King George III has died, Peter recalls that the last royal entry into Heaven was by the beheaded King Louis XVI, who was admitted as a martyr by playing on the sympathy of the saints.

While the Archangel Michael and Satan debate over who will get the soul of George III, witnesses are called. These include one who praises George, obviously to flatter him, and the anonymous letter writer known as "Junius" who criticized George and who refuses to recant his writings. Then Southey arrives and starts to recite his *A Vision of Judgment.* By the fourth line, the angels and devils have fled in terror. At the fifth line, Saint Peter uses his keys to knock Southey into his lake. In the confusion, George slips unobserved into Heaven.

Summary

Lord Byron's impact on nineteenth century European and American culture, both as a personal cultural figure and as a poet and satirist, cannot be exaggerated. Stylistically and formally, his work is more diverse than that of his fellow Romantics. Byron's curious and perhaps confusing blend of idealism and cynicism accounts in part for critical reluctance to assign to him the same label of Romantic as easily as to Wordsworth or Shelley. Yet in his idealistic, steadfast determination to pursue truth, to strip away the surface to expose cant, hypocrisy, and oppression, Byron was at once a reflection of his culture and an iconoclast.

Bibliography

Boyd, Elizabeth F. *Byron's "Don Juan": A Critical Study.* New Brunswick, N.J.: Rutgers University Press, 1945.

Calvert, William J. *Byron: Romantic Paradox.* New York: Russell & Russell, 1962.

Chew, Samuel. *The Dramas of Lord Byron.* Baltimore: The Johns Hopkins University Press, 1915.

Lovell, Ernest J., Jr. *Byron: The Record of a Quest.* Austin: University of Texas Press, 1949.

McGann, Jerome J. *"Don Juan" in Context.* Chicago: University of Chicago Press, 1976.

Marchand, Leslie. *Byron's Poetry: A Critical Introduction.* Boston: Houghton Mifflin, 1965.

Rutherford, Andrew. *Byron: A Critical Study.* London: Oliver & Boyd, 1962.

Thorslev, Peter, Jr. *The Byronic Hero: Types and Prototypes.* Minneapolis: University of Minnesota Press, 1962.

Trueblood, Paul G. *Lord Byron.* Boston: Twayne, 1977.

West, Paul, ed. *Byron: A Collection of Critical Essays.* Englewood Cliffs, N.J.: Prentice-Hall, 1963.

Lou Thompson

PEDRO CALDERÓN DE LA BARCA

Born: Madrid, Spain
January 17, 1600
Died: Madrid, Spain
May 25, 1681

Principal Literary Achievement

Author of more than one hundred full-length plays and many one-act *autos sacramentales* (religious, often allegorical plays), Calderón is considered one of the truly great dramatists of Spain's Golden Age.

Biography

Pedro Calderón de la Barca was born in Madrid, Spain, on January 17, 1600, into a well-established Castilian family of the lesser nobility. He was the third child of Ana María de Henao and Diego Calderón de la Barca, who held a post at the Spanish Court. The family therefore followed the king to Valladolid and then back to Madrid, where Calderón attended the Colegio Imperial, a Jesuit school, from 1608 to 1613. In 1610, his mother died suddenly, and his father died in 1615. His mother had wanted her son to become a priest, and his father encouraged him strongly to complete his studies. In 1614, Calderón had enrolled at the University of Alcalá de Henares. Then, in the years 1616 to 1620, he divided his time between Alcalá and the University of Salamanca, where he probably completed the degree in canonical law. His study of theology, logic, and scholastic philosophy may well have influenced his intellectual approach to the ideas presented in his plays. His early verses, which he entered in a poetry contest in 1620 in honor of the beatification of Saint Isadore, were considered worthy of praise by his great contemporary, the dramatist Lope de Vega, and his first play *Amor, honor y poder* (1623; *love, honor, and power*) was performed in Madrid in 1623. During the next two years, he was probably a soldier in Italy and Flanders. This period is followed by a very productive period of playwriting. By 1630, he had written fifteen plays, including *La dama duende* (1636; *The Phantom Lady*, 1664) and *El príncipe constante* (1629; *The Constant Prince*, 1853).

Although the record of his life is quite sketchy for someone who lived within the Court society, two stories appear in discussions of Calderón's life. One is from his university period, when he is said to have been fined for having killed a relative of

D. PETRVS CALDERON
DE LABARCA.
Ætat sua 81.

the duke of Frias (a case later settled out of court); the other tells of an escapade in which Calderón followed an actor, who had wounded his brother in a duel, into a convent. Complaints from the nuns caused him to be placed under house arrest for a few days.

By 1637, he had written almost all of his well-known secular plays, including his famous philosophical play *La vida es sueño* (1635; *Life Is a Dream*, 1830), and when Lope de Vega died in 1635, Calderón became his successor as Court dramatist. Twelve of his dramas were published in 1636 and another twelve in 1637. At the same time, he was appointed to the Order of Santiago. During a revolt against Spain in 1640, he was sent with his Order to Catalonia. His portrayals in *El alcalde de Zalamea* (1643; *The Mayor of Zalamea*, 1853) may have their origin in his experiences there. When ill health forced him to return to Madrid in 1642, he became a member of the household of the duke of Alba for four years. After his two brothers were killed and his mistress died within a short period, he resigned his post at Court in 1650 and entered the priesthood in 1651. In the following period, he wrote many *autos sacramentales*, medieval allegorical dramas. He was chaplain in Toledo for a time and then was persuaded by the king to return to Court in 1663, where he remained until his death. His plays were collected and edited: the third part with twelve plays in 1664, the fourth in 1672, and the fifth in 1677, which contains four plays that he disowned. His own list of dramas written in 1680 includes 110 secular plays and 70 *autos sacramentales*. It is said that at the time of his death he was in the process of writing a new *auto sacramentale*. He died on May 25, 1681, in Madrid, very much esteemed by his contemporaries as a great dramatist.

Analysis

Calderón's literary productions fall squarely within a period in Spain during which the arts and literature reached their greatest glory, a period often referred to as the Golden Age and associated with the reign of Philip IV (1621-1665). When he began writing his plays, the great dramatist, and Calderón's predecessor at Court, Lope de Vega had already developed the prescribed form of the *comedia*, a three-act drama (not necessarily a comedy) written in verse. His guidelines for composing the *comedia* are explained in *El arte nuevo de hacer comedias en este tiempo* (1609; *The New Art of Writing Plays*, 1914). Because of the tremendous influence of Lope de Vega on the theater of his time, Calderón also wrote using the established rules, composing carefully written plots and polished verse.

His style is marked by ornamentation, sometimes to the point of obscurity. A popular technique of this period, referred to as Gongorism (after a leading poet, Luis de Góngora y Argote), this style of writing was highly artificial and refined, using many figures of speech, mythological allusions, hyperbole, and archaic words, in addition to a complex syntax based on the Latin form. This style is often combined with conceptism, a cultivated play with ideas. Although this style presents difficulties for the modern audience, the seventeenth century Spanish audience expected and appreciated the skill behind such usage.

The *comedia* was a popular form of entertainment, involving questions of love, honor, and patriotism. In addition, the comic character provided comic relief in even serious dramas with scenes of mistaken identity or bumbling inability to understand a problem. The key, however, was action. Action was always preferred over subtle character development, and the plot itself involved major events of violence, such as murder, battles, even natural disasters. The conflict often set up a situation of good versus evil—for example, the peasant mayor defending his family's honor against an aristocratic captain's base actions in *The Mayor of Zalamea*, or the conflict between father and son in *Life Is a Dream*, successfully resolved when the son adopts the approved values of his father.

The plays of Calderón cover a whole range of variations. His poetic skill and religious sensitivity made him master of the *auto sacramentale*. In these allegorical plays, Calderón continued in the tradition of the medieval morality play, raising its artistic level. His scholastic background and dramatic skill combined to enable him to dramatize abstract theological concepts in a convincing way. A fine example of an earlier *auto sacramentale* is *El gran teatro del mundo* (1649; *The Great Theater of the World*, 1856). Throughout his life, these plays develop greater complexity, and late in his life the themes of the Fall and Redemption appear to be presented with a mature understanding and compassion toward human beings in their weakness. Some of Calderón's plays—*The Constant Prince*, about the devotion of Prince Ferdinand of Portugal, or the famous *El sitio de Breda* (1625), based on events also depicted in Diego Velásquez's painting *Las Lanzas*—present themes from history or a legend.

The court drama grew out of popular drama, and with the construction of the palace in the Buen Retiro, with its special theater, Calderón, too, wrote plays with spectacular staging effects and elaborate machinery and settings. Successfully developed court plays went beyond popular drama in combining drama with dance, music, and visual arts. Perhaps the best of these is *La hija del aire, Parte I and II* (1653; *The Daughter of the Air, Part I* and *II*, 1831), a play of violence and passion based on the legend of a warrior queen of Babylon. Mythological themes dominate this art form, as can be seen by some of the titles, *Eco y Narciso* (1661) and *El estatua de Prometeo* (1669).

Calderón's bloody tragedies of honor were very popular with seventeenth century audiences, even if audiences today find the resolution of some of the honor conflicts shocking. For example, in *El médico de su honra* (pb. 1637; *The Surgeon of His Honor*, 1853), an innocent wife is murdered by her husband on the mere suspicion of dishonoring his name. The whole issue of honor and its defense must be seen in its seventeenth century context in order to be understood, but this play was intended to shock, showing perhaps Calderón's rejection of the rigid assumptions of the honor code, which led to such excesses.

Although Calderón was known for many types of serious plays, he was also a master of the light, amusing *comedia de capa y espada* (cloak-and-sword play). The name derives from the cloak and sword that were the mark of a gentleman of the time.

These plays were pure entertainment—the theme was usually love along with its obstacles, intrigues, and misunderstandings, all written in charming, natural dialogue. The characters are paired sets of two or three gentlemen with their respective ladies and servants (confidants to their masters). The humorous *Casa con dos puertas, mala es de guardar* (1636; *A House with Two Doors Is Difficult to Guard*, 1737) is a good example.

Through the various forms that his dramas took, Calderón used the structure and poetic devices popular in his time, and, under Lope de Vega's influence, the development of characters was always subordinate to the action, producing a fast-moving, entertaining spectacle. In the case of the court play, especially, these elements often became quite elaborate. His plots are skillfully constructed, often with a struggle between opposing forces, and the themes are rarely simple; they are, rather, a group of related themes, all of which contribute to the plot.

Calderón's writing is characterized by various types of verse or meter depending on the use: soliloquies, for example, were often written in sonnet form; one of two types (called the *romance* and *redondilla*) were employed for dialogue and narration. Each change of meter changed the mood. Within his poetic style, baroque techniques appear, such as the use of visual images drawn from nature and mythology, the use of simile and metaphor, parodies and plays on words, the contrast of light and shadow (chiaroscuro) and self-contradictory images (oxymorons). In all of his works, Calderón's skillful use of the themes, techniques, and style of his period mark him as a truly masterful dramatist.

LIFE IS A DREAM

First produced: *La vida es sueño*, 1635 (first published, 1636; English translation, 1830)
Type of work: Play

A young prince, imprisoned from childhood, is tested by his father to see if his reason and prudence will triumph over base instincts.

Usually recognized as Calderón's finest drama, *Life Is a Dream* premiered at the Royal Court of Spain. Its theme, revealed in the title, focuses on the instability of life and the illusory nature of the world. The story opens one night in the countryside between Poland and Russia, where Rosaura, a noblewoman disguised as a man, and her servant are journeying on foot after the loss of their horses. The opening lines give an example of Calderón's imagery and language:

Are you the fabulous hippogriff running in harness with the wind?
Flameless thunderbolt, featherless bird, fish without scales,
Monster of the four elements without instinct to check your headlong flight?

Rosaura's questions include mythological references and images of nature described out of character. The landscape itself reflects Rosaura's emotional upheaval. Amid the turbulence, she finds Segismundo's prison cave and hears his soliloquy of distress at the loss of his freedom. His guardian, Clotaldo, shown throughout the drama to be a man of integrity, sends the visitors away, but not before recognizing Rosaura as his daughter by the sword that she carries (which acts as a symbol of her family honor).

From the beginning, the first of several themes grouped together in this complex philosophical drama are introduced. Segismundo had been imprisoned by his father, King Basilio, who feared the predictions of the stars that his son would humiliate him and rule as a tyrant. Now, years later, he wonders if he has done right and decides to test the young man by drugging him and bringing him to the palace. In these luxurious surroundings, the inexperienced Segismundo shows his base nature by following his own pleasure and acting in a violent and insulting manner. When returned to his prison, he is told by Clotaldo that it was all a dream—a development that sets up a second theme complex in which dream and reality are confused, and in which deception and truth are indistinguishable to the protagonist. As Segismundo says in his famous lines:

> What is life? a delirium!
> What is life? illusion,
> A shadow, a fiction
> Whose greatest good is nothing,
> Because life is a dream!
> Even dreams are only dreams.

When freed by soldiers later, Segismundo proves that he has learned from his experience to control his passions and to do good, as Clotaldo has counseled, even in his dreams. At the end of the play, the prophecy has been fulfilled, as his father kneels at his son's feet—showing the strength of predestination. Yet a moment later, Segismundo wins his father's forgiveness and demonstrates forbearance and prudence in his final actions—showing his ability to use his freedom and free will wisely to counterbalance the pull of his destiny.

A second theme throughout the play, introduced in the first act, is the question of honor. Rosaura has been deceived and abandoned by Astolfo, nephew of the king. The two main characters meet in their hour of need and help each other: Rosaura inspires love in Segismundo and shows him the way to appropriate princely conduct, while he, in turn, restores her honor by marrying her to Astolfo, thus sacrificing his own wishes to the demands of society by restoring each person to his or her rightful place.

THE MAYOR OF ZALAMEA

First produced: *El alcalde de Zalamea*, 1643 (first published, 1651; English
                    translation, 1853)
Type of work: Play

The mayor of Zalamea, a wealthy peasant, executes an aristocratic captain in
the royal army for having dishonored his (the mayor's) daughter.

The theme of honor is central to the action of Calderón's much-admired play *The
Mayor of Zalamea*. The plot is constructed around a conflict based on the contrast
between the honorable and just peasant Pedro Crespo and the dishonorable deeds of
the aristocratic Captain Álvaro. As the play opens, Crespo agrees to quarter Captain
Álvaro in his home, but he takes the precaution of hiding his beautiful, unmarried
daughter, Isabel, in the attic with a female companion. His curiosity aroused, Don
Álvaro later manages to see Isabel and abduct her. She is rescued by her brother, but
only after she has been raped and abandoned by the captain. In an effort to satisfy
the requirements of the honor code, Crespo tries every means to get Don Álvaro to
marry Isabel, even offering all of his wealth. The dramatic scene is particularly moving as Crespo acts sincerely and humanely to try to obtain justice. Yet even as he
shows his nobility of character, the captain arrogantly refuses his offer and rejects his
authority.

The question of legal jurisdiction now enters the play, as the aristocratic captain
declares himself exempt from civilian authority. Coupled with this question is the
theme of honor, which Crespo argues is a property of the soul, which belongs to
God, even though Álvaro's life and possessions are in the service of the king. The
honor question crosses the lines of rank and jurisdiction in his argument. At the
height of the action, the commander, Don Lope de Figueroa, confronts Crespo an-
grily on the question of legal authority over Don Álvaro. The verse form expresses
the anger as threats are exchanged.

The development of Pedro Crespo's character and demonstration of the qualities of
prudence and a sense of justice is central to this play. The audience watches through
the first two acts as his true character begins to emerge, until in act 3 he becomes an
agent of social justice. In deciding to execute Don Álvaro, Crespo debates whether he
should act as a father (in defense of family honor) or as the mayor of Zalamea (to
obtain justice at a higher level). When he acts, he does so as mayor, and in his argument at the end he maintains that the two spheres of justice, military and civilian, are
really all part of a higher law, the king's justice (representative of God's law).

Summary

Pedro Calderón de la Barca proved himself a master of the many variations of dramatic art of his time. His style can be ornate, with imagery and mythological references, or simple and more direct, to reflect characters of society's lower classes. His varied verse forms are suited to their use within the dialogue, and his plots are carefully constructed for dramatic effect.

Calderón's themes range from the religious and theological in his *autos sacramentales* to the witty and fast-moving stories of love and misadventure in his *comedias de capa y espada*. In his serious dramas, he focuses on larger issues, such as the problem of honor, dream and reality, deception and truth, freedom and predestination. With all of his dramas clearly anchored in the Spanish Golden Age, the force of allegory is often evident—showing the characters their rightful position within a society believed to be ordained by God.

Bibliography

Hesse, Everett W. *Calderón de la Barca*. New York: Twayne, 1967.

Honig, Edwin. *Calderón and the Seizures of Honor*. Cambridge, Mass.: Harvard University Press, 1972.

McGaha, Michael D., ed. *Approaches to the Theater of Calderón*. Washington, D.C.: University of America Press, 1982.

Parker, Alexander A. *The Allegorical Drama of Calderón: An Introduction to the Autos Sacramentales*. Oxford, England: Dolphin Books, 1962.

——————. *The Mind and Art of Calderón: Essays on the Comedias*. Cambridge, England: Cambridge University Press, 1988.

Ter Horst, Robert. *Calderón: The Secular Plays*. Lexington: University Press of Kentucky, 1982.

Wardropper, Bruce W., ed. *Critical Essays on the Theatre of Calderón*. New York: New York University Press, 1965.

Susan L. Piepke

ITALO CALVINO

Born: Santiago de las Vegas, Cuba
October 15, 1923
Died: Siena, Italy
September 19, 1985

Principal Literary Achievement

With quirky humanism and imaginative style, internationally acclaimed story-teller Calvino breathed life into traditional and innovative narrative forms by skillfully blending reality, fantasy, and wit.

Biography

Italo Calvino was born in Santiago de las Vegas, Cuba, near Havana, on October 15, 1923, to parents who were well into middle age. Agricultural scientists, they returned to the ancestral farm on the Italian Riviera when Calvino was two. Their intellectual openness, enlightened skepticism, and enthusiasm for scientific method deeply influenced Calvino's later artistic development.

After a rather lonely adolescence, Calvino left San Remo to study agronomy at the University of Turin in 1941. Drafted into the national army two years later, he immediately deserted to join the Italian Resistance and fight Fascism. When the war ended in 1945, he decided to return to Turin, change his major from agronomy to English literature (his thesis was on Joseph Conrad), complete his degree, and begin writing fiction. His first novel, *Il sentiero dei nidi di ragno* (1947; *The Path to the Nest of Spiders*, 1956), a realistic story about an orphan's wartime adventures with a band of partisans, appeared in 1947. It won the Riccione literary prize in 1947 and much critical praise. His many short stories, some of which appear translated in *Gli amore difficili* (1970; *Difficult Loves*, 1984), also earned acclaim.

In his mid-twenties, Calvino took a position with the Einaudi publishing house. The staff there included novelists Elio Vittorini, Cesare Pavese, and Natalia Ginzburg—all leaders in Italy's intellectual vanguard. They introduced Calvino to the neo-realist literary movement and encouraged his increasingly active participation in politics. Under their tutelage, Calvino found the late 1940's and the 1950's especially productive.

Besides his editorship at Einaudi (a position he kept until his death), he directed a literary journal with Vittorini, served on the staff of Italy's official Communist newspaper, and contributed many polemical articles to *Il Politecnico.* He also produced an

332

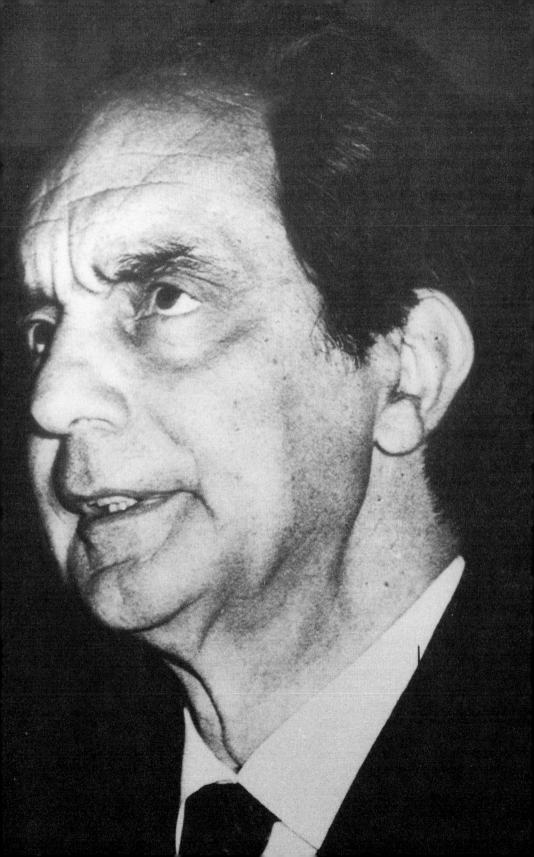

amazing amount of fiction, most of which boldly entered fantastic territory. Three of his four historical fantasy novels—*Il visconte dimezzato* (1952; *The Cloven Viscount*, 1962), *Il barone rampante* (1957; *The Baron in the Trees*, 1959), and *Il cavaliere inesistente* (1959; *The Non-Existent Knight*, 1962)—are from this period. They constitute some of his most celebrated and characteristic works.

Calvino took special delight in reading and studying fables. By editing and retelling some two hundred regional folktales in *Fiabe italiane* (1956; *Italian Fables*, 1959), he entertained readers of all ages and contributed significantly to folklore scholarship. This absorption in storytelling's ancient roots also stimulated him to produce some modern counterparts; several of these are collected in *La giornata d'uno scrutatore* (1963; *The Watcher and Other Stories*, 1971). These contemporary parables testify to Calvino's own political and social disenchantment (he quit the Communist Party around 1958).

Realistic and popular elements also pervade the comic vignettes of *Marcovaldo: Ovvero, Le stagioni in città* (1963; *Marcovaldo: Or, The Seasons in the City*, 1983), in which Marcovaldo, an impoverished peasant, moves his family to the big city. Ironically, he spends more time and money trying to recapture the life he abandoned than in improving his lot. As in much of Calvino's work, an essentially tragic view of life underlies the humorous and gently resigned spirit of the narratives.

Calvino moved to Paris in 1964, where he met and married an Argentinean translator for UNESCO (United Nations Educational, Scientific, and Cultural Organization) that same year; they had a daughter in 1965. Calvino remained in Paris for sixteen years, during which time friendships with internationally recognized intellectuals such as anthropologist Claude Lévi-Strauss and literary critic Roland Barthes greatly inspired his critical and creative writing. The finely crafted works from this period— *Le cosmicomiche* (1965; *Cosmicomics*, 1968), *Ti con zero* (1967; *t zero*, 1969), *Il castello dei destini incrociati* (1973; *The Castle of Crossed Destinies*, 1976), and *Le città invisibili* (1972; *Invisible Cities*, 1974)—are remarkable for their intellectual playfulness and literary inventiveness. In 1972, *Invisible Cities*, Calvino's final historical fantasy, captured the prestigious Feltrinelli Prize—Italy's equivalent of the Pulitzer Prize. The last novel Calvino wrote in Paris, a spirited parody of literary experiments such as the French *nouveau roman* (New Novel), appeared in 1979. The international success of *Se una notte d'inverno un viaggiatore . . .* (1979; *If on a Winter's Night a Traveler . . .* , 1981) secured Calvino's reputation as a major twentieth century author.

In 1980, Calvino and his family relocated to Rome. *Palomar*, his last novel, was published in 1983; the English version, *Mr. Palomar*, appeared around the time of his death on September 19, 1985, in Siena, Italy, from cerebral hemorrhage. As personal in its own way as his first novel was, *Mr. Palomar* is essentially an extended meditation on man and the cosmos. Its meticulous investigation of the complexities of human experience—whether physical, mental, or spiritual—is similar to the short stories in the posthumous *Sotto il sole giaguaro* (1986; *Under the Jaguar Sun*, 1988), where the senses of taste, hearing, and smell provide entry into the magical, ineffable, and grotesque dimensions of mundane existence.

Analysis
Calvino's reputation as a master storyteller and innovative writer rests primarily on his success in fusing the traditional and original, the magical and mundane, the grotesque and ineffable—elements that are disparate, even contradictory. Generally, this literary alchemy is seen in two basic ways: If the story relates something real, Calvino will introduce magical or fantastic elements; if it describes the incredible or imaginary, he will present it in a nonchalantly realistic manner.

Because of the intricate interrelationship of the actual and the imaginary in his work, Calvino is considered both a realist and a fantasist. His brand of realism, however, is best described as neorealistic. Like realism and naturalism, neorealism depicts the world in an unidealized, concrete manner. Unlike these, neorealism does not do so in order to present an impartial picture of reality; rather, it seeks to communicate a particular experience of that reality. Neorealism achieves this effect by revealing the elusive, intangible aspects of experience—the psychological, symbolic, or metaphysical dimensions, for example—residing within the physical and actual.

Calvino's imaginative perception of the real world is complemented by his rational interpretation of the fantastic. As he observes in an essay from *Una pietra sopra: Discorsi di letteratura e societa* (1980; *The Uses of Literature*, 1986):

> For me the main thing in a narrative is not the explanation of an extraordinary event, but the order of things that this extraordinary event produces in itself and around it; the pattern, the symmetry, the network of images deposited around it, as in the formation of a crystal.

Calvino refers frequently to the crystal to describe his own way of thinking and writing. In *Sulla fiaba* (1988; *Six Memos for the Next Millennium*, 1988), a collection of lectures that he was preparing at the time of his death, he remarks that the precision and geometric faceting of the crystal, and its ability to refract light are what make it, for him, a model of perfection and an emblem of his work. Calvino mimics its rationality, its symmetry and its ability to combine endlessly, in his writing to explore all the possible variations and alternatives of a given idea or argument. For him, the possible is as important as the real.

The "crystalline" features of Calvino's fiction are especially pronounced in works from his Parisian years. The complex permutations in *t zero*, the multiplicity of phenomena and interpretation in *Invisible Cities*, and the intricately woven interrelationships of characters, events, images, and ideas in *The Castle of Crossed Destinies* are clearly analogous to the faceted structure and systematic self-organization of crystals. Simultaneously rational and organic, this system offers Calvino a satisfying intellectual and artistic means of expressing and illuminating the entanglements of human life within an increasingly complex and unpredictable world.

The crystal's almost magical relationship with light is another significant quality. Applied to Calvino's fiction, lightness—one of the literary values he admired and discusses in *Six Memos for the Next Millennium*—suggests luminosity, elucidation, and weightlessness. Luminosity refers to visibility, or the exactness of Calvino's images. After observing that his stories generally grow out of an image or visualized concept, Calvino affirms that the visual image is "a way of attaining knowledge of the most profound meaning." In order to arrive at that meaning, he uses a procedure that strives to unite spontaneously generated images with the sequential logic of discursive thought. That is, in order to interpret images into words and then mold them into a narrative, he synthesizes intuition and reason, spontaneity and calculation, fantasy and fact.

Calvino's talent for elucidating contemporary reality often finds paradoxical expression in his historical novels. He sometimes takes a remarkable event as his departure point, such as Italian merchant Marco Polo's thirteenth century visit to Mongol emperor Kublai Khan's court in *Invisible Cities*, and interprets it in an original manner, which sheds light on contemporary issues. He also uses the literature of the past, Ludovico Ariosto's Renaissance epic *Orlando Furioso* (1516, 1521, 1532; English translation, 1591) and Miguel de Cervantes' satiric novel *El ingenioso hidalgo don Quixote de la Mancha* (1605, 1615; better known as *Don Quixote de la Mancha*, 1612-1620), for example, to inspire and form his modern visions.

Calvino's respect for the past and for literary tradition rarely translates into mere imitation. In *Cosmicomics* and *t zero*, for example, he reverses the usual premise of the historical novel: Instead of using the past as a means for understanding the present, and instead of evoking a real, specific time and place from history, he employs modern scientific theories to fashion a fantastic, impossible past. This reconstruction achieves its unity through its first-person narrator, Qfwfq, an ageless, protean being who describes the formation of the cosmos, the evolution of life, and the perplexities of consciousness. With Qfwfq, Calvino not only gives abstract ideas such as time and space a narrative form but, more importantly, elucidates important questions about the character of existence and the essence of being human.

It is this last question that raises the idea of light as weightlessness; while the tone of his work is accurately described as "light," it can hardly be called frivolous. This quality he prefers to characterize as a buoyant thoughtfulness adopted to ease the

> desperate and all-pervading oppression . . . in a human condition common to us all. . . .
> Whenever humanity seems condemned to heaviness . . . I have to change my approach,
> look at the world from a different perspective, with a different logic and with fresh
> methods of cognition and verification. . . . I look to [literature and] science to nourish
> my visions in which all heaviness disappears.

Literature for Calvino is thus not a body of traditions or a special, artistic way of using words; it is rather "the search for lightness as a reaction to the weight of living." This search not only expresses our existential needs but also affirms our distinctly human values.

THE CLOVEN VISCOUNT

First published: *Il visconte dimezzato*, 1952 (English translation, 1962)
Type of work: Novel

Split lengthwise by a cannonball, Medardo's good and evil halves generate various kinds of conflict, try to destroy each other, and are finally reunited.

The Cloven Viscount was rereleased in 1960 as part of the trilogy *I nostri antenati* (1960; *Our Ancestors*, 1980). Although the novels have no specifics in common, they are nonetheless connected by their similar exploration of concepts illuminating contemporary cultural crises. *The Cloven Viscount* probes ethics by interpreting literally the division of human good and evil; *The Baron in the Trees* explores the isolation and egocentricity of individuals; and *The Non-Existent Knight* examines the clash between the ideal and the real, between image and actuality.

The Cloven Viscount is deceptively simple. Participating in his first battle, Medardo is cloven in two by a cannonball. Patched by doctors, the recovered half returns to Terralba, immediately causes his father's death, and terrorizes the countryside; it is Medardo's evil self. Soon his good side returns. Inevitably, the two sides meet, duel, and, because of their wounds, are finally fused into "a whole man again, neither good nor bad, but a mixture of goodness and badness."

Clearly a parable on human nature, Medardo's division alludes to the archetypal struggle between good and evil. Yet Calvino offers alternate interpretations of this central dichotomy. In this story and its seventeenth century setting (the twentieth century's philosophical and scientific "forefather"), Medardo's division refers to philosophical dualism—the human being perceived as mind and body, subject and object—a view formulated around 1640 by French philosopher René Descartes. Moreover, with the motifs of science and technology, Calvino further alludes to a twentieth century variation: human being and machine. Technology, like its creator, is both gift and curse: Like Dr. Jekyll and Mr. Hyde, it possesses a formidable, ambiguous power.

To explore divisiveness and the ambiguities of duality, many other characters also contain contradictions: Pamela is chaste but earthy; Pietrochiodo is a destructive creator; Medardo's nephew, the narrator, is a high-born bastard. These variations and juxtapositions direct attention to what dualism, by nature, disregards—the inevitable "shades of gray." Such permutations also serve to effect a reversal in the sense of the terms of the dichotomy, as when the good Medardo is considered a worse evil than his counterpart. By exposing the complexity behind the supposed simplicity, Calvino emphasizes the integral unity of dichotomies: "Thus the days went by at Terralba, and our sensibilities became numbed, since we felt ourselves lost between an evil and a virtue equally inhuman." The paradoxical relationship of the two Medardos to Terralba's unusual members, especially the dour Huguenots and hedonistic lepers, provides a good example of the intersection of theme, structure, and technique in Calvino's work.

Unfortunately, "a whole Viscount is not enough to make all the world whole." Novels, like the situations they depict and the life they emulate, are, at least for this author, complex things incapable of giving easy answers. As the narrator melancholically reflects at the end: "I, though, amid all this fervor of wholeness, felt myself growing sadder and more lacking. Sometimes one who thinks himself incomplete is merely young."

THE BARON IN THE TREES

First published: *Il barone rampante*, 1957 (English translation, 1959)
Type of work: Novel

A young baron, rebelling against the restraints of family and society, climbs into the treetops to live freely, vowing never to descend.

Calvino appropriately sets *The Baron in the Trees*, his tale of the rebellious and eccentric Baron Cosimo Rondo, in the late eighteenth century—the uneasy transitional period from Enlightenment to Romanticism, the twentieth century's intellectual and spiritual "forefathers." The elegance, inventiveness, and practicality with which Cosimo (only twelve when he climbs into the trees) adapts to and improves upon his condition illustrate the Enlightenment's faith in reason, progress, and perfectibility. Cosimo's self-indulgence, "superhuman tenacity," and feral lifestyle, on the other hand, suggest the egotism, extravagance, and primitivism of Romantic sensibility.

Elevated above the world, Cosimo enters a familiar reality made strange, in which "branches spread out like the tentacles of extraordinary animals, and the plants on the ground opened up stars of fretted leaves like the green skins of reptiles." Stranger yet are the people he encounters: ragamuffin fruit thieves, murderous Moors, plotting Jesuits, literate brigands, exiled Spaniards, even the great Napoleon himself. Each seems more curious than the other.

It is Cosimo who is the most unusual of the lot. As Biagio, the narrator and Cosimo's brother, remarks, the locals consider him mad: "I am not talking only of his determination to live up there, but of the various oddities of his character; and no one considered him other than an original." Original in his persistent aloofness and nonconformity, he is also unique for the many guises he assumes. Sometimes, for example, he portrays a savior, as when he extinguishes fires and assists peasants. Other times he is a destroyer, as when he causes his uncle's decapitation, his bandit-friend's hanging, and his aged tutor's lifelong imprisonment. Most usually, however, he is a subversive: insurrection, a "Project for the Constitution of an Ideal State in the Trees," Freemasonry—all play parts in his revolt against human organization.

Cosimo's eccentric individualism arouses both admiration and contempt, sympathy and incomprehension—an ambivalence particularly pronounced in his love affairs. His most complicated affair is with the perverse and haughty aristocrat Violante (Viola). Throughout the novel, these two collide, mingle, and separate like a pair of natural, primeval forces. Cosimo's obstinate pride and ignorance of human feeling finally, irrevocably, clash with Viola's insatiable emotional appetite. As fiercely independent as Cosimo, Viola's individuality becomes too much for the customarily distant Cosimo; the inability to communicate and to accept another's individuality ultimately destroy their union.

Alone as never before, Cosimo vacillates between utterly wild, animalistic behavior and elaborately rational plans "for installing a world republic of men—equal, free, and just." Well past the age of sixty, he finally encounters a death that is as curious as his life and maintains his childhood vow. Although touchingly lyrical, his memorial, "Lived in trees—Always loved earth—Went into sky," only emphasizes his essential detachment from human life.

Paradoxically, however, Cosimo contributes his own special legacy to humanity. Restless spirit and witness to a great age, the "patriot on the treetops" achieves mythic stature. As his brother/biographer comments:

> [Cosimo] understood something else, something that was all-embracing, and he could not say it in words but only by living as he did. Only by being so frankly himself as he was till his death could he give something to all men.

Summary

Like his own forefathers, the Renaissance humanists, Italo Calvino finds material for his art wherever eye and mind pause, absorbed in contemplation or delight, and poses ageless questions about the nature of world and humanity. Calvino's own answer to the question "Who are we?" significantly reveals his artistic vision: "Who is each one of us, if not a combinatoria of experiences, information, books we have read, things imagined? Each life is an encyclopedia, a library, an inventory of objects." His translation of this comprehensive perception into vital new literary forms makes him one of the most original—and classical—authors of the modern age.

Bibliography

Adler, Sara Maria. *Calvino: The Writer as Fablemaker.* Potomac, Md.: Porrúa Turanzas, North American Division, 1979.

Cannon, JoAnn. *Italo Calvino: Writer and Critic.* Ravenna: Longo, 1981.

Carter, Albert H. *Italo Calvino: Metamorphoses of Fantasy.* Ann Arbor: UMI Research Press, 1987.

Olken, I. T. *With Pleated Eye and Garnet Wing: Symmetries of Italo Calvino.* Ann Arbor: University of Michigan Press, 1984.

Re, Lucia. *Calvino and the Age of Neorealism.* Stanford, Calif.: Stanford University Press, 1990.

Ricci, Franco, ed. *Calvino Revisited.* Ottawa: Dovehouse Editions, 1989.

Woodhouse, J. R. *Italo Calvino: A Reappraisal and an Appreciation of the Trilogy.* Yorkshire, England: University of Hull Publications, 1968.

Terri Frongia

ALBERT CAMUS

Born: Mondovi, Algeria
November 7, 1913
Died: near Villeblevin, France
January 4, 1960

Principal Literary Achievement

A major force in France's intellectual life by the middle of the twentieth century, especially among those associated with existentialism, Camus was a leading novelist, short-story writer, philosopher, and playwright.

Biography

Albert Camus was born on November 7, 1913, in Mondovi, a village in the interior of Algeria, which, since 1830, had been under the administration of France. Albert's father, Lucien, was a winery worker. His mother, Catherine Sintès, could not read or write. Shortly after the outbreak of World War I, Lucien Camus was mobilized in a North African regiment. Wounded at the First Battle of the Marne, he died on October 11, 1914, before Albert's first birthday. Catherine took the family to Belcourt, a working-class section of Algiers, to live with her mother, Marie Catherine Sintès. Catherine, who worked in a munitions factory and then as a cleaning woman, suffered a stroke that left her deaf and partially paralyzed. Albert lived with his mother, his older brother Lucien, and several relatives in a three-room apartment without electricity or running water, sharing a toilet with two other apartments.

At the local primary school, a teacher named Louis Germain took an interest in young Albert, providing him with extra instruction and entering him into competition for scholarships. As a subsidized day-boarder at a secondary school, Camus excelled in sports and began a lifelong friendship with teacher Jean Grenier, who encouraged him in his study of philosophy. In 1930, Camus developed the first symptoms of tuberculosis and moved out of his family apartment. In 1932, he published four articles in the Algerian journal *Sud*.

In 1934, Camus married Simone Hié, a fellow student, and also joined the Communist Party, which assigned him the task of proselytizing Muslims. Exempt from military service because of his lungs, he studied philosophy at the University of Algiers, financing his education through loans and a variety of odd jobs that included auto accessory salesman, municipal clerk, and research assistant with the university's meteorological service. Poor health, however, prevented him from pursuing a teach-

ing career. His marriage was dissolved in 1936.

Cofounder of the blue-collar Théâtre du Travail, Camus collaborated in 1936 in writing the play *Révolte dans les Asturies* (revolt in the Asturias), which was banned for performance but published. As an actor for Radio Algiers, he toured the countryside. In 1937, he began writing for the liberal newspaper *Alger-Républicain* and was expelled from the Communist Party in a dispute over policy. His first book, *L'Envers et l'endroit* (1937; *The Right Side and the Wrong Side*, 1968), a collection of essays, was also published in 1937. In 1939, Camus cofounded the literary review *Rivages* and, when France declared war on Germany, attempted to enlist but was turned down because of his tuberculosis. He moved to Paris to work on the staff of *Paris-Soir*, relocating in the South of France when the Germans occupied the North. In December, 1940, he quit his job at *Paris-Soir* and returned to Algeria with his new wife, Francine Faure, a math teacher from Oran.

In 1942, to recover from an attack of tuberculosis, he traveled with Francine to Chambon-sur-Lignon, in the mountains of central France. Camus remained there while Francine returned to Oran, and, after the Allied landing in North Africa, he became separated from her until the liberation of France. He joined the Resistance network Combat in the Lyons region. In 1942, he published his first novel, *L'Étranger* (1942; *The Stranger*, 1946), and his philosophical work *Le Mythe de Sisyphe* (1942; *The Myth of Sisyphus*, 1955). Camus moved to Paris, where he joined the editorial staff of Gallimard and worked on the underground newspaper *Combat*, becoming its editor. He became acquainted with Jean-Paul Sartre and other influential intellectuals. His play *Le Malentendu* (*The Misunderstanding*, 1948) was produced in Paris in 1944, after the city's liberation from German occupation. In 1945, his play *Caligula* (English translation, 1948) was produced, and he visited Algeria to report on atrocities committed by the colonial French government. He also became father to twins, Jean and Catherine.

Camus visited the United States in 1946 and, the following year, published *La Peste* (*The Plague*, 1948) to great acclaim. A 1948 production of *L'État de siège* (*State of Siege*, 1958), written in collaboration with actor-director Jean-Louis Barrault, was not successful. Camus spoke out against French repression of a popular rebellion in Madagascar and in defense of Greek Communists who were sentenced to death. Through written deposition, he testified for the defense in a trial of Algerian nationalists. In 1951, publication of *L'Homme Révolté* (*The Rebel*, 1956) provoked heated controversy and led to Camus' break with Sartre and other Marxist critics of his work.

After the 1954 outbreak of armed rebellion by Muslim Algerians against French administration, Camus became increasingly distraught over the escalating cycle of violence and reprisals. In 1955, he attempted to mediate a truce but was rebuffed. In 1956, he protested Soviet repression of the Hungarian Revolution and published *La Chute* (*The Fall*, 1957). In 1957, he published *L'Exil et le royaume* (*Exile and the Kingdom*, 1958), a volume of short stories, and "Réflexions sur la guillotine" ("Reflections on the Guillotine"), a plea for the abolition of capital punishment. On October 17 of that year, Camus became the ninth Frenchman and second youngest author of any nationality to be awarded the Nobel Prize in Literature.

His health and mood fluctuating, Camus worked on "Le Premier Homme" (the first man), a novel he never completed. On January 4 1960, he was killed instantaneously when a car driven by his publisher Michel Gallimard crashed into a tree near the French village of Villeblevin.

Analysis

When Camus received the Nobel Prize in 1957, the citation lauded him "for his important literary production, which with clear-sighted earnestness illuminated the problems of the human conscience in our times." Camus died less than three years later without augmenting what was a relatively meagre oeuvre: three novels and a handful of plays, short stories, and essays. It is possible to read his entire life's work in less time that it takes to absorb one novel by some of his more hermetic contemporaries.

Yet Camus is widely read and fervently admired in a way few other twentieth century writers are. In a memoir of Robert Kennedy, journalist Jack Newfield recalls that the senator always traveled with a copy of Camus' writings: "He discovered Camus when he was thirty-eight, in the months of solitude and grief after his brother's death. By 1968 he had read, and re-read, all of Camus essays, dramas and novels. But he more than just read Camus. He memorized him, meditated about him, quoted him and was changed by him."

Heir to the French tradition of literary crusaders, of activist authors like Michel de Montaigne, Voltaire, Victor Hugo, and Émile Zola, Camus is the lucid moral conscience of his era. His fiction, drama, and essays pose fundamental questions about individual identity and social bonds that cannot be ignored in the century that produced Auschwitz and Hiroshima. Camus served in the underground Resistance to the Nazi occupation of France and after the war refused to confine himself to a purely literary role. Willy-nilly, he became embroiled in many of the most tumultuous political controversies of the time—colonialism, capital punishment, racism, and East-West alliances. Even posthumously, he remains a public figure challenging his readers to a stringent standard of candor and compassion.

"A novel," wrote Camus in his review of Jean-Paul Sartre's novel *La Nausée* (1938; English translation, 1949), "is never anything but a philosophy expressed in images." Camus' own novels are probably much more than just a philosophy expressed in images but they are never anything less. *The Stranger, The Plague*, and *The Fall* are among the most popular and esteemed books ever published in France; translated into dozens of languages, they remain not only in print but also in demand long after most other books of their era have been forgotten. Their appeal is less in plot and characterization than in the utter honesty with which they pose questions of personal, social, and cosmic identity. The scrupulously austere style that Camus honed was an embarrassment to the temptations of bogus rhetoric.

Camus came to Paris in the 1940's with a proletarian and Algerian background that set him apart from the erudite middle-class French intellectuals who befriended him. Along with Jean-Paul Sartre, Simone de Beauvoir, and Maurice Merleau-Ponty, Camus emerged as one of the leaders of existentialism, a philosophical movement that was extremely popular following World War II. Existentialism has its roots in the writings of recent German philosophers, particularly Edmund Husserl, Karl Jaspers, and Martin Heidegger, though its legacy can be traced back through Freidrich Wilhelm Nietzsche and Søren Kierkegaard to as far as the pre-Socratic Greek Heraclitus. Never a systematic philosophy, existentialism was, in fact, a product of skepticism toward the intellectual arrogance of rational systems. Existentialism was the embodiment of a post-War *Zeitgeist* cynical toward the shibboleths and values that had facilitated and camouflaged global catastrophe. It insisted that existence precedes essence, that nothing is given—nothingness is the given. In the vast, indifferent universe, the individual is ineluctably responsible for creating his or her own identity. Five A's—alienation, absurdity, angst, anomie, and anxiety—seemed indispensable to the vocabulary of anyone who aspired to speak the language of existentialism, and there were many.

For a while, particularly in philosophical writings such as *The Myth of Sisyphus*, Camus was a very prominent existentialist voice, and the Algerian newcomer whom Sartre later called a "Cartesian of the absurd" became a frequent companion of Sartre and de Beauvoir during the heady days following the liberation of Paris. Camus, however, became increasingly uncomfortable in the role of high priest of the new cult of the posthumous God. Rejecting the faddishness of it all, he began emphasizing differences between his ideas and those of Sartre and insisted that he was not an existentialist. Following their feud in 1951, he no longer even called himself a friend of Sartre's.

Whether or not they are technically "existentialist," and whether or not the term has ceased to have any clear definition, Camus' books are an embodiment of the attitudes of many Europeans at the middle of the twentieth century. Behind novels that are tolerant of everything but falsehood lies widespread bitterness over the failure of the crusade to save democracy in Spain, the fall of France's Third Republic, the Nazi genocide, and the prospects of nuclear annihilation.

"Phony" is Holden Caulfield's favorite term of derision in J. D. Salinger's *The Catcher in the Rye*, a popular novel published in 1951 during the peak of Camus' career, and the term applies as well to everything that Meursault, Rieux, and Clamence despise in Camus' fictional worlds. Camus, for whom metaphysical mutiny was a starting point for full awareness, saw a development in his own writings "from an attitude of solitary revolt to the recognition of a community whose struggles must be shared." The evolution of his work was cut short by a fatal automobile accident. What he did leave behind is a legacy that Sartre recognized in the eulogy he published three days after his erstwhile comrade's shocking death: "Camus could never cease to be one of the principal forces in our cultural domain, nor to represent, in his own way, the history of France and of this century."

THE STRANGER

First published: *L'Étranger*, 1942 (English translation, 1946)
Type of work: Novel

This terse account describes how a man kills a stranger and suffers the consequences of actions that he never intended or even understood.

The Stranger offers one of the most striking openings in modern fiction: "Mama died today. Or yesterday maybe, I don't know." Immediately introduced is a character, Meursault, so disconnected from chronology and other human beings that he is one of twentieth century literature's most memorable embodiments of alienation, of an absurdist world where social bonds are a sham. The British edition of Camus' first published novel translates the title as *The Outsider*, and Meursault indeed finds himself a marginal figure in a decentered universe where private and immediate sensations have displaced objective norms.

Meursault, an employee of a shipping company, participates in the rituals of his mother's funeral and, though he realizes he is supposed to be playing the role of bereaved son, cannot feel anything for the old woman's corpse. Shortly after returning to Algiers, Meursault goes to the beach, picks up a woman, Marie Cardona, and takes her to the movies and then to bed.

The following Sunday, Meursault and Marie are invited by Raymond Sintès, a raffish neighbor, to spend the day at the beach. During the outing, they are trailed and menaced by two Arab men who are apparently resentful of the way in which Raymond has abused a woman. During a solitary walk along the shore, Meursault encounters one of the Arabs again. It is oppressively hot, and the knife that the Arab wields glistens blindingly in the sun. Without premeditation or reflection, Meursault takes the gun that Raymond has given him and fires five shots into the stranger.

Narrated in Meursault's own affectless voice, *The Stranger* consists of two sections. The first recounts the events leading up to the fatal shooting, and the second reports its aftermath—Meursault's imprisonment, trial, conviction, and impending execution. Part 2 is in effect a commentary on Part 1, an attempt to find coherence in one man's random actions. Marie, Raymond, the owner of the café that Meursault frequents, his mother's elderly friend, and others testify in court about the events in Part 1. Both attorneys attempt to find some pattern. In the story that Meursault's lawyer tells, all the details paint the portrait of an innocent man acting in self-defense.

Yet the prosecutor finds a different design. For him, Meursault's callousness about his mother's death is symptomatic of a cold-blooded murderer, and it is that reading that the jury accepts when it sentences Meursault to death by guillotine. Meursault, however, rejects the specious patterns that both attorneys impose on events. He also refuses consolation from the prison chaplain, who offers him a kind of cosmic narrative in which everything is linked to a vast providential scheme.

Alone in his cell, Meursault realizes that despite the lies people tell to camouflage the truth, all are condemned to death. Uncomfortable with the florid rhetoric that distracts a reader from stark realities, he becomes a champion of candor. In his spare, honest style and his recognition that life is gratuitous and resistant to human attempts to catalog and rationalize it, Meursault is prepared to face extinction liberated from all illusions. He is, wrote Camus in 1955, "not a piece of social wreckage, but a poor and naked man enamored of a sun that leaves no shadows. Far from being bereft of all feeling, he is animated by a passion that is deep because it is stubborn, a passion for the absolute and for truth."

THE PLAGUE

First published: *La Peste*, 1947 (English translation, 1948)
Type of work: Novel

Inhabitants of Oran, Algeria, are tested by an epidemic that devastates the city.

The Plague, which propelled Camus into international celebrity, is both an allegory of World War II and a universal meditation on human conduct and community. Organized into five sections, *The Plague* recounts the collective ordeal of Oran, Algeria, in the throes of an outbreak of bubonic plague. At the outset, even before the sudden proliferation of dead rats and sick humans that persuades reluctant officials to declare an epidemic, Oran is described as a drab, ugly city whose inhabitants are preoccupied with commerce.

Trapped within Oran after a quarantine is imposed are the novel's principal characters: Bernard Rieux, a physician separated from the ailing wife he sent to a sanatorium before the outbreak of the plague; Raymond Rambert, a Parisian journalist on assignment in Oran; Jean Tarrou, a stranger who takes an active part in opposing the epidemic; Joseph Grand, a municipal clerk obsessed with composing a perfect sentence; Paneloux, a Jesuit priest who delivers two crucial sermons during the course of the plague; and Cottard, a black-market opportunist.

Camus begins his novel with an epigraph from Daniel Defoe's *Robinson Crusoe* (1719) that invites readers to read the book as a veiled representation of something other than merely an epidemic in Oran. In a 1955 letter to critic Roland Barthes, the author specified the terms of the allegory; "*The Plague*, which I wanted to be read on a number of levels, nevertheless has as its obvious content the struggle of the European resistance movements against Nazism. The proof of this is that although the specific enemy is nowhere named, everyone in every European country recognized it."

The book is, moreover, a meditation on human solidarity and individual responsibility. What is the logical and ethical response to a universe in which suffering prevails and effort seems futile? In the first of two sermons strategically positioned in part 2 and part 4 of the five-part chronicle, Paneloux posits an anthropomorphic God who has sent the plague as retribution for human sin. After witnessing the agonizing death of an innocent child, however, Paneloux revises his theodicy, to reconcile unmerited torment with belief in a logical and benevolent Providence.

Tarrou, a magistrate's son who left home in revulsion over state executions, remains forever opposed to a scheme of things in which cruelty triumphs. His selfless, if hopeless, dedication to the struggle against the plague—both the actual disease and the metaphorical plague he contends is the human condition—offers a sharp contrast to the egoism of Cottard, who exploits the misfortunes of Oran for personal advantage. Rambert's initial reaction to the quarantine is concern for his personal happiness, for how he can escape from the city and return to Paris to the woman he loves. He learns, however, that his lot is also Oran's, and he stays in the city to make common cause with the victims of the plague.

Under such circumstances, the flamboyant individualism that enlivens traditional fiction is inappropriate, and the novel, conceding that readers crave heroes, nominates the lackluster Grand, whose grandness resides in selfless, bootless dedication to writing a perfect sentence and ending the plague:

> Yes, if it is a fact that people like to have examples given them, men of the type they call heroic, and if it is absolutely necessary that this narrative should include a 'hero,' the narrator commends to his readers, with, to his thinking, perfect justice, this insignificant and obscure hero who had to his credit only a little goodness of heart and a seemingly absurd ideal.

One of the novel's most striking features is its handling of narrative point of view. The story is told in meticulously neutral prose, from a perspective that seems detached from the experiences it recounts. Less than a dozen pages from the end, however, when the plague has subsided and the gates of Oran have been reopened, Rieux steps forward to confess that he has been the narrator all along. Though the text's preoccupation with exile and isolation are clearly the result of Rieux's own enforced separation from his ailing wife, he as narrator has taken great pains to present an impersonal "chronicle," the objective account of an honest witness. Writing himself into the story of his community is another way in which Rieux tries to overcome the solitude that is his lot as a widower and a human being.

In a universe in which "plague" is inexplicable and gratuitous, Rieux realizes that physicians are as ineffectual as anyone else. Yet he finds value in collective struggle, regardless of the outcome. The plague is never defeated. It merely, and mysteriously, recedes, and the reader is left with Rieux's realization that eternal vigilance is necessary against an indomitable foe.

THE FALL

First published: *La Chute*, 1956 (English translation, 1957)
Type of work: Novel

In an Amsterdam bar, a French lawyer imparts to a stranger his lessons in misanthropy.

The Fall is an extended monologue conducted over the course of five days by a man who calls himself Jean-Baptiste Clamence. The setting is Amsterdam, whose fogginess is miasmic and whose canals are likened to the concentric circles of hell. Like some infernal Ancient Mariner, the speaker attaches himself to a stranger who happens to wander into a raffish bar incongruously named Mexico City. A master of guile, Clamence deliberately piques the curiosity of his listener, who remains an unnamed "you." Gradually, cunningly, he implicates him—and the reader—in his diabolical tale. Clamence infers that his auditor is a successful Parisian lawyer in his forties, and he tailors his story to appeal to and expose the weaknesses of the stranger.

Clamence claims that he, too, used to live in Paris, where, as a widely respected magistrate, he exuded self-confidence. He then recounts an incident that forever undermined his certainties about personal worth. One November evening, walking across a bridge, he heard the cry of a woman who had thrown herself into the river. His reaction was to deny that he had heard anything and to continue walking. He remains, however, haunted by that dying cry and the fact that he evaded responsibility toward another human being.

Written at a troubled time in Camus' own life, *The Fall* is the bitter fictional tirade of a brilliant misanthrope who dismisses civilization with a mordant epigram: "A single sentence will suffice for modern man: he fornicated and read the papers." Clamence admits that his name is a cunning alias. Like the biblical *vox clamans in deserto*, the narrator is a voice crying in the wilderness mocking specious hope for clemency toward universal guilt. "Every man testifies to the crime of all the others—that is my faith and my hope," declares Clamence. It is also the rationale for his narrative, a strategy of confessing his culpability and coercing the listener—and reader—into acknowledging and sharing it.

Duplicitous Clamence has assumed the function of what he calls "judge-penitent," a deft way of being both condemner and condemned. He eventually lures his listener to his apartment, where he reveals a stolen Van Eyck on the wall. Our knowledge of the purloined painting now implicates the reader, too, in the crime. The subject of the work, "The Just Judges," reinforces the novel's theme of judgement even as it mocks the possibility of justice. It is not merely perverse bravado that impels Clamence to entrust his felonious secret to a stranger; he realizes that in a world devoid of innocence, no one dare judge anyone else. Yet he dreams of being apprehended, of finding release from his personal burden by a stroke of the guillotine. Jean-Baptiste longs for the decapitation that was the fate of his namesake John the Baptist:

> I would be decapitated, for instance, and I'd have no more fear of death; I'd be saved. Above the gathered crowd, you would hold up my still warm head, so that they could recognize themselves in it and could again dominate—an exemplar. All would be consummated; I should have brought to a close, unseen and unknown, my career as a false prophet crying in the wilderness and refusing to come forth.

Such redemption never comes. *The Fall* portrays all as trapped in a fallen world. Like Sisyphus, Clamence is condemned to repeat his futile gestures. Every time he encounters another listener (and reader), he is compelled anew to spread his gospel of universal guilt, to confirm it by his very success in persuading us to share his story.

THE MYTH OF SISYPHUS

First published: *Le Mythe de Sisyphe*, 1942 (English translation, 1955)
Type of work: Essays

The Myth of Sisyphus is a meditation on an ancient Greek figure who, condemned for eternity to a futile task, is seen by Camus as representative of the human condition.

The Myth of Sisyphus, Camus' most explicit philosophical pronouncement, begins by dismissing all reflection that evades the question of why we live. "There is but one truly serious philosophical problem, and that is suicide," he declares. "Judging whether life is or is not worth living amounts to answering the fundamental question of philosophy."

The Myth of Sisyphus includes several miscellaneous pieces—a discussion of Franz Kafka, a self-interview on the responsibility of the artist, and four personal evocations of the landscape of Algeria that were also published elsewhere. The most remarkable and influential section of *The Myth of Sisyphus*, however, is its title essay. In it and the supporting chapters, Camus appropriates the ancient Greek story of the king of Corinth who was punished by the gods for failing to show them sufficient respect. Sisyphus is condemned for eternity to push a boulder up the side of a steep mountain. Whenever he is about to reach the summit, the boulder rolls back to the base, and Sisyphus is obliged to begin his endless, pointless task again.

Camus seizes on this myth as an emblem of the human condition. Life, he contends, is absurd. Devoid of purpose, existence is an endless, empty series of compulsive repetitions with no possibility of attaining a goal. Sisyphus becomes the prototype of the "absurd hero," a figure whose variations Camus traces in the roles of the philanderer, the actor, and the conqueror. Like Rieux, who rebels against a scheme of things he cannot accept but cannot change, Camus' Sisyphus is a figure of admirable futility. "His scorn of the gods, his hatred of death, and his passion for life won him that unspeakable penalty in which the whole being is exerted toward accomplishing nothing. This is the price that must be paid for the passions of this earth."

A literary meditation rather than a work of rigorous formal philosophy, *The Myth of Sisyphus* offers a vision of human contingency and self-authentication popularly associated with the term existentialism. It assumes a post-Nietzschean universe in which the obituary for God has been written. Refusing to accept external validation, Camus contends that individuals are responsible for their own situations. He insists that such responsibility begins with awareness, a consciousness that *The Myth of Sisyphus* is itself designed to encourage.

The essay "The Myth of Sisyphus" concludes with the provocative assertion that despite the futility and dreariness of his punitive task, Sisyphus is a figure of felicity:

> Sisyphus teaches the higher fidelity that negates the gods and raises rocks. He too concludes that all is well. This universe henceforth without a master seems to him neither sterile nor futile. Each atom of that stone, each mineral flake of that night-filled mountain, in itself forms a world. The struggle itself toward the heights is enough to fill a man's heart. One must imagine Sisyphus happy.

Sisyphus possesses the satisfaction of awareness, the modest pleasure of honest confrontation with the bleak conditions of his existence. It is a gloss on the life and works of Camus himself, an obsessively lucid author who refused the spurious consolations of actions and expressions that divert us from the truth.

Summary

More than most other authors, Albert Camus both reflected and shaped his *Zeitgeist*, the spirit of an era plagued by tyranny, invasion, genocide, and colonialism. A child of the Algerian proletariat living among the Parisian intelligentsia and writing about human alienation, he stood both inside and outside history. He was a champion of lucidity and honesty in an age whose public rhetoric camouflaged savage realities. The sparely styled fiction, drama, and essays that Camus produced during a relatively brief career offer the paradox of tonic disillusionment, an exhilaration over candid contemplation of the absurd. In North America, perhaps even more than in France, Camus remains read and loved long after the works of many of his contemporaries have fallen out of favor and print.

Bibliography

Bloom, Harold, ed. *Albert Camus*. New York: Chelsea House, 1989.

Brée, Germaine, *Camus*. Rev. ed. New York: Harcourt, Brace & World, 1964.

Kellman, Steven G., ed. *Approaches to Teaching Camus's "The Plague."* New York: Modern Language Association of America, 1985.

Knapp, Bettina L., ed. *Critical Essays on Albert Camus*. Boston: G. K. Hall, 1988.

Lazere, Donald. *The Unique Creation of Albert Camus*. New Haven, Conn.: Yale University Press, 1973.

Lottman, Herbert R. *Albert Camus: A Biography*. Garden City, N.Y.: Doubleday, 1979.

McCarthy, Patrick. *Camus*. New York: Random House, 1982.

O'Brien, Conor Cruise. *Albert Camus of Europe and Africa*. New York: Viking, 1970.

Quilliot, Roger. *The Sea and Prisons: A Commentary on the Life and Thought of Albert Camus*. Translated by Emmett Parker. Tuscaloosa: University of Alabama Press, 1970.

Rhein, Phillip H. *Albert Camus*. New York: Twayne, 1969.

Thody, Philip. *Albert Camus, 1913-1960*. New York: Macmillan, 1962.

Steven G. Kellman

LEWIS CARROLL

Born: Daresbury, England
January 27, 1832
Died: Guildford, England
January 14, 1898

Principal Literary Achievement

World-renowned for his two Alice books, Carroll not only reshaped the genre of children's literature but also, in pioneering the art of nonsense, influenced the course of modern absurdist literature.

Biography

Charles Lutwidge Dodgson was born on January 27, 1832, in the parsonage of Daresbury, Cheshire. The third child and the eldest son of the eleven children of the Reverend Charles Dodgson and Frances Jane Lutwidge, he was descended from two North Country families with a long tradition of service to church and state. The world has come to know Charles Dodgson as Lewis Carroll, a pseudonym he chose in 1856 for his fictional and poetical works. He reserved his family name for his academic books and essays.

When he was eleven years old, his family moved from Daresbury to the rectory at Croft, just inside the Yorkshire boundary, where his father assumed his new duties as rector. During his years at Croft, Carroll revealed his early genius for nonsense by editing and writing for a series of family magazines titled *The Rectory Umbrella* and *Mischmasch*. Carroll matriculated at Christ Church, Oxford, on May 23, 1850. At the end of four years of study he distinguished himself by taking first-class honors in the Final Mathematical School and received his B.A. in 1854. During that same year, he published his first poem and story in the *Whitby Gazette*. Although he was ordained deacon in 1861, Carroll decided not to go on to take holy orders but instead to teach mathematics at Oxford, where he was to spend the rest of his life.

In 1856, Carroll purchased a camera and soon developed into one of the foremost portrait photographers of his day. His work includes numerous photographs of children as well as of such famous contemporaries as Alfred, Lord Tennyson, John Ruskin, the Rossetti family, Michael Faraday, John Everett Millais, and Holman Hunt. He is acknowledged as a pioneer in British amateur photography and the most outstanding photographer of children in the nineteenth century.

It was also in 1856 that Carroll first met the children of the dean of Christ Church,

Henry George Liddell. He immortalized these children—Alice, Edith, and Lorina—not only in his photographs but also in his classic story *Alice's Adventures in Wonderland* (1865). Alice was the inspiration for the story, and her two sisters appear in the tale as the Eaglet (Edith) and the Lory (Lorina). On July 4, 1862, Carroll, accompanied by his friend Robinson Duckworth, made a rowing expedition on the river with the three Liddell sisters. It was during this trip that he told them the story of Wonderland. He later wrote out the story and illustrated it with his own drawings. In February, 1863, he completed this original version of the story, which he titled *Alice's Adventures Underground.* Two years later he published an expanded version of the original story as *Alice's Adventures in Wonderland,* illustrated by the *Punch* artist John Tenniel.

In 1869, he published a collection of his comic and serious verse under the title *Phantasmagoria and Other Poems* (1869), the title poem being about a charming ghost that haunts a country gentleman. He then followed up the success of *Alice's Adventures in Wonderland* with the publication of *Through the Looking-Glass and What Alice Found There* in 1871. His long nonsense poem *The Hunting of the Snark,* illustrated by Henry Holiday, was published in 1876, followed by his last collection of comic verse, *Rhyme? and Reason?* in 1883.

Despite his innovative excursions into the world of nonsense and the absurd, Carroll did not neglect his traditional studies. He continued to publish a number of serious and traditional studies in mathematics and logic, including *Euclid and His Modern Rivals* (1879), *The Game of Logic* (1887), *Curiosa Mathematica, Part I* (1888), *Curiosa Mathematica, Part II* (1893), and *Symbolic Logic, Part I* (1896).

On January 14, 1898, Carroll died at his sisters' home in Guildford and is buried there. A memorial plaque has subsequently been placed in the floor of Westminster Abbey to honor this remarkable man. *Three Sunsets and Other Poems,* a collection of his serious verse, was published posthumously in 1898.

Analysis

In his serious poetry, collected in *Phantasmagoria* and *Three Sunsets and Other Poems,* Carroll reveals some of his heartfelt emotions of grief, anxiety, and love, but not without maintaining a firm control over those emotions. By writing in conventional poetic forms, alluding to established poets such as Samuel Taylor Coleridge, John Keats, and Alfred, Lord Tennyson, and modeling his poems upon theirs, and by adopting an accepted sentimental tone, Carroll carefuly modulated and refined the raw emotions that threatened his sense of order and psychological integrity, making them socially agreeable to his audience and to himself. He was especially attracted to and influenced by such poems as Coleridge's *The Rime of the Ancient Mariner,* Keats's "La Belle Dame sans Merci," and Tennyson's *In Memoriam* and "Mariana," all of which dwell upon such disturbing themes as guilt, depression, or sexual temptation. In short, Carroll attempted to shape his anxieties within a poetic tradition and to guard them against the riotous swirl of fear, chaos, and despair.

Carroll's nonsense verse, on the other hand, is much more complex and paradoxical than his serious poetry. Much as he relaxed and allowed his imagination to blossom in the presence of his young girlfriends, Carroll ignored and even challenged some of the conventional literary constraints in writing his comic poetry. The poetry in the two Alice books, such as "Twinkle, Twinkle, Little Bat," "Speak Roughly to Your Little Boy," "Beautiful Soup," "Jabberwocky," and "The Walrus and the Carpenter," are rebellious in the way that children are. These poems are visceral, instinctive, and free in their confrontation of authority and convention. While they assume the poetic forms and meters of traditional English poetry, they undermine that tradition by their comic tone, bizarre logic, and unsettling assumptions. Carroll's nonsense verse embodies his primal feelings about the possible meaninglessness of life, his repressed violence and sexuality, and his growing awareness that order and meaning within the context of a poem do not necessarily reflect a corresponding order in the terrifying void of cosmic reality.

Carroll's long poem *The Hunting of the Snark* is his comic defense against the unthinkable idea of the meaninglessness of life and his fear of annihilation after death. Under the leadership of the Bellman, a madcap crew sets forth to hunt the Snark. The hero of this mock epic is the Baker, who has been warned that he will be annihilated if the Snark is a Boojum. As the center of authority and truth, the Bellman constantly rings his bell (which is depicted in every illustration), reminding the crew of the passage of time and of their mortality. He defines truth by announcing at the outset that whatever he repeats three times is true. Carroll's questers, therefore, design their own world, for that is all they have. The mythical Snark is actually a booby trap, and the Baker vanishes away forever, thus destroying all order, hope, and meaning.

Carroll's strong Christian faith, however, would never allow him consciously to think along these lines. There was a God, a clear purpose in life, and an afterlife awaiting the righteous. Yet even as the Snark hunters manufactured some form of order as a buffer against madness, Carroll created a comic ballad with the bravado of an English adventurer in order to contain his greatest fear.

Carroll's sense of the absurd anticipates the work of the existentialists and Surrealists. The trial of the Knave of Hearts in *Alice's Adventures in Wonderland*, for example, points to Franz Kafka's *Der Prozess* (1925; *The Trial*, 1937). The decapitating Queen calls for the Knave of Hearts to be sentenced before the jury submits its verdict. The only evidence brought against him for stealing the tarts is a nonsense poem that is impervious to interpretation. In *The Hunting of the Snark*, Carroll presents another absurd trial, in which a pig is sentenced to transportation for life for leaving its pen. By the time the sentence is handed down, it is discovered that the pig has long been dead. The blank map that the Snark hunters use in their quest for the Snark also anticipates the existentialist view of the human will seen in Jean-Paul Sartre's counsel to leap before you look. Finally, given the fluidity of time and the dreamlike atmosphere of Wonderland, it is not surprising that Salvador Dalí chose to illustrate *Alice's Adventures in Wonderland* and that other surrealists find Carroll's own illustrations and prose a fertile ground for their own productions.

The great humor of the two Alice books, however, is what gives them their energy and immortality. It is a humor that transcends parody, satire, social wit, and slapstick—though to be sure those elements are all there—in order to fight the terrifying and incomprehensible issues of time, space, injustice, violence, self-identity, death, and the cosmic void. Rather than face these Medusa-like issues directly, Carroll circles and jabs at them with his comedy. His Christian faith gives a structure and meaning to his conscious life, and his humor protects that meaning from the threatening fears and uncertainties of his unconscious.

ALICE'S ADVENTURES IN WONDERLAND

First published: 1865
Type of work: Novella

After falling down a rabbit hole, Alice experiences a series of bizarre adventures that threaten to undermine her sense of order and control.

Although Carroll wrote *Alice's Adventures in Wonderland* explicitly to entertain children, it has become a treasure to philosophers, literary critics, biographers, clergy, psychoanalysts, and linguists, not to mention mathematicians, theologians, and logicians. There appears to be something in this work for everyone, and there are almost as many interpretations of it as there are commentators.

Alice's dream becomes her nightmare. A novelty at first, Wonderland becomes increasingly oppressive to Alice as she is faced with its fundamental disorder. Everything there, including her own body size, is in a state of flux. She is treated rudely, is bullied, is asked questions with no answers, and is denied answers to asked questions. Her recitations of poems turn into parodies, a baby turns into a pig, and a cat turns into a grin. The essence of time and space is called into question, and her romantic notion of an idyllic garden of life becomes a paper wasteland. Whether Alice, as some critics argue, is an alien who invades and contaminates Wonderland or is an innocent contaminated by it, one important fact remains the same: She has a vision that shows the world to be chaotic, meaningless, a terrifying void. In order to escape that oppressive and disorienting vision, she denies it with her outcry that "You're nothing but a pack of cards!" and happily regains the morally intelligible and emotionally comfortable world of her sister, who sits next to her on the green banks of a civilized Victorian countryside.

The assaults upon Alice's sense of order, stability, and proper manners wrought by such characters as the Hatter, Cheshire Cat, and March Hare make it clear that Wonderland is not the promised land, a place of sleepy fulfillment. Rather, Wonderland stimulates the senses and the mind. It is a *monde fatale,* so to speak, one that seduces Alice into seeking new sights, new conversations, new ideas, but it never satisfies her. Conventional meaning, understanding, and the fulfillment that comes with illumination are constantly denied her. That is the secret of Wonderland: Its disorienting and compelling attractions make it a "Wanderland" and Alice herself an addicted wanderer, free of the intellectual and moral burden of ordering her experiences into some meaningful whole. She is never bored because she is never satisfied.

Significantly, she is presented with a stimulating, alluring vision early in her adventures. Alice finds a tiny golden key that opens a door that leads into a small passage. As she kneels down and looks along the passage, she sees a beautiful garden with bright flowers and cool fountains. She is too large, however, to fit through the door in order to enter the attractive garden. Alice's dream garden corresponds to a longing for lost innocence, for the Garden of Eden. Her desire invests the place with imagined signifcance. Later, when she actually enters the garden, it loses its romantic aspect. In fact, it proves to be a parodic Garden of Life, for the roses are painted, the people are playing cards, and the death-cry "Off with her head!" echoes throughout the croquet grounds.

Alice's dream garden is an excellent example of Carroll's paradoxical duality. Like Alice, he is possessed by a romantic vision of an Edenic childhood more desirable than his own fallen world, but it is a vision that he knows is inevitably corrupted by adult sin and sexuality. He thus allows Alice's dream of the garden to fill her with hope and joy for a time but later tramples that pastoral vision with the hatred and fury of the beheading Queen and the artificiality of the flowers and inhabitants.

THROUGH THE LOOKING-GLASS

First published: 1871
Type of work: Novella

> After passing through a looking-glass, Alice is manipulated by the rules of a chess game until she becomes a queen.

Through the Looking-Glass and What Alice Found There abandons the fluidity and chaos of *Alice's Adventures in Wonderland* for artifice and strict determinism. In the first book, the emphasis is upon Alice's adventures and what happens to her on the experiential level. In the sequel, the reader accepts Alice and with detachment examines nature transformed in Looking-Glass Land's chessboard landscape. The voyage has shifted from the Kingdom of Chaos, with its riotous motion and verbal whirlpool, to the land of stasis, where the landscape is geometrical and the chesspieces are carefully manipulated by the rules of a precise game. In Wonderland every character says and does whatever comes into his or her head, but in the Looking-Glass world life is completely determined and without choice. Tweedledum and Tweedledee, the Lion and the Unicorn, the Red Knight and the White Knight must fight at regular intervals, whether they want to or not. They are trapped within the linguistic web of the poems that give them life, and their recurrent actions are forever predestined.

Whereas *Alice's Adventures in Wonderland* undermines Alice's sense of time, space, and commonsense logic, *Through the Looking-Glass* questions her very reality. Tweedledum and Tweedledee express the view developed by George Berkeley that all material objects, including Alice herself, are only "sorts of things" in the mind of the sleeping Red King (God). If the Red King were to awaken from his dreaming, they warn Alice, she would expire as quickly as a candle. Alice, it would seem, is a mere fiction shaped by a dreaming mind that threatens her with annihilation.

The ultimate question of what is real and what is a dream, however, is never resolved in the book. In fact, the story ends with the perplexing question of who dreamed it all—Alice or the Red King? Presumably, Alice dreamed of the King, who is dreaming of Alice, who is dreaming of the King, and the process continues. The question of dream versus reality is appropriately set forth in terms of an infinite regression through mirror facing mirror. The apprehension of reality is indefinitely deferred, and the only reality may be one's thoughts and their well-ordered expression. Were Alice to wake the Red King she would share the Baker's fate in *The Hunting of the Snark*. The cool geometry of Looking-Glass Land offers only a temporary oasis in a mutable, biological, and moral wasteland. Carroll recognized that the machinery of conventions and customs, mathematics and logic, and reality and dreams helped to define, and momentarily sustain and comfort, the frightened, imperfect, and comic adventurer.

In the final chapter, Alice rebels against the constraints of her chessboard existence. Having become Queen, she asserts her human authority against the controlling powers of the chessboard and brings both the intricate game and the story to an end. In chess terms, Alice has captured the Red Queen and checkmates the sleeping Red King. In human terms, she has matured and entered that fated condition of puberty, at which point Carroll dismisses his dreamchild once and for all from his remarkable fiction.

Summary

In contrast with the seeming placidity and orderliness of his life at Oxford, Lewis Carroll's writings exhibit considerable violence and disorder and a powerful struggle to control and contain those forces underground. This contrast, which gave rise to his two masterpieces—*Alice's Adventures in Wonderland* and *Through the Looking-Glass and What Alice Found There*—marks a fundamental conflict within Carroll himself, a ruthless battle between emotion and reason, sentiment and satire, chaos and control. Carroll was sometimes an intensely lonely man who needed the nonthreatening company of children to buoy his spirits and distract him from thoughts of death and the void. His books on mathematics and logic, which document the life of his mind, pale in comparison with his two Alice books and nonsense poetry, which document his obsession with the child girl and his unique comic battle with the great human fears that possess all human beings.

Bibliography

Greenacre, Phyllis. *Swift and Carroll: A Psychoanalytic Study of Two Lives.* New York: International Universities Press, 1955.

Guiliano, Edward, ed. *Lewis Carroll: A Celebration.* New York: Clarkson N. Potter, 1982.

_____, ed. *Lewis Carroll Observed.* New York: Clarkson N. Potter, 1976.

Hudson, Derek. *Lewis Carroll: An Illustrated Biography.* New illustrated ed. New York: New American Library, 1978.

Kelly, Richard. *Lewis Carroll.* Boston: Twayne, 1990.

Lennon, Florence Becker. *Victoria Through the Looking-Glass: The Life of Lewis Carroll.* London: Cassell, 1945.

Phillips, Robert S., ed. *Aspects of Alice: Lewis Carroll's Dreamchild as Seen Through the Critics' Looking-Glasses, 1865-1971.* New York: Vanguard Press, 1971.

Sewell, Elizabeth. *The Field of Nonsense.* Darby, Pa.: Arden Library, 1978.

Taylor, Alexander L. *The White Knight.* Edinburgh, Scotland: Oliver & Boyd, 1952.

Richard Kelly

MIGUEL DE CERVANTES

Born: Alcalá de Henares, Spain
September 29, 1547
Died: Madrid, Spain
April 23, 1616

Principal Literary Achievement

The creator of Don Quixote, one of the most original characters in world literature, Cervantes is known for his many-sided humor and his insight into the nature of reality.

Biography

Nothing is known of the first twenty years of Miguel de Cervantes Saavedra's life except that he is believed to have been born on September 29, 1547, and christened on October 9, 1547, in the church of Santa María in Alcalá de Henares, a small university town a little more than twenty miles northeast of Madrid. His father was Rodrigo de Cervantes, a ne'er-do-well surgeon who moved frequently from town to town while the mother probably remained in Alcalá with the children. Rodrigo's was an old family that had seen better days, claiming hidalgo rank but now heavily in debt. Cervantes' education seems to have been limited. In 1568, he was a student in the City School of Madrid, but he may have interrupted his studies to serve in the army in Flanders.

In December, 1569, he traveled to Rome as chamberlain in the household of Cardinal Acquaviva. Restless, he soon applied for a certificate of legitimacy to prove that he came from "Old Christian stock" so that he might, with his brother Rodrigo, enlist as a soldier in the Spanish army under Don Juan of Austria, an experience that gave him a chance to visit Italian cities. He fought in the Battle of Lepanto (1571). Sick below with a fever on the battleship *Marquesa*, he insisted on being brought on deck. In command of a longboat with twelve men, he continued to fight even after being wounded twice in the chest and having his left hand shattered, rendering it useless for the rest of his life. Later, he took part in the capture of Tunis in 1573.

He left the army in 1573, planning to return to Spain. En route, he and his brother were captured by the Turks and taken to Algiers, where Cervantes was imprisoned and enslaved for five years. After several attempts to escape, he was ransomed and returned to Madrid, where he tried to satisfy his ambitions as a writer, trying his

hand at sonnets and plays for the then-burgeoning theater. Between twenty and thirty plays were rejected by producers. In 1584, with Ana de Villafranca, probably an actress, he had an illegitimate daughter, Isabel. In December of that same year, he married Catalina de Salazar y Palacios, daughter of a prosperous peasant of Esquivas, who, however, brought him little dowry.

For all of his life, Cervantes was financially insecure. After his marriage, he was burdened with the responsibility for two sisters, an illegitimate daughter, a niece, and a maidservant, besides his wife, and his attempts at a literary career met with little or no financial success. In 1585, however, he wrote and published a pastoral romance, *La Galatea* (1585; *Galatea: A Pastoral Romance*, 1833), which had considerable popular reception. In that same year, his historic tragedy *El cerco de Numancia* (1784; *Numantia: A Tragedy*, 1870)—the story of the collective suicide of a Celtiberian city encircled by the Roman army in 133 B.C., which chose death rather than surrender—was successfully produced.

In 1588, he found employment collecting wheat and oil for the Spanish armada, roaming the countryside of Andalusia and becoming familiar with folk speech and folklore. Again he met with misfortune, was excommunicated for seizing wheat belonging to the cathedral of Seville, and was imprisoned for a shortage in his accounts. He wrote two sonnets on the armada that met with popular approval. In May, 1590, he applied for a post in the New World but was refused and told to seek something nearer home. He turned again to writing and in 1595 won first prize in a poetry contest. In 1598, his sonnet *Soneto al túmulo de Felipe II*, on the funeral of that monarch, attracted attention.

In 1603, after imprisonment for debt, he moved to the Calle del Rastro in Valladolid after the Court transferred there; he began work on *El ingenioso hidalgo don Quixote de la Mancha* (1605; *Don Quixote de la Mancha, Part 1*, 1612, hereinafter referred to as *Don Quixote*). Published in 1605, it was an immediate popular success, not only in Spain but abroad, quickly translated and published in England, Brussels, France, and Italy. Yet fate intervened again when, that same year, a neighbor was murdered, and Cervantes and his family were imprisoned for a time, an experience that embittered him and seems to have prompted him to withdraw from the limelight until 1608, when he moved back to Madrid. In 1613, Cervantes published *Novelas ejemplares* (1613; *Exemplary Novels*, 1846) and a collection of his comedies and interludes, *Ocho comedias y ocho entremeses* (1615; English translation, 1807). His long burlesque poem, *Viage del Parnaso* (1614; *The Voyage to Parnassus*, 1870), appeared in 1614. In 1614, a copy of a spurious and vicious so-called sequel to *Don Quixote* appeared, written by a mysterious Alonso Fernández de Avellaneda. Cervantes, angered, hurried to finish his own *Segunda parte del ingenioso cavallero don Quixote de la Mancha* (1615; *Don Quixote de la Mancha, Part 2*, 1620).

In his last year, Cervantes joined the Tertiary Order of St. Francis. Ill, he hurried to finish *Los trabajos de Persiles y Sigismunda* (1617; *The Travels of Persiles and Sigismunda: A Northern History*, 1619), a prose romance, which was not published until 1617, after his death. On April 18, 1616, Cervantes sent for the almoner of the Franciscan monastery to administer the last sacraments. The next day, somewhat improved, he wrote the dedication to *The Travels of Persiles and Sigismunda*, now finished. On Wednesday, he penned a final "Farewell, witticisms; farewell, jests; farewell, cheerful friends."

Cervantes died in Madrid on April 23, 1616—on the same day as William Shakespeare. He was buried in the Trinitarian monastery, wearing the Franciscan rough habit. His remains were scattered at the end of the seventeenth century during the rebuilding of the monastery. He left no children except for Isabel, and there are no descendants today.

Analysis

The strongest and most immediate impression one gets from most of Cervantes' work is his unique gift for humor, especially for burlesque, but also for irony. Besides *The Voyage to Parnassus* and some of the interludes, there is that kind of humor in *Don Quixote*: the dubbing of Don Quixote as a knight, the tournament at the duke's, the marvels such as the talking head and the enchanted bark, the visit of Altisidora to Hell. There is also burlesque of literary conventions: "sonnets, epigrams, or eulogies . . . bear[ing] the names of grave and entitled personages" that are "commonly found at the beginning of books"; the citation of authorities; segments in the pastoral and picaresque modes; sonnets and love tales.

Irony appears in the contrast between the grandiose expectations of Sancho Panza for the governorship of Barataria and the actual experience. There is a special irony, however, in the ending of the novel, when the dreams of Don Quixote come to nothing, and he resigns himself to being just Alonso Quijano.

There are other forms of humor, such as playfulness when Cervantes avenges himself on the spurious *Don Quixote* by placing that book in Hell, and in the confusion of Don Alvaro over meeting two Don Quixotes, the spurious one and the real one. There is also a playful humor of Cervantes' account of Don Quixote's discomfiture at the amorous advances of Altisidora. There is slapstick in Don Quixote's battle with the bagful of cats, and in the trampling of Sancho under the feet of the supposed defenders against the phony attack on Barataria.

Don Quixote, however, transcends humor. It borrows the experiences of Cervantes: his imprisonment and slavery in Algiers, his service in the army, his wanderings in Andalusia, his associations with the underworld during his imprisonments. Out of these experiences come most of the themes and motifs of his literary works.

Like many of his contemporaries, Cervantes had certain ideas about the nature and responsibilities of those who govern, ideas that he deftly wove into the fabric of his literary work, especially *Don Quixote*, where he frequently contrasts the ideals of chivalry with modern decadence. The tenure of Sancho as governor of Barataria gave Cervantes added opportunity to express those ideas: The common individual is as well equipped to govern as a noble; the governor should beware bribery and entreaties, be suave and mild in fulfilling duties, let the tears of the poor find compassion, and seek to uncover the truth in his or her judgments.

Cervantes also had certain standards for his literary profession, and he judged his contemporaries by those standards, especially in *The Voyage to Parnassus* and "Song of Calliope," standards that he applied not only to chivalric romances but also to the pastorals, love poetry, and comedy: verisimilitude, consistent structure, and the avoidance of supernatural elements, trivialities, and playing to the pit. He returns to this theme frequently in *Don Quixote*.

Cervantes shows an interest in, and sympathy for, the peasants, although he never idealizes them. He incorporates them into his comedies as well as in *Don Quixote*. Sancho is such a peasant, who repeatedly quotes folk proverbs. Several of the scenes in *Don Quixote* are village or countryside scenes like those Cervantes knew in Andalusia. Not surprising, then, is the presence of the pastoral elements, notably the love story of Grisótomo and Marcela in part I, and Don Quixote's decision to become a shepherd when he is compelled to forsake knight-errantry. The picaresque element, influenced by Cervantes' knowledge of the Sevillean underworld, appears in the beggar and other characters in his *Exemplary Novels*. In *Don Quixote*, it appears when Don Quixote tries to free a chain gang of galley slaves, criminals, who then turn on him and rob him. The most sharply delineated rogue is Ginés de Pasamonte, who appears twice in the novel.

The absorbing concern of *Don Quixote*, however, is the interplay between the delusions of Don Quixote and reality. This theme probably reflects an inner conflict within Cervantes himself, considering his youthful regard for the idealism of the chivalric, then for the pastoral romance, and considering his belief in the need for charm and imagination in poetry, tempered by his developing regard for artistic truth.

This dichotomy is dramatized by the play between Don Quixote, a well-read, highly imaginative but deluded individual, and Sancho Panza, an illiterate peasant with a store of common sense and folk wisdom but with little or no imagination or vision. At the beginning, the line of demarcation is clear-cut, but as the story progresses, the line becomes more and more blurred. There are times when the grand delusions of Don Quixote are so powerful that even Sancho has his doubts; in one instance, Quixote accepts the delusion that Dulcinea is enchanted. Sancho has his own illusions—that he will become the governor of an island and wealthy. At times, the roles are reversed, as when Sancho tries to deceive Quixote into believing that three peasant girls are princesses riding palfreys, and Quixote corrects him: "They are donkeys."

There are other distortions of reality for Sancho, as when he and Quixote encounter a carter with two docile lions in a cage, and Sancho, exaggerating their size and ferocity, flees. There are times when other people, sensible persons, also distort the truth: biased parents boast of their children, their lovers, their beloved. Persons, such as the innkeeper's daughter, who has illusions of bruises after dreaming that she has fallen from a tower, can be deluded by dreams. There is a difference, however, between their illusions and Quixote's, the difference between a transforming faith and absurd conclusions.

At the end of *Don Quixote*, sadly, Don Quixote no longer believes in his delusions, in his visions, and again he becomes Alonso Quijano. Yet, even then, the skeptic

Sancho Panza will protest: "Who knows but behind some bush we may come upon the lady Dulcinea, as disenchanted as you can wish."

DON QUIXOTE DE LA MANCHA, PART 1

First published: *El ingenioso hidalgo don Quixote de la Mancha*, 1605
                    (English translation, 1612)
Type of work: Novel

A certain Alonso Quijano fancies himself a modern knight-errant righting every manner of wrong and takes the name of Don Quixote.

Don Quixote is a parody of the romance of chivalry, as Aubrey F. G. Bell has described it, "a multiplicity of heterogeneous thoughts, events, episodes, scenes, and characters" welded together in a harmonious whole and bound together by "humor and the consistency of two chief characters," Alonso Quijano of the village of La Mancha, and an illiterate peasant whom he recruits as his squire.

Quijano, or Don Quixote, as he renames himself, is close to fifty, lean and gaunt, and has spent most of his time reading books of chivalry, selling many acres of his land to buy more of these books. Finally, his wits weakened, he decides to put into practice all that he has read. He polishes old pieces of armor and doctors a piece of a helmet with cardboard reinforced with iron strips, and he sets out to find someone to dub him a knight. The innkeeper at a nearby inn humors him. Alarmed at his absence, his niece finds him and brings him back to his village, where she and the curate decide to burn Quixote's library of more than one hundred books.

Quixote chooses as his lady a good-looking farm girl who lives nearby, Aldonza Lorenzo, whom he renames Dulcinea. Since a squire is necessary, Quixote persuades a neighboring farmer, Sancho Panza, to follow him, with promises of adventure and the prospect of winning an island, over which Sancho is to become governor. Embarked upon his second sally, they find windmills, which Quixote imagines to be giants. Despite Sancho's warnings, Quixote charges them and is unhorsed by one of the wings. Now seeing that these are really windmills, Quixote explains them as the work of a magician who has changed what are truly giants into windmills. There follow a series of episodes, many of them derived from folklore, in which Quixote suffers setbacks. Two flocks of sheep are imagined to be a Christian army fighting a pagan army—the bleating of the sheep mistaken for the neighing of horses, the sound of trumpets, and the roll of drums.

They meet a man on horseback with something on his helmet that gleams like gold. Quixote is convinced that it is the gold helmet of Mambrino, a famous enchanted helmet of folklore. Bearing down upon the horseman, who is a barber traveling from one village to another to perform some bloodletting for one man and to trim the beard of another, Quixote dismounts and puts to flight the barber, who abandons his headgear, which is actually a basin atop his head to protect it from the rain. Quixote picks it up and proceeds to wear it on his own head.

When Quixote and Sancho meet a chain gang of galley slaves, all criminals, Quixote concludes that now is the time to right wrongs and aid the wretched. When the guards refuse to unshackle them, Quixote charges, and in the turmoil the criminals break their chains and the guards alternate their blows between Quixote, Sancho, and the thieves. In the confusion, the guards flee, abandoning their weapons. The criminals now turn upon Quixote and Sancho and steal their clothing. Chagrined at the succession of defeats and fearing further pursuit, Quixote and Sancho retreat to the mountains of Sierra Moreno, where, Quixote reasons, there is a setting better adapted to the adventures that he seeks, a place for the marvels like those of which he has read.

There, Don Quixote meets a double pair of lovers, Cardenio and Luscinda, Fernando and Dorotea. Cardenio is betrayed by his friend Fernando, who tries to win Luscinda away from Cardenio while breaking his engagement to Dorotea. Cardenio becomes mad, a foil to Don Quixote's madness. Don Quixote, as helper of damsels in distress becomes involved, and the lovers are all eventually reunited. This preoccupation with love inspires Quixote to send a love letter and a love poem to Dulcinea with Sancho, who returns to the home village. There, he joins the curate and the barber in a plot to bring Quixote back home. Dorotea will pretend that she is a distressed princess who has come from Guinea to seek redress for an injury done to her by a giant, and to seek Don Quixote's help.

En route to the village, they stop at an inn, where Don Quixote goes to sleep in the garret where wineskins are kept. Dreaming that he is engaged in a struggle with a giant, he begins to slash at the wineskins. Half awake, he mistakes the wine for the flow of blood. Even after thoroughly waking, he continues the battle and begins to look for the giant's head on the floor, persuaded that he has cut it off. Sancho is so convinced that he looks for it too and assures the innkeeper's daughter that he saw the monster.

Among the persons at the inn are a student and a former soldier with a Morisco maiden. Both soldier and student inspire lengthy discourses from Don Quixote on war and peace, on the treatment of students, on the treatment of soldiers, and on the comparisons between the professions of arms and letters. Artillery, Don Quixote says, is a diabolic device by which an infamous arm may take the life of a valiant knight without his knowing from where the blow came. Peace is the greatest blessing desirable in this life. The end of war is peace.

The student's chief hardship is poverty. He must suffer hunger, cold, destitution, nakedness. The soldier is the poorest of the poor, dependent upon wretched pay, which comes late or never, and upon such booty as he can amass, to the peril of his life and conscience. On the day of battle, they place upon his head a doctor's cap to heal the wound inflicted by some bullet that may have passed through his temple or left him mutilated. It is far easier to reward scholars than soldiers, for the former may receive posts, while the latter receive any compensation that their master has a disposition to give. Men of letters argue that, without them, arms cannot support themselves; men of arms reply that, without them, there can be no letters, since by their efforts states are preserved. To attain eminence in letters requires time, loss of sleep, hunger, headaches, indigestion. To be a good soldier costs as much and more. The former soldier, pressed to tell his story, is revealed as a former captive of the Moors and enslaved by them. The Captive's Tale has many elements derived from Cervantes' own experiences in Algiers, at one time appearing briefly as a character in the tale.

Don Quixote's audience is impressed at seeing this apparently sensible man discussing topics rationally, a man so obsessed, however, when it comes to the subject of chivalry.

Sancho, the curate, and the barber finally get Quixote home. Back home, he is warmly greeted by the townsfolk and taken to his house, where the niece and the housekeeper care for him. Quixote and Sancho do mention the possibility of a third sally, but the author does not know what will happen.

DON QUIXOTE DE LA MANCHA, PART 2

First published: *Segunda parte del ingenioso cavallero don Quixote de la Mancha*, 1615 (English translation, 1620)
Type of work: Novel

Don Quixote embarks with Sancho Panza on his third sally, which takes him into a larger and more variegated world.

Responding to criticism of part 1 and stung by the spurious sequel to *Don Quixote* by Alonso Fernández de Avellaneda, Cervantes restricts this novel more to the protagonists, with fewer interpolations and digressions. Don Quixote and Sancho are never lost to view, and the bonds between them are kept strong, even when they are separated.

In part 2, there is a refinement of the character of Don Quixote and a development of his saner nature, moments of sanity when he comments on society in a mixed picture of madness and idealism. There is a corresponding refinement in the character of Sancho, as his understanding of and sympathy for Don Quixote develop. The world of part 2 is a much expanded world, in which Don Quixote travels much farther from his native village, as far as Barcelona and the Mediterranean coast. It has a wider range of characters: peasants, bandits, traveling actors, shepherds, country squires, dukes, Moriscos. Part 2 begins about a month after the end of part 1. Two new characters are introduced: Cid Hamete Benengeli, the Moorish author of *Don Quixote*, whom Cervantes frequently pretends to cite, and Sansón Carrasco, recent graduate of the University of Salamanca.

To cure Don Quixote's madness, the curate and barber consult frequently with the niece and housekeeper. Finally satisfied that he has come to his senses, they come to the house and begin a discussion of statecraft, in which Don Quixote impresses them with his good sense, until the subject turns to chivalry and he again defends the old knightly virtues found in the romances against the sloth, arrogance, and theory over practice of the present age, persuading his auditors of a return of his madness. When Don Quixote asks Sancho's opinions regarding criticisms of him, Sancho refers him to a book by Cid Hamete Benengeli, then mentions Sansón Carrasco, the student, who knows all about the book. Thus, Quixote and Sancho meet Sansón, who wins them over with flattery, although he is secretly allied with the curate and the barber, plotting stratagems to discourage Quixote as a knight.

The first concern of Don Quixote is to see his lady Dulcinea, so they set out for Toboso, Dulcinea's hometown. Stopping just outside, Quixote sends Sancho into town to find her. Sancho, however, has no idea what she looks like, so Quixote decides on a trick of his own: He (Quixote) will approach the first farm girl he meets. Don Quixote sees only a farm girl and is bewildered. Sancho is hard pressed to convince him. The girl, annoyed, rides off. Sancho explains the snub nose, mole on lip, and the odor of garlic as enchantments, an explanation that satisfies Quixote.

Arriving at a woods, the two meet Sansón, disguised as a knight. His plan is to challenge Quixote's mistress and in an ensuing clash of arms, defeat Don Quixote, who then by the rules of knighthood would be obligated to follow the bidding of the victor—in this case, to return to his village. Sansón's plot fails, and Don Quixote and Sancho leave him behind in the care of a bone-setter. In the woods, Don Quixote also meets the Knight of the Wood, who, not recognizing him, boasts of having met and defeated all Spanish knights. Further discussion reveals that the Knight of the Wood had really met the spurious Don Quixote that Avellaneda had conceived.

Don Quixote meets a traveler, Don Diego de Miranda, with whom he engages in his favorite subject, knights-errant. Don Diego, intrigued by this now sensible, now mad man, invites him to his home. En route, they meet a carter bearing two lions in a cage on his way to the king. Ordered to get out of the way and warned that the lions are dangerous, Quixote, feeling a threat to his courage, orders the carter to open the cages. His companions retreat to a far distance, while he approaches one of the lions, braces his buckler, draws his sword, and faces the lion, which then turns around, stretches, yawns, washes its face, and then enters its cage and lies down. God upholds true chivalry, Quixote shouts, and then fixes the white cloth of victory on his lance. Quixote is a crazy sane man, an insane man on the verge of sanity, Don Diego concludes.

Later, Don Quixote meets a duke and a duchess on a hunt in the forest and is invited to their palace, where the hosts keep Quixote and Sancho for their amusement, proceeding to play a series of "jests" at their expense. At a dinner, Quixote speaks of the giants whom he has conquered and the enchanters whom he has met. An ecclesiastic at the table recognizes Quixote and answers him with a sermon about Don Quixote's experiences, ridiculing his belief in these creatures. Angered, Quixote answers with a discourse on the high and narrow path of knight-errantry that rights wrongs and does good. The duke, to irritate the ecclesiastic, offers Sancho the governorship that Quixote had promised him.

Sancho's tenure as governor of the Island of Barataria, actually a village in the duke's domain, lasts but seven days, in which Don Quixote offers him much advice, and where Sancho very astutely settles petitions brought to him. Yet since this was another of the duke's jests, the latter arranges a mock invasion, in which Sancho is badly bruised and decides that he has had enough.

Slapstick humor is provided by the account of a hunt, where Sancho, frightened by a boar, scrambles up a tree and is stuck until his screams are heard and he is freed. In another incident, Dulcinea's disenchantment requires three thousand and some lashes on Sancho's back, which Sancho performs on himself, out of sight but not out of hearing, so that he lashes the trees, with proper sound effects.

Sansón attempts one more time to best Don Quixote in knightly encounter, this time disguised as the Knight of the White Moon. He is successful. Quixote agrees to return to La Mancha for a year. Since he can no longer be a knight-errant, however, he will become Quixotic, a shepherd, with Sancho as Pancino, living among shepherds and shepherdesses, restoring the Arcadia of old. Back home, Don Quixote calmly announces that he is no longer Don Quixote but Alonso Quijano, the Good, and the enemy of the romances. The curate declares that Quijano, the Good, is dying but also sane. After writing his will, Quixote dies. The curate sends for a notary to witness that he is truly dead, lest some author other than Cid Hamet Benengeli try to resurrect him falsely.

Summary

As a writer, Miguel de Cervantes aimed to move his reader to laughter. He also had serious concerns about excesses in literary art. A logical result was *Don Quixote*, a parody on chivalric romances.

An assemblage of heterogeneous elements welded together by humor and the consistency of two characters, *Don Quixote* is Cervantes' masterpiece. It depicts one of the world's best-known fictional characters, a madman who sets out to right wrongs, and a squire with much common sense but little or no vision. Between Don Quixote and Sancho Panza, Cervantes probes human delusions and the conflict between idealism and realism.

Bibliography

Bell, Aubrey F. G. *Cervantes*. Norman: University of Oklahoma Press, 1947.
Canavaggio, Jean. *Cervantes*. Translated by J. R. Jones. New York: W. W. Norton, 1990.
Church, Margaret. *Don Quixote: Knight of La Mancha*. New York: New York University Press, 1971.
Durán, Manuel. *Cervantes*. New York: Twayne, 1976.
Frank, Bruno. *A Man Called Cervantes*. New York: Viking Press, 1935.

Kelly, James Fitzmaurice. *Miguel de Cervantes Saavedra: A Memoir.* Oxford, England: Clarendon Press, 1913.

Madariaga, Salvador de. *"Don Quixote": An Introductory Study in Psychology.* London: Oxford University Press, 1966.

Mondadori, Arnoldo, ed. *Cervantes: His Life, His Times, His Works.* Translated by Salvator Attanasio and selections by Thomas G. Bergin. New York: American Heritage Press, 1970.

Predmore, Richard. *The World of "Don Quixote."* Cambridge, Mass.: Harvard University Press, 1967.

Schevill, Rudolph. *Cervantes.* New York: Duffield & Company, 1919.

Thomas Amherst Perry

BRUCE CHATWIN

Born: Sheffield, England
May 13, 1940
Died: Nice, France
January 18, 1989

Principal Literary Achievement

Widely recognized as one of England's most brilliant essayists, novelists, and journalists, Chatwin wrote semiautobiographical travel books that secured for him a permanent place among travel writers of the twentieth century.

Biography

Bruce Chatwin was born in Sheffield, England, on May 13, 1940. His mother was Margharita Turnell Chatwin and his father, Charles Leslie Chatwin, was a lawyer. His family regularly moved around England, but he attended a private secondary school in Marlborough. He did not pursue a formal university degree, choosing to read on his own and travel throughout the world to places that fascinated him. His writings about these locations became his first published works and established him as an expert on their history, geography, and culture.

He did, however, work for eight years at Sotheby's, the famous art auction house in London. Beginning as a porter there, he worked his way up to art consultant and picture expert and, finally, became a director and member of Sotheby's board of directors in 1965. His rise to such a high position in his early twenties has become one of the art world's most famous success stories. Though starting work still in his teens, he suggested that a newly acquired Picasso painting was really a fake. When highly paid experts were asked to authenticate the painting, they found that it was, indeed, just that. Chatwin was then offered a job as an expert in paintings. His career at Sotheby's was so successful that he was actually given, at age twenty-five, a partnership in the company, becoming the youngest man in the history of Sotheby's to be appointed director of modern art.

In the meantime, Chatwin had used his self-taught expertise to begin his own antiquities collection. Disaster struck, however, when he suddenly lost his eyesight at the age of twenty-five by, according to his eye doctor, studying too closely the details of paintings and other art objects. Though it was considered a psychosomatic disorder, his physician suggested that he find landscapes with long horizons so that he could physiologically expand the parameters of his vision. Upon the return of his

eyesight, Chatwin immediately sailed to the African Sahara and became deeply involved not only in the physical landscape but also with the nomadic tribes that traveled throughout the land and domesticated its enormous spaces. Initially, he had become interested in the relationship between the physical geography and the spiritual lives of those who live there and how that combined into a geography of the imagination.

Chatwin never returned to the rarefied atmosphere and financially successful world of art criticism and auctioneering, preferring the nomadic existence of the people that he studied for the remainder of his life. He then began his career as a journalist in London, journeying to the most remote parts of the earth and reporting on the strange nomadic peoples who lived in places that at first seemed barely habitable. What he discovered was that those places that seemed most barren actually possessed the most elaborate, complex, and richly detailed spiritual cosmologies. Yet he also discovered that even in remote areas, such as Patagonia and the outback of Australia, Western "civilization" and values had done enormous damage both to the natives of the region and to the delicate ecological balance between the human, animal, and plant life that cohabit in vital symbiotic relationships.

After becoming interested in anthropology and archaeology through his journalistic assignments, Chatwin began writing in earnest. His visit to the southern tip of South America known as Patagonia became the subject matter of his first full-length book, called *In Patagonia* (1977). It was highly praised by many critics as a worthy successor to the travel journals of both D. H. Lawrence and Evelyn Waugh. It won several prestigious awards at the time, namely the Hawthornden Prize in 1978 and the E. M. Forster Award in 1979. His ability to amalgamate facts with fictional techniques raised the level of discourse from mere reportage to a serious examination of the spiritual lives of a variety of European and indigenous groups in the desolate areas of the world.

His next major critical success was a novel titled *The Viceroy of Ouidah* (1980), which he had initially intended as a nonfictional biography about a notorious nineteenth century Brazilian slave trader, Francisco Felix de Souza. Chatwin's arrest and imprisonment as an illegal mercenary in the West African nation of Dahomey, the setting of de Souza's atrocities, became the occasion of the novel. The book mixed fact and fiction so compellingly that the German film director Werner Herzog decided to make it into a film. Having successfully garnered international acclaim as both a travel writer and a nonfiction novelist, Chatwin then proceeded to write a conventional novel about identical twin brothers who spend eighty years on a remote Welsh farm. The novel was called *On the Black Hill* (1982) and elicited high praise from such artists as John Updike, who compared it favorably to both Ernest Hemingway and Lawrence.

Chatwin's fifth book became his most renowned travel journal and received unusually high praise. *The Songlines* (1987) is a quasi-documentary account of his trip to Australia to study Aboriginal culture. Again, he intermixes an adventure narrative with philosophical meditations on the damage done to the instinctual lives of the natives of the area. The book has become a virtual model for the work of other concerned students of how Western culture has systematically destroyed the spiritual foundations of so-called savage cultures.

Chatwin's final novel, *Utz* (1989), was a product of his deep knowledge of antiquities. It documents, fictionally, the life of Caspar Utz, a Czech aristocrat who collected priceless Meissen figurines during World War II. His final work was a collection of essays titled *What Am I Doing Here* (1989), which was published posthumously. He died in Nice, France, on January 18, 1989, of a rare bone marrow cancer possibly contracted during a visit to China, but there were some reports that he actually died of complications from AIDS (acquired immune deficiency syndrome).

Analysis

The key to understanding the complex world of Chatwin is that he combined a number of identities that manifest themselves in his writings. He was a respected and highly accomplished novelist, a writer of critically acclaimed travel books, and a superb essayist. What distinguished him from others who write novels, travel literature, or essays was that he interwove genres in exceptionally imaginative ways. By amalgamating these genres, he was able to keep the content of his books open and multifaceted. *In Patagonia* is primarily a journalistic assignment that he recorded in ninety-seven journal entries. It documents a trip to the southern tip of South America but tells much more than the mere literal events of that trip. He consciously does not call it a diary, since that word suggests a simple recording of daily events. Since he is highly conscious of the etymologies of crucial words, he calls it a journal and stresses the connection between the words "journey" and "journal"; he thus establishes a two-part structure consisting of the physical journey and, as importantly, the spiritual journey he is taking into his own psyche as well as the spiritual history of the place itself.

The ostensible reason for the trip is to find the origin of a primitive relic that had been in his family for many years. What he serendipitously discovers is a deeper understanding of himself, his family, and the heart of Patagonia itself. By varying his methods of inquiry, he was able to bring into his book enormous amounts of information that include religious, historical, mythical, archaeological, and personal data. What emerges, then, are cultural investigations that reveal radical differences in his Eurocentric value system and the so-called primitive societies that had flourished until the arrival of Western exploiters. His physical explorations become metaphysical ones, since he is always interested in the earliest signs of some kind of common human nature. Chatwin, like writers such as the poet Ezra Pound and the fiction writer Guy Davenport, was keenly interested in how the archaic imagination reasserts itself in modern society, and how it can be used to salvage humankind from its self-destructive practices.

Since Chatwin possessed a highly attuned romantic imagination that trusted impulse and embraced risk, he believed that avenues other than fact and data contribute to a comprehensive understanding of humanity's problematical plight. His novel, *The*

Viceroy of Ouidah, combines the facts about the life of a Brazilian slave trader with Chatwin's own starkly dramatic recreations of the sadistic conditions under which the slaves suffered. Some critics called it a mock-heroic fantasy full of exotic, even surrealistic scenes. He uses fictional techniques to shape and organize the bare facts into cinematic images that demand attention and make their points with shattering impact.

After receiving worldwide acclaim for a travel book (*In Patagonia*) and a nonfiction novel (*The Viceroy of Ouidah*) that became a movie, Chatwin produced a conventional novel, fully fictional as far as anyone knew, of identical twin brothers who spend their lives on a remote Welsh farm. It is called *On the Black Hill* and is as explicitly detailed in miniature as his earlier works were grandly exotic.

The Songlines, perhaps his most brilliant and respected book, revisits the genre of the travel book as it details his explorations of one of the oldest cultures of the world, the Aboriginals in the dry heart of central Australia. Chatwin loved extremes and was especially enamored with where extremes converged. What interested him most were those locations, geographical and cultural, where the aggressively linear West meets the cyclical ever-renewing "primitive" imaginations of the Aboriginals.

In his last major work, he returned to the nonfiction novel. *Utz* combines techniques from detective fiction with James Bond-like adventures in its depiction of lost treasures of rare miniature figurines in central Europe. Chatwin was able to use his encyclopedic knowledge of the antiquities that he had collected during and after his career with Sotheby's.

IN PATAGONIA

First published: 1977
Type of work: Travel literature

The narrator journeys to the southern tip of South America to authenticate a lost family relic but discovers, instead, the disturbing riches of Patagonia.

One of the difficulties that critics had when *In Patagonia* first appeared in print was what to call it. It was certainly a travel book that treated that remote area with the same serious attention that classic travel writers such as D. H. Lawrence and Evelyn Waugh treated the locations that they wrote about. Indeed, Chatwin's style is every bit as literary and novelistic as the best of either Lawrence or Waugh, both of whom were known primarily as novelists.

Though the structure of the book is quite obviously the journal of a trip, Chatwin varies his methods throughout the work. He uses anecdotes about people he met and adventures he had and interweaves them, sometimes seamlessly, with anecdotes, adventures, and stories he had earlier read about in books and articles about Patagonia. Though the book opens with the narrator's call to adventure as he vows to find and authenticate the origin of a family relic from Patagonia (a piece of giant animal skin from prehistoric times), the narrator quietly removes himself as an active participant in the action of the venture. He prefers to record what he sees and hears and also to connect that data with the many sources he studied before embarking on his trip.

The book becomes, then, a mélange of diverse methods of presentation that include biography, autobiography, anthropology, myth, geography, religion, portrait, strange encounters, family history, and philosophical speculation. He uses all of these methods not only to describe a sense of the place but also, more importantly, to evoke the spirit of the actual geography and its relationship to the original natives, the Araucanian Indians. While the book celebrates the diversity of that part of the world, it also, just as vividly, laments what has been lost as a result of the invasions of other cultures into its precincts. The narrator spends considerable time meditating on the ruins of Patagonia and on what it had once been as a culture unsullied by Western materialistic values.

Chatwin is also involved in the ultimate journey South; that is, a Dantean journey into hell. Indeed, at the tip of Patagonia is Tierra del Fuego, or the Land of Fire. He meets a variety of wise and not-so-wise guides as he pursues both his actual and his mythological journeys to the underworld. What keeps the reader involved is the sense that he or she is witnessing and recording a fall from the Edenic timeless innocence of the native Patagonians into the time-bound, linear world of divided consciousness—that Western imperative that separates the world into categories of sacred and profane.

Chatwin uses dramatic juxtapositions to show how a variety of European immigrants such as the Welsh, the Germans, Scots, the Boers, and others had left the stultifying atmospheres of their native countries while yet ironically and unconsciously re-creating the same cultural restrictions they thought they were fleeing. What fascinates Chatwin about this urge to find satisfaction in radically new landscapes is the suspicion that the source of this desire has a genetic basis. In chapter 44, he encounters some scientists who have been studying the migration patterns of Jackass Penguins: "We talked late into the night, arguing whether or not we, too, have journeys mapped out in our central nervous systems; it seemed the only way to account for our insane restlessness." In short, the quest—the basic plot of most Western literature—can be explained as physiological law. Indeed, such questions tortured Chatwin in many of his other examinations of nomadic cultures. He suspected that humankind's fall consisted in abandoning his natural, biologically determined impulse to move throughout the world continuously; settling into a permanent place was therefore unnatural.

Chatwin's most convincing form of historical and anthropological inquiry always comes, however, in the form of his etymological research. Linguistically, the name "Patagonia" refers to a tribe of Tehuelche Indians who were hunters of great size, speed, and endurance. He extrapolates from these characteristics that Caliban, of William Shakespeare's *The Tempest* (1611), was probably a Patagonian, an idea that he pursues into Gnostic and Hermetic interpretations of Patagonia that had found their way into a number of Renaissance texts. Throughout the work, Chatwin identifies himself with the mythic Abel, the wanderer, as opposed to Cain, the horder of property. He also uncovers historical accounts of American heroes such as Butch Cassidy, and British scientist Charles Darwin, whose early associations with Patagonia were disturbing and repulsive.

One of Chatwin's most convincing arguments for looking upon Patagonia as a place of Edenic innocence is the language of one of its indigenous tribes, the Yaghans. He notes that there are no abstractions in that language for moral ideas such as "good" or "beautiful" unless they are rooted to actual things. The tribe's territory is always a paradise that could never be improved upon, and hell was the outside world.

The last stop on this odyssey through the visionary south is the cave in which his grandmother's cousin, Captain Charley Milward, had probably found the piece of prehistoric animal skin that became the central relic of his family. Nearing the end of his visit, he states that he has accomplished "the object of this ridiculous journey." Chatwin leaves Patagonia convinced that humankind lost its innocence when it ceased its nomadic existence and settled into one place, and that Cain derived his reputation for villainy principally because he founded the first city.

THE SONGLINES

First published: 1987
Type of work: Travel literature

The narrator, Chatwin, journeys throughout the Australian outback in search of Aboriginal sacred sites.

The Songlines is generally considered Bruce Chatwin's masterpiece, even though its form is difficult to categorize. It certainly is an adventure story, but it is also a novel of ideas; it combines, although to a lesser extent than *In Patagonia*, many of the identical literary, historical, and philosophical techniques such as anecdote, biography, autobiography, anthropological case study, and other similar methods of inquiry. The book includes a previously unpublished anthropological study called "The Nomadic Alternative," which had arisen from Chatwin's journeys to Africa and South America.

Some critics have labeled *The Songlines* a metaphysical novel that interweaves Chatwin's experiences in the Australian outback with philosophical meditations on the dark future of Western civilization. It resembles *In Patagonia* in that it can be read as a long meditation upon the ruins of the prelogical civilization of the Aboriginals who now dwell in the fallen world of time and permanent location and, as a result, have lost their visionary consciousness. Their reaction to being restricted to a particular space has resulted in alcoholism of epidemic proportions.

Readers familiar with Chatwin's recurring concern will encounter it again in this work. As in *In Patagonia*, Chatwin believes that humankind's original pristine state was as nomadic travelers rather than as settlers in a permanent location. What obsessed him for more than twenty years was the destructive territorialism that permanent ownership breeds. Mircea Eliade demonstrated in dozens of books that humankind has derived its sense of the sacred from symbolic centers in which the divine and the human intersect. These points of intersection (Calvary, for example) then become permanent centers of significance or shrines around which civilizations are built. People, then, derive their identities from their proximity to permanent sacred places.

What troubled Chatwin was that the definition of the sacred among the natives of the Australian outback differs radically from Christian theologians insofar as Aboriginal sacred places cover the earth and derive their sacred status and identity from the human imaginations that "sing" them into existence. The poetry of that idea and the idea of that kind of poetry drove him to pursue an arduous and sometimes dangerous trip into one of the world's most remote and desolate areas.

The narrator finds a brilliant Russian, Arkady Volchok, an Australian citizen, to guide him through the outback. Arkady's job is to map the sacred sites of the Aboriginals so that the national railroad system will not infringe upon those areas. Volchok becomes Chatwin's highly informed guide throughout the journey. What he discovers is in enormous contrast to the usual Judeo-Christian creation narrative, and the narrator's dramatic confrontation with these stunning differences becomes the energy that drives the story along. Volchok leads Chatwin through the elaborate cosmology of the natives consisting of the "Dreaming-tracks," or "Songlines," that are the footprints of the ancestors as they crisscrossed the land for ten thousand years singing the world into existence. As these ancient totemic ancestors traveled nomadically through the land, they scattered a trail of words and songs along their footprints, known as "Dreaming-tracks," which became paths of communication among the most distant tribes. By naming in song all significant objects or features of the landscape, the ancestors called all things into existence. Chatwin found that, once again, nature followed art in that the Greek word from which "poem" derives is "poesis," which means "to make or create." The "Walkabout" became, then, a ritual journey to keep the land in its original condition and, thus, re-create Creation. Nothing was there until the Ancestors, the great poets and singers, brought it into existence from out of their own minds and souls. The narrator delights in both the similarities and the differences between the primary wisdom of the European Holy Grail quest ("The king and the land are one") and the core of the Aboriginal cosmology ("The song and the land are one").

Later, in talking to an ex-Benedictine Aboriginal named Father Flynn, Chatwin finally hears articulated what he has suspected for twenty years: Once people settled into one place, everything began to disintegrate. The people had to keep moving in such barren land: "To move in such landscape was survival: to stay in the same place was suicide." A good third of the book consists of Chatwin's notes from his journal, most of which are quotations from a range of philosophers, spiritual leaders, and writers such as the Buddha, Meister Eckehart, the biblical writers, Shakespeare, Martin Buber, Arthur Koestler, William Blake, and many, many others. He concludes the book with salient quotations from Giambattista Vico, the linguistic philosopher Otto Jespersen, and finally the great German existentialist Martin Heidegger. Arkady takes him to witness the final hours of three ancient Aboriginals who are dying together on their shared totemic songline behind a large rock in the middle of a desert. They are "going back" into the place of their conception so that they may become "the Ancestor."

The author was terminally ill as he finished his book, and though the book's organization is weakest at its conclusion, Chatwin's sensual writing style is as lucid as anything he ever wrote.

Summary

Few writers went to such great lengths in pursuing their passionate obsessions as Bruce Chatwin. Suspecting that a nomadic existence was humankind's original and most natural condition, he journeyed to the farthest points on the planet to test his theory. If he was not as great a stylist as the other two distinguished travel writers Waugh and Lawrence, he certainly brought a more precise and varied brand of scholarship to his work. Compared with Lawrence, Chatwin documented even more brutally the disastrous consequences that modern industrialization and mechanization had on so-called primitive societies. His works truly celebrate the idiosyncratic diversity of the world while simultaneously lamenting the damage done to the instinctual lives of those, such as the Aboriginals, who have no methods of protecting themselves.

Bibliography

Ackerman, Diane. "Home Was Where the Road Was." *The New York Times Book Review*, September 10, 1989, p. 9, 11.

Clarke, Roger. "Walkabout." *The Listener* 118, no. 3019 (July 9, 1987): 29.

Enzensberger, Hans Magnus. "Much Left Unsaid." *The Times Literary Supplement*, June 16, 1989, p. 657.

Keneally, Thomas. "Going for a Songline." *The Observer*, June 28, 1987, 23.

Rieff, David. "The Wanderer's Wisdom." *The New Republic* 197 (November 30, 1987): 36-39.

Rushdie, Salman. "Before the Voice We Lost Fell Silent." *The Observer*, May 14, 1989, 48.

Patrick Meanor

GEOFFREY CHAUCER

Born: London(?), England
c. 1343
Died: London, England
October 25(?), 1400

Principal Literary Achievement

Generally agreed to be the most important writer in English literature prior to William Shakespeare, Chaucer retains a central position in the development of English literature and the English language.

Biography

While historians have been able to reconstruct much about Geoffrey Chaucer's life from the 493 documents, mostly office records, that mention him, these documents cast light only on the public life of a prominent civil servant; not one refers to him as an author. That is not to say that he was not recognized or appreciated as a poet by his contemporaries: In Chaucer's day, poetry was considered to be a leisure pastime of talented men, a valuable skill, but not in itself a career. Chaucer, too, probably thought of himself primarily in terms of his public duties rather than his poetry.

The exact date and even year of Chaucer's birth are unknown; the year 1340 has become traditionally accepted, but 1343 may be a more accurate guess. He was probably born in London, where his parents, John and Agnes, held property. His father was a prosperous wine merchant with business ties to the court of King Edward III.

Despite his middle-class origins, he was to have a distinguished public career as a courtier, soldier, diplomat, and civil servant. No records of his early childhood or schooling have survived, but in 1357 Chaucer received an appointment to serve as a page in the household of Elizabeth de Burgh, countess of Ulster and wife of Edward III's son Lionel, duke of Clarence. Chaucer apparently went along with Prince Lionel's forces when England invaded France in 1359, was captured by the French, and then ransomed in 1360.

No direct evidence survives concerning Chaucer's activities between 1360 and 1366, but Thomas Speght, who edited Chaucer's works in 1598, claimed to have seen records establishing that Chaucer was studying among the lawyers of the Inner Temple, one of the four great Inns of Court. As expensive academies for the sons of rich or noble families, the Inns were more convenient than the universities for a grounding in common law because of their proximity to the law courts in Westminster and

also because common law was studied in three languages, English, French, and Latin, at a time when only Latin was used at the universities. A period of study at one of the Inns would account for the training in record keeping and legal procedures that would have been considered prerequisite for many of the posts that Chaucer later held.

In 1366 he married Philippa de Roet, a woman well above his own social class, the daughter of a knight and sister of Katherine Swynford. (Swynford was to become the mistress and eventually the third wife of Edward III's son John of Gaunt, duke of Lancaster, who would become one of the most powerful men in England.) About 1367, Chaucer began working as a member of the household of Edward III and was soon advanced from the status of yeoman to that of esquire (just below a knight). He apparently had no specific duties and may have been valuable to the household in part for his storytelling abilities. He was engaged in four diplomatic missions to France between 1366 and 1370, and an extended mission to Italy in 1372-1373. In 1374, having been made financially independent with a yearly grant and a rent-free house, he left the royal household and became controller of customs for the Port of London. It was the first of a series of responsible administrative positions that he would hold through the reigns of three monarchs—a tribute both to his competence and to his ability to remain on good terms with the members of opposing factions.

Chaucer's busy life in public affairs was apparently never a serious obstacle to his creative work. Indeed, most of his poetry seems to have been written during the years of his most active public service, and relatively little after his retirement. Since Chaucer's works were all written before the introduction of the printing press into England and existed only in his manuscripts and copies made of them by scribes, there are no exact dates of "publication" of any of his works. Dating the works is further complicated by evidence that he left several of them unfinished and worked on others over long periods of time. Still, various kinds of evidence suggest that, by this stage of his career, he had translated much of the French *Roman de la rose* (eleventh century) into English as the *Romaunt of the Rose* (c. 1370), had written several short poems, and also had written the first of his "major minor poems," *Book of the Duchess* (c. 1370), an elegy almost certainly written to commemorate the death of Blanche of Lancaster, the first wife of John of Gaunt. The date of her death, probably in 1368 or 1369, has allowed literary historians to assign a fairly secure date to this particular work, although even in this case it may be that the poem was written well after the event.

Chaucer was sent again to France to conduct peace negotiations several times in 1376 and 1377. One of the goals of these talks may have been to arrange a marriage between ten-year-old Richard, heir to the English throne, and eleven-year-old Marie, daughter of the king of France. It has been suggested that the second of Chaucer's major minor poems, *Parlement of Foules* (1380), satirizes these discussions and was written during this period, but the date and occasion of the poem have been much disputed. He continued to hold positions of influence when Richard II came to the throne in 1377, traveling to Italy again in 1378 to negotiate with the ruler of Milan.

In 1380, Chaucer completed his translation of *De consolatione philosophiae* (c. 523; *The Consolation of Philosophy*), by the Roman philosopher Boethius, from Latin into English. This translation, known usually by the title *Boece* (1380), would have provided access to a work of great literary, as well as philosophical, value for those who could not read Latin, and it is also seen as having had a strong influence on Chaucer's own ideas. In 1382, he published *Troilus and Criseyde*, a poem that includes discussions of Boethian ideas about free will and determinism. In 1385, Chaucer was allowed to appoint a permanent deputy to handle his duties in the customs office, and in 1386 he was elected to Parliament, resigning the office of controller of customs shortly thereafter. The period between 1386 and 1389 seems to have been relatively quiet, and it is thought that during these years he wrote the General Prologue to *The Canterbury Tales* (1387-1400), as well as several of the individual tales themselves. He was appointed to the important post of clerk of the king's works in 1389, in charge of the maintenance and supervision of several royal forests, parks, and public buildings, including Westminster Palace and the Tower of London, until 1391, when he was appointed deputy forester of one of the royal forests, still a responsible position, but far less demanding than his clerkship had been. About this time, he must have written the fourth of his major minor poems, *Legend of Good Women* (1380-1386), and a technical manual on the use of the astrolabe, a scientific instrument used for astronomical observations, which Chaucer says he wrote for his ten-year-old son, Lewis, *A Treatise on the Astrolabe* (1387-1392). When Henry IV came to the throne in 1399, he doubled Chaucer's annuity, a sign of his continued favor with the court. Chaucer's tomb in London's Westminster Abbey, which marks the first burial in what has come to be called Poets' Corner, gives the date of his death as October 25, 1400.

Analysis

One of the keys to Chaucer's continued critical success is the scope and diversity of his work, which extends from romance to tragedy, from sermon to dream vision, from pious saints' lives to bawdy fabliaux. Each century's readers have found something new in Chaucer and have learned something about themselves, as well.

Chaucer was recognized even in his own time as the foremost of English poets. A ballad written by the French poet Eustache Deschamps in 1386, well before the writing of the works for which we now remember Chaucer, identifies him as the "great translator, noble Geoffrey Chaucer" (probably thinking of his translation of the *Romaunt of the Rose*) and praises his work extravagantly, as do the contemporary English writers Thomas Usk and John Gower. Chaucer's most important creative output consists of six major narrative poems, although his translations and short poems are also of high quality and considerable interest. These six are *The Canterbury Tales* and *Troilus and Criseyde*, his two masterpieces, and the four "major minor" poems, *Book of the Duchess, Parlement of Foules, Hous of Fame* (1372-1380) and *Legend of Good Women*.

All four of the major minor poems are structured by the devices of the dramatized first-person narrator and the dream vision. In the earliest of these poems, *Book of the Duchess*, the evidently lovesick and therefore (by the conventions of courtly love) insomniac narrator reads the classical myth of Ceyx and Alcyone to help him sleep. After finishing the tale, he does in fact fall asleep and has a dream in which he follows a group of hunters on a chase. He is eventually led by a small dog into a clearing in the woods, where he comes upon a grieving knight dressed all in black. At first uncomprehending, the narrator comes to realize that the Black Knight's grief has been caused by the death of his incomparable lady-love and the end of their blissful life together. The poet then wakes and resolves to write the story of his experience, presumably the very poem that the reader has just read. The poem is a sensitive elegy on the death of John of Gaunt's wife Blanche, but it is also of great interest in its own right as a work of art.

While the framing device of the dream vision had long been a standard tool for medieval poets, especially for the presentation of allegorical subjects, Chaucer's innovative grafting of the character of the narrator onto this stock technique creates additional levels of psychological and dramatic depth. The narrator's naïve questions, the result of his failing to understand the Black Knight's poetic and allusive speeches about his loss, provide the knight with a sympathetic, if obtuse, listener and enable him to talk his way through his grief and achieve a measure of consolation. Some critics prefer to read the poem with a slightly different emphasis, arguing that the dreamer-narrator only pretends to be naïve in order to help the knight work through his grief to a catharsis. Some see the dramatic irony as the effect of the distance between Chaucer the author and his naïve narrator; others interpret it as a result of the distance between the sophisticated narrator and the bumbling persona that he creates for the knight's benefit. In either case, the key narrative function—achieved through the unreliable persona who accurately records, but inaccurately interprets, the events that he narrates—is already present in Chaucer's first extended work. This narrative persona would appear in one guise or another in all Chaucer's major narratives and would become one of the poet's most distinctive stylistic trademarks.

Parlement of Foules follows *Book of the Duchess* closely in structure if not in time. Chaucer combines the motifs of the dream vision and limited narrator with the popular conventions of the council or parliament of birds and the *demande d'amour*, the "question of love," which calls for the solution of delicate and usually involved problems of etiquette in courtly love. As in the earlier poem, the narrator, having lamented his own inaptitude for love, reads a book (this time one on dreams) and falls asleep. After being shown around an allegorical landscape by one of the characters in the book that he had been reading, the narrator is taken to a beautiful park near the temple of Venus, where the birds of the parliament are gathered before the goddess of Nature on Saint Valentine's Day for the purpose of choosing their mates. A female "formel" eagle is claimed by three different suitors, who present in turn their arguments for deserving her love. The issue is then subjected to a lively debate among the general assembly of birds, which eventually deteriorates into bickering and name-calling. Nature takes charge at this point and leaves the decision to the formel eagle herself, who chooses to defer her choice until next year's Valentine's Day gathering. The shouting of the birds at this decision wakes the dreamer, who returns to his books, still hoping to learn from them something about love. Critics have been unable to agree about the interpretation of the poem. It has been read variously as a serious debate about the conventions of courtly love, as a satire mocking those conventions, as an allegory (either about love and marriage in general or, more specifically, about the suit of Richard II for the hand of Marie of France in 1377 or the hand of Anne of Bohemia in 1381), and as a political and social satire (with the birds representing different social classes).

Such diversity of critical opinion represents the norm, rather than the exception, in Chaucer studies, and there has been even less agreement about interpretation of his two remaining major minor poems, *Hous of Fame* and *Legend of Good Women*, at least in part because neither appears to have ever been completed. *Hous of Fame* presents an especially heterogeneous set of materials, recounting the dreamer's vision of the story of Dido and Aeneas in book 1, an airborne journey to the House of Fame in the talons of a talking eagle in book 2, and a visit to the House of Fame and the House of Rumor in book 3. None of the critical explanations offered of the poem's overall theme or meaning has been widely accepted, and the diversity of the different parts may preclude such unifying readings. The poem does succeed, however, as an often brilliantly comic literary experiment. *Legend of Good Women* presents a prologue, which exists in two versions, in which the god of love demands that the narrator write a series of tales about good women to atone for his many tales about unfaithful women. The nine tales that follow are not among Chaucer's best efforts, and he apparently lost interest and abandoned the idea without completing the poem. The device of a prologue and dramatic frame enclosing a series of stories, however, may well have helped him conceive the structure of *The Canterbury Tales*.

THE CANTERBURY TALES

First published: 1387-1400
Type of work: Poem

A motley group of travelers on a pilgrimage agree to take turns telling stories to one another along the way.

The Canterbury Tales, Chaucer's best-known and most important literary achievement, consists of twenty-four tales, some with prologues and epilogues, which range over a wide variety of styles, subjects, and genres. The work avoids becoming merely a loose collection of unrelated stories because of Chaucer's ingenious development of the framing device of the pilgrimage and his ability to suit his diverse tales to the personalities of their tellers. Chaucer's ideas about the book apparently evolved over a period of decades, with some tales (the Second Nun's Tale, parts of the Monk's

Tale) possibly written as early as the 1370's, and others (the Nun's Priest's Tale, the Parson's Tale) probably written in the later 1390's, not long before his death. The imaginative breakthrough that made the work possible, his conceiving of the framing narrative that lends coherence to the stories, seems to have occurred some time in the 1380's, when he must have written an early version of the General Prologue. The work is evidently unfinished, though the flexible nature of the framing device allows for considerable diversity of opinion as to Chaucer's final plans for the poem's over-all structure.

The Canterbury Tales begins with the General Prologue, which opens with a lyrical evocation of springtime in England, the time for folk to go on pilgrimages to holy shrines to thank the saints for their good fortune of the past year. It then proceeds to a series of portraits of a particular group of pilgrims assembled at the Tabard Inn in Southwark, near London, where they are preparing to leave on their pilgrimage to Canterbury. The ostensibly random assemblage of pilgrims actually provides a fairly complete spectrum of the middle classes of fourteenth century England, omitting the higher nobility and the poorer peasants but representing a substantial number of the social gradations between the Knight and the Plowman. These characters are not merely representative abstractions, however, but are provided with vividly individual traits to the degree that they become distinct characters for the reader.

One of the most interesting of the characters is the unnamed first-person narrator, who meets the group at the inn on his way to Canterbury, decides to join their party, and describes them for the reader. Critics usually call the narrator "Chaucer the Pilgrim" to differentiate him from the author, whose point of view often seems to diverge considerably from that of his mouthpiece. While the naïve narrator approves of the worldly Prioress and Monk and is amused by the villainous Shipman, the reader is able to see beyond his uncritically approving point of view to their serious faults. The technique of the unreliable narrator leaves all direct storytelling and commentary to speakers whose point of view is suspect to various degrees and calls for the reader to infer the implicit truth from the information provided. If Chaucer did not originate this method of narration, he certainly developed it to a greater extent than any other writer before him. The device of the unreliable narrator has had an influence on later narrative writing, especially in the twentieth century, that would be difficult to overestimate, and much of this influence may be traced directly to Chaucer's own refinement of the technique.

The proprietor of the Tabard Inn, Harry Bailly, is so struck by the conviviality of the group that he decides to join them on the condition that they agree to participate in a storytelling contest, with himself as leader and judge of the contest. Each pilgrim will tell four stories, two on the way to Canterbury and two on the way back, and the winner will get a free dinner at the inn at the other pilgrims' expense. The travelers agree and draw lots for the telling of the first tale. The lot falls to the Knight, who begins the sequence of tales. No pilgrim actually tells more than one tale (with the exception of Chaucer the Pilgrim, discussed below), and at one time it was thought that Chaucer must have originally planned some 120 tales (four each for thirty pilgrims). More recently, critics have argued that the scheme for 120 tales is proposed by Harry Bailly, not Chaucer, and that *The Canterbury Tales* as a whole may be fairly close to its final form. While the work is clearly not finished in a strict traditional sense (the pilgrims never arrive at Canterbury or return, and the winner of the contest is never revealed), it does seem to have a coherence of effect that is just as satisfying aesthetically as a more rigid closure would have been.

The Knight tells one of the longest and most formal tales, a chivalric romance with philosophical overtones set in ancient Thebes, treating of courtly love and ceremonial combat among the nobility. This somewhat idealized tale of aristocratic life is followed by an abrupt change of pace when the Miller, so drunk that he can hardly sit on his horse, insists on telling the next tale, which addresses the rather less courtly love of a college student and his elderly landlord's young wife. The tale is one of the finest examples of the fabliau, a short comic tale, usually obscene, depicting illicit love and practical jokes among lower- and middle-class characters. The tale contains a number of parallels to the Knight's Tale and may be viewed in part as a parody of it. In addition to connecting with the preceding tale, the Miller's Tale provides the impetus for the next. The Reeve, who bears a number of similarities to the foolish carpenter cuckolded by the student, takes the Miller's Tale personally and repays him with another fabliau, this one about a miller whose wife and daughter are comically seduced by two college students. The Cook's Tale, which follows, is an incomplete fragment that would evidently have been another fabliau.

These four tales follow the General Prologue and one another in all the major manuscripts of *The Canterbury Tales* and are collectively referred to as part (or fragment) 1 (or A). Depending on the manuscripts followed, modern editions usually recognize ten distinct parts; while the order of tales within each part is fixed, the parts themselves are not always arranged in the same order. None of the arrangements offered is without its problems, and it may well be the case that Chaucer had not decided on a final order. The most commonly followed arrangement is that of the Ellesmere manuscript, and that will be observed here, as well.

After part 2, which consists of the Man of Law's tale of the saintly Constance and her several tribulations, come parts 3 through 5, a textually and thematically connected series that has come to be called the Marriage Group, as several of the tales seem to be pursuing what amounts to a running debate on the proper roles of the man and woman in marriage. In the Wife of Bath's lengthy prologue, as well as in her tale, she argues that the woman should have the mastery of the man in marriage. While most of her arguments are drawn from traditional antifeminine satire, and while the stock character type of the bawdy older woman had existed since classical times, Chaucer combines these elements to original effect. Alison of Bath is developed into a much more rounded and sympathetic character than any of her predecessors, and her humorous and lively account of her methods of outwitting and dominating men seems, at least to modern readers, more feminist than antifeminist. After an exchange of fabliaux between the Friar and the Summoner (each telling a tale that degrades the other's profession), the Clerk tells a tale about a pure and virtuous wife, perhaps by way of replying to the Wife of Bath, and then the Merchant tells a tale of an unfaithful wife. After a short and incomplete attempt at a chivalric romance by the youthful Squire (whose tale does not measure up to that of his accomplished father, the Knight), the Franklin tells a tale of mutual respect and forbearance by a married couple, a tale that is usually seen as concluding the marriage debate with a compromise. Part 6, one of the more difficult to place in the sequence, contains the brief Physician's tale of Appius' sacrifice of his daughter Virginia and the justly renowned Pardoner's prologue and tale of greed and murder, frequently anthologized and often called one of the first great short stories in English literature.

Part 7 is the longest and most varied of the parts. It contains the Shipman's crude fabliau, the Prioress' sentimental saint's legend, Chaucer the Pilgrim's inept romance, Sir Thopas (so bad that he is interrupted and told to stop), and lengthy prose sermon, the Tale of Melibee, a series of brief tragic anecdotes by the Monk (also interrupted), and finally the Nun's Priest's tale. The latter is based on the popular stories of Reynard the Fox, in which the fox tries to outwit and capture the cock, Chauntecleer. Chaucer fuses the genre of the beast fable with that of the mock epic, telling his story of barnyard animals in the elevated rhetoric of courtly romance, and makes the cock into a somewhat bombastic orator whose digressive and encyclopedic argument with his wife over dreams almost overshadows the plot of the story. Because of its comedy and stylistic range, the Nun's Priest's Tale is widely considered by modern readers to be the one that ought to have been awarded the prize at the end of the pilgrimage. In 8, the Second Nun tells a saint's legend, and the Canon Yeoman delivers an exposé of the fraudulent practices of medieval alchemists. Part 9 contains only the Manciple's version of a tale from the *Metamorphoses* (c. A.D. 8) by Ovid, Chaucer's favorite classical author. Part 10 contains the Parson's long prose sermon and, perhaps, Chaucer's Retraction, a listing and retraction of his worldly writings, which some critics see as a part of the text and an ironic advertisement for the works, and which others see as a sincere extrafictional address to posterity.

While *The Canterbury Tales* may be unfinished, the very openness of its structure has increasingly come to be seen as one of the sources of the work's complexity and richness. The poem is unified to the degree that, read as a whole, it can draw the reader into the creative process of interpretation and discovery that it demands. Yet it is designed freely enough that the tales may also be appreciated as individual works outside the context of the frame.

TROILUS AND CRISEYDE

First published: 1382
Type of work: Poem

Troilus and Criseyde meet and fall in love in the besieged city of Troy but after three years of happiness are separated.

Troilus and Criseyde is Chaucer's longest complete work and in many ways his most polished; he wrote it at the peak of his creative powers and may well have expected it to endure as his most important literary achievement. Indeed, it has only been in the last century or two that readers have come to rank it a step beneath the incomplete and somewhat experimental *The Canterbury Tales*. His combining of the conventional setting and plot of medieval romance with realistic insights into character and motivation have led critics to debate whether it is more properly considered a sophisticated medieval romance or the first modern psychological novel.

The story of the Trojan War had long been a popular one in England, partly because of the popular legend that Britain had been founded by the Trojan hero Brut. It is not surprising, therefore, that Chaucer, like many of his contemporaries, wrote a book dealing with aspects of the Troy story. Chaucer's interest lies not so much in the Trojan War itself (though political events caused by the siege affect the personal events that constitute his focus) as in the love story between the two title characters, both members of the Trojan aristocracy. Troilus and Criseyde do not appear as characters in the original version of the legend of Troy, Homer's *Iliad* (c. 800 B.C.); Chaucer's immediate source is the contemporary Italian poet Giovanni Boccaccio's *Il filostrato* (c. 1335; *The Filostrato*, 1873), but Chaucer expands the poem considerably (from 5,740 to 8,239 lines) and changes the plot and characters so freely that the poem becomes distinctively his own creation.

The bare outline of the plot is relatively simple: The young nobleman Troilus, son of the Trojan king Priam, falls in love with the widow Criseyde, suffering all the pains of unrequited love specified in the courtly love tradition. He reveals his love for her to his friend Pandarus, who is also Criseyde's uncle and whose machinations eventually unite the two as lovers. Criseyde's father, Calchas, a soothsayer who has foreseen the Trojan defeat and has deserted to the Greek camp, arranges for his daughter to be exchanged for a Trojan prisoner and to be sent to join him. His well-intentioned effort to save his daughter from the destruction of the city has tragic consequences for the two lovers. Before leaving Troy, Criseyde promises to Troilus that she will escape and return to him; this proves difficult, however, and in time her resolve weakens, and she takes a new lover, the Greek soldier Diomede. Troilus eventually recognizes that she has been unfaithful and, having been killed by the Greek hero Achilles, looks down from the heavens and laughs at the mutability of earthly love as compared to the more durable joys of divine love.

The roles of Pandarus and Criseyde are far more complex in Chaucer's version than in Boccaccio's, and their treatment shifts the emphasis of the plot. Chaucer changes Pandarus from a nondescript comrade of Troilus to Criseyde's elderly uncle, creating tension between his dual roles as Troilus' friend and adviser and Criseyde's guardian. Criseyde is the most complex of the characters, and her actions are less clearly reprehensible. Whereas Boccaccio's tale is focused on Troilus, who represents the author's own disappointment in love, the role of Criseyde comes to dominate Chaucer's poem. The greater insight offered into Criseyde's character creates for the reader a balance between the effects that the outside pressures of fate and society have and those that result from Criseyde's own free will. While she does prove unfaithful to Troilus, the narrator is generally sympathetic to her, and it is difficult to see what else she could have done to survive under the circumstances in which she finds herself. As a result, critics are divided over whether her portrayal is meant to be admired and pitied or condemned as faithless and perhaps immoral.

Summary

Geoffrey Chaucer was recognized even in his own time as one of the greatest of English poets and is now regarded as the foremost writer in English literature before the time of William Shakespeare. The outstanding characterisics of Chaucer's work include its diversity—covering a spectrum of genres extending from pious saints' lives to bawdy fabliaux, from romance to tragedy—and its consistently humorous quality, allowing Chaucer to combine the serious treatment of moral and philosophical questions with a pervasively comic and entertaining style. His masterpiece, *The Canterbury Tales*, has proven to be one of the truly inexhaustible classics of world literature, appealing to each new generation of readers in new ways.

Bibliography

Bowden, Muriel. *A Commentary on the General Prologue to the Canterbury Tales.* 2d ed. New York: Macmillan, 1967.

Donaldson, E. Talbot. *Speaking of Chaucer.* New York: W. W. Norton, 1970.

Howard, Donald R. *Chaucer.* New York: E. P. Dutton, 1987.

Muscatine, Charles. *Chaucer and the French Tradition: A Study in Style and Meaning.* Berkeley: University of California Press, 1957.

Payne, Robert O. *Geoffrey Chaucer.* 2d ed. Boston: Twayne, 1986.

Rowland, Beryl, ed. *Companion to Chaucer Studies.* Rev. ed. New York: Oxford University Press, 1979.

Shoeck, Richard, and Jerome Taylor, eds. *Chaucer Criticism.* 2 vols. Notre Dame, Ind.: University of Notre Dame Press, 1960-1961.

William Nelles

ANTON CHEKHOV

Born: Taganrog, Russia
January 29, 1860
Died: Badenweiler, Germany
July 15, 1904

Principal Literary Achievement
Chekhov was both a great writer of short fiction and a superb dramatist.

Biography

Anton Pavlovich Chekhov was born on January 29, 1860, into a family of trades-men in the southern Russian port town of Taganrog, a stiflingly provincial place where he spent his first nineteen years. Chekhov despised Taganrog and used the adjective "Taganrogish" for behavior that he regarded as dull, boorish, squalid, or vulgar. An-ton's father, Pavel Egorovich, was a despotic grocer who terrorized his wife, five sons, and one daughter, overworked them, eventually went bankrupt, and had to flee town to escape his creditors. Anton's mother was the soul of kindness, but too timid and deferential to protect her children against an abusive father who beat his offspring, ordered them to attend church services daily, but forbade them the luxury of play. "We felt like little convicts at hard labor," Chekhov wrote in an 1892 letter about his childhood—though he did manage to fish and swim and to become a great practical joker. It is nonetheless crucial to note that he was deprived of an adequate portion of familial love in his formative years. That may account for the central flaw in Chekhov's character: his marked tendency to avoid emotional (and with women, physical) inti-macy with family, friends, and lovers.

Chekhov's Taganrog schooling coincided with tremendous socioeconomic revolu-tionary ferment incited by the writings of Mikhail Bakunin, Aleksandr Herzen, and others, culminating in the assassination of Czar Alexander II in 1881. Yet he was sheltered from these winds of modernity and showed no particular inclination, in either his youth or his manhood, to espouse or oppose radical causes. He did show early signs of the poor health that would cost him his life at the age of forty-four: peritonitis, malaria, hemorrhoids, migraines, and other ailments. His symptoms may well have indicated an early tubercular infection, with the bacillus aided in its assault on Chekhov's body by his hard boyhood regimen of schooling, churchgoing, and shopminding.

In July, 1876, the elder Chekhovs and all the children but Anton fled Taganrog

Антонъ Павловичъ
ЧЕХОВЪ
род. 16-го Января 1860 г.

for Moscow, leaving him to finish grammar school and giving him a theme, dispossession, that he was to feature in both *Tri Sestry* (1901; *Three Sisters*, 1920) and *Vishnyovy sad* (1904; *The Cherry Orchard*, 1908). For three years, the lad supported himself alone in his hometown, burdened with economic worries but relieved of his tyrannical father. Astonishingly, Chekhov not only took care of his own needs but also was able to send small sums to his family. He seems to have been born with a maturity and a fastidious sense of order and responsibility that never deserted him.

In August, 1879, Chekhov joined his family in Moscow and lived there for the next twenty years. He began a demanding five-year grind to become a physician, began his literary career in 1880 with comic sketches published in periodicals, and soon established himself as the de facto head of the Chekhov household. Chekhov was enormously prolific in his early years as a writer. He wrote not only stories and short plays but also sketches, comic calendars and captions for cartoons, and even a detective novel, *Drama na okhote* (1884; *The Shooting Party*, 1926). When he reviewed his achievements for the *Collected Works* (1899-1902), he excluded 342 of his early titles, calling them "my literary excrement," but only six of his later ones. The major source for Chekhov biographers is his enormous and often eloquent correspondence; the total number of his extant letters is about forty-four hundred.

In June, 1884, Chekhov passed his medical school examinations and was to practice medicine sporadically during the remaining twenty years of his life, though always as a profession secondary to writing. He often claimed medicine for his "wife," literature for his "mistress"; but the mistress had little trouble supplanting the wife. Chekhov's medical training enabled him to become acquainted with people on diverse social levels and reinforced his sensible, pragmatic (or diagnostic) view of life. Chekhov often attested in his letters to the harmony of his two callings, claiming that familiarity with the scientific method had enriched his literary skills: "To the chemist nothing in this world is unclean. The writer must be as objective as the chemist."

In one respect, ironically, Chekhov's medical knowledge proved to be of no value: his care, or rather neglect, of his own health. As early as December, 1884, he suffered a serious attack of chest pains and blood spitting. In October, 1888, he wrote of these bleedings and chronic coughing fits but refused to characterize them as tubercular symptoms. Hemorrhoids afflicted him with maddening torments, but he rejected a medical colleague's offer to remove them by an operation. Gastritis, phlebitis, migraine headaches, dizzy spells, defective vision, heart palpitations—all these were frequent afflictions.

In the 1890's, with Chekhov established as a highly eligible bachelor, many women sought his affections, while he usually managed to evade them. A highly productive, hardworking writer, he both used his writing as a shield against amorous involvements and insisted that sexual energy (of which he had very little) bore no relation—except perhaps an inverted one—to creative energy (of which he had a ceaseless supply). He frequently linked artistic creativity with erotic self-denial. Sensual, fleshly women in Chekhov's fiction and drama are almost invariably predatory, distasteful, and villainous, with Chekhov-the-author idealizing, as romantically desirable, pallid women with thin arms and flat breasts. Yet Chekhov-the-man, when interested in women at all, preferred them robust, hearty, and earthy. While love is the dominant theme of Chekhov's mature work, it is almost never happily consummated love: He prefers to collapse illusions rather than fulfill hopes, to stress romantic frustration and forlornness rather than union and bliss.

Before his marriage at the age of forty-one, Chekhov had only one incontestable mistress, the actress Lydia Yavorsky. Olga Knipper was Chekhov's second certain mistress, then his wife for what were to be his last three years. She had taken drama lessons from Vladimir Ivanovich Nemirovich-Danchenko, cofounder of the Moscow Art Theater, and graduated into leading roles with his company, including Masha in *Three Sisters* and Lyuba Ranevskaya in *The Cherry Orchard*. Olga was Chekhov's opposite rather than duplicate: lusty in contrast to his asceticism, insecure and manic-depressive compared to his stable, steady temperament. By July, 1900, she was creeping into his Yalta bedroom at night, stepping on creaking stairs that awakened his old mother and spinsterish sister. The forthright, determined Olga took the initiative in courting the evasive, elusive author, and they were married on May 25, 1901.

In June, 1904, Anton and Olga traveled to the German spa of Badenweiler, near the Black Forest, to attempt his cure. On July 15 he died there, first taking the time to explain to his wife that he was about to die, then draining a glass of champagne, turning calmly to his left side, and expiring. Chekhov's corpse was delivered to Russia in a railway wagon labeled "Fresh Oysters"—an incongruous effect that he would have loved to have used in one of his stories.

Analysis

Chekhov is the gentlest, subtlest, most modest, and most complex of the nineteenth century's major authors. In an era when such titans as Leo Tolstoy and Fyodor Dostoyevski are concerned with the conflict of good against evil, Chekhov sees mainly the conflict of simplicity against pretension and finds the consequences depressing. In the Russia of his time, choked with morality tales, nourished on progressive theories of history, lashed with messianic messages, Chekhov was ahead of his age, a lonely, restrained, melancholy man who remains, despite extensive scholarship and criticism, an ambiguous and elusive figure.

Chekhov is the moralist of the venial sin, seeing a soul damned not for murder, robbery, or adultery but for the small, universal faults of ill-temper, untruthfulness, miserliness, and disloyalty. In his short story "Poprygunya" ("The Grasshopper"), Olga Iranovna, who cheats on her dull doctor husband by having an affair with a mediocre, flashy painter, will not be damned for her adultery. Rather, she will be damned for her shallowness, superciliousness, and narcissism. Be truthful to yourselves and to others, Chekhov says in his art.

With his penchant for understatement and irony, Chekhov has had an overwhelming influence on both short-story writers and dramatists. He does not commit himself to any particular stance, does not issue moral imperatives to his public, bequeaths no mystical enlightenment to a darkling humanity. Neither a prophet nor a system builder,

Chekhov is a diagnostician who works unobtrusively and dispassionately but with great care and delicacy through the materials that life presents. He has no religion, accepting a world of comfortless indifference. He is averse to metaphysics and politics, romanticism and sentimentality. Unlike Tolstoy, he refuses to idealize the peasant class; he is disgusted by the crass materialism of the middle class; and he chronicles the drift, inertia, and self-pity of the upper class.

Yet Chekhov's bleak vision of modern life does not lead him to regard existence as meaningless or people as absurd. Humane to the very marrow of his bones, he never loses sight of the qualities that make his characters affective beings even when analyzing them with tough and apparently impersonal candor, and he refuses to entertain false hopes about them or their world. In what has become a famous letter, Chekhov writes in October, 1889:

> I am not a liberal, a conservative, an evolutionist, a monk, or indifferent to the world. I should like to be a free artist—and that is all. . . . I regard trademarks or labels as prejudices. My holy of holies are the human body, health, intelligence, talent, inspiration, love, and the most absolute freedom—freedom from violence and falsehood in whatever form these may be expressed.

Chekhov is passionately addicted to what he vaguely labels "culture," by which he means an indefinable union of humanity, decency, intelligence, education, will, and accomplishment. Yet his tough intelligence tells him—and his audience—that such people constitute a dwindling minority. Consequently, he afflicts most of his characters with such flaws as laziness, hypocrisy, pretentiousness, and self-destructiveness.

In everything that Chekhov writes, he refuses to claim for himself the brilliant, commanding powers that are often considered the essence of literary genius. His art is indirect, muted, and apparently casual; he loves to pose as an ideal eavesdropper who communicates an overheard conversation to the jury of his readers or spectators. He excludes whatever is maneuvered, subjective, theatrical, or otherwise grand. He is modest in both his matter and his manner, dealing with the pains of isolation and loneliness, frustrated ambitions, agonizing misunderstandings, forlorn hopes, boredom and listlessness. He consistently questions the heroic mode, with his best fiction and drama representing lives from which the possibility of valor has been removed, with pathos and desolation displacing honor, admiration, or dignity. Even when his scenes are comic, the sound of heartbreak's snapping strings is never distant.

Chekhov's techniques are those of suggestion and implication, with the author meticulously invisible yet miraculously present. He has a remarkable gift for psychological acuteness and absolute control of tone—a subtle and unique blend of the melancholy, the farcical, the lyrical, and the ironic. He evokes atmosphere with marvelous skill, portrays elusive states of mind, renders fleeting sensations and subtle effects by a masterful selection of telling details. Like a pointillist painter, Chekhov's brush strokes may seem, at close range, monotonous and drab. Yet once readers step back to view the work from the proper distance, they will respond to the irresistible art of a supreme stylist and creator of mood.

Chekhov knows that both the tragedy and the comedy of life are precisely that they do not usually lead to a large crisis but dissolve in small ones. Thus, he avoids, in both his stories and his plays, the cumulative action that Henrik Ibsen, August Strindberg, Émile Zola, and Fyodor Dostoevski favor. He insists on observing his characters in the apparently commonplace routine of their everyday lives.

THE KISS

First published: "Potseluy," 1887 (English translation, 1915)
Type of work: Short story

Lieutenant Ryabovich, a timid artillery officer, finds his life significantly changed as the result of a kiss in the dark.

The setting of "The Kiss" is a Russian village on a May evening. The officers of an artillery bridgade encamped nearby are invited by a retired lieutenant general, the leading landowner in the village, to spend an evening dining and dancing in his residence. After describing a panoramic scene of aristocratic society, Chekhov focuses on one of the officers, Ryabovich, an inarticulate conversationalist, a graceless dancer, a timid drinker, and an altogether awkward social mixer. During the evening, he strays into a semidark room, which is soon entered by an unidentifiable woman, who clasps two fragrant arms around his neck, whispers, "At last!" and kisses him. Recognizing her mistake, the woman then shrieks and runs from the room.

Ryabovich also exits quickly and soon shows himself to be a changed man: He no longer worries about his round shoulders, plain looks, and general ineptness. He begins to exercise a lively romantic fancy, speculating who at the dinner table might have been his companion. Before falling asleep, he indulges in joyful fantasies.

The artillery bridgade soon leaves the area for maneuvers. Ryabovich tries to tell himself that the episode of the kiss was accidental and trifling, but to no avail: His psychic needs embrace it as a wondrously radiant event. When he tries to recount it to his coarse fellow officers, he is chagrined that they reduce it to a lewd, womanizing level. He imagines himself loved by, and married to, the woman, happy and stable; he can hardly wait to return to the village, to reunite with her.

In late August, Ryabovich's battery does return. That night, he makes his second trip to the general's estate, but this time he pauses to ponder in the garden. He can no longer hear the nightingale that sang loudly in May; the poplar and grass no longer exude a scent. He walks a bridge near the general's bathing cabin and touches a towel that feels clammy and cold. Ripples of the river rip the moon's reflection into bits. Ryabovich now realizes that his romantic dreams have been absurdly disproportionate to their cause. When the general's invitation comes, he refuses it.

It is a masterful tale, as Chekhov demonstrates his vision of life as a pathetic comedy of errors, with misunderstanding and miscommunication rooted in the psychic substance of human nature. Lieutenant Ryabovich, the least dashing and romantic of men, is transformed by the kiss meant for another into a person with a penchant for an intense inner life that runs its dreamy course virtually separate from the dreariness of external reality. He inflates an insignificant incident into an absurd cluster of fantasies centering on ideal love and beauty. All the more embittering, then, is his plunge from ecstasy to despair as he recognizes, in the story's anticlimatic resolution, the falseness of his hopes, the frustration of his yearnings.

Chekhov dramatizes two of his pervasive themes in "The Kiss." One is the enormous difficulty, often the impossibility, of establishing a communion of feelings between human beings. Ryabovich discovers that he cannot explain to his fellow officers his happiness that an extraordinary event has transformed his life. Lieutenant Lobytko regards Ryabovich's experience as an opportunity to parade and exaggerate his own sexual adventures. Lieutenant Merzlyakov dismisses the lady in the dark as "some sort of lunatic." The brigade general assumes that all of his officers have his own preference for stout, tall, middle-aged women.

The other great Chekhovian theme (which he shares with Nikolai Gogol) is the contrast between beauty and sensitivity, and the pervasiveness of the elusive characteristic best expressed by the Russian word *poslost'*. The term is untranslatable, but it suggests vulgarity, banality, boredom, seediness, shallowness, suffocation of the spirit. Ryabovich, surrounded by the coarseness of his comrades, depressed by the plodding routine of artillery maneuvers, poignantly tries to rise above this atmosphere of *poslost'* by caressing an impossible dream.

When Ryabovich returns to Lieutenant General von Rabbeck's garden in late summer, "a crushing uneasiness took possession of him." His exultant mood disappears as he confronts the prospect of a nonexisting reunion with a nonexisting beloved. Chekhov symbolizes Ryabovich's feelings of rejection and disillusionment. As Ryabovich touches the general's cold, wet bathing towel and observes the moon's reflection, this time torn by the river waters, he has a shattering epiphany of heartbreak: "How stupid, how very stupid!" he exclaims, interpreting the endless, aimless running of the water as equivalent to the endless, aimless running of his life—of all lives. "To what purpose?"

THE LADY WITH THE DOG

First published: "Dama s sobachkoi," 1899 (English translation, 1917)
Type of work: Short story

Two people married to other partners fall in love, only to face an uncertain future.

Alternately titled "The Lady with the Dog" or "The Lady with the Little Dog," this story treats the theme of adultery, akin to Leo Tolstoy's *Anna Karenina*, (1875-

1878; English translation, 1886), and has a heroine with the same first name. Yet whereas Tolstoy pursues and punishes his Anna for having violated a social and moral law, Chekhov treats his Anna gently and compassionately in one of his most accomplished tales.

The plot can be briefly summarized. The banker Dmitry Dmitrich Gurov, a married but philandering man of almost forty, spends a vacation alone in the seaside resort of Yalta, where he meets and skillfully seduces a much younger lady, Anna Sergeyevna, who is also on holiday without her spouse. Their first encounter leads to a furtive and sporadic liaison, with Anna, who lives in a provincial town, having trysts with him in Moscow once every two or three months. Now deeply in love, the couple faces an unpredictable future. Chekhov ends the story on this indeterminate note.

Like a play, the narrative is divided into four parts, each of which deftly dramatizes a different phase of Anna and Dmitry's romance. The first, of course, deals with their meeting in Yalta. The reader makes Dmitry's acquaintance as a type: He is a cold-blooded roué, contemptuous of women as easy conquests yet compulsively erotic. He approaches Anna by fondling her dog, discovers that Anna is a gentlewoman who, like himself, is bored on holiday, and finds himself charmed by her shyness, slimness, and "lovely gray eyes."

In part 2, they walk on the pier, Gurov kisses her passionately, they have sex back at the hotel, and Anna is immediately remorseful, while he calmly cuts himself a section of watermelon. The alternation of Gurov's feelings between cynicism and lyricism recurs rhythmically. Chekhov treats Anna tenderly, rendering her shame and penitence as genuine, with her unconsciously assuming the posture of a classical Magdalen. When she leaves for home, both lovers assume that the brief affair has ended. He reflects that she overestimated his character in calling him "kind, exceptional, high-minded," while his treatment of her was arrogantly condescending.

Section 3 starts with Gurov busily immersed in his Moscow life and expecting Anna's image to have filtered out of his memories within a month. Not so. He discovers himself in love with her and finds life without her "clipped and wingless." He travels to Anna's town to see her, only to find her house virtually sealed off by "a long gray fence studded with nails." That is the first of a series of images of hardness, constriction, and enclosure. They symbolize the difficulty and sadness of a love between people both married to others. Anna's town is the apotheosis of grayness: the fence, a gray carpet in the hotel room, a gray cloth covering the bed, the inkwell on the desk gray with dust.

Gurov finds Anna attending a first night performance in the local theater. In the scene describing their reunion there, the tone of the tale assumes dramatic tension. Both speak in anxious, short, urgent exclamatory phrases. Gurov, now realizing that his heart belongs to Anna, treats her deferentially and no longer worries whether onlookers can see them embracing. The best that they can do, however, is to meet on the theater's narrow and gloomy staircase. She swears that she will visit him in Moscow and does so in chapter 4.

In Moscow, Anna and Dmitry find a pathetically marginal happiness together. Chekhov contrasts the scene in her hotel room there with that in part 2. Gurov is now soft and considerate with Anna, no longer slightly bored and irritated. For the first time, he finds himself loving a woman unselfishly. The story's concluding mood is one of gentle melancholia, of mingled joy and pain and sadness.

THREE SISTERS

First produced: *Tri sestry*, 1901 (first published, 1901; English translation, 1920)
Type of work: Play

The Prozorov family of three sisters and one brother leads lives of quiet desperation in a provincial town.

Nowhere in modern drama is there greater majesty or fuller substance than in *Three Sisters*. These qualities issue from Chekhov's incomparable ability to make physical data yield moral truth, domestic irritation dilate into the great cage of cosmic suffering, and a single moment beat with the immeasurability of all time. Almost nothing "happens" in the play: His characters transmit no urgency, create no suspense, feel little tension. Yet *Three Sisters* offers a psychic and spiritual eventfulness so dense, yet also so delicately organized, as to make the work one of the miracles of drama and certainly Chekhov's masterpiece. No play has ever conveyed more subtly the transitory beauty and sadness of the passing moment. None has ever expressed more shatteringly the defeat of sensitive minds and generous hearts, the pathos of frustrated personal aspirations.

The play's structure is woven of several separate strands of narrative, resulting in a complex dramatic texture. A highly educated Moscow family, the Prozorovs, were geographically transplanted eleven years earlier than the beginning action when the father, a brigadier general, took command of an artillery unit in a provincial town. The first scene opens on the first anniversary of his death, with the three daughters and one son living in their inherited house but wishing they were in Moscow. That city is seen by them through a haze of delusions as a center of sunshine, refinement, and sensibility, in contrast to the banality, stupidity, and dreariness of their town. This vision of Moscow is, of course, a mythical opiate. The Prozorovs never move there, preparing the reader/spectator for the play's principal motifs of nonattainment, nonfulfillment.

Olga, the eldest sister, teaches school; Masha has married a dull local teacher, Kulygin; Irina, the youngest, has a position in the telegraph office; Andrey, the family's pride, is expected to continue his studies at Moscow University and become a professor. All four are wonderfully reared, highly educated, sensitive, and unhappily stranded in a mediocre small town where only the officers of the garrison are of their class. Chekhov concentrates on the wasting away of this superior family in a coarse and sordid environment.

This milieu is personified by Natasha, a local girl whom Andrey marries, a pretentious, bourgeois, vicious, and vengeful person who is Chekhov's most malevolent character. She dispossesses the Prozorovs by steady degrees in the drama's course, taking control of the house's mortgage money and shifting the family from room to room, until she has finally evicted them from the house. In the last act, Olga is installed in a municipal apartment, Irina has moved to a furnished room, and even Andrey is ejected from his section of the residence to make way for a baby sired by Natasha's lover, Protopopov.

In typically Chekhovian manner, the conflict is usually kept indistinct. Andrey and his sisters are too polite or too deeply involved in their own problems or simply too weak to confront Natasha directly. Nevertheless, the contrast between the town's natives (not only Natasha but also Kulygin and, offstage, Protopopov) and the Muscovites (the Prozorovs and certain artillery officers) provides the basic theme of the clash between culture and vulgarity. The Prozorovs permit the dreary town to brutalize them. Masha tries to find happiness through a liaison with a lieutenant colonel, Vershinin, also unhappily married; then his brigade must leave, and she is again sentenced to her unbearable pedant of a husband. Olga, doomed to spinsterhood, suffers from migraine headaches. Andrey, drained of his youthful vigor, resigns himself to a minor bureaucratic post and loses heavily at cards.

Irina's story is more complicated: The most beautiful of the sisters, she is desired by a lieutenant, Baron Tusenbach, a cheerful soul despite a gloomy philosophy of life, and Captain Solyony, a disagreeable, menacing bully. For a while, Irina is tormented by dreams of Moscow and a perfect romance. Then she resigns herself to marrying the likable, decent Tusenbach, who has abandoned his commission to seek salvation through hard work in a brickyard, even though she does not love him. In act 4, however, Solyony, having sworn that if he cannot have Irina, nobody else shall, challenges Tusenbach to a duel and kills him.

Everything fails the Prozorovs. As their culture fades, Masha forgets her piano-playing skills, Irina is perpetually tired, Andrey trails through life aimlessly—the forces of darkness move in on them like carrion crows, slowly and relentlessly withdrawing all that once promised them contentment. The question that the play finally asks, articulated by Olga in her last speech, is whether the Prozorovs' defeat has any ultimate meaning. According to Vershinin, it does: He has faith in the future, whose generations will be more productive and progressive, as civilization marches toward perfection. In a friendly debate, Tusenbach disagrees:

> Life will be just the same as ever not merely in a couple of hundred years' time, but in a million years. Life . . . follows its own laws, which don't concern us, which we can't discover anyway.

Even gloomier is Chebutykin, a sixty-year old physician who had once been in love with the mother of the Prozorov family and who has transferred that affection to

Irina, having installed himself in the family circle. He takes refuge from his disappointment through alcohol, neglect of his medical knowledge, and a profound nihilism.

In the last act, Chebutykin does not raise a finger to prevent the Solyony-Tusenbach duel—he sees everything that comes to hurt the Prozorovs but never intervenes. With the family's hopes shattered, the sisters huddle together, statuesque, motionless, defeated, listening as Olga muses, if we wait a little longer, we shall find out why we live, why we suffer. . . . Oh, if we only knew, if only we knew!"

THE CHERRY ORCHARD

First produced: *Vishnyovy sad*, 1904 (first published, 1904; English
                         translation, 1908)
Type of work: Play

The decline of the aristocracy is symbolized by Lyuba Ranevskaya's loss of her cherry orchard.

Whereas Chekhov depicts the defeat of the cultured elite in one of drama's saddest works, *Three Sisters*, he examines the same problem from a more comic-ironic view in *The Cherry Orchard*. While Konstantin Stanislavsky staged the premiere of the play as a somber tragedy, Chekhov insisted, in letters about this production, on calling it "not a drama but a comedy, in places almost a farce." Nontheless, it has most often been performed as pathethic drama. Surely, its subjects are depressingly serious: the loss of an ancestral estate, the rise of a semiliterate, ambitious middle class to replace the aristocracy, the dispossession and scattering of the Ranevskaya family and household, the guilt and remorse of Lyuba, who cannot resist her attachment to an unworthy man. The play's concerns are loss, the failure to communicate and comprehend, and the death of an old order.

The Cherry Orchard presents a dilemma: The Ranevskaya family, which includes landowner Lyuboff (Lyuba) Andreena Ranevskaya and her brother Gayev, daughter Anya and adopted daughter Varya, faces two alternatives that it finds equally unacceptable: either to lose the estate on the auction block because of the unpaid mortgage, or to destroy its uniqueness by chopping down its cherry trees and razing the residence to replace it with summer cottages. The second option, which will be exercised by the business man who buys the orchard at auction, Yermolay Alexeevich Lopahin, offers what the gentry considers a vulgar economic solution at the expense of its cherished values of beauty and inspiration. In this situation, Mme Ranevskaya chooses not to act—thereby forfeiting the property.

Before the reader/spectator laments the losses dramatized, it would be well to understand precisely what is being lost, and why. Chekhov softens the act of dispossession by qualifying sympathy for the victims and complicating the character of the despoiler. Certainly, both Lyuba and Gayev, while charming and well-intentioned, are a good deal less pathetic and attractive than their predecessors, the Prozorovs. Lyuba is irresponsible, negligent, and self-destructive. Her indolence and uncontrollable extravagance bring her house tumbling down. Granted, to her the orchard emblematizes childhood innocence, the elegance of the old, leisured, manorial nobility, culture, grace, purity, and beauty. Yet Lyuba's visions of innocence and childhood have had to yield to her tarnished adulthood with its reckless adultery, her girlishness, and inertia. Once the symbol of a vigorous way of life, the orchard now represents the decay and rottenness that have overtaken that life.

While the orchard reminds Lyuba of her pure childhood, it strikes the student-tutor Trofimov as a memento of slavery. He tells the seventeen-year-old Anya of the guilty dreams of Russia's decaying upper class:

> Just think . . . you grandfather . . . and all your forefathers were serf owners—they owned living souls. Don't you see human beings gazing at you from every cherry tree in your orchard . . . don't you hear voices?

Eloquently idealistic though Trofimov is, he has his less engaging side. Chekhov is usually ironic at the expense of the activist, and he shows Trofimov as slothful, superficial, fatuous, and undersexed. The volatile Lyuba lashes out at him for urging her to confront the truth of her miserable situation; she stabs cruelly at his immaturity. Horrified, he rushes out of the room and tumbles down the stairs. After a remorseful Lyuba begs his pardon and dances with him they forgive each other. Chekhov shows how his characters can lapse from dignity only to accentuate their humanity.

The self-made merchant/developer Lopahin plays a profoundly ambiguous role in the drama. He is the despoiler of the old order, who cannot restrain his class-conscious sense of triumph when he has acquired the orchard at the auction: He rightly calls himself "a pig in a pastry shop," is brisk with the servants, pitiless with Gayev, and insensitive to Varya, who would like to marry him. Yet he is the most positive character in the play. He labors, with increasing exasperation, to bring the befuddled gentry to their senses. He is alone in having energy, purpose, dedication, and shrewdness enough to suggest how the estate can be converted into a profitable operation. He worships Lyuba and can refuse her nothing, though he despairs of her ability to survive. Most likely, she is the secret love of his life, furnishing the real reason why he will not marry Varya. Chekhov shows Lopahin as generous, unpretentious, and free of malice; Lopahin's motives are innocent, though his impact is destructive. In sum, Chekhov markedly softens the act of dispossession.

Moreover, he shows that what is being lost is not, in truth, an order of stability, familial love and unity, innocence and usefulness—these are already long gone. The destruction of the estate is the destruction of illusions, and the drama explores this double negative at many ambivalent and ironic levels of action, characterization, and theme. The governess Charlotta soliloquizes about her rootlessness and life's emptiness then muffles her words by chewing on a cucumber and clowning. Gayev vows that the estate will not be sold, while continually popping candy into his mouth.

Lyuba's valet Yasha parodies her French manners, while her maid Dunyasha mimics her passionate nature. The rivalry of the clumsy clerk Yepihodov and the insolent Yasha for the affected Dunyasha is a travesty of romantic love. Old, deaf Firs, neglected and abandoned at the play's end, is a relic of the obsolete days when the orchard's cherries were abundant and sweet.

Summary

"You ask me what life is?" Anton Chekhov once wrote his wife. "It is like asking what a carrot is. A carrot is a carrot, that's all we know." Chekhov records facts: people, places, things, words, actions. Held in his artist's vision, they catch the comic, pathetic, sometimes frightening, other times loving but always vulnerable and lonely human pose between birth and death. Chekhov is the subtlest, quietest, most indirect of storytellers and dramatists, capable of examining his characters' darkest despair with calm sympathy, gentle irony, and restrained affection. As an author, he seeks to be an impartial witness to the human condition, careful not to indulge in moral fervor, messianic dogma, or anything that smacks of theatricality. A hater of lies and delusions, he has no remedy for the disease of modern life and refuses to arouse false hopes about the future of humankind.

Bibliography

Bruford, W. H. *Anton Chekhov*. London: Bowes & Bowes, 1957.

Hahn, Beverly. *Chekhov: A Study of the Major Stories and Plays*. New York: Cambridge University Press, 1977.

Hingley, Ronald. *Chekhov: A Biographical and Critical Study*. London: Unwin, 1950.

Jackson, R. L., ed. *Chekhov: A Collection of Critical Essays*. Englewood Cliffs, N.J.: Prentice-Hall, 1967.

Karlinsky, Simon. *Anton Chekhov's Life and Letters*. Berkeley: University of California Press, 1973.

Magarshack, David. *Chekhov the Dramatist*. New York: Hill & Wang, 1960.

Rayfield, Donald. *Chekhov: The Evolution of his Art*. New York: Harper & Row, 1975.

Gerhard Brand

MAGILL'S
SURVEY
OF
WORLD
LITERATURE

GLOSSARY

Aesthetics: The branch of philosophy that studies the beautiful in nature and art, including how beauty is recognized in a work of art and how people respond to it. In literature, the aesthetic approach can be distinguished from the moral or utilitarian approach; it was most fully embodied in the movement known as aestheticism in the late nineteenth century.

Alienation: The German dramatist Bertolt Brecht developed the theory of alienation in his epic theater. Brecht sought to create an audience that was intellectually alert rather than emotionally involved in a play by using alienating techniques such as minimizing the illusion of reality onstage and interrupting the action with songs and visual aids.

Allegory: A literary mode in which characters in a narrative personify abstract ideas or qualities and so give a second level of meaning to the work, in addition to the surface narrative. Two famous examples of allegory are Edmund Spenser's *The Faerie Queene* (1590, 1596) and John Bunyan's *The Pilgrim's Progress* (1678). For modern examples, see the stories and novels of Franz Kafka.

Alliteration: A poetic technique in which consonant repetition is focused at the beginning of syllables, as in "Large mannered motions of his mythy mind." Alliteration is used when the poet wishes to focus on the details of a sequence of words and to show the relationships between words in a line.

Angry young men: The term used to describe a group of English novelists and playwrights in the 1950's and 1960's, whose work stridently attacked what it saw as the outmoded political and social structures (particularly the class structure) of post-World War II Britain. John Osborne's play *Look Back in Anger* (1956) and Kingsley Amis' *Lucky Jim* (1954) are typical examples.

Angst: A pervasive feeling of anxiety and depression often associated with the moral and spiritual uncertainties of the twentieth century, as expressed in the existentialism of writers such as Jean-Paul Sartre and Albert Camus.

Antagonist: A character in fiction who stands in opposition or rivalry to the protagonist. In William Shakespeare's *Hamlet* (c. 1600-1601), for example, King Claudius is the antagonist of Hamlet.

Anthropomorphism: The ascription of human characteristics and feelings to animals, inanimate objects, or gods. The gods of Homer's epics are anthropomorphic, for example. Anthropomorphism occurs in beast fables, such as George Orwell's *Animal Farm* (1945). The term "pathetic fallacy" carries the same meaning: Natural objects are invested with human feelings. *See also* Pathetic fallacy.

Antihero: A modern fictional figure who tries to define himself and establish his own codes, or a protagonist who simply lacks traditional heroic qualities, such as Jim Dixon in Kingsley Amis' *Lucky Jim* (1954).

Aphorism: A short, concise statement that states an opinion, precept, or general truth, such as Alexander Pope's "Hope springs eternal in the human breast."

III

Apostrophe: A direct address to a person (usually absent), inanimate entity, or abstract quality.

Archetype: The term was used by psychologist Carl Jung to describe what he called "primordial images" that exist in the "collective unconscious" of humankind and are manifested in myths, religion, literature, and dreams. Now used broadly in literary criticism to refer to character types, motifs, images, symbols, and plot patterns recurring in many different literary forms and works. The embodiment of archetypes in a work of literature can make a powerful impression on the reader.

Aristotelian unities: A set of rules for proper dramatic construction formulated by Italian and French critics during the Renaissance, purported to be derived from the *De poetica* (c. 334-323 B.C.; *Poetics*) of Aristotle. According to the "three unities," a play should have no scenes irrelevant to the main action, should not cover a period of more than twenty-four hours, and should not occur in more than one place or locale. In fact, Aristotle insists only on unity of action in a tragedy.

Assonance: A term for the association of words with identical vowel sounds but different consonants: "stars," "arms," and "park," for example, all contain identical *a* (and *ar*) sounds.

***Auto sacramental*:** A Renaissance development of the medieval open-air Corpus Christi pageant in Spain. A dramatic, allegorical depiction of a sinful soul wavering and transgressing until the intervention of Divine Grace restores order. During a period of prohibition of all secular drama in Spain, from 1598 to 1600, even Lope de Vega Carpio adopted this form.

Autobiography: A form of nonfiction writing in which the author narrates events of his or her own life. Autobiography differs from memoir in that the latter focuses on prominent people the author has known and great events that he has witnessed, rather than on his own life.

Ballad: Popular ballads are songs or verse that tell dramatic, usually impersonal, tales. Supernatural events, courage, and love are frequent themes, but any experience that appeals to ordinary people is acceptable material. Literary ballads— narrative poems based on the popular ballads—have frequently been in vogue in English literature, particularly during the Romantic period. One of the most famous is Samuel Taylor Coleridge's *The Rime of the Ancient Mariner* (1798).

Baroque: The term was first used in the eighteenth century to describe an elaborate and grandiose type of architecture. It is now also used to refer to certain stylistic features of Metaphysical poetry, particularly the poetry of Richard Crashaw. The term can also refer to post-Renaissance literature, 1580-1680.

***Bildungsroman*:** Sometimes called the "novel of education," or "apprenticeship novel," the *Bildungsroman* focuses on the growth of a young protagonist who is learning about the world and finding his place in life; a typical example is James Joyce's *A Portrait of the Artist as a Young Man* (1916).

GLOSSARY

Blank verse: A term for unrhymed iambic pentameter, blank verse first appeared in drama in Thomas Norton and Thomas Sackville's *Gorboduc*, performed in 1561, and later became the standard form of Elizabethan drama. It has also commonly been used in long narrative or philosophical poems, such as John Milton's *Paradise Lost* (1667, 1674).

Bourgeois novel: A novel in which the values, the preoccupations, and the accoutrements of middle-class or bourgeois life are given particular prominence. The heyday of the genre was the nineteenth century, when novelists as varied as Jane Austen, Honoré de Balzac, and Anthony Trollope both criticized and unreflectingly transmitted the assumptions of the rising middle class.

Burlesque: A work that by imitating attitudes, styles, institutions, and people aims to amuse. Burlesque differs from satire in that it aims to ridicule simply for the sake of amusement rather than for political or social change.

Capa y espada: Spanish for "cloak and sword." A term referring to the Spanish theater of the sixteenth and seventeenth centuries dealing with love and intrigue among the aristocracy. The greatest practitioners were Lope de Vega Carpio and Pedro Calderón de la Barca. The term *comedia de ingenio* is also used.

Catharsis: A term from Aristotle's *De poetica* (c. 334-323 B.C.; *Poetics*) referring to the purgation of the emotions of pity and fear in the spectator aroused by the actions of the tragic hero. The meaning and the operation of the concept have been a source of great, and unresolved, critical debate.

Celtic romance: Gaelic Celts invaded Ireland in about 350 B.C.; their epic stories and romances date from this period until about A.D. 450. The romances are marked by a strong sense of the Otherworld and of supernatural happenings. The Celtic romance tradition influenced the poetry of William Butler Yeats.

Celtic Twilight: Sometimes used synonymously with the term Irish Renaissance, which was a movement beginning in the late nineteenth century which attempted to build a national literature by drawing on Ireland's literary and cultural history. The term, however, which is taken from a book by William Butler Yeats titled *The Celtic Twilight* (1893), sometimes has a negative connotation. It is used to refer to some early volumes by Yeats, which have been called self-indulgent. The poet Algernon Charles Swinburne said that the Celtic Twilight manner "puts fever and fancy in the place of reason and imagination."

Chamber plays: Refers to four plays written in 1907 by the Swedish dramatist August Strindberg. The plays are modeled on the form of chamber music, consisting of motif and variations, to evoke a mood or atmosphere (in these cases, a very sombre one). There is no protagonist but a small group of equally important characters.

Character: A personage appearing in any literary or dramatic work. Characters can be presented with the depth and complexity of real people (sometimes called "round" characters) or as stylized functions of the plot ("flat" characters).

Chorus: Originally a group of singers and dancers in religious festivals, the chorus evolved into the dramatic element that reflected the opinions of the masses or commented on the action in Greek drama. In its most developed form, the chorus consisted of fifteen members: seven reciting the strophe, seven reciting the antistrophe, and the leader interacting with the actors. The chorus has been used in all periods of drama, including the modern period.

Classicism: A literary stance or value system consciously based on the example of classical Greek and Roman literature. While the term is applied to an enormous diversity of artists in many different periods and in many different national literatures, it generally denotes a cluster of values including formal discipline, restrained expression, reverence of tradition, and an objective, rather than subjective, orientation. Often contrasted with Romanticism. *See also* Romanticism.

Comédie-Française: The first state theater of France, composed of the company of actors established by Molière in 1658. The company took the name *Comédie-Française* in 1680. Today, it is officially known as the *Theatre Français* (*Salle Richelieu*).

Comedy: Generally, a lighter form of drama (as contrasted with tragedy) that aims chiefly to amuse and ends happily. The comic effect typically arises from the recognition of some incongruity of speech, action, or character development. The comic range extends from coarse, physical humor (called low comedy) to a more subtle, intellectual humor (called high comedy).

Comedy of manners: A form of comedy that arose during the seventeenth century, dealing with the intrigues (particularly the amorous intrigues) of sophisticated, witty members of the upper classes. The appeal of these plays is primarily intellectual, depending as they do on quick-witted dialogue and clever language. For examples, see the plays of Restoration dramatists William Congreve, Sir George Etherege, and William Wycherley. *See also* Restoration comedy/drama.

Commedia dell'arte: Dramatic comedy performed by troupes of professional actors, which became popular in the mid-sixteenth century in Italy. The troupes were rather small, consisting of perhaps a dozen actors who performed stock roles in mask and improvised on skeletal scenarios. The tradition of the *commedia*, or masked comedy, was influential into the seventeenth century and still exerts some influence.

Conceit: A type of metaphor, the conceit is used for comparisons that are highly intellectualized. When T. S. Eliot, for example, says that winding streets are like a tedious argument of insidious intent, there is no clear connection between the two, so the reader must apply abstract logic to fill in the missing links.

Conversation poem: Conversation poems are chiefly associated with the poetry of Samuel Taylor Coleridge. These poems all display a relaxed, informal style, quiet settings, and a circular structure—the poem returns to where it began, after an intervening meditation has yielded some insight into the speaker's situation.

Cubism: A term borrowed from Cubist painters. In literature, cubism is a style of poetry, such as that of E. E. Cummings, Kenneth Rexroth, and Archibald Mac-Leish, which first fragments an experience, then rearranges its elements into some new artistic entity.

Dactyl: The dactylic foot, or dactyl, is formed of a stress followed by two unstressed syllables, as in the words "Washington" and "manikin." "After the pangs of a desperate lover" is an example of a dactylic line.

Dadaism: Dadaism arose in France during World War I as a radical protest in art and literature against traditional institutions and values. Part of its strategy was the use of infantile, nonsensical language. After World War I, when Dadaism was combined with the ideas of Sigmund Freud, it gave rise to the Surrealist movement.

Decadence: The period of decline that heralds the ending of a great age. The period in English dramatic history immediately following William Shakespeare is said to be decadent, and the term "Decadents" is applied to a group of late-nineteenth and early twentieth century writers who searched for new literary and artistic forms as the Victorian Age came to a close.

Detective story: The "classic" detective story (or "mystery") is a highly formalized and logically structured mode of fiction in which the focus is on a crime solved by a detective through interpretation of evidence and clever reasoning. Many modern practitioners of the genre, however, such as Raymond Chandler, Patricia Highsmith, and Ross Macdonald, have placed less emphasis on the puzzlelike qualities of the detective story and have focused instead on characterization, theme, and other elements of mainstream fiction. The form was first developed in short fiction by Edgar Allan Poe; Jorge Luis Borges has also used the convention in short stories.

Dialectic: A philosophical term meaning the art of examining opinions or ideas logically. The dialectic method of Georg Wilhelm Friedrich Hegel and Karl Marx was based on a contradiction of opposites (thesis and antithesis) and their resolution (synthesis). In literary criticism, the term has sometimes been used by Marxist critics to refer to the structure and dynamics of a literary work in its sociological context.

Dialogue: Speech exchanged between characters, or even, in a looser sense, the thoughts of a single character. Dialogue serves to characterize, to further the plot, to establish conflict, and to express thematic ideas.

***Doppelgänger*:** A double or counterpart of a person, sometimes endowed with ghostly qualities. A fictional *Doppelgänger* often reflects a suppressed side of his personality, as in Fyodor Dostoevski's novella *Dvoynik* (1846; *The Double*, 1917) and the short stories of E. T. A. Hoffmann. Isaac Bashevis Singer and Jorge Luis Borges, among other modern writers, have also employed the *Doppelgänger* with striking effect.

Drama: Generally speaking, any work designed to be represented on a stage by actors (Aristotle defined drama as "the imitation of an action"). More specifically, the term has come to signify a play of a serious nature and intent that may end either happily (comedy) or unhappily (tragedy).

Dramatic irony: A situation in a play or a narrative in which the audience knows something that the character does not. The irony lies in the different meaning that the character's words or actions have for himself and for the audience. A common device in classical Greek drama. Sophocles' *Oidipous Tyrannos* (429 B.C.; *Oedipus Tyrannus*) is an example of extended dramatic irony.

Dramatic monologue: In dramatic monologue, the narrator addresses a persona who never speaks but whose presence greatly influences what the narrator tells the reader. The principal reason for writing in dramatic monologue is to control the speech of the major persona by the implied reaction of the silent one. The effect is one of continuing change and often surprise. The technique is especially useful for revealing characters slowly and for involving the reader as another silent participant.

Dramatic verse: Poetry that employs dramatic form or technique, such as dialogue or conflict, to achieve its effects. The term is used to refer to dramatic monologue, drama written in verse, and closet dramas.

Dramatis personae: The characters in a play. Often, a printed listing defining the characters and specifying their relationships.

Dream vision: An allegorical form common in the Middle Ages, in which the narrator or a character falls asleep and dreams a dream that becomes the actual framed story.

Dystopian/Utopian novel: A dystopian novel takes some existing trend or theory in present-day society and extends it into a fictional world of the future, where the trend has become more fully manifested, with unpleasant results. Aldous Huxley's *Brave New World* (1932) is an example. The utopian novel is the opposite: It presents an ideal society. The first utopian novel was Sir Thomas More's *Utopia* (1516).

Elegy: A long, rhymed, formal poem whose subject is meditation upon death or a lamentable theme. The pastoral elegy uses a pastoral scene to express grief at the loss of a friend or important person. *See also* Pastoral.

Elizabethan Age: Of or referring to the reign of Queen Elizabeth I of England, lasting from 1558 to 1603, a period of important developments and achievements in the arts in England, particularly in poetry and drama. The era included such literary figures as Edmund Spenser, Christopher Marlowe, William Shakespeare, and Ben Jonson. Sometimes referred to as the English Renaissance.

English novel: The first fully realized English novel was Samuel Richardson's *Pamela* (1740-1741). The genre took firm hold in the second half of the eighteenth century, with the work of Daniel Defoe, Henry Fielding, and Tobias Smollett, and reached its full flowering in the nineteenth century, in which great novelists such as Jane Austen, Charles Dickens, William Makepeace Thackeray, Anthony

Trollope, Thomas Hardy, and George Eliot produced sweeping portraits of the whole range of English life in the period.

Enlightenment: A period in Western European cultural history that began in the seventeenth century and culminated in the eighteenth. The chief characteristic of Enlightenment thinkers was their belief in the virtue of human reason, which they believed was banishing former superstitious and ignorant ways and leading to an ideal condition of human life. The Enlightenment coincides with the rise of the scientific method.

Epic: Although this term usually refers to a long narrative poem that presents the exploits of a central figure of high position, the term is also used to designate a long novel that has the style or structure usually associated with an epic. In this sense, for example, Herman Melville's *Moby Dick* (1851) and James Joyce's *Ulysses* (1922) may be called epics.

Epigram: Originally meaning an inscription, an epigram is a short, pointed poem, often expressing humor and satire. In English literature, the form flourished from the Renaissance through the eighteenth century, in the work of poets such as John Donne, Ben Jonson, and Alexander Pope. The term also refers to a concise and witty expression in prose, as in the plays of Oscar Wilde.

Epiphany: Literally, an epiphany is an appearance of a god or supernatural being. The term is used in literary criticism to signify any moment of heightened awareness, or flash of transcendental insight, when an ordinary object or scene is suddenly transformed into something that possesses eternal significance. Especially noteworthy examples are found in the works of James Joyce.

Epistle: The word means "letter," but epistle is used to refer to a literary form rather than a private composition, usually written in dignified style and addressed to a group. The most famous examples are the epistles in the New Testament.

Epistolary novel: A work of fiction in which the narrative is carried forward by means of letters written by the characters. Epistolary novels were especially popular in the eighteenth century. Examples include Samuel Richardson's *Pamela* (1740-1741) and *Clarissa* (1747-1748).

Epithet: An adjective or adjectival phrase that expresses a special characteristic of a person or thing. "Hideous night," "devouring time," and "sweet silent thought" are epithets that appear in William Shakespeare's sonnets.

Essay: A brief prose work, usually on a single topic, that expresses the personal point of view of the author. The essay is usually addressed to a general audience and attempts to persuade the reader to accept the author's ideas.

Everyman: The central character in the work by the same name, the most famous of the English medieval morality plays. It tells of how Everyman is summoned by Death and of the parts played in his journey by characters named Fellowship, Cousin, Kindred, Goods, Knowledge, Confession, Beauty, Strength, Discretion, Five Wits, and Good Deeds. Everyman has proved lastingly popular; there have been many productions even in the twentieth century. More generally, the term means the typical, ordinary person.

Existentialism: A philosophy or attitude of mind that has gained wide currency in religious and artistic thought since the end of World War II. Typical concerns of existential writers are humankind's estrangement from society, its awareness that the world is meaningless, and its recognition that one must turn from external props to the self. The works of Jean-Paul Sartre and Franz Kafka provide examples of existentialist beliefs.

Experimental novel: The term is associated with novelists such as Dorothy Richardson, Virginia Woolf, and James Joyce in England, who experimented with the form of the novel, using in particular the stream-of-consciousness technique.

Expressionism: Beginning in German theater at the start of the twentieth century, expressionism became the dominant movement in the decade following World War I. It abandoned realism and relied on a conscious distortion of external reality in order to portray the world as it is "viewed emotionally." The movement spread to fiction and poetry. Expressionism influenced the novels of Franz Kafka and James Joyce.

Fable: One of the oldest narrative forms, usually taking the form of an analogy in which animals or inanimate objects speak to illustrate a moral lesson. The most famous examples are the fables of Aesop, who used the form orally in 600 B.C.

Fabliau: A short narrative poem, popular in medieval French literature and during the English Middle Ages. Fabliaux were usually realistic in subject matter and bawdy; they made a point of satirizing the weaknesses and foibles of human beings. Perhaps the most famous are Geoffrey Chaucer's "The Miller's Tale" and "The Reeve's Tale."

Fairy tale: A form of folktale in which supernatural events or characters are prominent. Fairy tales usually depict a realm of reality beyond that of the natural world in which the laws of the natural world are suspended.

Fantasy: A literary form that makes a deliberate break with reality. Fantasy literature may use supernatural or fairy-tale events in which the ordinary commonsense laws of the everyday world do not operate. The setting may be unreal. J. R. R. Tolkien's fantasy trilogy, *The Lord of the Rings* (1955), is one of the best-known examples of the genre.

Farce: From the Latin *farcire*, meaning "to stuff." Originally an insertion into established Church liturgy in the Middle Ages, farce later became the term for specifically comic scenes inserted into early liturgical drama. The term has come to refer to any play that evokes laughter by such low-comedy devices as physical humor, rough wit, and ridiculous and improbable situations and characters.

Femme fatale: The "fatal woman" is an archetype that appears in myth, folklore, religion, and literature. Often she is presented as a temptress or a witch who ensnares, and attempts to destroy, her male victim. A very common figure in Romanticism, the fatal woman often appears in twentieth century American literature.

Figurative language: Any use of language that departs from the usual or ordinary meaning to gain a poetic or otherwise special effect. Figurative language embodies various figures of speech, such as irony, metaphor, simile.

First person: A point of view in which the narrator of a story or poem addresses the reader directly, often using the pronoun "I," thereby allowing the reader direct access to the narrator's thoughts.

Folklore: The traditions, customs, and beliefs of a people expressed in nonliterary form. Folklore includes myths, legends, fairy tales, riddles, proverbs, charms, spells, and ballads and is usually transmitted through word of mouth. Many literary works contain motifs that can be traced to folklore.

Foreshadowing: A device used to create suspense or dramatic irony by indicating through suggestion what will take place in the future. The aim is to prepare the reader for the action that follows.

Frame story: A story that provides a framework for another story (or stories) told within it. The form is ancient and is used by Geoffrey Chaucer in *The Canterbury Tales* (1387-1400). In modern literature, the technique has been used by Henry James in *The Turn of the Screw* (1898), Joseph Conrad in *Heart of Darkness* (serial, 1899; book, 1902), and John Barth in *Lost in the Funhouse* (1968).

Free verse: Verse that does not conform to any traditional convention, such as meter, rhyme, or form. All poetry must have some pattern of some kind, however, and there is rhythm in free verse, but it does not follow the strict rules of meter. Often the pattern relies on repetition and parallel construction.

Genre: A type or category of literature, such as tragedy, novel, memoir, poem, or essay; a genre has a particular set of conventions and expectations.

German Romanticism: Germany was the first European country in which the Romantic movement took firm grip. Poets Novalis and Ludwig Tieck, philosopher Friedrich Wilhelm Joseph Schelling, and literary theorists Friedrich and August Wilhelm Schlegel were well established in Jena from about 1797, and they were followed, in the second decade of the nineteenth century, by the Heidelberg group, including novelist and short-story writer E. T. A. Hoffmann and poet Heinrich Heine.

Gnomic: Aphoristic poetry, such as the wisdom literature of the Bible, which deals with ethical questions. The term "gnomic poets" is applied to a group of Greek poets of the sixth and seventh century B.C.

Gothic novel: A form of fiction developed in the late eighteenth century that focuses on horror and the supernatural. An example is Mary Shelley's *Frankenstein* (1818). In modern literature, the gothic genre can be found in the fiction of Truman Capote.

Grand Tour: Fashionable during the eighteenth century in England, the Grand Tour was a two- to three-year journey through Europe during which the young aristocracy and prosperous, educated middle classes of England deepened their knowledge of the origins and centers of Western civilization. The tour took a standard route; Rome and Naples were usually considered the highlights.

Grotesque: Characterized by a breakup of the everyday world by mysterious forces, the form differs from fantasy in that the reader is not sure whether to react with humor or with horror. Examples include the stories of E. T. A. Hoffmann and Franz Kafka.

Hagiography: Strictly defined, hagiography refers to the lives of the saints (the Greek word *hagios* means "sacred"), but the term is also used in a more popular sense, to describe any biography that grossly overpraises its subject and ignores his or her faults.

Heroic couplet: A pair of rhyming iambic pentameter lines traditionally used in epic poetry; a heroic couplet often serves as a self-contained witticism or pithy observation.

Historical fiction: A novel that depicts past historical events, usually public in nature, and that features real, as well as fictional, people. Sir Walter Scott's Waverley novels established the basic type, but the relationship between fiction and history in the form varies greatly depending on the practitioner.

Hubris: Greek term for "insolence" or "pride," the characteristic or emotion in the tragic hero of ancient Greek drama that causes the reversal of his fortune, leading him to transgress moral codes or ignore warnings.

Humanism: A human-centered, rather than God-centered, view of the universe. In the Renaissance, Humanism devoted itself to the revival of classical culture. A reaction against medieval Scholasticism, Humanism oriented itself toward secular concerns and applied classical ideas to theology, government, literature, and education. In literature, the main virtues were seen to be restraint, form, and imitation of the classics. *See also* Renaissance.

Iambic pentameter: A metrical line consisting of five feet, each foot consisting of one unstressed syllable followed by one stressed syllable: "So long as men can breathe or eyes can see." Iambic pentameter is one of the commonest forms of English poetry.

Imagery: Often defined as the verbal stimulation of sensory perception. Although the word betrays a visual bias, imagery, in fact, calls on all five senses. In its simplest form, imagery re-creates a physical sensation in a clear, literal manner; it becomes more complex when a poet employs metaphor and other figures of speech to re-create experience.

Impressionism: A late nineteenth century movement composed of a group of painters including Paul Cézanne, Édouard Manet, Claude Monet, and Pierre-Auguste Renoir, who aimed in their work to suggest the impression made on the artist by a scene rather than to reproduce it objectively. The term has also been applied to French Symbolist poets such as Paul Verlaine and Stéphane Mallarmé, and to writers who use the stream-of-consciousness technique, such as James Joyce and Virginia Woolf.

Irony: Recognition of the difference between real and apparent meaning. Verbal irony is a rhetorical trope wherein *x* is uttered and "not *x*" is meant. In the New Criticism, irony, the poet's recognition of incongruities, was thought to be the master trope in that it was essential to the production of paradox, complexity, and ambiguity.

Jacobean: Of or pertaining to the reign of James I of England, who ruled from 1603 to 1623, the period immediately following the death of Elizabeth I, which saw tremendous literary activity in poetry and drama. Many writers who achieved fame during the Elizabethan Age, such as William Shakespeare, Ben Jonson, and John Donne, were still active. Other dramatists, such as John Webster and Cyril Tourneur, achieved success almost entirely during the Jacobean era.

Jungian psychoanalysis: Refers to the analytical psychology of the Swiss psychiatrist Carl Jung. Jung's significance for literature is that, through his concept of the collective unconscious, he identified many archetypes and archetypal patterns that recur in myth, fairy tale, and literature and are also experienced in dreams.

Kafkaesque: Refers to any grotesque or nightmare world in which an isolated individual, surrounded by an unfeeling and alien world, feels himself to be caught up in an endless maze that is dragging him down to destruction. The term is a reference to the works of Austrian novelist and short-story writer Franz Kafka.

Leitmotif: From the German, meaning "leading motif." Any repetition—of a word, phrase, situation, or idea—that occurs within a single work or group of related works.

Limerick: A comic five-line poem employing an anapestic base and rhyming *aabba*, in which the third and fourth lines are shorter (usually five syllables each) than the first, second, and last lines, which are usually eight syllables each.

Linear plot: A plot that has unity of action and proceeds from beginning to middle to end without flashbacks or subplots, thus satisfying Aristotle's criterion that a plot should be a continuous sequence.

Literary criticism: The study and evaluation of works of literature. Theoretical criticism sets forth general principles for interpretation. Practical criticism offers interpretations of particular works or authors.

Lyric poetry: Lyric poetry developed when music was accompanied by words, and although the "lyrics" were later separated from the music, the characteristics of lyric poetry have been shaped by the constraints of music. Lyric poems are short, more adaptable to metrical variation, and usually personal compared with the cultural functions of narrative poetry. Lyric poetry sings of the self; it explores deeply personal feelings about life.

Magical Realism: Imaginary or fantastic scenes and occurrences presented in a meticulously realistic style. The term has been applied to the fiction of Gabriel

García Márquez, Jorge Luis Borges, Günter Grass, John Fowles, and Salman Rushdie.

Masque: A courtly entertainment popular during the first half of the seventeenth century in England. It was a sumptuous spectacle including music, dance, and lavish costumes and scenery. Masques often dealt with mythological or pastoral subjects, and the dramatic action often took second place to pure spectacle.

Melodrama: Originally a drama with music (*melos* is Greek for "song"). By the early nineteenth century, it had come to mean a play in which characters are clearly either virtuous or evil and are pitted against one another in suspenseful, often sensational situations. The term took on a pejorative meaning, which it retains: any dramatic work characterized by stereotyped characters and sensational, improbable situations.

Metafiction: Refers to fiction that manifests a reflexive tendency, such as Vladimir Nabokov's *Pale Fire* (1962), and John Fowles's *The French Lieutenant's Woman* (1969). The emphasis is on the loosening of the work's illusion of reality to expose the reality of its illusion. Such terms as "irrealism," "postmodernist fiction," and "antifiction" are also used to refer to this type of fiction. *See also* Postmodernism.

Metaphor: A figure of speech in which two dissimilar objects are imaginatively identified (rather than merely compared) on the assumption that they share one or more qualities. The term is often used in modern criticism in a wider sense, to identify analogies of all kinds in literature, painting, and film.

Metaphysical poetry: A type of poetry that stresses the intellectual over the emotional; it is marked by irony, paradox, and striking comparisons of dissimilar things, the latter frequently being farfetched to the point of eccentricity. Usually used to designate a group of seventeenth century English poets, including John Donne, George Herbert, Andrew Marvell, and Thomas Traherne.

Meter: Meter is the pattern of language when it is forced into a line of poetry. All language has rhythm, but when that rhythm is organized and regulated in the line so as to affect the meaning and emotional response to the words, then the rhythm has been refined into meter. The meter is determined by the number of syllables in a line and by the relationship between them.

Mock epic: A literary form that burlesques the epic by taking a trivial subject and treating it in a grand style, using all the conventions of epic, such as invocation to the deity, long and boastful speeches of the heroes, and supernatural machinery. Alexander Pope's *The Rape of the Lock* (1712, 1714) is probably the finest example in English literature. The term is synonymous with mock heroic. *See also* Mock hero.

Mock hero: The hero of a mock epic. *See also* Mock epic.

Modernism: A term used to describe the characteristic aspects of literature and art between World War I and World War II. Influenced by Friedrich Nietzsche, Karl Marx, and Sigmund Freud, modernism embodied a lack of faith in Western civilization and culture. In poetry, fragmentation, discontinuity, and irony were common; in fiction, chronological disruption, linguistic innovation, and the stream-of-consciousness technique; in theater, expressionism and Surrealism.

Morality play: A dramatic form in the late Middle Ages and the Renaissance containing allegorical figures (most often virtues and vices) that are typically involved in the struggle over a person's soul. The anonymously written *Everyman* (1508) is one of the most famous medieval examples of this form.

Motif: An incident, situation, or device that occurs frequently in literature. Motif can also refer to particular words, images, and phrases that are repeated frequently in a single work. In this sense, motif is the same as leitmotif. Motif is similar to theme, although the latter is usually more abstract.

Myth: An anonymous traditional story, often involving supernatural beings, or the interaction between gods and humans, and dealing with the basic questions of how the world and human society came to be. Myth is an important term in contemporary literary criticism. The critic Northrop Frye, for example, has said that "the typical forms of myth become the conventions and genres of literature." He means that the genres of comedy, romance, tragedy, and irony (satire) correspond to seasonal myths of spring, summer, autumn, and winter.

Narrative: An account in prose or verse of an event or series of events, whether real or imagined.

Narrator: The character who recounts the narrative. There are many different types of narrator. The first-person narrator is a character in the story and can be recognized by his use of "I"; third-person narrators may be limited or omniscient. In the former, the narrator confines himself to knowledge of the minds and emotions of one or at most a few characters. In the latter, the narrator knows everything, seeing into the minds of all the characters. Rarely, second-person narration may be used (an example can be found in Edna O'Brien's *A Pagan Place*, published in 1970).

Naturalism: The application of the principles of scientific determinism to fiction. Although it usually refers more to the choice of subject matter than to technical conventions, conventions associated with the movement center on the author's attempt to be precise and objective in description and detail, regardless of whether the events described are sordid or shocking. Naturalism flourished in England, France, and America in the late nineteenth and early twentieth centuries.

Neoclassicism: A term used to describe the classicism that dominated English literature from the Restoration to the late eighteenth century. Modeling itself on the literature of ancient Greece and Rome, neoclassicism exalted the virtues of proportion, unity, harmony, grace, decorum, taste, manners, and restraint. It valued realism and reason over imagination and emotion. *See also* Rationalism, Realism.

Neorealism: A movement in modern Italian literature, extending from about 1930 to 1955. Neorealism was shaped by opposition to Fascism, and by World War II and the Resistance. Neorealist literature therefore exhibited a strong concern with social issues and was marked by pessimism regarding the human condition. Its practitioners sought to overcome the gap between literature and the masses, and its subject matter was frequently drawn from lower-class life. Neorealism is associated preeminently with the work of Italo Calvino.

Nonsense literature/verse: Nonsense verse, such as that written by Edward Lear and Lewis Carroll, makes use of invented words that have no meaning, portmanteau words, and so-called macaroni verse, in which words from different languages are mingled. The verse holds the attention because of its strong rhythms, appealing sounds, and, occasionally, the mysterious atmosphere that it creates.

Novel of education: See *Bildungsroman*.

Novel of ideas: A novel in which the characters, plot, and dialogue serve to develop some controlling idea or to present the clash of ideas. Aldous Huxley's *Eyeless in Gaza* (1936) is a good example.

Novel of manners: The classic example of the form might be the novels of Jane Austen, wherein the customs and conventions of a social group of a particular time and place are realistically, and often satirically, portrayed.

Novella: An Italian term meaning "a little new thing" that now refers to that form of fiction longer than a short story and shorter than a novel.

Objective correlative: A key concept in modern formalist criticism, coined by T. S. Eliot in *The Sacred Wood* (1920). An objective correlative is a situation, an event, or an object that, when presented or described in a literary work, expresses a particular emotion and serves as a precise formula by which the same emotion can be evoked in the reader.

Ode: The ode is a lyric poem that treats a unified subject with elevated emotion, usually ending with a satisfactory resolution. There is no set form for the ode, but it must be long enough to build intense emotional response. Often the ode will address itself to some omnipotent source and will assume a spiritual hue.

Oxford Movement: A reform movement in the Church of England that began in 1833, led by John Henry (later Cardinal) Newman. The Oxford Movement aimed to combat liberalism and the decline of the role of faith in the Church and to restore it to its former ideals. It was attacked for advocating what some saw as Catholic doctrines; as a result, Newman left the Church of England and became a Roman Catholic in 1845.

Panegyric: A formal speech or writing in praise of a particular person or achievement; a eulogy. The form dates back to classical times; the term is now often used in a derogatory sense.

Parable: A short, simple, and usually allegorical story that teaches a moral lesson. In the West, the most famous parables are those told in the Gospels by Christ.

Parody: A literary work that imitates or burlesques another work or author, for the purpose of ridicule. Twentieth century parodists include E. B. White and James Thurber.

Pastoral: The term derives from the Latin "pastor," meaning "shepherd." Pastoral is a literary mode that depicts the country life in an idealized way; it originated in classical literature and was a popular form in English literature from 1550 to 1750. Notable pastoral poems include John Milton's "Lycidas" and Percy Bysshe Shelley's *Adonais*.

Pathetic fallacy: The ascribing of human characteristics or feelings to inanimate objects. The term was coined by John Ruskin in 1856, who disapproved of it, but it is now used without any pejorative sense.

Persona: *Persona* means literally "mask": It is the self created by the author and through whom the narrative is told. The persona is not to be identified with the author, even when the two may seem to resemble each other. The narrative persona in Lord Byron's *Don Juan* (1819-1824, 1826), for example, may express many sentiments of which Byron would have approved, but he is nonetheless a fictional creation who is distinct from the author.

Personification: A figure of speech that ascribes human qualities to abstractions or inanimate objects.

Petrarchan sonnet: Named after Petrarch, a fourteenth century Italian poet, who perfected the form, which is also known as the Italian sonnet. It is divided into an octave, in which the subject matter, which may be a problem, a doubt, a reflection, or some other issue, is raised and elaborated, and a sestet, in which the problem is resolved. The rhyme scheme is usually *abba abba ced cde, cdc cdc*, or *cde dce*.

Philosophical dualism: A theory that the universe is explicable in terms of two basic, conflicting entities, such as good and evil, mind and matter, or the physical and the spiritual.

Picaresque: A form of fiction that revolves around a central rogue figure, or picaro, who usually tells his own story. The plot structure of a picaresque novel is usually episodic, and the episodes usually focus on how the picaro lives by his wits. The classic example is Henry Fielding's *The History of Tom Jones, a Foundling* (1749).

Pindaric ode: Odes that imitate the form of those composed by the ancient Greek poet Pindar. A Pindaric ode consists of a strophe, followed by an antistrophe of the same structure, followed by an epode. This pattern may be repeated several times in the ode. In English poetry, Thomas Gray's "The Bard" is an example of a Pindaric ode.

Play: A literary work that is written to be performed by actors who speak the dialogue, impersonate the characters, and perform the appropriate actions. Usually, a play is performed on a stage, and an audience witnesses it.

Play-within-the-play: A play or dramatic fragment performed as a scene or scenes within a larger drama, typically performed or viewed by the characters of the larger drama.

Plot: Plot refers to how the author arranges the material not only to create the sequence of events in a play or story but also to suggest how those events are connected in a cause-and-effect relationship. There are a great variety of plot patterns, each of which is designed to create a particular effect.

Poem: A unified composition that uses the rhythms and sounds of language, as well as devices such as metaphor, to communicate emotions and experiences to the reader.

Poet laureate: The official poet of England, appointed for life by the English sovereign and expected to compose poems for various public occasions. The first official laureate was John Dryden in the seventeenth century. In the eighteenth century, the laureateship was given to a succession of mediocrities, but since the appointment of William Wordsworth in 1843, the office has generally been regarded as a substantial honor.

Polemic: A work that forcefully argues an opinion, usually on a controversial religious, political, or economic issue, in opposition to other opinions. John Milton's *Areopagitica* (1644) is one of the best known examples in English literature.

Postmodernism: The term is loosely applied to various artistic movements that have succeeded modernism, particularly since 1965. Postmodernist literature is experimental in form and reflects a fragmented world in which order and meaning are absent.

Pre-Raphaelitism: Refers to a group of nineteenth century English painters and writers, including Dante Gabriel Rossetti, Christina Rossetti, and William Morris. The Pre-Raphaelites were so called because they rebelled against conventional methods of painting and wanted to revert to what they regarded as the simple spirit of painting that existed before Raphael, particularly in its adherence to nature; they rejected all artificial embellishments. Pre-Raphaelite poetry made much use of symbolism and sensuousness, and showed an interest in the medieval and the supernatural.

Prose poem: A type of poem ranging in length from a few lines to three or four pages; most occupy a page or less. The distinguishing feature of the prose poem is its typography: it appears on the page like prose, with no line breaks. Many prose poems employ rhythmic repetition and other poetic devices not found in prose, but others do not; there is enormous variety in the genre.

Protagonist: Originally, in the Greek drama, the "first actor," who played the leading role. The term has come to signify the most important character in a drama or story. It is not unusual for there to be more than one protagonist in a work.

Proverb: A wise and pithy saying, authorship unknown, that reflects some observation about life. Proverbs are usually passed on through word of mouth, although they may also be written, as for example, the Book of Proverbs in the Bible.

Psychological novel: Once described as an interpretation of "the invisible life," the psychological novel is a form of fiction in which character, especially the inner life of characters, is the primary focus, rather than action. The form has characterized much of the work of Henry James, James Joyce, Virginia Woolf, and William Faulkner. *See also* Psychological realism.

Psychological realism: A type of realism that tries to reproduce the complex psychological motivations behind human behavior; writers in the late nineteenth century and early twentieth century were particularly influenced by Sigmund Freud's theories. *See also* Psychological novel.

Pun: A pun occurs when words with similar pronunciations have entirely different meanings. The result may be a surprise recognition of an unusual or striking connection, or, more often, a humorously accidental connection.

Quest: An archetypal theme identified by mythologist Joseph Campbell and found in many literary works. Campbell describes the heroic quest in three fundamental stages: departure (leaving the familiar world), initiation (encountering adventures and obstacles), and return (bringing home a boon to transform society).

Rabelaisian: The term is a reference to the sixteenth century French satirist and humorist François Rabelais. "Rabelaisian" is now used to refer to any humorous or satirical writing that is bawdy, coarse, or very down to earth.

Rationalism: A system of thought that seeks truth through the exercise of reason rather than by means of emotional response or revelation, or traditional authority. In literature, rationalism is associated with eighteenth century neoclassicism. *See also* Neoclassicism.

Realism: A literary technique in which the primary convention is to render an illusion of fidelity to external reality. Realism is often identified as the primary method of the novel form; the realist movement in the late nineteenth century coincided with the full development of the novel form.

Renaissance: The term means "rebirth" and refers to a period in European cultural history from the fourteenth to the early seventeenth century, although dates differ widely from country to country. The Renaissance produced an unprecedented flowering of the arts of painting, sculpture, architecture, and literature. The period is often said to mark the transition from the Middle Ages to the modern world. The questing, individualistic spirit that characterized the age was stimulated by an increase in classical learning by scholars known as Humanists, by the Protestant Reformation, by the development of printing, which created a wide market for books, by new theories of astronomy, and by the development of other sciences that saw natural laws at work where the Middle Ages had seen occult forces. *See also* Humanism.

Restoration comedy/drama: The restoration of the Stuart dynasty brought Charles II to the English throne in 1660. In literature, the Restoration period extends from 1660 to 1700. Restoration comedy is a comedy of manners, which centers around complicated plots full of the amorous intrigues of the fashionable upper classes. The humor is witty, but the view of human nature is cynical. Restoration dramatists include William Congreve, Sir George Etherege, and William Wycherley. In serious, or heroic, drama, the leading playwright was John Dryden. *See also* Comedy of manners.

Roman à clef: A fiction wherein actual persons, often celebrities of some sort, are thinly disguised. Lady Caroline Lamb's *Glenarvon* (1816), for example, contains a thinly veiled portrait of Lord Byron, and the character Mark Rampion in Aldous Huxley's *Point Counter Point* (1928) strongly resembles D. H. Lawrence.

Romance: Originally, any work written in Old French. In the Middle Ages, romances were about knights and their adventures. In modern times, the term has also been used to describe a type of prose fiction in which, unlike the novel, realism plays little part. Prose romances often give expression to the quest for transcendent truths.

Romanticism: A movement of the late eighteenth century and the nineteenth century that exalted individualism over collectivism, revolution over conservatism, innovation over tradition, imagination over reason, and spontaneity over restraint. Romanticism regarded art as self-expression; it strove to heal the cleavage between object and subject and expressed a longing for the infinite in all things. It stressed the innate goodness of human beings and the evils of the institutions that would stultify human creativity. The major English Romantic poets are William Blake, Lord Byron, Samuel Taylor Coleridge, John Keats, Percy Bysshe Shelley, and William Wordsworth.

Satire: A form of literature that employs the comedic devices of wit, irony, and exaggeration to expose, ridicule, and condemn human folly, vice, and stupidity. Justifying satire, Alexander Pope wrote that "nothing moves strongly but satire, and those who are ashamed of nothing else are so of being ridiculous."

Scene: A division of action within an act (some plays are divided only into scenes instead of acts). Sometimes, scene division indicates a change of setting or locale; sometimes, it simply indicates the entrances and exits of characters.

Science fiction: Fiction in which real or imagined scientific developments or certain givens (such as physical laws, psychological principles, or social conditions) form the basis of an imaginative projection, frequently into the future. Classic examples are the works of H. G. Wells and Jules Verne.

Sentimental novel: A form of fiction popular in the eighteenth century in which emotionalism and optimism are the primary characteristics. The best-known examples are Samuel Richardson's *Pamela* (1740-1741) and Oliver Goldsmith's *The Vicar of Wakefield* (1766).

Shakespearean sonnet: So named because William Shakespeare was the greatest English sonneteer, whose ranks also included the earl of Surrey and Thomas Wyatt. The Shakespearean sonnet consists of three quatrains and a concluding couplet, rhyming *abab cdcd efef gg*. The beginning of the third quatrain marks a turn in the argument.

Short story: A concise work of fiction, shorter than a novella, that is usually more concerned with mood, effect, or a single event than with plot or extensive characterization.

Simile: A type of metaphor in which two things are compared. It can usually be recognized by the use of the words "like," "as," "appears," or "seems."

***Skaz*:** A term used in Russian criticism to describe a narrative technique that presents an oral narrative of a lowbrow speaker.

Soliloquy: An extended speech delivered by a character alone on stage, unheard by other characters. Soliloquy is a form of monologue, and it typically reveals the intimate thoughts and emotions of the speaker.

Song: A lyric poem, usually short, simple, and with rhymed stanzas, set to music.

Sonnet: A traditional poetic form that is almost always composed of fourteen lines of rhymed iambic pentameter; a turning point usually divides the poem into two parts, with the first part (octave) presenting a situation and the second part (sestet) reflecting on it. The main sonnet forms are the Petrarchan sonnet and the English (sometimes called Shakespearean) sonnet.

Stanza: When lines of poetry are meant to be taken as a unit, and the unit recurs throughout the poem, that unit is called a stanza; a four-line unit, a quatrain, is one common stanza. Others include couplet, *ottava rima*, and the Spenserian stanza.

Story line: The story line of a work of fiction differs from the plot. Story is merely the events that happen; plot is how those events are arranged by the author to suggest a cause-and-effect relationship. *See also* Plot.

Stream of consciousness: A narrative technique used in modern fiction by which an author tries to embody the total range of consciousness of a character, without any authorial comment or explanation. Sensations, thoughts, memories, and associations pour forth in an uninterrupted, prerational, and prelogical flow. For examples, see James Joyce's *Ulysses* (1922), Virginia Woolf's *To the Lighthouse* (1927), and William Faulkner's *The Sound and the Fury* (1929).

***Sturm und Drang*:** A dramatic and literary movement in Germany during the late eighteenth century. Translated as "Storm and Stress," the movement was a reaction against classicism and a forerunner of Romanticism, characterized by extravagantly emotional language and sensational subject matter.

Surrealism: A revolutionary approach to artistic and literary creation, Surrealism argued for complete artistic freedom: The artist should relinquish all conscious control, responding to the irrational urges of the unconscious mind. Hence the bizarre, dreamlike, and nightmarish quality of Surrealistic writing. In the 1920's and 1930's, Surrealism flourished in France, Spain, and Latin America. (After World War II, it influenced such American writers as Frank O'Hara, John Ashberry, and Nathanael West.)

Symbol: A literary symbol is an image that stands for something else; it may evoke a cluster of meanings rather than a single specific meaning.

Symbolism: A literary movement encompassing the work of a group of French writers in the latter half of the nineteenth century, a group that included Charles Baudelaire, Stéphane Mallarmé, and Paul Verlaine. According to Symbolism, there is a mystical correspondence between the natural and spiritual worlds.

Theater of Cruelty: A term, coined by French playwright Antonin Artaud, which signifies a vision in which theater becomes an arena for shock therapy. The characters undergo such intense physical and psychic extremities that the audience cannot ignore the cathartic effect in which its preconceptions, fears, and hostilities are brought to the surface and, ideally, purged.

Theater of the Absurd: Refers to a group of plays that share a basic belief that life is illogical, irrational, formless, and contradictory, and that humanity is without meaning or purpose. Practitioners, who include Eugène Ionesco, Samuel Beckett, Jean Genet, Harold Pinter, Edward Albee, and Arthur Kopit, abandoned traditional theatrical forms and coherent dialogue.

***Théâtre d'avant-garde*:** A movement in late nineteenth century drama in France, which challenged the conventions of realistic drama by using Symbolist poetry and nonobjective scenery.

Third person: Third-person narration occurs when the narrator has not been part of the event or affected it and is not probing his own relationship to it but is only describing what happened. He does not allow the intrusion of the word *I.* Third-person narration establishes a distance between reader and subject, gives credibility to a large expanse of narration that would be impossible for one person to experience, and allows the narrative to include a number of characters who can comment on one another as well as be the subjects of commentary by the participating narrator.

Tragedy: A form of drama that is serious in action and intent and that involves disastrous events and death; classical Greek drama observed specific guidelines for tragedy, but the term is now sometimes applied to a range of dramatic or fictional situations.

Travel literature: Writing that emphasizes the author's subjective response to places visited, especially faraway, exotic, and culturally different locales.

Trilogy: A novel or play written in three parts, each of which is a self-contained work, such as William Shakespeare's *Henry VI* (*Part I*, 1592; *Part II*, c. 1590-1591; *Part III*, c. 1590-1591). Modern examples include C. S. Lewis' Space Trilogy (1938-1945) and William Golding's Sea Trilogy (1980-1989).

Trope: Trope means literally "turn" or "conversion"; it is a figure of speech in which a word or phrase is used in a way that deviates from the normal or literal sense.

***Verismo*:** Refers to a type of Italian literature that deals with the lower classes and presents them realistically using language that they would use. Called *verismo* because it is true to life, and, from the writer's point of view, impersonal.

Verse: Verse is a generic name for poetry. Verse also refers in a narrower sense to poetry that is humorous or merely superficial, as in "greeting-card verse." Finally, English critics sometimes use "verse" to mean "stanza," or, more often, to mean "line."

Verse drama: Verse drama was the prevailing form for Western drama throughout most of its history, comprising all the drama of classical Greece and continuing to dominate the stage through the Renaissance, when it was best exemplified by the blank verse of Elizabethan drama. In the seventeenth century, however, prose comedies became popular, and in the nineteenth and twentieth centuries verse drama became the exception rather than the rule.

Victorian novel: Although the Victorian period extended from 1837 to 1901, the term "Victorian novel" does not include works from the later decades of Queen Victoria's reign. The term loosely refers to the sprawling works of novelists such as Charles Dickens and William Makepeace Thackeray, which are characterized by a broad social canvas.

Villanelle: A French verse form assimilated by English prosody. It is usually composed of nineteen lines divided into five tercets and a quatrain, rhyming *aba*, *bba*, *aba*, *aba*, *abaa*. The third line is repeated in the ninth and fifteenth lines. Dylan Thomas' "Do Not Go Gentle into That Good Night" is a modern example of a successful villanelle.

Well-made play: From the French term *pièce bien faite*, a type of play constructed according to a "formula" that originated in nineteenth century France. The plot often revolves around a secret known only to some of the characters, which is revealed at the climax and leads to catastrophe for the villain and vindication or triumph for the hero. The well-made play influenced later dramatists such as Henrik Ibsen and George Bernard Shaw.

Weltanschauung: A German term translated as "worldview," by which is meant a comprehensive set of beliefs or assumptions by means of which one interprets what goes on in the world.

Zeitgeist: A German term meaning the spirit of the times, the moral or intellectual atmosphere of any age or period. The *Zeitgeist* of the Romantic Age, for example, might be described as revolutionary, restless, individualistic, and innovative.

LIST OF AUTHORS